PARTICIPATION IN EU RULE-MAKING

Participation in EU Rule-Making

A Rights-Based Approach

JOANA MENDES

OXFORD
UNIVERSITY PRESS

OXFORD
UNIVERSITY PRESS

Great Clarendon Street, Oxford OX2 6DP

Oxford University Press is a department of the University of Oxford.
It furthers the University's objective of excellence in research, scholarship,
and education by publishing worldwide in

Oxford New York

Auckland Cape Town Dar es Salaam Hong Kong Karachi
Kuala Lumpur Madrid Melbourne Mexico City Nairobi
New Delhi Shanghai Taipei Toronto

With offices in

Argentina Austria Brazil Chile Czech Republic France Greece
Guatemala Hungary Italy Japan Poland Portugal Singapore
South Korea Switzerland Thailand Turkey Ukraine Vietnam

Oxford is a registered trade mark of Oxford University Press
in the UK and in certain other countries

Published in the United States
by Oxford University Press Inc., New York

First published 2011

British Library Cataloguing in Publication Data
Data available

Library of Congress Cataloging in Publication Data
Data available

Typeset by SPI Publisher Services, Pondicherry, India
Printed in Great Britain
on acid-free paper by
CPI Antony Rowe, Chippenham, Wiltshire

ISBN 978–0–19–959976–9

1 3 5 7 9 10 8 6 4 2

eu conhecia já o rebentar do mar
das páginas dos livros que já tinha lido
(. . .)
era só ouvir o sonhador falar
da vida como se ela houvesse acontecido

(Ruy Belo, *E tudo era possível*)

aos meus pais

ACKNOWLEDGEMENTS

This book comes to print two years after I defended it as a PhD thesis at the European University Institute, in Florence. Starting this note in reverse chronological order, I would like to thank my friends and colleagues with whom I have had the opportunity to discuss my ideas on participation since March 2009. José Eduardo Dias, Guilherme Vilaça, Larisa Dragomir, Christina Eckes, Madalina Busuioc, and Ronald van Ooik have contributed in different ways to consolidating and challenging some of the ideas in the book. I would also like to thank my professor and friend José Carlos Vieira de Andrade of the University of Coimbra for a very helpful discussion that dissipated my last remaining hesitations on my theoretical construction. The anonymous OUP reviewers gave me important suggestions and comments that contributed decisively to sharpen some of my arguments. I am grateful for this. I am particularly indebted to Deirdre Curtin, who has warmly supported me in many ways during my rather eventful first year in the Netherlands. Without her, revising and bringing this book to publication would certainly have been a much harder task. Still in Amsterdam, Angela Moisl and Diana Hamidzai provided me with valuable help, at different stages, with some of the technical aspects of the manuscript.

A particular word of gratitude goes to the members of my PhD committee: my supervisor Jacques Ziller, Bruno de Witte, Paul Craig, and Loïc Azoulai. Their reviews of my doctoral thesis and the discussion we held during the defence, in particular the way they have disputed my arguments, were extremely important to refine my views on participation and to transforming the thesis into a book.

Florence was where my work began. The initial idea of my thesis received a great impulse in December 2004, following a round table organized by Jacques Ziller, the subject of which was 'What's new in European administrative law?' and, in particular, the vivid discussion between Paul Craig and Edoardo Chiti on the matter of participation. Until then, I was not at all certain about what my initial intention of discovering a 'principle of participation in European administrative law' could mean. This discussion, in a way, was a starting point for the work now presented to you.

Throughout the research, Jacques Ziller's supervision gave me room for creativity and the freedom to make the fundamental choices involved in writing a doctoral dissertation. I suspect, however, that he understood better, and certainly earlier, than me the potentialities and perils of my endeavour. His understanding of supervision has proven crucial to the final outcome of this work. In the meetings with Bruno de Witte I was firmly questioned about the ultimate reasons for my choices, and thereby challenged to rethink and strengthen them. At the same time, these conversations were safe harbours in the midst of my doubts. In contrast, the discussions I had with Christian Joerges, still at an early stage of development of this work, made me doubt the very reason for undertaking this task. Little of what I sought to defend passed his criticism with approval. The fact that he was nonetheless interested in the broad underpinnings of the thesis added weight to his sceptical views on my yet to be born dissertation. Joerges' vigorous disagreement helped me define the purpose of this work and thereby contributed to its final results. With Marise Cremona, Neil Walker, and Miguel Poiares Maduro I had single but fruitful discussions for the development of the initial chapters. At a later stage, Paul Craig's advice not to fight lost battles was quite valuable. I hope I have been successful in steering this work away from the more slippery grounds to which he implicitly referred. Edoardo Chiti and Matteo Ortino were willing to read some of my manuscripts and scrutinized them critically. Their views were quite important for me. Finally, Alun Gibbs helped me in correcting some of my most obscure uses of his mother tongue.

I would like to mention the kindness and promptness of Ruth Gbikpi and Emir Lawless at the EUI library. Ruth, apart from taking care that many inter-library loans always reached my hands on time, was tireless in finding books of which I had only bare references. Emir discovered for me the less accessible documents of the EU institutions. Many do not show up in the final work that is now before you, but were nevertheless important for developing my research.

Most of this work was written in the quietness of the Palagetto, where I had the blissfulness of sharing my life with Jan and the great joy of receiving our friends and family. Their presence, there and elsewhere, has helped us to endure the more difficult moments of our work. The Palagetto also brought us the friendship of James, with whom we discovered some of the mountains of the Alpi Apuane. Our hikes were an important form of catharsis in the writing period of the dissertation now transformed into this book and remain a warm and vivid memory of those days.

Lastly, writing the dissertation that originated this book would have not been possible without the funding of two Portuguese entities: the *Direcção-Geral de Assuntos Comunitários* and the *Fundação para a Ciência e Tecnologia*. The dissertation defended at the European University Institute in March 2009 has been revised and updated. The law is as stated on October 2010, and the website addresses cited were last visited on 31 October 2010.

CONTENTS

ABBREVIATIONS

Cedefop	European Centre for the Development of Vocational Training
CESR	Committee of European Securities Regulators
CFCA	Community Fisheries Control Agency
CFI	Court of First Instance of the European Communities (General Court, after Lisbon)
CPVO	Community Plant Variety Office
EASA	European Aviation Safety Agency
EC	European Community
ECDC	European Centre for Disease Prevention and Control
ECHA	European Chemicals Agency
ECJ	European Court of Justice
ECOSOC	Economic and Social Committee
ECSC	European Coal and Steel Community
EEC	European Economic Community
EFSA	European Food and Safety Authority
EMSA	European Maritime Safety Agency
ENISA	European Network and Information Security Agency
ERA	European Railway Agency
ESMA	European Securities and Markets Authority
EU	European Union
EU-OSHA	European Agency for Safety and Health at Work
Euratom	European Atomic Energy Community
Eurofund	European Foundation for the Improvement of Living and Working Conditions
FSAP	Financial Services Action Plan
OHIM	Office for Harmonisation in the Internal Market
TEU	Treaty on the European Union (consolidated version, 2010)
TFEU	Treaty on the Functioning of the European Union (consolidated version, 2010)
UCITS	Undertakings for Collective Investment in Transferable Securities

TABLE OF CASES, LEGISLATION AND OTHER ACTS

Judgments

Opinions

Decisions of the European Ombudsman

Treaties

Directives

Regulations

Decisions

Recommendations

Inter-institutional agreements

Council

European Commission

European Council

European Parliament

Committee of the Regions

Economic and Social Committee

European bodies

Other European documents

Press

Press releases

Newspaper articles

Chapter 1

Introduction

1.1 Approach and Aims

This book addresses the procedural position of natural and legal persons whose rights and legally protected interests are affected by the regulatory acts adopted by the European institutions. It is based on a rights-based approach to participation, in that it analyses participation as a procedural right grounded in the impact regulatory acts have on substantive rights and interests. It is a normative endeavour since it aims to redefine the current scope and meaning of participation rights in European Union (EU) administrative law.[1] This is based on a firm understanding of the origins and rationales of participation rights as well as of the participatory mechanisms that pervade EU decision-making. The legal analysis is as such situated in the broader political context of European integration.

This book puts forward and demonstrates two main propositions. First, the current scope of participation rights in EU administrative law is too narrow in the face of regulatory reality. It follows that, as they stand, European decisional procedures are not faithful to the values of the rule of law that the EU claims as their own and seeks to promote. Secondly, the scope of participation rights should be extended to new situations and new types of procedures, in particular those that generally fall within the

[1] The term 'participation rights' is used here as an equivalent to 'rights of participation' referring to the right of natural and legal persons to be heard in the decisional procedures that concern them, not to the set of rights associated with participation (such as access to information or the duty to give reasons). The term 'participation rights' is preferred to that of 'right to be heard'. The latter will be reserved to refer to the Courts' stance on this procedural right, which will be criticized in this book, and the former to the broader conception that will be defended here. Moreover, the use of the plural ('participation rights' instead of 'participation right') is justified by the differences that will be delineated among different types of participants.

category of rule-making, i.e. procedures that lead to the adoption of general norms, whichever their form, that affect an undetermined number of persons. This extension is required by a paradigm of EU administrative law that is consonant with the constitutional underpinnings of EU law, in particular those that have enhanced the position of the individual in the EU legal system.[2]

Participation rights are too narrow in two different senses. First, they are too narrow when compared with the effects that Union acts produce, directly or indirectly, in the legal sphere of natural and legal persons who are the subjects of the accrued regulatory powers of the EU institutions.[3] Secondly, they are too narrow when compared with the legal values and principles endorsed by the EU legal system.[4] As such, as a first step, the book points out the limits of participation rights in EU administrative law, which have contributed to the neglect of the procedural position of natural and legal persons in regulatory procedures. Moreover, participation rights should be distinguished from the different forms of participation that imbue the EU regulatory structures. In fact, although the use of participation has become more explicit and systematic under the so-called 'new governance' developments, these have not, in general, improved the legal protection of subjective rights and legally protected interests of the persons affected by the Union regulatory action. The specific meaning attributed to the concept of participation in this book is implicit in these statements: participation refers here to the procedural rights of intervention in decisional procedures grounded in substantive rights or interests that are affected by these same procedures. This concept, the various forms of participation in EU decision-making, and the limits of participation rights are developed in the following four chapters and concretized in the sector studies presented in the last three chapters.

[2] The term 'Union' or the abbreviation EU will be used throughout this work to refer to the law, processes, acts, and institutions of the European Union as a single entity that encompasses the former three pillars. Also the 'Community' designation will be used. The resort to one or other term will depend on the context, namely on the period and segment of law or policy to which each part of the analysis refers. The term 'Community' is preferred when drawing on the developments which occurred before the Maastricht Treaty entered into force. This is particularly the case in Chapter 3.

[3] 'Legal sphere' refers to the entire set of advantageous legal positions (among which rights) and disadvantageous positions (among which duties) that are granted to and impinge upon legal and natural persons.

[4] These are indicated below.

The study goes one step further: it puts forward a different construction for participation rights, which is deemed to surmount these limits without exceeding the legal boundaries within which participation can still be conceived as a procedural right. The rights-based concept of participation defended in the book both enables an extension of participation rights in EU law and provides for the limits of such an extension. This leads us to the second proposition. It is contended that participation rights should exist where the legal spheres of private persons are affected by a regulatory act adopted by the EU administration, independently of the form of the latter and irrespective of their being in an analogous position to that of the addressee of the act. Therefore, among other consequences, the rule according to which no participation rights should be recognized in procedures that lead to the adoption of general acts, should be cast away. The bases of this construction are presented in the next chapter. The conception of participation rights that is developed there guides the analyses undertaken throughout this work.

The aims of the book are revealed by this short introduction. Demonstrating both the current limits and the possibilities of extension of participation rights are its core aims. Two ancillary tasks embody two further objectives. The first consists of the identification of a legal concept of participation that is capable of grounding the proposed extension of participation rights. This means that the construction put forward will stress the legal values in which participation is grounded and will seek to explore the potentialities and limits of participation as a legal concept. Secondly, one should be able to relate the proposed extension to the broader institutional developments that have brought participation to the fore of EU governance. Therefore, the various participation mechanisms that pervade the EU institutional and legal system will be considered in terms of what connects them to, and separates them from, participation rights, as they are understood in this book.

The construction proposed is deemed to yield results that are more consonant with the rule of law than the current *status quo* on this matter. Rule of law is meant here as the imposition of substantive and procedural limits to the exercise of public power. The rule of law has been heralded as one of the foundations of EU law, to the extent that its institutions and bodies are submitted to legal norms and that judicial review by the EU Courts ensures respect for these norms.[5] Legal developments such as the

[5] This was the sense of the Court's judgment in *Les Verts* (Case 294/83, *Parti écologiste 'Les Verts' v European Parliament* [1986] ECR 1339, paragraph 23). On this point, Jean Paul Jacqué (2006) *Droit institutionnel de l'Union Européenne*, 4th edn, Paris: Dalloz, pp. 51–4. As is widely known the principle is enshrined in Article 2 of the Treaty on the European Union (TEU, OJ C 83/13, 30.3.2010.).

respect for fundamental rights have stressed the protection of the individual as being an inherent dimension of this principle.[6] Nevertheless, concern for the protection of the substantive rights and legally protected interests of the persons affected by the exercise of public powers has arguably not been transposed to the design of regulatory procedures and structures set up in the EU context, beyond the realm now covered by Article 41 of the Charter of Fundamental Rights.[7] Moreover, one may argue that this contrasts with the 'empowerment' of private persons vis-à-vis Member States and the respective administrations, by way of the principles of direct effect and primacy, as well as state liability for breach of EU law.[8] Further, it may also be held that this tends to ignore the case law that establishes the importance of procedural law in protecting fundamental rights.[9] Indeed, by an argument *a maiori ad minus*, procedural law is equally relevant for the protection of subjective rights and legally protected interests that do not have the status of fundamental rights.

It follows from these last arguments that the propositions of the book are also congruous with specific features of the EU legal system. These stem not only from the principles mentioned, but also from four other characteristics. To begin with, the various forms of cooperation between national and European administrations—which tend to blur the distinction between direct and indirect administration—are very likely to boost situations in which the rights and interests of private persons are affected by the combined action of national and EU administrative entities. This may require a perspective on the issue of the legal protection of these persons different from the one inherent in the principle of procedural autonomy. Further, a typology of acts of the Union, grounding the distinction

[6] See, in this regard, Armin von Bogdandy (2006) 'Constitutional principles' in Armin von Bogdandy and Jürgen Bast (eds), *Principles of European Constitutional Law*, Oxford and Portland: Hart Publishing, pp. 3–52 at pp. 15–20; Jacqué, *op. cit.*, pp. 51–74; Jürgen Schwarze (2006) *European Administrative Law*, Revised 1st edn, London: Sweet and Maxwell, p. cxvi; on the various elements of the rule of law principle that have been recognized by the EU Courts, Schwarze, *ibid*, p. cxviii, on their more recent developments see, among others, *ibid*, pp. cxix–clxii.

[7] OJ C 83/389, 30.3.2010.

[8] On the impact of these principles on the relationship between persons and their national administrations, see Alberto Massera (2007) 'I principi generali', in Mario P. Chiti and Guido Greco (eds), *Trattato di diritto amministrativo europeo*, Tomo I, 2nd edn, Milano: Giuffrè, pp. 285–414, at pp. 379–89.

[9] E.g. Case 222/86, *Union nationale des entraîneurs et cadres techniques professionnels du football v Georges Heylens and others* [1987] ECR 4097, paragraph 14, referring to the duty to state reasons as a means of ensuring the right to effective judicial protection.

between legislative and administrative rule-making on substantive criteria is still found wanting, despite the new rules of the Treaty on the Functioning of the European Union.[10] Moreover, it is doubtful whether the distinction between general and individual acts will ever be able to grasp the reality of the forms of Union action, in particular with regard to the effects of the acts. In addition, the modes of production of EU rules are very much determined by a combination of representative and participatory elements. This is arguably an important systematic element to understand and reflect upon EU decisional procedures, providing a possible 'constitutional basis' for the furtherance of participation rights. While the first feature reinforces the relevance of the topic chosen as an object of analysis, the second, third, and fourth aspects mentioned incline us to question the influence of some of the arguments which have been deployed to delimit the scope and meaning of participation rights in EU administrative law.

This book is based on two premises. First, the forms of procedural participation which have been developed with regard to administrative procedures, both in national legal systems and in EU administrative law, are the most appropriate to test the legal protection of natural and legal persons affected by public regulatory action. From this premise derive two important tools of analysis used in this work: the construction of the concept of participation proposed and the reliance on the theory of legal administrative relationships, both embedded in doctrines of national administrative law.[11] The topic of procedural administrative participation recalls that the issue of authority–liberty, which has been at the core of the development of administrative law in national legal systems, has been largely absent from EU administrative law. This is due to the persistent but erroneous assumption that, with the exception of competition law, the action of the EU institutions drawing on an administrative function bears upon relationships among public authorities, not with the rights and interests of natural and legal persons. Nevertheless, this was arguably the core concern that pushed for the development of procedural entitlements of interested persons in EU administrative law, in particular in the areas of direct administration. Secondly, the exercise of the administrative function that may justify the recognition of participation rights pervades different levels of decision-making. In the EU legal system, the identification of the administrative function is essentially a matter of interpretation of the

[10] Articles 289 to 291 TFEU (OJ C 83/1, 30.03.2010).

[11] On the methodology of translation, see the section below.

Treaty and primary norms that define the competences of the decisional bodies and, with it, the subject matter of regulation and the goals to be achieved.[12]

1.2 Method and Sources

The book is essentially an interpretation of the principle according to which 'a person whose interests are perceptibly affected by a decision taken by a public authority must be given the opportunity to make his point of view known' before the adoption of the act.[13] This is its point of departure and its point of arrival. In fact, as mentioned, the main purpose of this work is to redefine the scope and meaning of participation rights and this principle, in particular its current judicial interpretation, decisively conditions these two elements in current EU administrative law.

The method is one of legal interpretation. The wording of the norms where this principle is enshrined, whether judicial or legislative, is the first step of the legal analysis. This provides its core empirical ground. Nevertheless, the aims of legal analysis stray far beyond the understanding of positive law based on the syntax of norms. In this case, as stated, the study of participation rights intends to assess critically their scope and meaning with a view to proposing a different normative solution to the problem of the procedural protection of substantive rights and legally protected interests in the realm of EU administrative law. Therefore, the scope and meaning of participation rights need to be understood in light of the rationales of these rights, both as they have been developed in EU law and as they may be interpreted in light of general principles of law accepted in the EU legal system. Furthermore, this legal interpretation will include a consideration of the historical development of participation rights and mechanisms in the EU legal and political system, as well as of their current features.

The core arguments of the book are thus grounded in a hermeneutics that combines the teleological, historical, and systematic elements of legal interpretation. The rationales of the principle according to which persons

[12] On the difficulties in identifying the administrative function of the EU, see Dominique Ritleng (2009) 'L'identification de la fonction executive dans l'Union', in Jacqueline Dutheil de la Rochère (ed.), *Exécution du droit de l'Union, entre mécanismes communautaires et droits nationaux*, Bruxelles: Bruylant, pp. 27–51.

[13] Case 17/74, *Transocean Marine Paint Association v Commission* [1974] ECR 1063, paragraph 15.

affected in their rights and interests by an act of public authority should be heard before the adoption of the act yields a reference point for elaborating a more comprehensive understanding of participation than the one strictly enshrined in positive law. This understanding is capable of grounding a broader scope of participation rights than the one currently accepted in EU administrative law. Further, the knowledge of the origins of this principle and of the way it has been perceived, interpreted, and applied contributes to characterizing it and to clarifying the reasons for its current scope. In addition, this analysis is situated in the context of the EU legal and political system. This brings to this work elements of the 'normative whole' in which participation rights and mechanisms are embedded as well as the consideration of related norms and practices that may shed new light on the principle under analysis. In particular, the pervasiveness of participatory mechanisms in the EU regulatory structures leads one to question the strict legal-formal conceptions of participation, conveyed by the Courts' jurisprudence.[14] Moreover, this calls into question whether, as imparted by the Commission, there is effectively no room for law in the configuration of some of these mechanisms, and compels one to consider which, if any, the role of law could be. At the very least, the study of non-legal forms of participation allows us to consider other meanings of participation, which are not wholly deprived of legal significance, even if detached from the core concern for the dignity of the person that has underpinned the judicial developments on this matter. Additionally, it calls the interpreter's attention to other dimensions of the relationships that intervene between natural and legal persons concerned by European law and the actions of the EU institutions. Therefore, understanding the meaning of different participation mechanisms in the EU setting is an important systematic element of the analysis undertaken in this book. Participation emerges thus as a feature that is embedded in the institutional-constitutional tradition of European integration and this stresses the inadequacy of the current legal scope of participation rights in view of the constitutive features of the EU polity.

This work relies on three different groups of sources. First, the leading cases of the European Court of Justice and of the Court of First Instance

[14] Jurisprudence is used throughout this work in the sense of a body of case law with authoritative value. Unless otherwise specified, the terms 'Courts' and 'EU Courts' refer here to the Court of Justice (for which the abbreviation ECJ is still used) and to the General Court, which will still be designated Court of First Instance (or CFI) when referring to judgments issued before the Lisbon Treaty entered into force (cf. Article 19(1) TEU).

(now General Court) on participation rights, as well as relevant EU legislative norms. Secondly, the administrative laws of Member States and doctrinal works thereon. Thirdly, political science studies, policy documents, and preparatory acts of EU legislation.

The case law of the EU Courts is the main source to understand the origins and the historical developments of the *audi alteram partem* principle in EU administrative law, as well as the current scope and meaning of participation rights. This analysis provides one of the pillars of the book. The study of the case law is complemented by a cursory resort to the EU legislative norms that enshrine the right to be heard and other procedural rights of participation in sector legislation, in particular in competition law, that have been the object of judicial interpretations. In fact, the current scope and meaning of participation is the result of the interplay between the legislative and judicial developments. The Courts' stance is both conditioned by the legislative options and conditions them also in areas in which these matters have not been the object of a consistent body of case law.

The resort to sources of national law has a threefold purpose. First, they provide an overview of rules and conceptions that are very likely to have influenced EU law in this matter, and, thus, contribute to a better understanding of participation rights from a *de lege lata* perspective. In fact, the principle according to which affected persons should be heard before the adoption of an act that affects their rights and interests stems from the laws and common constitutional traditions of Member States. These shed light on the origins, scope, and meaning of participation rights. The assumption that the conception of participation rights in EU administrative law was influenced by the national legal orders is confirmed by the Courts' methodology in creating general principles of law. It is worth mentioning that the judgment of the European Court of Justice and the Opinion of Advocate General Warner in *Transocean Marine Paint Association* are conspicuous examples of this methodology.[15] Secondly, the study of national legal rules

[15] Loïc Azoulai (2000) *Les garanties prodédurales en droit communautaire. Recherches sur la procedure et le bon gouvernement*, PhD Thesis, European University Institute: Florence, pp. 110–15, where the case is discussed (also Takis Tridimas (2006) *The General Principles of EU Law*, 2nd edn, Oxford: Oxford University Press, p. 372). See, equally, Adelina Adinolfi (1994) 'I principi generali nella giurisprudenza comunitaria e la loro influenza sugli ordinamenti degli Stati membri', *Rivista Italiana di Diritto Comunitario*, pp. 521–79, at p. 543–4; Xavier Groussot (2000) 'The general principles of Community law in the creation and development of due process principles in competition law proceeding: from Transocean Marine Painting (1974) to Montecatini (1999)', in Ulf Bernitz and Joakim Nergelius (eds), *General Principles of European Community Law*, The Hague: Kluwer Law International, pp. 185–204, at p. 188.

on participation rights provides some valuable normative indications for the construction of legal solutions addressing problems that might arise as a result of the proposed extension of participation rights in EU administrative law. In this sense, rules of national law yield useful normative elements from a *de lege ferenda* perspective.[16]

The relevance of national sources from a *de lege ferenda* perspective unveils an additional, deeper, and more decisive reason to resort to rules and principles of national law when analysing certain aspects of EU law: this provides a second level of analysis, a benchmark to assess critically the current state of EU law, which is the purpose of this book. In our case, this benchmark is grounded in a common understanding of what participation means and which values it conveys in the specific context of the procedural protection of persons and legally protected interests before the exercise of public power. A common understanding of participation, which is acceptable across different legal systems, may be deduced from monographic studies that analyse the features of participation rights in different national contexts, as well as from the few comparative works that cover this subject matter.[17] These allow us to identify the legal and political foundations of participation rights. On this basis, one may sustain that certain concepts or conceptions developed in national legal contexts may circulate from national to EU law, provided that they yield an explanatory basis for the understanding of the legal issues that emerge in the EU legal order, have a sufficient normative capacity to deal therewith, and are consonant with other features of the EU legal and political system.[18] Two important

[16] On the influence of national laws in the construction of EU law, see, *inter alia*, Pierre Pescatore (1980) 'Le recours dans la jurisprudence de la Cour de Justice des Communautés Européennes a des normes déduites de la comparaison des droits des États membres', *Revue Internationale de Droit Comparé*, Vol. 32, n. 2, pp. 337–59, at pp. 354–8. This recalls the functions of general principles in European law and the Courts' methodology in their creation. On this, see Adinolfi, *op. cit.*, pp. 528–33; Yves Galmot (1997) 'L'apport des principes généraux du droit communautaire à la garantie des droits dans l'ordre juridique français', *Cahiers de Droit Européen*, Vol. 33, n. 1–2, pp. 67–79, at p. 78; Tridimas, *op. cit.*, pp. 29–35; Massera, *op. cit.*, p. 291.

[17] Michel Fromont (2006) *Droit administratif des États européens*, Paris: Presses Universitaires de France, pp. 215–22; Schwarze, *op. cit.*, n. 6, pp. 1243–371; Stefano Battini, Bernardo G. Mattarella, and Aldo Sandulli (2007) 'Il procedimento' in Giulio Napolitano (ed.) *Diritto Amministrativo Comparato*, pp. 107–74. A comparison between the French and the German system is provided by Ewald Eisenberg (2000) *L'audition du citoyen et motivation des décisions administratives individuelles. Étude comparative en France et en Allemagne*, Paris: L'Harmattan. The references to the monographic works or articles on specific national systems are found throughout the book, in particular in Chapter 2.

[18] These considerations on the possibility of translating national concepts to the European setting draw on Neil Walker (2003) 'Postnational constitutionalism and the problem of

aspects of the conceptual framework of the book, presented in Chapter 2, derive from this approach: the concept of participation proposed and the resort to the concept of legal administrative relationship as an important support for the construction of participation rights set forth.

The choice of national legal orders from which legal sources were selected was determined by the linguistic capacities of the author and is, therefore, confined to England, France, Italy, Spain, and Portugal. It should be noted that, although this work includes references to the German legal system, the author's knowledge in this regard is only based on translated works.[19] From a *de lege ferenda* perspective, the sources of the Italian legal system have been particularly influential in this work. Italian studies on participation in administrative procedures are abundant and the debates on this topic are prolific, not least due to the discussions that preceded the entering into force of the general law on administrative procedure, but also given the relevance attributed to the legal subjective positions of individuals in the Italian system of judicial review.[20]

The third type of source mentioned—political science studies, policy documents, and preparatory acts of EU legislation—is required to analyse participation as a feature of the EU institutional form and of its regulatory structures. This strand of participation (strictly, non-legal dimensions of participation), when approached by lawyers, tends to be considered independently of the problem of procedural protection of persons affected by the exercise of public powers (due process rights in administrative procedures). Nevertheless, as pointed out above, this is an important systematic element of the interpretation of participation rights undertaken in this work. It is in this respect that the interdisciplinary nature of the topic of this book becomes more pressing. Political science studies—mostly articles, published both in journals and in working paper series, such as the EUROGOV, as well as monographic studies included in collective works—have helped the author to navigate the functioning and other related problems of some of the participatory structures in place at the EU level, thereby acquiring knowledge of

translation' in Joseph H.H. Weiler and Marlene Wind (eds), *European Constitutionalism beyond the State*, Cambridge: Cambridge University Press, pp. 27–54, at pp. 35–38.

19 In particular, Galetta's translation and commentary of the German *Verwaltungsverfahrensgesetz* was a valuable source in understanding the basic standpoint of the German legal system in this matter (Diana-Urania Galetta (2002) *La legge tedesca sul procedimento amministrativo (Verwaltungsverfahrensgesetz). Traduzione con testo a fronte e commento introduttivo*, Milano: Giuffrè).

20 For a flavour, see Massimo Occhiena (2002) *Situazioni giuridiche soggettive e procedimento amministrativo*, Milano: Giuffrè, Chapters 2 and 3.

facts of potential legal relevance, or at least, facts that may be valued from a legal standpoint. Admittedly, the author's lack of deeper knowledge of this discipline has limited the use of its sources in this work. Additionally, the consultation of websites in which participatory practices can be followed was relevant from this perspective (for example, the website of the Committee of European Securities Regulators was particularly useful for the study undertaken in Chapter 6). The Commission's COM documents were also a source for understanding the rationales and features of certain participatory practices. Furthermore, these documents were equally important to comprehend the legal strand of participation: given the Commission's prerogatives to initiate legislation, its general stance is likely to transpire into legislative provisions.

Finally, the conception and extension of participation rights propounded are tested in the sector analyses. The choice of sectors was meant to cover the different dimensions of participation in the European legal and political setting and to shed light on the differences and continuities between the two strands of participation mentioned. In addition, they also cover different modes of EU administration: implementation by national administrations, notwithstanding the strong European shaping of national decisions (securities markets regulation under the Lamfalussy process); implementation both by national and European entities, permeated by composite administrative procedures which in fact lead to an integrated administration (food law);[21] a form of direct administration, in which the administrative decisions are primarily within the competence of the European Commission (state aid). It will be demonstrated that the specific division of executive powers which is intrinsic to the EU administration does not need to—and indeed should not—contend with the granting or otherwise of participation rights to the persons affected by administrative regulatory acts.

The approach is different in each case, since the respective objects of analysis are also different. The study on the sector of state aid elaborates the interpretation of Article 108(2) TFEU. In essence, it focuses on the study of the Courts' case law regarding this Article, but it also relates it to regulatory developments which have occurred in this field beyond the framework of the Treaty. It brings together different cases, on the assumption that this is

[21] The term integrated administration refers here to the inter-linkages between national and EU administration, which are reflected in and embodied by the decisional procedures that combine their respective contributions in the regulatory decisions adopted in the realm of EU administrative law.

an essential task to build up a doctrinal approach to the subject matter under analysis.[22] The object of the chapter dedicated to food law is the examination of selected procedures that are deemed to be representative of the decisional powers of the EU institutions in this field and that are likely to impact on the private legal sphere. It draws on the analysis of the respective directives and regulations, and situates this in the development of this EU policy. The analysis of the regulatory structure set up in the area of financial services is the one that most deviates from a strict method of legal interpretation, given its object. It examines a regulatory process that results in the enactment of legal norms but is essentially informed by considerations that stray beyond the strict legal realm. It is also not a sector analysis proper, but a study of one regulatory process. Its sources are mostly the several policy documents that delineate this process and the related participatory procedures, as well as those which display their functioning and evaluation.

1.3 Existing Literature and the Contribution of this Book

The use of a method of legal interpretation combined with the scope and purposes of this book define its province in relation to other EU legal studies on participation. It is submitted that, given the very ambiguity of the term participation, delimiting the purview of this work in relation to previous studies undertaken on this subject matter is useful to clarify the approach adopted here. The existing studies may be grouped within two main bodies of literature: roughly, one combines a legal-political approach to the topic, while the other adopts essentially a strictly legal standpoint of analysis. It is worth considering these two perspectives in turn.

In the first strand, participation has been analysed from the perspective of its potentials and limitations as a source of legitimacy of EU decision-making, capable of countering, at different levels, the EU's democratic shortcomings. As a result of this approach, these studies stand at the intersection between law and political science, combining also legal and political theory in different degrees and variances. The origins of this strand can be traced back to the first academic debates on the EU democratic deficit which shifted the discussions on this topic from the institutional

[22] In this sense, Schwarze, *op. cit.*, n. 6, p. 9.

realm to the role of 'non-institutional' actors in EU governance; in particular, to those studies which have argued for the introduction of deliberative democratic processes in the EU modes of governance.[23] A different variant of this approach, perhaps more inspired by a republican model of democracy, suggested the creation of notice and comment rules resembling those envisaged in the US Administrative Procedure Act of 1946.[24] Also in this case the underlying idea seems to have been that pluralist participation, filtered by such rules, would foster democracy within the EU. In a similar direction, another perspective of analysis has focused on the question of participation through the lens of citizenship.[25]

This strand of literature was nourished by the focus given to participation in the Commission's White Paper on Governance and by the subsequent inclusion of the principle of participatory democracy in the Constitutional Treaty signed in Rome in 2004, reiterated after Lisbon in the Treaty of the European Union.[26] It also branched in different directions. In particular,

[23] See, for example, Deirdre M. Curtin (1996) '"Civil society" and the European Union: opening spaces for deliberative democracy?', *Collected Courses of the Academy of European Law*, Vol. VII, Book 1, The Hague: Kluwer Law International, pp. 185–280. For an illustration of a more theoretically oriented approach, Joshua Cohen and Charles Sabel (1997) 'Directly-deliberative polyarchy', *European Law Journal*, Vol. 3, n. 4, pp. 313–42.

[24] Paul Craig (1997) 'Democracy and rulemaking within the EC: an empirical and normative assessment', *European Law Journal*, Vol. 3, n. 2, pp. 105–30. Similar concerns with the legitimacy of EU administrative decision-making led to the debates on the possible codification of EU administrative procedures, in which such notice and comment rules could be enshrined (e.g. Carol Harlow (1996) 'Codification of EC administrative procedures? Fitting the foot to the shoe or the shoe to the foot', *European Law Journal*, Vol. 2, n. 1, pp. 3–25; Martin Shapiro (1996) 'Codification of administrative law: the US and the Union', *European Law Journal*, Vol. 2, n. 1, pp. 26–47). These ideas were taken up and debated in the specific context of the comitology procedures: Francesca Bignami (1999) 'The democratic deficit in European Community rulemaking: a call for notice and comment in comitology', *Harvard International Law Journal*, Vol. 40, n. 2, pp. 453–515 (defending the existence of a dubious 'right of civil society participation' as a third generation of participation rights; see Bignami (2005) 'Creating European rights: national values and supranational interests', *Columbia Journal of European Law*, Vol. 11, n. 2, pp. 241–353 at pp. 315–36); Stijn Smismans (2004) *Law, Legitimacy, and European Governance. Functional Participation in Social Regulation*, Oxford: Oxford University Press, pp. 448–56. Ellen Vos (1999) 'EU committees: the evolution of unforeseen institutional actors in European product regulation' in Christian Joerges and Ellen Vos (eds), *EU Committees: Social Regulation, Law and Politics*, Oxford: Hart Publishing, pp. 19–47, at p. 46.

[25] Carol Harlow (1999) 'Citizen access to political power in the European Union', EUI Working Paper RSC No. 99/2; Stijn Smismans (2007) 'New governance—the solution for active citizenship, or the end of citizenship?', *Columbia Journal of European Law*, Vol. 13, n. 3, pp. 595–622.

[26] Article 11 TEU (OJ C 83/13, 30.03.2010).

these constitutional and 'para-constitutional' developments fuelled the studies on the role of civil society participation in democratizing the EU governance structures. This is a burgeoning literature the threads of which are difficult to grasp in this short account. Most academic studies on the White Paper published after its adoption tended to be critical of the Commission's conceptions regarding participation.[27] More recent studies tend to focus on the assessment of the democratic potential of the Commission's participatory practices,[28] as well as on the 'participatory promises' announced as accompanying the so-called new modes of governance.[29] Other works also draw on the legitimacy debate and on ways of going about the EU's claimed 'legitimacy problem', even if they have a different focus from the broader political role of civil society in democratizing governance.[30] On the other hand, the EU constitutional developments motivated some legal scholars to attempt a different legal outlook concerning these matters.[31]

27 A limited sample is provided in Chapter 3, Sub-section 3.3.2, where the analyses of Kenneth Armstrong, Paul Magnette, Olivier De Schutter, and Stijn Smismans are cited.

28 See Beate Kohler-Koch and Barbara Finke (2007) 'The institutional shaping of EU-society relations: a contribution to democracy via participation?', *Journal of Civil Society*, Vol. 3, n. 3, pp. 205–21, and the sector studies included in this special issue; B. Kohler-Koch, D. De Bievre, and W. Maloney (eds) (2008) *Opening EU Governance to Civil Society—Gains and Challenges*, Connex Report Series, no. 5 (<http://www.connex-network.org/series>); Sandra Kröger (2008) 'Nothing but consultation: the place of organised civil society in EU policy-making across policies', European Governance Papers (EUROGOV) no. C-08-03, <http://www.connex-network.org/eurogov/pdf/egp-connex-C-08-03.pdf>.

29 Stijn Smismans (2008) 'New modes of governance and the participatory myth', *West European Politics*, Vol. 31, n. 5, pp. 874–95 (first published as a EUROGOV Working Paper).

30 See, for example, Smismans' monograph on functional participation in social regulation (Stijn Smismans (2004) *Law, Legitimacy, and European Governance*, *cit.*, Chapter 1). Smismans focuses on 'the role of law in structuring interest group participation' always with an eye to assessing whether institutionalized forms of participation might be an additional source of EU legitimacy (*op. cit.*, p. 42).

31 Some analyses included in legal commentaries to the Constitutional Treaty are illustrative of this standpoint (e.g. Eric Meisse (2005) 'La démocratie administrative dans le Traité établissant une Constitution pour l'Europe', in Vlad Constantinesco, Yves Gautier, and Valérie Michel (eds), *Le Traité établissant une Constitution pour l'Europe. Analyses et commentaires*, Strasbourg: Presses Universitaires de Strasbourg, pp. 397–417). From an administrative law perspective, see Carol Harlow (2006) 'Civil society organisations and participatory administration: a challenge to EU administrative law?', in Stijn Smismans (ed.), *Civil Society and Legitimate European Governance*, Cheltenham, Northampton: Edward Elgar, pp. 115–40). Harlow notes that 'as yet there has been no real response from administrative law to the problems of participatory administration and new governance', although, according to her, the measures that the Commission has been experimenting have the potential to cause a transformation of EU administrative law (p. 135).

The second strand of literature has older and deeper roots in EU legal studies. It studies participation rights from the strict perspective of 'hard law', as they have been developed by the Courts and enshrined in EU legislation. With the exception of studies undertaken in certain fields—such as some environmental law studies, which tend to display approaches that come close to the ones described above—these are, in the main, positive-legal analyses of participation rights which essentially examine the norms in force, explicating the Courts' stance on these matters. In this body of literature, two main approaches may be identified. Many studies focus on the procedural rights in force in specific fields of law, chiefly the rights of the defence in competition law, which is generally considered the archetype of the administrative activity of the Commission and a privileged field of analysis of the right to be heard.[32] Others have a broader approach which covers the different fields where the Courts' case law has developed—staff disciplinary procedures, state aid, anti-dumping, customs, and financial assistance through structural funds.[33] In this second group, some focus on re-constructing the main developments of the Courts' case law, with a view to identifying general principles, rules, and tendencies embodied

[32] The archetypal character of competition procedures is expressly mentioned by Maria C. Baruffi (2001) *La tutela dei singoli nei procedimenti amministrativi comunitari*, Milano: Giuffrè, p. 65. In this sense also Damien Chalmers, Christos Hadjiemmanuil, Giorgio Monti, and Adam Tomkins (2006) *European Union Public Law: Texts and Materials*, Cambridge: Cambridge University Press, p. 441. This approach is taken in the following works: Léon Goffin (1980) 'La jurisprudence de la Cour de Justice sur les droits de la défense', *Cahiers de Droit Européen*, pp. 127–44; Valentine Korah (1980) 'The rights of the defence in administrative proceedings under Community Law', *Current Legal Problems*, Vol. 33, pp. 73–97; P.J. Kuyper and T.P.J.N. van Rijn (1982) 'Procedural guarantees and investigatory methods in European law, with special reference to competition', *Yearbook of European Law*, Vol. 2, pp. 1–55; Asteris Pliakos (1987) *Les droits de la defense et le droit communautaire de la concurrence*, Bruxelles: Bruylant; R.H. Lauwaars (1994) 'Rights of the defence in competition cases', in Deirdre Curtin and Ton Heukels (eds), *Institutional Dynamics of European Integration. Essays in Honour of Henry G. Schermers*, Vol. II, Dordrecht: Martinus Nijhoff Publishers, pp. 497–509; Julian M. Joshua (1991) 'The right to be heard in EEC competition procedures', *Fordham International Law Journal*, Vol. 15, n. 1, pp. 16–91; Georges Karydis (1997) 'Le contrôle des concentrations entre entreprises en vertu du règlement 4064/89 et la protection des intérêts légitimes des tiers', *Cahiers de Droit Européen*, n. 1–2, pp. 81–139, in particular pp. 85–93.

[33] See Ole Due (1987) 'Le respect des droits de la défense dans le droit administratif communautaire', *Cahiers de Droit Européen*, Vol. 23, n. 4–5, pp. 383–96 (with an emphasis on competition law and state aid procedures); Schwarze, *op. cit.*, n. 6, pp. 1320–71; Baruffi, *op. cit.*, Chapters II and III (excluding staff cases and customs procedures); Tridimas, *op. cit.*, n. 15, pp. 394–406; Paul Craig (2006), *EU Administrative Law*, Oxford: Oxford University Press, pp. 314–30, 360–73; Massera, *op. cit.*, n. 15, pp. 345–78.

therein and providing an outlook for possible future developments.[34] Some insert the legal analysis in the broader institutional and political context that has been the purview of the first strand of literature mentioned above, thereby yielding a more comprehensive view on the normative choices that built up the current legal regime of participation.[35] Others, drawing on the mutual influence between national administrative laws of the Member States and EU administrative law, analyse the topic of participation rights from the viewpoint of comparative law, inquiring how far they have been enshrined in these different sites as a result of this interplay.[36] Naturally, as is implicit in some of the above considerations, these different approaches are in part determined by the different periods in which they were produced. For example, the adoption of the Charter of Fundamental Rights, given its Article 41 on the right to a good administration, has encouraged analyses of participation which tends to take away from the developments which have occurred in the specific bodies of substantive law, even if the analyses are perforce still very much embedded in the latter.[37]

As stated in the previous section, the book endorses the view that, in relation to this subject matter and in the current state of development of EU administrative law, the strict procedural and substantive legal realm cannot be isolated from the broader political, institutional, and constitutional developments that have shaped the EU as it now stands.[38] The first strand of literature described, which tends to focus on the political significance of

[34] See Meinhard Hilf, Gritta Ciesla, and Eckhard Pache (1991) 'Rights vis-à-vis the administration at the Community level', in Antonio Cassese, Andrew Clapham, and Joseph Weiler (eds), *Human Rights and the European Community: Methods of Protection*, Baden-Baden: Nomos, pp. 455–91; Koen Lenaerts and Jan Vanhamme (1997) 'Procedural rights of private parties in the Community administrative process', *Common Market Law Review*, Vol. 34, n. 3, pp. 531–69. Hanns Peter Nehl (1999) *Principles of Administrative Procedure in EC Law*, Oxford: Hart Publishing, pp. 71–91. This approach underlines Craig's analysis (*op. cit.*, pp. 314–30) and, partially, Tridimas's (*op. cit.*, n. 15, pp. 378–94). See also Azoulai, *op. cit.*, n. 15, particularly Part I and Chapter 2 of Part II, and Barbier de la Serre (2006) 'Procedural justice in the European Community case-law concerning the rights of the defence: essentialist and instrumental trends', *European Public Law*, Vol. 12, n. 2, pp. 225–50.

[35] Azoulai, *op. cit.*, n. 15, Part II, through his analysis of procedures of social regulation (see in particular, Chapter 2 of Part II). Craig, *op. cit.*, *loc. cit.*

[36] Schwarze, *op. cit.*, n. 6, pp. 1320–71.

[37] For example, Alberto Zito (2002) 'Il diritto ad una buona amministrazione nella Carta dei Diritti Fondamentali dell'Unione Europea e nell'ordinamento interno', *Rivista Italiana di Diritto Pubblico Comunitario*, Vol. 12, n. 2–3, pp. 425–44; Denys Simon (2006) 'Le principe de « bonne administration » ou la « bonne gouvernance » concrète', in *Le droit de l'Union Européenne en principes. Liber amicorum en l'honneur de Jean Raux*, Éditions Apogée, pp. 155–76.

[38] In this sense, it shares the approaches of Azoulai and Craig.

participation, is therefore useful to the extent that it reflects and builds on these developments. The perspective of analysis is, nonetheless, a quite different one. Participation rights are not seen in this work as the legal (or political) solution to the problem of the democratic legitimacy of EU decision-making. They are studied, both from an empirical (*de lege lata*) and normative (*de lege ferenda*) perspective, with a view to building up a doctrinal contribution to the problem of the legal protection of natural and legal persons when affected in their rights and interests by the regulatory action of the EU institutions and bodies.

The issue of legitimacy crops up to the extent that the proposals put forward in this work lead to a claim of procedural legitimacy. Procedural legitimacy derives from procedures designed to ensure both the protection of the persons affected, the material justice, and the technical appropriateness of the decisions adopted by the EU administrative bodies.[39] This is in any case a different claim from the one underpinning the studies mentioned above. The extension of participation proposed in this work is not based on an argument drawn from a principle of participatory,[40] deliberative, economic, and social democracy, or administrative democracy.[41] Even if the book's propositions might be relevant from these standpoints, they are grounded in a reconstruction of the concept of participation which draws on values of the rule of law and on a conception of the relationships between decision-makers and recipients of decisions that abstracts from the form of the act adopted. These two aspects constitute the backbone of the proposed extension of participation rights to rule-making procedures.

The approach followed in this work brings it closer to the legal analyses that form the second strand of literature mentioned above, specifically to those that have attempted to provide broader views on participation, straying beyond the realm of sector specificities. The problem that grounds the topic of this book—the legal protection through the decisional procedure of

[39] On the fundamental ambiguity of the term procedural legitimacy, see Azoulai, *op. cit.*, n. 15, pp. 403–4. Material justice is used throughout this work to refer to the substantive quality of a decision that embodies a composition of interests which results from taking due consideration and balancing the different public and private legally protected interests that the decision-maker is bound to take into account.

[40] On the ambiguity of the term in particular in relation to the topic of this study, see João Baptista Machado (1982) *Participação e descentralização. Democratização e neutralidade na Constitutição de 76*, Coimbra: Almedina, pp. 136–9.

[41] These last two forms of democracy ground Azoulai's proposals for an extension of participation rights (*op. cit.*, n. 15, pp. 484–50).

the persons who are confronted with the public regulatory powers of the EU institutions—is addressed in a 'horizontal' way, across sectors, therefore abstracting from, but not ignoring the developments which have occurred in the specific areas of substantive law. As such, the book will not offer a detailed account of the procedural rules which have tended to be the focus of legal studies (for example, competition law), but will refer to these studies in developing a wider approach to participation rights. Rather, it builds up a conceptual framework on the basis of general theories of administrative law that are valid in the EU context, and tests it in sector studies, the choice of which was explained above. Therefore, the analysis of the limits and possibilities of expanding participation rights in EU administrative law takes as a starting point previous works that have embraced this perspective.[42] At the same time, another feature defines the approach adopted: as mentioned, elements drawn from national administrative laws are crucial both to understanding current features of participation rights in EU law and to providing tools for a critical analysis of the *status quo*. Nevertheless, it was considered that there was no need to undertake in this book a comparative study proper, given that existing works provide enough elements for these purposes.

The approach described situates this work as a conceptual analysis undertaken in the field of EU administrative law, understood as the part of EU law that one may consider to be administrative law.[43] As endorsed here, this is not defined by reference to a typology of acts or of functions grounded in the 'traditional' separation of powers.[44] In accordance with the view of administrative law as an instrument to curb the exercise of public power to the rule of law, in particular in its relationships with private persons, the administrative law of the EU is delimited by identifying the scope of the regulatory action of the EU institutions which is capable of impacting directly on the legal sphere of private persons and, thus, creating legal links between these two poles.[45] There are admittedly considerable pitfalls in such an endeavour, but it is nonetheless believed that this might be a valuable path to define in the realm of EU law the area of law dealing with what, at the national level, is usually termed

[42] Namely the works of Paul Craig and Loïc Azoulai mentioned.

[43] Schwarze, *op. cit.*, n. 6, pp. 3–10. This also underlines Craig's *EU Administrative Law*.

[44] Jean-Bernard Auby and Jacqueline Dutheil de la Rochère (2007) 'Introduction générale', in Auby and Dutheil de la Rochère (eds), *Droit administratif européen*, Bruxelles: Bruylant, pp. 1–22, at pp. 4–7.

[45] Cf. the second premise pointed out above, Section 1.1.

implementation or '*exécution de la loi*'. A second aspect of EU administrative law—the mutual interferences between the national and the EU administrative legal orders[46]—is muted in this study, in the sense that it is taken merely as a methodological premise which allows the author to resort to national law for the purposes stated above.

At the same time, the book sustains a paradigm of EU administrative law which propounds the adoption of rules and principles directed at ensuring the material justice and technical appropriateness of administrative decisions while respecting the subjective rights and legally protected interests of private persons, in the segment of EU administrative law which relates to the exercise of regulatory power by the EU institutions and bodies. This is consonant with the developments which have occurred in European law and which have enhanced the position of the individual in the European legal system.[47]

One final word is due, before presenting the structure of the book. The author does not ignore the political connotations of the topic. Participation—as a fact and as a topic of an academic study—is hardly ever ideologically neutral.[48] However, this aspect is not pursued in the analysis. The choice of 'ignoring' this dimension of participation follows from the aims of this work. In particular in the framework of EU legal-political studies, and given the more recent debates on the role of participation in the EU polity,[49] this choice is deemed to be important, in order to bring to light the legal values in which participation is grounded and to dwell upon the potentialities and limits of participation as a legal concept. This is the key to the book's contribution to the theory of EU administrative law.

1.4 Structure

The conceptual framework on which the book is based is presented in Chapter 2. This characterizes the concept of participation adopted in the book. A legal-technical approach is proposed, since this work addresses mostly the legal dimensions of participation, even if these are analysed in

[46] Schwarze, *op. cit.*, n. 6, pp. 3–10; Auby and Dutheil de la Rochère, *op. cit.*, n. 44, pp. 3–4 and 6–7.

[47] See Section 1.1 above.

[48] Mario Nigro (1980) 'Il nodo della partecipazione', *Rivista trimestrale di diritto e procedura civile*, Vol. 34, pp. 225–36, at p. 229.

[49] See Chapter 3.

the context of its political significance and developments. The concept of participation adopted allows us to single out a rights-based approach to participation from other forms of participation. It is built by reference to the functions of participation and to the persons who are entitled to access the procedure. Furthermore, an overview of the basic rules and principles of some national legal orders provides a solid basis to understand the reasons and limits of the distinction between rule-making and individual determinations, which delimits the scope of participation rights both in national and in EU law. The chapter assesses the limits of this approach and this opens the way to proposing the concept of legal administrative relationship as the framework for the recognition and interpretation of participation rights. Finally, participation rights are characterized as relative rights, given that, in justified circumstances, incompatible requirements of decision-making may prevail; in any case, this contingency needs to be framed within specific limits, an aspect which is also addressed in this chapter.

As mentioned above, the legal analysis undertaken in this book is embedded in the political and institutional contexts of European integration. Thus, Chapter 3 seeks to understand the development and meaning of participatory mechanisms in the EU, thereby providing a broader view on the role of participation in the EU legal and political system. Based on an historical-institutional analysis, this chapter highlights the origins of interest representation in the European integration process, covering both the European Coal and Steel Community (ECSC) and the European Community (EC). Furthermore, it describes the forms of participation that permeate the EU institutional set-up and in each case draws attention to the underlying rationales of participation. Chapter 3 reveals, in particular, the continuity between the long-standing practices of interest representation and the participation practices that have been developed under the so-called new modes of governance. Moreover, it characterizes interest representation as a constitutive feature of the EU institutional set-up, revealing its constitutional significance. In addition, the various forms of participation mentioned in Chapter 2, which are different from the rights-based participation endorsed in this book, are illustrated here, namely consultation, forms of involvement of private persons that lead to power-sharing, and organic participation. The analysis of their meaning shows the contrast between these forms and the rights-based participation defended in this work.

Chapters 4 and 5 are the core of the book. Together, they reveal the strengths and weaknesses of the Courts' case law in relation to the scope of protection afforded to natural and legal persons through participation rights in decisional procedures that might have an adverse effect on their legal sphere. Both chapters approach participation from a rights-based perspective and present how participation is and may be legally conceived in EU law. In the main, Chapter 4 examines and points out the limits of the Courts' stance in relation to procedures leading up to the adoption of individualized decisions. This study is introduced by a brief overview of how the procedural protection of the individual has been devised in EU law. This draws on the relation between procedural protection and judicial review and characterizes the general approach of the EU legislator in this regard. This overview highlights the importance of the Courts' role in the development of participation rights, and, at the same time, defines the context that frames the Courts' jurisprudence. The analysis of the Courts' case law on the right to be heard constitutes then the main part of the chapter. It shows, in particular, how the right to be heard has been conceived and approached by the Courts and it demonstrates how their stance is predetermined by the conception of the procedure as entailing a bilateral relationship between the deciding body and the addressee of the decision or, more generally, the persons thereby affected.

Chapter 5 complements Chapter 4, insofar as it examines the Courts' approach to participation in rule-making procedures. It is argued that the different positions of the Court on the right to be heard in individual procedures, on the one hand, and rule-making procedures, on the other, are grounded in the same premise, in particular on the preconception regarding the structure of the procedure that is identified and characterized in Chapter 4. Although intertwined with other factors, this was determinant in the *Atlanta* judgment, the Courts' leading ruling on participation rights in rule-making procedures. In this chapter, the rule according to which participation rights cannot be recognized in rule-making procedures is deconstructed. The reasons why the Courts excluded general acts from the realm of participation rights are scrutinized and criticized, including both the arguments invoked in *Atlanta*, which were limited to acts adopted on the basis of a Treaty article, and the extension of this exclusion operated by subsequent judgments. In fact, the same arguments were then used to cover other acts of a general nature, but no further reasons were given to support this extension. After having dissected the Courts' stance with regard to participation rights, this chapter assesses how the concept of participation rights proposed in Chapter 2 may contribute to surmount the shortcomings of the Courts' approach with regard to the legal protection of the individual confronted with the regulatory intervention of the European Union. Finally, the last part of the chapter considers how the modifications proposed could impact on the scope of other procedural guarantees that are ancillary to the right to be heard, namely the right to access information, the duty to state reasons, the duty of careful and impartial examination, and language rights.

The sector studies undertaken in Chapters 6 to 8 illustrate the limitations of the current *status quo*. In addition, they explain which type of situations should give rise to the recognition of participation rights, according to the proposed construction, and to whom these should be granted. The problems that could result from the extended scope of participation rights that is defended in the book are also considered.

Chapter 6 addresses the role of consultation procedures in the context of the Lamfalussy process, contrasting it with the rights-based approach to participation that underpins the book. Therefore, in a way, it builds a bridge between the political and the legal strands of participation. The Lamfalussy process is of particular interest in this work because participation—in the form of consultation procedures—has a prominent role in this regulatory structure. The study undertaken in this chapter has a threefold purpose. First, admitting that some of the reasons that ground consultation are also present in other sectors of EU policy-making, this chapter contributes to clarifying the reasons why participation has become one of the principles of EU governance. At the same time, the specificities of consultation in the field of financial services are highlighted, as well as the features that distinguish them from the rules and standards of consultation defined in the Commission White Paper and in its Communication 'Towards a reinforced culture of consultation'. This study, therefore, relates to and concretizes some of the themes developed in Chapter 3. Secondly, it clarifies the distinction between, on the one hand, the rights-based participation put forward in the book and, on the other, consultation procedures as they have been designed and conceived in the context of EU governance and developed especially by the Commission's governance initiatives. The analysis of rule-making following the Lamfalussy process illustrates the differences but also the points of contact between consultation and rights-based participation. This chapter shows how the latter has been quite a distant concern in the setting up of the consultative procedures, specifically, in the area of financial services, and, in general, of the consultation practices that pervade European governance. Thirdly, one specific decisional procedure covered by the Lamfalussy process—the one ruling the adoption of accepted market practices—is analysed. This illustrates one of the aspects of rights-based participation presented in Chapter 2: the contingency of participation in the face of general conditions and functions of decision-making. In this respect, Chapter 6 addresses the problems ensuing from the recognition of participation rights in rule-making procedures and elaborates on the solutions to circumvent these problems that are proposed in Chapter 2.

Chapter 7 analyses selected legal regimes in the sector of food law. These have in common the fact that they frame the adoption of decisions that impact directly on the legal sphere of private persons. The procedures analysed in this chapter also illustrate how the growing decisional powers of the Commission in these matters contrast with scant concern for ensuring procedural guarantees to persons affected by its decisions. This chapter dwells particularly upon two threads of the book. First, the distinction between general and individual acts should not ground the scope of participation rights. In other words, the form of the act adopted should not be the criterion to determine in absolute terms when they are recognized or not. This is demonstrated by characterizing a specific type of act: the market authorizations of foodstuffs. Depending on the legislative technique chosen in each case, these may be adopted either through an individual decision or a general act, both having similar regulatory effects. Secondly, Chapter 7 illustrates the type of regulatory intervention that originates legal administrative relationships and analyses the consequences that should ensue in terms of participation rights. In addition, it is argued that two different layers of participation rights may be identified in the procedures leading to the adoption of market authorizations. This difference will be further examined and clarified in Chapter 8, namely by highlighting the different procedural status attendant on the exercise of participation rights.

Chapter 8 examines the only provision of the Treaty that makes the decisional powers of the Commission dependant on a participatory procedure (Article 108(2) TFEU). The study of the Courts' case law regarding the rationales of the procedural intervention of persons concerned, as well as the very concept of persons concerned for the purposes of this norm will test four essential aspects of the construction of participation rights presented: the functions of participation as inseparably encompassing a dignitarian and an instrumental rationale (even though they may have different weight in different circumstances);[50] the distinction between two categories

[50] The term 'dignitarian' is used in this book to refer to the fundamental dignity of the person when subject to an administrative intervention.

of interested persons which grounds different procedural status; the claim that the scope of those entitled to participate needs to pay heed to the rationales of participation and is dependent on the substantive link of the person concerned with the underlying material situation; and the inconsistencies of the general/individual divide to ground participation rights, illustrated by the fact that state aid decisions may impinge upon general acts adopted by Member States. This sector study demonstrates that, despite the Courts' hesitations and some contradictions, there are enough indications in the jurisprudence to ground the distinction between the two layers of participation rights that are defended in this work: those of holders of subjective rights and those of holders of legally protected interests. Furthermore, the analysis of the Courts' case law on these matters illustrates how the rules on standing have influenced the way participation rights have been conceived in EU law. Finally, this chapter also tests whether the provision of Article 108(2) TFEU should be extended by analogy to rule-making procedures that have become an acquired competence of the Commission. This examination is made on the basis of the following assumption: one can deduce from the Treaty that, in the field of state aid, the powers expressly assigned to the Commission that may impact on private persons' legal spheres were intended to be framed by a participatory procedure. This assumption is backed up by an overview of the preparatory works of the Treaty in this regard.

Chapter 2

Unravelling Participation: A Rights-based Approach

This chapter elucidates the defining elements of the rights-based concept of participation and elaborates the theoretical framework that grounds the critical analysis of the current scope of participation rights in EU law as well as the normative proposals defended in this book.

Participation is far from being an unequivocal concept. As conceived in this book, it refers to the procedural intervention of natural and legal persons whose substantive rights and interests are potentially affected by EU regulatory measures, irrespective of the form in which the latter are adopted. The functions and the underlying values of participation as well as the definition of the persons whose intervention is legally relevant are the basic elements of the rights-based concept of participation that grounds the normative approach of this book. They are explained in Sections 2.2 and 2.3, respectively. Before embarking on this analysis, Section 2.1 endeavours to single out the concept of participation adopted from other senses and connotations of the term, in order to better delimit what, in this work, is meant by 'rights-based participation'.

As defended here, participation rights arise in the legal sphere of those implicated in the legal relationships that emerge from the adoption of regulatory measures. They are the reflection of the substantive rights and interests that are affected by public intervention. This allows us to identify the types of measures the adoption of which gives rise to participation rights: its content needs to be such that it effectively shapes the rights and duties of the persons it affects. In other words, the concreteness of the act needs to be such that, after its adoption, the possibility of it affecting those persons who fall within its realm is effective and not merely potential. From this perspective, it is not the distinction between individual and general acts—one of the perennial themes ancillary to a legal approach to participation—which should guide the granting or otherwise of participation rights (Section 2.4). An alternative framework for the recognition and understanding of participation rights, more adequate to a rights-based approach, is built on the basis of the concept of a legal administrative relationship (Section 2.5). Finally, the role of participation is balanced against factors that are often pointed out as opposing or restricting the remit of participation and that may militate against extending participation rights to rule-making procedures. The circumstances under which participation rights might need to be limited or conditioned are explained in Section 2.6.

Both the concept of participation and the theoretical approach explained in this chapter are constructed by resorting extensively to conceptions of general administrative law developed in national administrative legal systems. These have influenced the fundamental traits of the current EU legal regime of participation rights, in particular the Courts' case law, albeit in an unsystematic, inconsistent, and patchy way. As such, some of the conceptions presented in this chapter are echoed in the reconstruction of current EU law undertaken at a later stage in this book (in particular in Chapter 4). In this chapter, the loose threads of a rights-based approach to participation present and absent from EU law are woven together in order to build the conceptual framework of the book. This will serve as the normative background against which current EU law will be critically assessed and freed from its current limits.

2.1 Participation: What's in a Word?

Participation, in a simple and general form, can be presented as the possibility of taking part in decision-making processes.[1] In this broad sense, it comprises the participation of public entities in decision-making processes that are attributed to the competence of a different entity or administration (inter-administrative participation), as well as the involvement of the public or of interest holders in the exercise of public functions. Inter-administrative

[1] Mario Chiti (1977), *Partecipazione popolare e pubblica amministrazione*, Pisa: Pacini Editore, pp. 34–5. For various forms of participation, other than those mentioned in the text, underlining their diversity and different embeddings, Franco Levi (1977), 'Partecipazione e organizzazione', *Rivista Trimestrale di Diritto Pubblico*, Vol. 27, n. 4, pp. 1625–47, at 1625–30 and 1634–5.

participation is particularly frequent in composite, multilayered administrative systems and stems from the need to ensure administrative collaboration among different services and different levels of administration, or, more strictly, to respect the allocation of competences among them when they are implicated in any given decision. When referring to the involvement of natural and legal persons in the exercise of public functions, participation encompasses different forms. These are reflected in the undefined concept of participatory democracy now enshrined in the Treaty on European Union (TEU), following the provision first envisaged in the Constitutional Treaty.[2] Participation in decision-making processes can take place in a variety of ways: consultations open to whoever wishes to have a say in the matter at issue; more selective forms of involvement, namely 'dialogue with representative associations and civil society'; citizens' legislative initiatives, by which citizens urge the adoption of a legislative act. All these ways of accessing the procedure imply the involvement of persons situated outside the formal, public decision-making structures typical of a representative system and have further in common the fact that the 'external input' is ultimately filtered by the latter, albeit in different forms and to different degrees. Whenever participation in this broad sense is mentioned in the book, it will be termed 'participation at large', in the sense that it does not refer specifically to any of the precise forms that it may encompass. This broader, somewhat vague concept is distinct from the concept adopted in the book, characterized by the traits briefly enunciated in the introduction to this chapter.

The term participation acquires a more precise sense when referred to decisional processes where persons 'external' to the institutional setup, different from those entrusted with decision-making powers, are formally associated therewith *by reason of specific interests* which those persons embody and which are considered legally relevant for the subject matter being decided. This more restricted meaning is the basis of the concept of participation defended here. Forms of participation in which citizens or groups of citizens initiate a decision-making process (in a similar way to the citizens' legislative initiative) are excluded from this notion of participation,

[2] Article 11 of the Treaty on European Union (TEU), as envisaged in the Treaty of Lisbon (consolidated version, OJ C 83/13, 30.03.2010). Cf. Article I-47 of the Treaty establishing a Constitution for Europe (OJ C 310/1, 16.12.2004). Both versions endorse participatory democracy as a complement to representative democracy (cf. Article 10 TEU and Article I-46 (1) of the Constitutional Treaty).

since the latter presupposes that they are called into an already initiated decision-making process.[3] Moreover, non-legally mediated forms of participation also remain outside: the association with the decisional process takes place during one of its formalized stages and gives rise to procedural rights. More importantly, access requires a certain connection to the subject matter at issue, expressed by the notion of 'legally relevant interest'. This specification excludes from the concept of participation the intervention of experts whose legal position is not touched by the subject matter under appreciation in the procedure: they introduce the specific technical or scientific knowledge needed to ground the content of the act adopted, in a supposedly 'neutral' position in relation to the matter being decided.[4] Furthermore, access is thus restricted, since the reference entity of this concept of participation is not the citizen (the public or civil society without distinction), but the person situated in a social group or the person as holder of a specific, legally protected interest that is touched by the decisional process.[5] In this sense, participation is similar to interest representation, defined as a system which ensures that specific interests are voiced in decisional processes by groups which represent them, politically or legally. To the extent that interest representation may encompass some of the traits of a rights-based participation, these two modalities of participation may, in certain cases, overlap. Nevertheless, interest representation disposes of, or at least is not consistent with, a substantive affecting of subjective rights and legally protected interests of the participants, which is one of the defining characteristics of rights-based participation.

Participation and consultation are often taken to be synonyms. In fact, seeking a dividing line between these two terms often means treading on slippery ground.[6] Consultation is a form of 'participation at large', if it is

[3] Sabino Cassese (1970) 'Il privato e il procedimento amministrativo', in *Archivio Giuridico Filippo Serafini*, pp. 25–147, at p. 27.

[4] Where the legal position of holders of specific knowledge brought into the procedure is particularly affected by its final outcome, 'potential experts' do not intervene as such but as interest holders. On this, see the discussion of Case T-326/99, *Nancy Fern Olivieri v Commission and the European Agency for the Evaluation of Medicines (EMEA)* [2003] ECR II-6053, below in Chapter 7, Section 7.3.

[5] Distinguishing two systems of representation (representative democracy and interest representation) by reference to the citizen and to 'l'homme situé', Jean Boulouis (1986) 'Représentation et participation dans la vie politique et administrative', in *La participation directe du citoyen à la vie politique et administrative. Travaux des XXI*[es] *Journées d'études juridiques Jean Dabin sous la direction de Francis Delpérée*, Bruxelles: Bruylant, pp. 49–67, at pp. 50–1.

[6] The characterization of consultation that follows is based on how this has been perceived in EU law and governance. The points sketched here are resumed below in Chapter 6, Section 6.5.

defined as the intervention in a decisional procedure of natural and legal persons who are deprived of formal decisional power and are therefore external to the public structure of decision-making. It involves the creation of public discussion fora in which either the public in general or particularly interested persons are asked to express their views on a given regulatory proposal. It is different from rights-based participation since the procedural intervention is not necessarily grounded in the substantive rights and interests of the participants (although consultation may be restricted to the so-called stakeholders). Moreover, these are not granted procedural rights that, following their exercise, would require the decision-maker to adopt a specific conduct subject to judicial control (although, in some instances where consultation is mandatorily determined, the set of duties that the latter is bound to comply with, by legal imposition, coincide with those usually associated with a rights-based participation).[7] In EU law, it is quite common for the legislator to define that certain decisional procedures need to be subject to public consultation or to consultation of specific groups. However, frequently, these rules have a thin prescriptive content: they simply require that consultation take place. The requirements to render it effective are adopted and observed by the decision-maker on a voluntary basis.[8] They tend to accommodate policy concerns (e.g. responsiveness). Therefore, the choices of who, when, and how to consult are often left to the discretion of the decision-maker.

In other instances of 'participation at large', participants associated with the decision-making process acquire decision-making powers, which they either share with the public body or exercise autonomously under predefined conditions. In these situations, participation in decision-making acquires specific forms: co-regulation, delegated private regulation, publicly recognized self-regulation.[9] The rule-making power provided to social

[7] In EU law, this is especially the case of the rules regarding public participation in respect of the drawing up of certain plans and programmes relating to the environment (Article 2(2) of the Directive No. 2003/35/EC of the European Parliament and of the Council of 26 May 2003, OJ L 156/17, 25.6.2003).

[8] This is, for example, the case of consultation procedures for the authorization of genetically modified food and feed (Articles 6(7) and 18(7) of Regulation No. 1829/2003, of the European Parliament and of the Council, of 22 of September 2003, on genetically modified food and feed, OJ L 268/1, 18.10.2003, as amended). On this see, Chapter 7, Sub-section 7.2.3.

[9] These concepts represent various types of combination of public and private regulation, which are distinct from a rights-based concept of participation. See, further, Fabrizio Cafaggi (2006) 'Rethinking private regulation in the European regulatory space', in Fabrizio Cafaggi (ed.), *Reframing Self-regulation in European Private Law*, The Netherlands: Kluwer Law International, pp. 3–75, at pp. 21–35.

partners under Articles 154(4) and 155 TFEU is one example of power sharing between EU institutions and entities representative of the interests concerned.[10] These forms of participation are distinct from rights-based participation, to the extent that they are not necessarily the reflection of the substantive rights and interests affected by the act adopted. Moreover, unlike rights-based participation, they endow the participants with decision-making power. In a rights-based participation, participants are informed, they are heard, their views might be taken into consideration, they may require explanations, but the final act adopted is not required to reflect the interests voiced in the procedure. It should be noted that the rationales of a rights-based participation apply when the procedure is conducted by a private regulator in fact exercising public authority (e.g. in cases of delegation) and its outcome is legally binding on persons who do not share decision-making power. Arguably, in these cases, impartiality as well as full representation and consideration of interests affected that are not encompassed by the cooperative arrangements are of even more importance to countervail privileges of stronger groups.[11]

Another relevant distinction contributes to defining the meaning of participation for the purposes of this book: the difference between organic participation and procedural participation. The first, of corporatist origin, takes place when the persons affected by the decision-making processes are included in the institutional structures with a consultative role (e.g. advisory bodies) or as interest representatives in decisional bodies.[12] Procedural participation implies that participants remain outside institutional structures. The universe of participants is not *a priori* delimited. Participants are defined in relation to the subject matter of the specific decision-making procedure in which they intervene.[13] Organic participation is present at the

[10] See, in this regard, Case T-135/96, *Union européenne de l'artisanat et des petites et moyennes entreprises (UEAPME) v Council* [1998] ECR II-2335. In this judgment, the Court denied the existence of an individual right to enter the negotiations leading to the adoption of collective agreements that have the rank of legislative acts (paragraphs 75 to 80).

[11] According to Schmidt-Assmann, one of the functions of administrative law is to counter the action of stronger groups in the face of phenomena of 'collaborative administration' (Eberhard Schmidt-Assmann (2003) *La teoría general del derecho amministrativo como sistema*, Madrid: Marcial Pons, pp. 23–5, see also pp. 36–40).

[12] It is also referred to as institutionalized participation (e.g. Franco Levi, *op. cit.*, n. 1, p. 1642). The term organic is preferred here, since procedural participation, being formalized by specific decisional structures, is also institutionalized.

[13] In similar terms, Sabino Cassese (1986) 'Les conditions de participation du citoyen à la vie administrative', in *La participation directe du citoyen à la vie politique et administrative. Travaux des XXIes Journées d'études juridiques Jean Dabin, cit.*, n. 5, pp. 273–82, at p. 277.

EU level. Think of the Economic and Social Committee (with origins in analogous national consultative bodies), whose core advisory activity pertains to primary legislation; of participatory bodies created within EU agencies, as well as of consultative committees composed of interests' representatives.[14] Compared to organic participation, procedural participation at the administrative level has clear advantages. The procedure is the ideal site for the composition of interests and thus for the acquisition of interests external to institutionalized decisional structures. Participation ensures the 'widest openness' of the latter while guaranteeing their stability and ensuring the 'distinction of roles which is essential both to the certainty and impartiality of the organization and to the [richness] of participation'.[15] Arguably, procedural participation is more appropriate to fulfil both the subjective and the objective functions of participation, respectively, the procedural protection of the legal sphere of the persons affected by a regulatory measure, and the contribution to the achievement of an accurate decision that reflects an impartial representation of the underlying factual situation and a due consideration and balancing of the interests involved.

Therefore, the rights-based concept of participation propounded in the book is a form of procedural participation in which access to the procedure is limited to holders of substantive rights and interests who are affected by the respective outcome. It gives rise to a set of procedural rights (notice, access to information, reason-giving) directed at ensuring the fulfilment of the subjective and objective functions of participation. While participation may engender forms of collaboration between the decision-maker and the decision's recipients, the final decision is the sole responsibility of the body legally entrusted with the decision-making competence. In other words, the fact of participation does not endow interveners with formal decisional powers.[16]

[14] These and other forms of organic participation are analysed in Chapter 3.

[15] Mario Nigro (1980) 'Il nodo della partecipazione', *Rivista Trimestrale di Diritto e Procedura Civile*, Vol. 34, pp. 225–36, at p. 231 (author's translation). In pursuance of the administrative function, the distance and impartiality of the decision-maker to the interests at stake is an essential guarantee against reducing participation to an 'instrument of preservation' of private interests contrary to the demands of public interest (Jean Rivero, 'Introduction' in *La participation directe du citoyen à la vie politique et administrative. Travaux des XXIes Journées d'études juridiques Jean Dabin*, *cit.*, n. 5, pp. 7–19, at p. 17.

[16] In this sense, Vasco Pereira da Silva (1996) *Em busca do acto administrativo perdido*, Coimbra: Almedina, pp. 403–4. The author underlines that 'responsibility [of the administration] for the decisions taken must be the limit to participation in the procedure' (*loc. cit.*).

2.2 Collaboration, Defence, and the Rule of Law

On the basis of the functions of participation—accurate exercise of decisional discretion and procedural protection of the substantive rights and legally protected interests affected by authoritative acts—legal scholars tend to separate what they consider to be two distinct forms of participation.[17]

On the one hand, the intervention in the procedure of parties external to the institutionalized decisional structure is directed at facilitating the fulfilment of the decisional function. Participation assumes a function of collaboration with the decision-maker, as the information brought into the administrative procedure facilitates and enriches the task of pondering the factual situation under appraisal, and is thus relevant for the accuracy of the final choices and for the concretization of the public interest. The participant in the procedure voices their own interests. These, however, are only legally relevant insofar as they are manifestations of the public interests that are linked to the subject matter of the procedure and, as such, need to be considered by the decision-maker.[18] The applicable rules determine in each instance these sets of interests. Participation is justified both by the principle of care, according to which the decision-maker has the duty to carefully and impartially examine and balance all the relevant circumstances of the factual situation before them, and by the contribution of the participants to the effectiveness of decisional processes. 'Effectiveness' sums up different advantages usually associated with the collaboration between decision-makers and recipients of decisions ensuing from participation: responsiveness, compliance, and implementation are considered to be enhanced or facilitated by participation.

[17] See, for example, Denis J. Galligan (1996) *Due Process and Fair Procedures: A Study of Administrative Procedures*, Oxford: Clarendon Press, p. 130; Schmidt-Assmann, *op. cit.*, n. 11, p. 118; Sabino Cassese (2007) 'La partecipazione dei privati alle decisioni pubbliche. Saggio di diritto comparato', *Rivista Trimestrale di Diritto Pubblico*, Vol. 57, n. 1, pp. 13–41, at pp. 13–15 (the same distinction appears in Cassese (1970) 'Il privato . . .', *cit.*, n. 3, pp. 31–4 and Cassese (1986) 'Les conditions . . .', *cit.*, n. 13, p. 279). In a slightly different approach, Eduardo García de Enterría (1989) 'Principios y modalidades de la participation ciudadana en la vida administrativa', in Rafael Gómez-Ferrer Morant (ed.), *Libro homenaje al Profesor José Luís Villar Palasí*, Madrid: Civitas, pp. 437–52, at p. 441–3.

[18] Fabrizio Fracchia (1996) 'Manifestazioni di interesse del privato e procedimento amministrativo', *Diritto Amministrativo*, Vol. 4, n. 1, pp. 14–50, at p. 48; Enzo Cardi (1995) 'Procedimento amministrativo', *Enciclopedia Giuridica*, Roma: Treccani, Vol. XXIV, pp. 1–8, at p. 6.

On the other hand, the intervention of persons concerned by the procedure is grounded in the 'moral imperative' of allowing them to defend their subjective rights and interests before the adoption of a decision with potential negative impact in their regard. Participation guarantees that the persons who are affected by a given decision are not 'treated purely as an object of the administration's action'.[19] Allowing them to intervene in the procedural decision and to put across their views is essential in order to respect their human dignity, in particular in cases where an assessment of the person's conduct is the basis of the decision taken in their regard. In this sense, participation has a defence function: it affords anticipated procedural protection to affected persons. Thus, it is also seen as a complement to judicial review, since the participant is able to contradict the possible future decision, invoking errors, flaws, or mistakes which could ultimately lead to the illegality of the final act.[20] Participation is grounded in a principle of justice and it is a formality required by the rule of law, being typical of individual procedures from which sanctions or penalties may emerge or in which a potentially advantageous position is denied to an applicant.

It is generally assumed that this distinction grounds two separate realities. In the first case, participants are said to intervene in a social function as active members of the community or of specific communities to which they belong, defending collective interests that may coincide with public interests (*uti cives*). Participation is, thus, 'often associated with a sense of citizenship'.[21] In the second case, participants intervene to defend their own private rights and interests as a direct result of the interference of public powers in their legal sphere (*uti singuli*). In this sense, participation arises in the context of a bilateral relationship established by force of the procedure between legal or natural persons, on the one hand, and the decision-maker, on the other, and is grounded in the degree to which the substantive rights and legal interests of the former are affected.[22]

[19] Meinhard Hilf, Gritta Ciesla, and Eckhard Pache (1991) 'Rights vis-à-vis the administration at the Community level', in Antonio Cassese, Andrew Clapham, and Joseph Weiler (eds), *Human Rights and the European Community: Methods of Protection*, Baden-Baden: Nomos, pp. 455–91, at p. 459.

[20] Refering to Italian administrative law, but of general relevance, Massimo Occhiena (2006) 'Partecipazione al procedimento amministrativo', in Sabino Cassese (ed.), *Dizionario di Diritto Pubblico*, Vol. V, Milano: Giuffrè, pp. 4128–38, at p. 4134.

[21] Galligan, *op. cit.*, n. 17, p. 128.

[22] On this distinction, David Duarte (1996) *Procedimentalização, participação e fundamentação: para uma concretização do princípio da imparcialidade administrativa como parâmetro decisório*, Coimbra: Almedina, pp. 135–6.

According to one position, only the former may be considered participation, since the latter is merely a form of defence of the individual before the exercise of public power and cannot be pinned down to a principle of participatory democracy.[23] Two arguments contradict this view. First, participation need not be grounded in the principle of participatory democracy, at least not exclusively. Admittedly, enhanced legitimacy may derive from a participated procedure as a result of the plural configuration of the content of the act, but this does not necessarily mean that its democratic quality is enhanced.[24] Indeed, participation is often perceived as a complementary source of democracy given the 'approximation of the citizen to decision-making', but it is not always clear how this contributes to the democratic nature of decision-making. While the political relevance of the participatory phenomenon rests largely on these assumptions, the ultimate legal reason for the procedural intervention resides elsewhere: in the respect for the autonomy of the participant, of their rights and legally protected interests, and, therefore, in a particular relation of the participant with the material situation which motivated the procedure.[25] Beneath political justifications, a rights-based participation in the sense defended in this work is grounded in basic requirements of the rule of law, which, as will be seen below, cannot be reduced to a perspective of defence.

Secondly, the clear-cut distinction between the two categories mentioned does not withstand closer scrutiny. To begin with, participation as collaboration also entails the protection of the interests voiced in the procedure and, when intervening to defend their interests, the participant also collaborates in the decision-making process by providing information

[23] García de Enterría, *op. cit.*, n. 17, p. 442. Implicit also in Cassese (1986), 'Les conditions . . .', *cit.*, n. 17, p. 279. In Cassese's latest writing, however, this restrictive notion of participation was replaced by a tripartite classification of participation, either grounded in a principle of justice (participation as defence), on a principle of effectiveness (participation as collaboration), or on a principle of democracy (where 'civil society is allowed to express its own opinion in a process of collective decision-making')—Cassese (2007) 'La partecipazione . . .', *cit.*, n. 17, p. 14. This tripartite classification, established by other authors, refers to a concept of participation broader than rights-based participation, since it embraces the intervention of the 'public', 'the civil society', or 'the citizens' irrespective of any further qualification that is capable of making the intervention in the procedure legally meaningful.

[24] Schmidt-Assmann, *op. cit.*, n. 11, p. 121.

[25] This factor is also present in the concept of participation alluded by García de Enterría, to the extent that the author justifies it on the basis of an 'intention of including in the administrative decisions or actions the references to the general interest that the citizens *in direct relation to it* may uphold' (*op. cit.*, n. 17, p. 442, author's translation, emphasis added).

and alternative interpretations of the facts under assessment.[26] Thus, the difference between the two types is not qualitative, but rather a matter of degree, measured in each case by the predominance of one function over the other. In the end, this depends on the relevance of the personal factor in the underlying material situation. In addition, the enhancement of procedural rules that are likely to lead to adequate outcomes is also a requirement of the rule of law insofar as material justice is a value to be upheld beyond the formal correctness of the decision-making procedure.[27] As underlined by Nigro, the procedural protection and the collaboration of interested persons in the definition of the composition of interests that justifies the final decision are 'two aspects of the same phenomenon, a demand of justice'.[28] This applies also to the participation of collective entities: their intervention in the procedure ensures respect for their autonomy as well as for the interests they were created to pursue, thereby also contributing to the achievement of materially just decisions.[29] Therefore, this distinction distorts and overly simplifies the conceptual and effective reality of participation. Nevertheless, it may be useful for analytical purposes, since it underlines the diversity of situations covered by procedural participation.[30] As highlighted by Cassese, the 'non-unity' of the theme of participation derives from the diversity of the position of the participant in relation to the subject matter of the procedure, which is 'sometimes external or marginal to the procedure and to the function which the latter performs, sometimes, on the contrary, central and dominant'.[31] In any case, beyond this diversity, it is the same legal principle—

[26] This seems to be corroborated by the observations of Riccardo Villata (1992) 'Riflessioni in tema di partecipazione la procedimento e legittimazione processuale', *Diritto Processuale Amministrativo*, Vol. 9, pp. 171–205, at pp. 181–2; Massimo Occhiena (2002) *Situazioni giuridiche soggettive e procedimento amministrativo*, Milano: Giuffrè, pp. 377–8; Stefano Battini, Bernardo G. Mattarella, and Aldo Sandulli (2007) 'Il procedimento' in Giulio Napolitano (ed.), *Diritto Amministrativo Comparato*, pp. 107–74, at p. 131, although the authors maintain the duality of participation.

[27] On both arguments, Duarte, *op. cit.*, n. 22, pp. 137–9, and, further, p. 166. In a similar sense, defending participation as serving the purpose of the principle of justice, João Baptista Machado (1982) *Participação e descentralização. Democratização e neutralidade na Constituição de 76*, Coimbra: Almedina, pp. 134 and 136. For the notion of material justice endorsed in this book see n. 36 of Chapter 1.

[28] Mario Nigro (1980) 'Procedimento amministrativo e tutela giurisdizionale contro la pubblica amministrazione (il problema di una legge generale sul procedimento amministrativo)', *Rivista di Diritto Processuale*, Vol. 35, pp. 252–78, at p. 262.

[29] Baptista Machado, *op. cit.*, n. 27, pp. 137–8.

[30] It is used as such in Chapter 3.

[31] Cassese, 'Il privato ...', *cit.*, n. 3, p. 31 (author's translation).

the rule of law—and the values thereby warranted that ground a rights-based participation.

It follows from these considerations that procedural participation encompasses both functions. It structures the exercise of the decisional function along the procedural rules that, deriving from participation, ensure the plural configuration of the content of the act. These are deemed to favour the achievement of accurate and adequate results. At the same time, it safeguards—and anticipates in relation to eventual judicial review—the procedural protection of the private and public interests that may be affected by the outcome of the procedure. It is noteworthy that the element of procedural protection that derives from participation is especially relevant in legal systems where the mechanisms of judicial review are insufficient, especially given restrictive access rules. Participation has, in this respect, a non-negligible compensatory function.[32]

On the whole, even if participation is, in a sense, always political,[33] it is possible to identify one specific legal meaning grounded in the respect and pursuance of distinct legal values—the rule of law inseparable from a goal of material justice—from other participatory phenomena with stronger a political connotation. In this sense, as mentioned above, the enhanced procedural legitimacy of participated decision-making may be an effect, important nevertheless, of opening the procedure to the persons affected by it, but not the ultimate legal reason to create participatory procedures.

2.3 Rights' Holders

The rights-based concept of participation adopted in this book requires that access to the procedure is restricted to holders of subjective rights and legally protected interests who have some connection to the subject matter under appreciation. In other words, participants should be holders of rights and interests that are eventually touched by the outcome of the procedure and are protected by the legal system. Arguably, this is the only way of making the fact of participation legally relevant, i.e. amenable to procedural

[32] Duarte, *op. cit.*, n. 22, pp. 166–7. Nigro, 'Il nodo…', *cit.*, n. 15, p. 262. This point is developed in Chapter 4, Sub-section 4.1.1.

[33] Nigro, 'Il nodo…', *cit.*, n. 15, p. 229.

guarantees and to judicial review. How restrictive or how broad this curb is in the end, depends on what is meant by relevant interest.

At the outset, it should be noted that, in this strict sense, participation has been mainly perceived as a right to be heard in adjudicative administrative procedures, in relation to individual determinations, both in national administrative systems and in EU administrative law, as established by the EU Courts' jurisprudence.[34] This is due, in part, to the parallelism of this category of procedures with trial-type procedures and, mainly, to the traditional conception of administrative law, according to which the administrative procedure creates a bilateral relationship between the administration and the person concerned by the decision (usually its addressee). In these cases, the interference in the private sphere of the latter by an authoritative decision requires compensation by procedural rules that structure the power of the decision-maker. These two factors combined ground the view of participation rights as rights of defence that have been received in EU administrative law as a principle common to the laws and constitutional traditions of Member States.[35] In this view, the persons legitimated to intervene in the procedure are, first and above all, the addressees of the administrative act and, secondly, holders of related interests on whom the outcome of the procedure will, very likely, negatively impact (these are usually the persons whose interests are contrary to those of the addressee of the act).

The above considerations on the rationales of participation unfold a different view on the delimitation of potentially interested persons. The procedure may touch the interests of persons other than the addressee of the act and those who have an interest contrary to the latter's. In other words, the procedure may also affect the legal position of persons, whose specific situation is not necessarily differentiated from that of others affected in a similar way. This is particularly so in the areas where EU action bears upon diffuse interests, such as consumer, environmental, or public health protection. Moreover, like the addressee of the decision and the persons who may be treated similarly, the persons concerned may equally have a potentially valuable contribution to make to the content of

[34] Paul Craig (2006), *EU Administrative Law*, Oxford: Oxford University Press, pp. 314–22; Jürgen Schwarze (2006 [1992]), *European Administrative Law*. Revised 1st edn, London: Sweet and Maxwell, pp. 1243–371. For more developments on national laws, see the section below; on the stance of the EU Courts, see also Chapter 4, Sections 4.2 and 4.3.

[35] Battini *et al.*, *op. cit.*, n. 26, p. 132.

the decision. Arguably, opening the procedure to other interested persons—whose entitlement to access it may be *also* assessed on the basis of their own contribution to the outcome of the procedure—may be a means of 'avoiding resistances and negative reactions' as well as consensuses created between the decision-maker and a 'few carefully selected persons'.[36]

The question remains: who are interested or concerned persons? A first answer would be, all those implicated in the legal relationship that emerges from the public intervention, i.e. persons whose legal sphere is affected by the outcome of the procedure. The legal positions of those affected may be valued differently by the legal system. Following this idea, one may identify two categories of persons concerned. Firstly, holders of subjective rights affected by the final decision or persons who, in light of the applicable norms, may aim to acquire a certain good or advantage through the decision that is being adopted or to prevent a specific public interference in their legal sphere. Secondly, holders of legally protected interests also touched by the final decision. These persons voice 'objectivized interests' that are protected by the legal system insofar as their fulfilment is, at the same time, one of the goals of the latter and should therefore be considered in the exercise of the decisional function. By reason of a certain proximity to the material situation at issue, it is possible to ascertain that the decision touches their legal sphere. They have therefore a differentiated position: theirs is not merely a general interest in the legality of the decision and in the pursuance of the public interest. Their proximity to the material situation may be assessed on the basis of their belonging to a social or professional group concerned by the decision, or of their material connections to the procedure—either to the person targeted by the procedure or to the objective situation under examination.[37]

[36] Boulouis, *op. cit.*, n. 5, p. 66.

[37] This notion essentially draws on the concept of legitimate interest developed in Italian administrative law (although it is not exclusive to this legal order). Nevertheless, it does not fully coincide with this concept. In this legal system, the concept of legitimate interest serves to qualify both access to the decisional procedure and access to justice, delimiting the realm of the ordinary and the administrative jurisdictions. It is nevertheless discussed in the literature whether the entitlement to participate should be considered a subjective right, a legitimate interest, or a procedural interest. Being at the core of the Italian administrative justice system, this concept has been widely discussed in the literature. On this, Massimo S. Giannini (1981) *Istituzioni di diritto amministrativo*, Giuffrè: Milano, pp. 257–60; Aldo Sandulli (1989) *Manuale di Diritto Amministrativo*, 15th edn, Napoli: Jovene, pp. 107–14; Mario Nigro (1994) *Giustizia amministrativa*, 4th edn, Bologna: Il Mulino, pp. 87–117 (and underlining the diversity of legitimate interests as well as the challenges the concept poses, Mario Nigro (1987) 'Ma che cos'è questo interesse legittimo?

In both cases, access to the procedure grants interested persons an advantageous position that is linked to substantive rights or to legally relevant substantive interests. This advantageous position is conferred upon a natural or a legal person, allowing the respective holder to influence the exercise of the decisional power, with a view to fulfilling the underlying substantive interest.

In each case, the relation of the natural or legal persons to the underlying substantive position differs and their legal positions are valued in different ways by the legal system, mostly because the relevance of the personal factor is stronger in the first case. This may justify a difference in the legal treatment of the participant, that is, the procedural guarantees which attend participation may be stronger in relation to those who intervene in the procedure to defend a subjective right or interest than in relation to holders of legally protected interests.[38] As argued above, the functions of participation are the same in both situations, although in the first case the rationale of defence may be predominant and, in the second, the rationale of collaboration (intended as contribution to the fulfilment of the public interest) may prevail. In any case, the effective differentiation pertains not to the function of participation, but to the underlying subjective position which grounds and legitimates the intervention in the procedure as well as the way this is valued by the legal system. While, in relation to the first category of interested persons mentioned, the legal system protects their individual legal position as such, in relation to the second category, their interest is considered legally relevant essentially because it needs to be balanced by the decision-maker during the procedure, insofar as it coincides with a relevant public interest. However, the procedural position of the latter is not merely a reflection of the objective protection conferred by the legal system, since access to the procedure depends not only on the existence of a legally

Interrogativi vecchi e nuovi punti di riflessione', *Il foro italiano*, pp. 469–83); Alberto Zito (1996) *Le pretese partecipative del privato nel procedimento amministrativo*, Giuffrè: Milano, pp. 19–38; Occhiena, *Situazioni giuridiche soggettive . . .*, *cit.*, n. 20, Chapters III and V (on the various doctrinal positions defended in relation to the nature of the entitlement to participate in the procedure); Aldo Sandulli (2000) 'Il procedimento', in Sabino Cassese (ed.) *Trattato di diritto amministrativo. Diritto Amministrativo Generale*, Vol. II, Milano: Giuffrè, pp. 927–1215, at p. 1024–30; Bernardo G. Mattarella (2000) 'L'attività' in Sabino Cassese (ed.), *Trattato di Diritto Amministrativo. Diritto Amministrativo Generale*, Vol. I, Milano: Giuffrè, pp. 629–703, at pp. 629–37.

[38] Defending that, *inter alia*, the design of the procedure should vary according to the relevance of the personal factor in the underlying material situation, see Galligan, *op. cit.*, n. 17, pp. 63–70.

relevant interest: as pointed out above, the interest of the participant also needs to be qualified by a particular connection to the subject matter being decided, i.e. the participant's legal sphere needs to be affected by the procedure.

The relevance of the personal factor may determine a different procedural treatment afforded to each category, more protective in relation to holders of subjective rights.[39] This amounts to recognizing them as having a stronger procedural position in relation to other interested persons. Note that this effect is grounded in the person's relation to the subject matter under appreciation—in particular in the relevance of the person's conduct to the decision eventually adopted and in the way their legal sphere is implicated in the material situation being regulated—as well as in the normative configuration of the subject matter. If the issue is, for example, the application of a penalty or sanction to an enterprise for violation of competition rules, it is justified that the person whose conduct is being assessed and the person who gave rise to the procedure have an enhanced procedural protection as against the position of the administration.[40] The public interests involved may justify the intervention of other persons concerned. However, irrespective of other interests implicated in the decision that need to be balanced against the interests of the infringer and those of the complainant, or of other subjective rights that might require consideration, the decision is very much grounded in the assessment of the conduct of the undertakings targeted by the Commission's investigation. When, for example, the issue concerns the funding of a power plant with potential negative effects on the environment or the release of a trading authorization for a product potentially harmful to public health, an assessment of the persons involved or of their conduct is not at stake. More than in the previous situation, the applicant's position cannot be detached from, and needs to be balanced against, other public and legally protected private rights and interests which must be safeguarded and may require the definition of restrictive conditions to the activity that is being assessed. Several contradictory and heterogeneous interests come together in the procedure and need to be examined and balanced on an equal footing by the decision-

[39] See Section 2.6 below, Chapter 5, Sub-section 5.3; Chapter 7, Sub-section 7.3.3; Chapter 8, Sub-section 8.2.3.

[40] It is known that in EU competition law the position of the complainant is different from the position of the addressee of an individual decision (Joined Cases 142 and 156/84, *British-American Tobacco Company Ltd and R. J. Reynolds Industries Inc. v Commission* [1987] ECR 4487, paragraph 20, and Case T-17/93, *Matra Hachette SA v Commission* [1994] ECR II-595, paragraphs 34 and 35).

maker, in light of the principles and norms which regulate the substance of the subject matter. Ultimately, these principles and norms define the range of interests which need to be considered in the procedure and will stipulate the eventual differences of procedural treatment of the persons wishing to have a say in the procedure.

This distinction between two different categories of participants does not reflect an *a priori* judgment regarding the relative importance of subjective rights over legally protected interests, but rather the fact that, *where justified* in the circumstances of the case and in light of the applicable legal norms, the consideration of the individual and their subjective legal sphere may be necessary to respect their dignity. Nor does this distinction reflect a dividing line between property and liberty rights that mostly require the non-interference of public powers, on the one hand, and rights that require active protection by public powers, on the other. The transformation of legal interests, protected mostly in their objective dimension as public interests, into subjective rights—i.e. individual entitlements associated with the possibility of taking action against illegitimate consequences produced in the individual legal sphere—depends on concrete legislative choices. In other words, the 'subjectivation' of legally protected interests is not limited to the sphere of legal interests traditionally protected by civil codes. It can encompass social, consumer, and environmental rights.[41] This effect depends also on the interpretation of such legislative choices. As such, depending on the circumstances of the case and the relevant legal rules applicable, persons adversely affected or likely to be adversely affected by environmental damage may be considered holders of subjective rights entitled to defend their personal position in decisional procedures. Other persons voicing environmental interests in the procedure will most likely be considered holders of legally protected interests, if they intervene in an objective capacity, i.e. they defend aspects of legally relevant interests that could otherwise not be sufficiently taken into consideration by the decision-maker (e.g. associations whose scope is by statute the protection of the environment and which are concerned by the decision at issue).

The distinction between holders of subjective rights and of legally protected interests is not a clear cut one, in the sense that it is hardly possible to identify *a priori* two clearly distinct groups of persons concerned by a given

[41] In a similar sense, Norbert Reich (1998) '"System der subjectiven öffentlichen Rechten" in the Union: A European Constitution for citizens of bits and pieces', *Collected Courses of the Academy of European Law*, Vol. VI, Book 1, pp. 157–236, at pp. 164–5, 169, 177.

decision. As a result of the above, this differentiation stems essentially from the way in which the material situation is assessed by the decision-maker within the limits of the legal criteria by which they are bound. In this sense, it is part of a balancing exercise, through which the decision-maker assesses the private and public interests at stake, as well as the relation of the interested persons with the procedure at issue. In complex regulatory situations that contend with varied interests and legal positions—the most likely scenario in modern administrations—different degrees of procedural protection are likely to be considered both by the decision-maker and the courts when assessing the conduct of the latter. The criteria that ground the distinction referred to, as they are defended here, should then be understood as legal criteria that guide the decision-maker and the judge in assessing each material situation. Given the underlying values of participation, this assessment should be directed at ensuring the adoption of procedurally fair and materially just decisions, both ensuring the legal protection of those affected and a sound consideration of the interests that need to be balanced in each case.

It should be noted that the proposed distinction between subjective rights and legally protected interests certainly does not have the maturity in EU law that it has in the national legal orders of some Member States (such as Italy, Spain, and Germany). However, the protective intention of EU law norms—or, more precisely, the possibility of interpreting a norm as intended to confer rights on individuals—is determinant for core issues such as direct effect and the non-contractual liability of the EU institutions. On this basis, it may also be possible to distinguish between specific aims of protection and degrees of legal protection.[42]

'Participation rights' is therefore a broad term that encompasses the advantageous positions granted to persons whose subjective rights and legally protected interests are affected by the outcome of a decisional procedure. As mentioned, participation rights allow their holders to influence the exercise of the decisional power, with the intention of satisfying the underlying substantive interest that is voiced in the procedure. It was

[42] This aspect will be developed in Chapter 8, where it will be shown that a basis for the distinction mentioned can be found in the case law regarding the procedure of Article 108(2) TFEU. See, further, Sacha Prechal (2008) 'Protection of Rights: How Far?' in Sacha Prechal and Bert van Roermund (eds), *The Coherence of EU Law. The Search for Unity in Divergent Concepts*, Oxford: Oxford University Press, pp. 155–82, in particular pp. 163–70 and 178–82. See also, in the same volume, Saša Beljin (2008) 'Rights in EU Law', pp. 91–122, exploring the interconnections between national and EU legal concepts.

defended that the content of this advantageous position may differ according to the substantive position that the interested persons occupy in the underlying material situation as well as the way in which this is assessed by the legal system. This aspect will be taken up again at a later point in this chapter and will be developed in other parts of this work, in particular in the sector analyses.[43] For now, two other aspects require further elaboration. First, as stated, participation rights have been traditionally restricted to the right to be heard recognized in relation to individual determinations. Since this has also determined the conception of participation rights in EU law, it is important to have an overview of how participation rights are regulated in some national legal systems, in order to better understand the EU rules on this matter. Secondly, interest holders have been defined above as those who are involved in the legal relationship stemming from the decision adopted. This suggests a specific way of conceiving participation rights, which dispenses with the form of the act as a criterion to ground participation rights. These two aspects will be examined in turn, in the following two sections.

2.4 Participation, Individual Acts, and Regulations

Participation in administrative procedures in European national legal systems assumes primarily the form of a right to be heard in individual determinations, in most cases limited to holders of subjective rights or individual legally protected interests that are negatively affected by an administrative act.[44] In general, procedures leading up to the adoption of general administrative acts and regulations do not compulsorily entail a right to participate, this being left to the discretion of the decision-maker, unless otherwise determined in specific legislation.

As is well known, exactly what administrative regulations are differs according to the systems of government of each country. In the United

[43] See n. 39.

[44] The Italian and the Spanish general rules of procedure are exceptions in this respect, envisaging also the participation of holders of public interests and of diffuse interests (Michel Fromont (2006) *Droit administratif des États européens*, Paris: Presses Universitaires de France, pp. 218–19; see the reference to these legal systems, below). On the restrictiveness of German law in this matter, Diana-Urania Galetta (2002) *La legge tedesca sul procedimento amministrativo (Verwaltungsverfahrensgesetz). Traduzione con testo a fronte e commento introduttivo*, Milano: Giuffrè, p. 29.

Kingdom, delegated legislation is considered a part of administrative rule-making, whereas this is not the case in other legal systems.[45] In some legal systems, regulations are considered to be norms enacted by administrative authorities in the exercise of an administrative function. Therefore, they are subject to the general procedural principles applicable also to the adoption of other administrative decisions, even if specific provisions are envisaged for the respective decisional procedure. In other legal systems, regulations are excluded from the general rules of administrative procedure, arguably because they are considered to pertain more to a function of government than to the realm of the administrative function.[46]

Notwithstanding the different formal cloaks, it is fair to define regulations by contrast with administrative acts, the former corresponding to general norms that affect an undetermined number of persons, and the latter to individual decisions issued to regulate a concrete situation and addressed to identified addressees. This is, admittedly, a bare-bone definition that hides the diversity of forms of normative acts.[47] To underline the distinction between the two forms of administrative action, the function of norm creation, or the capacity to produce innovation in the legal system,

[45] For example in Italy, Spain, and Portugal, where governments are entitled both to pass laws under delegation of the Parliament (*decreti legislativi*, under Article 77 of the Italian Constitution; *decretos legislativos*, under Articles 82 to 85 of the Spanish Constitution; *decretos-lei autorizados*, under Articles 165(2) to (5) and 198(1)(b) and (c) of the Portuguese Constitution) and autonomous legislative acts (*decreti-legge*, under Article 77 of the Italian Constitution; *decretos-leys*, Articles 86 of the Spanish Constitution; *decretos-leis*, under Article 198(1)(a) of the Portuguese Constitution). All have the value of law. For the UK, see Paul Craig (2008) *Administrative Law*, 6th edn, London: Sweet and Maxwell, p. 715.

[46] Portugal and Italy are in the first group (according to Mattarella, the Italian law on administrative procedure also applies to regulations, although they are subject to specific rules—Mattarella (2000) 'Il provvedimento', in Sabino Cassese (ed.), *Trattato di Diritto Amministrativo. Diritto Amministrativo Generale*, Vol. I, Milano: Giuffrè, pp. 705–925, at p. 757). Germany and Spain are in the second group. In Spain, the exclusion mentioned raises legal problems and doctrinal discussions (Francisco López Menudo (1993) 'Los principios generales del procedimiento administrativo', in Javier Barnés Vázquez (ed.), *La justicia administrativa en el derecho comparado*, Madrid: Civitas, pp. 91–158, at pp. 150–1; José Luis Bremejo Latre (2004) 'Procedimiento administrativo común y elaboración de disposiciones administrativas', *Revista Española de Derecho Administrativo*, n. 124, pp. 611–29, at pp. 612–13; Luciano Parejo Alfonso, Antonio Jiménez-Blanco, and Luis Ortega Álvarez (1998) *Manual de derecho administrativo*. Vol. 1. 5th edn, Barcelona: Ariel, p. 487). In Germany, the definition of administrative procedure enshrined in the German law on administrative procedure is limited to the preparation and adoption of administrative acts and contracts (§ 9 of the *Verwaltungsverfahrensgesetz*). Nevertheless, Schmidt-Assmann argues that the regulation has always been considered as a third form of administrative action next to the categories defined in this law (Schmidt-Assmann, *op. cit.* n. 11, p. 339).

[47] On this, see Sub-section 2.4.3 below.

is also invoked to define regulations. Another criterion also sometimes used pertains to the aim of regulations: contrary to administrative acts, regulations do not aim to define the public interest in a concrete situation, but are intended to regulate in the abstract an undefined number of legal relationships.[48]

In this section, the relevance of this divide for purposes of participation in the legal orders of six Member States (United Kingdom, France, Germany, Italy, Spain, and Portugal) is explained and criticized. This synopsis has a double purpose. First and foremost, it sheds light on the origins of this divide in EU law and explains its resilience. Secondly, contrasting different solutions found in national systems indicates innovative paths to deal with potential problems posed by participation. This does not mean that the brief study that follows is intended to find *the* normative solution that could be transposed to EU law and overcome the limitations that will be identified in subsequent chapters. The normative proposals of this book are not based on a comparative study, but, as explained, on a rights-based approach to participation that is lacking, as such, in EU law, against which current EU law is assessed, and which is required by the values that the EU legal system purports to uphold. Nevertheless, an overview of selected legal orders might provide useful insights also from a *de lege ferenda* perspective.

What follows is not a comparative study proper, but an overview of different legal systems guided by the stated purposes.[49] It is essentially limited to the relevance of the divide between individual acts and administrative regulations in defining the applicability of rules on participation.[50] Moreover, in coherence with the concept of participation expounded above, only participation during an already initiated procedure is considered here. Another limitation is noteworthy: only the national general rules of procedure are taken as reference to the observations that follow and these do not exhaust the normative spectrum regarding participation, which should also take into account sector legislation as well as, in federal and regional political systems, federate and regional rules on the administrative procedure.

[48] On these different criteria and their insufficiencies, see Juan Alfonso Santamaria Pastor (1988) *Fundamentos de derecho administrativo*, Vol. I, Madrid: Ramon Areces, pp. 720–23.

[49] Legal comparisons require a specific method that was not followed in this overview.

[50] On other aspects, namely the circle of people to whom a right to be heard is recognized and the content of participation rights, see Fromont, *op. cit.*, n. 44, pp. 216–22, who refers to the French, German, Italian, and Spanish general rules of procedure.

2.4.1 *Beneath and beyond EU law: selected national legal systems*

The intervention of private persons in adjudicative, trial-type procedures has a long-standing tradition in common law systems, under the *audi alteram partem* premise of natural justice. In English law, the scope of this maxim has in the past been quite restricted, namely to judicial or quasi-judicial procedures. However, its applicability has been extended to other fields under the term 'procedural fairness'.[51] In a nutshell, it can be said that it applies to administrative acts where the deprivation of an individual's right, interest, or legitimate expectation without a prior hearing would be an unfair result.[52] However, whether procedural fairness requires a right to an oral hearing or, for example, merely the submission of written observations, depends on the circumstances of the case and, specifically, on the impact that the decision might have upon the individual.[53] Despite the looser requirements of the principle, administrative rule-making has largely been excluded from its scope. However, mandatory participation is envisaged by statute for rule-making procedures in certain policy areas, e.g. town and country planning, through the realization of public inquiries. Public inquiries, an important institution of English law in matters related to land use, entail public discussions.[54] Moreover, a few judicial decisions have held that there is a duty to act fairly (that is, adequately to consult and consider submitted comments) also in relation to decisions entailing economic policy choices.[55] Nevertheless, these remain an exception and there is no presumption in favour of a duty to act fairly in relation to acts of general scope. On the contrary: in principle, the duty to act fairly does not apply where the decision involves policy or rule-making.[56] It should, however, be

[51] Paul Craig, *op. cit.*, n. 45, pp. 371–6 and, on the disputable distinction between natural justice and procedural fairness, pp. 376–9 (more synthetically, Galligan, *op. cit.*, pp. 73–2). See also Stanley A. de Smith, Harry Woolf, and Jeffrey L. Jowell (1995) *Judicial Review of Administrative Action*, 5th edn, London: Sweet and Maxwell, Chapter 7.

[52] Paul Craig, *op. cit.*, n. 45, p. 375–87. See also De Smith, Woolf, and Jowell, *op. cit.*, pp. 401–30.

[53] De Smith, Woolf, and Jowell, *op. cit.*, p. 402 and Chapter 9.

[54] For problems posed by public inquiries, Tony Prosser (2007) 'Administrative procedure and the protection of citizen's rights: report from the United Kingdom' in Alberto Massera (ed.), *Le tutele procedimentali. Profili di diritto comparato*, Napoli: Jovene Editore, pp. 71–95, at pp. 83–5.

[55] De Smith, Woolf, and Jowell, *op. cit.*, n. 51, pp. 407, 414–15.

[56] Craig, *op. cit.*, n. 45, p. 397 ('There is no general duty to consult imposed by common law where the order is of legislative nature'), De Smith, Woolf, and Jowell, *op. cit.*, n. 51, pp. 486–8, and also Paul Craig (1990) *Public Law and Democracy in the United Kingdom and in the United States of America*, Oxford: Clarendon Press, pp. 160–2. For a criticism, see Craig, *op. ult. cit.* pp. 162–6, Craig, *Administrative Law*, *cit.*, n. 45, pp. 736 and 739 (also De Smith, Woolf, and Jowell, *op. cit*, n. 51, pp. 405 and 488). On political developments on the duty to consult, Craig, *Administrative Law*, *cit.*, n. 45, p. 738–9.

noted that while the common law does not impose any requirement of participation in the absence of a legislative requirement, it might ground the need to participate on legitimate expectations (e.g. where a body has in the past established a practice of consultation, where it has given an undertaking to consult, or where it has established a rule which is relied upon by an individual or a group which it proposes to change or to depart from).[57]

In France, the scope of applicability of the right to be heard has also been expanded, though on quite different legal grounds. The principle according to which a hearing should be held before the adoption of an act, as an essential element of the rights of the defence in administrative procedures (*les droits de la défense*), was originally quite restricted. As a rule, it was limited to the adoption of measures such as sanctions. In other cases where a decision impacted negatively upon individual rights and interests but was taken to pursue a general interest (*intérêt général*) or in view of a reason of public order (*ordre public*), there was no legal need to invite affected parties to submit observations and objections to the likely outcome of the procedure, unless otherwise determined by a specific legislative determination.[58] The opportunities to participate in the administrative procedure were, however, enlarged by jurisprudence and by law.[59] First, the *Conseil d'État* extended the right to be heard to cases where a decision is taken having a person in consideration (*intuitu personae*). Nonetheless, this line of jurisprudence is applicable in the realm of civil service cases and has not been extended to other areas.[60] Secondly, by legislative determination, individual decisions (*décisions individuelles*) that require the giving of reasons must be adopted after the submission of written observations by the person concerned, or oral observations if so required.[61] The law enumerates which

[57] Robert Baldwin (1995), *Rules and Government*, Oxford: Clarendon Press, p. 75; Craig, *Administrative Law*, *cit.*, n. 45, p. 397.

[58] René Chapus (2000) *Droit administratif général*, Tome I, 14th edn, Paris: Monchrestien, pp. 1095–9, in particular pp. 1098–9. Also André de Laubadère, Jean-Claude Venezia, and Yves Gaudemet (1996) *Traité de droit administratif*, Tome 1, 14th edn, Paris: LGDJ, pp. 682–3.

[59] On the difficulties of this process, regarding the judicial developments, see Guy Isaac (1968) *La procédure administrative non contentieuse*, Paris: LGDJ, pp. 388–98, and Ewald Eisenberg (2000) *L'audition du citoyen et motivation des décisions administratives individuelles. Étude comparative en France et en Allemagne*, Paris: L'Harmattan, pp. 55–9.

[60] Chapus, *op. cit.*, n. 58, p. 1100, and Isaac, *op. cit.*, pp. 396–8.

[61] Article 24 of Law No. 2000-321, of 12 April 2000, regarding citizens' rights in their relationships with the administration (*Journal Officiel* No. 88, 13 April 2000; it replaced a previous act of 1983, where this solution was envisaged for the first time). On this, Chapus, *op. cit.*, n. 58, pp. 1100–4. This provision does not apply when the procedure was initiated upon private initiative, in case of urgency or exceptional circumstances, when the hearing could compromise

individual decisions require reason-giving. They include those that impact negatively on the legal sphere of the person concerned (among which those denying an authorization) and decisions derogating from general rules.[62] While the right of interested parties to be heard is thus limited to individualized procedures, other forms of participation envisaged by French law (*consultation-enquête*) can be said to replace the exercise of this procedural right in relation to the elaboration of general rules, insofar as they allow the integration of collective interests in the exercise of the administrative function.[63] One of the modalities of consultation of persons and bodies representative of social and professional interests affected by a particular determination includes the confrontation of opinions of the different actors involved (*consultation-enquête contradictoire*). Public consultations (*enquêtes publiques*) may in certain cases be followed by public debates (*débats publics*), essentially in the areas of land planning and environment.[64] Both *consultation-enquête* and *enquêtes publiques* are conceived as means of acquiring information in the elaboration of general determinations and, as such, they do not entail individual procedural rights.[65]

Germany, in contrast to France, has a general law on administrative procedure, where its basic rules regarding administrative acts (and administrative contracts) are defined. The legal treatment afforded to the right to be heard is enshrined therein. Accordingly, before adopting an act that interferes with the rights of a person (*eingreifend Verwaltungsakt*), the decision-maker must give this person the opportunity to submit observations

public order or international relations and, finally, when a specific procedure has been envisaged by law (Article 24).

[62] Articles 1 and 2 of Law No. 79-587, of 11 July 1979, on the duty to give reasons for administrative acts and the improvement of the relationships between the administration and the public (*Journal Officiel*, 12 July 1979). On this, Eisenberg, *op. cit.*, n. 59, pp. 115–17.

[63] Isaac, *op. cit.*, n. 59, pp. 459–63, in particular p. 461.

[64] Law No. 2002-276, of 27 February 2002 on the 'democracy of proximity' (*démocratie de proximité*; *Journal Officiel*, 28 February 2002), Articles 132–134 and 138–143. Public debates are organized by the *Commission nationale du débat public*, in the terms defined in Article L. 121-1 of the code on the environment, modified by Article 134 of Law No. 2002-276, *cit.* Comparing the English public inquiries and the French *enquêtes publics*, Fromont, *op. cit.*, n. 44, pp. 220–1.

[65] Isaac, *op. cit.*, n. 59, pp. 474–7, distinguishing and underlining the similarities between *consultation-enquête* and *enquête publique*. For a critique of the effectiveness of participatory mechanisms in France, see Jean-Bernard Auby (2007), 'Procédure administrative et garantie des droits des citoyens en droit français', in Alberto Massera, *op. cit.*, n. 54, pp. 31–49, at p. 48. The author underlines that the centrality of judicial review in the French administrative system continues to overshadow the role that the administrative procedure could have in ruling the relationships between citizens and administration (*op. cit.*, p. 45).

regarding the relevant facts for the adoption of the decision.[66] This rule is subject to exceptions. Among others, a hearing need not be given where 'the authority wishes to issue a general order [...]'.[67] This term includes, for example, general administrative acts (*Allgemeinverfügungen*), i.e. acts which, containing a concrete ruling, are addressed to several persons who are determined or determinable on the basis of general characteristics, or relating to the public law aspect of a matter, or to its use by the collectivity.[68] Different from these are administrative acts which, having a concrete addressee, contend nonetheless with several interests whose holders may intervene in the procedure. Participation, in these cases, is subject to specific rules, embodying *Massenverfahren*: persons interested in intervening in the procedure, voicing the same interests, may be urged to nominate a common representative.[69] Rule-making procedures, on the other hand, are not regulated by the general procedural law or any other general federal law. They are regulated by sparse, sectoral legislation. Rules on participation in rule-making procedures, where they exist, should be found there.[70] Nevertheless, provisions regulating the formation and adoption of urban plans are defined in the law on administrative procedure. This procedure entails a participatory phase. In particular, the municipalities (*Gemeinden*) concerned must release the plan for public consultation, except when the circle of interested parties is known, in which case publicity may be restricted to these, and every person whose interests may be affected by the plan can submit observations; moreover, a report on this hearing needs to be transmitted to the decision-maker.[71]

[66] The term used to define those entitled to intervene is 'party' (*Beteiligt*), who may be any person whose legally protected interests may be affected. Hans Meyer (1993) 'El procedimiento administrativo en la Republica Federal de Alemania', in Barnés Vázquez, *op. cit.* n. 46, pp. 281–316, at pp. 295–300 and pp. 307–9.

[67] § 28(2), 4 of the *Verwaltungsverfahrensgesetz*, which also excludes the need to comply with a right to be heard in cases where a 'administrative acts in considerable numbers or administrative acts using automatic equipment' are to be adopted (translation according to the German Federal Ministry of the Interior, Section V II 1, 01.01.2009).

[68] § 35 of the *Verwaltungsverfahrensgesetz*. On this, see Hartmut Maurer (1994 [1992]) *Droit administratif allemand* (traduit par Michel Fromont), Paris: LGDJ, pp. 202–4.

[69] §§ 17 to 19 and 67 of the *Verwaltungsverfahrensgesetz*, in particular § 18(1). On this Meyer, *op. cit.*, n. 66, p. 300 and Fromont, *op. cit.*, n. 44, p. 221.

[70] Meyer, *op. cit.*, n. 66, pp. 286 and 293–4. Comparing the French and the German administrative law on the right to be heard and on the duty to motive administrative decisions, Eisenberg, *op. cit.*, n. 59, pp. 117–73.

[71] § 73(3), (4) and (9) of the *Verwaltungsverfahrensgesetz*.

Italian administrative law follows a similar line regarding the consequences attached in terms of participation to the distinction between general acts and individual acts. The law on administrative procedure determines that its rules on participation are not applicable to normative procedures or to those leading up to the adoption of general administrative acts, programmes, plans, or fiscal acts, but remits to specific legislation the regulation of participation in these cases.[72] In other words, the rules according to which, firstly, decision-makers need to hear the addressees of their decisions, the persons adversely affected by administrative acts who are sufficiently individualized in the procedure, as well as persons whose hearing is determined by law, and, secondly, persons voicing public, private, and diffuse interests who may be adversely affected by the procedure, are only applicable to administrative acts.[73] This category includes acts which, being addressed to legal persons and pertaining to their internal and external rules, affect social or professional groups represented by them (*atti colletivi*) and acts which may themselves be decomposed into different single acts since they embody decisions which are directed at several persons at the same time (*atti plurimi*).[74] According to one commentator, there is no principled exclusion of compulsory participation in relation to normative acts, the presumption being that this matter is regulated on a sector basis.[75] Moreover, Caranta and others point out that the Italian administrative courts have, in certain instances, limited the scope of the exclusion, considering that the rules on participation are applicable when the normative and general acts indicated in Article 13(1) of the Italian procedural law impose charges (*vincoli*), as well as to cases in which acts modify previous general or planning decisions.[76]

The Spanish rules on procedural participation are particularly open when compared with the national legal orders surveyed so far. Procedures leading up to the adoption of individualized administrative acts must, by constitutional determination, entail hearings (*audiencia*) where the parties concerned (*los interesados*) defend their rights and interests which may be

[72] Article 13 of the Law of 7 August 1990, No. 241 (*Giornale Ufficiale*, 18 August 1990, No. 192), as amended. On this Roberto Caranta, Laura Ferraris, and Simona Rodriguez (2005) *La partecipazione al procedimento amministrativo*, 2nd edn, Milano: Giuffrè, pp. 31–42.

[73] Articles 7(1) and 9(1) of the Law of 7 August 1990, No. 241, as amended. On these provisions, *inter alia*, Sandulli, 'Il procedimento', *cit.*, n. 26, pp. 1022–9, Caranta *et al.*, *op. cit.*, Chapter 4.

[74] Caranta *et al.*, *op. cit.*, p. 32. '*Atti collettivi*' and '*atti plurimi*' are defined by Massimo S. Giannini (1993) *Diritto Amministrativo*, Vol. II, 3rd edn, Milano: Giuffrè, pp. 287–8.

[75] In this sense, Sandulli, 'Il procedimento', *cit.*, n. 26, p. 1032.

[76] Caranta *et al.*, *op. cit.*, n. 72, p. 37.

affected by the outcome of the administrative procedure.[77] '*Interesados*' are holders of rights and of individual or collective legitimate interests that may be hindered by the adoption of the final decision. Associations and organizations representative of economic and social interests may be considered holders of collective legitimate interests in the terms defined by law.[78] This is considered to have the double function of defence and collaboration.[79] In addition, public consultation through which natural or legal persons may present claims and comments (*información pública*) may also be held. Unless otherwise determined by law, whether an *información pública* takes place or not is a matter to be decided by the decision-maker, depending on the concrete appreciation of whether the subject matter at issue requires or advises the opening of the procedure to public scrutiny.[80] According to the Spanish Constitutional Court, *informaciónes públicas* do not embody a simple right of political participation, since they grant participation in administrative decision-making (either directly or through collective entities) to citizens thereby affected. They ensure both the compliance with the principle of care in the exercise of the administrative function and the protection of rights and interests of affected interests. In fact, the Court underlines that: '[...] its purpose is [...] to urge those who have an interest or wish to express their opinions to serve as a source of information to the administration and, thereby, favour the measure's adequacy and opportunity, as well to provide a channel for the defence of individual or collective rights of those potentially affected'.[81] The procedural intervention as such does not accord

[77] Article 105, a) of the Constitution and Article 84 of the Law No. 30/1992, of 26 November, on the legal regime of public administrations and of the common administrative procedure (*Boletín Oficial* No. 285, 27 November 1992). According to the Spanish Constitution, the right to be heard in administrative procedures has a constitutional basis (Article 105, c)).

[78] Article 31 of the law quoted in the note above.

[79] Judgment of the Supreme Court (STS) 3ª 4ª 6.10.1993, pertaining to the function of the *audiencia*, quoted in the CD-ROM annexed to José Garberi Llobregat (ed) (2007) *El procedimento administrativo común (comentarios, jurisprudencia, formularios)*, Vol. II, Valencia: Tirant Lo Blanch (Jurisprudencia, Parte Septima, p. 18).

[80] Article 86(1) determines that the decision-maker may decide to open this procedural phase 'when the nature of the procedure thus requires' ('*quando la naturaleza [del procedimiento] lo requiera*'). Some examples of compulsory consultations are provided by Isabel Gallego Córcoles (2007) 'La instrucción del procedimiento administrativo común' in Garberi Llobregat, *op. cit.*, pp. 1305–88, at p. 1339. They include, for example, the procedure for the classification of heritage sites ('*bienes integrantes del patrimonio*').

[81] Judgment of the Constitutional Court (Sentencia Tribunal Constitucional) No. 119/1995 (*Sala Segunda*), 17th July, II, 6 (author's translation). The judgment refers not to the general rule enshrined in the general law on administrative procedure, but to one of the sectoral legal regimes

participants the condition of *interesados*, but they are granted the right to obtain from the administration a reasoned answer to the questions raised.[82] These two forms of participation envisaged in the general law on administrative procedure do not preclude other modalities of citizens' participation that might be put in place by public administrations.

The scope of these rules is confined to the procedure for the adoption of administrative acts. They do not apply to rule-making procedures. However, procedural participation in the adoption of acts of general scope is a constitutional determination. According to Article 105, a) of the Spanish Constitution, the law must regulate the terms in which citizens affected by administrative measures of general scope (*disposiciones administrativas*) may participate in the respective procedure, directly or through legally recognized organizations and associations. Most authors interpret the constitutional term *disposiciones administrativas* as referring to administrative regulations.[83] According to the constitutional provision, those who participate do not need to have a specific interest in order to access the procedure (the norm refers to *ciudadanos* and not to *interesados*), but need nonetheless to have a certain connection to it: they need to be 'affected' by the regulations adopted.[84] There is no general law on rule-making procedures concretizing this constitutional norm.[85] One law applies this provision to the regulations enacted by the Government and determines that participation is a general rule in the elaboration of regulations that affect citizens' rights and interests. Both citizens, directly, or legally recognized organizations

that determine the compulsory realization of *informaciones públicas*. At any rate, commentators tend to underline the double nature of this procedural phase, both ensuring political participation and a principle of care in the exercise of the administrative function (Gallego Córcoles, *op. cit.*, p. 1338, quoting Ramón Parada; in a similar sense, Josep Mª Castellà Andreu (2001) *Los derechos de constitucionales de participación política en la Administración Pública*, Barcelona: Cedecs Editorial, p. 441). On the effects of breach of the corresponding rules, see Gallego Córcoles, *op. cit.*, pp. 1343–4.

[82] Article 86(3) of the law quoted above, n. 77. It is further specified that the administrative reply to the comments submitted may be common to all the interventions which have raised the same questions (Article 86(4)).

[83] Castellà Andreu, *op. cit.*, n. 81, pp. 471–4.

[84] Castellà Andreu, *op. cit.*, n. 81, p. 467–71, underlining the difficulties that the constitutional provision raises.

[85] Criticizing this solution, also for the problems that it raises in terms of complying with the constitutional requirement of participation, see Bremejo Latre, *op. cit.*, n. 46 Another author underlines that some independent regulatory authorities have not been fully compliant in this respect (Gerardo García Álvarez (2006) 'Los poderes normativos de las Administraciones independientes en el ámbito economico', *Revista de Administración Pública*, n. 171, pp. 139–79, at p. 158).

representative of the interests affected are entitled to intervene in the rule-making procedure.[86] Only in two cases is the Government exempted from hearing them: when serious reasons of public interest thus demand or when the legal persons at issue have already participated in the procedure through other forms.[87] In addition to the participation of affected citizens, public consultations may be held. As in relation to individual determinations, this is not a compulsory requirement of rule-making procedures.[88]

The Portuguese rules on administrative procedure yield similar opportunities of participation. As with Spanish administrative law, Portuguese administrative law has departed, in this respect, from the French and German influences that have shaped its administrative legal system.[89] The general law on administrative procedure envisages different rules for procedures leading up to the adoption of administrative acts and those culminating in regulations. Regarding the first, interested persons—including, where applicable, citizens who may be adversely affected in their rights to public health, housing, education, cultural heritage, environment, land planning, and quality of life, as well as legal persons defending these rights and interests—have the right to be heard in the procedure before the adoption of the final decision and must be informed of its probable outcome (*audiência dos interessados*).[90] This implements the constitutional determination according to which citizens should be able to participate in the

[86] Article 24(1)(c) of Law No. 50/1997, of 27 November 1997, on the organization, competences and functioning of the Government (*Boletín Oficial* No. 285, 28 November 1997). Contrary to Law No. 30/1992, *cit.*, n. 77, this law does not apply to the *Comunidades Autónomas*, although many of them have adopted similar rules on participation. On this Castellà Andreu, *op. cit.*, n. 81, pp. 425–34.

[87] Article 24(1)(c), last sentence and paragraph (d) of the law quoted.

[88] Article 24(1)(c), *idem*.

[89] Fromont, *op. cit.*, n. 44, pp. 49–56.

[90] Article 100(1) and 53 of the Decree-Law No. 442/91, of 15 November (*Diário da República* n.º 263, I-A), as amended (henceforth, law on administrative procedure). According to the latter provision, the following persons are entitled to intervene in the procedure: holders of subjective rights and legally protected interests which are affected by the procedure, associations whose constitutive aim is the defence of those rights and interests, as well as citizens affected by an administrative action which hampers diffuse interests, residents in the area where a public commodity affected by the administrative actions is located, associations that have as a constitutive aim the defence of those interests, and pertinent local authorities that are entitled to intervene in the administrative procedure. While notice of the procedure is only directed at holders of rights and legally protected interests who may be adversely affected by acts adopted after the procedure and who may be identified by name (Article 55 of the law on administrative procedure), the procedural intervention of other interested persons under the law on so-called popular procedural participation determines that the procedure is publicly open to comments (Article 5 of Law No. 83/95, of 31 August, *Diário da República* n.º 201, I-A).

decisional procedures and deliberations that concern them.[91] The law identifies the situations in which this procedural requirement does not take place and also those cases where it may be dispensed with. Thus, the hearing does not take place when the decision is urgent, when participation might hinder the effectiveness of the procedure, and when the large number of interested parties makes its realization unfeasible. In these latter cases, however, the decision-maker must, when possible, replace the *audiência* with a public consultation (*consulta pública*). The hearing may be dispensed with when interested persons have had the opportunity to put forward their views on the relevant aspects of the procedure and when the decision is likely to be favourable to interested parties.[92] In all these cases, reasons need to be given for the decision not to open the procedure to participation.[93]

Rule-making procedures, on the other hand, may entail two participatory mechanisms. Firstly, an *audiência* is also envisaged in relation to rule-making procedures, although in different terms. The decision-maker must hear representatives of the interests affected, in the terms defined in specific legislation, when the project of regulation imposes duties or charges (*deveres, sujeições ou encargos*) thereon and there are no duly justified reasons of public interest which impede the hearing. According to one interpretation, the fact that this is envisaged as a rule means that specific legislation should treat as exceptional the cases in which an *audiência* is dispensed with.[94] Contrary to the Spanish rules of procedure applicable to governmental regulations, the hearing of natural persons is not envisaged as a general rule. However, this is determined by the law on popular procedural participation, in relation to plans that set the agenda of the public administration and to urban plans. This is equally applicable to decisions on the localization and realization of public works with environmental, social, and economic impacts on the population.[95] In these cases, when participation may require more than twenty hearings, direct participation may be replaced by a collective procedure (*procedimento colectivo*) in which the

[91] Article 267(5) of the Portuguese Constitution. On this norm and the interpretations that have been put forward, see Pedro Machete (1995) *A audiência dos interessados no procedimento administrativo*, Lisboa: Universidade Católica Editora, pp. 371–86.

[92] Article 103 of the law on administrative procedure.

[93] In this sense Mário Esteves de Oliveira, Pedro Costa Gonçalves, and João Pacheco de Amorim (1999) *Código do Procedimento Administrativo Comentado*, 2nd edn, Coimbra: Almedina, p. 463 and p. 465.

[94] Esteves de Oliveira *et al.*, *op. cit.*, p. 525.

[95] Article 4(1) of Law No. 83/95, *cit.*, n. 90.

decision-maker urges the interested persons to nominate representatives.[96] Secondly, also according to the terms defined in specific laws, the project of the regulation may need to be submitted to public appreciation (*apreciação pública*), whenever the nature of the subject matter thus allows. The notice of an *audiência* is notified personally to the entities that represent the affected interests. In contrast, the *apreciação pública* is open to any person who would like to intervene. In both cases, participation is based on the project of the regulation accompanied by the respective justification.[97]

2.4.2 *Common grounds, different solutions*

This overview of the basic rules of participation in selected national administrative laws evinces the different degree of protection afforded by each legal system, in terms of the range of acts covered by process rights and, cursorily, of the range of persons who may be entitled to intervene in the procedure. These different normative solutions cannot be fully understood if isolated from the legal traditions in which they emerge. Nevertheless, common features may be identified.

Prima facie, the prevailing rationale for participation rights seems to be that of ensuring respect for the rights and legally protected interests of persons affected by administrative decisions. Nevertheless, at least the Spanish and the Portuguese rules indicate that the separation between the function of defence and that of collaboration is ever more blurred.

Clearly, the means by which interested parties may intervene in administrative procedures are different in procedures for the elaboration of administrative acts and those leading to the adoption of regulations. The latter are usually ruled by specific legislation, most commonly in the areas of urban planning, land use, or environment. However, both the Spanish and the Portuguese legal systems envisage similar processes of participation for both types of acts. The broad scope for participation rights recognized in these two countries is explained by their constitutional context: their rules on participation are the concretization of constitutional norms which, despite different formulation, scope, and content, have in common a concern for the democratization of an

[96] Article 10 of Law No. 83/95, *cit.*, n. 90.

[97] Article 116 of the law on administrative procedure. On these and other differences between the two figures, see Esteves de Oliveira *et al.*, *op. cit.*, n. 93, pp. 523–34. These authors are of the opinion that the motivation of the regulation only needs to be disclosed in the *audiência* and not in the *apreciação pública* (p. 532).

authoritarian and corporative administration, emphasizing the rupture with the legal systems existing until the mid to late 1970s.[98]

Several arguments come together in the identification of a possible common ground for the sharp differentiation between the legal treatment afforded to individual determinations and general measures, common to the English, French, Italian, and German legal systems, although their relative relevance may differ from case to case. To begin with, considerations of practical order seem to weigh in favour of this option. It is usually deemed that the need to hear a large number of persons involved in the procedure would constitute too heavy a burden for the administration.[99] Notwithstanding the strength of this argument, both the German and the Portuguese rules of procedure provide a solution that may counter this inconvenience (*Massenverfahren* and *procedimentos colectivos*). Two other reasons may add normative justification to excluding participation entitlements from rule-making procedures: the lack of individual differentiation and the fact that administrative rules are usually adopted by bodies which are accountable to a representative assembly.[100] Related to this last ground is the argument that administrative rules pertain to a regulatory activity that, being mainly programmatic, is closer to a political function than to a

[98] On the constitutional foundations of administrative participation in Spanish administrative law, see Miguel Sanchéz-Moron (1979) 'El principio de participación en la Constitución española', *Revista de Administracíon Pública*, n. 39, pp. 171–205; and in Portuguese administrative law, Machete, *op. cit.*, n. 91, pp. 337–90. To a certain extent, the constitutional framework in which the Spanish and Portuguese rules of procedure were created—namely the combination of representative and participatory democracy entailed in the respective Constitutions—resembles the current EU constitutional context. This could be an indication for a possible transposition of the rules on participation of the Portuguese and Spanish systems in the EU legal order. As mentioned, this is not the path taken in this book in order to propose a different normative outlook on participation rights in the EU. It should in any case be noted that the reception of normative solutions found in the legal systems of one Member State that are considered useful and adequate for reinforcing the rule of law in the EU legal system is a valid approach in EU law. This is one of the possible results of the methodology of the EU Courts when resorting to comparative law. See, in particular, Pierre Pescatore (1980) 'Le recours, dans la jurisprudence de la Cour de Justice des Communautés Européennes, à des normes déduites de la comparaison des droits des États membres', *Revue Internationale de Droit Comparé*, Vol. 32, n. 2, pp. 337–59, at pp. 353–4. See also, for an overview of this approach to normative development in the EU legal order, Koen Lenaerts (2003) 'Interlocking legal orders in European and comparative law', *International and Comparative Law Quarterly*, Vol. 52, n. 4, pp. 873–906.

[99] In this sense, for the German case, Schwarze, *op. cit.*, n. 34, p. 1260 and De Smith, Woolf, and Jowell, *op. cit.*, n. 51, p. 416, referring to English law. This is also the reason advanced by Eisenberg for the French and the German rules of procedure (*op. cit.*, n. 59, p. 118).

[100] This is mentioned by De Smith, Woolf, and Jowell, *op. cit.*, *loc. cit*, n. 51.

strict administrative function.[101] Again, these are not insurmountable contentions, even if the respective political and constitutional contexts are determinant in this respect. The fact that regulations affect the rights and legally protected interests of private persons led the Spanish legislator to grant access to the procedure to the natural and legal persons who represent their affected interests and the Portuguese legislator to envisage the participation of the entities representing the interests concerned, in the terms mentioned above. Given the characteristics of the respective political systems, the possible political nature of the decisions at issue and the prevailing model of democracy did not have the effect of excluding regulations from the general provisions on participation.

Finally, another reason for the strength of the distinction between general and individual acts in national legal orders lies in the roots of participation in administrative procedures, which emerged by analogy with judicial procedures. This explains the predominance of the defence rationale. This is perhaps more evident in the English and French cases, which have nevertheless diverged in the legal treatment given to participation. In Germany, the influence of fundamental rights in the administrative system has also led to the predominance of the individual protection as a rationale of participation. It follows that the dominance of an 'adversarial-adjudicative conception of process rights'[102] is imprinted in the administrative law of some European states, which have so far influenced the shaping of EU administrative law. The judicial origin of the right to be heard in administrative procedures is well expressed by the use of the term '*droits de la défense*' or 'rights of the defence', often used in the EU Courts' jurisprudence.

Different combinations of these factors have very likely contributed to keeping the intervention of interested parties within the boundaries of individual decision-making, hampering its possible expansion.[103] Nevertheless, contrasting with the clear-cut distinction between general and individual acts, both at the national and at the EU level, the modes of the exercise of the administrative function are increasingly complex and diverse,

[101] Arguing that this is the reason for the exclusion of regulations from the scope of the Italian rules of procedure on participation, Caranta *et al.*, *op. cit.*, n. 72, pp. 38–9.

[102] Craig, *Administrative Law*, *cit.*, n. 45, p. 373. Tracing the evolution of the *audi alteram partem* principle, Craig underlines that 'process rights are modeled on those of the ordinary courts' (*ibid*, p. 378).

[103] Isaac, *op. cit.*, n. 59, pp. 389 and 396. According to the author, the difficulties found by the French courts in expanding the right to be heard to fields different from the application of sanctions is especially due to this judicial imprint.

and not easily amenable to the general–individual divide that has so far determined the legal regime of administrative participation in both contexts.

2.4.3 *Challenging the individual–general divide*

The clear-cut distinction between individual administrative acts and regulations is challenged by the plethora of diverse forms of administrative action. As a result, the definitions of regulation and administrative act built by reference to their general or individual character and to their abstract or concrete nature are likely often to be unsatisfactory and, as such, unsuitable to determine the legal regime of participation.

Regulations have a relatively undefined legal nature. They are situated at the intersection between the legislative and the administrative function, being both a source of general rules and an instrument of administration.[104] They are usually second-level norms, although in some legal systems they can be directly grounded in constitutional norms. The similarities with the legislative function justified the epithet of materially legislative acts (*actes matériellement législatifs*) used by some authors; others emphasize their similarities with individual decisions.[105] Adding to this complexity, the term regulation encompasses a wide variety of instruments ranging from purely organizational norms defining the composition and functioning of public bodies to norms that regulate the activity and entitlements of private persons. Notwithstanding their general nature, i.e. the absence of identified addressees, these norms can define very precise entitlements and duties, either dispensing with individual acts that concretize them in relation to defined addressees or still requiring an act that eventually specifies whether an activity or person is subject to the previously defined regulatory regime.[106] As underlined by Santamaria Pastor, normative power is not expressed merely through texts drafted in normative form, enacting general and abstract rules as surrogates of laws. It conveys 'extremely varied contents, of atypical symbolic expression (plans, graphs, chemical or mathematical formulae, etc.) and of varied subjective range, which makes the difference between the norm and the single (or plural) act

[104] Maurer, *op. cit.*, n. 68, p. 351.

[105] For the first, Laubadère *et al.*, *op. cit.*, n. 58, p. 582; Fromont indicates that the French doctrine tends to consider regulations as administrative acts (*actes administratifs*), even if they are subject to different rules (*op. cit.*, n. 44, p. 276).

[106] Parejo Alfonso *et al.*, *op. cit.*, n. 46, p. 487–8.

that implements it an extremely fuzzy one'.[107] Independent regulatory authorities have furthered the use of this instrument and, frequently, expanded the cases in which they impact directly upon individuals' legal sphere.[108] Recognizing this individual effect of regulations, some legal systems afford access to courts to persons affected or liable to be affected in the near future by a regulation, in order to control the legality of administrative norms.[109]

Also, administrative acts cannot only be defined by reference to their individualized and concrete nature. Indeed, there are administrative decisions which, ruling a concrete situation, are addressed to a determined or determinable circle of people defined on the basis of general criteria (e.g. the producers of a certain type of cereal or the importers of a product) or acts which determine a legal status (e.g. the declaration of emergency situations). These are termed general administrative acts. Administrative lawyers seem to agree that the determinant element in identifying these acts is the absence of determined or determinable addressees.[110] This is, at least, their distinctive characteristic with relation to 'typical' administrative acts (*actes administratifs*). Being directed at an undetermined group of individuals, they 'promulgate concrete norms [*norms d'espèce*], which refer to one situation or one particular process'.[111] They have the 'ability of producing

[107] Santamaria Pastor, *op. cit.*, n. 48, p. 712. In EU law, numerous examples could be given. Among many others, this is the case of regulations which define the list of tradable products to the exclusion of all others, establishing the chemical, biological, and physical parameters that ground their safety for human health and, hence, their tradability. On this type of act, see below, Chapter 7.

[108] Parejo Alfonso *et al.*, *op. cit.*, n. 46, p. 488. Edoardo Chiti (2004) 'La disciplina procedurale della regolazione', *Rivista Trimestrale di Diritto Pubblico*, Vol. 54, n. 3, pp. 679–736, at p. 685.

[109] This is the case in Germany, although limited to regulations enacted by the *Länder*, where this is envisaged in their respective laws, and restricted to certain types of subject matters (Maurer, *op. cit.*, n. 68, pp. 357–8). In France this possibility is broader: a person claiming to be harmed in their interests by a regulation may contest its validity on the basis of its illegality (*recours en annulation*; see Fromont, *op. cit.*, n. 44, p. 275–6, who mentions Belgium, Italy, and Greece as countries that have followed the French model). In Portugal, the declaration of illegality of a regulation may be requested by whoever has suffered prejudice or might, in the near future, be harmed by its application (Article 73 of Law No. 15/2002, of 22 February, *Diário da República* n.º 45, I-A, as amended).

[110] Maria Chiara Romano (2006) 'Atti amministrativi generali', in Cassese (ed.), *Dizionario di Diritto Pubblico*, *cit.*, n. 20, Vol. I, pp. 491–8; Bernardo G. Mattarella, 'L'attività', *cit.*, n. 37, pp. 663–8; Giannini, *Diritto Amministrativo*, *Dizionario di Diritto Pubblico*, *cit.*, n. 20, p. 288; José Ramón Parada Vasquez (2007), *Derecho Administrativo. Vol. I, Parte general*, 16th edn, Madrid: Marcial Pons, p. 70; Parejo Alfonso *et al.*, *op. cit.*, n. 46, p. 712; Réné Chapus (2001) *Droit administratif général*, Tome I, 15th edn, Paris: Montchrestien, pp. 527–33; André de Laubadère *et al.*, *op. cit.*, n. 58, pp. 584–5.

[111] Chapus, *op. cit.*, n. 58, pp. 516–22 (author's translation).

effects vis-à-vis an open group of people [...], behaviours and circumstances', the category of 'addressees' remaining therefore open.[112] The normative nature of this type of act is contested.[113] In any case, in view of the varied content of regulations, it is not easy to distinguish general administrative acts from this other type of regulatory act. Some authors prefer a formal criterion, proposing to define the nature of the act according to the administrative procedure followed for its adoption. Others deny that administrative acts may be normative and resort to the distinction between norms and acts; they point out that normative acts remain in the legal system and produce legal effects after their application, while the efficacy of administrative acts, even if addressed to an undeterminable number of people, is limited to one application in time.[114] In German administrative law, general administrative acts are considered a sub-species of administrative acts, which are nonetheless regulated by some specific rules: for example, as was seen above, according to the German law on administrative procedure they need not be subject to a participatory procedure. A similar stance prevails in Italian administrative law, which for the purposes of participation treats general administrative acts as regulations.[115] French authors have used the term *décisions d'espèce* to refer to acts which are neither individual nor general (also referred to as *actes non-réglementaires*). This term, however, is not used by the French courts and these acts can be considered both as administrative acts and as regulations, with the corresponding legal consequences, namely regarding whether a participatory procedure should be followed or not.[116]

General administrative acts are possibly the best example of the continuity between regulations and administrative acts. It results from the above that, in between these traditional categories of forms of administrative action, there are regulations that may impact directly on the individuals' legal sphere and *prima facie* administrative acts that have general effects and

[112] Giacinto della Cananea (2000) *Gli atti amministrativi generali*, Cedam: Padova, p. 172 (author's translation).

[113] There seems to be unanimity among French and Spanish authors that these are not normative acts (*opera et loc. cit.*, n. 110). This is less peaceful among Italian authors (in this sense Romano, *op. cit.*, n. 110, p. 492; attributing them a normative character, Cananea, *op. cit.*, pp. 172–5).

[114] For an example of the first stance, see Giannini, *Diritto Amministrativo*, *cit.*, pp. 288–9 (the author considers this to be the safest criterion); defending the second position, Ramón Parada, *op. cit.*, n. 110, p. 59 and Parejo Alfonso *et al.*, *op. cit.*, n. 46, p. 712.

[115] See above, Sub-section 1.4.1. The Italian doctrine tends to consider general administrative acts as a type of administrative act (see, for example, Giannini, *Diritto Amministrativo*, *cit.*, n. 74, *loc. ult. cit.*).

[116] Laubadère *et al.*, *op. cit.*, n. 58, pp. 584–5; Chapus, *op. cit.*, n. 58, pp. 516–22.

cannot be defined by reference to their addressees. Informal acts, such as information, guidelines, and directives, which may have similar effects to legally binding acts, add to the difficulties of the distinction. Where they are legally treated as binding acts, they may be subject to the regime of administrative acts or to that of regulations, depending on the content of the act.

Given the difficulties in defining the effects of an administrative decision purely on the basis of the legal form chosen for the administrative action, two related conclusions can be drawn. First, the legal divide between general and individual acts rests largely on a legal fiction. Effectively, there is a continuum between rule-making and individual administrative decisions. Secondly, as a result, using this formal classification of acts as *the* basic criterion to determine whether participation should be a legal requirement of a decision-making procedure limits excessively the procedural protection of individuals directly affected, excluding it in cases in which it would be required in view of the effects of the act. Simultaneously, it limits the cases in which the collaboration of private parties in decisional procedures is legally regulated. This is one of the main threads of the book, which, given the scope of this work, will be developed only in relation to EU law. At the same time, the suggested abandonment of the general–individual divide as the main premise for delimiting the scope of participation rights requires an alternative frame that delimits a legally meaningful scope of participation. The concept of legal administrative relationship will serve this purpose, while enabling an extension of participation rights more consonant with rule of law requirements.

2.5 Participation and Legal Administrative Relationships

One of the main arguments of this book is that the legal regime of participation should be rooted in the concept of legal administrative relationship and not in the forms of administrative action. Legal administrative relationship may be defined as a '"framework concept" which allows us to explain the legal bonds established between the administration and private persons' that emerge during the procedure followed for the enactment of a legal act and remain after its adoption.[117]

[117] See Vasco Pereira da Silva (1996) *Em busca do acto administrativo perdido*, *cit.*, n. 16, pp. 160–1, drawing on Otto Bachof ('Die Dogmatik des Verwaltungsrechts vor den Gegenwartsaufgaben der Verwaltung' in *Veröffentlichungen der Vereinigung der Deutschen Staatsrechtslehrer*, Berlin, 1972).

For the reasons presented above, grounding the legal regime of participation in the forms of administrative action is unsatisfactory. On the contrary, the concept of legal administrative relationship is more suitable to understand participation as a legally relevant occurrence. The argument is based on two related assertions. First, participation in decisional procedures gives rise to a legal relationship, in which the interveners are confronted with the decision-maker, both to defend their subjective positions eventually affected by the procedure and to contribute to a better representation of the reality that is subject to regulatory intervention. Secondly, given the functions of participation and the values in which it is grounded, access to the procedure should reflect, as far as possible, the material relationship which is envisaged as a result of the decision adopted. This relationship encompasses the several legal spheres that are touched by the outcome of the procedure, i.e. those on which rights, privileges, duties, and charges emerge from the administrative decision. Arguably, the creation of such a relationship can emerge also from acts of general scope. These assertions are substantiated in the two sub-sections below (2.5.2 and 2.5.3). First, however, it is pertinent to briefly elaborate on this concept and on its relevance for this book.

2.5.1 *Theories of administrative action*

The theory of the legal administrative relationship and the theory of the legal forms of administrative action convey two different ways of structuring the administrative action, by focusing on two different aspects of it.[118] The former selects, as an element of analysis, the relationships that are established between different actors by effect of the administrative action and regulates them as legal relationships, which consist of a reciprocity of rights and duties, or, more precisely, of a reciprocity of advantageous and disadvantageous legal positions. The latter propounds that the forms of the acts issued by the administration, chosen according to the effects envisaged, condition the legal regime to which they are subject, namely the procedural rules for their elaboration, and their legal consequences. Its objects of analysis are the results of the administrative action, i.e. the types of decisions, according to the form chosen for their adoption (typically, act, regulation, or contract).

[118] On this Schmidt-Assmann, *op. cit.*, n. 11, pp. 305–47, on which the following observations draw.

The theory of the forms of administrative action has been dominant in most administrative legal systems and has influenced the system of acts of the EU.[119] Despite its shortcomings in grasping the complexity of the administrative action, it is an inexorable element of positive law, essential to the rationality, clarity, and stability of legal actions.[120] Its shortcomings, however, may be usefully supplemented by the concept of legal administrative relationship.

The defenders of an alternative way of structuring the administrative action convincingly argue that the concept of legal administrative relationship has the advantage of focusing on the rights of natural and legal persons affected by an administrative act, whichever its form. This contributes to a better grasp of the relationships of collaboration that often intervene between them. More importantly, it better highlights the various aspects of the material situation under regulation, since it underlines the connections between the different advantageous and disadvantageous legal positions emerging from the administrative action that benefit and are incumbent upon the legal spheres of the persons concerned. Therefore, the concept of legal administrative relationship helps in distinguishing the different levels of legal relationships and the intertwinement between different norms and legal situations that come together in the regulated situation. As such, it is submitted, this is the most suitable perspective of analysis to achieve a desirable balance between the realization of the public interest—the administration's *raison d'être*—and the protection of the rights and interests of those affected by the administrative action in the pursuance of the public interest.[121]

The role of the theory of the legal administrative relationship in administrative law has been widely debated at the national level, in particular in the German legal system. The debates concerned not so much the validity of the theory, but its scope. Specifically, it is disputed whether this theory

[119] In the EU legal system, the dominance of the legal form in structuring the effects of the public action is both furthered and softened: on the one hand, the choice of legal acts is determined by the Treaty provisions regarding each policy area, the institutions not being free to choose the legal instrument which they consider more appropriate in each case; on the other hand, the Court has constantly held that the form of the act is not necessarily determinant of its legal regime, indicating its content as the decisive factor for defining the applicable rules.

[120] Santamaria Pastor, *op. cit.*, n. 48, p. 724.

[121] On this Pereira da Silva, *op. cit.*, n. 16, pp. 186–7 and Schmidt-Assmann, *op. cit.*, n. 11, pp. 312–17. Pereira da Silva underlines the technical advantages emerging from the concept of legal administrative relationship (pp. 188–206).

should become the *fil conducteur* of a general theory of administrative law, thereby replacing the theory of the forms of administrative action—and, therefore, the structuring role that the *acte administratif* has had in the French and German systems of administrative law, as well as in those under their influence—or whether it should be restricted to specific sectors of administrative law, or simply be regarded as a conceptual tool which provides an explanatory and normative basis for dealing with particular problems.[122] The theory of the legal administrative relationship is endorsed in this work in this last sense. First, it is submitted that its core concept contributes to emphasizing the fact that the EU legal order affects not only the relationships among public authorities but also the rights and interests of natural and legal persons. Secondly, it is argued that it does not introduce a 'strange' element into the EU legal order, but rather, it is coherent with its fundamental traits.[123]

2.5.2 *Procedural and material legal administrative relationships*

The concept of administrative relationship may be used in a material and in a procedural sense.[124] The procedural administrative relationship emerges during the decisional procedure, before the adoption of the act that crystallizes the material legal relationship. It consists of the entitlements of intervention of public and private persons in the procedure and the correlative duties of respect and collaboration. The material administrative relationship is composed of the legal bounds of advantageous and disadvantageous positions that link the persons concerned to the administration by the effect of the decision adopted.

The concept of procedural administrative relationship contributes to a better understanding of the intervention of natural and legal persons in the administrative procedure and, particularly, of the relationships established between decision-makers and persons concerned by their decisions in the forging of the latter. There are two different views on how this operates. In one perspective, participation may be seen as the procedural reflection of individual subjective rights, allowing both the administration and those potentially affected by the future decision to uphold their reciprocal rights

[122] On this see Maurer, *op. cit.*, n. 68, pp. 171–3; José Joaquim Gomes Canotilho (1994) 'Relações jurídicas poligonais, ponderação ecológica de bens e controlo judicial preventivo', *Revista Jurídica do Urbanismo e Ambiente*, n. 1, pp. 55–65, at pp. 55–6.

[123] See above, Section 1.1.

[124] Pereira da Silva, *op. cit.*, n. 16, p. 161, pp. 189–90, p. 435, and Schmidt-Assmann, *op. cit.*, n. 11, pp. 375–6.

and duties.[125] The procedure thus emerges as an instrument of regulation of material administrative relationships and participation as a means of defending subjective legal positions.[126] However, while it may be desirable to conceive the procedure as an instrument regulating the administrative relationships, this view needs to be tempered by also considering the objective function of the administrative procedure.[127] In fact, the latter should ensure at the same time the correct and efficient performance of administrative action. As explained, participation is also relevant in connection with this objective function of the procedure. In addition, the legal sphere of persons other than holders of subjective rights may also be touched by the procedure in such a way that they are encompassed in the material relationships that stem from the adoption of the act. Therefore, procedural administrative relationships also include persons who, neither being affected in their subjective rights nor being directly targeted by the envisaged act, are affected in their legally protected interests and voice concerns that are pertinent to the composition of interests that ground the final decision. The range of interests that are legally pertinent (i.e. those that, by the force of law, need to be taken into account in each case) is defined by the applicable rules and principles. In this sense, procedural administrative relationships should be conceived also in light of the substantive regime that it serves. Furthermore, the persons establishing a procedural relationship with the decision-maker are not necessarily only those who intervene in the procedure to exercise participation rights. Other persons take part in the procedure without being concerned by the envisaged act—in the sense that their rights and interests will not be touched by the final decision—because their intervention is considered relevant for the correctness of the procedure. They also enter into a relationship with the decision-maker. This includes both public entities that have decisional or advisory competences connected to the matter under appreciation and natural or legal persons who intervene in the capacity of experts.

This broader view, specifically in what refers to interested persons[128] is particularly relevant in the context of complex administrative decisions which involve multiple and contradictory interests.[129] These result mostly

[125] This is the conception prevailing in German administrative law (Pereira da Silva, *op. cit.*, n. 16, p. 419). On this, see Maurer, *op. cit.*, n. 68, p. 167.

[126] Pereira da Silva, *op. cit.*, n. 16, p. 161.

[127] In a similar sense, Pereira da Silva, *op. cit.*, n. 16, p. 441.

[128] See Section 1.3.

[129] Maurer, *op. cit.*, n. 68, p. 170. Canotilho, *op. cit.*, p. 170, n. 122, pp. 56–8.

from a 'steering' administrative activity, i.e. that through which the administration controls and regulates socio-economic sectors. The ensuing administrative decisions, even if formally destined to specific addressees, often have effects which stray beyond the legal sphere of the latter, having wider consequences in a 'given environment or market situation'.[130] These decisions regulate a complex set of divergent and convergent interests and the decision-maker has the duty to consider them impartially and on an equal footing in the respective procedure. At the same time, the interested persons admitted to the procedure have duties of collaboration and respect.[131] According to Schmidt-Assmann, 'the procedural administrative relationship expresses an idea of "equality of arms" between interested parties'. Thus, it ensures 'a correct balance of the interests voiced by the interveners, taking into consideration what the substantive law has defined for the resolution of the conflict'.[132] In fact, it results from what was stated above that the interests voiced in the procedure need to be evaluated in light of the criteria defined in the applicable substantive law.

The previous observations highlight that the concept of procedural administrative relationship, as such, does not enable us to grasp fully the advantages entailed in grounding the legal regime of participation in the concept of legal administrative relationship. It needs to be put in context both with the material situation being regulated and with the relevant substantive rules that shape the ensuing material relationship. The ability of the act to change the legal positions of the persons affected—i.e. its legal effects—is the basis on which to identify the persons who will be granted access to the decisional procedure. In turn, the criteria for assessing the interests voiced in the procedure, and hence for identifying the different procedural status of participants, are contained in the substantive law regulating the matter. The procedure becomes a projection of the material situation that is the object of administrative intervention. First, even if the two concepts do not coincide, the procedural administrative relationship should, to the greatest extent possible, reflect the material administrative relationship that is envisaged to result from the procedure. Secondly, as mentioned, it should be framed by the legal criteria defined in the applicable substantive norms.

[130] Schmidt-Assmann, *op. cit.*, n. 11, p. 184, author's translation.
[131] Schmidt-Assmann, *op. cit.*, n. 11, pp. 25 and 184–5.
[132] Schmidt-Assmann, *op. cit.*, n. 11, p. 376.

Thus, the concept of procedural administrative relationship structures, according to an idea of equality, the legal links that emerge in the administrative procedure between the decision-maker, on the one hand, and the different natural and legal persons, on the other. It reflects both the rights and the legally protected interests of the persons affected by the ensuing decision and it is shaped in light of the relevant substantive norms. In this way, participation is grounded in the material effects produced by the decisions in the legal sphere of private persons, and is assessed in light of the legal criteria applicable to the subject matter at issue. Arguably, this ensures that the deployment of the administrative function respects not only the rights and interests of the affected persons but also the set of interests that have been defined as legally protected in the applicable substantive norms.

It follows that the procedure, more than an instrument of regulation of administrative relationships, is a projection of the different aspects implicated in the material situation being regulated. This perspective ties in with a pluralist conception of the administrative procedure, according to which this is the ideal site for the composition of private and public interests that come together in the administrative action and are thereby affected.

2.5.3 *The case of regulations*

This conception of the procedure applies to acts of both an individual and a general nature. Admittedly, the concrete procedural steps are different in each case. Nevertheless, both types of acts should be adopted according to parameters that ensure a correct exercise of the administrative function with respect for the rights and legally protected interests of the persons concerned. It is possible that in the case of regulations or, more broadly, in the adoption of acts of a general nature, the function of the procedure is predominantly to ensure the objective and due consideration of interests that need to be balanced by the decision-maker, in view of the public interests to be achieved. Precisely because in theory this type of act is not directed at producing immediate effects in the legal sphere of natural and legal persons, procedural protection of the legal interests of those affected becomes a secondary concern. However, where such effects are in fact produced, the distinctions between individual administrative acts and acts of a general nature, as well as between the functions of the procedure in each instance, are considerably blurred.

The possibility of analysing regulations in a relational framework is not unproblematic. Some authors claim that material administrative relationships cannot emerge from rules as such.[133] This assertion is grounded in the general and abstract nature of regulations. A norm cannot give rise to an administrative relationship: this only comes about when concretized by an individual administrative decision, by a contract established between the administration and private parties, or by another legally relevant behaviour, which effectively links two or more people by reciprocal rights and duties. By analogy, the same observation is valid for general administrative acts.

Whereas in principle one would agree that the abstract and general provision of the rights and duties is not enough to give rise to an administrative relationship, it should nonetheless be acknowledged that there are different shades of the general and abstract characteristics of regulations. It follows that only an analysis of the content of the act can reveal the veracity of the assumption that no administrative relationship may emerge from general and abstract acts. In certain circumstances, this will be proven untrue.

Despite the absence of individualized addressees, regulations or general administrative acts may impact directly on private legal spheres, in a similar way to individual administrative acts. Two situations need to be distinguished in this respect. It might occur that the regulation effectively contains an individual decision, adopted under the form of regulation. In this case, an administrative relationship emerges directly from the regulation. This however should be subject to the legal regime of administrative decisions. In EU law, this possibility was explicitly recognized in Article 230(4) EC, according to which a decision adopted under the form of a regulation could be of direct and individual concern to a natural or legal person. The new wording of Article 263(4) TFEU covers this situation: an act 'which (. . .) is of direct and individual concern to them' may be either a decision addressed to another person or a general act.[134] In any event, the fact that a general act may directly and individually concern certain persons, thereby effectively containing a decision, does not mean that the act

[133] Schmidt-Assmann, *op. cit.*, n. 11, pp. 316–17, and Pereira da Silva, *op. cit.*, n. 16, pp. 149–86 and pp. 202–3, referring to the German legal doctrine.

[134] In the scheme of Article 263(4) TFEU, regulatory acts that do not entail implementing measures need to be considered separately from other general acts, given that, in the latter case, standing only depends on direct concern. On the difficulties in interpreting the expression 'regulatory acts', see references below in Chapter 4, Sub-section 4.1.1.

changes its nature.[135] A clear example is the terrorist lists inserted in Council regulations. According to the Courts, the fact that persons and entities who are subject to the restrictive measures imposed by these regulations are expressly named in one of its annexes 'does not mean that the act is not of general application within the meaning of the second paragraph of Article 249 EC [current 288 TFEU] or that it is not to be classified as a regulation'.[136]

Alternatively, the regulation may define intensively the contours of the material situation in a way that it decisively conditions the content of the administrative relationships that will fall within its realm. The norm defines precise rights and duties, which will emerge as such in the legal sphere of individuals, by the effect of a legally relevant fact (e.g. the application for inserting a given good in a Union list of tradable products). In these cases, even if no administrative relationship emerges as such from the enactment of the regulation, the rules that it contains shape the content of the administrative relationship which will emerge between the public decision-makers and the legal or natural persons who are subject to this regulation.[137] In these circumstances, after the adoption of the regulation, the possibility of it affecting the persons who fall within its realm is effective and not merely potential. In a way, this possibility is today recognized by Article 263(4) TFEU, if one assumes that the expression 'regulatory acts' refers to regulations (i.e. acts of general nature).[138]

That general provisions may directly create rights and duties in the legal spheres of individuals is demonstrated, in EU law, by the cases in which EU institutions incur non-contractual liability as a result of the adoption of regulations. In these cases, a direct link must be established between the adoption of an unlawful norm and actual and certain damage.[139] Thus, legal

[135] Case C-358/89, *Extramet Industrie v Council* [1991] ECR I-2501, paragraph 13. For a recent application, see for example, Case T-16/04, *Arcelor SA v European Parliament and Council* [2010] nyr., paragraph 94).

[136] Joined Cases C-402/05 P and C-415/05 P, *Yassin Adbullah Kadi and Al Barakat International Foundation v Council and Commission* [2008] ECR I-6351, paragraph 241.

[137] This idea resulted from a discussion that the author had with Vasco Pereira da Silva, for whose kindness she would like to thank him.

[138] On the doubts that this expression raises, see, among others, Michael Dougan (2008) 'The Treaty of Lisbon 2007: Winning minds, not hearts', *Common Market Law Review*, Vol. 45, n. 3, pp. 617–703, at pp. 677–8. See further Chapter 4, Sub-section 4.1.1.

[139] As is known, the three requirements of non-contractual liability are unlawful conduct on the part of the Union, actual and certain damage, and a causal link between the unlawful conduct and the damage alleged.

or natural persons may suffer an unlawful charge as a result of the adoption of the norm. For example, a regulation defining the level of production aid to processed tomato products which is adopted without consideration of the criteria defined in the basic regulation, and which, as a result, conduces to a lower amount of aid, hinders the beneficiaries' entitlements.[140] From this decision emerges a concrete administrative relationship between the Commission—who will pay the amount defined—and the beneficiaries of the aid—whose legal entitlements are hence concretely defined. According to EU law, participation rights are excluded in these instances, given the form of the act and its generality. And yet, this act may produce actual and certain damage in the legal sphere of natural and legal persons.

The fact that a material administrative relationship may emerge directly from the enactment of a general act strengthens the claim for the recognition of participation rights in the respective decisional procedures. When rules have external effects liable to affect identifiable persons in their rights and interests, the subjective rationale of participation comes to the fore: participation in rule-making procedures is also grounded in the need to protect subjective rights and interests that might be particularly affected by the outcome of the procedure. There is no valid reason why, in cases such as these, those affected by the general act should not *a priori* be given an opportunity to express their views in the course of the respective administrative procedure.

2.6 Hurdles and Limits of Participation

The previous sections have mapped the rights-based approach to participation that grounds this book. In this conception, participation rights are instrumental in two related ways. First, their recognition depends on the underlying substantive positions. The ultimate reason for the procedural intervention resides in a particular relation of the participant with the material situation that motivated the procedure. This essentially follows from the fact that a public decision resulted in an interference in the legal sphere of legal or natural persons, creating or reshaping their respective advantageous or disadvantageous positions. In other words, participation rights are justified where the regulatory activity of the EU institutions and bodies amounts to shaping legal administrative relationships between

[140] Case C-243/05 P, *Agraz SA and others v Commission* [2006] ECR I-10833.

public and private entities, in the sense that they either define or decisively determine the content of the rights, interests, duties, and charges recognized to or impinging upon the persons concerned. Secondly, given the convergence between the subjective and the objective functions of participation, participation rights are an instrument to ensure both the fair treatment of the persons affected by the procedure and the protection of the private and public interests which, being legally relevant for the decision at issue, need to be considered in the respective procedure. As stated above, both favour the achievement of materially just decisions.

The instrumentality of participation makes it contingent. A first manifestation of this contingency is the argument that the bearing of participation may vary according to the type of power exercised, namely depending on whether this is a discretionary power or not. Although this variable is likely to be less relevant when considering participation in rule-making procedures—indeed, most likely the definition of rules involves the exercise of discretion—it is worth making a few observations in this regard. Certainly, participation is all the more important when the administration uses a discretionary power, since it contributes to structuring the process of defining which solution is best compatible with the interests the decision-maker needs to satisfy by law, while ensuring respect for the persons' rights and interests. It should be noted that participation is equally pertinent in cases of 'technical discretion', that is in cases in which the decision-maker's choice is bound by objective parameters (the decision does not result from a discretionary assessment, in a narrow sense) but where the final decision entails an evaluation of technical or specialized knowledge.[141] But participation is also relevant when discretion is virtually absent. One may argue that, in these cases, the exercise of participation rights is legally significant only to the extent that it ensures respect for the dignity of the persons affected. Indeed, the final composition of interests is determined by the applicable rules. Yet, an instrumental logic still applies, since the intervention of the persons affected may be useful in order to better define the contours of the factual situation under examination, especially in cases in which these are contentious.[142]

[141] On this distinction, Bernardo G. Mattarella (2006) 'Discrezionalità amministrativa', in Cassese (ed.), *Dizionario di Diritto Pubblico*, *cit.*, n. 20, Vol. III, pp. 1993–2003, at p. 1006.

[142] This is particularly true when the facts on the basis of which the administration decides are controversial. Referring to Italian law, but of general relevance, Giovanni Virga (1998) *La partecipazione al procedimento amministrativo*, Milano: Giuffrè, pp. 55–7.

In addition, a series of conditions of decision-making may influence the bearing of participation and, at the same time, pose problems to the possible extension of participation rights to rule-making procedures. First, participation may become undesirable in contexts of socio-economic or scientific complexity and uncertainty in which decision-making processes may be embedded. On certain occasions, participation may be detrimental to the very function of the procedure or to the protection of legally relevant interests. For example, it may be argued that the consideration of the interests voiced, which follows from the exercise of participation rights, may conflict with the need to base decision-making on technical and scientific assessments. These conditions may require that the decision-maker is left with enough margin of manoeuvre to decide on whether or not to open the procedure to interested persons, an effect that the recognition of participation rights would in principle prevent. Secondly, especially when participation rights are granted in rule-making procedures, the range of interested persons may be such that it is impossible to hear them without blocking the whole decisional procedure. Thirdly, in some situations, celerity is the core of the administrative action and this may not be compatible with the hearing. The difficulties or even impracticalities of participation come to the fore in situations in which being expeditious is a necessary requirement to the utility of the public intervention. Swiftness is required, for example, when the protection of public health compels the immediate withdrawal of a suspect product from the market, irrespective of the consequences that this might have for the respective producers. Fourthly, in other situations, secrecy may be the key to the effectiveness of the measures envisaged. This was one of the contending aspects involved in the judicial conflict regarding the legality of the terrorist lists adopted by the Council.

These possible hurdles to participation are different manifestations of the classic opposition between participation and effectiveness of decision-making. They may impact both on the scope of participation and on the forms of exercising these rights. At first sight, some militate against broadening the scope of participation, a possibility that is opened by grounding participation rights in legal administrative relationships. However, it is possible to accommodate in different ways the requirements of decision-making explained above and the need to ensure respect for the values underlying participation rights.

Beginning with the last two hurdles mentioned, how celerity and secrecy of decision-making may impact on the exercise of participation rights is a matter that has already been decided by the EU Courts. In these situations, it is justified that the persons concerned are not heard before the adoption of the decision, but they need to be given the opportunity to put forward their views at a subsequent stage, namely during judicial procedures.[143] This option should, in any case, be duly grounded and justified.

The second hurdle mentioned—the difficulties or impracticalities of participation resulting from a great number of participants—might be countered by making access to the procedure dependent on previous aggregation of interests. Similarly to solutions found in national law, concerned persons voicing the same interests may be required to nominate a representative, or to produce one single document that may include a statement of divergent opinions. The choice of interlocutors on the part of the decision-maker should be backed by their duty to aggregate the interests they represent.

Not being the ideal situation, the possibility of representation—hence, indirect participation—does not necessarily deny the values of participation. The conditions under which representation should be accepted avoid this effect. First, the need for a representative ought to be justified in light of the conditions of decision-making (e.g. an otherwise excessive number of participants). An additional way to ensure that resort to this possibility is not abused to the detriment of participants is to allow for a mechanism of opposition or contestation during the procedure. The practice of EU decision-makers in this regard could be scrutinized by the Courts and by the Ombudsman. Secondly, the nomination of a representative does not necessarily mean that possible specific situations of those represented are not taken into account by the decision-maker. Admitting representation does not mean that the decision-maker may require that interested persons, independently of their views, need to 'speak with one voice'. Different groups should be entitled to nominate different representatives. As mentioned, the common positions communicated to the decision-maker by the representative may include statements of dissent by those represented. This could be seen as a way of sharing the burden of participation between participants and decision-maker. Precise rules need to be defined in order to avoid the situation where, instead of sharing the burden, the decision-maker transfers it to the participants. Thirdly, the representative should have the duty to act fairly in relation to the represented, namely the duty to

[143] Case C-28/05, *G.J. Dokter and others v Minister van Landbouw, Natuur en Voedselkwaliteit* [2006] ECR I-5431, paragraph 76; Kadi and Al Barakat, *cit.*, n. 136, paragraphs 338–342, 344, and 348.

report, and the decision-maker could be charged with controlling this. Finally, the decision-maker needs to check the mandates of the representative or representatives in order to control whether they cover the range of persons possibly affected by the measure at issue. This control of representativeness applies also in cases where the representative is a collective person.

The first hurdle mentioned above is perhaps the one with the most far-reaching impact on participation rights. Undoubtedly, the recognition of participation rights implies limiting the action of the decision-maker, since it bounds the exercise of discretionary powers to the observance of procedural rules which are directed at ensuring the procedural protection and due consideration of the persons and interests affected by the decision. In certain areas, this may disrupt the decisional procedure beyond acceptable limits.

At this point, one should recall the distinction between the procedural status of the two circles of interested persons sketched above as well as the fact that their procedural position is influenced by the way their underlying subjective position is valued by the legal system.[144] On this basis, one way to accommodate participation and effectiveness of decision-making, where these become incompatible, is to accept that the intervention of the second circle of interested persons—holders of legally protected interests that, in light of the applicable norms, need to be taken into account by the decision-maker—may be facultative, i.e. not imposed on the decision-maker. While they are entitled to access the procedure because their legal sphere is affected by the decision, their personal position is not protected as such by the legal system. This is not the case with respect to holders of affected subjective rights, who, as mentioned before, in light of the applicable norms, may aim at acquiring a good or an advantage granted by the administration, or at preventing a specific public interference in their legal sphere, and whose specific situation needs therefore to be considered by the decision-maker. The dignitarian rationale of the intervention of holders of subjective rights prevails over instrumental considerations and the decision-maker is bound to hear them even if this conflicts with the effectiveness of the decisional procedure. Nevertheless, given the objective conditions that give rise to participation—i.e. the existence of an act the content of which is precise enough to give rise to a material administrative

[144] See, further, Chapter 5, Sub-section 5.3; Chapter 7, Sub-section 7.3.3; Chapter 8, Sub-section 8.2.3.

relationship—and the requirement that grounds the intervention of these persons—i.e. the fact that their legal sphere is implicated in that material administrative situation—the decision not to hear this group of interested persons needs to be justified. This decision is detrimental to the interests of the potential participants. While this may be justified on the basis of the very requirements of decision-making in the given circumstances, the values that underpin the recognition of participation rights ought not to be fully depleted. Therefore, not only should the decision-maker be bound to motivate this decision, but also they should be able to demonstrate that sufficient heed was paid to the relevant legally protected interests. In other words, the decision-maker needs to show prudence and diligence in consideration for the affected legal positions of the putative participants. This is, nonetheless, one important aspect that contributes to the stronger procedural position of holders of subjective rights in relation to holders of legally protected interests.[145]

The respect of subjective rights is, therefore, the ultimate limit to the contingency of participation. This includes cases where restrictions to fundamental rights may emerge from the final decision, but also situations in which a person's conduct or entitlements are under scrutiny.

Now, these considerations influence and further the proposed forms to accommodate participation rights in cases in which celerity and secrecy clash therewith and also in cases in which direct participation may be replaced by indirect participation. Considering that standing may be more restricted than access to decisional procedures, the possibility of compensating for the lack of a hearing by granting interested persons an opportunity to put forward their views in judicial proceedings may be limited to holders of subjective rights. This is still the case in EU law, should an extended view of participation rights be accepted, with the apparent exception of self-executing regulatory acts.[146] Regarding the choice between direct participation and representation, the aggregation of interests should only be required

[145] This point is developed below (cf. n. 144 above).

[146] It remains to be seen how the new Article 263(4) TFEU will effectively impact on standing, in particular, how restrictive the Courts will be in granting access to natural and legal persons directly but not individually affected. At the time of the writing, the Courts had not yet addressed this issue, having decided that actions pending at the time of the entry into force of the Lisbon Treaty should be decided in light of previous Article 230(4) EC (see, for example, Case T-539/08, *Etimine SA v Commission* [2010], nyr., paragraphs 73–80). The expression 'self-executing' regulatory acts is taken from Dougan, n. 138, p. 676.

in cases in which the decision-maker is not bound to consider the individual position of interested persons.

2.7 Rights-based Participation

It follows from the above that rights-based participation refers to the intervention during a decision-making procedure of holders of subjective rights or of legally protected interests potentially affected by the outcome of the procedure. This substantive relation to the procedure is the basis for granting participation rights. Their recognition is, therefore, dependent on the underlying substantive positions. As conceived in this book, participation rights are grounded in the rule of law in a double sense: not only do they allow for the procedural protection of the persons and interests affected, but they also enhance the conditions for the achievement of materially just decisions to the extent that they favour the consideration and balancing of interests involved, in light of the criteria legally defined in the applicable norms.

The concept of legal administrative relationship is the most suitable to understand this type of participation. First, this concept contributes to better identifying, beyond the strict formality of the act, both types of situation in which participation rights are justified—those in which the act adopted effectively shapes the links between the advantageous and disadvantageous positions of the persons affected—and the several legal spheres potentially touched by the outcome of the procedure, as well as to ordering the different links established between them. Therefore, it is conducive to a better representation of the material situation underlining the procedure and helps to circumscribe the persons who should be entitled to access it, i.e. those involved in the material administrative relationship that, predictably, will emerge from the final decision. This includes those who, being touched by the procedure, voice interests that need to be considered by the decision-maker insofar as they are public interests that, according to the applicable norms, need to be pursued in that instance. Their connection to the procedure gives them, however, a qualified position to defend such interests and this should be legally recognized. Secondly, resort to the concept of administrative relationship contributes to structuring the roles of participants during the procedure, in accordance with their relation to the respective subject matter and with legally binding substantive criteria. Overall, the recognition of participation rights should be framed by the concept of legal administrative relationship, rather than being dependent on the forms of administrative action. In fact, in view of the blurred distinction between general and individual acts, a rule determining the exclusion of participation rights from procedures leading up to the adoption of general acts overlooks the cases in which the exercise of participation rights would be justified. This limits the scope of the latter without consideration for the values that underpin such rights or for the functions that rights-based participation fulfils in the procedure.

From a procedural perspective, participation rights may be broadly defined as advantageous positions that allow their holders to influence the exercise of the decisional power. These procedural rights are the correlative of the duty of the decision-maker to carefully and impartially examine the factual situation before them. This requires both the consideration of the substantive rights and interests of the persons whose legal spheres are concerned by the decision at issue and of the set of legally protected interests that, according to the applicable rules, should be pursued in each instance.

While participation rights have the same ground and functions, the underlying material positions of the persons affected (i.e. the person's position in relation to the subject matter being decided) may be differently protected by the legal system. This different substantive legal position of the participant determines a different evaluation of their procedural role and also of the content of their procedural rights. As such, a stronger procedural position may be granted to holders of subjective rights when compared to that of holders of legally protected interests. This is reflected also in the possible ways of accommodating participation with competing decision-making requirements that may clash with participation rights.

Chapter 3

Participation beyond Procedural Rights

This chapter provides an account of the institutional practices of participation in EU decisional processes. It returns to the relatively undefined meaning of 'participation at large' characterized at the beginning of the previous chapter, in particular to the forms of interest representation and consultation fostered by the EU institutions. Its purpose is twofold. First, participation, in this broad sense, is characterized as a constitutive feature of EU decision-making. This statement is grounded, in part, in Treaty provisions, namely those on the EU advisory bodies, and, in part, in institutional practices that have developed beyond the Treaties. Current Article 11 of the Treaty on the European Union has acknowledged the constitutional relevance of these practices, which have contributed 'to shaping the EU's emergent constitutional form and nature'.[1] Secondly, the characterization of participatory practices, which are both backed up by or dispense with legal rules, clarifies the differences between these and rights-based participation. In a way, this chapter contributes to delimit negatively the concept of participation that will ground the subsequent chapters of the book, by clarifying what a rights-based participation is *not*. At the same time, it shows that the latter has been absent from the EU decisional processes. More importantly, by demonstrating how participation is embedded in European integration, the consideration of the more political forms of participation stresses the inadequacy of the current legal scope of participation that will be the object of the following chapters.

The first section surveys the role of the advisory bodies created by the Treaties, together with the relevant provisions on participation that were envisaged in the Treaty establishing the European Coal and Steel

[1] Gráinne de Búrca (2003) 'The constitutional challenge of new governance in the European Union', *European Law Review*, Vol. 28, n. 6, pp. 814–39, at p. 817.

Community. This provides an overview of the roots of interest representation in European integration and reveals some of the reasons that turned interest representation into a constitutive feature of the EU legal and institutional setting. The second section analyses the institutional practice of decision-making in the EU, focusing on the instances of participation present in first pillar committees and agencies. The choice of committees and agencies to illustrate the institutional practice of decision-making is not random. Committees permeate through decision- and rule-making procedures. EU agencies embody a form of deploying administrative functions that has acquired renewed relevance in the recent years. In addition, both have been at the core of the legitimacy and accountability discussion, which has embedded most recent developments on 'participation at large' in EU decision-making. This section will be completed with a brief account of the role of interest groups beyond the formalized instances of consultation.

Participation in EU decision-making has undergone a transformation process, which accompanied the constitutional transition of the Community from the completion of market integration to a more encompassing political Union with widened competences in social and political areas. The third section analyses the meaning of participation in the context of the EU governance discourses, in particular the Commission's stance revealed in the White Paper on Governance, where participation was heralded as one of the good governance principles.[2] This 'governance approach' to participation represented a turning point in the meaning attributed to participation in the EU political and legal system. Insofar as the White Paper can be seen as a 'constitutional episode' in the wider EU constitutional process,[3] participation acquired with it a renewed constitutional significance, later reflected in the Constitutional Treaty and, subsequently, in the Treaty of Lisbon. In this respect, the White Paper is the most visible point of a line of

[2] Commission of the European Communities, 'European Governance. A White Paper', COM (2001) 428 final, Brussels, 25.7.2001 (hereinafter, White Paper on Governance or, simply, White Paper).

[3] Neil Walker (2001), 'The White Paper in constitutional context', in Christian Joerges, Yves Mény, and Joseph H.H. Weiler (eds), 'Symposium: Mountain or Molehill? A critical appraisal of the Commission White Paper on Governance', Jean Monnet Working Paper No. 6/01 (the quoted expression is withdrawn from p. 2; see below, note 186). Suggesting the emergence of a new model of European constitutionalism premised on new systems of governance and perceived in recent developments, including 'the mobilization and gradual recognition of civil society in the European policy debate', see de Búrca, *op. cit.*, n. 1, pp. 815, 830.

normative development which intersects with the long-standing, more traditional, and silent strand of interest representation.

This chapter is based on an institutional-functional approach to the different forms of participation currently in place. The form of presenting the various themes differs. The first section, as well as the first part of the third section, presents the evolution of participation rules and mechanisms. The second section is more descriptive of the participation mechanisms currently in place.

3.1 Participatory Governance in the Making

3.1.1 *At the roots of integration: the ECSC Treaty*

At first sight, tracing to the 1950s the beginning of participatory governance in the EU might seem far-fetched. In this context, the term is certainly anachronistic. Nevertheless, the following analysis of participation under the ECSC Treaty illustrates the different forms and roles participation acquired throughout European integration. If by participatory governance one means policy-making underpinned by participation,[4] its roots can undoubtedly be found in the early days of integration, as will be shown below. Indeed, analysing the instances of participation in the realm of the ECSC Treaty not only contributes to explaining the relevance participation later acquired but also demonstrates that participation is a genetic feature of European integration.

Both the Treaty of Paris and the Treaties of Rome fostered forms of institutionalized interest representation through the creation of advisory bodies, a Consultative Committee in the first case, and the Economic and Social Committee in the second, common to the European Economic Community (EEC) and to the European Atomic Energy Community (Euratom). Even if influenced by the constitutional traditions of most

[4] See Beate Kohler-Koch (2008) 'Does participatory governance hold its promises?' in B. Kohler-Koch and F. Larat (eds), *Efficient and Democratic Governance*, Connex Report Series n. 9 pp. 265–95, at p. 282, contrasting participatory governance to participatory democracy. As Koch argues, participatory democracy is normatively a more demanding concept: it requires compliance with normative standards that are not necessarily ensured by 'participatory engineering' (this term is used by T. Zittel (2008) 'Participatory Engineering: Promises and Pitfalls', in B. Kohler Koch, D. de Bievre, and W. Moloney, *Opening EU-Governance to Civil Society—Gains and Challenges*, CONNEX Report Series No. 5, pp. 119–44).

Member States at the time, this institutionalization of interest representation was a response to specific regulatory needs of the newly created organizations, calling for collaboration with interested parties.

In the case of the European Coal and Steel Community (ECSC), the relevance of collaboration and support of those affected by the Community's action was explicitly recognized in the Treaty. Indeed, Article 5, while defining in broad terms the competences of the Community, determined that these were to be carried out by the institutions 'with a minimum of administrative machinery and *in close co-operation with the parties concerned*'.[5]

There is an essential difference between the EEC Treaty and the ECSC Treaty with regard to participation. While the former in its inception granted formalized participation only through the Economic and Social Committee,[6] the latter's provisions on the respective Consultative Committee were only one aspect of the formal possibilities of participation of interested parties in the Community's decision-making procedures. This is possibly due to the markedly supranational nature of the ECSC combined with the concrete nature of the Treaty (*traité-loi* or 'legislative Treaty' as opposed to the 'framework' Treaty—*traité-cadre*—establishing the EEC).[7] In fact, in building the common market, the High Authority established direct contacts with undertakings the activity of which fell within the realm of the Treaty. In addition, several provisions of the ECSC Treaty created rights and duties in the legal sphere of the persons concerned by its rules.[8] This introduces a different value of participation beyond the general framework of participatory governance: other than the policy reasons that justified the involvement of interested persons in policy-making, participation could also be grounded in the legal constraints that result from authoritative decisions of a public entity and affect the legal sphere of the persons concerned. This bridge between participation grounded in policy reasons and participation grounded in the procedural

[5] Emphasis added.

[6] With the exception of the intervention of parties concerned in state aid procedures (today, ruled by Article 108(2) TFEU, consolidated version, OJ C 83/47, 30.03.2010) which will be analysed in Chapter 8.

[7] In this sense, Jürgen Schwarze (2006) *European Administrative Law*. Revised 1st edn, London: Sweet and Maxwell, p. 1321.

[8] E.g. the High Authority could demand undertakings to provide information on their individual investment plans (Article 54, paragraph 3 ECSC); moreover, the undertakings had the right to benefit from the results of technical and economic research promoted by the High Authority and financed with the product of the levies charged (Article 55(2) ECSC).

protection of the interests affected by regulatory measures can be detected in the ECSC Treaty, even if it might not have been consistently assumed.

Procedural participation

Three different situations should be distinguished when analysing instances of procedural participation envisaged in the ECSC Treaty. First, the Treaty determined that individual decisions imposing pecuniary sanctions or determining periodic penalty payments had to be adopted after giving the person concerned the opportunity to submit comments (Article 36, first paragraph). Given the nature of the powers involved and the legal traditions of Member States, one can surmise that participation had, in this case, a predominantly defensive function. This provision ensured, at the Treaty level, the respect for the inalienable due process right to be heard.

Secondly, the procedure of elaboration of some measures of general scope required the previous consultation of interested persons. In fact, in all cases where consultation of the Consultative Committee was compulsory within the terms of the Treaty, associations of undertakings had 'the right to submit to the High Authority . . . the comments of its members on the proposed action'.[9] To this extent, associations of undertakings had a relevant collaborative function in the performance of the High Authority's functions. This feature was intrinsically linked to the intention of maintaining a reduced administrative machinery, but, arguably, also ensured the procedural protection of the interests affected by the decision of the High Authority.

This enlarged considerably the possibilities of participation in decisions affecting the interests of undertakings, since the Consultative Committee needed to intervene in decisions regarding quite a few relevant matters. Among these were the publication of general objectives and programmes by the High Authority, the determination of minimum and maximum prices, the initiation or support for research related to the production and increased use of coal and steel, the establishment of a system of production quotas in cases of market crises, the adoption of recommendations in cases in which undertakings would charge abnormally low prices as a result of paying abnormally low wages, or decisions adopted following Member States' practices having harmful effects on competition.[10] Associations of

[9] Article 48(2) ECSC.

[10] Respectively, Article 46(4); Article 61, a) and b); Article 55(2); Article 58(1); Article 68(2); Article 67(2) and (3), all of the ECSC Treaty.

undertakings thus had a privileged position in relation to associations of other potentially interested persons. However, in order to counterbalance this weight, the Treaty demanded that the High Authority, when seeking information or striving to facilitate the performance of its tasks, would resort to associations of undertakings which ensured the representation of workers and consumers in their organization.[11]

In other instances, the Treaty simply enshrined the right of persons concerned to submit comments, without the mediation of associations. This was defined, for example, in relation to the adoption of reasoned opinions regarding individual financial aid programmes.[12]

In a third group of cases, participation of concerned parties was not a compulsory procedural requirement for the adoption of the acts envisaged in the Treaty. First, the High Authority, in the performance of its functions, could at any time consult 'Governments, the various parties concerned (undertakings, workers, consumers and dealers) and their associations, and any experts'. Secondly, undertakings, workers, consumers, and dealers, as well as their associations, could present any suggestions or comments to the High Authority on questions affecting them.[13] This norm may be seen as a logical consequence of the collaboration which the Treaty intended to establish between the High Authority, on the one hand, and the persons affected by its activity, on the other.[14]

There is still another side to this collaboration. The High Authority was entitled to obtain from the persons concerned the information needed for the fulfilment of its decisional functions. It could unilaterally determine which information should be provided by the undertakings concerned and, in case of an infringement, the latter could be subject to a pecuniary sanction.[15]

These different ways of involving interested parties in the decision-making procedures of the High Authority gave rise to a constant flow of

[11] Article 48, paragraph 3 ECSC. For the legal and practical problems that this provision raised, see Paul Reuter (1953) *La Communauté Européenne du Charbon et de l'Acier*, Paris: LGDJ, pp. 111–12.

[12] Article 54, paragraph 4 ECSC.

[13] Article 46, paragraphs 1 and 2 ECSC, respectively.

[14] On these provisions, see Sergio Neri (1970) 'Diposizioni generali. Articoli 46 e 47', in Rolando Quadri, Riccardo Monaco, and Alberto Trabucchi (eds), *Trattato istitutivo della Comunità Europea del Carbone e dell'Acciaio: Commentario, Vol. II, Articoli 45–100*, Milano: Giuffrè, pp. 597–642, at pp. 623–4.

[15] Reuter, *op. cit.*, n. 11, p. 111. Cf. Articles 47, 54(3) and 65(3) ECSC.

information and negotiations between them. One commentator noted at the time: '[T]here seems to be a policy of information and persuasion in Luxembourg'.[16]

The Consultative Committee

The creation of the Consultative Committee responded to the political will to give institutional voice to the concerns of interested parties in the integration process, not least due to the pressure exerted by trade unions. While some authors suggest the intention of compensating for the feeble political control exercised by an insufficiently representative Assembly provided with weak powers,[17] technically, the Committee was created as an auxiliary body to the High Authority, not as a supplementary source of political control.[18]

According to the Treaty, the Committee should 'comprise equal numbers of producers, of workers and of consumers and dealers', all appointed by the Council in their personal capacity. Producers and workers were appointed on the basis of lists drawn by their organizations, previously chosen by the Council. Consumers and dealers were appointed directly by the Council, given the absence of representative organizations.[19] The Committee members were not bound by 'any mandate or instructions from the organisations which nominated them'.[20] Moreover, contrary to what the Treaty of Rome determined in relation to the Economic and Social Committee, there was no partition of seats among Member States, which, in principle, allowed dissociation of national interests from the representation of 'functional' interests.[21] These features, together with the fact that the Consultative Committee had self-regulatory power—it adopted its rules of procedure without any need for external approval—

[16] Jean de Soto (1958) *La Communauté européenne du charbon et de l'acier (C.E.C.A.)*, Paris: Presses Universitaires de France, p. 41 (author's translation).

[17] Elio Fanara (1970) 'Alta autorità', in Quadri, Monaco, and Trabucchi (eds), *Trattato istitutivo della Comunità Europea del Carbone e dell'Acciaio: Commentario, Vol. I, Articoli 1–45*, Milano: Giuffrè, pp. 226–75, at pp. 227 and 228.

[18] Article 7 ECSC.

[19] Article 18, first to fourth paragraphs ECSC and Fanara, *op. cit.*, p. 234.

[20] Article 18, fourth paragraph. This arguably avoided the transformation of the Committee 'from advisory *supra partes* body, providing technical collaboration to the High Authority... into a "corporative parliament"', contrary to intentions conveyed by the Committee (Fanara, *op. cit.*, p. 239. De Soto, *op. cit.*, n. 16, p. 44).

[21] However, both De Soto and Reuter indicate that nationality was a factor considered in the designation of the members, as well as the representativeness of different labour organizations (De Soto, *op. cit.*, n. 16, pp. 42–3; Reuter, *op. cit.*, n. 11, p. 57).

and could be convened by a majority of its members, made it institutionally stronger than its twin, the Economic and Social Committee.[22] However, the Treaty did not envisage the Committee's financial autonomy nor the autonomy of its services vis-à-vis the High Authority and the initial maximum limit of fifty-one members posed problems of effective representation of the interests affected.[23]

As mentioned, the Treaty determined, in several instances, the compulsory consultation of the Committee before the adoption of an act by the High Authority. In all other cases, the High Authority could consult the Committee whenever it deemed appropriate. In addition, the Treaty required that the Committee should be continuously informed of the broad lines of the High Authority's action regarding investment and financial aid as well as agreements and concentration.[24]

Despite these features, which could indicate that the Committee had a strong institutional relevance, the effective role played by the Consultative Committee seems to have been weak, at least in its first years of activity. Fanara gives an account of tense relationships between the High Authority and the Committee in a first phase of their work, the latter complaining of the High Authority's unwillingness to ensure the Committee's consultative role. This was followed by a second period (since 1955) of more intense collaboration between the two institutions.[25] According to Haas, participation through informal lobbying channels was soon considered by interest groups to be more effective than representation at the Committee.[26] In the same line, De Soto considered that the role of the Committee was 'more relevant at the political and psychological level' and that, technically, its utility was 'mediocre', the bulk of the technical collaboration residing in the contacts established directly between the High Authority and interested parties, as well as in working groups set up by the former.[27] The weaknesses

[22] Article 19, fourth paragraph, for the last aspect mentioned (see the sub-section below).

[23] Reuter, *op. cit.*, n. 11, p. 58. Given the lack of financial autonomy, Reuter considered the Committee to be a semi-autonomous body. The same lack of financial autonomy characterizes the Economic and Social Committee. The maximum limit of fifty-one members was raised as a result of the accession of new Member States.

[24] Article 19, paragraphs 1 and 2 ECSC.

[25] Fanara, *op. cit.*, n. 17, pp. 270–2.

[26] Ernst B. Haas (1958 [1968]) *The Uniting of Europe. Political, Social, and Economic forces 1950–1957*, Stanford: Stanford University Press, p. 340.

[27] De Soto, *op. cit.*, n. 16, p. 44. According to him, 'trade unions are thus ensured to be associated to the more important questions of Community life ... and ... this psychological value should not be neglected' (author's translation).

of the Committee might have been attributed to the existence of other channels of communication established between interested persons and the deciding institutions. As will be seen below, the Economic and Social Committee met similar difficulties.

In any event, participation was undoubtedly a strong institutional feature of the ECSC. Arguably, this derives from the concrete powers of intervention that were granted to the High Authority, from the intention of keeping its administrative apparatus within minimum dimension and, therefore, reliant on the cooperation of interested parties, as well as from the establishment of a particular form of interaction between the High Authority and the economic and social actors within its realm of influence, which was considered favourable to the integration process.

3.1.2 *Between corporatism, interest representation, and civil society*

As mentioned above, the creation of the Economic and Social Committee, like that of ECSC's Consultative Committee, has its origins in the constitutional traditions of the Member States. In fact, the representation of socio-economic interest groups in the formal political-institutional framework was common to the large majority of the Member States.[28] Nevertheless, this representation assumed specific features in the EC institutional set-up, the evolution of which influenced the transformation of the role of the Economic and Social Committee.

The inclusion of a body representative of the economic and social interests advisory to the decision-making institutions of the EEC and Euratom was a controversial issue in the respective negotiations.[29] Initially excluded from the intergovernmental debates, it entered the negotiations at the end of 1956 by way of a Dutch proposal, supported by the Belgian delegation. It was refuted by France and strongly contested by Germany (influenced by the negative experience of the Weimar Republic and by a liberal view of the

[28] Elena Calandri indicates that the existence of similar bodies in the six countries (with the exception of the German Federation) was a factor that weakened the position of those that contested its creation (Elena Calandri (2000) 'Le genesi del Comitato Economico e Sociale: forze professionali e strategie nazionali' in Antonio Varsori (ed.), *Il Comitato Economico e Sociale nella costruzione europea*, Marsilio Editori: Venezia, pp. 47–65, pp. 56–7).

[29] 'One of the most controversial issues', according to Gerda Zellentin (1962) 'The Economic and Social Committee', *Journal of Common Market Studies*, Vol. 1, n. 1, pp. 22–28, at p. 26. Giving rise merely to a 'skirmish without traumas', according to Calandri, *op. cit.*, p. 47 (author's translation).

process of economic integration).[30] The limits placed on the Committee's power have their origin here:[31] the lack of a right of initiative, the need to be convened at the request of the Commission and the Council, and the requirement for unanimous approval of its rules of procedure by the Council.[32] Moreover, being absent from the list in Article 7(1) EC (originally Article 4(1)), it was not recognized as a Community institution, a trait that remains unchanged until today.[33] In the end, the creation of the Economic and Social Committee was 'trapped' by factors both external and internal to the negotiations: divergent positions of European trade unions and trade union confederations regarding such a Committee and the process of integration itself, on the one hand, and different views defended by the national delegations on its existence and role, on the other.

This had a decisive influence on the Committee's role, still visible today. Namely, despite drawing inspiration from similar national institutions, the Economic and Social Committee deviated from their characteristics. Two traits made it difficult to characterize it as a purely corporate body. First, together with 'representatives of the various categories of economic and social activity, in particular, representatives of producers, farmers, carriers, workers, dealers, craftsmen, professional occupations', it encompassed 'representatives of the general public'.[34] Secondly, its members were appointed 'in their personal capacity and [could] not be bound by any mandatory instructions'. According to Lodge and Herman, 'the diffuseness of the Committee's membership . . . partly accounts for discrepant views as to its appropriate role in EEC decision-making', somewhere between a parliamentary-type institution representing economic and social interests

[30] Antonio Varsori (2000) 'Per una storia del Comitato Economico Sociale', in Antonio Varsori (ed), *op. cit.*, n. 28, pp. 3–23, at p. 6–7; Elena Calandri, *op. cit.*, n. 28, pp. 51–7.

[31] Zelletin, *op. cit.*, p. 23. See, in detail, Calandri, *op. cit.*, n. 28, pp. 60–3.

[32] Articles 198, first paragraph, 196, third paragraph and 196, second paragraph of the EEC Treaty, respectively, in the original numeration.

[33] Article 13 TEU, Lisbon (consolidated version, OJ C 83/13, 30.03.2010).

[34] Article 193, second paragraph of the EEC Treaty. The Treaty of Rome determined that its composition should ensure 'adequate representation' of the various categories of interests (Article 195 (1), second paragraph of the EEC Treaty), which was found in a tripartite composition: one-third trade unions, one-third business, commerce, and industry, one-third general interests. (Leon N. Lindberg, (1968) [1963] *The Political Dynamics of the European Economic Integration*, Stanford: Stanford University Press, p. 91; Juliet Lodge and Valentine Herman (1980) 'The Economic and Social Committee in EEC decision-making', *International Organisation*, Vol. 34, n. 2, pp. 265–84, at p. 268). A proposal for a tripartite composition had been put forward by the Confédération Internationale des Syndicats Chrétiens to the Spaak Commission in 1955 (on this see Calandri, *op. cit.*, n. 28, p. 51).

and the more corporate-like national economic and social committees, not representing the interest groups' view alone nor those of the general public.[35]

The Economic and Social Committee was conceived as having a purely advisory function, deprived of an active role in shaping the Community's action. In practice, it had—and still has—too limited a capacity to effectively influence decision-making.[36] Throughout the years of European integration, the Economic and Social Committee struggled for a meaningful existence in the face of various pressures. The proliferation of other consultative bodies and the existence of other, possibly more effective means of access by interest groups to European decision-making was one of them.[37] The direct election of the European Parliament was a major institutional challenge.[38] The creation of the Committee of the Regions and the formalization of social dialogue, both issuing from the Maastricht revision, were more recent changes that equally impacted on the Committee's function. The Committee of the Regions absorbed some of the Committee's scope of action, while the institutionalization of social dialogue at the Community level ignored the potential role that the Economic and Social Committee could have had in this respect.[39]

Nevertheless, instances of compulsory consultation of the Committee increased with the successive revisions of the Treaty, in particular due to the expansion of the Community competences.[40] At the same time, the

[35] Lodge and Herman, *op. cit.*, p. 268. Today, the members of the Committee are no longer 'appointed in their personal capacity'. However, while this could be seen as an attempt to enhance its corporate nature, the independent status of the Committee's members vis-à-vis 'mandatory instructions' was maintained. The Treaty determines, moreover, that the Committee members are 'completely independent in the performance of their duties, *in the Union's general interest*' (Article 300(4) TFEU, ex-Article 258 EC, third paragraph; emphasis added).

[36] This was favoured by the fact that there was no reference in the Treaty concerning the need for the Commission and the Council to take the Committee's opinion into account, as well as by the abovementioned constraints on the Committee's autonomy (Lodge and Herman, *op. cit.*, pp. 269–73). This disproved the more optimistic views that saw the Committee's intervention as a source of democratic legitimation for measures adopted by a Community supranational bureaucracy (Zelletin, *op. cit.*, n. 29, p. 28).

[37] On this, Willem van der Voort (1997) *In the Search of a Role. The Economic and Social Committee in European Decision Making*, PhD Thesis, Leiden University, pp. 131–71.

[38] Varsori, *op. cit.*, n. 30, pp. 14–15.

[39] See Articles 154 and 155 TFEU (ex-Articles 138 and 139 EC). Raffaele Cadin (2004) 'Il Comitato Economico e Sociale', in Antonio Tizzano, *Trattati dell'Unione europea e della Comunità europea*, Milano: Giuffrè, pp. 1206–20, at p. 1207. For a more detailed account of the Committee's difficulties, see Varsori, *op. cit.*, n. 30, pp. 8–21.

[40] See Jean-Paul Jacqué, Rolin Bibier, Marcel Haag *et al.* (2000) *Commentaire J. Mégret. Le Parlement européen, le Conseil, la Commission, la Cour des comptes, le Comité économique et social, le*

Maastricht Treaty introduced fundamental changes in the Committee's status, which indicated the intention to reinforce its role: among other changes, its power of initiative was formally recognized (although this was an established practice for almost twenty years),[41] as were the competences to meet on its own initiative and to adopt its rules of procedure.[42] This greater autonomy, however important, was likely a poor compensation for a body which was struggling for its relevance. A cynic could argue that these changes were directly correlated with the verification of the long-established weaknesses of the Committee.

Maastricht was also the milestone of subsidiarity, of European citizenship, of 'bringing the EU closer to the citizens', and of the EU legitimacy crisis discourse.[43] In the quest for its own identity, the Committee saw here a new opportunity: henceforth, it aspired to become the institutional bridge between the 'civil society' and the EU.[44] The Nice Treaty formalized the Committee's aspirations, today solidified in the TFEU.[45] Moreover, the Committee's members need to act in the general interest of the Union. According to one commentator the notion of 'organized civil society' became 'the minimum common denominator of the Committee's different facets'.[46] If the reference to the 'general public' in the original version and the guarantees of the independence of its members introduced awkward elements in an otherwise fully-fledged corporative body, with

Comité des régions, la Banque européenne d'investissement, le fonds européen d'investissement, Vol. 9, 2nd edn, Bruxelles: Editions de l'Université de Bruxelles, pp. 380–2.

[41] Lodge and Herman, *op. cit.*, n. 34, p. 274.

[42] Respectively, current Article 304, first paragraph TFEU (ex-262, first paragraph EC) and Article 303, third and second paragraphs TFEU (ex-260, third and second paragraphs EC).

[43] The Maastricht Treaty was a turning point in the Community's legitimacy problems. Predicting this, see Joseph H.H. Weiler (1991) 'Problems of legitimacy in post 1992 Europe', *Aussenwirtschaft*, Vol 46, n. 3/4, pp. 411–37, at pp. 413–14. See also Carol Harlow (1999) 'Citizen access to political power in the European Union', EUI Working Paper RSC No. 99/2, p. 5 and Anthony Arnull (2002) 'Introduction: the European Union's accountability and legitimacy deficit', in Anthony Arnull and Daniel Wincott (eds), *Accountability and legitimacy in the European Union*, Oxford: Oxford University Press, pp. 1–12, at p. 7.

[44] Varsori, *op. cit.*, n. 30, pp. 21 and 23; Stijn Smismans (1999) 'An Economic and Social Committee for the citizen, or a citizen for the Economic and Social Committee?', *European Public Law*, Vol. 5, n. 4, pp. 557–82 (note pp. 561–2).

[45] See former Article 257(2) EC. The wording of the corresponding Article 300(2) of the TFEU seems to return to the tripartite composition—employers, employed, and other parties representative of civil society.

[46] Cadin, *op. cit.*, n. 39, p. 1209 (author's translation). Demonstrating concerns about the capacity of the Committee to develop this new role, see Stjin Smismans (2004) *Law, Legitimacy and European Governance. Functional Participation in Social Regulation*, Oxford: Oxford University Press, p. 138–9.

hindsight it is possible to trace therein a faint embryo of what the Committee would seek to become. Nevertheless, the ambiguity of the Committee's nature persists. Described in the sixties as an 'economic parliament' that laid the foundations for 'the formation of a new type of supranational corporatism',[47] it remains today an 'assembly-type body of corporatist nature' under the guise of an '"assembly of associations" of the post-modern society capable of synthesising the "civil dialogue" (no longer merely "social") in the framework of a model of "participatory democracy"'.[48] While it was stronger in the Nice formulation, this trait was arguably maintained in the TFEU.

As Varsori maintains: 'the changes the [Committee] went through during its forty years of existence reflect in a precise and meaningful way the more general transformations of the European construction'.[49] As such, it could not but reflect also 'the rediscovery of civil society'.[50] At a deeper level, however, in its search for a role in a new institutional framework, it departed more and more from the model of the national economic and social committees from which it derived its existence and acquired a constitutional function specific to the political and institutional problems of the European integration process. This became more evident when political union became a goal of integration.

3.1.3 *Bringing the regions in*

The Committee of the Regions was created by the Maastricht Treaty as a response to the progressive impact of the integration process on regional and local government. In fact, by the time of its creation, European integration had both strengthened and weakened these lower levels of government.[51] In particular, the goal of 'economic and social cohesion' introduced in the Single European Act as a result of the accession of Southern European countries in the late 1970s and mid-1980s, as well as the creation of the corresponding regional policy, placed European regions as interlocutors of

[47] Zelletin, *op. cit.*, n. 39, p. 28.

[48] Cadin *op. cit.*, n. 39, p. 1208 (author's translation).

[49] Varsori, *op. cit.*, n. 30, p. 4 (author's translation).

[50] The expression is from Kenneth A. Armstrong (2002) 'Rediscovering civil society: the European Union and the White Paper on Governance', *European Law Journal*, Vol. 8, n. 1, pp. 102–32. On this, see below Sub-section 3.3.2.

[51] Liesbet Hooghe and Gary Marks (1995) 'Channels of subnational representation in the European Union', in Renaud Dehousse and Thomas Christiansen (eds) (1995), 'What model for the Committee of the Regions? Past experiences and future perspectives', EUI Working Paper EUF No. 95/2, Florence: European University Institute, pp. 6–33, at pp. 11–21.

the Community institutions, even if through the Member States' filter.[52] Concomitantly, the expansion of Community competences to areas other than regional policy had begun to touch upon competences of certain regions and federal sub-national units, as well as those of local government in unitary states.[53] This effect had been further enhanced by a parallel movement, the reasons of which lay beyond European integration: the ongoing transferral of central competences to sub-national units. Stronger regions thus claimed to have an institutional say in the Community decision-making processes concerning them.[54]

The creation of the Committee of the Regions also met the main concerns of the Community institutions. It served the purpose of according added legitimacy to EU policy-making, in particular to Community action in regional policy. Involving representatives of regional and local government—the public authorities that are closer to the citizens—in the Community decision-making procedures was intended to help in 'closing the gap' between the citizens and the Community.[55] The desired legitimation effect was reinforced by the Nice amendment which determined that these representatives 'either hold a regional or local authority electoral mandate or are politically accountable to an elected assembly', thereby underlining the connection between the regional representatives and their respective constituencies.[56] Nevertheless, the political intention behind the creation

[52] Following the partnership principle, then enshrined in Article 4 of Council Regulation No. 2052/88 on the tasks of the Structural Funds (OJ L 185/9, 15.07.1988), today in Article 11 of Council Regulation No. 1083/2006 (OJ L 210/25, 31.7.2006). For an account of the progressive importance of regions in European integration, underlining the Single European Act as a turning point, see Théophile M. Margellos (1997), 'L'émergence de la 'région' dans l'ordre juridique communautaire', in Georges Vandersanden, *L'Europe et les régions. Aspects juridiques*, Bruxelles: Éditions de l'Université de Bruxelles, pp. 19–63 (in particular, pp. 20–35). On the use of the term 'Community' rather than 'Union' in this sub-section see Chapter 1, note 2.

[53] Thomas Christiansen (1995), 'Second thoughts—The Committee of the Regions after its first year', in Dehousse and Christiansen, *op. cit.*, n. 51, pp. 34–64, at p. 35.

[54] Christiansen emphasizes the role of the German Länder in pushing for its creation, *op. cit.*, pp. 34–64, at pp. 34–5. See also Jim Cloos, Gaston Reinesch, Daniel Vignes, and Joseph Weyland (1993) *Le Traite´de Maastricht. Genèse, analyse, commentaries*, Bruxelles: Bruylant, pp. 408–9.

[55] Christiansen, *op. cit.*, p. 49–52. The author quotes Jacques Delors' opening speech at the first plenary session of the Committee, where he stated 'the task of [the Committee] is nothing less than to enhance the democratic legitimacy of the Union' (*op. cit.*, p. 51).

[56] Current Article 300(3) of the TFEU (ex-Article 263, first paragraph EC). This was mostly the recognition of a previous practice. Although the wording before Nice gave rise to different interpretations, since the outset most Member States nominated elected members to the Committee. In fact, this was perceived as a means of strengthening the Committee's role within the EU institutional system. On this, see Catherine Schneider (1997) 'Morceaux choisis sur la

of the Committee contrasted with fact that, at the outset, the cases in which the Treaty determined the compulsory intervention of the Committee did not cover the exercise of Community functions that may considerably affect regional or local competences, such as agriculture.[57] This suggests that, at least initially, Member States did not fully pursue the claimed goal of involving political representatives of the local and regional constituencies in the areas of Community decision-making that impact upon their competences. Nevertheless, the intervention of the Committee is not limited to cases of compulsory intervention: it may adopt own-initiative opinions and it may issue facultative opinions at the request of the Council, the Commission, or the Parliament. In addition, it has the prerogative of being informed by these institutions when the Economic and Social Committee has requested an opinion, and it is entitled to intervene if it considers that specific regional interests are involved.[58]

The Committee of the Regions is similar to the Economic and Social Committee in most of its institutional features—an 'unjustified mimicry', according to some authors.[59] Namely, its members are appointed following the logic of national representation by proposal of the Member States, which limits its legitimacy as representative of the sub-national units in EU procedures and hinders the intended 'proximity effect'.[60] Formally, the

composition du Comité des Régions', in Jacques Bourrinet (ed.), *Le Comite´des Re´gions de l'Union Europe´enne*, Paris: Economica, pp. 15–45, at pp. 25–8.

[57] This feature is pointed out, *inter alia*, by Marie-Françoise Labouz, Laurence Burgorgue-Larsen, and Thierry Daups (1994) 'Le Comité des Régions: « gardien de la subsidiarité »?', *Europe*, Octobre 1994, pp. 1–4, at p. 2 and Christian Mestre (1997) 'Radioscopie du Comité des Régions: organisation, fonctionnement, compétences', in Jacques Bourrinet, *op. cit.*, pp. 47–83, at pp. 59–70 referring to the period prior the Amsterdam Treaty. This Treaty extended the instances of compulsory intervention of the Committee, to the fields of transport (Article 71 EC, now Article 91 TFEU), employment (Articles 128(2) and 129 EC, now Articles 148(2) and 149 TFEU), social policy (Article 137(2) EC, now Article 153(2) TFEU), European Social Fund (Article 148 EC, now Article 164 TFEU), and environment (Article 175(2) and (3), now Article 192(2) and (3) TFEU). Agriculture remains excluded from the Committee's compulsory advice (Article 43(2) of the TFEU).

[58] Article 307 TFEU (ex-Article 265, first, second, fourth, and fifth paragraphs EC).

[59] Labouz, Burgorgue-Larsen, and Daups, *op. cit.*, p. 1.

[60] Article 305, third paragraph TFEU (ex-Article 263 EC, fourth paragraph). On this contradiction, and other critical points, see Tony Cole (2005) 'The Committee of the Regions and subnational representation to the European Union', *Maastricht Journal of European and Comparative Law*, Vol. 12, n. 1, pp. 49–72, at p. 51. Also pointing out the incoherences of the representation system set up by the Treaty of Maastricht, see Mestre, *op. cit.*, n. 57, pp. 52–7. Schneider also points out the limits to legitimacy derived from the rules of appointment (*op. cit.*, n. 56, p. 31).

Committee's members enjoy guarantees of independence and have the duty to act in the general interest of the Community (now, Union). Like the Economic and Social Committee, the Committee of the Regions is convened at the request of the Council, the Commission, or on its own initiative, and has self-regulatory power, adopting its own rules of procedure (since the Amsterdam Treaty, these are no longer subject to approval by the Council).[61]

Like the Economic and Social Committee, the Committee of the Regions has sought to solidify and strengthen its role in the Community institutional system; in particular it has strived to acquire a more important political status. For this purpose, and in other ways, it has resorted widely to its own-initiative opinions and has used the inter-linkages between different matters to include in its compulsory opinions statements on issues that fall outside the range of those policy areas where the Treaty makes its intervention compulsory.[62] The pressures from the Committee to alter its institutional status, together with its insistence on a self-claimed role as guardian of the subsidiarity principle, have resulted in two important changes envisaged in the Treaty on the Functioning of the European Union (following what had been foreseen in the Constitutional Treaty). In fact, two of its main aspirations are now satisfied: first, the subsidiarity principle received a new formulation, embracing the reference to the regional and local level as adequate levels of action for the exercise of shared competences; secondly, the Committee was recognized as having the *locus standi* to bring actions for annulment of European legislative acts on grounds of infringement of the principle of subsidiarity in the cases where its intervention in the respective procedure is required by the Treaty.[63]

[61] See, respectively, Articles 300(4) TFEU (ex-Articles 263, fifth paragraph EC); 306, third paragraph TFEU (ex-Article 264, third paragraph EC); 306, second paragraph TFEU (ex-Article 264, second paragraph EC).

[62] On these and other strategies used by the Committee to expand its role within the Community institutional system, see Laurence Burgorgue-Larsen (1997) 'L'élaboration d'une doctrine consultative par le Comité des Régions', in Bourrinet, *op. cit.*, n. 56, pp. 191–229.

[63] Article 5(3) of the TFEU (cf. Article I-11(3) of the Constitutional Treaty); Article 263(3) TFEU (Article III-365(3) of the Constitutional Treaty) Article 8, second paragraph of the Protocol on the application of the principles of subsidiarity and proportionality (protocol no. 2, drafted in the same terms in the Lisbon Treaty and in the Constitutional Treaty). These claims date back to 1995: they were expressed in the opinion of the Committee on the revision of the Treaties presented at the Intergovernmental Conference that approved the Amsterdam Treaty, although in more ambitious terms (reported by Jordan Pujol I Soley; reproduced at Bourrinet, *op. cit.*, n. 56, see pp. 240–1). On the Committee's claim to become the guardian of subsidiarity, see Mestre, *op. cit.*, n. 57, pp. 80–2.

3.1.4 *From neo-functionalism to legitimacy*

The creation of advisory bodies in the Treaties establishing the Communities signed in the 1950s resulted from political concerns inherent in the specific dynamics of the integration process. Involving societal groups in decision-making was perceived as a possible guarantee of further integration. This can be seen as an expression of neo-functionalism, which inspired the Community method, insofar as involving societal groups in decision-making was perceived as a possible guarantee of further integration. Moreover, the resort to technical advice provided by members external to the executive institutions was also a consequence of the reduced size that the respective administrations were required to have.[64] The Communities' executives therefore needed to rely on the collaboration of the parties concerned by their action. The influence of national traditions of social dialogue was, originally, an additional factor in favour of the creation of such bodies.

Interest representation as defined in the Treaties was, however, conditioned by two antagonistic forces: the aim of involving interested parties in the Community rule-making activity, on the one hand, and the fear of corporatism, on the other. The guarantees of independence of their members, the logic of national representativeness, their mission to act in the Community's general interest, as well as weaknesses of their institutional status contributed to the ambiguity of these bodies and, arguably, to their difficulties in fulfilling their role.

Member States and Community institutions turned to advisory bodies when the need to reinforce the Community's legitimacy came more strongly to the fore. The changes in the role of the Economic and Social Committee and the creation of the Committee of the Regions were expressly intended to fulfil this purpose.

[64] As was seen above, in the case of the ECSC High Authority, this was a Treaty requirement. Although no reference to the size of the Commission's administrative apparatus is mentioned in official documents, it may be surmised that the same concern was valid for the EEC (both France's resistance to strong supranational institutions and the fact that the High Authority's model served as an example to design the Commission's administration reinforce this assumption—see Marie-Thérèse Bitsch (2004) *Histoire de la construction europeénne*, Bruxelles: Editions Complexe, pp. 117–18; see, in addition, the chart on the staff members of the Commission in its first years, in Michel Dumoulin (ed.) (2007) *The European Commission 1958–72. History and Memories*, Luxembourg: Office for Official Publications of the European Communities, p. 220).

Irrespective of their limitations and of the 'political interpretations' of their role, the presence of advisory bodies in the Union's institutional setting reflects the rule according to which interested parties should have a say in Union decision-making procedures concerning them. This is clearer in the creation of the Committee of the Regions, which in part resulted from the expansion of (then) Community competences in areas that contended with regional and local competences. In addition, it is interesting to note that organic participation was complemented by instances of procedural participation in the ECSC Treaty, where the powers of the High Authority were markedly more akin to an administrative function and the Treaty provisions more suitable to create rights and duties in the legal sphere of those falling within their realm of influence. This feature suggests that participation is a genetic institutional characteristic of Community (now, Union) decision-making processes, even if the ECSC rules were sector-restricted and deemed *lex specialis* in Community law.[65]

As now enshrined in the TFEU, interest representation through the advisory bodies of the Union is essentially limited to policy orientations and to interventions in legislative procedures (e.g. the adoption of guidelines which Member States must take into account in their employment policies, according to Article 148 TFEU; or the several instances in which a regulation or a directive is to be adopted following the co-decision procedure, after consultation of the Committees). Despite the possibilities of intervening in decision-making at the request of one institution, or on their own initiative, institutional practice seems to focus on this segment of policy- and rule-making.[66] This leaves out a wide scope of regulatory activity, where a plethora of advisory committees and formal and informal instances of participation were accommodated over the years. At the same time, the express provisions regarding interest representation in European decision-making were, since the inception of the integration process, only a small part of the institutional reality of interest representation.

[65] On the connections between the two Treaties, Koen Lenaerts and Piet van Nuffel (2005) *Constitutional Law of the European Union*, 2nd edn, London: Sweet and Maxwell, p. 11.

[66] A cursory consultation of implementing regulations adopted by the Commission, though not necessarily representative of the Committees' activity, has not given any indication on the Committees' intervention in the realm of non-legislative rule-making.

3.2 Institutional Practice: Participation Pervades

3.2.1 *Committees: embedded interest representation*

Interest, expert, and comitology committees

It is widely known that the Commission and the Council are daily assisted by committees, entrusted with a variety of functions at the same time similar to and different from the ones assigned to the consultative committees just mentioned. This is a deep-rooted feature of the EU polity.[67] Emil Noël, writing in 1963, as executive secretary of the Commission, described the working methods of the Commission in the following terms. When the Commission defines the guiding lines of a certain policy, it does so 'after having conducted the broadest consultations, and gathered the opinions of governments, administrations, professional organizations'. When it has to determine the practical conditions of application of a previously defined policy or when it issues decisions of an essentially technical nature, the Commission 'resorts, in a systematic way, to the collaboration of national experts... designated by each of the concerned national administrations'. These meetings 'are completed by numerous consultation meetings that the members of the Commission or its services organize regularly with the leading figures of the professional organizations (trade unions, employers' organizations, agriculture organizations, groupings of traders...)'.[68] This practice gave rise to the proliferation of committees, at both ends of rule-making, i.e. when deciding policy lines and when fleshing out the practicalities of their implementation. These committees may be set up by the Commission, by the Council act, or by an act of the Council and the Parliament which defines the legal regime of a given subject matter. Very few have their legal bases in Treaty articles.[69] Many are not created by a formal act.

[67] On the origins of the comitology system, see Carl Fredrik Bergström (2005) *Comitology: Delegation of Powers in the European Union and the Committee System*, Oxford: Oxford University Press, pp. 43–57.

[68] Emil Noël (1963) 'Comment fonctionnent les institutions de la Communauté Économique Européenne', *Revue du Marché Commun*, Vol. 6, pp. 14–21, at p. 20 (author's translation).

[69] These are envisaged in Article 99 (ex-79 EC, transport), Article 134 (ex-114 EC, (2), (3), and (4), economic and financial committee), Article 150 (ex-130 EC, employment Committee), Article 163 (ex-147 EC, European Social Fund), Article 207(3) (ex-133(3) EC commercial policy), and Article 218(4) (ex-300(1) EC, international agreements), all from the TFEU.

The relevance of these committees in terms of participation differs from case to case. In fact, the rationales of committees are as varied as their composition. Only interest committees, that is, those composed of representatives from the social and economic sectors concerned, were specifically established to ensure interest representation (i.e. to secure the input of concerned sectors into decision-making). Expert (or scientific) committees and comitology committees do not have this primary purpose. The former, composed of specialists from public and private organizations, are destined to compensate for the lack of internal expertise and guarantee the technical appropriateness of decision-making. The latter, composed of representatives of national governments, ensure the presence of Member States in decision-making procedures.[70] It should be noted that some committees have a mixed composition, entailing national government representatives alongside representatives of interests affected, or scientists and representatives of the socio-economic sectors concerned. Moreover, it is not always easy to draw the line between experts and interest representatives.[71] Only comitology committees seem to escape possible mixed composition.[72] Nevertheless, contrary to what is statutorily defined, there may be cases in which representatives from interest groups take part in the committees'

[70] This tripartite classification draws on Ellen Vos (1999), 'EU committees: the evolution of unforeseen institutional actors in European product regulation' in Christian Joerges and Ellen Vos (eds), *EU Committees: Social Regulation, Law and Politics*, Oxford: Hart Publishing, pp. 19–47, at p. 22. See also Peter van der Knaap (1996) 'Government by committee: legal typology, quantitative assessment and institutional repercussions of committees in the European Union', in Robin H. Pedler and Günther F. Schäfer, *Shaping European Law and Policy. The Role of Committees and Comitology in the Political Process*, Maastricht: European Institute of Public Administration, pp. 83–116, at pp. 85–6, 90. For the sake of clarity, a narrow definition of comitology committees (referring only to those which, prior to Lisbon but still at the time of writing allow the Council to control the Commission's exercise of the implementing powers conferred on it under former Article 202 of the EC Treaty, following predefined procedures) is preferred in the text.

[71] Some authors prefer to include interest committees in the wider group of expert committees, considering that their members are 'interested experts', on the basis that the criteria to define their composition are not only the representativeness of the interest groups but also the expertise of the persons assigned to represent them (see Mario Savino (2005) *I comitati dell'Unione europea: la collegialità amministrativa negli ordinamenti compositi*, Milano: Giuffrè, p. 289 and pp. 377–9). This is, however, not a common characteristic of interest committees (see, for example, the selection criteria for members of the Advisory Committee on Safety and Health at Work—Council Decision of 22 July 2003, OJ C 218/1, 13.9.2003).

[72] Cf. Articles 3(1), 4(1) and 5(1) of the Council Decision No. 1999/468/EC, of 28 June 1999 laying down the procedures for the exercise of implementing powers conferred on the Commission (OJ L 184/23, 17.7.1999), amended by Council Decision No. 2006/512/EC, of 17 July 2006, OJ L 200/11, 22.7.2006 (the so-called 'comitology decision', still in force at the time of writing).

discussions and negotiations.[73] It remains true, however, that despite the enormous relevance of comitology in non-legislative rule-making, the instances of participation in these committees are virtually non-existent. These will, therefore, not be treated in detail in this chapter.

Contrary to the intervention of comitology committees in rule-making procedures, that of interest and expert committees is not, as a rule, compulsory.[74] Also unlike comitology committees, the composition and procedural rules of interest and expert committees are not pre-defined in a uniform act, which makes it more difficult to characterize their specific role and functioning.[75] Regarding these committees, 'the only general rule is that there is no rule'. This was stated by a Commission official, who, referring to consultative committees established by the Commission, explained their role as follows:

> The Commission's wish to be firmly rooted in the reality of social and business life explains the wide diversity of types and membership of committees. They may be ad hoc or standing committees, their members may be independent experts or national civil servants (attending in a personal capacity), and the social partners may be involved (on an equal-representation basis).[76]

[73] Van der Knaap, warning against over-simplifications that may arise from distinguishing non-comitology and comitology committees, gives some examples of this practice (*op. cit.*, n. 70, p. 101). See also Annette Töller (1998) 'The 'Article 19 Committee': the regulation of the environmental management and audit scheme', in M.P.C.M van Schendelen (ed.), *EU Committees as Influential Policymakers*, Aldershot: Ashgate, pp. 179–206, at pp. 181–2. No mention of this practice is found in the successive Reports from the Commission on the working of committees (COM (2010) 354 final, Brussels, 2.7.2010; COM (2009) 335 final, Brussels, 3.7.2009; COM (2008) 844 final, Brussels, 15.12.2008; COM (2007) 842 final, Brussels, 20.12.2007; COM (2006) 446 final, Brussels, 9.8.2006; COM (2005) 554 final, Brussels, 10.11.2005; COM (2004) 860, OJ C 65 E/1, 17.3.2005; COM (2003) 530 final, OJ C 223 E/16, 19.9.2003; COM (2002) 733 final, OJ C 223 E/1, 19.9.2003).

[74] There are exceptions: see, for example, Articles 6(1), 77, and 78 of Council Regulation No. 1698/2005, of 20 September 2005, on support for rural development by the European Agricultural Fund for Rural Development, (OJ L 277/1, of 21.10.2005).

[75] This is not to say that a strictly legal view on committees through the lens of the legal norms which regulate their risks is adequate to perceive their role and functioning. The plasticity of committees and their potential to stray beyond legally assigned tasks has been widely reflected in the literature. See, for example, Joseph H.H. Weiler (1999), 'Epilogue—comitology as revolution: infranationalism, constitutionalism and democracy' in Joerges and Vos (eds), *op. cit.*, n. 70, pp. 339–50, at p. 342 and Carol Harlow (2000) *Accountability in the European Union*, Oxford: Oxford University Press, p. 175.

[76] Giuseppe Ciavarini Azzi (1999) 'Comitology and the European Commission' in Joerges and Vos (eds), *op. cit.*, n. 70, pp. 51–7, at p. 52. See also Günther F. Schäfer (1996) 'Committees in the EC policy process: a first step towards developing a conceptual framework', in Pedler and Schäfer (eds), *op. cit.*, n. 70, pp. 3–23, at pp. 6–10.

Nonetheless, it is possible to draw a few general traits of interest committees, which allow us better to understand their scope as well as the meaning of the interest representation that they convey. These will be presented in the following pages.

Representation in the hands of the Commission

Interest committees, like expert committees, may operate both in the ascendant phase of rule-making, i.e. in the preliminary phase of the legislative process, and in the implementation phase, being involved in the drafting of non-legislative rule-making and in the adoption of individual decisions.[77] The Advisory Committee on Fisheries and Aquaculture, for example, may intervene in 'questions concerning the rules of the common fisheries policy and in particular measures that the Commission may take in the framework of such rules'.[78] This vague formulation seems to encompass the adoption of administrative rules and decisions. On the contrary, interest committees set up in relation to the organization of markets of specific agricultural products, generally gathering representatives of agriculture, industry, trade, workers, and consumers, operate mostly at the implementation level, assisting the Commission on 'all matters relating to common agricultural policy and to the policy of rural development and its implementation, and in particular the common organizations of the market and the measures which the Commission is called on to take in that context'.[79]

At both levels, the rules regarding their functioning reveal that, generally, interest committees are under tight control of the institution that creates them, usually the Commission (but also the Council, in the case of committees established to assist it). The appointment of their members, their logistics, and functioning are substantially, if not absolutely, determined by the Commission. Their members are appointed by the Commission (or the Council), usually on the basis of a proposal made by organizations established at Union level, or by the Member States.[80] The Commission

[77] Economic and Social Committee, General Secretariat (1980) *Community Advisory Committees for the Representation of Socio-economic Interests*, Westmead, Farnborough, Hampshire: Saxon House, Teakfield Limited, p. 9; Josef Falke (1996) 'Comitology and other committees: a preliminary empirical assessment', in Pedler and Schäfer (eds), *op. cit.*, n. 70, pp. 117–65, at pp. 151, 154. The functions of some of them go beyond the involvement in concrete decision-making processes (some examples in Savino, *op. cit.*, n. 71, p. 370).

[78] Article 2 of Commission Decision No. 1999/478/EC, of 14 July 1999, reviewing the Advisory Committee on Fisheries and Aquaculture (OJ L 187/70, 20.7.1999).

[79] Article 1(2) of Commission Decision No. 2004/391/EC on the advisory groups dealing with matters covered by the common agricultural policy (OJ L 120/50, 24.4.2004).

[80] Cf. Article 4(1) of Commission Decision No. 1999/478/EC, *cit.*, n. 78; Article 3 of Commission Decision No. 2004/391/EC, *cit.*, note above; and Article 3(3) of Council Decision of 22

provides committees with a secretarial service and meeting rooms.[81] As a rule, the committees intervene if called to do so by the Commission; there are, however, exceptions in which the initiative is given to the committee.[82] Commission representatives or observers designated by the Commission may, or in certain cases must, attend the meetings.[83] These are convened by the Commission, or at least in agreement with the Commission.[84] In addition, the agenda and the annual work programme may need to be defined by, or in agreement with, the Commission.[85] In some cases, the Commission's control goes even further. For example, in the case of the Advisory Committee on Fisheries and Aquaculture, it is defined that its agreement is needed in drawing up 'rules concerning the implementation of the work programme, the preparation of meetings, the location of meetings, reports, positions or conclusions and the formulation of opinions or recommendations'.[86]

In general, one may assume that interest committees are created with a twofold aim. First, they permit access to information held by interest representatives and thus contribute to improving the Commission's regulatory proposals. They also constitute a way of testing possible reactions to the Commission's regulatory choices by those on whom the success of regulatory measures ultimately depends. In a way, interest committees may be seen as imperfect precursors of impact assessment analyses. The committees' opinions give the Commission an indication of the concerns of represented interests, allowing it to accommodate them and eventually facilitate or ensure support for its measures.

further feature reveals an additional intent: to forge political consensus. In fact, while in some cases the views of the various interest groups that compose them must be displayed in the report they forward to the Commission, allowing it to perceive the different stances expressed, in

July 2003 (setting up an Advisory Committee on Safety and Health at Work, OJ C 218/1, 13.9.2003).

[81] Also in the case of committees created by the Council (Article 6(5) of Council Decision of 22 July 2003, *cit.*, n. 71).

[82] Article 2 of Commission Decision No. 1999/478/EC, *cit.*, n. 78.

[83] Article 6 of Commission Decision No. 2004/391/EC *cit.*; Article 8(2) of Commission Decision No. 1999/478/EC *cit.*, n. 78,; Article 6(5) of the Council Decision of 22 July 2003, *cit.*, n. 71.

[84] Article 7(1) of Commission Decision No. 2004/391/EC *cit.*; Article 8(1) of Commission Decision No. 1999/478/EC *cit.*; Article 6(1) and (2) of Council Decision of 22 July 2003, *cit.*, n. 71.

[85] Article 8(1) of Commission Decision No. 1999/478/EC *cit.*, n. 78; Article 8 of Commission Decision No. 2004/391/EC *cit.*, n. 79.

[86] Article 8(4) of Commission Decision No. 1999/478/EC *cit.*, n. 78.

others the committees may be required to reach a unanimous agreement and formulate joint conclusions.[87]

According to a 1980 study of the Economic and Social Committee, where some of the characteristics just highlighted are also mentioned,

> the guiding principle behind [the consultation of advisory committees on the implementation of Community policies] is that *all interest groups* in a particular industry which have Community umbrella organizations and are *directly affected* by a Community Regulation must have the opportunity to be involved in its implementation.[88]

This statement is resonant, for example, in the preamble of the Commission decision that defined the composition and functioning of the advisory groups operating in the common agricultural policy, according to which: '*[a]ll the economic sectors directly involved* in the operation of the market organizations and *affected by agricultural policy decisions*, as well as consumers, should have an opportunity to participate in drafting the opinions requested by the Commission'.[89]

Considering the features underlined above regarding the composition and functioning of interest committees, one may argue that such a statement conveys, at best, an excessively optimistic view of the role of interest committees. The opportunity of all those affected by Union policies to be involved in decision-making procedures through interest committees may be more a fiction than a reality. The choice of the interests that are to be represented and of those who are considered representative of these interests is exclusively in the hands of the Commission. In view of the functions pointed out above, the Commission is, in principle, interested in creating bodies which are effectively representative, but this does not necessarily guarantee representation of all interests concerned.[90] Moreover, the Commission decides when

[87] Cf. Article 9 of Commission Decision No. 2004/391/EC, *cit*, n. 79; Article 9 of Commission Decision No. 1999/478/EC, *cit.* and Article 7(2) of the Council Decision of 22 July 2003, *cit.*

[88] Economic and Social Committee, *op. cit.*, n. 77, p. 6 (emphasis in the original). The fact that Community (now Union) umbrella organizations are given the opportunity to participate in these committees is as such an incentive for interest groups to create European level organizations (p. 7).

[89] Preamble, recital 2 of Commission Decision No. 2004/391/EC, *cit.*, n. 71, emphasis added.

[90] Vos underlines the exclusion of representatives of environmental organizations from the Advisory Committee on Foodstuffs (Ellen Vos (1999) *Institutional Frameworks of Community Health and Safety Legislation: Committees, Agencies, and Private Bodies*, Oxford: Hart Publishing, p. 176).

it needs the advice of these representatives. In certain cases, this may ultimately lead to paralyzing of the committees' activity. In fact, in view of the committees' functions explained above, consultation of interest committees may easily be superseded by publication of consultative documents, Internet consultations, and hearings of specific groups (workshops, conferences, and seminars are alternative means of gathering technical information). Likewise the Commission can easily dispense with consultation.

This general characterization reveals that these forms of interest representation are quite distant from the rule of law logic that underlines the recognition of participation rights defended in this book. In addition, when compared to procedural participation, interest committees present the general drawbacks of organic participation. Namely, they risk excluding the interests that have not been selected to sit in the committee, and they contribute to diminishing or eliminating the distance between decision-makers and recipients of decisions chosen to form the committee, thus annulling the possibilities of dissent or favouring collusion. The institutional set-up and the rules to which interest committees are subjected (if formalized) are likely to make them particularly susceptible to the last effect.

3.2.2 *EU agencies: covering the spectrum of participation*

So far, only one form of participation in EU decision-making processes has been identified: interest representation in decision-making bodies through consultative or advisory bodies, both envisaged in the Treaties and taken up in the institutional practice of decision-making beyond the strict formality of the Treaties. EU agencies present a more varied picture in this regard. In fact, the analysis of participatory structures in agencies and procedures involving them reveals the spectrum of different forms and functions of participation present in the EU institutional and legal setting. Different forms of organic and procedural participation have been created, respectively, in the structure of some agencies and in the legal regime under which they operate. At the same time, it is possible to trace different functions of participation envisaged in the decisional procedures in which the agencies intervene: administrative collaboration, defence of the rights and interests of the persons concerned akin to the *audi alteram partem* principle, and transparency of decision-making with a view to avoiding public disaffection.

This variety reflects the diversity of the EU agencies. They are endowed with different functions and powers in accordance with the goals of integration pursued in the fields in which they operate.[91] Their creation was in part intended to offset the administrative deficit of the former European Community, which became particularly acute as its competences expanded, some requiring the deployment of highly technical knowledge. At the same time, agencies responded to the need to respect the principle of executive federalism while avoiding excessive centralization of administrative tasks (determined by political and practical reasons), and, at the same time, interlocking Member States' administrations among themselves, as well as interlocking the administrations and the Commission.[92] Administrative collaboration between Community (now Union) institutions and Member State administrations was the inexorable compromise between these competing needs.[93]

This is reflected in the organic structures of agencies, which entail representatives appointed by the different entities or institutions whose collaboration or input is considered necessary to carry out the function entrusted to these bodies. Theoretically, 'the [organizational formula of] representativeness can be applied in different ways depending on the case in question, at times increasing the proportion of supranational interests involved in relation to intergovernmental interests, and at others, favouring the predominance of Member States' interests over those of the

[91] Edoardo Chiti (2000) 'The emergence of a Community administration: the case of European agencies', *Common Market Law Review*, Vol. 37, n. 2, pp. 309–43, at pp. 311–17. Edoardo Chiti (2002) *Le agenzie europee. Unità e decentamento nelle amministrazioni comunitarie*, Padova: Cedam, p. 339. See also, in particular on the growth of agencies, Deirdre Curtin (2009) *Executive Power of the European Union. Laws, Practices and the Living Constitution*, Oxford: Oxford University Press, pp. 146–50.

[92] Chiti, *Le agenzie . . .*, *cit.*, pp. 48–58, in particular, pp. 56–8, and Edoardo Chiti (2009) 'An important part of the EU's institutional machinery: features, problems and perspectives of European agencies', *Common Market Law Review*, Vol. 46, n. 5, pp. 1395–442, at 1408–13. Also Renaud Dehousse (2002) 'Misfits: EU Law and the Transformations of European Governance', in Christian Joerges and Renaud Dehousse (ed.), *Good Governance in Europe's Integrated Market*, Oxford: Oxford University Press, pp. 207–29, at pp. 216–17 (in a similar way, Dehousse (1997), 'Regulation by networks in the European Community: the role of European agencies', *Journal of European Public Policy*, Vol. 4, n. 2, pp. 246–61, at pp. 251–4). Other rationales for the creation of EU agencies have been pointed out in the literature: see Damien Geradin and Nicolas Petit (2004) 'The development of agencies at the EU and national levels: conceptual analysis and proposals for reform', Jean Monnet Working Paper 01/04, p. 36 (available at <http://www.jeanmonnetprogram.org/papers/papers04.html>).

[93] Chiti, *Le agenzie . . .*, *cit.*, p. 56.

supranational administration'.[94] In some instances, this was extended to representatives of the interests affected by the activity of agencies, when they are involved, in different ways, in the agencies' organic structures.[95]

Organic participation

Administrative collaboration grounds three forms of interest representation in the agencies' organic structure. To begin with, interest representatives sit on the management, governing, or administrative boards (the different names used to designate the body in charge of the agencies' political control). This began in agencies that operate in fields related to social policy—the European Centre for the Development of Vocational Training (Cefedop), the European Foundation for the Improvement of Living and Working Conditions (Eurofund), and the European Agency for Safety and Health at Work (EU-OSHA)—thereby ensuring the involvement of social partners in the development of the European social policy, as determined in the Treaty.[96] This model was followed in four other agencies created more recently: the European Maritime Safety Agency (EMSA), the European Network and Information Security Agency (ENISA), the European Railway Agency (ERA), and the European Chemicals Agency (ECHA).[97]

[94] Edoardo Chiti (2004) 'Decentralisation and integration into the European administrations: a new perspective on European agencies', *European law Journal*, Vol. 14, n. 3, pp. 402–38, p. 422. In practice, however, management boards are dominated by Member State representatives that usually outnumber the Commission representatives (the management board of the European Food and Safety Authority—EFSA—with fourteen members appointed by the Council in consultation with the European Parliament from a list drawn up by the Commission, is the exception; Article 25(1) of Regulation No. 178/2002, of the European Parliament and of the Council, of 28 January 2002, OJ L 13/1, 1.2.2002). In some cases also the European Parliament is entitled to nominate a member, usually an 'independent person'. This is the case of the European Centre for Disease Prevention and Control—ECDC— (Article 14(1) of Regulation No. 851/2004, of the European Parliament and of the Council, of 21 April 2004, OJ L 142/1, 30.4.2004) and of the European Chemicals Agency (Article 79(1) of Regulation No. 1907/2006, of the European Parliament and of the Council, of 18 December 2006, OJ L 396/1, 30.12.2006).

[95] For a critical view, see Chiti, 'An important part of the EU's institutional machinery . . .', *cit.*, n. 92, p. 1402.

[96] Respectively, Article 4(2) of Council Regulation No. 337/75, of 10 February 1975 (OJ L 39/1, 13.2.1975); Article 6(1) of Council Regulation No. 1365/75, of 26 May 1975 (OJ L 139/1, 30.5.1975); Article 8 of Council Regulation No. 2062/94, of 18 July 1994 (OJ L 216/1, 20.8.1994), as amended by Council Regulation No. 1112/2005, of 24 June 2005 (OJ L 184/5, 15.7.2005). The preamble of Regulation No. 1112/2005 emphasizes the political relevance of a tripartite composition of the management of the three agencies (recitals 9 to 12).

[97] Respectively, Article 11 of Regulation No. 1406/2002, of the European Parliament and the Council, of 27 June 2002 (OJ L 208/1, 5.8.2002); Article 6(1) of Regulation No. 460/2004, of the European Parliament and the Council, of 10 March 2004 (OJ L 77/1, 13.3.2004), as amended;

Also advisory boards and working groups, which in certain cases are part of the agencies' organic structures, may include representatives of interests affected. This is a second method of ensuring participation in EU agencies. Only in one case, however, is an agency's advisory body exclusively composed of interested parties: the advisory body of the European Aviation Safety Agency (EASA), which assists, among other matters, in budgetary matters, in the adoption the agency's work programme, and the definition of procedures for issuing individual decisions, certification specifications, opinions, and guidance material for the implementation of the aviation safety legal regime approved by the executive director.[98] The advisory bodies of other agencies are either exclusively composed of representatives of national or regional authorities competent in the respective field (EFSA and the Community Fisheries Control Agency (CFCA), or predominantly constituted by representatives of competent national authorities alongside a minority of representatives of interested parties deprived of a right to vote (the Advisory Forum of the ECDC).[99]

One may consider that networks established or pooled by the agencies that comprise interested parties constitute a third form of ensuring participation in EU agencies. Networks are another manifestation of administrative collaboration that permeates this form of administration. In some cases, they form the core of the agencies' mission.[100] When they involve interested parties external to the administrative structure this is tantamount to

Article 26(1) of Regulation No. 881/2004, of the European Parliament and the Council, of 29 April 2004 (OJ L 164/1, 30.4.2004); Article 79(1) of Regulation No. 1907/2006, *cit.*, n. 94.

[98] Article 33(4) of Regulation No. 216/2008, of the European Parliament and the Council, of 20 February 2008 (OJ L 79/1, 19.3.2008). According to the agency's website, these interested persons are 'organizations representing aviation personnel, manufacturers, commercial and general aviation operators, maintenance industry, training organizations and air sports' (<http://www.easa.eu.int/ws_prod/g/g_org_main.php>). Nothing was said regarding forms of appointment of the advisory body's members.

[99] Article 27(1) and (3) of Regulation No. 178/2002, *cit.* n. 94 (EFSA); Article 31(1) of Council Regulation No. 768/2005, of 26 April 2005, OJ L 128/1, 21.5.2005 (CFCA); Article 18(1) of Regulation No. 851/2004, *cit.* n. 94 (ECDC). For advisory groups, see the case of ERA's working parties, which need to be representative of 'those sectors of the industry and of those users which will be affected by measures which might be proposed by the Commission on the basis of the recommendations addressed to it by the Agency' (Article 3(1) of Regulation No. 881/2004, *cit.*, n. 97).

[100] See Craig, *EU Administrative Law*, Oxford: Oxford University Press, pp. 176–9. The rationales of networks vary according to the functions that the agency performs and the concrete 'organizational architecture' (to borrow Chiti's term) in which they are placed—see Chiti 'The emergence...', *cit.*, n. 91, pp. 317–28.

bringing interests affected into the realm of the agencies' action and involving them in the discharge of these functions. This is the case, for example, in fields where private organizations have had a long-standing active role, e.g. the European Environment Information and Observation Network and the Fundamental Rights Platform.[101]

However, the purposes of these forms of interest representation are quite different from the functions of rights-based participation, explained in the previous chapter. They are essentially a means of fostering the collaboration of professionals and experts as well as the adherence of relevant professional groups encompassed in the agencies' action, pooling support and ensuring agreement with the agencies' action at the 'macro' political level. Considering the political function of management boards—they essentially have powers of political control over the agencies' executive or regulatory activity[102]—interest representation in this case is patently not directed at involving affected persons or their representatives in decision-making processes susceptible of shaping legal relationships.[103]

This is also the case with advisory bodies. Either these are not involved in the actual decision-making processes in which the agency participates—for example, the EASA's advisory body[104]—or they assist directly in the performance of the agencies' administrative functions but are not participatory bodies proper. For instance, the advisory bodies of the EFSA, the CFCA,

[101] Article 4 of Regulation No. 401/2009, of the European Parliament and of the Council, of 23 April 2009 (OJ L 120/1, 11.5.1990) and Article 10 of Council Regulation No. 168/2007, of 15 February 2007 (OJ L 53/1, 22.2.2007).

[102] See, for example, Articles 8, 10, 11 (2), 13, and 14 of Regulation No. 2062/94, as amended, *cit.*, n. 96 (EU-OSHA); Article 14 of Regulation No. 851/2004, *cit.*, n. 94 (ECDC); Article 25(2) of Regulation No. 881/2004, *cit.*, n. 97 (ERA).

[103] See, in more detail, Joana Mendes, *Rights of Participation in European Administrative Law. A Rights-based Approach to Participation in Rulemaking*, PhD Thesis, European University Institute: Florence, pp. 76–7.

[104] See note 98, above. The EASA's decisions which may impact on the legal spheres of persons falling under its realm of action are taken by the executive director (Articles 38(3) and 18 of Regulation No. 216/2008, *cit.*, n. 98). When the agency defines airworthiness specifications or issues environmental certificates under Article 20(1), it is shaping the duties of the concerned operators in the field of civil aviation; when it issues opinions, preparing drafts of implementing rules to be adopted by the Commission, under Article 19(1), it contributes to that effect, particularly because 'where [implementing measures] comprise technical rules and in particular rules relating to construction and design and operational aspects, the Commission may not change their content without prior coordination with the Agency' (Article 17(2)(b)). However, as will be seen below, participation in EASA's decision-making is far from being restricted to organic participation through its advisory body.

and the ECDC, which assist the agencies' directors, are intended 'to constitute a mechanism for an exchange of information ... the pooling of knowledge [and] to ensure close cooperation between the [agency] and the competent bodies in the Member States' (EFSA and ECDC), as well as 'to ensure close cooperation with stakeholders' (CFCA).[105] Expertise, combined on occasion with an element of representativeness, and involvement of the relevant public entities operating at different territorial levels seem to be the essential ingredients to ensure the quality of decision-making or a successful enforcement of the legal regime in question. These are the two concerns underlying the set-up of advisory bodies. Interest representation is a secondary matter.[106] Similarly, ERA's working groups are expert groups that, at the same time, constitute a sort of 'interface' between professionals from the railway sector and the competent national authorities.[107]

Interest representation is also far from being the main purpose of networks, even where these comprise representatives of interested persons. They are mainly directed at ensuring information gathering, the creation of 'Community-wide epistemic communities' (e.g. the networks promoted by EFSA),[108] as well as cooperation in implementation and enforcement of EU policies.[109] Admittedly, the inclusion of private persons in networks established by agencies may have the side effect of ensuring interest representation in decision-making processes—for example, when the information gathered by the network is the direct foundation of binding administrative decisions.[110] It would, however, be far-fetched to consider them as participatory structures proper.[111] As in the case of advisory groups, interest representation is an accidental effect of mechanisms directed at ensuring the effectiveness of the agencies' functions.

[105] Respectively, Article 27(4) of Regulation No. 178/2002, *cit.*, n. 94 (EFSA); Article 18(4) of Regulation No. 851/2004, *cit.*, n. 94 (ECDC); recital 30 of the preamble of Council Regulation No. 768/2005, *cit.*, n. 99 (CFCA).

[106] See Mendes, *Rights of participation ...*, *cit.* n. 103, pp. 78–80.

[107] Article 3(1) of Regulation No. 881/2004, *cit.*, n. 97. This is true even if it is specified that the members of these groups are chosen from lists drawn by concerned organizations naming the 'most qualified experts mandated to represent them in each working party' (Article 3(2) of Regulation No. 881/2004, *cit.*, n. 97).

[108] Article 36 of Regulation No. 178/2002, *cit.*, n. 94. The expression is Dehousse's, 'Regulation by networks ...', *cit.*, n. 92, p. 256.

[109] Article 77(4) and 86 of Regulation No. 1907/2006, *cit.*, n. 94.

[110] Chiti, 'The emergence ...', *cit.*, n. 91, p. 317.

[111] See Mendes, *Rights of participation ...*, *cit.* n. 103, pp. 80–1.

Procedural participation

Where agencies were empowered to adopt directly individual decisions binding on the persons to whom they are addressed, the latter were granted participation rights before the adoption of such decisions. This is the case of the procedures followed by the Office for Harmonisation in the Internal Market (OHIM), the Community Plant Variety Office (CPVO), and the EASA. These three agencies have certification functions. The OHIM and the CPVO follow adjudicative procedures, in which not only the addressee of their decisions, but also other interested persons have the right to be heard—in the latter case in the form of submitting written observations—and are granted the related ancillary guarantees (such as the right to access documents or to appeal, or be party to appeal procedures filled before an agency board).[112] The EASA, among other competences, is entitled to issue binding decisions pertaining to airworthiness specifications for products, parts, or appliances of aircrafts and to the definition of the respective environmental requirements.[113] The rules of the EASA's decisional procedures are not as sophisticated as those followed by the other two agencies.[114] In any case, according to the applicable legal framework, the procedure for the adoption of individual decisions needs to be transparent and must accommodate the 'hearing of the natural or legal person to be addressed in the decision and of any other party with a direct and individual concern'; the duty to provide reasons, notification, and publication of the decision; and provision of information on the legal remedies available to the addressee and other parties to the proceedings.[115] These procedural rights of intervention allow the respective holders to express their views on decisions

[112] On the procedures of OHIM, see Chiti, *Le agenzie . . .* , *cit.*, n. 91, pp. 137–50. They are similar to those of the CPVO—cf. Article 56 of Council Regulation No. 874/2009 of 17 September 2009 establishing implementing rules for the application of Council Regulation No. 2100/94 as regards proceedings before the Community Plant Variety Office (OJ L 251/3, 24.9.2009); Articles 59, 77, 75, and 68 of Council Regulation No. 2100/94, of 27 July 1994, on Community variety plant rights (OJ L 227/1, 1.9.1994), as amended.

[113] Article 20(1)(a) to (d) of Regulation No. 216/2008, *cit.*, n. 98.

[114] Article 53 of Regulation No. 216/2008, *cit.*, n. 98.

[115] Article 53(1) of Regulation No. 216/2008, *cit.*, n. 98. See also Articles 4, 11, and 13(2) of the Decision of the management board concerning the general principles related to the certification procedures to be applied by the agency for the issuing of certificates for products, parts and appliances ('products certification procedures') EASA MB Decision No. 7–2004, 30 March 2004, available at <http://www.easa.eu.int/ws_prod/g/doc/About_EASA/Manag_Board/2004/mb_decision_072004_pcp.pdf>.

that may negatively impact on them and seem to have been conceived essentially as a means of ensuring respect for their substantive rights and interests. Their meaning is therefore considerably different from the forms of interest representation analysed above.

Other types of participatory procedures attend the exercise of the EU agencies' functions in cases where these do not have formal or direct decision-making power, but their action is nonetheless directed at influencing private conduct and conforming it in light of the public interest. Thus, some of the EU agencies that have essentially advisory functions are obliged by the legislator to follow consultation procedures open to the submission of comments from the public in general, or restricted to interested persons. These procedures—carried out either by the agencies themselves or by the body to whom the decisional competence has been formally attributed—have different meanings, but ultimately express an instrumental approach to participation. They are both conceived as an enhanced form of transparency and as a means to ensure collaboration of the persons involved in the regulatory activity.

Duties of consultation are envisaged in the regulation establishing the EFSA. In this case, 'open and transparent' consultation procedures cover the preparation, evaluation, and revision of food law, i.e. the whole regulatory cycle, save when incompatible with the urgency of the matter.[116] They are, therefore, not dependent on the nature of the acts to be adopted, encompassing both general and individual acts, as well as, one would argue, both binding and non-binding acts.[117] Consultation, in the context of food law, assumes a specific function: as an additional facet of transparency, it is aimed at ensuring the confidence of the public in food regulation. Coherently, there is no indication that persons particularly affected by decisions adopted in this field should be granted specific procedural guarantees on the basis of the degree to which their rights and legally protected interests are affected (e.g. the right to have access to non-publicized information or the duty of the decision-maker to take their observations into account).[118]

[116] Article 9 of Regulation No. 178/2002, *cit.*, n. 94.

[117] Note, however, that the definition of food law in Article 3(1) of Regulation No. 178/2002, *cit.*, n. 94, does not seem to include non-binding acts.

[118] This is, nevertheless, a matter to be defined in specific legislation regarding the authorization of food and feedstuffs. Whether these specific regimes respond to needs of procedural protection of affected interests, and the extent to which there is a mismatch between the type of power exercised by the agency and the procedural guarantees afforded to those whose legal

Consultation is also an essential procedural step in the adoption of opinions, certification specifications, and guidance material issued by the EASA,[119] but here it has a different meaning. The provision for consultation in the EASA regulation regards the issuing of opinions, certification specifications, and guidance material. The EASA's management board must establish transparent procedures which must 'whenever necessary involve appropriate experts from relevant interested parties' and include wide consultation with interested parties following a procedure 'which includes an obligation on the agency to make a written response to the consultation process'.[120] The reference to interested parties (contrary to 'the public' as in the EFSA's regulation), the possibility that 'interested experts' are involved in the drafting of the agency's opinions and rules, as well as the duty of the EASA to respond to the consultation process (though not requiring that this is taken into account in the motivation of the opinion) indicate a certain degree of consideration for those affected by the agency's regulatory action and, possibly, a more consequent involvement of interested persons in the decision-making process than the one envisaged in the EFSA regulation. Nevertheless, nothing in the written provisions supports the belief that the intent of consultation goes beyond collaboration in the discharge of the decisional competences.

At the end, participation in these cases is a response to the regulatory needs present in each field and to the substantial aims of the corresponding legal regime.[121] It is not correlated with the fact that the powers exercised by the agency may impinge directly or indirectly upon the legal spheres of the individuals that fall within its realm and is not directed at ensuring procedural protection to concerned persons. On the contrary, the assumption that the agencies' decisions are incapable of affecting directly the legal sphere of natural and legal persons is a reason to exclude procedural rights from the corresponding procedures. However, the distinction between advisory functions and true decision-making power can easily be a legal fiction.[122]

spheres are affected or shaped by the agency's regulatory decisions, is analysed below, in Chapter 7.

[119] Article 52(1)(b) and (c) of Regulation No. 216/2008, *cit.*, n. 98. On the EASA's participatory practices, see Craig, *op. cit.*, n. 100, pp. 179–80.

[120] Article 52(1)(b) and (c) of Regulation No. 216/2008, *cit.*, n. 98.

[121] On the relevance of this factor, Chiti, 'The emergence…', *cit.*, n. 91, pp. 317 and 340.

[122] See further, Chiti, 'An important part of the EU's institutional machinery…', *cit.*, n. 92, pp. 1405–06, 1418, 1426.

3.2.3 *Interlocking interests: the Commission and interest groups*

A chapter dedicated to highlighting how the institutional practice of Union decision-making is permeated by participatory rules, structures, and practices could not be complete without a reference, albeit brief, to the role of organized interests in the Union decisional processes.

Since its outset, the European process of integration has attracted interest groups. The supranational institutions, the Commission in particular, prompted this attention.[123] On the one hand, the wide purview of the integration project, and the Communities' powers, meant the creation of rights and duties that bear directly upon individuals without the filter of the state, and made it clear that these powers would likely be 'important and of immediate significance'.[124] On the other hand, the Commission, eager to solidify its role as guardian of the Community interest, sought support for deepening economic integration beyond the will resulting from interstate agreements, thus providing the process of integration 'with its own motive power'.[125] Beyond the realm of institutionalized participation, it found in organized interests its 'natural constituency'.[126]

There are dissent interpretations as to whether predictions of neo-functionalist theories, according to which relevant interest groups would shift their focus and their loyalties to the supranational level of policy-making and drive the process of integration forward, were revealed in fact to be true.[127] Nevertheless, neo-functionalism seems adequately to explain at

[123] The following observations will focus on the relationships between the Commission and interest groups, since the Commission is 'the foremost venue for interest representation at the EU level' (Justin Greenwood (2007) *Interest Representation in the European Union*, 2nd edn, Houndmills: Palgrave Macmillan, p. 24). Moreover, its initiatives on the regulation of interest representation, together with those adopted by the European Parliament, represent the most significant developments in this regard. For a comprehensive view on access points of organized interests to European decisional processes, see Greenwood, *op. cit.*, Chapter 2.

[124] David Coombes (1970) *Politics and Bureaucracy in the European Community*, London: George Allen and Unwin Ltd, pp. 25–6. See also Joël Rideau (1993) 'Les groupes d'intérêt dans le système institutionnel communautaire', *Revue d'Affaires Européens*, n. 3, pp. 49–73, at pp. 50–3.

[125] David Coombes, *op. cit.*, p. 98, confronting Spinelli's (Altiero Spinelli (1966) *The Eurocrats, Conflict and Crisis in the European Community*) and Lindberg's analyses on the success of this strategy (Leon N. Lindberg (1963) *The Political Dynamics of European Economic Integration*).

[126] Justin Greenwood (2003) *Interest Representation in the European Union*, Houndmills: Palgrave Macmillan, p. 4.

[127] According to Beate Kohler-Koch, 'theoretical reasoning and empirical evidence confirm that European organization of interests grew in response to, and not in advance of integrative steps . . . [;] European interest groups were not driving forces of regional integration', as neo-functionalists had

least some of the historical turning points of the integration process.[128] At any rate, interest groups diversified their access points to decision-making processes and established organizations at all levels of a 'multi-layered system of government'. On the other hand, the Commission, disposing of limited resources, has since the outset resorted largely to external expert advice. Organized interest groups not only represent an important source of specialized information, but also provide the Commission with opportunities to scrutinize beforehand the way its policies are perceived by market participants and with information about the impact and implementation of adopted measures.[129] As it expressly stated:

> The Commission has always been an institution open to outside input. The Commission believes this process to be fundamental to the development of its policies. This dialogue has proved valuable to both the Commission and to interested outside parties. Commission officials acknowledge the need for such outside input and welcome it.[130]

This genetic intertwining has been inbuilt in the Union's political system up until today. A legal analysis of the mechanisms of participation needs to take into account that, behind the legal scene, informal mechanisms of participation are often more influential and determinant of the content of Union decisions than those enshrined in legal texts. At the same time, the relationships between the Commission and interest groups are often the substratum of the participation procedures envisaged in legal provisions, even if these may seek to insulate the decisional procedure from informal interventions.[131] The practices of consultation—through green papers and the like—the origins of which can be traced back to the beginning of the

predicted (Kohler-Koch (1997) 'Organized interests in European integration: the evolution of a new type of governance', in Helen Wallace and Alasdair R. Young (eds), *Participation and Policy-making in the European Union*, Oxford: Clarendon Press, pp. 42–68, at p. 46).

[128] See Wolfgang Streeck and Phillippe Schmitter (1991) 'From national corporatism to transnational pluralism: organised interests in the Single European Market', *Politics and Society*, Vol. 19, n. 2, pp. 133–64, at p. 148. This is corroborated by Helen Wallace (in her Introductory chapter included in Helen Wallace and Alasdair R. Young (eds), *op. cit.*, pp. 1–16, at p. 5) and by Justin Greenwood (in the second edition of his book *Interest Representation in the European Union*, *cit.*, n. 123, pp. 1–2).

[129] Beate Kohler-Koch, *op. cit.*, p. 48. Justin Greenwood, *op. cit.*, n. 123, pp. 5–6.

[130] These are the opening statements of the Commission Communication 'An open and structured dialogue between the Commission and special interest groups' (Communication 93/C63/02, of 12 of December 1992, SEC/92/2272 final) available at <http://www.ec.europa.eu/civil_society/interest_groups/index_en.htm>). See, also, Justin Greenwood, *op. cit.*, n. 123, p. 7, quoting the same passage. On this communication, see observations below.

[131] Rideau, *op. cit.*, n. 124, p. 64.

integration process, rest largely on the interaction described by the Commission in the quoted passage. Their rationales are similar to some of the forms of participation analysed above. All in all, these and other 'inclusive practices' represented a means of securing the efficient performance of the Commission's decision-making functions. They were also intended as a source of legitimacy grounded in support and confidence in policy-making processes, as well as on the technical appropriateness of its decisions.[132] In the main, they have remained politically institutionalized patterns of interaction immune to legal recognition.

The relations between the Commission and interest groups have suffered a process of transformation, when transparency came to the fore both as an essential dimension of 'good administrative conduct' and as a legal principle. Since the beginning of the 1990s transparency has become part of the legitimacy and regulatory strategies of the Commission's governance initiatives.

A first sign of change occurred when the Commission made an attempt to regulate the behaviour of interest groups and of Commission officials in their respective relations. Following a similar step that had been taken by the European Parliament,[133] the Commission adopted a communication entitled 'An open and structured dialogue between the Commission and special interest groups'.[134] The significance of this initiative is more revealing if seen in the political context of the time, which explains its adoption. In the wake of the negative results of the Danish referendum on the Maastricht Treaty, the Community, and the Commission in particular, was more than ever under pressure to ensure transparency, granting access to information and equal access to policy-making procedures.[135] Openness became an impetus for the Commission to change its image and practices.[136] An additional thrust behind this process was the exponential growth of European interest groups, which occurred in the latter half of the 1980s, as a result of the Single European Market

132 On this latter aspect, Greenwood, *op. cit.*, n.123, p. 1.

133 On this, Andrew M. McLaughlin and Justin Greenwood (1995) 'The management of interest representation in the European Union', *Journal of Common Market Studies*, Vol. 33, n. 1, pp. 43–156, at pp. 144–5.

134 For references, see n. 130 above.

135 See Curtin, *The Executive Power of the European Union . . . , cit.*, n. 91, p. 206.

136 John Peterson (1995) 'Playing the transparency game: Consultation and policy-making in the European Commission', *Public Administration*, Vol. 73, n. 3, pp. 473–92. On how theuse of information and communication technology fostered openness of the Commission's practices, as well as those of other institutions, see Curtin, *The Executive Power of the European Union . . . , cit.*, n. 91, p. 218–33.

programme. This also called for a different strategy to deal with interest representation.[137]

In its communication, the Commission essentially called for self-regulation of interest groups, exhorting them to adopt codes of conduct, along the lines of the minimum requirements defined by the Commission in the said communication. Moreover, it stated its intention to create a directory with all relevant information on interest groups. However, this did not amount to any official recognition nor did it have a licensing effect that could lead to selective access. According to the Commission, this directory did not 'confer ... the granting of any ... privileges such as special access to information, buildings, officials, etc.'.[138] As will be seen below, this is still today the Commission's approach to a register of interest representatives.

Transparency was undoubtedly the driving force behind these measures. Nevertheless, they seemed to be too feeble to accomplish this goal. Commenting on the Commission's communication, McLaughlin and Greenwood pointed out, in 1995, that: 'regulating "lobbying" cannot restructure the complex patterns of interest intermediation in which the Commission is involved with private interests'. They rightfully defended the position that a change in the '"lobbying" environment' would only come about if the EU institutions would revise their procedures on access to information and the rules for handling confidential documents.[139] A first step in this direction had already been taken: in 1994 the Commission issued a communication on 'Improved access to documents', which, together with similar documents of the Council and the Parliament, were the forerunners of the current regulation on access to documents.[140]

[137] This is referred in the said communication (p. 1). See also Beate Kohler-Koch, *op. cit.*, n. 127, p. 46, and the data presented by the Committee of the Regions in this respect: Committee of the Regions (2003) 'The regional and local dimensions in establishing new forms of governance', Luxembourg: Office for Official Publications of the European Communities, pp. 41–2.

[138] Communication, 'An open and structured dialogue ...', *cit.*, n. 130, p. 2.

[139] McLaughlin and Greenwood, *op. cit.*, n. 123, pp. 151–2. In addition to these original flaws, the recommendations of the Commission for self-regulation of lobbying had little success. The rather slow reaction to its communication in the following years (McLaughlin and Greenwood, *op. cit.*, n. 133, pp. 152–4) seems to have developed into an extremely low adherence (see Daniela Obradovic and Jose M. Alonso Vizcaino (2006) 'Good governance requirements concerning the participation of interest groups in EU consultations', *Common Market Law Review*, Vol. 43, n. 4, pp. 1049–85, at p. 1068). See, further below, n. 147.

[140] Regulation No. 1049/2001, of the European Parliament and of the Council, 30 May 2001, regarding public access to European Parliament, Council and Commission documents (OJ L 145/43, 31.5.2001). On the history of this regulation, see Ian Harden (2009) 'The revision of Regulation n. 1049/2001 on public access to documents', *European Public Law*, Vol. 15, n. 2,

In addition, from the point of view of ensuring equal access of interest groups to decision-making procedures, the measures proposed by the Commission were certainly ill-adapted to address the imbalance between representation of business interests and consumer interests, traditionally under-represented.[141] In this respect, McLaughlin and Greenwood warned: '[I]nstitutional arrangements have developed so far that it might now be too late to consider the creation of a "level playing field".'[142] More recently, Greenwood highlighted that the practice of establishing partnership agreements with certain groups in some policy sectors, endorsed in the Commission's White Paper on Governance, hinders the attempts to establish a desirable 'level playing field'.[143] These observations are all the more relevant as equal access is a persistent problem in the way the Commission relates to organized groups.[144]

At any rate, this communication represented the inception of the regulation of interest representation that culminated in the Commission's 2006 Transparency Initiative. This resumed the two veins of the 1992 Communication. First, it proposed the setting up of a voluntary registration system containing information about 'interest groups and lobbyists who wish to be consulted on EU initiatives' (namely, the interests and persons they represent, their mission, and their funding sources). Secondly, it advocated the promotion of self-regulation of lobbyists, on the basis of minimum criteria for codes of conduct defined by the Commission, preferably accompanied by monitoring and sanctions potentially applied in cases of incorrect registration and breach of the code of conduct.[145] These initiatives were

pp. 239–56, at pp. 239–40. At the time of writing, the debates on the reform of the regulation were still ongoing: see European Parliament resolution of 17 December 2009 on improvements needed to the legal framework for access to documents following the entry into force of the Lisbon Treaty (P7_TA(2009)0116). See also, 'EU institutions struggle to adapt openness principle', *EuropeanVoice.com*, 14.10.2010.

141 On the bias favouring organized interests as a 'persistent [feature] in agency policies' and on the problems of effective representation of unorganized interests, see, referring to a different setting, Richard Stewart (1975) 'The reformation of American administrative law', *Harvard Law Review*, Vol. 88, n. 8, pp. 1667–813, at pp. 1684–7.

142 McLaughlin and Greenwood, *op. cit.*, n. 133, *loc. cit.*

143 Greenwood, *op. cit.*, n. 133, p. 4. In his opinion, '[t]here are incentives for the European Commission to pursue a system of privilege for certain preferred partner organisations.... [All public administrations] prefer to engage with those who keep to the rules of the game, rather than aggressive outsiders who create conflict beyond the confines of bureaucratic capacity to deal with it' (*op. cit., loc. cit.*).

144 Greenwood, *op. cit.*, n. 133, p. 45.

145 Green Paper 'European Transparency Initiative', COM (2006) 194 final, Brussels, 3.5.2006 (first launched in November 2005, by a 'Communication to the Commission from the

effectively accompanied by self-regulatory initiatives of some organizations, but they were, and still are, considered to be quite limited in comparison with the wide range of lobbyists.[146] A register of interest representatives was effectively established, but has had comparatively low adherence.[147] Moreover, its usefulness has been largely contested, not least due to the voluntary nature of the register.[148]

This is part of a major change, which led to an apparently more structured incorporation of organized interests in EU decision-making, endorsed namely in the Commission's 2001 White Paper on Governance and the follow-up initiatives on minimum standards for consultation and better regulation.[149] The political context in which the Commission operates and the pressure for ensuring legitimacy, transparency, and

President, Ms Wallström, Mr Kallas and Ms Fischer Boel proposing the launch of a European Transparency Initiative', available at <http://ec.europa.eu/archives/commission_2004–2009/kallas/doc/etik-communication_en.pdf>), pp. 6–10. For feedback and follow up, see Communication from the Commission 'Follow-up to the Green Paper "European Transparency Initiative"', COM (2007), 127 final, Brussels, 21.3.2007. Here, among other measures, the Commission proposed the revision of the 1992 minimum criteria for a code of conduct and that subscription to this renewed code becomes a requirement for registration. The code of conduct has been adopted in its Communication 'European Transparency Initiative—A framework for relations with interest representatives (Register and Code of Conduct)' (COM(2008) 323 final, Brussels, 27.5.2008).

[146] On this, Greenwood, *op. cit.*, n. 123, pp. 46–7.

[147] The register for interest representatives was set up in June 2008 (Commission Communication, 'European Transparency Initiative: the Register of Interest Representatives, one year after', COM (2009) 612 final, Brussels, 28.10.2009), but of an estimated 15,000–20,000 lobbyists only 303 had registered in the beginning of September 2008 ('EU lobbyists shun European Commission register', *EUObserver*, 05.09.2008), a number that rose to 1,600 at the end of June 2009 ('EU lobbyist register boosted by "market forces"', *EUObserver*, 22.06.2009) and to over 2,000 in October 2009, according to the Commission. See Communication from the Commission, 'European Transparency Initiative: the Register of Interest Representatives, one year after', *cit.* For a different view on the success of the register, see 'Most EU lobbyists are "not registering"', *EuropeanVoice.com*, 11.03.2010, referring to a survey by the Alliance for Lobbying Transparency and Ethics Regulation (ALTER-EU), available at <http://www.alter-eu.org/sites/default/files/documents/eu-lobby-firms-registration-2010-03–22.pdf>. In 29 October 2010, the register's website indicated 3,167 lobbyists registered (<https://webgate.ec.europa.eu/transparency/regrin/welcome/do.locale?=en#en>). The stress placed on numbers on both sides of the dispute reveals the political salience of this issue.

[148] On the criticisms directed at the register see the *EUObserver* article, 'EU lobbyist register boosted . . .', *cit.*, note above. See also 'Unveiling EU transparency' *European Voice*, 14.10.2010 for an overview on the reforms envisaged in October 2010.

[149] These are analysed below, Sub-sections 3.3.2 and 3.3.3. The expression 'structured incorporation of organized interests in European decision-making' is withdrawn from Obradovic and Vizcaino, *op. cit.*, n. 139, p. 1049.

accountability no longer permitted it to keep its intertwining with interest groups fully in the shade. Part of the Commission's strategy to enhance the legitimacy of Union decisional processes relied therefore on demanding standards of representativeness and accountability adopted by the organizations with which it interacts.

Apart from the regulation on access to documents, these changes have largely and deliberately remained outside the realm of 'hard' legal rules. On the other hand, fostering the involvement of a wide range of actors in decision-making processes has given rise to new decisional processes entailing power sharing between public and private actors at the margin of the traditional Community method. These issues will be dealt with below.[150]

3.2.4 *Participation: a constitutive feature of decision-making*

The establishment of links of administrative collaboration between public and private entities determined both the spread of the wide plethora of committees that assist the EU institutions in various decisional processes and the creation of EU agencies. Administrative collaboration meant also the association of interested parties or their representatives with decision-making, both through formalized structures or procedures and through informal contacts with interest groups. In the main, the pervasiveness of participation in the Community, and now in the Union institutional practice resulted from the need to acquire information essential for an appropriate delivery of the EU regulatory functions, to ensure responsive regulation, and facilitate compliance. Formal interest representation grounded in a rationale of collaboration assumed different shapes: from the restricted form of organic participation embodied in interest committees—which are at the service of the Commission and the Council—to other forms of insertion in more or less formalized decisional organic structures, such as the agencies' management boards, advisory boards, and networks. Administrative collaboration also inspired a number of the instances of procedural participation present in some agencies' regimes.

Two other forms of participation can be detected in EU institutional practice, both of a procedural nature, both straying beyond a rationale of administrative collaboration. One can be pinned down to a concept of rights-based participation: in cases where agencies were granted formal

[150] Section 3.3.

decision-making powers in adjudicative procedures, interested parties were given a say in EU decision-making procedures concerning their rights and interests. The other reveals a third meaning of participation, which can be termed participation as 'public-making'.[151] In this sense, participation is directed at creating a channel of 'communication' between decision-makers and the 'public', opening the decisional procedures to comments, as a means of enhancing their transparency and 'visibility' and, ultimately, creating a 'sense of belonging' to a given polity. In this last case, participation often takes the form of consultation phases inserted in decisional procedures and no legal guarantees are attached to the fact of participation. Transparency, in this sense, does not refer to the right to access documents the regime of which is contained in the relevant regulation,[152] but to a practice of openness that consists of enabling 'the public', as an abstract and undefined entity, to take part in decisional processes. Whether this is merely a means of letting 'the public' know which proposals are on the table or leads to a deeper involvement in these processes, depends on the consequences the Commission wishes to draw from the comments received. Admittedly, the Commission often publishes a general report on the results of the consultation and indicates whether changes are envisaged as a result of the comments forwarded to it.[153] These three different meanings of participation constitute the three different strands of participation present in the Union institutional and legal setting.

In synthesis, two conclusions can be drawn. First, participation in the vein of interest representation is a long-standing constitutive feature of EU decisional processes. The involvement of interested parties in EU decision-making procedures recognized in the founding Treaties was reproduced, widened, and furthered by the committees' practice and by specific legal regimes created to fulfil the goals of integration, accompanied by the redefinition of the administrative bodies competent in the

[151] This expression was suggested by Neil Walker (recognizing the lack of a more adequate term) in a discussion with the author.

[152] Regulation No. 1049/2001, *cit.*, n. 140.

[153] Yet, there are flaws in following this self-imposed conduct, namely 'weaknesses in providing general feedback explaining how and to what extent the comments have been taken into account by the Commission' (Communication from the Commission, 'Follow-up to the Green Paper "European Transparency Initiative"', *cit.*, n. 145, p. 6). For a general assessment, see C. Quittkat and B. Finke (2008) 'The EU Commission Consultation Regime', in B. Kohler Koch, D. de Bievre, and W. Moloney, *Opening EU-Governance to Civil Society—Gains and Challenges*, CONNEX Report Series No. 5, pp. 183–222.

respective fields. It is thus present at different levels of decision-making and across different regulatory fields, powers, and forms of delivering the EU administrative functions. Even though the involvement of interested parties remains dependent on the regulatory specificities of each policy field, it is undoubtedly a widespread practice which has common origins in the institutional and political features of the EU administration, namely its reduced size, the lack of direct enforcement powers in certain areas and its contested nature in certain historical periods. These features determined the need to establish links of administrative collaboration both with other competent administrative authorities and with interested parties. Secondly, it follows from the above analysis that ensuring the procedural protection of the rights and interests of concerned persons was only an issue in relation to procedures leading up to individual determinations. In cases where agencies advise the institutions on regulatory decisions adopted under the form of general acts, the impact that EU decisions can have in defining or determining duties or rights of individuals does not seem to have been a regulatory concern, or, at least, did not lead to the creation of similar procedural guarantees.

Other than formally institutionalized modes of interest representation or participation, the informal activity of interest groups is equally a relevant feature of the EU polity. The way it has evolved is largely linked to the Commission's own interpretation of its institutional role. The changes which occurred at this level not only mirror deeper transformations verified in the integration process but are also a sign of one noticeable development in Union institutional practices: the furtherance of practices of participation based on administrative collaboration and transparency.

It results from the above analysis that the institutional context of European integration has determined the pervasiveness of participation in EU decisional structures. As indicated above, changes in the EU institutional context have created changes in the way some of the forms of participation which have characterized the European polity since its beginning are perceived. The next section will focus upon the two institutional milestones in the integration process which were simultaneously turning points in the institutional practice of participation: the Commission's programme for the completion of the internal market and its consequences in terms of regulatory strategies, on the one hand; and, on the other, the institutional reforms undertaken by the Commission since 2001, some of which were later partially accepted into the Constitutional Treaty, and now consolidated in the Lisbon Treaty.

3.3 The Turn to Participatory Governance

3.3.1 *Participation and 'new' regulatory approaches*

The completion of the internal market, in the period between 1985 and 1992, produced far-reaching institutional and administrative changes within the Community.[154] For the purposes of this work, two main points deserve notice, both pertaining to regulatory innovations. First, the Commission's strategy for the acceleration of the removal of trade barriers led, *inter alia*, to a systematic resort to private standardization bodies in the field of technical harmonization, departing from the regulatory techniques of harmonization that had been used until then. Secondly, the completion of the internal market brought to the fore concerns relating to Community over-regulation, to the impact of Community legislation on business, as well as to the transparency of regulatory processes. This led to a reform of the Community's regulatory policy. A few patchy and fragmented initiatives adopted in the beginning of the 1990s ultimately resulted in the Commission's better law-making programme, comprising systematic consultation processes inserted in impact assessment analyses.[155]

These two aspects—increased resort to forms of private regulation and consultations in impact assessment analyses—were later included in the White Paper on Governance and in the respective follow-up Commission initiatives.[156] Moreover, they were taken up in the 2003 Inter-institutional agreement on better law-making, in which the Parliament, the Council, and the Commission endorsed the use of co-regulation and self-regulation as 'alternative methods of regulation', defining the conditions thereof, and

[154] For an overview of the process, see, among others, Kenneth Armstrong and Simon Bulmer (1998), *The Governance of the Single European Market*, Manchester and New York: Manchester University Press, Chapter 1; Helmut Schmitt von Sydow (1988) 'The basic strategies of the Commission's White Paper', in Ronald Bibier, Renaud Dehousse, John Pinder, and Joseph H.H. Weiler (eds), *1992: One European Market? A critical analysis of the Commission's internal market strategy*, Baden-Baden: Nomos, pp. 79–106. For an account of its problematic points, see Bibier, Dehousse, Pinder, and Weiler (1988) 'Back to the future: policy, strategy and tactics on the White Paper on the creation of a single European market' in the same volume (pp. 13–31). On the related institutional changes, see Renaud Dehousse (1988) 'Completing the internal market: institutional constraints and challenges', still in the same publication, pp. 311–36.

[155] On these initiatives, see Armstrong and Bulmer, *op. cit.*, pp. 290–9.

[156] Commission of the European Communities, 'European Governance. A White Paper', COM (2001) 428 final, Brussels, 25.7.2001 (hereinafter, White Paper on Governance). For references, regarding the follow-up initiatives, see below Sub-section 3.3.2.

purported to engage in consultative processes as a means of improving the quality of legislation.[157] In this context, they became the pillars of a systematic institutional practice aimed at involving interested parties in Community decision-making procedures in a more structured way than before, albeit with different functions. This is the theme of the following pages. First, the 'new approach to harmonization' is taken as one example of the varied mixed forms of public and private regulation that mushroomed at EU level.[158] Given the purposes of this work, the analysis focuses on how this 'new' form of regulation contends with the participation of persons excluded from the regulatory arrangements. Secondly, the origins of the 'better law-making' policy are analysed and put in context with the first signs of the EU legitimacy crisis in the aftermath of the first Danish referendum on the Maastricht Treaty. This sets the scene for the study of the meaning of participation in the realm of the Commission governance initiatives developed thereafter, examined below (Sub-section 3.3.2).

Participation under the 'new approach to harmonization'

The 'new approach to harmonization' was designed to address the *lourdeur* of the Community legislative procedures in the field of technical harmonization.[159] It embodies a form of co-regulation,[160] in which private entities (European standardization bodies) set voluntary rules ('technical specifications') in accordance with legislatively defined general principles and requirements as well as contractually agreed requirements. Compliance with such rules is tantamount to compliance with the legislative act.[161]

[157] OJ C 321/1, 31.12.2003.

[158] Presenting the new approach to harmonization as a landmark in the establishment of the internal market, see Christian Joerges, Harm Schepel, and Ellen Vos (1999) 'The law's problems with the involvement of non-governmental actors in Europe's legislative processes: the case of standardisation under the '"New Approach"', EUI Working Paper No. 99/9, pp. 7–8.

[159] The expression is Dehousse's, 'Misfits...', *cit.*, n. 92, p. 216.

[160] Fabrizio Cafaggi (2006) 'Rethinking private regulation in the European regulatory space', in Fabrizio Cafaggi (ed.), *Reframing Self-regulation in European Private Law*, The Netherlands: Kluwer Law International, pp. 3–75, at pp. 27–8. Harm Schepel (2005) *The Constitution of Private Governance. Product Standards in the Regulation of Integrating Markets*, Oxford, Portland: Hart Publishing, p. 240 (on the nature of technical specifications, see p. 52).

[161] The basic principles were set out in Annex II of the Council Resolution on a new approach to technical harmonization and standards, the so-called 'Model Directive' (OJ C 136/1, 7.5.1985). Harm Schepel underlines that the new approach was in fact revealed to be more differentiated than this account suggests (Harm Schepel, *op. cit.*, p. 227). On this, see, *inter alia*, Jacques Pelkmans (1987) 'The new approach to technical harmonisation', *Journal of Common Market Studies*, Vol. 25, n. 3, pp. 249–69; von Sydow, *op. cit.*, n. 154, pp. 94–6; Richard H. Lauwaars (1988) 'The "Model

The ensuing collaboration between public and private decision-makers therefore blurs the divide between rule-definition and rule-application, as well as between the rule-maker and the persons subject to the rule—later identified as one of the characteristics of the so-called 'new modes of governance'.[162] In this case, the intervention of private persons in the decisional process clearly has a different meaning from the 'weaker' forms of participation that have been mentioned in the sections above. Although this is equally informed by considerations of administrative collaboration and efficiency, they intervene in the decisional procedures with decision-making powers. The resulting decisions have external effects vis-à-vis third parties not involved in these procedures.[163]

This led the Commission to engage in a series of attempts to harness their activity to principles of public decision-making, moulding their decisional processes.[164] Among these was the concern to ensure participation of the 'regulated': the Commission pushed the European standardization entities to involve all interested parties in the definition of technical standards, in particular to ensure the participation of diffuse interests, excluded from the bodies of these standardization entities. This confirms the Commission's commitment to ensuring respect for interest representation in regulatory structures, possibly entailing the consideration for societal interests that would otherwise risk being marginalized.

First mentioned in the 'General guidelines for co-operation' signed by the Commission and the European Committee for Standardization (CEN) in November 1984, the need to ensure the involvement of interested parties was further emphasized in subsequent documents. The Council in its 2002 'Conclusions on standardization' stressed 'the importance it attaches to the ability of *all relevant interested parties* to participate *effectively* in standardization'; it requested 'that national standards bodies ensure the involvement of such parties in the process at national level, and [invited] the European

Directive" on technical harmonisation', in Bibier, Dehousse, Pinder, and Weiler (eds), *op. cit.*, pp. 151–73; Christian Joerges (1988) 'The new approach to technical harmonisation and the interests of consumers: reflections in the requirements and difficulties of a Europeanisation of product safety policy' in Bibier, Dehousse, Pinder, and Weiler (eds), *op. cit.*, n. 154, pp. 175–225, in particular pp. 206–15; Harm Schepel, *op.cit.*, n. 160, pp. 63–7 and pp. 225–58.

[162] Joanne Scott and David M. Trubek (2002) 'Mind the gap: law and new approaches to governance in the European Union', *European Law Journal*, Vol. 8, n. 1, pp. 1–18, at p. 8.

[163] On the relativity of the adjective 'weaker' and on the need to evaluate 'weaknesses and strengths . . . by looking at current practices together with an examination of formal rules', Cafaggi, *op. cit.*, n. 160, p. 26.

[164] See Joerges, Schepel, and Vos, *op. cit.*, n. 158, pp. 17–24 and Harm Schepel, *op. cit.*, n. 160, pp. 242–6.

standards bodies to foster the exchanges of information with the relevant interested parties at European level'.[165] The 2003 'General guidelines for the cooperation between CEN, CENELEC and ETSI, the European Commission and the European Free Trade Association' defined the involvement of interested parties as one of the European standardization policy objectives. In particular, 'economic and social partners in Europe and other relevant interest groups, namely NGOs, that might not otherwise be involved but who have a legitimate interest in the outcome, [should] be involved in the process of standardization'.[166] Moreover, standardization entities should ensure that their structures and procedures are representative and 'increase the participation of interested circles, especially public authorities, manufacturers, small and medium-sized enterprises, consumers, workers and environmental interest groups, at the national and European level in the drafting of standards and other deliverables' as well as ensure that 'their views are adequately taken into account' and that they have access to documents in order to 'effectively participate'.[167] More recently, the Commission stressed again the importance of ensuring 'fair and balanced representation of all stakeholders of standardization', in particular 'small and medium enterprises, but also users/consumers and researchers'.[168] In practice, the Commission has striven for the inclusion of consumers in the process of standardization by funding private associations such as ANEC (European Association for the co-ordination of consumer representation in standardisation) and NORMAPME (European Office of

[165] Council conclusions of 1 March 2002 on standardization, OJ C 66/1, 15.3.2002 (emphasis added). On the difficulties and results of the Commission's pressure on European standardization bodies to ensure participation, see Josef Falke (1997) 'Achievements and unresolved problems of European standardisation: the ingenuity of practice and the queries of lawyers' in Christian Joerges, Karl-Heinz Ladeur, and Ellen Vos (eds), *Integrating Scientific Expertise into Regulatory Decision-making. National Traditions and European Innovations*, Baden-Baden: Nomos, pp. 187–224, at pp. 208–15. See, equally, his proposals for securing a balanced involvement of all parties concerned, at pp. 219–20 and pp. 222–3. Harm Schepel underlines the feebleness of the Commission's attempt, given that 'the integration of European wide interest groups in European standardization conflicts with the [European standard bodies] cardinal organizational principle of national delegations' (*op. cit.*, n. 160, p. 245).

[166] General guidelines for the cooperation between CEN, CENELEC and ETSI, the European Commission and the European Free Trade Association, 28 March 2003 (OJ C 91/7, 16.4.2003), p. 9.

[167] *Idem*, p. 10.

[168] Communication from the Commission to the Council, the European Parliament and the European Economic and Social Committee, 'Towards an increased contribution from standardisation to innovation in Europe', COM (2008) 133 final, Brussels, 11.3.2008, pp. 8–9.

Craft/Trades and Small and Medium-sized Enterprises for Standardisation), which are associate members of, or have been given an equivalent status by, the European standardization bodies.[169]

Arguably, this could indicate that, from the institutions' perspective, one decisive criterion for ensuring participation is whether regulatory practices have potentially binding effects vis-à-vis third parties, independently of the nature and origin of the regulatory power. Technical standards, whether defined by public or private rules, affect the market positions of undertakings and impact on the protection of employees, consumers, and the environment.[170] In this sense, the rationales for ensuring a rights-based participation of interested parties—consideration for the rights and legally protected interests externally affected by the regulatory activity, both from a perspective of defence and care of administrative action—are present in private modes of regulation which are incorporated in public regulatory processes.[171] Nevertheless, a rights-based participation seems to be distant from the possible forms of participation envisaged so far with regard to standardization processes. Acceptability of standards, as well as forging consensuses among interested persons and thereby facilitating the success of the standardization process, but also transparency and accountability, seem to be the prevailing rationales for the Commission to endorse participation in these regulatory processes and urge standardization bodies to do so.[172]

An incipient new framework for consultation processes

The fulfilment of the internal market legislative programme brought to the fore the Commission's concern for ensuring the adequacy and effectiveness of its policy strategies, as well as to respond to anxieties of excessive regulation. The abolition of the physical and technical barriers to trade having been achieved at the legislative level, the Community needed not only to ensure the smooth functioning of the internal market through an effective uniform application and enforcement of the Community legislation,

[169] See, respectively, <http://www.anec.org> and <http://www.normapme.com>.

[170] Falke, *op. cit.*, n. 165, p. 219.

[171] For the various types of regulatory processes combining public and private regulation, see Cafaggi, *op. cit.*, n. 160, pp. 21–35.

[172] See 'General guidelines…', *cit.*, n. 166, p. 9 and Communication from the Commission to the Council, the European Parliament and the European Economic and Social Committee, 'Integration of Environmental Aspects into European Standardisation', COM (2004) 130 final, Brussels, 25.02.2004, p. 14.

but also to make sure that firms and consumers would feel its economic effects. How to guarantee that the existing administrative mechanisms were adapted to the new situation created by the abolition of internal border controls, on the one hand, and how to achieve a sufficient degree of reciprocal trust to answer the needs of economic operators and consumers, on the other, became pressing issues. The diagnosis was made by the Sutherland Report, which was presented to the Commission in October 1992 and endorsed subsequently by the latter.[173] Among other recommendations, the committee stressed the need to ensure the proportionality and transparency of Community policy-making, in particular of its legislative proposals. To that effect, it recommended, respectively, that:

> All proposals for Community action should be based on a wide-ranging analysis of its political, social and economic impact, comparing the advantages and disadvantages of intervention and of non-intervention. This analysis should be based on the five criteria of need, effectiveness, proportionality, consistency and communication.[174]
>
> Wide and effective consultation on Commission proposals is essential. The Commission should introduce a better procedure for making people aware, at the earliest possible stage, of its intention to propose legislation, making available the background analysis, particularly in the light of the principles of subsidiarity and proportionality. Discussions should be held with a wide range of interested parties.[175]

Stressing that this would represent a continuation of previous institutional practices, the Commission pledged to follow these recommendations.[176] It stated its commitment to systematically precede its proposals by impact

[173] 'The internal market after 1992: meeting the challenge', Report presented to the Commission by the High Level Group on the operation of the internal market, President: Peter Sutherland, SEC(92)2044, Brussels, 26 of October 1992 (hereinafter, 'the Sutherland Report'). Apart from the tasks mentioned in the text, the group was mandated to consider the optimal distribution of responsibilities and competences within the Community for those effects and to suggest to the Commission a strategy to ensure that all the benefits from the internal market would be in practice after 1992 (the Sutherland Report, p. 1).

[174] Recommendation No. 1, pp. 20–1 of the Sutherland Report (the page numbering corresponds to the French version of the Report).

[175] Recommendation No. 8, pp. 26–7 of the Sutherland Report.

[176] The Commission's reaction can be assessed essentially on the basis of the two documents: Communication from the Commission to the Council and to the European Parliament, 'The operation of the Community's internal market after 1992. Follow-up to the Sutherland report', SEC (92) 2227 final, Brussels, 2 December 1992; and Communication from the Commission, 'Follow-up to the Sutherland Report: legislative consolidation to enhance the transparency of Community law in the area of the internal market', COM (93) 361 final, Brussels, 16 December 1993.

assessment analyses and undertook to make a more systematic use of consultation documents (green papers), even proposing to adopt a procedure that bears a strong resemblance to the US notice and comment procedure: it would publish its 'legislative intentions' in the Official Journal, including the information of the legislative impact assessment, and invite interested parties 'to make known any observations or comments they could have'.[177]

At stake was not only the effectiveness of the internal market regulation, but also the need to tackle the legitimacy crisis exacerbated by the difficulties faced in the ratification process of the Maastricht Treaty. With the expansion of social and political competences—embracing more sensitive issues than before by the effect of the Single European Act—and under the very likely perspective of the creation of a political union, the legitimacy of the Community powers became more than ever a disputed issue. This rapidly developed into a deeper social legitimacy crisis.[178] Involvement of 'the public' or of 'citizens' in decision-making procedures, through consultations held transparently at an earlier stage of these procedures, was taken as part of the recipe for ensuring closeness, responsiveness, representativeness, and accountability, the yardsticks of democracy that were perceived as fading away as the integration process moved forward.[179] In fact, a similar insistence on consultation to that contained in the Sutherland Report is found in the Conclusions of the European Councils of Birmingham and Edinburgh, held in October 1992 and December 1992 respectively.[180] These documents suggest that there was a need to 'reassure a

[177] Communication, 'The operation of the Community's internal market after 1992 . . .', *cit.*, pp. 5–6.

[178] On the distinction between formal and social legitimacy and the legitimacy problems of the integration process, see Weiler, 'Problems of legitimacy in post 1992 Europe', *cit.*, n. 43. Also building on this distinction, Amaryllis Verhoeven (2002) *The European Union in Search of a Democratic and Constitutional Theory*, The Hague, London, New York: Kluwer Law International, pp. 63–70. For a recent account of the academic debates on this matter, see Beate Kohler-Koch and Berthold Rittberger (2007), 'Charting crowded territory: debating the democratic legitimacy of the European Union' in Kohler-Koch and Rittberger (eds), *Debating the Democratic Legitimacy of the European Union*, Lanham: Rowman & Littlefield Publishers, pp. 1–29.

[179] Weiler, *op. cit.*, n. 43, p. 416–18.

[180] See Point I.8 of the 'Birmingham Declaration—A Community close to its citizens', Annex I to the Conclusions of the Presidency of the Birmingham European Council (*Bulletin of the European Communities*, No. 10, 1992, p. 9), welcoming a Commission proposal to make a more systematic use of consultation papers. Also, European Council of Edinburgh, Conclusions of the Presidency, Annex 3 to Part 1: 'Transparency – Implementation of the Birmingham Declaration' (in *Bulletin of the European Communities*, No. 12, 1992, pp. 18–20, also p. 10), referring in particular to the

concerned public', 'restore the confidence of its citizens in the European venture', or simply to 'demonstrate more clearly the benefits of Community integration'.[181] Moreover, in the 1993 'Inter-institutional declaration on democracy, transparency and subsidiarity', where the institutions defined the law-making rules they should follow, the Commission resumed the proposal it had put forward in its reaction to the Sutherland Report: the creation of 'a notification procedure, consisting of the publication in the Official Journal of a brief summary of any measure planned by the Commission, with the setting of a deadline by which interested parties may submit their comments'.[182]

Henceforth, participation was intended to ensure citizens' closeness to the Community and, now, to the Union. Consultation practices of the Commission thus acquired a new cloak. Nevertheless, with the exception of access to documents of the EU institutions, and apart from a more systematic resort to mechanisms of consultation already in place, few substantial changes effectively occurred in the Commission's practice in this respect.[183] These threads were taken up again in the 2001 White Paper on Governance and the follow-up papers, where they were more consistently developed. The analysis of some of these documents will allow us to assess this 'renewed' meaning of participation.

transparency of the work of the Council and to measures to make the Community legislation clearer and simpler and of easier access, in line with some of the measures suggested by the Sutherland Report.

[181] The expressions are taken from the introductory notes to the Conclusions of the European Councils of Birmingham and of Edinburgh (points I.1 of both, *Bulletin of the European Communities*, No. 10, 1992, p. 7 and *Bulletin of the European Communities*, No. 12, 1992, p. 7).

[182] OJ C 329/133, 6.12.1993 (Annex to the European Parliament 'Resolution on democracy, transparency and subsidiarity', A3–0356/93), p. 134. For a comment, see Paul Craig (1997) 'Democracy and rulemaking within the EC: an empirical and normative assessment', *European Law Journal*, Vol. 3, n. 2, pp. 105–30, at pp. 121–2.

[183] Significantly, Gráinne de Búrca highlighted the ambiguities and disparities behind the apparently consensual conceptions of citizenship, democracy, subsidiarity, and transparency (openness and accessibility) in the official reports presented to the 1996 Amsterdam Intergovernmental Conference as well as their somewhat shallow use. She commented: 'it is not clear from reading some of the reports whether the official participants in the reform process genuinely believe that the Union lacks essential legitimacy and requires fundamental reform, or whether their principal aim is to placate the public' (Gráinne de Búrca (1996) 'The quest for legitimacy in the European Union', *The Modern Law Review*, Vol. 59, n. 3, pp. 349–76, at p. 372).

3.3.2 *Revamping participation: 'interest representation' meets 'civil society'*

Under the thrust of legitimation and tied by a lagged process of constitutional reform bound to produce results only in 2004,[184] the Commission issued in 2001 the White Paper on Governance, proposing 'a series of initial actions' for 'the reform of European governance'.[185] While it conveys the Commission's official view on the desirable future developments of the EU, this paper may be considered as part of a wider administrative and constitutional reform process.[186] Among other aspects, and following from the developments mentioned above, this reform process entailed an emphasis on the role of private actors in European decision-making processes, ranging from 'pure participation' to power sharing between public and private actors. Not intending to enter into a comprehensive analysis and meaning of the paper's proposals, it is important, for current purposes, to note the reasons why participation appears as one of its core notions, given the meaning of the so-called 'principle of participation' as well as to characterize the Commission's stance regarding participation. Some authors confirm the prominence of participation also in the preliminary works of the White Paper.[187]

The long acknowledged reasons for the involvement of interested persons in public decision-making, namely ensuring their collaboration in the making and implementation of Community decisions as a means of

[184] That is, at the end of the mandate of the Prodi Commission that had came into office in late 1999. More extensively on the context that gave momentum to reform, see, among others, Paul Magnette (2003) *Contrôler l'Europe. Pouvoirs et responsabilité dans l'Union Européene*, Bruxelles: Éditions de l'Université de Bruxelles, pp. 10–15.

[185] White Paper, *cit.*, n. 2, p. 3. On the reasons for the use of the term governance, see Christian Möllers (2006) 'European governance: meaning and value of a concept', *Common Market Law Review*, Vol. 43, n. 2, pp. 313–36, at pp. 324–5.

[186] On the constitutional significance of the White Paper, see Walker, 'The White Paper in constitutional context', *cit.*, n. 3. He underlines the White Paper's 'constitutional resonance' and considers it 'an episode within, and a contribution to, an extended constitutional narrative' (p. 2). These interpretations find textual support in the White Paper, which, referring to the 2004 Intergovernmental Conference, called for 'urgent action to adapt governance under the existing treaties' (p. 3) and started a process of reform 'preparing for further institutional change' (p. 8).

[187] Bernard Gbikpi and Jürgen R. Grote (2002), 'From democratic government to participatory governance', in Jürgen R. Grote and Bernard Gbikpi (eds), *Participatory Governance. Political and Social Implications*, Leske and Budrich, Opladen, pp. 17–34, at p. 18. This is also referred to by Paul Magnette (2003) 'European governance and civic participation: beyond elitist citizenship?', *Political Studies*, Vol. 51, n. 1, pp. 144–60, at p. 147.

compensating the latter's administrative deficit, were present in the White Paper. However, in line with the developments mentioned above, they were now dressed up with the Commission's rhetoric of '[connecting] Europe more closely with its citizens'.[188] The insistence on involving concerned parties in the Community's regulatory process meant, in the Commission's discourse, a turn to a 'European civil society'. In an optimistic view, this could be seen 'primarily as an attempt to complete a process of democratisation of which the development of representative democracy through the European Parliament marked the initial transformation of the élite system of technocratic governance'.[189] Notwithstanding the added values of the governance initiative and its follow-ups, the following analysis will reveal the predominance of less value-laden results.

Far from being innovative, the involvement of 'civil society' pursued in the White Paper basically meant refurbishing the forms of interest representation that the Commission had long since fostered. In other words, the purported 'principle of participation' essentially perpetuated former practices of consultation and interest representation, eventually retouched and better structured due to the Commission's search for social legitimacy. The limits of this approach have been underlined by both Kenneth Armstrong and Paul Magnette.[190] According to them, despite fostering an apparently 'universalistic conception of participation', as suggested by the use of the notion of civil society—'civil society plays an important role in giving voice to the concerns of citizens and delivering services that meet people's needs'[191]—most of the White Paper's proposals were directed at organized interests. It aimed at '[structuring] existing relationships between the Commission and organized civil society' more than 'seeking to provide new

[188] On the one hand, it stressed that the already existing practices help 'the Commission and the other Institutions to arbitrate between competing claims and priorities and [assist] in developing a longer term policy perspective.' (p. 14). On the other, it highlighted that '[the goal of reforming governance] is to open up policy-making to make more inclusive and accountable . . . [,] connect the EU more close to its citizens and lead to more effective policies.' (p. 8).

[189] Armstrong, 'Rediscovering civil society . . .', *cit.*, n. 50, p. 109.

[190] Armstrong, *op. cit.*, n. 50, p. 109, 113–15, 128–32. Magnette, *op. cit.*, n. 184, in particular pp. 147–50. For more positive views on the meaning of participation in the context of the White Paper, see, among others, Olivier De Schutter (2002) 'Europe in search of its civil society', *European Law Journal*, Vol. 8, n. 2, pp. 198–217 (still critical, proposing forms for better involvement of civil society in the regulatory process) and Deidre M. Curtin (2003) 'Private interest representation or civil society deliberation? A contemporary dilemma for European governance', *Social Legal Studies*, Vol. 12, n. 1, pp. 55–75.

[191] White Paper, *cit.*, n. 2, p. 14.

forms of access to civil society actors' were present in the White Paper.[192] In addition, the added legitimacy allegedly sought through these participatory processes is intended to be attained by an enhanced quality of the regulatory outcome, more than by the intrinsic representativeness and 'democratic quality' of the participatory processes.[193] In fact, the orientation towards efficiency or output, inherent in a governance approach,[194] is clear in the formulation of the 'principle of participation'. Participation is an instrument to better policy delivery and social legitimacy a desired effect of enhanced efficiency.[195]

These and other related issues have been widely debated in the literature. It suffices to underline here that the Commission's stance on participation positions itself as an alternative to what could be termed a 'rule of law approach to participation', which would consist in the recognition of participation rights and the corresponding administrative and judicial procedural guarantees. The Commission dismisses any role that law could have in structuring the relationships between 'civil society' and the Commission, thus:

> What is needed is a reinforced culture of consultation and dialogue; a culture which is adopted by all European [i]nstitutions...[196]

> Creating a culture of consultation cannot be achieved by legal rules which would create excessive rigidity and risk slowing the adoption of particular policies. It should rather be underpinned by a code of conduct that sets minimum standards, focusing on what to consult on, when, whom and how to consult. Those standards will reduce the risk of the policy-makers just listening to one side of the argument or of particular groups getting privileged access on the basis of sectoral interests or

[192] Magnette, *op. cit.*, n. 184, p. 147, and Armstrong, *op. cit.*, n. 50, p. 119, respectively. The quotation is taken from the White Paper (*cit.*, n. 2, p. 14).

[193] On this, see Xénophon A. Yataganas (2002), 'La gouvernance européenne: entre reformes administrative et institutionelle. Articolation cohérente ou bricolage fortuit?' in Christian Joerges, Karl-Heinz Ladeur, and Jacques Ziller (eds), 'Governance in the European Union and the Commission White Paper', EUI Working Paper Law No. 2002/8, pp. 2–9, at p. 8.

[194] Möllers, *op. cit.*, n. 185, p. 317. Denouncing the White Paper's 'performance bias', Walker, *op. cit.*, n. 3, pp. 35–6.

[195] This is demonstrated by the following passage: 'The quality, relevance and effectiveness of EU policies depend on ensuring wide participation throughout the policy chain—from conception to implementation. Improved participation is likely to create more confidence in the end result and in the [i]nstitutions which deliver policies. Participation crucially depends on central governments following an inclusive approach when developing and implementing EU policies.' (White Paper, *cit.*, n. 2, p. 10.)

[196] White Paper, *cit.*, n. 2, p. 16.

nationality, which is a clear weakness with the current method of ad hoc consultations. These standards should improve the representativity of civil society organizations and structure their debate with the [i]nstitutions.[197]

This stance was buttressed in the Commission's Communication that approved the code of conduct mentioned and defined the principles and standards of consultation:

[A] situation must be avoided in which a Commission proposal could be challenged in the Court on the grounds of alleged lack of consultation of interested parties. Such an over-legalistic approach would be incompatible with the need for timely delivery of policy, and with the expectations of the citizens that the European Institutions should deliver on substance rather than concentrating on procedures.[198]

A legal grip of consultation processes was, therefore, overtly excluded. The new effective contribution that the White Paper brought in terms of participation was the stated intention of a better structure and framework for previously existing practices of interest representation and consultation, which, in the Commission's view, was intended to improve the transparency, openness, and equity of consultation procedures. Although these are eminently legal-administrative values, legal rules and remedies are considered undesirable to ensure them.[199]

Some have seen in this 'formalization' the creation of a 'new mode of governance', in which 'private activity does not merely seek to influence government decision-making but is actually involved'.[200] Although the Commission's approach, first stated in the White Paper and then developed in its code of conduct on consultation practices, was intended to induce a change, one should be wary of qualifying it as a 'new mode of governance' without further specification. On the one hand, if one may define 'new governance' as referring to regulatory processes that depart from the classic

[197] *Idem.*, p. 17.

[198] Communication from the Commission, 'Towards a reinforced culture of consultation and dialogue—General principles and minimum standards for consultation of interested parties by the Commission', COM(2002) 704 final, Brussels, 11.12.2002, p. 10. For a synthetic, yet thorough analysis of this document, its background and practices that followed it, see Paul Craig, *EU Administrative Law*, *cit.*, n. 100, pp. 324–7.

[199] The standards are set to be revised in 2011, but none of the reforms envisaged seems to modify this aspect (Commission Communication, 'Smart Regulation in the European Union', COM (2010) 543 final, Brussels, 8.10.2010, p. 10).

[200] Obradovic and Alonso Vizcaino, 'Good governance requirements . . .', *cit.*, n. 139, p. 1050.

Community method,[201] the Commission's governance approach to consultation does not hold this qualification, since it mostly represents a refurbishing of practices that have always been attendant to the Community method (the added value in terms of rationalization and transparency notwithstanding). The interaction between interest groups and the Commission has been crucial for the functioning of the system since the outset of the integration process.[202] On the other hand, if 'new governance' broadly refers not to the 'originality or temporality' but to the 'increasingly widespread, deliberate and explicit use' of 'processes and practices that have a norm-setting or regulatory dimension but do not operate primarily or at all through the conventional mechanisms of command-and-control-type legal institutions',[203] it is not at all evident that this approach to consultation can receive the epithet of 'new governance'. Admittedly, consultation practices are now more structured and blatant, possibly more widespread,[204] but they do not necessarily lead to a deviation from command-and-control modes of regulation. Calling it a 'new mode of governance' is, in any case, far-fetched, if the analysis is not accompanied by an emphasis on the continuities with 'older forms of governance' and by further specifications.[205]

3.3.3 *'From conception to implementation': the gaps*

More importantly, one should bear in mind the limited scope of application of the principles and standards of consultation spelt out by the Commission

[201] Neil Walker (2006) 'EU constitutionalism and new governance' in Gráinne de Búrca and Joanne Scott (eds), *Law and Governance in the EU and the US*, Oxford, Portland: Hart Publishing, pp. 15–36, at pp. 21–2. Scott and Trubek use this criterion as a starting point for analysis, to then enumerate the characteristics of new governance: participation and power sharing, multi-level integration, diversity and decentralization, deliberation, flexibility and revisability, experimentation and knowledge creation (Scott and Trubek, *op. cit.*, n. 162, pp. 1–2, 5–6).

[202] Above, Sub-section 3.2.3.

[203] Gráinne de Búrca and Joanne Scott (2007) 'Introduction', *Columbia Journal of European Law*, Vol. 13, n. 3, pp. 513–17, at p. 514, as well as David Trubek and Louise Trubek (2007) 'New governance and legal regulation: complementarity, rivalry, and transformation', *Columbia Journal of European Law*, Vol. 13, n. 3 pp. 539–64, at p. 543, n. 9.

[204] See Quittkat and Finke, *op., cit.*, n. 153.

[205] Criticizing the oppositional logic between 'old' and 'new', Walker, 'EU constitutionalism and new governance', *cit* n. 201, pp. 22–4. For quite a different perspective, Möllers, *op. cit.*, n. 185, who, more than underlining continuities, considers that the use of the term governance by the Commission merely 'repeats an old debate in the administrative law community about the status of interest representation in administrative rule-making' (p. 325).

in the 2002 Communication.[206] This reveals the focus of participation. To begin with, these principles and standards are primarily applicable to the legislative initiatives that are subject to impact assessment, which restricts their scope of application to the legislative initiatives that the Commission *chooses* to submit to impact assessment. These are not only those defined in the Commission's annual policy strategy and annual work programme, but also those 'decided each year by the Secretariat General/Impact Assessment Board and the departments concerned'.[207] Non-legislative initiatives covered by impact assessments are restricted to 'white papers, action plans, expenditure programmes, negotiating guidelines for international agreements . . . which define future policies' and to 'certain implementing measures (so called "comitology" items) which are likely to have significant impacts'.[208] As noted by Craig, this is far from ensuring consultation in cases where normative provisions can impact upon the individual's legal sphere.[209] Clearly, these consultation rules provide no guarantee of involvement of affected parties in decisional procedures that concern them. The application of consultation standards is expressly excluded in the following cases: special consultation procedures defined in the Treaty (namely, consultations of consultative committees or bodies and undertaken under the social dialogue), those determined by Community legislation or convened

[206] The general principles of consultation are the general principles of governance expounded in the White Paper: participation, openness and accountability, effectiveness, coherence (Communication from the Commission, above note 198, pp. 16–18). The minimum standards are listed in the Communication 'Towards a reinforced culture of consultation', *cit.*, above, n. 198, pp. 19–22, and refer to the clarity and provision of information that forms the basis for consultation processes, to the openness, effectiveness, and time-frames of such consultations, as well as to the publicity of the respective results.

[207] Communication 'Towards a reinforced culture of consultation', *cit.*, n. 198, p. 15. European Commission, 'Impact Assessment Guidelines', 15 January 2009, SEC(2009) 92, p. 6 (available at <http://ec.europa.eu/governance/impact/commission_guidelines/docs/iag_2009_en.pdf>). For an empirical analysis of the first three years of the practice of impact assessment in the EU, see Francis Chittenden, Tim Ambler, and Deming Xiao (2007) 'Impact assessment in the EU', in Stephen Weatherill (ed.), *Better Regulation*, Oxford: Oxford University Press, pp. 271–86, indicating, among richer findings, the relatively small number of proposals that have been submitted to impact assessment in 2005 (p. 281), although in the same year the Commission purported to extend it to all regulatory proposals included in its work programme (p. 277). See also Report from the Commission, 'Better lawmaking 2005, pursuant to article 9 of the protocol on the application of the principles of subsidiarity and proportionality (13th report)' COM(2006) 289 final, Brussels, 13.06.2006, p. 3.

[208] European Commission, 'Impact Assessment Guidelines', *cit.*, n. above, p. 6.

[209] Craig, *EU Administrative Law*, *cit.*, n. 100, p. 325, n. 55.

under international agreements.[210] Consultations held during comitology procedures were initially excluded from the scope of the standards defined in the 2002 Communication, but these may now be applicable in the context of impact assessments to implementing measures with significant impacts. Nevertheless, the rules set by the Commission's Communication are essentially meant to be applied to policy initiatives and, in particular, in the pre-legislative phase, preceding the Commission's proposal to the Council, or to the Council and the Parliament.[211]

Other references in the Communication confirm this interpretation. First, the Commission states that 'a clear dividing line must be drawn between consultations launched on the Commission's own initiative *prior to the adoption of a proposal*, and the subsequent formalized and compulsory decision-making process according to the Treaties'. Secondly, it stresses that 'the scope of the standards should [not] be generally widened, [nor should they be] separated from the Commission's approach to extended impact assessments', for this could impair the principle of proportionality and impede the Commission from '[assessing] its consultation needs on a case-by-case basis in line with its right of initiative'.[212] Thus, a more structured and improved participation covered by the code's standards does not cover 'the policy chain—from conception to implementation', the remit of the principle of participation as spelt out in the White Paper.[213] Hence, the standards thought to enhance transparency and accountability are lacking where compliance with these values has been considered to be particularly feeble, leaving largely untouched the wide regulatory activity inherent in the Commission's implementing and delegated powers.[214] Even if the Commission encourages its services to apply those principles and standards 'to any other consultation exercises they intend to launch',[215] the added legitimacy sought by the Commission

[210] It is not fully clear whether consultation requirements under international agreements' (p. 16) refers to consultations held by force of international agreements or to consultations of interested parties carried out in the process of negotiating international agreements, or both.

[211] Similarly, Obradovic and Alonso Vizcaino, *op. cit.*, n. 139, pp. 1066–7.

[212] Communication 'Towards a reinforced culture of consultation', *cit.*, n. 198, pp. 10–11 (emphasis added).

[213] White Paper *cit.*, n. 2, p. 10.

[214] See Sub-section 3.2.1, above. This is noted by Peter Strauss (2006) 'Rulemaking in the ages of globalization and information: what America can learn from Europe, and vice versa', *Columbia Journal of European Law*, Vol. 12, n. 3, pp. 645–94, at p. 663, comparing the realms of notice and comment in the US and the EU. The term 'implementing' is used here in a broad sense, not with the specific meaning it acquired by force of Article 291 TFEU.

[215] *Idem.*, p. 15.

through improving its consultation procedures is primarily limited to the earlier non-decisional phase legislative procedures and thus, to agenda-setting. Nothing in the envisaged reform of the Commission's consultation standards—set to take place in 2011—seems to extend this to the non-legislative procedures, with the exception of those mentioned above.[216] As pointed out by Möllers, consultation practices envisaged in the White Paper constitute 'the missing link between the political agenda-setter and society', being surrogates for the absent structures of representative government that ensure the acquisition of factual information and the articulation of different interests essential to policy definition.[217]

Finally, consequences deriving from the insertion of consultation practices as a component of impact assessment analysis procedures should be noted. First, the meaning and relevance of consultation in legislative processes depends essentially on the perceived function of impact assessment in Union decision-making, which is still ambiguous, partially due to the lack of procedural rules.[218] In fact, as it stands at the moment, impact assessment can either be reduced to a forum for different interested parties to express their political preferences, potentially instrumentalizing the decisional process (or at least one of its phases), or amount to an economic and scientific 'objective' analysis of the possible impacts of legislation. Voiced interests are diluted in reports grounded in measurable criteria which define the societal gains and losses of legislative acts. Secondly, consultation potentially shares some of the features and criticisms that can be pointed out to better regulation processes, namely it is part of a strategy for achieving 'efficient allocation of scarce resources' and risks being a 'device for confirming preconceptions and for dressing them up with the veneer of rational

[216] Communication, 'Smart Regulation in the European Union', *cit.* n. 199, p. 6. Although this Communication stresses the importance of including implementing legislation in better regulation programmes (broadly speaking), this concern seems to target the implementation by Member States and not non-legislative procedures carried out by the Commission (see Communication quoted, pp. 3, and 7–8).

[217] Möllers, *op. cit.*, n. 185, p. 325. In this light, Smismans' conclusion according to which 'new governance contributes to participation practice rather than to ensuring equal participation rights' is not surprising (Stijn Smismans (2007) 'New governance—the solution for active European citizenship, or the end of citizenship?', *Columbia Journal of European Law*, pp. 595–622, at pp. 622 and 611; on the issue of identity, naturally raised by the concept of citizenship, pp. 614–21).

[218] On the ambiguity of impact assessment as adopted by the European Union, see Anne C.M. Meuwese (2007) 'Inter-institutionalising EU impact assessment', in Stephen Weatherill (ed.), *Better Regulation*, Oxford: Oxford University Press, pp. 287–309, in particular pp. 287–90 and 298–302.

inevitability'.[219] Thirdly, as part of the Commission's better regulation strategy, consultation is related to the question of the application of the principle of subsidiarity, and, thus, to the issue of the vertical distribution of competences,[220] but not the balancing of interests implicated in administrative rule-making.

3.3.4 *Shifting lenses*

The strands of participation that have long since underlined the various forms of interest representation pervading the European decisional structures were woven together in the White Paper on Governance and cloaked with the motto of creating a European public space, or a European public, by 'connecting the European institutions to its citizens' or, more vaguely, to the European civil society. Indeed, participation in the context of the Commission's governance approach contains an additional normative claim, clearly revealed by the following passage:

> Providing more information and more effective communication are a pre-condition for generating a sense of belonging to Europe. The aim should be to create a transnational 'space' where citizens from different countries can discuss what they perceive as being the important challenges for the Union. This should help policy makers to stay in touch with European public opinion, and could guide them in identifying European projects which mobilize public support.[221]

From the three rationales of participation identified above—participation grounded in administrative collaboration, which strives to ensure the acquisition of information, responsiveness and compliance; participation grounded in a dignitarian rationale; and participation as 'public making'—the latter seems to have been at the forefront of the more recent institutional discourses. This 'transformation' accompanied the transition of the integration process from the completion of the internal market to the creation of a political union, from an essentially economic and utilitarian focus of the integration process, grounded in functional efficiency, to the

[219] Stephen Weatherill (2007) 'The challenge of better regulation', in Weatherill, *op. cit.*, pp. 1–17, at pp. 8–9.

[220] 'Interinstitutional agreement on better lawmaking' (OJ C 321/1, 31.12.2003), points 2 and 26. See also Communication from the Commission, 'European Governance: Better Lawmaking, COM (2002) 275 final, Brussels, 5.6.2002; Communication from the Commission, 'On impact assessment', COM (2002) 276 final, Brussels, 5.6.2002, in particular pp. 5 and 7–9; and, e.g., the Report from the Commission 'Better lawmaking 2005 . . .', *cit.*, n. 207.

[221] White Paper, *cit.*, n. 2, pp. 11–12.

configuration of a European polity concerned with improving the intrinsic, value-based legitimacy of its governing structures and with its acceptance by European citizens.[222] Yet, it results from the foregoing analysis that the emphasis placed on participation as 'public-making' in this context represented more a systematic than a substantive change: a change from a resort to participation in a case-by-case and unsystematic manner to a structured, legitimacy-laden approach. Participation grounded in administrative collaboration and participation as 'public-making' were intertwined under the auspices of a European governance reform in a somewhat ambiguous manner, in which the latter represents more a cloak of the former than a substantive innovation. In fact, under the new legitimacy garment participation remains, as before, essentially output-oriented. In addition, in the main this 'incremental innovation' tends to exclude one important segment of EU rule-making: the adoption of non-legislative acts.

A different trend may be identified: the technical complexity of the regulatory processes deriving from new forms of knowledge generation determined an increased resort to private regulation and to hybrid forms of public and private regulation. In the face of technical complexity and scarce knowledge resources held by public administrations, administrative collaboration required private parties' intervention in the regulatory process sharing decisional powers with public decision-makers. In this context, the need to ensure responsiveness to interests affected but not represented in the regulatory collaborative scheme brings the concern for consideration of the societal interests implicated in the regulatory process shyly to the fore. Not that this was absent before: in a way, it was present in the emergence of some of the forms of interest representation present in the European institutional framework (e.g. the representation of regions in EU decisional processes when their interests became more obviously affected

[222] On this, see, among others, Richard Bellamy and Dario Castiglione (2004) 'Normative theory and the EU: legitimising the Euro-polity and its regime', in Lars Trägardh (ed.), *After National Democracy. Rights, Law and Power in America and the New Europe*, Oxford and Portland Oregon: Hart Publishing, pp. 9–40. According to Walker, 'as the performative scope and ambition of an entity increases, clearly the legitimacy of the institutional regime which sustains the entity becomes a salient consideration in its own terms, and not just as an instrument for performance delivery. The more the European Union's regulatory sphere has expanded to cover decisions bearing upon the allocation of key resources and the balance between fundamental political values, and the more it has come to challenge the dominance of the State in these matters, the greater has become the concern that its institutional regime is fully and fairly representative of the range of constituencies affected by its actions.' (Walker, 'The White Paper in constitutional context', *cit.*, n. 3, p. 6).

by the integration process). It is, in any case, noticeable in the attempts of the delegating EU institutions to shape private decisional processes in this sense, as shown in relation to the new approach to harmonization. As regulation moves away from a command-and-control model, the need to ensure a balanced representation of interests in the regulatory process acquires a reinforced thrust given the need to compensate for the possible over-representation of the interests involved.

The roots of these more recent developments lie, as signalled above, in the institutional and administrative changes linked to the fulfilment of the internal market and to the 'constitutional' transition of the integration process. Their net result may be summarized as follows. There is perhaps a broader, more explicit and systematic use of participation, which certainly did not lose its multifaceted nature. Having evolved from long-standing practices and traditions, participation is now an outspoken feature of 'pragmatic governance'.[223] There is possibly also a more intensive usage of participation, as a result of the combination of different forms that come together in one legal regime or procedure (public consultations, consultations of stakeholders, networks, combined with participation in interest committees). In any case, the resilient strength of participation grounded in a rationale of collaboration overshadows the other possible meanings of the term. In fact, many of the 'new' forms of participation rely on an essentially strategic, policy-oriented use of participation. They are 'thin' forms of participation disconnected from the consideration of rights and legally protected interests of the persons affected by the regulatory processes.

3.4 From the 1950s to Lisbon

This extensive account of the institutionalized forms of participation in European integration displays participation as a pervasive feature of the EU, not only in the more recent institutional developments following the Commission's White Paper on Governance, but since the outset of the integration process. The involvement of interested persons in the EU regulatory processes, as it is now perceived in European governance, is a

[223] The expression is Gráinne de Búrca's ('The constitutional challenge of new governance in the European Union', *cit.*, n. 1, p. 816).

result of a steady process of gradual change and development in which different meanings of participation converge.

Since the inception of European integration, interest representation has been a response to the reduced administrative apparatus of the Communities. The connection between 'a minimum of administrative machinery' and the cooperation of the persons concerned by the regulatory processes was expressly stated in the ECSC Treaty and may be deemed to be also at the origin of similar mechanisms of participation in the EEC, this time mostly of an informal nature. Arguably, the different nature of the two founding Treaties accounts for the reduced instances of formal participation envisaged in the latter. The collaboration of concerned persons provided technical information needed to support decisional procedures, facilitated the enactment of responsive rules and decisions, and thereby adherence to the latter. Therefore, it favoured compliance and eased implementation. At the same time, the Commission found in its links with interest groups a basis to strengthen its institutional role. These rationales underlay the implicit guiding rule according to which affected interests should have a say in the respective procedures. However, with the exception of formal instances of interest representation in agencies, as well as, naturally, the composition and intervention of the 'grand' advisory bodies, the decisions as to who was considered to be representative of the relevant interests, as well as to when and how these entities should intervene is a matter to be decided by the Commission (or by the Council) in each case.

The White Paper on Governance, itself the result of the political-institutional context dominated by legitimacy concerns, marked the passage from an instrumental use of participatory procedures and structures grounded in the 'utility' of the involvement of interested persons in the Community regulatory processes—in the senses mentioned above—to an instrumental use of, in essence, the same procedures and structures with a view to reaching out to the public. Reaching out to the public would create a sense of belonging that would underpin the legitimacy of the Union, or at least diminish the perceived gap between the citizens and the EU institutions, and undermine the legitimacy of the Union. This turn is illustrated by the 'new' role assumed by the Economic and Social Committee. However, in essence there was little innovation in this claimed change.

The prominence of interest representation in the EU institutional setting, which has been illustrated in this chapter, suggests the 'constitutional resonance' of participation in the EU. The analysis of the institutional practice of EU decision-making revealed that participation has been a reflexive and a constitutive feature of the EU polity throughout the integration process.[224] With different variants, interest representation has moulded the EU institutional setting, not so much due to the formalization of interest representation in the founding Treaties, but mainly because it has been intrinsic to the way the EU institutions—particularly the Commission—have perceived their institutional role embedded in the socio-economic context of European integration.

The institutional practices presented in this chapter are the substratum of the 'principle of participatory democracy', now enshrined in the Treaty on the European Union.[225] In this respect, with the exception of the provision on the citizens' legislative initiative, the enshrinement of this provision in the Treaty is more a symbolic recognition of a long-established custom than an innovation in the democratic foundations of the European Union. It represents, nonetheless, the recognition that this 'custom' is a constitutional feature of the Union, forming part of its political and institutional foundations. The fact that it is now a Treaty norm is not without consequences. At least, what was in essence a discretionary choice of the institutions is now a norm of conduct by which the institutions need to abide, irrespective of the means chosen to give it effect.

From these developments, and from the constitutional connotation of participation, is excluded a denser meaning of the term that could underpin a different, 'thicker' or material constitutional dimension to participation. Namely, the values of the rule of law—procedural protection of the persons affected by the administrative action and care in the deployment of the decisional function based on the consideration and balancing of the interests involved in respect for the rights and legally protected interests of the persons concerned—which ultimately base participation on the respect of the dignity of the person and on the achievement of material justice, are left

[224] This remark, as well as the distinction presented below between a symbolic and a material meaning of constitutionalism to qualify participation, results from a discussion I had with Neil Walker, whom I would like thank for clarifying my ideas regarding participation and constitutionalism. The expression 'constitutional resonance' is also his (see above n. 186).

[225] Article 11(1) to (3) EU, following the Lisbon Treaty. The heading 'Principle of participatory democracy' figured in the Constitutional Treaty (Article I-41 of the Treaty establishing a Constitution for Europe, OJ C310/1, 16.12.2004) and disappeared from the version of this norm that finally made it into the Lisbon Treaty. The content of both provisions is, however, identical, and nothing in Article 11 indicates that the teleological meaning of this norm could be other than enshrining the principle of participatory democracy as one of the democratic pillars of the democratic life of the Union. Whether or not the norms of this provision may be considered to embody forms of participatory democracy is a different issue. See n. 4 above.

unanswered by the 'new' and old forms of participation presented in this chapter. In these contexts, the persons who are called upon or allowed to participate are seen in an objective role, as holders of a specific function, determined by the needs of the political system. They are not considered in their subjectivity, as holders of rights and legally protected interests that compose their legal sphere, ultimately grounded in the dignity of the person. This is possibly due to the fact that the regulatory activity in which they participate has not been perceived as capable of touching personal legal spheres, even if that may in fact happen. The exceptions are the cases in which the decision-making body has undisputedly the power to shape the rights and duties of the persons to whom the final act adopted is addressed, as in the adjudicative procedures led by some of the EU agencies. Depending on the regulatory options of the legislator, the procedural protection may be extended to other persons concerned who are entitled to intervene in the procedure. At any rate, this thicker meaning of participation is restricted to individualized procedures, i.e. those leading to the adoption of formal individual decisions. The fact that such a meaning of participation is envisaged in these cases is very likely due to the influence of the *audi alteram partem* principle that, on the basis of the common constitutional traditions of Member States, had been raised to the category of a general principle of Community law in the mid-1970s. Whether these are the only instances where such a meaning of participation is justified and how the procedural protection of the individual has been perceived in EU law are the main threads of the next chapters.

Chapter 4

EU Administrative Action, Procedural Guarantees, and Participation

This chapter focuses on how the procedural protection of natural and legal persons affected in their rights and interests has been conceived in EU law. In particular, it explains the EU Courts' approach to participation in individual decision-making procedures.[1] The theme of procedural protection is resumed in the following chapter, which analyses the Courts' case law on participation in rule-making procedures. Together with Toth, natural and legal persons are defined for current purposes as all those 'whether set up under private or public law and whether owned privately or publicly, who/which may possess substantive or procedural rights, obligations and capacities under Community law and which are not Member States'.[2] Procedural protection is ensured through the administrative guarantees that are granted during the decisional procedure, in particular, the right to be heard. As has been explained above, in the context of this work the procedural protection of persons concerned is intrinsically linked to the protection of the substantive rights and legally protected interests to which they are entitled under the confluence of the applicable legal systems.

The first part of the chapter provides a general overview on the administrative procedural guarantees present in the EU legal system (Section 4.1),

[1] As mentioned in Chapter 1, unless otherwise specified, the terms 'Courts' and 'EU Courts' are used in the book to refer to the Court of Justice (for which the abbreviation ECJ is still used) and to the General Court, which will still be designated 'Court of First Instance', expect when referring to judgments issued after the TFEU entered into force.

[2] Akos G. Toth (1978) *Legal Protection of Individuals in the European Communities. Volume I, The Individual and Community Law*, Amsterdam: North-Holland Publishing Company, p. 99. For the sake of convenience, the term 'individuals' is sometimes used in this chapter to refer to natural and legal persons who come within the realm of EU law.

which allows us better to situate and understand the Courts' approach to participation rights. Such an analysis needs to take into account the control mechanisms that may be deployed for the enforcement of substantive rights and interests, specifically the judicial remedies available and the control exerted by the European Ombudsman over instances of maladministration. A wide literature has dwelt upon these issues.[3] In particular, the limits of the EU judicial system in light of the principle of effective judicial protection have been widely debated.[4] While these matters are too broad to be analysed comprehensively in this book, a few observations are due in order to stress the relevance of participation rights as an anticipated form of legal protection of the person (Sub-section 4.1.1). Sub-sections 4.1.2 and 4.1.3 analyse how the problem of administrative procedural protection has been generally conceived in the EU legal system and the limits of this system in this regard.

This first part sets the scene for defining and characterizing the scope and meaning of participation rights in EU administrative law. This is best perceived through the analysis of the Courts' case law. Indeed, they have had a central role in the development of these rights. In general, as the administrative powers of the EU institutions and bodies have expanded, the Courts have adjusted the flaws of the EU legal system on this matter, thereby defining the contours of procedural rights.[5] In essence, the second

[3] Among others, Angela Ward (2007), *Judicial Review and the Rights of Private Parties in EU Law*, Oxford: Oxford University Press; Giandomenico Falcon (2007) 'La tutela giurisdizionale', in Mario Chiti e Guido Greco (eds) *Trattato di Diritto Amministrativo Europeo*, Vol. II, 2nd edn, Milano: Giuffrè, pp. 697–785; Thomas Eilmansberger (2004) 'The relationship between rights and remedies in EC law: in search of the missing link', *Common Market Law Review*, Vol. 41, n. 5, pp. 1199–246; Walter van Gerven (2000) 'Of rights, remedies and procedures', *Common Market Law Review*, Vol. 37, n. 3, pp. 501–36. Several works have also been published on the role of the European Ombudsman. Among others, Katja Heede (2001) *European Ombudsman: Redress and Control at the European level*, The Hague: Kluwer Law International, in particular Chapters 3, 5, and 8; Peter Bonnor (2001) *The European Ombudsman: A Novel Rule-source in Community Administrative Law*, PhD Thesis, European University Institute, Florence, especially Part II, in particular Chapters 1 and 3; Simone Cadeddu (2004) 'The proceedings of the European Ombudsman', *Law and Contemporary Problems*, Vol. 68, n. 1, pp. 161–80; Claude Blumann (2005) 'Article II-103: Médiateur européen' in Laurence Burgorgue-Larsen, Anne Levade, and Fabrice Picod (eds), *Traité établissant une Constitution pour l'Europe. Part II. La Charte des droits fondamentaux de l'Union, Vol. 2*, Bruxelles: Bruylant, pp. 551–66; Alexandros Tsadiras (2007) 'The position of the European Ombudsman in the Community system of judicial remedies', *European Law Review*, Vol. 32, n. 5, pp. 607–26.

[4] In particular, with regard to private *locus standi* in actions for annulment. See notes 7 and 10, below.

[5] On this point, Renaud Dehousse (1999) 'Towards a regulation of transnational governance? Citizen's rights and the reform of comitology procedures' in Christian Joerges and Ellen Vos

part of the chapter scrutinizes the Courts' reasoning on the right to be heard and, through the analysis of leading cases, traces the evolution of the case law in this matter (Sub-sections 4.2.1 and 4.2.2). The examination of this case law reveals the scope and rationales of the right to be heard, as this has been understood by the Courts (Sub-section 4.2.3), and, concomitantly, allows us to identify the limits of the judicial reasoning on participation rights (Section 4.3).

4.1 Legal Protection of Persons in EU Administrative Law

4.1.1 *Effective judicial protection and participation rights*

Access to judicial review and access to decisional procedures through participation rights interplay in a number of ways.[6] Restrictive access to courts has an impact on the way access to decisional procedures is judicially perceived, since it limits the scope of persons who could claim participation rights before the courts and could thereby instigate further developments on the matter. On the other hand, generous rules of access to decisional procedures strain restrictive standing rules. In this sense granting participation rights is likely to create pressure for the recognition of corresponding

(eds), *EU Committees: Social Regulation, Law and Politics*, Oxford, Portland: Hart Publishing, p. 122. Loïc Azoulai notes a continuous expansion of legal protection not exempted from regressions and contradictions (Azoulai (2000) *Les garanties procédurales en droit communautaire. Recherches sur la procédure et le bon gouvernement*, PhD Thesis, European University Institute, Florence, p. 103). See also Maria C. Baruffi (2001) *La tutela dei singoli nei procedimenti amministrativi comunitari*, Milano: Giuffrè, pp. 12–13, 64, and Takis Tridimas (2006), *The General Principles of EU Law*, Oxford: Oxford University Press, p. 370.

[6] The following considerations do not aim to define an ideal model of interaction between administrative procedure and judicial review in the EU legal system, based on the functions that should be assigned to the former. Such a task would require a complex analysis that strays beyond the scope of this work (on this, see Mario Nigro (1980) 'Procedimento amministrativo e tutela giurisdizionale contro la Pubblica Amministrazione (il problema di una legge generale sul procedimento amministrativo)', *Rivista di Diritto Processuale*, Vol. 35, pp. 252–78, at p. 253). Instead, the following study focuses on the *practical* interactions between the two access points that natural and legal persons have to the public law system. Nevertheless, underlying this section is the idea that, to a certain extent, and in particular in circumstances in which access to judicial review is limited, the administrative procedure has or should have sufficiently similar characteristics to those of judicial procedures, and eventually compensate for the deficiencies of judicial review. On three possible models along which it is possible to conceive the relationships between decisional procedure and judicial process, see Nigro, *op. cit.*, pp. 252–78. For a preliminary account of the applicability of these models to EU law, see Azoulai, *op. cit.*, pp. 299–307.

remedies that ensure compliance with such rights. However, there is no *a priori* need for standing rules to mirror rules of access to decisional procedures: different logics of access may be defended as a result of the different functions of access rules in each case. Access to decisional procedures should be grounded in the enhancement of the procedural conditions for material justice. Material justice results from due consideration for, and balancing of, the relevant contrasting public and private interests, in light of the public interest that the final act should uphold, while respecting the rights and legally protected interests of the persons affected. This requires not only that persons more directly affected are accorded the possibility of defending their own interests in the face of public intervention, but also that access allows for contributions that facilitate an accurate representation of the matters of fact and law involved in the situation to be regulated. Access to courts is based on the need to ensure that the substantive and procedural rules of law have been observed in this process. Broader or more restrictive access depends on a fundamental choice of the legal system: on whether it is conceived to primarily ensure 'objective legality' or the judicial protection of individuals' rights.

Nevertheless, an inverse relationship might be established between effective judicial protection and the procedural protection that follows from participation rights. In particular when rules of standing are restrictive, limitations on access to courts and effective judicial protection may be compensated for by exercising participation rights during the decisional procedure. This is the aspect of the interplay between the two rights (effective judicial protection and procedural participation) that will be highlighted in this section. It will be argued that, in view of the limitations of access of private parties to judicial review in the EU legal system, participation rights during decisional procedures are an essential aspect of the legal protection of rights and interests of persons affected by the Union legal acts.

The shortcomings of the EU judicial system with regard to effective judicial protection have been chiefly pointed out in relation to standing in actions of annulment. As has been copiously stressed in the literature, individuals have only limited access to judicial review of Union acts, given the Courts' interpretation of the requirement of 'individual concern' under former Article 230(4) EC. This requirement has been maintained by Article 263(4) TFEU—also under the Lisbon Treaty the direct challenging of decisions by persons other than their addressees and of decisions in the form of regulations depends on their individual concern. There is, however, one important exception: individual concern no longer applies to the standing of private persons for the annulment of self-executing regulatory acts (i.e. those not entailing implementing measures).[7] At any rate, the Courts' interpretation of 'individual concern', it is argued, impairs effective judicial protection of persons adversely affected by the conduct of EU institutions.[8] It is submitted that the limitations of the EU system of judicial protection are especially obvious in relation to Union acts of general application.[9] As will be argued below, this has remained mostly unchanged under Article 263(4) TFEU. As a rule, natural or legal persons affected in their rights and interests by an act of a general nature (a regulation or a directive) need to prove that their specific circumstances allow one to consider them as being affected by the measures at issue in similar terms to an addressee of a

[7] Article 263(4) TFEU distinguishes for the purposes of standing acts addressed to the person concerned, acts of individual and direct concern (which, arguably, can be both decisions and general acts), and regulatory acts that do not entail an implementing measure, regarding which the applicant only needs to prove direct concern (Treaty on the Functioning of the European Union, consolidated version, OJ C 83/47, 30.03.2010). On the innovations of Article 263(4) TFEU, see below, n. 12 and text.

[8] Despite subsequent developments, the leading case in this matter remains Case 25/62, *Plaumann & Co. v Commission* [1963] ECR 95, at 107 (recently reiterated in Case T-16/04, *Arcelor SA v European Parliament and Council* [2010] nyr., paragraphs 99 to 116). The general principles defined by this jurisprudence have, on occasion, been given a less rigid interpretation in order to avoid blunt denials of justice. On this, José Carlos Moitinho de Almeida (1995) 'Le recours en annulation des particuliers (article 173, deuxième alinéa, du traité CE): nouvelles réflexions sur l'expression « la concernent... individuellement »', in Ole Due, Marcus Lutter, and Jürgen Schwarze (eds) *Festshrift für Ulrich Everling*, Vol. I, Baden-Baden: Nomos, pp. 849–74; also Albertina Albors-Llorens (2003) 'The standing of private parties to challenge Community measures: has the European Court missed the boat?', *Cambridge Law Journal*, Vol. 62, n. 1, pp. 72–92, at pp. 76–81. However, the Court has been resilient to change (see Anthony Arnull (2001) 'Private applicants and the action for annulment since *Codorniu*', *Common Market Law Review*, Vol. 38, n. 1, pp. 7–52). Authors have differed on the possibility of a different interpretation of former Article 230(4) EC. Some have argued that this would not necessarily infringe the boundaries set by the Treaty, others have considered that the judicial interpretation of the requirement of individual concern is the only possible one given the Treaty access limitations (compare the opposing opinions of Paul Craig and Jürgen Schwarze in the articles quoted below, note 10, p. 505 and pp. 296–7, respectively).

[9] Despite the breakthroughs in *Codorniu* (Case C-309/89, *Codorniu v Council* [1994] ECR I-1853) and *Extramet* (Case C-358/89, *Extramet Industrie v Council* [1991] ECR I-2501). On the impact of these judgments see Arnull, *op. cit.*, p. 31 (reiterated in Arnull (2006) *The European Union and its Court of Justice*, Oxford: Oxford University Press, p. 77). On the problems posed by the EU system of direct challenge of normative acts, see, in particular, Denis Waelbroeck and A.-M. Verheyden (1995) 'Les conditions de recevabilité des recours en annulations des particuliers contre les actes normatifs communautaires', *Cahiers de Droit Européen*, Vol. 31, n. 3–4, pp. 399–441. For a different view, Paul Nihoul (1994) 'La recevabilité des recours en annulation introduits par un particulier à l'encontre d'un acte communautaire de portée générale', *Revue Trimestrielle de Droit Européen*, Vol. 30, n. 35, pp. 171–94, at pp. 186–94.

decision. This proof is clearly more difficult in relation to general acts. This came forcefully to the fore in the *Jégo-Quéré* and *UPA* judgments, and in particular in the assertive opinion of Advocate General Jacobs on the *UPA* case.[10] Among other aspects, the Advocate General highlighted that, under the Courts' interpretation of former Article 230(4), 'the greater the number of persons affected by a measure the less likely it is that judicial review... will be made available', irrespective of the harm caused. This is, undoubtedly, a perverse effect of the current access rules. While it may be counter-argued that it is unlikely that an act of general application will have effects similar to those of an individual decision, it will be shown below that this is not necessarily the case.[11]

The criticisms of Article 230(4) EC have been partially taken on board by the Treaty on the Functioning of the European Union. The fact that Article 263(4) TFEU enlarges standing of natural and legal persons—insofar as they may bring proceedings against 'regulatory acts' which, being of direct concern to them, do not entail implementing measures—tackles the most obvious case of denial of justice under the rules of the EU system of judicial review (i.e. that in which the parties concerned cannot have any remedy before national jurisdictions for the only act to challenge is an act adopted by the EU institutions or other entities). Nevertheless, undue limitations remain in other cases.[12] Effective judicial protection continues to rely on an

[10] Opinion of Advocate General Jacobs, delivered on 21 March 2002, on Case C-50/00 P, *Unión de Pequeños Agricultores v Council* [2002] ECR I-6677, Case T-177/01, *Jégo-Quéré and Cie SA v Commission* [2002] ECR II-2365, paragraphs 47 to 53, Case C-263/02 P, *Commission v Jégo-Quéré and Cie SA* [2004] ECR I-3425, paragraphs 36 to 39. For a discussion of these cases, and the problems they raise in terms of judicial protection of the persons concerned, see Paul Craig (2003) 'Standing, rights and the structure of legal argument', *European Public Law*, Vol. 9, n. 4, pp. 493–508; Albors-Lorens, *op. cit.*, pp. 81–92. Jürgen Schwarze (2004), 'The legal protection of the individual against regulations in European Union law', *European Public Law*, Vol. 10, n. 2, pp. 285–303. Other Advocates General before had highlighted the problems raised by the access rule of Article 230(4); see Hjalte Rasmussen (1980) 'Why is Article 173 interpreted against private plaintiffs?', *European Law Review*, Vol. 5, pp. 112–27, at p. 113 and n. 7, p. 114.

[11] On normative acts and the distinction between these and individual acts, see, below, Chapter 5, Sub-section 5.2.5.

[12] In this sense (regarding the Constitutional Treaty signed in Rome in 2004, but equally applicable to the Lisbon Treaty), Cornelia Koch (2005) '*Locus standi* of private applicants under the EU Constitution: preserving gaps in the protection of individuals' right to an effective remedy', *European Law Review*, Vol. 30, n. 4, pp. 511–27, at pp. 519–27. See also Michael Dougan (2008) 'The Treaty of Lisbon 2007: Winning minds, not hearts', *Common Market Law Review*, Vol. 45, n. 3, pp. 617–703, at pp. 676–79. Both authors highlight the uncertainty of what is meant by 'regulatory act'. According to the preparatory works, this expression seems to be intended to embrace binding non-legislative acts (Koch, *op. cit.*, pp. 520–1; for a criticism of this choice

imperfect decentralized system, in particular on the duty of national courts to ensure effective legal protection under EU law, by completing their national legal systems with the necessary remedies and procedures. Outside the realm of acts not entailing implementing measures, and given the individual concern requirement that remains applicable in all other cases,[13] the system continues not to ensure standing of private persons for direct challenge of Union acts in cases where this could be justified in light of the adverse effects that certain measures might have in their regard. Indirect challenge of normative acts is possible by resorting to the plea of illegality granted under Article 277 TFEU (ex-Article 241 EC, now extended to any 'act of general application adopted by an institution, body, office or agency of the Union'). However, the availability of this remedy depends on the adoption of implementing acts that can be challenged before the EU Courts.[14] Therefore, it still leaves uncovered cases where adverse effects emerge directly from general acts.[15]

The insufficiencies of direct action to challenge the validity of EU legal acts are not offset by the possibility of resorting to national courts and referring questions of validity to the EU Courts through preliminary rulings. The imperfections of this solution in terms of effective judicial protection have been highlighted by Advocate General Jacobs in his opinion on the *UPA* case. In particular, he pointed out the limited competence of national courts when assessing the validity of EU law, the inadequacy of access to court through preliminary references as a remedy capable of protecting the applicants' rights, and the disadvantages of proceedings before national courts.[16]

Nor are the deficiencies of the EU judicial system compensated for by the possibility of resorting to action for damages under Article 340(2) TFEU

Dougan, *op. cit.*, 677–9). See also Paul Craig (2006) *EU Administrative Law*, Oxford: Oxford University Press, pp. 344–7.

[13] Note that the persons to whom the act is addressed do not need to prove individual and direct concern.

[14] The term 'implementing acts' is used to refer generally to secondary acts complementing or executing primary acts. It is not used with the specific meaning the term has acquired under Article 291 TFEU.

[15] On the scope and purpose of this remedy, see Matthias Vogt (2006) 'Indirect judicial protection in EC law—the case of the plea of illegality', *European Law Review*, Vol. 31, n. 3, pp. 364–77; Dimitrios Sinaniotis (2001) 'The plea of illegality in EC law', *European Public Law*, Vol. 7, n. 1, pp. 103–25, at pp. 105–17.

[16] *Cit.*, n. 10, paragraphs 40 to 44. The Advocate General further confronted these drawbacks with the advantages of direct challenge (paragraphs 45 to 48).

(ex-Article 288(2) EC). In theory, a person who has been denied access to an action of annulment of harmful acts may have the alternative of resorting to an action for damages. However, the success of liability claims is dependent upon the verification of demanding conditions that have been strictly applied by the Courts, which have been wary of excessively curtailing the decision-makers' discretion.[17] Hence the limited success of liability claims, in particular in relation to acts of a general nature that have normative effect.[18] As a result, despite the more generous rules of access—there is no need to demonstrate individual concern—the utility of resorting to this action remains uncertain.[19] In any event, this type of action cannot be seen as a surrogate of direct challenges of the validity of Union acts for three main reasons: first, it does not allow for preventive protection;[20] secondly, the only remedy it provides is the payment of compensation for loss; thirdly, the unlawfulness of the act, by itself, does not lead to an award of damages and, since the requirements of substance of this action are different from those of the action for annulment, the review carried out by the Courts in an action for damages 'does not cover all the factors which may affect the legality of [the] measure'.[21]

As a whole, the 'scrutiny of judicial review under Article 230(4) [263(4) TFEU], Article 234 [267 TFEU] (validity) and Article 288 [340(2) TFEU] shows that concern for the interests of private parties has penetrated less forcefully when the legality of measures emanating from Community institutions is at issue'.[22] In these circumstances, procedural protection ensured during decision-making is of even more fundamental importance.

[17] David Bailey (2007) 'Damages actions under the EC merger regulation', *Common Market Law Review*, Vol. 44, n. 1, pp. 101–39, at p. 109. These conditions are worth recalling: a *sufficiently serious* breach of a rule of law *intended to confer rights on individuals*; a causal link between this breach and the claimed damages; proof of the existence and extent of these damages. These conditions, their interpretation by the Courts, and the problems they pose have been discussed, *inter alia*, by: Bailey, *op. cit.*, pp. 109–12, Takis Tridimas (2001) 'Liability for breach of Community law: growing up and mellowing down?', *Common Market Law Review*, Vol. 38, n. 2, pp. 301–32, at pp. 322–3 and 326–31; Baruffi, *op. cit.*, n. 5, pp. 241–54.

[18] Ward, *op. cit.*, n. 3, p. 367; Bailey, *op. cit.*, p. 109; Tridimas, *op. cit.*, n. 4, pp. 481 and 485; Baruffi, *op. cit.*, n. 5, pp. 241–2.

[19] Ward, *op. cit.*, n. 3, p. 13.

[20] Moitinho de Almeida, *op. cit.*, n. 8, p. 872.

[21] Ward, *op. cit.*, pp. 368 and 372–5, and *Jégo-Quéré v Commission*, *cit.*, n. 10, paragraph 46, from where the quotation is taken (further, on other drawbacks of the damages action, see Ward, *op. cit.*, pp. 375–402).

[22] Ward, *op. cit.*, n. 3, p. 10 (also pp. 407 and 415–18).

It may be counter-argued that, as pointed out above, judicial remedies and procedural participation are two different realities, since the function of judicial review with regard to the protection of individuals' rights is different from the function of the decisional procedure designed for the adoption of measures of a legislative or administrative nature. Nevertheless, while participation contributes to a more suitable delivery of the decisional function, facilitating due and balanced consideration for the different public and private interests at issue, it also gives affected persons the possibility of contradicting potential errors which may possibly lead to the illegality of the final act. As such, and to this extent, participation anticipates judicial review and compensates for limitations in effective judicial protection. In a judicial system with the features alluded to above, the procedural intervention in the decisional process may well be the only guarantee from which the persons affected in their rights and interests by acts of the EU institutions and other entities may benefit in the face of the exercise of administrative power embodied in these acts.[23]

In addition to judicial remedies, one needs to consider a second limb of the system of control over the EU administrative action. In fact, natural and legal persons affected by misconduct of the EU institutions or bodies have an additional remedy: they may submit cases of maladministration to the appreciation of the Ombudsman, under Article 228 TFEU (ex-Article 195 EC). Indeed, the right to be heard is part of the European Code of Good Administrative Behaviour and compliance therewith has been scrutinized by the Ombudsman while assessing possible instances of maladministration.[24] Moreover, the Ombudsman has confirmed that it is within his powers to review compliance with the minimum standards on consultation adopted by the Commission, also in a pro-active way.[25] Nevertheless, by reason of the Ombudsman's powers, this remedy, however relevant, does not countervail the shortcomings of effective legal protection of the

[23] In this sense, also Baruffi, *op. cit.*, n. 5, p. 287, in her conclusions to a study on the protection of individuals in EU administrative procedures.

[24] Article 16 of the European Code of Good Administrative Behaviour (available at <http://www.ombudsman.europa.eu/resources/code.faces>). See, for example, cases quoted below, n. 27.

[25] See Decision of the Ombudsman on complaint 948/2004/OV against the Commission (4.5.2005), paragraphs 1.1 to 1.4, 3.8, and 3.18, as well as Decision of the Ombudsman on complaint 3617/2006/JF against the Commission (3.7.2008), where the Ombudsman reviewed thoroughly the Commission's compliance with its minimum standards on consultation (see, in particular, paragraphs 2.28 to 2.34). This encompasses mostly consultations conducted by the Commission prior to the adoption of legislative proposals, but not those possibly conducted in the adoption of non-legislative acts (see, above, Chapter 3, Sub-section 3.3.2).

individuals in the EU judicial system.[26] At the same time, the inquiry into instances of maladministration covers dimensions of proper administrative conduct that go beyond strict compliance with legal rules. This may lead to extended procedural protection of persons concerned.[27]

In short, in light of the limitations of posterior controls available to private parties in the EU legal system, procedural protection of the persons concerned during decisional procedures conducive to the adoption of Union acts becomes a crucial component of the rule of law. Concretely, restrictive rules of standing require particular care in the definition of rules of access that encompass those potentially affected by the acts adopted. The next section explains how this matter has been addressed in EU law.

4.1.2 *Administrative procedural guarantees*

On a first approach, the procedural protection of the individual vis-à-vis the EU administration through procedural guarantees provided during the administrative procedure can be analysed at two different levels, following the traditional distinction between indirect and direct administration. A segment of the literature contests (or tends to contest) the validity of a model of indirect administration, and hence of this distinction, in the current stage of European integration.[28] Not wanting to enter this debate

[26] Baruffi, *op. cit.*, n. 5, p. 257. The right to petition the European Parliament, which is broader in scope, could, in certain circumstances, constitute a guarantee of persons affected by actions of the European institutions (on this Baruffi, *op. cit.*, n. 5, pp. 256–7). Yet, one can hardly conceive it as a remedy equated to those available through judicial review.

[27] See, regarding the right to be heard, Decision of the Ombudsman on complaint 2449/2007/VIK against the Commission (16.12.2009), paragraphs 71 to 75, which extends the survey of the right to be heard beyond the instances where the administration has a legal duty to comply with it; Decision of the Ombudsman on complaint 375/2001/IJH against the European Parliament (23/04/2002), paragraphs 2.1. to 2.6, and Decision of the Ombudsman on complaint 1250/2000 (JSA)/IJH against the European Parliament (19/07/2001), paragraphs 3.7. to 3.9, both extending the duty to comply with the right to be heard in the adoption of acts that are not legal acts. See also Decision of the Ombudsman on complaint 406/2008/(WP)VIK against the Commission (16.12.2009), paragraphs 33, 35, and 36, where the Ombudsman considered that, in the circumstances of the case, consultation before the adoption of a policy document, while not being a legal obligation of the Commission, was good administrative practice.

[28] Edoardo Chiti e Claudio Franchini (2003), *L'integrazione amministrativa europea*, Bologna: Il Mulino (in particular Chapters 2 and 3), drawing on previous separate works of both authors: Claudio Franchini (1993) *Amministrazione italiana e amministrazione comunitaria. La coamministrazione nei settori di interesse comunitario*, Padova: Cedam (in particular Chapter 5); Edoardo Chiti (2002) *Le agenzie europee. Unità e decentramento nelle amministrazioni comunitarie*, Padova: Cedam; and, still, Edoardo Chiti (2009) 'The administrative implementation of European Union law: a taxonomy and its implications' in Herwig C.H. Hofmann and Alexander H. Türk (eds) (2009)

here, it is submitted that, underneath the thick links of administrative collaboration that connect national administrations to the centralized EU administration and lead to the identification of different modes of integrated administration, the distinction between direct and indirect administration remains the matrix of the EU administrative system.[29] It is, moreover, the one that best suits the analytical purposes of this research, since it continues to inform the way in which the procedural protection of the individual is conceived in EU law.

Thus, on a first level, the procedural protection of the individual is essentially a matter of national law. As such, it is conceived along the coordinates given by the principles of direct effect and supremacy, on the one hand, and the principle of procedural autonomy, on the other. If normative integration resulting from the interplay of the first set of principles makes natural and legal persons *'les sujets de droit communautaire'*,[30] their legal protection under EU law is provided by national rules of procedure, subject to the limits of effectiveness and non-discrimination.[31] Whereas this principle has been mostly developed in relation to the tasks of national courts in litigation involving rights stemming from EU law

Legal Challenges in EU Administrative Law. Towards an Integrated Administration, Cheltenham: Edward Elgar, pp. 9–33. See also Herwig Hofmann and Alexander Türk (2006) 'Conclusions—Europe's integrated administration', in Hofmann and Türk (eds), *EU Administrative Governance*, Cheltenham: Edward Elgar, pp. 573–96, at pp. 580–4 and Hofmann and Türk (2007) 'The development of integrated administration in the EU and its consequences', *European Law Journal*, Vol. 13, n. 2, pp. 253–71, at pp. 254–63.

[29] In this sense, highlighting the relevance of the distinction in legal terms, Jacques Ziller (2007) 'Introduction: les concepts d'administration directe, d'administration indirecte et de co-administration et les fondements du droit administratif européen', in Jean-Bernand Auby et Jacqueline Dutheil de la Rochère (eds), *Droit administratif européen*, Bruxelles: Bruylant, pp. 235–43, at p. 241–3; but also stressing its misleading simplicity, Jacques Ziller (2009) 'Exécution centralisée et exécution partagée: le fédéralisme d' exécution en droit de l'Union européenne', in Jacqueline Dutheil de la Rochère (ed.), *Exécution du droit de l'Union, entre mécanismes communautaires et droits nationaux*, Bruxelles: Bruylant, pp. 111–38, in particular, pp. 118–23. See also Karine Caunes (2007) 'Et la fonction exécutive européenne créa l'administration à son image... Retour vers le futur de la comitologie', *Revue trimestrielle de droit européen*, Vol. 43, n. 2, pp. 297–346, at pp. 300–12. This distinction is now for the first time reflected in the Treaty (namely in Article 291(1) and (2) of the TFEU).

[30] Philippe Manin (2005) *l'Union Européene. Institutions, ordre juridique, contentieux*, Paris: Pedone, p. 507.

[31] On the problems raised by this 'division of powers' to the principle of direct effect, see Deirdre Curtin and Kamiel Mortelmanns (1994), 'Application and enforcement of Community law by the Member States: Actors in search of a third generation script' in Deirdre Curtin and Ton Heukels (eds), *Institutional Dynamics of European Integration. Essays in Honour of Henry G. Schemers*, Vol. II, Dordrecht: Martinus Nijhoff Publishers pp. 423–66, at pp. 432–3.

(judicial procedural autonomy), it is equally applicable in the realm of national administrative procedures (administrative procedural autonomy).[32] In fact, early case law where the Court affirmed the principle later termed 'procedural autonomy' referred to national administrative procedures used as an instrument of Community law, namely in the field of customs and agriculture.[33] More recently, in a case with similar subject matter, the Court re-affirmed the principle in its current formulation.[34]

From this perspective, the legal protection of individuals under EU law obeys a logic of effectiveness of this legal order, namely of its enforcement in the relationships between individuals and Member States under EU influence. Individuals are endowed with substantive rights and remedies that enable them to be a vehicle for ensuring Member States' compliance, by resorting, if necessary, to national courts. To this extent, the Court has held that all organs of national administrations are required to apply the provisions of EU law that are unconditional and sufficiently precise to be relied upon by an individual against the state.[35] Further, the Court has stated that the legal protection that individuals derive from the direct effect of EU law provisions prevails over administrative acts imposing restrictions

[32] On the scope and limits of judicial procedural autonomy, see, among others, Mark Hoskins (1996) 'Tilting the balance: supremacy and national procedural rules', *European Law Review*, Vol. 21, n. 5, pp. 365–77; Constantinos N. Kakouris (1997) 'Do Member States possess judicial procedural "autonomy"?', *Common Market Law Review*, Vol. 34, n. 6, pp. 1389–412; Van Gerven, *op. cit.*, n. 3; Pascal Girerd (2002) 'Les principes d'équivalence et de l'effectivité: encadrement ou désencadrement de l'autonomie procédural des Etats membres', *Revue Trimestrielle de Droit Européen*, Vol. 38, n. 1, pp. 75–102; Eilmansberger, *op. cit.*, n. 3. Referring to the two branches of the principle, Ziller, *op. cit.*, n. 29, at p. 240.

[33] Case 39/70, *Norddeutsches Vieh- und Fleischkontor GmbH v Hauptzollamt Hamburg-St. Annen* [1971] ECR 49 (procedure regarding the application of special import terms for frozen meats for processing) and Case 94/71, *Schlüter & Maack v Haupzollamt Hamburg-Jonas* [1972] ECR 307 (procedure regarding export refunds on products subject to the same price system, in the realm of the common organization of the market in sugar).

[34] Case C-1/06, *Bonn Fleisch Ex- und Import GmbH v Hauptzollamt Hamburg-Jonas* [2007] ECR I-5609, paragraph 41: 'in the absence of Community legislation on the point, the detailed procedural rules intended to safeguard the rights which individuals derive from Community law fall within the internal legal order of the Member States by virtue of the principle of procedural autonomy of the Member States, they must, however, not be less favourable than those governing similar domestic situations (principle of equivalence) or render impossible in practice or excessively difficult the exercise of rights conferred by Community law (principle of effectiveness)'. See also, in relation to different subject matter, Case C-426/05, *Tele 2 Telecommunication GmbH v TeleKom-Control-Kommission* [2008] ECR I-685, paragraphs 54 to 56.

[35] Case 103/88, *Fratelli Costanzo SpA v Comune di Milano* [1989] ECR 1839, paragraphs 31 and 32.

contrary to EU law.[36] As far-reaching as these solutions may be, it is submitted that solely on this basis EU law adds little in terms of procedural guarantees afforded during the administrative procedure. In fact, these guarantees are those envisaged by national law only adapted in order to ensure the effectiveness of EU law.

However, at a second level, in the limited areas where EU institutions are directly in charge of the implementation or execution of EU law, rules and principles directed at the procedural protection of individuals affected by EU administrative action, or, at least, having this effect, have been both enshrined in the Treaties as well as in secondary legislation and, especially, have been developed by the case law of the Courts. Articles 108(2) TFEU (ex-Article 88(2) EC), 296(2) TFEU (ex-Article 253 EC), 297(2) third paragraph TFEU (ex-Article 254(3)), and 15(3) TFEU (ex-Article 255 EC) are relevant provisions of the Treaty for current purposes. The first determines that, in the procedure designed to structure the Commission's power of appraisal regarding new state aid, the Commission must give notice to parties concerned to submit their comments, before issuing a decision that finds a given aid incompatible with the common market or considers that an aid is being misused. The second establishes that legal acts of the Union need to state the reasons on which they are based. This provision, broader in range, encompasses acts of an administrative nature. Insofar as it is an important means of ensuring effective judicial review, it is a procedural guarantee that is granted to persons affected by Union acts.[37] The third, based on legal certainty, states that acts of individual nature must be notified to the persons to whom they are addressed, taking effect at that point. The fourth enshrines the right of access to documents, which, alongside its broader function of ensuring public scrutiny of public action (being as such 'of the essence of democracy'), may be also a means to secure the legal protection of individuals in the face of decisions that concern

[36] Case C-224/97, *Erich Ciola v Land Vorarlberg* [1999] ECR I-2517, paragraphs 33 and 34. On the constitutional problems that this raises, Bruno de Witte (1999) 'Direct effect, supremacy, and the nature of the legal order', in Paul Craig and Gráinne de Búrca (eds), *The Evolution of EU Law*, Oxford: Oxford University Press, pp. 177–213, pp. 192–3. On this, see Sacha Prechal (2005) *Directives in EC Law*, 2nd edn, New York: Oxford University Press, pp. 65–72.

[37] In this sense, Jürgen Schwarze (2006) *European Administrative Law*. Revised 1st edn, London: Sweet and Maxwell, pp. 1411–12 and p. 1414. Also Marina Franchi (2004) 'Articolo 253', in Antonio Tizzano (ed.), *Trattati dell'Unione Europea e della Comunità Europea*, Milano: Giuffrè, pp. 1194–6, at p. 1194. This point is developed in the next chapter (see, below, Sub-section 5.4.2).

them.[38] On the whole, one can argue that these provisions stem from the rule of law principle, according to which procedural guarantees should accompany powers of the institutions with a possible negative effect on the legal spheres of individuals.[39]

Further, secondary legislation that rules matters where EU institutions or bodies have executive powers sets out specific procedures that envisage procedural guarantees on behalf of the persons concerned. Notably, procedural rules in the field of competition law and those governing the relationships between civil servants and EU institutions and bodies—fields where the executive power of the EU is likely to be more 'intrusive' in the legal spheres of private persons—grant interested parties the right to access the file and the right to be heard before a decision is adopted in their regard.[40] Most importantly, these rights were developed, completed, and strengthened by the Courts' case law, through which the right to be heard—the acknowledged cornerstone of the rights of the defence—seconded by the right to access the file and the duty to give reasons, acquired the status of a general (or fundamental) principle of EU law.[41] Both the right to be heard and the other procedural guarantees mentioned are now enshrined in Article 41(1) and (2) of the Charter of Fundamental Rights, which crystallizes previous case law.[42] Moreover, as will be analysed below, the right to be heard was extended to the so-called composite procedures, which involve

[38] Craig, *EU Administrative Law*, *cit.*, n. 12, pp. 350–60 (the quotation in the text is from p. 350). This aspect is developed in the next chapter (see, below, Sub-section 5.4.1).

[39] The argument is reinforced if one bears in mind the scheme adopted in the ECSS Treaty and the links between the two former Treaty systems (on the relationships between the founding Treaties, see, for example, Koen Lenaerts and Piet Van Nuffel (2005) *Constitutional Law of the European Union*, London: Sweet and Maxwell, pp. 11). As analysed in Chapter 3, in the realm of the ECSC Treaty the enshrinement of procedural guarantees was ancillary to the Community's competences to adopt individual acts directed at specific persons. Provisions of this type enshrined in the EC Treaty were rare (and still are in the TFEU), given the nature of the Treaty as a 'framework Treaty'.

[40] Schwarze, *European administrative law*, *cit.*, n. 3, pp. 1321–4, and 1342. Among others, Article 27 of Council Regulation No. 1/2003, of 16 December 2002, on the implementation of the rules on competition laid down in Articles 81 and 82 of the Treaty (OJ L 1/1, 4.1.2003). See Articles 6, 11, and 13 of Council Regulation No. 773/2004, of 7 April 2004, relating to the conduct of proceedings by the Commission pursuant to Articles 81 and 82 of the EC Treaty (OJ L 123/18, 27.4.2004), as amended.

[41] On the connections between these different procedural guarantees, see Chapter 5, Section 5.4.

[42] See the 'Explanations relating to the Charter of Fundamental Rights', now in OJ C 303/17, 14.12.2007, p. 28. The European Ombudsman in its Decision on complaint 1250/2000(JSA)/IJH against the European Parliament (17.1.2001), under 'inquiry', considered that the Charter did more than crystallize previous case law (he stated: 'the drafters of the Charter did not limit themselves to a codification of existing rights').

decisions of both national and EU administrative bodies or entities and thus encompass one or more intertwined sub-procedures which are instrumental in the adoption of the final decision.[43]

This casts a different light on the contribution of EU law in terms of administrative procedural guarantees, especially if one takes into account that the two levels of analysis mentioned are not isolated. On the contrary, national and EU legal systems are under mutual influence, insofar as principles and institutes of national law inspire solutions adopted at EU level and principles and institutions of EU law impact upon national law.[44] In this second vein, the interplay between EU and national legal systems conditions the administrative procedural autonomy that in principle assists national administrations when implementing EU law. Specifically, the Court has held that national authorities in these circumstances must abide by the fundamental principles of EU law, in particular the rights of the defence, while it is within their competence to define which procedural rules warrant the rights of the persons concerned.[45] Furthermore, in accordance with the nature of the right to be heard as a general principle of EU law, the Court considered that this must be respected by Member States' authorities when following a procedure defined by a directive even if this procedural guarantee was not explicitly envisaged therein.[46] Moreover,

[43] The fact that the sub-procedures lose their autonomy is, according to Maseo Seco, a distinctive feature of composite procedures (Luis F. Maseo Seco (2004) 'I procedimenti composti comunitari: riflessioni intorno alla problematica della impossibilità di difendersi ed eventuali alternative', in Giacinto della Cananea and Matteo Gnes (eds), *I procedimenti amministrativi dell'Unione Europea. Un'indagine. Atti del convegno di Studio, Urbino, 14 Marzo 2003*, Torino: Giappichelli, pp. 11–32, at pp. 17–18). The author draws on categories of Spanish law (see Luciano Parejo Alfonso *et al.* (1998) *Manual de derecho administrativo*, Vol. I, Barcelona: Ariel, pp. 551–603 at p. 559). On composite administrative procedures and the ensuing legal problems in EU law, see Giacinto della Cananea (2004) 'The European Union's mixed administrative proceedings', *Law and Contenporary Problems*, Vol. 68, pp. 197–217 and Herwig C.H. Hofmann (2009) 'Composite decision making procedures in EU administrative law' in Hofmann and Türk (eds), *Legal Challenges in EU Administrative Law . . . , cit.*, n. 28, pp. 168–76.

[44] Schwarze, *European Administrative Law, cit.*, n. 37, pp. cxiii–cxvi; Jean-Bernard Auby and Jacqueline Dutheil de la Rochère (2007) 'Introduction générale', in Auby and Dutheil de la Rochère (eds), *cit.*, n. 29, pp. 1–22, at pp. 11–17.

[45] Case C-60/92, *Otto BV v Postbank NV* [1993] ECR I-5683, paragraph 14. In this case the national authorities involved were judicial authorities, but the framing of procedural autonomy by the fundamental principles of EU law is equally applicable to administrative authorities (this was argued by Advocate General Cosmas in his Opinion delivered on 14 November 1996, in Case C-97/95, *Pascoal & Filhos Ld^{a} v Fazenda Pública* [1997] ECR I-4209, paragraph 101).

[46] Case C-28/05, *G.J. Dokter and others v Minister van Landbouw, Natuur en Voedselkwaliteit* [2006] ECR I-5431, paragraphs 73 to 78. See also Joined Cases C-379/08 and C-380/08,

legal norms enshrined in EU legislation that do not ensure compliance with the right to be heard are invalid, and hence inapplicable by national authorities.[47] It follows from this case law that indirect application of EU law must not have the effect of depleting the procedural protection of the persons affected by administrative procedures under the influence of EU law. At least, there should be an equivalent procedural protection of persons affected by the direct powers of EU administrative bodies or entities and those affected by national procedures that apply EU law. It may, therefore, be deduced that respect for the rights of the defence is a limit to national procedural autonomy that Member States enjoy when implementing EU law. This is confirmed by the procedural rights enshrined in Article 41 of the Charter of Fundamental Rights,[48] and has been explicitly stated by the Court in a more recent judgment.[49]

In addition, in certain fields, EU legislation defines procedures to be followed by Member States, that may have the effect of protecting individuals' rights and interests and may be opposed by individuals against Member States, provided that the direct effect of the corresponding provisions may be ascertained.[50] Environmental law of EU origin is particularly rich in the set of procedural rights of the public and of parties concerned that Member States need to respect when implementing EU law. For example, the public concerned, i.e. 'that affected by or likely to be affected

Raffinerie Mediterranee (ERG) SpA and others v Ministero dello Sviluppo economico [2010] nyr., paragraphs 55 and 56.

[47] Case C-395/00, *Distellerie Fratelli Cipriani SpA v Ministero delle Finanze* [2002] ECR I-11877, paragraphs 53 and 54.

[48] OJ C 83/389, 30.3.2010. Underlying this statement is the assumption that Article 51(1) of the Charter prevails over the apparent limitation of the scope of Article 41 to institutions, bodies, offices, and agencies of the Union.

[49] Case C-349/07, *Sopropé v Fazenda Pública* [2008] ECR II-10369, paragraphs 37 and 38. Note that also the duty to motivate decisions is an explicit limit to the Member States' procedural autonomy: see Case 222/86, *Union nationale des entraîneurs et cadres techniques professionnels du football v Georges Heylens and others* [1987] ECR 4097, paragraph 15.

[50] See, for example, Case C-201/02, *The Queen on the application of Delena Wells v Secretary of State for Transport, Local Government and the Regions* [2004] ECR I-723, paragraphs 56–61, 66, and 70, where the Court defined that individuals may rely on the provisions of Directive No. 85/337/EEC requiring environmental impact assessment to challenge a Member State's act which infringes those provisions. It should be noted that, in the case of directives, the assessment of direct effect may be a source of legal uncertainty for private litigants. Referring to this problem in the specific field of the environment, Martin Hedemann-Robinson (2007) *Enforcement of European Union Environmental Law*, London and New York: Routledge-Cavendish, Chapter 6, in particular pp. 225–34.

by, or having an interest in the environmental decision-making procedures', is entitled to have access to the information relevant to the adoption of a decision with a potential environmental impact; it must 'be given early and effective opportunities' to participate in the relevant decision-making procedures; moreover, the main reasons and considerations on which the environmental impact assessment decision is based need to take into account the concerns and opinions expressed by the public concerned; finally, 'the public concerned [either] having a sufficient interest, or alternatively, ... maintaining the impairment of a right ...' must have access to judicial review to challenge the substantive or procedural legality of decisions, acts, or omissions subject to these rights.[51] In this case, the procedural status of persons concerned by administrative procedures is enhanced (provided that the corresponding legal regimes are effectively enforced).

In a sense, the case of participation in EU environmental law is peculiar, and to a certain extent unparalleled, given the acknowledged relevance of participation in environmental matters (the reason why participation is a long-standing principle of EU environmental law) and, specifically, because these procedural rights were formally created as a result of the Aarhus Convention on Access to Information, Public Participation in Decision-making and Access to Justice in Environmental Matters and of the EU obligations under it.[52] In any case, it illustrates how the EU may actively further procedural rights in specific policy fields, imposing them as duties of

[51] Respectively Articles 6(3) and (4) (as well as Article 7(3)), 9(1), and 10a of the Council Directive No. 85/337, of 27 June 1985 on the assessment of the effects of certain public and private projects on the environment, as amended (OJ L 175/40, 5.7.1985). The definition of public concerned is given in Article 1(2). Similar procedural rights were enshrined in Directive No. 2003/35/EC of the European Parliament and of the Council, of 26 May 2003, providing for public participation in respect to the drawing up of certain plans and programmes relating to the environment (OJ L 156/17, 25.6.2003), as well as in Directive No. 2008/1/EC of the European Parliament and of the Council, of 15 January 2008, concerning integrated pollution prevention and control (OJ L 24/8, 29.1.2008).

[52] There is a wide literature on this matter. For a flavour, see Maria Lee (2005) *EU Environmental Law. Challenges, Change and Decision-making*, Oxford: Hart Publishing, Chapters 5 and 6. It should be noted that similar provisions of participation of public concerned are envisaged in relation to plans and programmes relating to the environment of the responsibility of EU institutions or bodies (Article 9(2) to (5) of Regulation No. 1367/2006 of the European Parliament and of the Council, of 6 September 2006 on the application of the provisions of the Aarhus Convention on Access to Information, Public Participation in Decision-making and Access to Justice in Environmental Matters to Community institutions and bodies (OJ L 264/13, 25.9.2006).

Member States, thereby enhancing the procedural guarantees of individuals affected by decisions that fall within the realm of EU law.

In sum, while the legal protection of the individual anchored in the direct effect of EU law and in the principle of procedural autonomy leads to the assertion that this matter has been tackled in the EU legal system essentially through the lens of effectiveness, other normative developments place a different emphasis on the legal protection of the individual by EU law independent of an instrumental rationale. In particular, two features reveal this second facet of procedural protection: first, the procedural guarantees recognized to individuals when affected by decisions of EU institutions or bodies; secondly, the requirement for Member States to respect the right to be heard when applying EU law (especially when this is not explicit in the applicable written rules) as well as specific participatory procedures created in certain fields of EU law which may entail procedural guarantees to the persons affected.

4.1.3 *Limits of the legal protection of persons concerned*

To conclude on the basis of the above that EU law entails a complete procedural protection of the persons affected by the activity of the EU administration, which could compensate for the limitations of its judicial system, would be too rash. Undoubtedly, EU law may have a 'protective role' vis-à-vis persons concerned by administrative action within its realm. Yet, three observations condition such an assertion.

First, gaps in protection may arise due to the complex interaction between national and EU interventions in given procedures, which are the reflection of the administrative collaboration that pervades the EU administrative system. The confluence of national and EU procedural rules may prevent the procedural intervention of persons concerned at the moment at which it would be due, possibly hindering the effectiveness of participation. In this respect, it is submitted that it is not enough to envisage procedural guarantees at the EU level or to ensure that Member States comply with them when implementing EU law. In particular in relation to composite administrative procedures, developed in different phases at both levels, it would be desirable to mitigate the possible perverse effects of a formally divided administrative system by ensuring that the procedural intervention of the person concerned occurs in direct relation to the intervention of the deciding bodies that effectively determine the content of the final act.[53] This would imply a unitary conception of European procedures, irrespective of how each one is concretely designed and of how the competence for the adoption of the final act is allocated. It is noteworthy that the concern for the procedural moment in which the procedural rights are exercised has not been absent from the Courts' case law, both in what relates to different phases of 'purely EU procedures', and also in the realm of composite procedures.[54] Even though this indicates a tendency towards this unitary conception of the procedure, it is not certain whether the full consequences of this step in terms of participation rights have been assumed.[55]

Secondly, the recognition of participation rights in secondary law does not follow a logic according to which persons adversely affected in their rights and interests should be afforded procedural rights vis-à-vis the decision-maker. While it is common to find provision for the right to be heard in regulations and directives defining the legal regime for a certain matter, express provisions in this sense are lacking in other areas.[56] Moreover, in most cases where participatory procedures are imposed by EU law on Member States, or constitute a duty of the EU institutions or bodies themselves, the corresponding provisions, too broad in range, can hardly ever be interpreted as providing a fully-fledged procedural protection to persons concerned. This aspect will be developed elsewhere in the book.[57] For now, it suffices to underline that, in this respect, procedural protection

[53] The drawbacks of a divided system for the protection of the individual are clearly illustrated, in relation to judicial review, by *Borelli* (Case C-97/91, *Oleificio Borelli SpA v Commission* [1992] ECR I-6313; for a discussion, see Eduardo García de Enterría (1993) 'La ampliación de la competencia de las jurisdicciones conetncioso-administrativas nacionales por obra del Derecho Comunitario. Sentencia *Borelli* de 3 diciembre de 1992 del Tribunal de Justicia y el articulo 5 CEE', *Revista Española de Derecho Administrativo*, n. 78, pp. 297–314). Similar cases are discussed in Giandomenico Falcon (2004) 'Separazione e coordinamento tra giurisdizioni europee e giurisdizioni nazionali nella tutela avverso gli atti lesivi di situazioni soggettive europee', *Rivista Italiana di Diritto Pubblico Comunitario*, Vol. 14, n. 5 pp. 1153–77, at pp. 1172–5. In general, on the difficulties raised by composite procedures to the effective judicial protection of natural and legal persons, see in Alexander H. Türk (2009) 'Judicial review of integarted administration in the EU', in Hofmann and Türk (eds), *Legal Challenges in EU Administrative Law . . .* , *cit.*, pp. 218–56.

[54] See, for example, Joined Cases 46/87 and 227/88, *Hoechst AG v Commission* [1989] ECR 2859, paragraph 15. Also the judgments in *Technische Universität München* and *France-Aviation*, analysed below reveal this concern (see Sub-section 4.2.2).

[55] See note 130, below.

[56] In this sense, see Craig, *op. cit.*, p. 322, pointing out that this is especially the case in areas of shared administration between Member States and the EU institutions. He adds that 'many of the most prominent instances' where participation rights have been recognized, in particular in procedures for the adoption of acts of a general nature, have been enshrined as rights vis-à-vis national authorities pursuing EU legislation rather than EU institutions (pp. 322–4).

[57] Below, Chapter 7. As will be seen there, procedural protection was not the rationale that grounded the creation of some participatory procedures in the field of food law.

is partially perceived as a matter of political choice and is conditioned by the delicate balance that EU decision-making procedures often need to achieve between competing national and other interests.

Lastly, and crucially, the real meaning of the 'protective role' of EU law with regard to the persons affected by the regulatory action of the Union needs to be assessed in light of the scope of the right to be heard, and, more broadly, of participation rights, as they have been developed by the EU Courts. This will be examined next.

4.2 The Right to be Heard

There are quite a few accounts in the literature on the development and scope of the right to be heard as an effect of the EU Courts' case law.[58] From one perspective the meaning of the right to be heard in EU law can only be fully grasped if scrutinized in the context of specific fields of law.[59] This is true at least to the extent that it is (or should be) correlated with the types of powers exercised in each field. Nevertheless, the following analysis takes a different perspective for two main reasons. First, it is possible to trace the main hallmarks of the Courts' case law, with a view to identifying general rules and principles and determine the boundaries beyond which the Courts are unlikely to stray.[60] Secondly, the study presented next is undertaken with a view to setting the scene for one of the main arguments of this book, namely that, major breakthroughs notwithstanding, the Courts have been excessively restrictive in defining the scope of participation rights.

For this purpose, at the risk of some repetition, it is important to return to cases analysed by other authors. On occasion, different interpretations, meanings, or opinions on some of the leading cases are provided, adding value to yet another account of the Courts' positions on the matter. The analysis focuses on the right to be heard of natural and legal persons confronted with decisions of the EU administration or, in any case, affected by them. It encompasses both cases where final decisions are formally adopted by EU institutions or bodies (mainly the Commission) and

[58] See literature quoted on notes 32 to 34 of the introduction (Chapter 1).

[59] In this sense, Koen Lenaerts and Jan Vanhamme (1997) 'Procedural rights of private parties in the Community administrative process', *Common Market Law Review*, Vol. 34, n. 3, pp. 531–69, at p. 532.

[60] See, in this respect, the literature quoted in note 34 of Chapter 1.

decisions adopted following composite administrative procedures in which the latter intervene together with national administrations.

The following pages consider the right to be heard in isolation from other rights that are bundled together under the heading of rights of the defence (such as the right to be assisted by a lawyer, legal professional privilege, the right against self-incrimination, and protection against disproportionate investigations). This choice is certainly not grounded in considerations pertaining to the lack of relevance of these other rights, but rather stems from the purpose of the analysis of the right to be heard in the context of this book. It is submitted that the right to be heard taken as the core of the rights of the defence corresponds only to the stricter scope of application of participation rights, i.e. trial-type procedures which may lead to incriminatory decisions or culminate in the adoption of sanctions. Nevertheless, it should be borne in mind that procedural guarantees related to the right to be heard—namely, the right of access to information, the duty of careful and impartial examination of the facts at issue, the duty to motivate decisions, and the language rights of European citizens—are necessary conditions of the effectiveness and meaningfulness of participation rights, irrespective of their narrower or broader scope.[61] The following sub-section dwells upon the status of the right to be heard in the EU legal system, as well as upon the Courts' general approach (Sub-section 4.2.1). Next, the Courts' reasoning and its results are analysed by looking at the landmark cases on the matter (Sub-section 4.2.2). Subsequently, the limits to this right are highlighted (Sub-section 4.2.3) and, by way of conclusion, some critical remarks on the Courts' stance are put forward (Section 4.3).

4.2.1 *Fundamental principle, pragmatic approach*

The right to be heard in administrative procedures made its entrance into EU law as a 'general rule' of law drawing inspiration from Member States' national legal systems.[62] The common law principle of natural justice—*audi alteram partem*—grounded the recognition of this right in the EU legal system as a general rule of law.[63] Shaped and refined by the Courts' case law, it is today securely anchored in European law. From a 'general rule', it was raised to the category of 'fundamental principle of Community law'

[61] They are considered at later point in the book (see below, Chapter 5, Section 5.4).

[62] Case 17/74, *Transocean Marine Paint Association v Commission* [1974] ECR 1063.

[63] Opinion by Advocate General Warner, delivered on 19 September 1974 [1974] ECR 1082–92, at 1088.

(*Hoffman-La Roche*) and, subsequently, considered a part of the fundamental rights case law (*Al-Jubail*), as the cornerstone of the rights of the defence.[64] As such, it has an overarching position in the EU legal system. In particular, it 'cannot be excluded or restricted by any legislative provision... [and] must therefore be ensured both where there is no specific legislation and also where legislation exists which does not itself take account of that principle'.[65] Or, as has been repeatedly stated by the Courts, 'observance of the right to be heard is, in all proceedings initiated against a person which are liable to culminate in a measure adversely affecting that person, a fundamental principle of Community law which must be guaranteed even in the absence of any rules governing the proceedings in question'.[66]

Yet, despite this legal status, the Courts have shown some wavering, or reluctance, in providing the right to be heard with a consistent and coherent doctrinal basis.[67] They have maintained a pragmatic approach on this matter, the solution of each case depending fundamentally on the judicial stance adopted therein. This certainly has inconveniences in terms of legal certainty. Even if one accepts that procedural rules need to be adjusted to the substance of each case, while analysing the Courts' case law, one is led to conclude that it fails to provide basic criteria that would make the scope of

[64] Azoulai, *op. cit.*, n. 5, pp. 117–18. *Transocean, cit.*, paragraph 15; Case 85/76, *Hoffmann-La Roche & Co. AG v Commission* [1979] ECR 461, paragraph 9; Case C-49/88, *Al-Jubail Fertilizer Company (Samad) et Saudi Arabian Fertilizer Company (Safco) v Council* [1991] ECR I-3187, paragraph 15.

[65] Case T-260/94, *Air Inter v Commission* [1997] ECR II-997, paragraph 60 (a strong assertion that was not as such repeated in later judgments).

[66] Earlier, *inter alia*, Case 234/84, *Belgium v Commission* [1986] ECR 2263, paragraph 27; Case C-135/92, *Fiskano v Commission* [1994] ECR I-2885, paragraph 39. Recently, Joined Cases T-309/04, T-317/04, T-329/04, and T-336/04, *TV 2/Danmark A/S and others v Commission* [2008] ECR II-2935, paragraph 136, Case T-53/08, *Italy v Commission* [2010], nyr., paragraph 114 (though referring broadly to the 'rights of the defence'); Case T-189/02, *Ente per le Ville Vesuviane v Commission* [2007] ECR II-89, paragraph 88 (on this case, see, below, note 130); Case T-158/07, *Cofac v Commission* [2009] ECR II-237, paragraph 35. A stricter variant of this formulation is 'observance of the right to be heard is, in all proceedings in which *sanctions, in particular fines or penalty payments*, may be imposed, a fundamental principle of Community law which must be respected *even if the proceedings in question are administrative proceedings*' (for more recent examples, Case T-29/05, *Deltafina SpA v Commission* [2010] nyr, paragraph 113; Case C511/06 P, *Archer Daniels Midland Co v Commission* [2009] ECR I-5843, paragraph 84; and Joined Cases T-125/03 and T-253/03, *Akzo Nobel Chemicals Ltd and others v Commission* [2007] ECR II-3523, paragraph 120, emphasis added).

[67] Critically, Hanns Peter Nehl (1999) *Principles of Administrative Procedure in EC Law*, Oxford: Hart Publishing, p. 98; Barbier de la Serre upholds the pragmatism of the Courts, albeit with some reservations (Barbier de la Serre (2006) 'Procedural justice in the European Community case-law concerning the rights of the defence: essentialist and instrumental trends', *European Public Law*, Vol. 12, n. 2, pp. 225–50, in particular pp. 248–50).

the right to be heard more predictable.[68] Outside the core purview of the right to be heard—trial-type administrative procedures which, having been initiated against a given person, may produce adverse effects in their legal sphere, typically culminating in the application of a sanction or an equivalent measure—the Courts' case law on the matter has been inconsistent, unsystematic, and at times equivocal.[69]

According to one interpretation, the pragmatic stance of the Courts with regard to the right to be heard stems from oscillations between an 'essentialist' and an 'instrumentalist' approach to the rights of the defence.[70] These conceptions correspond to the two rationales of participation rights identified in Chapter 2 by reference to their main functions: participation as defence, enabling a person possibly affected by the outcome of a procedure to defend their rights and interests before the final decision is adopted; participation as collaboration, facilitating the achievement of accurate decisions insofar as the procedural intervention of the persons concerned contributes to taking into consideration the different facets of the factual situation which the decision-maker needs to appreciate. In other words, participation grounded in the dignity of the person and participation as a factor that contributes to the proper exercise of the administrative function. These two conceptions, at times taken as mutually exclusive antonyms, and at other times, apparently, as interconnected approaches, have unevenly underpinned the Courts' case law.[71]

Arguably, it is possible to identify situations in which more likely than not the right to be heard will be granted.[72] Yet, at the same time, they reveal the

[68] In this sense, Barbier de la Serre, *op. cit.*, p. 249.

[69] Tridimas, *op. cit.*, n. 5, p. 370; Barbier de la Serre, *op. cit.*, pp. 225–6, 237. This is without prejudice to its acknowledged contribution to the evolution of procedural rights in EU law (among others, Nehl, *op. cit.*, pp. 70–1; Craig, *EU Administrative law*, *cit.*, n. 12, p. 314).

[70] Barbier de la Serre, *op. cit.*, pp. 248 and pp. 228–9.

[71] They are taken as antonyms when the Court considers that, independently of the contribution that a person's procedural intervention may have to the matter under decision, they cannot access the procedure because they were not individually targeted by it (Case C-170/89, *Bureau Européen des Unions de Consommateurs v Commission* [1991] ECR I-5709, paragraphs 19–21; see also, on this case, the Opinion of Advocate General Mischo delivered on 13 March 1991, paragraph 9). They may be taken as intertwined concepts when the Court expressly mentions that participation of private persons in the administrative procedure is grounded both in procedural requirements of 'due process' or 'sound justice' and on demands of 'good administration' (earlier, in staff cases, in Case 32/62, *Maurice Alvis v Council* [1963] ECR 49; on this case, Tridimas, *op. cit.*, pp. 370–1 and Barbier de la Serre, *op. cit.*, p. 234) or, generally, when this convergence results from the reasoning of the Court (Case T-277/03, *Vlachaki v Commission* [2005] ECR CS I-A-57, II-243, paragraph 64).

[72] Barbier de la Serre, *op. cit.*, pp. n. 67, 248–9. The 'general rules' mentioned in the paragraph draw on this author's analysis.

contradictions of the Courts' stance on this matter. While the Courts have signalled that the right to be heard is of fundamental importance particularly when the decisions adopted mean an assessment of the persons' behaviour,[73] the CFI has denied the right to be heard in cases where the 'charges' imposed on certain persons heavily limited their fundamental rights invoking to this effect the absence of discretionary power of the decision-maker; it was not criticized in this point by the ECJ.[74] Whereas the right to be heard is more likely to be recognized in cases in which the persons concerned can contribute to the quality of the decision and the decision-maker has wide discretionary powers,[75] persons who are not targeted by the decision in a similar way to an addressee have been denied this right.[76] Whilst the right to be heard is expected to be refused where its exercise entails excessive material costs, the Court, refuting a similar argument invoked by the Commission, has stressed that 'an argument based on practical grounds is not sufficient to justify infringement of a fundamental principle such as the observance of the rights of the defence'.[77] Although

[73] For example, Case T-346/94, *France-Aviation v Commission* [1995] ECR II-2841, paragraphs 39 and 40; C-315/99 P, *Ismeri Europa Srl v Court of Auditors* [2001] ECR I-5281, paragraphs 28 to 30.

[74] Case T-306/01, *Ahmed Ali Yusuf and Al Barakaat International Foundation v Council and Commission* [2005] ECR II-3533, paragraphs 326 to 328, and Case T-315/01, *Yassin Abdullah Kadi v Council and Commission* [2005] ECR II-3649, paragraphs 256 to 258, later overruled by the Court of Justice: Joined Cases C-402/05 P and C-415/05 P, *Yassin Adbullah Kadi and Al Barakaat International Foundation v Council and Commission* [2008] ECR I-6351, paragraphs 333 to 348. The Court of Justice dismissed the grounds on which the Court of First Instance considered that the Community powers were bound in this case. Nevertheless, the existence or absence of a discretionary power for the recognition of the right to be heard was not considered in the analysis of the breach of the right. On this, see Chapter 5, Sub-section 5.1.3.

[75] Notably in *Technische Universität München v Hauptzollamt München-Mitte* [1991] ECR I-5469, paragraphs 14 and 24–25.

[76] Case C-170/89, *Bureau Européen des Unions de Consommateurs (BEUC) v Commission* [1991] ECR I-5709, paragraphs 19–21. Case T-167/94, *Detlef Nölle v Council and Commission* [1995] ECR II-2589, paragraph 63 (see also paragraph 76; as will be noted below, the procedural intervention of the person concerned was in this case ensured on different grounds—on this, Nehl, *op. cit.*, n. 67, pp. 76–7); Case T-326/99, *Nancy Fern Olivieri v Commission* [2003] ECR II-6053, paragraph 94. In a way, this can also be deduced from the Order of the Court of First Instance in Case T-369/03, *Arizona Chemical BV and others v Commission* [2005] ECR II-5839, paragraphs 79 and 80.

[77] Case C-32/95 P, *Commission v Lisrestal—Organização Gestão de Restaurantes Colectivos Ld*[a] [1996] ECR I-5393, paragraph 37. Yet, in a subsequent judgment the Court implicitly accepted the Court of First Instance ruling according to which practical reasons can justify the non-applicability of the right to be heard (Case T-109/94, *Windpark Groothusen GmbH & Co. Betriebs-KG v Commission* [1995] ECR II-3007, paragraph 48; Case C-48/96 P, *Windpark Groothusen v Commission* [1998] ECR I-2873, paragraph 46).

the Courts' stance has arguably been predominantly grounded in an 'essentialist' approach (to borrow Barbier de la Serre's expression and, for now, his opinion), they have repeatedly asserted that an infringement of the right to be heard can only lead to the annulment of the decision on procedural grounds if the applicant who challenges the validity of the irregular decision can prove that its content would otherwise have been a different one.[78] Finally, the right to be heard is strongly anchored in EU law as a general principle, and yet, the Court of First Instance has stressed that its application had been limited, up to that point in time, to the areas of economic law seemingly seeking in this an additional argument to deny the right to be heard outside that realm.[79]

This perspective on the Courts' case law, in particular this way of presenting it, may be contested. It may be argued that it is misplaced, that procedural issues should not necessarily overplay substantive considerations, that procedural rights cannot be guaranteed 'to an unlimited extent' since they encroach upon efficiency of administrative action and 'can thus negatively affect major public interests'.[80] Admittedly, in each of the cases mentioned, the Courts' final conclusion was grounded in their analysis of the particularities of the factual situation they were called upon to judge, without which the above statements cannot be fully understood.[81] These

[78] More recently, Case T-444/07, *Centre de promotion de l'emploi par la micro-entreprise (CPEM) v Commission* [2009] ECR II-2121, paragraph 53; and *Ville Vesuviane*, *cit.*, n. 66, paragraph 96. Also on this point the Court has not been consistent, dropping this position on occasion. On this Nehl, *op. cit.*, n. 67, p. 98 (also Tridimas, *op. cit.*, n. 5, pp. 391–2). For an intermediary stance, closer to the latter, see Case T-147/97, *Champion Stationery Mfg Co. Ltd and others v Council* [1998] ECR II-4137, paragraph 79 and Case C-194/99, *Thyssen Stahl v Commission* [2003] ECR I-10821, paragraph 31. Mentioning that the 'harmless error rule' tends to be used as a 'control device where breach of the process right might have far-reaching consequences', Craig, *EU Administrative Law*, *cit.*, n. 12, p. 373.

[79] *Yusuf*, *cit.*, n. 74, paragraphs 326 and 327 and *Kadi*, *cit.*, n. 74, paragraphs 256 and 257 (see note 73, above). On this, see, below, Chapter 5, Sub-section 5.1.3. The ECJ judgment did not explicitly criticize this point. Nevertheless such a statement would probably not occur nowadays, in particular due to the reiteration of the importance of the right to be heard in subsequent cases on counter-terrorist sanctions, and, especially, due to the connection between this right and the defence of fundamental rights such as the right to effective judicial review. See, in this respect, Case T-85/09, *Yassin Abdullah Kadi v Commission* [2010] nyr., paragraph 181. Nevertheless, the statement of the CFI in its first *Kadi* judgment demonstrates the possible limitations of the value of the right to be heard as a general principle of law.

[80] Hilf *et al.*, *op. cit.*, p. 459. Underlying these considerations is a markedly instrumental view on procedural rights. In essence, they highlight possible drawbacks of an exclusively dignitarian approach to procedural rights.

[81] Most of the cases mentioned are analysed below (in the following sub-sections and in the next chapter; *Nanci Olivieri* is discussed in Chapter 7).

are, therefore, pertinent criticisms. Undoubtedly, there are limits to the observance of the right to be heard. These first observations are not intended to suggest a possible heedlessness of the Courts in handling procedural matters, but to highlight the Courts' technique of deciding the case before it without elucidating 'legal matters of principle'.[82] One may argue that, having raised the right to be heard to the category of general or fundamental principle of EU law, the Courts have not engaged in a critical appreciation of the underlying principles that form its rationales. Such an analysis could provide a more solid ground on which to base a more consistent approach to participation rights in EU administrative law, from which both the criteria for application of the right to be heard and the methods used to combine them could be deduced with a higher degree of certainty.[83] Lastly, it should be added that this general setting makes the task of analysing the case law on the right to be heard independently of a sector analysis, as undertaken below, a riskier one.

4.2.2 *Scope and meaning*

The foundations

It has been said that the main criterion for applying the right to be heard consists of the adverse effect that an administrative decision might have vis-à-vis individual parties.[84] Yet, it is not always certain what exactly 'adverse effect' stands for.[85] Two main interpretations follow from early case law. The broader formulation used by the Court dates from the *Transocean* case. Here, it was held that 'a person *whose interests are perceptibly affected* by a decision taken by a public authority must be given the opportunity to make his point of view known.... [E]specially so in the case of conditions which... impose considerable obligations having far-reaching effects'.[86] At issue in this case was a decision of the Commission adopted under former Article 85 (3) EC (later re-numbered 81(3) EC, and now 101(3) TFEU), renewing the

[82] On this, Nehl, *op. cit.*, n. 67, p. 93.

[83] Barbier de la Serre, considering that 'the EC Courts do not necessarily need to confine the rights of the defence within over-rigid categories that could turn out to be, in certain cases, inconsistent with procedural justice', nevertheless argues that the criteria for application of the rights of the defence and 'the method used to combine and weigh up these criteria' should be made clearer (*op. cit.*, n. 67, p. 249).

[84] Nehl, *op. cit.*, n. 67, pp. 71 and 84; Baruffi, *op. cit.*, n. 5, p. 53. In a similar sense, Tridimas, *op. cit.*, n. 5, p. 379, Craig, *op. cit.*, n. 12, pp. 314–15 and Barbier de la Serre, *op. cit.*, n. 67, pp. 237–8.

[85] Barbier de la Serre, *op. cit.*, n. 67, pp. 238–9.

[86] *Transocean*, *cit.*, n. 62, paragraph 15.

exemption from the general prohibition on anti-competitive practices. This decision subjected the undertakings concerned to duties of information, which they considered to be prejudicial to their interests without being grounded in good reasons. Moreover, it had been adopted without the previous hearing of the persons concerned. The Court, considering that the decision was overall beneficial to the undertakings, annulled it only partially on the basis of the infringement of the right to be heard. In the reasons for the judgment, the Court added that in deciding this particular matter 'the Commission enjoys a large measure of discretion' and determined that, as such, 'the exercise of this discretionary power is linked to a preliminary canvassing of objections which may be raised by the undertakings'.[87] So, while the fact that the act is, in some tangible way, adverse to the interests of the persons affected is sufficient to ground the recognition of the right to be heard, their intervention is also linked to the power of appraisal of the deciding authority.

A few years later, the Court adopted a more restrictive formulation. In *Hoffman-La Roche*, it held that 'observance of the right to be heard is in all proceedings in which *sanctions, in particular fines or penalty payments, may be imposed* a fundamental principle of Community law which must be respected *even if the proceedings in question are administrative proceedings*'.[88] The Court thus confined the scope of the principle to administrative proceedings leading up to the imposition of sanctions. In *Transocean* not only did the wording not bear the same restrictiveness, but also the Court had analysed a decision that was overall favourable to the applicants.[89] Furthermore, the last part of the quoted passage also underlines this restrictive effect. Drawing a parallel with the judicial proceedings, the Court stresses the commonalities between judicial due process and trial-type adjudicative administrative proceedings, where similar procedural standards should apply since they are likely to produce analogous

[87] *Transocean*, *cit.*, n. 62, paragraph 16. The French version is more explicit in placing this requirement as a 'compensation' for the discretion of the Commission ('*en contrepartie*, l'exercice de ce pouvoir d'appréciation est lié a une large information préalable des objections que les entreprises pouvaient faire valoir', emphasis added).

[88] *Hoffmann-La Roche*, *cit.*, n. 64, paragraph 9, emphasis added.

[89] As pointed out by Nehl, 'this confinement [could not] be deduced from the general context of the judgment' (*op. cit.*, n. 67, p. 72). The *Hoffmann-La Roche* formulation is similar to the one of Article 36 of the ECSC Treaty and, in this sense, less 'daring' in terms of Community law development (it corresponded also to the sense of the right to be heard as enshrined in specific legislation at the time: for example, in Article 19(1) of Regulation No. 17 of 1962—OJ 13/204, 21.2.1962).

consequences in the legal sphere of the persons targeted. In other words, administrative decisions in this type of procedure entail assessments of the targeted persons' behaviour and the application of sanctions as a consequence of illegal conduct.[90] This was the type of procedure in the case under judgment: the Commission considered that *Hoffman-La Roche* had a dominant position in the market which it had abused, thereby infringing the Treaty competition rules, and, as such, was subject to the imposition of a fine.

The two different formulations have been repeatedly used by the Courts in subsequent judgments.[91] Apparently, the use of the more restrictive interpretation has not had the effect of limiting the scope of application of the right to be heard. Lenaerts and Vanhamme, for example, are of the opinion that the term 'sanction' must be understood as meaning 'any Community measure which inflicts a loss on a private party or, at least, imposes *restitutio* on such party' (i.e. imposes a 'compensation for the illegal obtainment or use of a right or financial benefit').[92] Nehl stresses that the Court was initially hesitant to give the concept of adverse effect a broad interpretation, but finally abandoned its stricter approach.[93] Craig notes that, despite the restrictive formulation of *Hoffman-La Roche*, 'the general trend of the case law has... been to require a hearing even where no sanction is imposed, provided that there is some adverse impact, or some significant effect on the applicant's interests'.[94] Nevertheless, it is submitted that repeated resort to the restrictive wording of *Hoffmann-La Roche* has influenced the Courts' stance regarding the right to be heard. This point

[90] This parallelism had more far-reaching consequences in the case at issue: the procedural irregularities having been 'put right during the proceedings before the Court, they do not necessarily lead to the annulment of the contested decision insofar as remedying them at a later stage has not affected the right to be heard' (paragraph 15). Consequently, the plea based on the infringement of this right was not successful. This argumentation had the result of depleting the breadth of the 'fundamental principle' in the realm of administrative proceedings. As pointed out by Ole Due, the legal guarantee then results from the judicial and not from the administrative proceedings (*op. cit.*, p. 391).

[91] For later examples, see n. 66 above.

[92] Lenaerts and Vanhamme, *op. cit.*, n. 59, p. 535, n. 12. Similarly, Marta Cartabia (1991) *La tutela nel procedimento amministrativo. La legge n. 241 del 1990 alla luce dei principi comunitari*, Milano: Giuffrè, p. 85, who considers that the broader formulation used by the Court is the predominant one, since the Court has applied the term sanctions to acts that did not have the character of a sanction. Yet, she invokes *Hoffman-La Roche* to demonstrate her argument. Also Baruffi, *op. cit.*, n. 5, p. 54 (stating that, of the two formulations, the broader is 'the correct one', *sic*).

[93] Nehl, *op. cit.*, n. 67, p. 71.

[94] Craig, *op. cit.*, n. 12, pp. 314–15.

will be developed below.[95] For now it suffices to underline that it has had at least the effect of circumscribing the core purview of application of the right to be heard. Outside this purview, persons upon whom a 'lesser harm' has been inflicted may still be granted this right, but there is also a broad range of decisions with an adverse impact on the private persons' legal sphere regarding which the respect for the right to be heard is not required.[96] In any event, in these outer circles, it is not certain which degree of adversity triggers the recognition of the right to be heard.[97]

Nevertheless, four features common to both cases allow us to better map the scope of this right. First, the right to be heard was recognized in procedures initiated against the applicant, in which an administrative authority carries out an investigation that bases the final individual decision.[98] Next, the bearers of the interests involved in the decision are easy to determine: they are the addressees of the acts adopted. Moreover, the final decision entails a bilateral administrative relationship that essentially involves the author and the addressee of the act. Finally, the right to be heard was upheld in an area where the Commission has a large power of appraisal, that is, the application of competition rules of Articles 101 to 103 TFEU (ex-Articles 81 to 83 EC). Roughly, the same characteristics are present in staff disciplinary procedures, the other field where at the time of these judgments, the right to be heard had also been recognized.

Not all these four features remained untouched by subsequent case law, which considerably expanded the scope of the right to be heard. In this process, the requirements of *Hoffman-La Roche* were loosened, their resilience notwithstanding. The formulation of *Transocean* allowed the scope of the right to widen. *Hoffman-La Roche*, however, stood as a reminder of the limits of this expansion.

'Hybrid' acts

The right to be heard was later expanded to procedures leading up to the adoption of anti-dumping regulations. Three main factors facilitated this

[95] Section 4.3.

[96] These two circles are identified by Barbier de la Serre (*op. cit.*, n. 67, pp. 238–9). Nehl points out another effect of the restrictive formulation of *Hoffman-La Roche*: according to him, it has contributed to shape the reduced degree of protection afforded to complainants in competition administrative procedures (*op. cit.*, n. 67, p. 73).

[97] In this sense, Barbier de la Serre, *op. cit.*, n. 67, p. 238.

[98] Although in *Transocean* the issue was the renewal of exemptions adopted under former Article 81(3) EC, now 101(3) TFEU.

transposition.[99] First, the similarities between competition and anti-dumping procedures both in terms of the investigative powers of the Commission and of the substantive interests involved. Secondly, Advocate General Warner had forcefully pleaded for this extension in 1979, in *NTN Toyo Bearing Company*.[100] Thirdly, the right to be heard had become expressly enshrined in the anti-dumping basic regulation and the corresponding implementing act: producers, exporters, and importers are recognized as possessing the right to intervene during the investigative procedures that precede the adoption of the regulation.[101]

The nature of the act adopted was simultaneously the obstacle preventing the recognition of the right to be heard in anti-dumping procedures and the reason why it was eventually recognized. The acts following such procedures are of a general nature, formally applicable to an indeterminate number of persons. Nonetheless, as underlined by Advocate General Warner in the said opinion, an anti-dumping regulation 'may lead to a finding that a particular exporter has been guilty of dumping and, on the basis of that finding, result in the imposition of an anti-dumping duty on his products *nominatim*'. As such, 'it has enough of the character of a procedure preparatory to a decision of individual and direct concern to him'.[102] In this reasoning, the essential element to trigger the applicability of the right to be heard lies in the fact that the act adopted, irrespective of its form, is of individual and direct concern to the applicant. Thereby the condition on which depends access to judicial review of private applicants, other than the addressee of an individual act (Article 263(4) TFEU ex-Article 230(4)) is transposed to the administrative procedure.[103] In turn, Advocate General

[99] Nehl, *op. cit.*, n. 67, pp. 73–4.

[100] Opinion of Advocate General Warner, delivered on 14 February 1979, on Case 113/77, *NTN Toyo Bearing Company Ltd and others v Council* [1979] ECR 1212.

[101] Article 7(1), a), b), and (4) of Council Regulation No. 2423/88, repealed. See current Article 6(5) to (7) of Council Regulation No. 1225/2009, of 30 November 2009, on protection against dumped imports from countries not members of the European Community (OJ L 343/51, 22.12.2009). See also Article 11(5) to (7) of Council Regulation No. 597/2009, of 11 June 2009, on protection against subsidised imports from countries not members of the European Community (OJ L 188/93, 18.7.2009).

[102] Opinion of Advocate General Warner, *cit.*, p. 1262.

[103] On this interplay, see further Chapter 8, Sub-sections 8.1.3 and 8.2.4. In a way, the Advocate General left the door open for a broader recognition of participation rights to persons other than those directly and individually affected, by stating that 'in general, no one has the right to be heard during the process of preparation of legislation *such as he has* in the process of preparation of an administrative decision affecting him individually and directly' (*ibid*, emphasis added). Reading between the lines, one could argue that he does not dismiss the possibility of

Darmon, in his opinion delivered on *Al-Jubail*, while recalling the differences between competition and anti-dumping procedures, underlined the similarities between the consequences deriving from the loss of a market as a result of the imposition of anti-dumping duties and from the imposition of a sanction on an undertaking.[104] Therefore, in both cases, the transposition of the right to be heard to anti-dumping procedures does not entail any deviation from the four characteristics pointed out above. The sufficient individualization of the persons concerned during anti-dumping investigations and the consequences that the final act may have in their regard allows us to consider that the procedure was initiated against them and that a bilateral relationship between the author of the act and the persons directly and individually affected emerges from the final act. Also in anti-dumping procedures the Commission has broad powers of appraisal in defining the final decision. In this respect, despite the undeniable widening of the scope of the right, nothing has fundamentally changed in the main factors that trigger the application of the right to be heard.

Seconding the opinion of the Advocate General, the Court held that

> [the requirements stemming from the right to a fair hearing] must be observed not only in the course of proceedings which may result in the imposition of penalties, but also in investigative proceedings prior to the adoption of anti-dumping regulations which, despite their general scope, may directly and individually affect the undertakings concerned and entail adverse consequences for them.[105]

Significant in the Court's judgment was the fact that the right to be heard was placed in the realm of the fundamental rights jurisprudence.[106] The

participation rights in procedures of general scope that would, in any case, have a different density than the right to be heard in administrative procedures leading to the adoption of individual decisions.

[104] Opinion of Advocate General Darmon delivered on 7 February 1991, in Case C-49/88, *Al-Jubail Fertilizer Company (Samad) et Saudi Arabian Fertilizer Company (Safco) v Council* [1991] ECR I-3187, paragraphs 73 and 74.

[105] *Al-Jubail*, *cit.*, n. 64, paragraph 15. For a recent application of this rule, see Case T-249/06, *Interpipe Niko Tube ZAP and Interpipe NTRP VAT v Council* [2009] ECR II-383, paragraph 64.

[106] '... fundamental rights form an integral part of the general principles of law, whose observance is ensured by the Courts. Consequently, it is necessary ... to take account in particular of the requirements stemming from the right to a fair hearing, a principle whose fundamental character has been stressed on numerous occasions in the case-law of the Courts ...' (*idem, ibidem*). On this Nehl, *op. cit.*, n. 67, p. 75; Craig, *op. cit.*, n. 12, p. 315. That the right to be heard is one of the fundamental rights of the EU legal order has been recently reiterated also in a judgment on anti-dumping: Case T-409/06, *Sun Sang Kong Yuen Shoes Factory (Hui Yang) Corp. Ltd v Council* [2010] nyr., paragraph 132.

wish expressed by the Court that EU law should provide a standard of judicial protection to individuals equal or at least comparable to the standards of certain national legal systems also deserves notice. In fact, acknowledging that 'as they stand at present, the rules in question [anti-dumping procedural rules] do not provide all the procedural guarantees for the protection of the individual which may exist in certain national legal systems', the Court held that 'the Community institutions must be all the more scrupulous' with regard to the right to a fair hearing.[107]

The bilateral scheme underlining the Court's reasoning in *Al-Jubail*, grounded in an analogy with competition procedures, came expressly to the fore in the *Nölle* judgment.[108] The Court considered that no right to be heard could be recognized to an independent importer in the realm of an anti-dumping procedure, on the ground that this 'was not against the applicant and could not for that reason result in a measure adversely affecting it'. However, not to leave an obviously affected person deprived of any guarantees, and on the basis of the applicable rules, the Court held that the applicant could access the procedure to the extent that they had demonstrated a 'sufficient interest as an "interested party"' for the purpose of taking part in the anti-dumping procedure. Accordingly, the Commission, respecting the principle of care, must 'consider seriously and in detail whether [the] arguments or proposals [invoked by the interested party] are well founded'. The principle of care was intended as 'a rule protecting individuals' and thereby avoided a blunt denial of procedural guarantees where they would in principle be fully justified.[109] A forced reasoning, without a doubt, which does not seem to have been followed in subsequent cases,[110] but one that reveals the difficulties of the Court in fully assuming a different 'structural setting' for the right to be heard.

In any event, *Al-Jubail* did establish the right to be heard in the field of anti-dumping procedures and thereby in relation to 'hybrid' regulations

[107] *Al-Jubail*, *cit.*, n. 64, paragraph 16. The Court thereby revealed 'its commitment to ensure that the highest standards of procedural protection are to be applied in anti-dumping procedures' (Nehl, *op. cit.*, n. 67, p. 75), confirming its concern in ensuring that procedural guarantees are not depleted as an effect of EU law.

[108] *Nölle*, *cit.*, n. 76. For a sharp criticism, see Nehl, *op. cit.*, n. 67, p. 76–7 (also pp. 129–32).

[109] *Nölle*, *cit.*, n. 76, paragraphs 63 and 78. Nehl notes that the realm of protection of the principle of care remains unclear, in particular if confronted with the purview of the right to be heard (*op. cit.*, n. 67, pp. 110–11, 131–2, 162–3).

[110] No results were given on searching the Eur-lex and Curia databases up to 31 October 2010. In general, on the case law on the principle of care, see Nehl, *op. cit.*, n. 67, Chapter 9.

(i.e. regulations of an individualized nature that can have an effect similar to the one entailed in an administrative decision) and to persons who, even though not formally targeted by the procedure, are substantially considered to be so, given their direct and individual concern in the matter being decided.[111]

Discretion and procedural guarantees

In the same year of the *Al-Jubail* judgment, the Court decided another important case for the development of the right to be heard. In *Technische Universität München*, a case concerning the possible exemption from customs duties, the Court found that:

> ... where the Community institutions have [a discretionary] power of appraisal [attached to complex technical evaluations], respect for the rights guaranteed by the Community order in administrative proceedings is *of even more fundamental importance*. Those guarantees include, in particular, the duty of the competent institution to examine carefully and impartially all the relevant aspects of the individual case, *the right of the person concerned to make his views known*, and to have an adequately reasoned decision. Only in this way can the Court verify whether the factual and legal elements upon which the exercise of the power of appraisal depends were present.[112]

The innovation of *Technische Universität München* lies not so much in the strong assertion of procedural guarantees as countervailing discretionary power. This, as was seen above, follows the line of *Transocean*, even though it is more assertively stated here. More relevant is the interpretation of the rationales of the right to be heard that grounded its recognition in this case. The applicant was considered a privileged vehicle of information for the attainment of a proper and accurate decision in light of the pursuance of

[111] The expression 'hybrid' to qualify anti-dumping regulations has been notably used by Advocate General Warner in his Opinion in *NTN Toyo Bearing*, *cit.*, n. 100, p. 1262. On the state of the art of the right to be heard in the field of anti-dumping after *Al-Jubail*, see Tridimas, *op. cit.*, n. 5, p. 404–5, who points out the limited success of claims regarding the breach of the right to be heard in this area.

[112] Case C-269/90, *Technische Universität München v Hauptzollamt München-Mitte* [1991] ECR I-5469, paragraph 14, emphasis added. Having returned to this judgment in a subsequent case, the Court clarified that 'it is not only the particularly technical nature of a case which is liable to give rise to a right on the part of the person concerned to be heard before the Commission, but the latter's power of appraisal in this connection' (*France-Aviation*, *cit.*, n. 73, paragraph 33). On the specific background of this case, see Nehl, *op. cit.*, n. 67, pp. 133–5.

the public interest.[113] This was enough reason to extend the right to be heard to procedures initiated *by* and *not against* the person concerned. There is, correlatively, an expansion of the interpretation of the requirement 'adverse effect', since this now encompasses the denial of an advantage sought by an applicant.[114] Together, these three aspects allow the interpreter to detach participation rights from the strict defensive perspective that had until then been adopted by the Court. Even if it does not fully depart from a dignitarian rationale (at the end, the intervention in the procedure is still ancillary to a purpose of defence), it is clear that what triggered the recognition of the right to be heard in this case was not the need to pay heed to the person's dignity and to enable its defence in the face of the administrative decision taken in their regard.[115] As a result, one of the fundamental characteristics mentioned above as defining the scope of the right to be heard was overstepped in this case. At the same time, this reasoning could, in principle, open the procedure to persons other than the addressee of a decision or the person directly and individually concerned by it, that is, those affected in their rights and interests by a Union act but not directly targeted by it. In fact, participation rights could be recognized on the basis of the position of the person concerned in relation to the material situation underlying the procedure *and* on the person's contribution to the correctness and accurateness of the act. Should the Court have followed this path, the recognition of the right to be heard could have been extended beyond the scheme of a bilateral relationship. This was not however the case, as will be seen below.

An additional feature confirms the importance of this judgment. The right to be heard was recognized in a procedure that falls in the realm of the EU indirect administration. In particular, the application of the common customs tariff regime requires a coordinated action between the national authorities of the Member States and the Commission. In the case at issue, the *Technische Universität München* had initiated an objection procedure

[113] *Technische Universität München*, *cit.*, paragraph 24: '... it is the importing institution which is best aware of the technical characteristics which the scientific apparatus must have in view of the work for which it is intended. The comparison between the imported apparatus and the instruments originating in the Community must, consequently, be made according to the information about the intended research projects and the actual intended use of the apparatus provided by the person concerned.'

[114] This same aspect is underlined by Azoulai, who considers that this case was the occasion for the Court to extend the right to be heard to non-repressive procedures (*op. cit.*, n. 5, p. 124).

[115] In this sense, Azoulai, *op. cit.*, n. 5, pp. 392–3.

against the decision of the national customs authority that had denied it the exemption of customs duties regarding the importation of scientific apparatus. By request of the national authority, the Commission was required to intervene in the procedure and decided along the same lines. In the sequence of the latter's decision, the national customs authority confirmed its initial decision and rejected the application for duty-free admission. The direct interlocutor of *Technische Universität München* was therefore the national customs authority. However, the Court considered that *Technische Universität München* should have been able to put its own case before the Commission, making its own views known before the decision was issued.

The stance adopted in *Technische Universität München* was followed in subsequent cases, as the cases analysed next will reveal. Namely, the recognition of the right to be heard exercised before the EU deciding body in the realm of composite procedures also conducted by national administrations was maintained in later judgements, as was, at least in some cases, the broad interpretation of the requirement of 'adverse measures', consisting of the denial of benefits. Yet, the approach to the right to be heard taken in this judgment remains an exception in the Courts' case law.[116] The Court has on several occasions applied the principle laid down in *Technische Universität München* according to which 'where a Community institution has wide discretion, observance of the procedural guarantees conferred by the Community legal order is of even more fundamental importance'.[117] However, in most cases, the application of this principle was not related to the recognition of the right to be heard or, in any event, did not ground the extension of the right's scope. In two conspicuous judgments where the principle was indeed related to the right to be heard, it was invoked in order to support the denial of the right in decisional procedures where the Community institutions were deemed not to have discretion in defining

[116] In this respect, Azoulai points out that the quantity of references to this decision is more due to 'the quality of its formulation than to its underlying logic' (*op. cit.*, n. 5, p. 128, author's translation).

[117] Among others, quoting only more recent judgments, Case T-74/08, *NowPharma EG v Commission* [2010] nyr., paragraph 87; *TV 2/Danmark*, *cit.*, paragraphs 179, 201, and 203; *Interpipe*, *cit.*, n. 105, paragraph 40; Case T-285/03, *Agraz SA and others v Commission* [2005] ECR II-1063, paragraph 49; Case T-413/03, *Sandong Reipu Biochemicals Co. Ltd v Council* [2006] ECR II-2243, paragraph 63. With a different wording but equivalent meaning, Case T-375/03, *Fachvereinigung Mineralfaserindustrie eV Deutsche Gruppe der Eurima v Commission* [2007] ECR II-121, paragraph 90. Before them, notably, Case T-13/99, *Pfizer Animal Health SA v Council* [2002] ECR II-3305, paragraph 171, and Case T-70/99, *Alpharma Inc. v Council* [2002] ECR II-3495, paragraph 182.

the content of the act.[118] In most cases, resort to the principle defined in *Technische Universität München* served to ground the principle of care involving the duty of the competent institution to examine carefully and impartially all the relevant aspects of the individual case.[119] As will be seen below, this duty has had the effect of reinforcing the procedural position of the persons concerned who were able to access the procedure either on the basis of the rules that result from the above analysis or under specific legislative provisions. However, it does not seem to provide grounds to broaden the scope of persons who are entitled to participate in decisional procedures.[120] In this sense one may say that the protective scope of the principle of care is limited to an 'internal dimension' of the procedure.

In particular, the logic of combination of the two rationales of the right to be heard and, especially, the possibility of granting the right also on objective grounds pertaining to the substantive quality of the decision adopted were not present in later Court decisions. The potential to expand the personal scope of the right on the basis of this reasoning, suggested above, remained thus unexplored. Or, to put it in different terms, it does not seem to have been an effect envisaged by the Court at the time, and certainly not later. The effective contribution of *Technische Universität München* to the right to be heard was, nonetheless, meaningful, since it did expand the scope of the right as to the type of procedures in which it is required. No less importantly, and from a broader perspective, it remains a landmark case in the procedural protection of individuals in EU administrative law. The path it opened in relation to the right to be heard is confirmed by the cases analysed in the next two sub-sections.

Composite procedures

In *France-Aviation*, a case on the remission of import duties, the Court pursued the stance adopted in *Technische Universität München*, enforcing

[118] '... [R]espect for the procedural rights guaranteed by the Community legal order, especially the right of the person concerned to make his point of view known, is correlated to the exercise of discretion by the authority which is the author of the act at issue', *Yusuf, cit.*, n. 74, paragraph 327, and *Kadi, cit.*, n. 74, paragraph 257 (see above n. 74).

[119] *NowPharma, cit.*, n. 117, paragraph 87; Case C-326/05 P, *Industrias Químicas des Vallés, SA v Commission* [2007] ECR I-6557, paragraph 77; *Sandong, cit.*, paragraph 63; Joined Cases T-376/05 and T-383/05, *TEA-CEGOS, SA and others v Commission* [2006] ECR II-205, paragraph 76; *Agraz, cit.*, paragraph 49. On the principle of care and the importance of *Technische Universität München* in this respect, see Nehl, *op. cit.*, n. 67, Chapters 8 and 9.

[120] In *Nölle*, briefly discussed above, the access of the importer to the procedure was based on a rule of secondary legislation (see note 100 above). Also in this case, the principle of care, as applied by the Court, had the effect of reinforcing his procedural position inside the procedure.

the right to be heard in the realm of composite administrative procedures.[121] It held that, in such procedures, the right to be heard must be ensured in the first place in the relations between the person concerned and the national administration. In fact, the applicable regulation 'provides only for contacts to take place between the person concerned and the administration, on the one hand, and between the administration and the Commission, on the other'. Yet, this does not exempt the Commission from analysing the information that is transmitted to it by the national authorities in order to assess that it has all the relevant information to ground its final decision.[122] In this case, in particular, the Commission's final decision had been adopted on the basis of insufficient information, since the national authorities had failed to submit to it all the relevant documentation.[123] The Court therefore analysed on which grounds and in which terms the right to be heard should be granted to the applicant.

The right to be heard was recognized on the following grounds. Not only did the Commission have 'a discretion at least equivalent to that which the Court of Justice recognized it as having in the judgment in *Technische Universität München*', but also its decision implied a valuation over the applicant's behaviour—contrary to the national administration's recommendation on the case, it accused the applicant of 'obvious negligence'. Therefore, respect for that right was 'even more necessary'.[124] The Court thus grounded the right to be heard directly in the power of appraisal of the Commission and, apparently, it invoked reasons pertaining to respect for the person's dignity only in an ancillary way. However, contrary to *Technische Universität München*, where the determinant factor basing the procedural intervention of the person concerned was the knowledge held by the

[121] The procedure for the remission of import duties has been described by the Court, in a case with similar subject matter, in the following way. '[It] involves two separate stages. The first is at national level. The person liable must submit his application for remission to the national administration.... [In the circumstances defined in the applicable Regulation, the national administration] must submit the application to the Commission for a decision. The second stage of the procedure is thus at Community level and the national authorities submit the file relating to the person liable to the Commission. After consulting a group of experts composed of representatives of all the Member States, the Commission then decides whether the application for remission is justified' (Case T-42/96, *Eyckeler & Malt AG v Commission* [1998] ECR II-401, paragraph 74). See further Articles 899, and 905 to 909 of Commission Regulation (EEC) No. 2454/93 of 2 July 1993 laying down provisions for the implementation of Council Regulation (EEC) No 2913/92 establishing the Community Customs Code (OJ L 1/253, 11.10.1993).

[122] *France-Aviation*, *cit.*, n. 73, paragraph 30.

[123] *France-Aviation*, *cit.*, n. 73, paragraph 35.

[124] *France-Aviation*, *cit.*, n. 73, paragraphs 34 and 36.

importing institution and, thus, its contribution to the appropriateness of the outcome, the reasons invoked by the Court to demonstrate the power of appraisal of the Commission in this case stress the power of appreciation that the Commission has in assessing the conduct of the person concerned. It follows that it is essentially a subjective rationale of the right to be heard that grounds the Court's judgment.[125] The Court therefore departs from the judgment on which it bases its ruling in *France-Aviation*. Nevertheless, in none of the subsequent judgments analysed does it rely so extensively on *Technische Universität München* for the purposes of recognizing participation rights.

On this basis, according to the Court, the Commission had 'a duty to arrange for the applicant to be heard by the French authorities'.[126] In the Court's assessment, the Commission should have used its right to require additional explanations to the national administration in order to trigger the right to be heard of the person concerned and, thereby, correct the failures of the procedure as it had been conducted by the national authorities.

This case is certainly illustrative of the Court's activism in the protection of the right to be heard. The Court clearly focused its analysis on the need to ensure the procedural protection of persons concerned irrespective of how Community procedures are designed and split between Community and national authorities. It was particularly concerned with the effective compliance with the right to be heard and, thus, sought to avoid that the complexity of the administrative procedure would in practice lower the level of procedural protection recognized to the individual.[127] This is reinforced by the fact that the harmless error principle was expressly

[125] See *France-Aviation*, *cit.*, n. 73, paragraph 34, in light of the applicable rules. The relevant norm in this case allows remission of import duties in 'special circumstances in which no negligence or deception may be attributed to the person concerned' (Article 13(1) and (2) of Council Regulation No. 1430/79, of 2 July 1979, on the repayment or remission of import or export duties—OJ 175/1, 12.7.1979, repealed). See Article 83 in current Regulation (EC) No. 450/2008, of the European Parliament and the Council, of 23 April 2008, laying down the Community Customs Code (Modernised Customs Code) (OJ L 145/1, 4.6.2008).

[126] *France-Aviation*, *cit.*, n. 73, paragraph 36.

[127] Nehl and, more cautiously, Azoulai, seem to consider this to be a first attempt to federalize the administrative procedure (Nehl, *op. cit.*, n. 67, pp. 80–1 and 90–1; Azoulai, *op. cit.*, n. 5, p. 148). Nehl is of the opinion that this is a first step towards 'a theory of imputability of procedural defects [that] could . . . contribute to achieving coherent individual protection in co-operative EC administrative proceedings' (*op. cit.*, n. 67, p. 90). The analysis of a recent case—*Ville Vesuviane*—reveals the dubious stance of the Court in this regard (see observations below).

rejected by the Court. Without much ado, it annulled the Commission's decision solely on the basis of the infringement of the right to be heard.[128] Still, the Court did not recognize the right to be heard directly before the Commission.[129] Subsequently, however, in *Eyckeler & Malt* and *Primex Produkte* (dealing with the same subject matter), the Court considered, on similar grounds, that the Commission should have provided for a hearing directly before it. These rulings confirm that the fact that the private party only establishes a direct relation with the national administrative authorities does not prevent the recognition of the right to be heard in the stage of the procedure that takes place before the Commission, where that is justified in the face of the content of the latter's decision.[130] Nevertheless, subsequently the CFI returned to the *France-Aviation* reasoning in cases concerning the application of structural funds, where the procedures are developed between the Commission and Member States. In such case the Court considered that given the effect of the decision in the applicant's legal sphere, the right to be heard should be ensured by the Commission. However, the Court seems to have rejected that this right ought to be exercised directly before the Commission. In a recent case, the Court went on to analyse whether the applicant had been heard by the Italian authorities, without considering if they should have been heard directly by the Commission. It should be noted that the latter is fully responsible for the decisions of granting, refusing, reducing, or suspending the benefit at issue, on the basis of information that is transmitted to it by the Member States. Moreover, the Court did not hesitate to apply the 'harmless error' principle in its stricter form. It concluded that it did not have enough elements to decide that the content of the decision would have been different had the applicant been properly heard by the Italian authorities, thereby rejecting their claim.[131] In another case, the Court (renamed General Court) reiterated that in such procedures it

[128] *France-Aviation*, *cit.*, n. 73, paragraphs 39 and 40.

[129] Criticizing this conclusion as a 'bureaucratic detour' that denied the right to be heard before the Commission itself, Nehl, *op. cit.*, n. 67, p. 79.

[130] *Eyceler & Malt*, *cit.*, n. 121, paragraphs 84 to 88; Case T-50/96, *Primex Produkte Import-Export GmbH & Co and others v Commission* [1998] ECR II-3773, paragraphs 67 to 71. In a similar vein, though in relation to different procedures and with different grounds, see the decision of the European Ombudsman on complaint 2449/2007/VIK, *cit.*, n. 27, paragraphs 73 to 75.

[131] *Ville Vesuviane*, *cit.*, n. 66, paragraphs 91, 93–100. The CFI's judgment on *Ville Vesuviane* was quashed on appeal by the ECJ (Joined Cases C-445/07 P and C-455/07 P, *Commission v Ente per le Ville Vesuviane* and *Ente per le Ville Vesuviane v Commission* [2009] ECR I-7993). However, the ECJ ruled solely on the admissibility of the action before the CFI, not entering the analysis of the substance of the case.

suffices that the Commission certifies that the beneficiary of EU funds has been given the possibility of effectively making their point of view known ('utilement' in the French version).[132] This sheds new light on the consequences that could be drawn from *Eyckeler* and *Primex Produkte*. Namely, it reveals that the Court vacillated in adopting a proper unitary conception of the procedure that would ensure participation before the authority that effectively defines the content of the act.[133]

On the basis of these cases, one could claim that the bilateral scheme of the procedure does not determine the recognition of the right to be heard. Indeed, even if the persons concerned do not have any direct contact with the Commission, the latter should either hear them before adopting the adverse decision or ensure that their right has been respected by national authorities in the segment in which they are responsible for the procedure. This observation is, however, tempered by the examination of other cases.

A 'direct link' grounding the right to be heard

In *Lisrestal*, the Commission, alleging misuse of aid, had decided to reduce the assistance that had been granted by the European Social Fund to the applicant undertakings, regarding an operation related to vocational training. The beneficiaries of the aid appealed, claiming, *inter alia*, that the Commission had infringed their right to be heard, since they had not had the opportunity of setting forth their views on the said reduction. Both the CFI and the ECJ on appeal gave reason to the beneficiaries of the funding.

They considered that, although Member States play the decisive formal role in the respective administrative procedures—according to the applicable regulation, they are the sole interlocutors of the European Social Fund—the contested decision adopted by the Commission directly concerned the applicants and adversely affected them. In fact, not only did the decision deprive the applicants of a part of the assistance granted, but it also named and expressly referred to them as the direct beneficiaries. Furthermore, in the Courts' interpretation, the applicable regulation, which defines the Commission's competence to suspend, reduce, or

[132] *Cofac v Commission*, *cit.*, n. 66, paragraphs 39 and 54 (note that the Court refers to the jurisprudence according to which the Commission either needs to ensure that the persons affected have been heard by the national authorities or needs to give them the possibility to be heard directly before the Commission—paragraph 37), following Case T-450/93, *Lisrestal—Organização Gestão de Restaurantes Colectivos Ld^{a} and Others v Commission* [1994] ECR II-1177.

[133] On this see, above, Sub-section 4.1.3.

withdraw aid and to order the refund of the amounts paid, establishes a '*direct link* between the Commission and the recipient of the assistance'.[134] This is because the Member State concerned does not have a power to make its own assessment on the matter (merely to comment on the Commission's decision) and, moreover, it only has secondary liability for the repayment of the sums unduly applied while primary liability falls on the beneficiaries. In addition, the Commission assumes full responsibility for the decision adopted.[135] The Courts therefore considered that the adverse effect, in this case, consisted of 'the economic consequences of the decision to reduce the assistance'.[136] In this sense, the procedure had been 'initiated against' the beneficiaries of the aid.[137] On appeal, the Court rejected the Commission's argument that the decision did not impose a sanction or a penalty (by which the Commission suggested that the right to be heard was not applicable).[138] The Commission further argued that, given the way the fund is administered, it was 'extremely difficult' to consult the beneficiaries directly. This argument was also rejected, since, in the Court's view, practical reasons could not ground an infringement of the right to be heard.[139]

This reasoning reveals the Courts' willingness to go beyond the formality of the decisional procedure and to decide on the basis of the effective links that the acts of the EU institutions create with the persons affected by them. Hence the stress put on the 'direct link' established between the

[134] *Lisrestal cit.*, paragraph 47, and *Commission v Lisrestal, cit.*, n. 77, paragraph 28. This was not the first ruling that asserted this direct link between the Commission and the 'third parties' directly concerned by the former's decisions when the immediate interlocutor of the Commission is the Member State. See Joined Cases C-48/90 and C-66/90, *Netherlands v Commission* [1992] ECR I-565, paragraphs 50 and 51. The reasoning in *Lisrestal* is, however, more elaborated in this regard.

[135] *Lisrestal v Commission, cit.*, paragraph 43 to 49; *Commission v Lisrestal, cit.*, n. 77, paragraphs 24 to 30. In a similar vein, see Decision of the European Ombudsman on complaint 709/2002/JMA against the European Commission (20.10.2003), paragraphs 1.5 and 1.7. Stressing the legal liability of the Commission as a ground of the right to be heard, see also Case T-102/00, *Vlaams Fonds voor de Sociale Integratie van Personen met een Handicap v Commission* [2003] ECR II-2433, para 60 and *Cofac v Commission, cit.*, n. 66, paragraph 37, although admitting, as mentioned above, that the Commission may only need to ensure that the right to be heard was effectively exercised, instead of giving the persons concerned the right to be heard before it.

[136] *Lisrestal v Commission, cit.*, n. 132, paragraph 48, and *Commission v Lisrestal, cit.*, n. 77, paragraph 33. A similar reasoning was adopted in *Air Inter, cit.*, n. 65, paragraph 62 (for a discussion of this case, see Nehl, *op. cit.*, n. 67, pp. 91–4).

[137] *Commission v Lisrestal, cit.*, n. 77, paragraph 24 (the inverted commas figure in the original).

[138] *Commission v Lisrestal, cit.*, n. 77, paragraphs 31 to 34.

[139] *Commission v Lisrestal, cit.*, n. 77, paragraphs 35 to 38.

Commission and the beneficiary of the aid. In doing so, the Court adopted a broad concept of 'adverse measures' and provided a possible yardstick to assess the degree of adversity that triggers the application of the right to be heard. Breakthroughs notwithstanding, the *Lisrestal* judgment is still very much indebted to an adversarial conception of the administrative procedure according to which this involves the decision-maker and the person targeted by the administrative decision in a bilateral relationship. The applicants were given the right to be heard because they were directly and individually concerned by the Commission's decision.[140] It is implicit that, for this purpose, they needed to be targeted by the act at issue in a similar way to the formal addressee of the decision.

In this respect, it is doubtful whether it is possible to see here an extension of the personal scope of application of that right. Strictly speaking, although in narrow formal terms the recipients are third parties in the administrative procedure and the Court does ignore this formality to be able to grant them procedural protection, in reality they are entitled to the right to be heard due to an especially strong charge that the decision produces in their regard (the suspension of the aid and the repayment of the previously accorded aid). In these circumstances, there can be little doubt that it is the analogy between this position and that of an addressee that justifies the recognition of the right to be heard.

4.2.3 *Where the Courts stand*

The judgments analysed in this section allow us to identify the main breakthroughs in the recognition and consolidation of the right to be heard. First, as a fundamental principle, the right to be heard must be recognized even in the absence of a written rule or when the existing rules do not ensure a sufficient degree of procedural protection (*Transocean*, *Hoffman-La Roche*). Secondly, a person has a right to be heard whenever an administrative act may have an adverse effect on their interests, for it entails negative

[140] *Lisrestal v Commission*, *cit.*, n. 132, paragraph 45. On appeal, the Court of Justice expressly stated that the circumstances of the case allowed to consider that 'the procedure which led to the decision at issue was "initiated against" [the applicants]' (*Commission v Lisrestal*, *cit.*, n. 77, paragraph 24). Arguably, this entails the requirement of direct and individual concern (which, moreover, results from the Court's reasoning in the subsequent paragraphs, namely paragraph 26). The Court's reasoning in a recent judgment confirms this analysis: see Case T-238/07, *Ristic and others v Commission* [2009] ECR II-117, paragraph 159. Here, invoking *Lisrestal*, the Court makes clear that where the procedure cannot be considered as having been initiated against a person, the latter is denied a right to be heard.

consequences in their legal sphere. These negative consequences are usually of an economic nature (e.g. application of a sanction or a penalty, or the denial of an advantage sought by the applicant), although unfavourable subjective evaluations of the person's behaviour associated with the measure adopted in their regard also ground their right to intervene in the procedure (*France-Aviation*). Thirdly, the right to be heard is recognized not only in procedures that lead to the adoption of administrative acts, but also before the adoption of 'hybrid' regulations (as mentioned above, these are regulations of an individualized nature that can have an effect similar to the one entailed in an administrative decision). This was notably recognized in *Al-Jubail*. Lastly, this right is also granted in composite procedures that evolve in two different stages where the Member State is the sole interlocutor of the Commission, as decided in *Technische Universität München*, *France-Aviation*, *Primex Produckte*, and others.

The initial judicial approach to this matter indicated that recognition of the right to be heard is mapped by four main characteristics of the underlying procedure: first, the procedure is initiated against a person; secondly, the bearers of the interests involved in the decision are easily identified; thirdly, the final decision entails a bilateral administrative relationship between the author and the addressee of the act; fourthly, the competent administrative body has fairly broad powers of investigation and of appraisal regarding the factual situation on which it needs to decide. As a result of the developments in the Courts' case law, two of these characteristics of the procedure have changed. To begin with, the procedure does not need to be formally initiated against a person. This results from the broader concept of adverse measures implicitly adopted, *inter alia*, by the Courts in *Technische Universität München* and *Lisrestal*. Adverse measures may be the refusal of an advantageous position or the reduction of a benefit that had previously been accorded. Further, the bilateral scheme can be identified not by reference to the applicable formal rules of procedure, but taking into account the effective links established between the decision-maker and the person concerned (as decided, most notably, in *Lisrestal*).

It follows from the observations made above that, despite these somewhat looser requirements, the recognition of the right to be heard still necessitates that the holder is sufficiently affected by the act at issue in a way that resembles the position of the addressee of a negative decision (this results, namely, from the judgments in *Al-Jubail* and *Lisrestal*). In other words, in order to access the procedure invoking their right to be heard, the persons concerned need to be in a position substantially equivalent to that of the persons against whom a procedure has been initiated. Accordingly, the bilateral relationship established between the decision-maker and the person concerned as a result of the act adopted remains the essential structural element underlying the right to be heard, as was shown in the analysis of the *Lisrestal* judgment.

In all the cases scrutinized, the persons concerned were easily identified and the Commission enjoyed considerable power of appraisal in deciding the subject matter before it. It also results from the above analysis that the Commission's power of appraisal is not the determinant factor underlying the right, but the circumstance that strengthens the need to ensure to the persons affected the possibility to intervene in the procedure before the final decision is adopted. While the judgment in *France-Aviation* seems to contradict this observation, the reasoning of the Court reveals that it is chiefly the respect for the person's dignity that grounded the applicant's right to be heard in this case. Overall, in the EU Courts' case law, this is the rationale that underlies the right to be heard and, consequently, delimits its scope.

Technische Universität München remains the exception. It stands out as the case that departs furthest from the traditional scheme underlying the right to be heard. The principle according to which wide discretionary powers should be compensated by the enhancement of procedural guarantees assumed a different role in this judgment. Objective considerations related to the quality of the decision adopted were the determinant factor in recognizing the right to be heard to the university involved in the judicial conflict. The Commission alone did not have enough information to exercise its power of appraisal in this case, given the technical complexity of the assessment it required. The contribution of the person concerned was considered essential to the appropriateness of the final decision and this determined their procedural status.

This objective approach enabled the expansion of procedural protection to administrative procedures initiated by the person concerned. This point was followed in subsequent cases and contributed to allowing the right to be heard to be considered as a principle compliance with which should not be hindered by the procedure's composite structure, even if this does not necessarily lead to recognizing the right to be heard before the authority that is effectively responsible for the content of the act. Nevertheless, the reasoning according to which the right to be heard may be mainly grounded in the potential contribution that the interested person may bring to the outcome of the procedure was not repeated in future cases.

As such, the right to be heard remained strictly bound to the adverse effect that an individual measure may have in regard to the person sufficiently targeted by it, in the meaning specified above. Such is, as a rule, the scope of the fundamental principle that must be recognized even in the absence of a written rule or when the existing rules do not ensure a sufficient degree of procedural protection. On occasion, the Courts' use of the stricter formulation found in *Hoffman-La Roche* reminds the legal community that not all adverse effects give rise to a right to be heard.[141]

4.3 Right to be Heard: Inner Formal Boundaries

It follows from the above analysis that the bilateral relationship established between a natural or a legal person and the decision-maker, irrespective of how it is manifested, is the decisive structural element of the right to be heard. If, as a direct effect of the act adopted by the competent institution, the person's legal sphere potentially suffers a negative impact, consisting either of a duty or charge imposed on them or of the denial of an advantage sought, they will be recognized as having a right to be heard. This is the substantive element of this right. Yet, in the Courts' position, the convergence of these two elements is only conceivable if the act is an individual decision and the person concerned is, formally or substantively, its addressee. Beyond this core purview, expansions of the personal or objective scope of the right to be heard are only possible if in some way they can still be brought within this basic framework. This is why one may argue that the decisive criterion is not the adverse effect of a measure in the legal sphere of a natural or legal person as such, but the production of this adverse effect within the framework of a bilateral relationship.[142] Perhaps because this structural element is easier to abstract from the concrete circumstances of each case, the Courts have not taken as much care in defining what type of adverse effect may justify the

[141] For example, in *Windpark Groothusen*, it can be argued that the Court of First Instance (which was not overruled by the Court of Justice) returned to the wording of *Hoffman-La Roche* to reinforce its conclusion that in this case there was not an adverse effect that could ground the right to be heard. It held that 'a person's right to a hearing before adoption of an act concerning that person arises only where the Commission *contemplates the imposition of a penalty* or the adoption of a measure likely to have an adverse effect on that person's legal position' (*cit.*, n. 64, paragraph 47, emphasis added). It therefore stressed the imposition of a penalty as a yardstick against which an adverse effect is measured.

[142] For a different view, Nehl (*op. cit.*, n. 67, pp. 71 and 84).

procedural intervention of the person concerned as they have in delimiting the boundaries by reference to the structural element underlying the right to be heard.[143] The right to be heard is thus essentially recognized to the addressees of individual measures, the possibilities of expansion being delimited by the permissible scope of extensive interpretation.

Three aspects in particular can be said to have influenced this approach. First, overall the Courts' approach underlines the subjective element inherent in the dignity of the person and the function of defence, i.e. the individual protection attached to the procedural intervention. Secondly, the influence of competition law procedures as the archetype of administrative procedures in EU law has arguably contributed to keep the right to be heard within the boundaries indicated above. Together with staff disciplinary procedures involving the institutions' civil servants and agents, competition law procedures following the infringement of EU law are the typical example of the bilateral relationship characterized above and have been the matrix from which the right to be heard has evolved. In particular, the detailed rules of procedure defined early on in Regulation No. 17 (the first regulation implementing Articles 85 and 86—later 81 and 82 of the EC Treaty, currently, Articles 101 and 102 TFEU)—especially those contained in Article 19 regarding the right to be heard, the hearing of persons demonstrating a sufficient interest, and of interested third parties (then developed in the corresponding implementing regulation)—are likely to have influenced this specific configuration of the procedure.[144] More broadly, the rationale of defence and the ensuing bilateral scheme underlying the procedural intervention of persons concerned in EU economic law have contributed to introducing a distinction between the rights of the defence and procedural rights of other persons, usually deprived of access to the file in the same terms as the addressee of the decision and excluded from a formal hearing.[145] This is largely due to the conception that the

[143] Underlining the uncertainties regarding what may be considered to be an adverse effect for the purposes mentioned, Barbier de la Serre, *op. cit.*, n. 67, pp. 238–9.

[144] OJ 13/204, 21.02.1962. Regulation No 17 was lastly complemented by Commission Regulation No. 2842/98, of 22 December 1998, on the hearing of parties in certain proceedings under Articles 85 and 86 of the EC Treaty (OJ L 354/18, 30.12.98). It was repealed by Council Regulation No. 1/2003 (*cit.*, n. 40) on the implementation of the rules on competition laid down in Articles 81 and 82 of the Treaty (now Articles 101 and 102 TFEU). Procedural rights of intervention are today defined in its Article 27 as well as in Articles 10 to 14 of Commission Regulation No. 773/2004, which replaced Commission Regulation No. 2842/98 (OJ L 123/18, 27.4.2004).

[145] On this distinction, see Azoulai, *op. cit.*, n. 5, pp. 261–2.

procedural rights of other persons should be limited by the need to protect the rights of the defence of those targeted by the procedure. In particular with regard to complainants, 'the limits of [their rights] are reached where they begin to interfere with [the targeted] companies' right to a fair hearing'.[146] The rule that complainants' procedural rights are not 'as far-reaching as the right to a fair hearing of the companies which are the object of the Commission's investigation',[147] originally resulting from Regulation No. 17, has been extended to other areas of economic law.[148] Underlying this conception is a presupposition regarding the role of the so-called 'third parties': while, as was seen above, the participation of the addressees of EU decisions in the respective decisional procedure ensues from a defence rationale, the procedural intervention of 'third parties' is considered to be an instrument to fulfil the goals of the procedure.[149] While the former is grounded in the fundamental need to respect the person's dignity, the latter is grounded in demands of good administration.[150] Nevertheless, it may be contested that persons whose economic activities may suffer injuries or losses as a result of an infringement of rules regulating economic activities should be treated differently from the person to whom the infringement is being imputed.[151] In any case, this underlying assumption has mainly had the effect of excluding certain persons from the scope of the right to be heard.

Thirdly, it is contended that the resort to the restrictive formula of the right to be heard as stated in *Hoffmann-La Roche* has contributed to strengthening the bilateral scheme within which the right to be heard is conceived by the EU Courts. Stressing the element of sanction as the

[146] Joined Cases 142 and 156/84, *British-American Tobacco Company Ltd and R. J. Reynolds Industries Inc. v Commission* [1987] ECR 4487, paragraph 20 and in Case T-17/93, *Matra Hachette SA v Commission* [1994] ECR II-595, paragraphs 34 and 35. On this, Azoulai, *op. cit.*, n. 5, p. 262.

[147] *BAT and Reynolds*, *cit.*, paragraph 20.

[148] It has influenced the procedural regime applicable to decisions pertaining to mergers (Azoulai, *op. cit.*, n. 5, p. 266), in state aid procedures (in *British Airways*, the Court quoted *BAT and Reynolds* to invoke the difference between holders of a right to be heard and interested parties for purposes of Article 108(2) TFEU (former 88(2) EC), who 'have only the right to be involved in the administrative procedure to the extent appropriate in light of the circumstances of the case'—Joined Cases T-371/94 and T-394/94, *British Airways and Others v Commission* [1998] ECR II-2405, paragraph 60), but also the distinction in *Nölle* between the holder of a right to be heard and interested parties that are able to intervene under the principle of care (see above p. 26).

[149] On this distinction, analysing in depth the corresponding procedures of economic law, see Azoulai, *op. cit.*, n. 5, pp. 259–78. Also in this regard the Courts' stance in ambiguous, as pointed out by the author at p. 277. On the same subject matter, Baruffi, *op. cit.*, n. 5, pp. 125–34.

[150] In this sense, Azoulai, *op. cit.*, n. 5, p. 278.

[151] On this, Nehl, *op. cit.*, n. 67, p. 73.

underlying reason for the recognition of the right to be heard, the use of this formula accentuates the parallels between administrative decisional procedures and judicial procedures. It thus favours the emphasis put on the dignitarian and defence rationale supporting the procedural intervention. Beneath the judicial developments analysed above, the formula mentioned helps to restrain further expansions that could break with the fundamental scheme that has been characterized in these pages.[152] This is, admittedly, a factor ancillary to stronger arguments, but one that nonetheless insists on the individuality of the harm resulting from the institutions' acts in the framework of a bilateral relationship established between them and the addressees of their decisions. As such, one may argue that this factor favoured the exclusion from the scope of the right to be heard of persons substantively affected by an act in a different way from that of an addressee of a decision.

These different factors are interrelated. Combined, they have arguably contributed to restraining the 'inherently dynamic exercise' of defining the procedural rights of persons concerned by the acts of the EU institutions.[153] The 'almost endless diversity of substantive settings' that require the procedural rights of persons concerned has been constrained into the formal boundaries that delimit the Courts' position in this matter: there needs to be an individual measure, or an act equivalent to an individual measure, and a person affected either as the addressee of the act or in a equivalent position.

On the basis of the above, and in light of what was defended in Chapter 2 regarding the rationales of participation rights that underlay a rights-based approach to participation, one may argue that the Courts' stance resulted in an excessive restriction of the scope of participation rights. This argument will be developed in the next chapter.

4.4 The Resilient Strength of Structure

This chapter has shown the formalistic approach that underlies the Courts' pragmatism with regard to participation rights. Underneath a case-by-case

[152] Nehl has held that the restrictive formula of *Hoffmann-La Roche* has 'restrained, at first, the scope of the application of the fundamental right to be heard to competition procedures'. Moreover, it 'seems to be largely responsible for the reduced degree of protection in favour of complaining competitors' (*op. cit.*, n. 67, p. 73).

[153] The cited expression is Lenaerts' and Vanhamme's, *op. cit.*, n. 59, p. 569, as is the one in the following paragraph.

approach which in some respects leads to inconsistent results, it was possible to identify the main features of the procedures that delimit the scope of participation rights in relation to individual decisions or to acts that can be equated thereto. On this basis, it was demonstrated that the bilateral relationship established between a person that is affected by an act as if it were its addressee, on the one hand, and the decision-maker, on the other, is the essential structural element that delimits the procedures where the right to be heard is applicable. The fact that, to have this effect, the procedure does not need to be formally initiated against the person concerned and that this bilateral scheme is not defined exclusively on the basis of the formal rules of procedure, does not contradict this conclusion. Insofar as it defines the boundaries of the right to be heard, this 'structural setting' arguably prevails over the substantive element that triggers the recognition of the right. In fact, the adverse effect that an act produces in the legal sphere of the persons concerned only triggers the recognition of the right to be heard if verified within this bilateral scheme. This, in turn, implies that the act is an individual decision and that the person concerned is or can be considered to be its addressee. This is the objective and personal scope of the fundamental principle that must be recognized irrespective of an applicable written rule. This formal scheme has underlain and delimited the expansion of participation rights, even where the Courts admitted them within the realm of procedures leading to the adoption of 'hybrid' acts, such as anti-dumping regulations. As will be demonstrated in the next chapter, this formalistic approach has ultimately led the Court to exclude participation rights from rule-making procedures.

Returning to the first part of the chapter, and in particular to the relationships between access to decisional procedures and standing, it may be argued that one of the reasons for the limits put by the Courts to the expansion of participation rights lies in the current rules of access to judicial review, in a double sense. First, these have limited the instances in which the Courts could have striven to extend participation rights. Secondly, by limiting access to decisional procedures, the Courts have avoided the possible pressure that would result to the rules of standing from enlarging the scope of participation rights solely on the basis of the adverse effect that a measure may produce on the rights and interests of concerned persons. By doing so, they have restrained the legal protection of persons affected by Union acts also with regard to access to decisional procedures, thereby limiting the compensatory function that participation rights could have in view of the limited access to justice. This might change as a result of the looser standing requirements that Article 263(4) TFEU defines for self-executing regulatory acts.[154]

In conclusion, while the Courts have indeed been active in extending the procedural guarantees of persons affected by the acts of the EU administration, and, in particular, the right to be heard—imposing it also as a limit to the procedural autonomy of Member States, as was seen in the first part of the chapter—they have kept this extension within tight formal boundaries. As a result, while EU law may have a 'protective role' vis-à-vis the persons concerned by administrative action within its realm, this is formally restricted to a certain type of procedure—those leading to the adoption of individual acts—and to a certain category of persons—those who are, or can be considered to be, the addressees of a decision, unless otherwise determined in a written norm.

[154] See below Chapter 5, Section 5.3 *in fine*.

Chapter 5

Participation Rights in EU Administrative Rule-making

This chapter critically analyses the rule according to which participation rights cannot be granted in the realm of rule-making procedures. First, the arguments that the Court has invoked to ground this rule are examined and deconstructed. Its scope covers both legislative and administrative normative acts, i.e. acts of a general nature that implement or develop the provisions of legislative acts.[1] Given their general nature, they cannot be considered to have specific addressees or to concern specific persons in view of their individual legal spheres; given their function, administrative normative acts are usually termed implementing acts (or secondary derivative acts). This rule will be analysed and criticized on the basis of the very arguments invoked by the Courts to justify it (Sections 5.1 and 5.2). As such, this analysis further demonstrates the Courts' restrictive stance that was, in part, characterized in the previous chapter. The fact that the Courts have adhered to the formal limits that they themselves have set to participation rights narrows decisively the potential scope of the fundamental principle according to which the right to be heard should be ensured even in the absence of any written rule. Concretely, it is argued that, as a result of this exclusion, participation rights are not granted in situations in which they could be justified in light of the rationales of participation, in particular if heed is paid to the rights and interests of persons affected by the acts of the EU administration. Furthermore, it is shown that this exclusion is based on a classification of legal acts that does not grasp the reality of the diversity of EU acts. While the arguments presented here are based on the interpretation of leading cases on participation

[1] On the definition of normative acts valid in EU law, see, further, Sub-section 5.2.5 below. Legislative acts are defined in Sub-section 5.2.2.

rights in rule-making procedures issued under the previous Treaty, these cases are still valid law. Moreover, should the Courts take the opportunities provided by the TFEU to revise their stance in this matter, it remains important to understand the reasons that, at the time of the writing, continue to block the recognition of participation rights in rule-making procedures.

Secondly, this chapter shows how the concept of participation defended in the book could contribute to overcoming the limitations of the judicial approach to participation rights (Section 5.3). The chapter closes with the analysis of the relationships between participation rights and other procedural rights and duties that, in their dimension of ancillary guarantees to participation rights, complete and define the procedural status of persons concerned by the acts adopted by the EU institutions (Section 5.4). These are access to information, the duty to give reasons, the duty of careful and impartial examination, and language rights. In particular, this last section considers the impact that a possible extension of participation rights, as defended in the book, could have in the scope of these other procedural guarantees.

5.1 Outer Formal Boundaries of Participation Rights

5.1.1 *The* Atlanta *rule*

The basic statements of the Court regarding the right to be heard in decisional procedures leading to the adoption of acts of a general nature are contained in *Atlanta*.[2] Atlanta and other companies, whose business consisted of importing third country bananas into the Community, brought an action before the Court of First Instance claiming the payment of compensation for the damages they had suffered as a result of the import restrictions on bananas stemming from the Council regulation that established the common organization of the banana market. Among other pleas on which the applicants sought to ground the unlawfulness of this regulation, they invoked a breach of their right to be heard before its adoption. They argued that 'as far as an individual is concerned, it makes no difference whether his legal situation is affected by the outcome of an administrative procedure or by the outcome of a legislative procedure', thus defending the view that the right to be heard should be transposed to the context of a

[2] Case T-521/93, *Atlanta AG and others v Council and Commission* [1996] ECR II-1707.

legislative procedure leading to the adoption of general acts.[3] They contended that the Commission had not taken into consideration the specific situation of a discrete group of traders, overlooking divergent interests when imposing that all should speak 'with one voice', and hence acting in breach of their procedural rights.[4] Further, they claimed that 'in a field such as that governed by agricultural law, in which the institutions have quite considerable power, the legislature must, before acting, give all the parties the chance to express their views'.[5]

The Court of First Instance dismissed the plea regarding the breach of the right to be heard on the basis of three main arguments. First, concerning the applicants' claim for an extension of the right to be heard to the realm of legislative procedures, the Court held that the case law on the right to be heard 'must be considered in its proper context' and should not be recognized in 'the context of a Community legislative process culminating in the enactment of legislation involving a choice of economic policy and applying to the generality of the traders concerned'.[6] Secondly, the Court held that 'in the context of a procedure for the adoption of a Community act based on a Treaty article, the only obligations of consultation incumbent on the Community legislature are those laid down in the article in question'. Thirdly, according to previous case law, 'the obligation to consult the Parliament, as laid down in various places in the Treaty, reflects at the Community level the fundamental democratic principle that the people should take part in the exercise of power through the intermediary of a representative assembly'.[7] Also according to the Treaty, the Court continued, representation of economic and social groups in the legislative procedure takes place through consultation of the Economic and Social Committee.[8] The Court did not limit itself to stating that the right to be heard was not applicable in respect to the concrete regulation under judgment. Rather, the wording of these paragraphs suggests the enshrinement of a general rule applicable to all legislative procedures.

[3] *Idem*, paragraph 65. They reaffirmed the same argument in the appeal before the ECJ, seeking the application of the *Al-Jubail* reasoning also in their case (Case C-104/97 P, *Atlanta AG and others v Commission and Council* [1999] ECR I-6983, paragraph 31).

[4] *Atlanta, cit.*, n. 2, paragraph 65.

[5] *Idem*, paragraph 67.

[6] *Idem*, paragraph 70.

[7] *Idem*, paragraph 71.

[8] *Idem*, paragraph 72. In direct response to one of the applicants' arguments, the Court added that the Council did not need to hear traders individually in order to take into account the particular situation of distinct categories of traders (paragraph 73).

The European Court of Justice upheld all arguments on appeal.[9] Moreover, this Court introduced one aspect absent from the judgment delivered at first instance: the regulation at issue, contrary to anti-dumping regulations such as that challenged in *Al-Jubail*, was not of direct and individual concern to the applicants, hence that line of case law could not be applied to the case under judgment. This observation may have been intended to safeguard the consistency of the Courts' case law, preserving the stance defended in *Al-Jubail*. It had, in any case, the effect of turning the requirement to define private parties' *locus standi* in actions for annulment also into a test in deciding the extension or otherwise of the right to be heard to the realm of acts of general scope. Arguably, this aspect of the ECJ's judgment could be a (narrow) gateway for admitting participation rights in procedures conducive to the adoption of general acts. Nevertheless, the Court did not enter the analysis of the act the unlawfulness of which was being argued, nor did it consider the way in which the applicant had been affected by it. The lack of direct and individual concern was simply assumed.[10]

This aspect of the Court's reasoning drew on the Advocate General's opinion on the case.[11] According to the latter, 'where an undertaking is affected by a *legislative act* which affects all operators in the same category alike, the link between its individual situation and the act in question becomes a different one', and the undertaking concerned can no longer be considered 'like a defendant in administrative proceedings'.[12] However, contrary to his conclusion, it does not necessarily follow that the persons concerned should not be entitled to voice their views in the procedure at all. This conclusion should rather depend on the impact that the act may have on the rights and

[9] *Atlanta v Commission*, *cit.*, n. 3, paragraphs 37 and 38. The first two were expressly sanctioned by the Court of Justice. There is no reference to the third argument, but one can surmise that it was considered to be an extension of the former.

[10] A possible justification may lie in the fact that this aspect had already been analysed in a previous action for annulment brought by the applicants against the same regulation. This is mentioned by the Advocate General (Opinion of Advocate General Mischo, delivered on 6 May 1999, in Case C-104/97 P, *Atlanta AG and others v Commission and Council* [1999] ECR I-6983, paragraph 67), but omitted by the Court in its judgment. The order quoted by the Advocate General has not been published in the European Court Reports and is not available in the Curia database (<http://curia.europa.eu/jurisp/cgi-bin/form.pl?lang=en>). In the absence of further reference in the Advocate General's Opinion and given the silence in the Court's judgment, the analysis will proceed on the presupposition that the lack of a direct and individual concern was simply assumed.

[11] See Opinion of Advocate General Mischo, *cit.*, paragraphs 62 to 69.

[12] Opinion of Advocate General Mischo, *cit.*, paragraph 66. Emphasis added. The Advocate General originally used the term '*act normatif*'.

interests of the persons affected, irrespective of its general nature. Not taking this effect into account, the Court simply relied on the bilateral scheme underlying its case law on the right to be heard and reinforced its stance invoking an argument based on the principle of representative democracy.[13]

As such, the Courts' reasoning amounted to a principled denial of rights of participation of interested parties in procedures conducive to the adoption of acts of general scope. Arguably, the Courts' concern was that of maintaining the purview of the EU institutions' discretion when adopting rules involving a policy choice. These should not be bound by procedural requirements that constrain them to take into account the position of persons with a particular connection to the rules in question. Underlying this stance is a clear distinction between individual and general acts, only nuanced by the ECJ's reference to the concept of individual and direct concern.

The act at issue in *Atlanta* was an act adopted by the Council. Nevertheless, the rule formulated in this judgment is not only applicable to acts adopted in direct application of the Treaty rules—legislative acts in the terminology of the Lisbon Treaty, if adopted following a legislative procedure—as one could be led to argue on the basis of the *Atlanta* judgment and by virtue of the reasoning followed by the Court in this case. Before *Atlanta*, the same principled exclusion of the right to be heard was stated in an action for annulment of a Commission's implementing regulation adopted on the basis of an act of the Council.[14] There the Court of First Instance held that:

> The very nature of the process of preparing *legislative acts* and of *such acts themselves, as measures of general application*, is such that the participation, by virtue of [general principles of Community law, such as the right to be heard], of the persons and/or associations affected is not required, their interests being deemed to be represented by the political authorities called upon under the Treaty to adopt those acts.[15]

[13] For a more complete critique of this judgment, see Section 5.2 below.

[14] The terminology used in this chapter to refer to legal acts remains the one accepted at the time at which the acts where adopted. Therefore, 'implementing regulation' in the sentence above does not refer to implementing regulation within the meaning of Article 291 TFEU.

[15] Case T-122/96, *Federazione Nazionale del Commercio Oleario (Federolio) v Commission* [1997] ECR II-1559, paragraph 74, emphasis added. One should not read too much into the use of the expression '*legislative acts*' in this case (as in others prior to the entering into force of the Lisbon Treaty). In fact, the Italian version—the language of the case—refers to 'il processo di elaborazione degli atti normativi' and to 'gli atti normativi medesimi, in quanto provvedimenti di portata generale'. The other language versions consulted (Italian, French, Spanish, Portuguese, and German) also do not contain in this paragraph any reference to 'legislative acts'. This rule has been subsequently reiterated: see Case T-30/07, *Denka International BV v Commission* [2008] ECR II-101, paragraph 63.

Furthermore, the Court clarified that

> the very nature of the *legislative process* ... does not, as such, require that all persons affected should be heard, although it does not rule out the possibility for the *legislature* to seek information from undertakings and/or associations concerned when the characteristics of the economic sector at issue so justify.[16]

In general, where applicants have sought the extension of the right to be heard to general measures, the Court has applied the *Atlanta* rule, invoking the normative character of the procedures leading to the adoption of such measures. Thus, in *Bergaderm*, the Court denied that the Commission had violated the *audi alteram partem* principle by not hearing the persons concerned. At stake was the adoption of a directive that determined the withdrawal of certain products from the market, as a result of the adaptation to technical progress of the annexes of the corresponding basic act. This directive was considered to be a normative act, hence the *audi alteram partem* principle could not validly be invoked in this case, since, according to the *Atlanta* rule, this principle does not apply 'in the context of *the legislative* process'.[17] In this judgment, the Court admitted that 'by way of an exception and subject to certain express provisions ... certain rights of the defence must be guaranteed during the adoption of a *legislative act*'.[18] But it also stressed that in the absence of such provisions, the right to be heard cannot be granted.[19]

[16] *Federolio*, *cit.*, paragraph 77, emphasis added. Also here the use of the 'legislative vocabulary' is not fully certain. While all language versions consulted coincide in using the equivalent to the term '*legislator*', the Italian reads '*natura stessa del processo normativo*' and the others refer to the nature of the '*legislative process*' (French, Spanish, Portuguese, German).

[17] Case T-199/96, *Laboratoires pharmaceutiques Bergaderm SA and Jean-Jacques Goupil v Commission* [1998] ECR II-2805, paragraphs 50 and 58, emphasis added. The English translation uses the expressions '*legislative measures*' and '*legislative character*' where the French—the language of the case—followed by the other language versions consulted, reads '*actes à caractère normatif*' and '*nature normative*' to refer to the norms at issue in this case (paragraph 50). Yet, the French version also, like the other translations mentioned, when invoking the *Atlanta* principle, refers to '*les procédures legislatives*' (paragraph 58). Here again the English translation, using the singular 'the legislative process', does not fully correspond to the original.

[18] *Bergaderm*, *cit.*, paragraph 59. There is the same discrepancy between the English version and the others, the latter referring to '*act normatif*' or the equivalent.

[19] In another case, the Court considered that the fact that the preamble of a directive refers that its implementation requires the close collaboration of the persons concerned is not a provision capable of grounding procedural rights of the latter (Case T-339/00 *Bactria Industriehygiene-Service Verwaltungs GmbH* v *Commission*[2002] ECR II-2287, paragraph 51, upheld on appeal: Case C-258/02 P, *Bactria v Commission* [2003] ECR I-15105, paragraph 43). *Bactria* makes it clear that the proviso of express conditions conferring procedural rights should not be broadly interpreted.

5.1.2 *The (ir)relevance of individual and direct concern*

In *Pfizer* and *Alpharma*, where the *Atlanta* rule was also applied, the Court dwelt upon the direct and individual concern of the applicants in detail, contrary to its approach in *Atlanta*. Since these were actions for annulment of a regulation initiated by private applicants, the fulfilment of this requirement was a condition for their admissibility. At issue in both cases was the annulment of a Council regulation that, as a result of the amendment to the annexes of a directive concerning additives in feedstuffs, withdrew the authorization to trade certain additives. Having established that the act under judgment was a general act, the Court resorted to the case law according to which the general application of an act does not preclude direct and individual concern.[20] Considering the effect of the act at issue, the Court concluded that the requirement of direct concern was fulfilled in this case: 'the effect of the measure, which applies directly to all the traders concerned without any need for intermediate rules to be adopted, is to remove [Pfizer's and Alpharma's] authorisation to market that substance'.[21] On the other hand, the individual concern of the applicants was grounded in the particular status of the applicants under the basic act. The Court considered that according to the applicable directive, there was a link between the applicants and the authorization of the additives, as the applicants were the persons responsible for placing them on the market for the first time and the only ones who were entitled to renew this authorization. Although this did not grant them an exclusive right to market the additive at issue, it endowed them with certain legal safeguards. Hence, the Court concluded that they enjoyed 'a particular legal situation'. In addition, the applicants had been involved in the procedure culminating in the adoption of the regulation: following the directive's rules, this procedure was triggered by the applicants who were, as a result, entitled to certain procedural guarantees. This 'particular legal situation' conferred certain peculiar attributes on the applicants that differentiated them from all other persons, according to the *Plaumann* case law.[22]

[20] Case T-13/99, *Pfizer Animal Health SA v Council* [2002] ECR II-3305, paragraphs 82 to 84, and Case T-70/99, *Alpharma Inc. v Council* [2002] ECR II-3495, paragraphs 74 to 76.

[21] *Pfizer, cit.*, paragraphs 86 and 87; *Alpharma, cit.*, paragraphs 78 and 79.

[22] *Pfizer, cit.*, paragraphs 88 to 105; *Alpharma, cit.*, paragraphs 80 to 97.

Nevertheless, the Court denied that Pfizer and Alpharma were entitled to a right to be heard in a 'legislative procedure'. This procedure, being defined in the basic directive, did not entail a participatory phase and the Court assertively upheld the *Atlanta* rule:

> ... the right to be heard in an administrative procedure taken against a specific person, which must be observed, even in the absence of any rules governing the procedure in question ..., cannot be transposed to a *legislative procedure* leading, as in the present case, to the adoption of a measure of general application .... *The fact that [Pfizer and Alpharma]—unlike the farmers in particular—[are] directly and individually concerned by the contested regulation does not alter that finding* ....[23]

The possible gateway, which according to the above interpretation of the ECJ's judgment in *Atlanta*, could have led to the recognition of participation rights in legislative procedures of interested parties holding a specific interest or right vis-à-vis these procedures was here bluntly denied.[24] In doing so, the Court of First Instance not only refused to extend the *Al-Jubail* ruling to situations other than anti-dumping procedures but also expressly contradicted it, since in this judgment the element which triggered the application of the right to be heard was the fact that the persons at issue were individually and directly concerned by the anti-dumping regulation.[25] By arguing that persons individually and directly concerned by a measure adversely affecting them are not entitled to a right to be heard solely because the measure at issue is an act of general nature, the Court also contradicted the status of general principle attributed to the right to be heard, at least in the broadest formulation of *Transocean Marine Paint Association*.[26] As it had done in *Atlanta*, the Court stuck to a strict distinction between general acts and individual acts, ignoring the need for procedural protection of the rights and interests of those who, by the Court's own

[23] *Pfizer, cit.*, paragraph 487; *Alpharma, cit.*, paragraph 388. Emphasis added. The term legislative procedure is reiterated in other language versions (*'procédure législative'*, *'procedimiento legislativo'*, *'procedura legislativa'*, *'processo legislativo'*, *'Gesetzgebungsverfahren'*).

[24] See Sub-section 5.1.1. The CFI did not quote *Al-Jubail* (possibly this was not invoked by the applicants) nor the paragraph of the ECJ's *Atlanta* judgment that sustained the abovementioned interpretation (paragraph 36: 'the case-law referred to by Atlanta relates to particular acts of direct and individual concern to the applicants, whereas, in the case before us, the order of the Court of Justice of 21 June 1993 referred to above held that Regulation No. 404/93 was not of direct and individual concern to the applicant'). It mentioned only the part of the *Atlanta* judgment where the ECJ upheld the reasoning of the Court of First Instance.

[25] See above, Chapter 4, Sub-section 4.2.2, under 'Hybrid acts'.

[26] Case 17/74, *Transocean Marine Paint Association v Commission* [1974] ECR 1063, paragraph 15.

reasoning, were directly and individually affected by the regulation at issue. As will be argued below, this amounts to a strictly formalistic position that, in addition, does not correspond to the nature of EU legal acts, both before and after the entering into force of the Lisbon Treaty. In any case, in a somewhat bizarre statement, the Court felt the need to highlight in both cases that the applicants had had the effective opportunity to make their views known in the procedure that led to the adoption of the regulation under judgment. One wonders about the relevance of this observation in the Court's overall reasoning: how would the lack of such an opportunity have changed the Court's decision in this respect?

One last aspect deserves to be mentioned. Both *Pfizer* and *Alpharma* invoked the violation of a Commission document entitled 'Guidelines on the Application of the Precautionary Principle, dated 17 October 1998', where the Commission undertook to involve all interested parties when considering the possible risk management options on the basis of the results of risk assessment. The Court considered that this document 'was neither adopted nor published by the Commission but is exclusively a working document, prepared by the Directorate-General Consumer Policy and Consumer Health Protection with a view to a communication being adopted by the Commission itself.' It had been expressly described by the Commission as 'a discussion paper which [did] not reflect [its position] but merely sought to obtain the views of the various interested parties straight away'. As such it could not be intended as entailing a self-imposed limitation on the Commission's discretion, so as to ground procedural rights of the persons concerned.[27]

5.1.3 *Back to direct and individual concern*

In *Yusuf*, the nature of the act adopted was again mentioned with regard to the plea on the breach of the right to be heard. As is broadly known, this was, together with *Kadi*, the first of a series of cases on the application of sanctions to persons deemed to have terrorist associations.[28] Many of these

[27] *Pfizer*, *cit.*, n. 20, paragraph 121; *Alpharma*, *cit.*, n. 20, para. 142.

[28] Case T-306/01, *Ahmed Ali Yusuf and Al Barakaat International Foundation v Council and Commission* [2005] ECR II-3533; and Case T-315/01, *Yassin Abdullah Kadi v Council and Commission* [2005] ECR II-3649 (hereinafter '*Kadi*'), later overruled by the Court of Justice: Joined Cases C-402/05 P and C-415/05 P, *Yassin Adbullah Kadi and Al Barakaat International Foundation v Council and Commission* [2008] ECR I-6351. (hereinafter, '*Kadi and Al Barakaat*)'. Similar questions regarding the right to be heard were raised in other cases: Case T-253/02, *Chafiq Ayadi v*

cases stand at the crossroads of the then first and second pillars, bringing together different decisional procedures and different powers of judicial review. In this case in particular, the Court enjoyed full jurisdiction to appreciate the validity of the contested act: concretely, under judgment in *Yusuf*, as subsequently in *Kadi*, was the legality of a Council regulation adopted on the basis of former Articles 60, 301, and 308 EC (see current Articles 75 and 215 TFEU) imposing that all funds and economic resources pertaining to the persons, groups, or entities listed in its annex, which had been identified by the United Nations Sanctions Committee as being related to terrorist organizations, should be frozen and no other funds or economic resources should be made available to them.[29] Among other pleas, the applicants claimed that this regulation had been adopted in breach of their right to be heard. Neither Yusuf, Al Barakaat International Foundation, nor Kadi had been given the opportunity to voice their views on the facts alleged and on the evidence adduced against them before the application of the economic sanctions determined by the contested regulation, nor—Yusuf and Al Barakaat also alleged—had they been informed of the reasons and justification for those sanctions.

Somewhat strikingly in light of *Atlanta*, *Pfizer*, and *Alpharma*, the Court contested that, as a matter of principle, the applicants could be denied a right to be heard before the adoption of the act under challenge 'on the sole ground, advanced by the Council and the United Kingdom, that neither the ECHR nor the general principles of Community law confer on individuals any right whatsoever to be heard before the adoption of an act of a legislative nature'.[30] In *Yusuf*, the Court was called upon to appreciate the nature of the act at issue, since the applicants invoked the violation

Council [2006] ECR II-2139 (see also the judgment on appeal Joined Cases C-399/06 P and C-403/06 P, *Faraj Hassan and Chafiq Ayadi v Council* [2009] nyr.; Case T-228/02, *Organisation des Modjahedines du peuple d'Iran (OMPI) v Council* [2006] ECR II-4665; Case T-47/03, *José Maria Sison v Council* [2007] ECR II-73; Case T-49/04, *Faraj Hassan v Council and Commission* [2006] ECR II-52 (as well as the judgment on appeal cited above); Case T-256/07, *Organisation des Modjahedines du peuple d'Iran v Council*, [2008] ECR II-3019; Case T-284/08, *People's Mojahedin Organization of Iran (PMOI) v Council* [2008] ECR II-3487; Case T-318/01, *Omar Mohammed Othman v Council and Commission* [2009] ECR II-1627; Case T-18/08, *Pye Phoy Tay Za v Council* [2010] nyr.; most recently, see Case T-85/09, *Yassin Abdullah Kadi v Commission* [2010] nyr. (*Kadi II*).

[29] In general, on judicial review of EU sanctions giving effect to UN lists of terrorist suspects (non-autonomous sanctions), see Christina Eckes (2009) *EU Counter-Terrorist Policies and Fundamental Rights. The Case of Individual Sanctions*, Oxford: Oxford University Press, Chapter 5.

[30] *Yusuf*, *cit.*, paragraph 322. Similarly, *Modjahedines*, *cit.*, paragraph 95, and *Sison*, *cit.*, paragraph 143.

of former Article 249 EC (now Article 288 TFEU). It considered that the identification of the persons in the annex to the regulation, 'so that they appear to be directly and individually concerned by it', did not object to the general nature of the act.[31] This was supported by the Court of Justice, holding that 'while it is true that the contested regulation imposes restrictive measures on the persons and entities whose names appear in [its] exhaustive list [...] [,] the fact remains that the persons to whom it is addressed are determined in a general and abstract manner'.[32] Nevertheless, this time, the nature of the act was a not a reason to apply the *Atlanta* rule. The Court of First Instance argued that the regulation at issue was not 'of an exclusively legislative nature', since it was of direct and individual concern to the applicants, 'to whom it refers by name, indicating that sanctions must be imposed on them'. As a result, the *Atlanta* case law was 'irrelevant'.[33] Having cast away the *Atlanta* rule, the case law grounding the right to be heard as a general principle of EU law was hence applicable.[34] Therefore, contradicting its stance in *Pfizer* and *Alpharma*, the Court recognized that the applicant's direct and individual concern could lead to the recognition of the right to be heard in this case. Without examining explicitly the nature of the acts, this stance underlined the Court's judgments in other cases regarding economic and financial sanctions directed at persons suspected of terrorist connections.[35]

One could legitimately argue that these two different approaches in *Pfizer* and *Alpharma*, on the one hand, and *Yusuf*, on the other, do not entail a contradiction. Although an explanation for this discrepancy is nowhere to be found in the Court's reasoning, the facts and the rights at issue in *Yusuf* are different enough from the substantive circumstances of *Pfizer* and

[31] *Yusuf*, *cit*., n. 28, paragraph 185. See also paragraphs 186 to 188.

[32] *Kadi and Al Barakaat*, *cit*., n. 28, paragraph 242 (see also paragraphs 243 and 244). According to the Courts, the decisive criterion to distinguish between a regulation and a decision seems to have been the concept of the addressee of the act, not that of the object of the act. As stated by the Court of First Instance, 'an act the object of which is to freeze the funds of the perpetrators of terrorist acts, viewed as a general and abstract category, would be a decision if the persons to whom it was addressed were one or more persons expressly named. On the other hand, an act the object of which is to freeze the funds of one or more persons expressly named is in fact a regulation if it is addressed in a general and abstract manner to all persons who might actually hold the funds in question. That is precisely the situation in this case' (paragraph 188).

[33] *Yusuf*, *cit*., n. 28, paragraph 324. Similarly, *Modjahedines*, *cit*., n. 28, paragraphs 97 and 98, and *Sison*, *cit*., n. 28, paragraphs 145 and 146.

[34] *Yusuf*, *cit*., n. 28, paragraph 325.

[35] See, for example, *OMPI*, *cit*., n. 28, paragraphs 95 to 98, and *Othman*, *cit*., n. 28, paragraphs 83 to 85.

Alpharma to justify a different approach. In fact, looking at the substance of the cases, these hardly seem to be comparable. *Yusuf* deals with restrictions that drastically limit the fundamental right to the property of the persons concerned to the point of depriving them of any economic means and, consequently, capable of preventing them to 'lead a normal social life',[36] for an indeterminate period of time (i.e. the period in which they are listed as having terrorist associations). Moreover, these measures are very likely to damage their reputation and possibly their fundamental right to private and family life. In contrast, in *Pfizer* and *Alpharma* only the applicants' interests in commercializing a certain product were at stake. In *Yusuf*, a blunt affirmation of the *Pfizer* or *Alpharma* type—the applicants are directly and individually concerned by the contested regulation, but this does not alter the finding that the right to be heard in administrative procedures cannot be transposed to a legislative procedure—would be even less acceptable as being clearly contrary to the rule of law.

However, the fact that in *Yusuf* and *Kadi* the far-reaching restrictions at issue concerned fundamental rights did not seem to have weighed heavily in the reasoning of the Court of First Instance regarding the right to be heard (nor, for that matter, regarding the right to effective judicial review).[37] The applicants' right to be heard was denied at first instance in *Yusuf* and *Kadi* on the basis of an argument that is puzzling in light of the circumstances of the case, an argument which, moreover, contradicts the dignitarian rationale that has predominantly underlain the Courts' case law on the right to be heard (as was demonstrated in the section above). According to the Court, the persons concerned should be denied a right to be heard because they could not change the outcome of the procedure. Giving a different meaning to the judgment in *Technische Universität München*, in particular of the correlation between the right to be heard and the discretionary powers of the deciding body, the Court of First Instance held that the right to be heard was not applicable in this case, since the EU institutions had acted under circumscribed powers. The conclusion of the CFI that the EU had acted under circumscribed powers was grounded in a wrong interpretation of the relationship between the international and the EU legal order and, on

[36] As acknowledged by the CFI in *Ayadi*, *cit.*, n. 28, paragraph 121, and *Hassan*, *cit.*, n. 28, paragraph 97.

[37] In this respect, the ECJ's approach in *Kadi and Al Barakaat*, on appeal, was considerably different and influenced subsequent judgments: see *Kadi and Al Barakaat*, *cit.*, n. 28, paragraphs 348 to 352, and *Othman*, *cit.*, n. 28, paragraphs 91 and 99, and, more recently, *Kadi II*, *cit.*, n. 28, paragraphs 171 to 184.

these grounds, was quashed by the Court of Justice on appeal.[38] The Court of Justice therefore rejected the premise on which the CFI had based its reasoning on the applicability of the right to be heard.[39] It upheld the right to be heard of the persons named in the contested regulation (albeit with limitations) essentially on the basis of the instrumentality of this right of the defence for purposes of effective judicial protection.[40] Nevertheless, the Court did not decide on the relevance of the existence or otherwise of a discretionary power for the recognition of the right to be heard and, therefore, did not contest this part of the CFI's judgment.

At the end, the nature of the act challenged became a secondary issue in the Court's reasoning in these two cases. The fact that the Court considered the regulation challenged to be of individual and direct concern to the applicants remits the analysis of this case to the realm of the right to be heard in individual administrative procedures. Nevertheless, the judgments analysed illustrate the continuum—or overlap—between 'abstract and general' EU acts, thus classified by the Court, and individual decisions, and shows where the Courts place the dividing line between one and the other for the purpose of determining the scope of participation rights.

5.1.4 *The dividing line*

These cases all deal with the question of the recognition or otherwise of the right to be heard in acts of general nature, but they are quite different from one another. The subject matter at issue is varied: common organization of agricultural markets and related consequences for traders, EU decisions concerning risk regulation essentially dependent on scientific or technical assessments affecting the producers of certain substances, limitations of fundamental rights of persons identified as being related to international

[38] *Yusuf, cit.*, n. 28, paragraphs 264, 265, 328; *Kadi, cit.*, n. 28, paragraphs 213, 214 and 258 (contrast to *Modjahedines, cit.*, n. 28, paragraphs 99 to 108, in particular paragraph 107 and *Sison, cit.*, n. 28, paragraphs 147 to 155, in particular paragraph 154). In *Technische Universität München*, the Court had held that respect for procedural guarantees is of '*even more* fundamental importance' where the Community institutions have a wide power of appraisal resulting from complex technical evaluations that need to underlie their decisions (Case C-269/90, *Technische Universität München v Hauptzollamt München-Mitte* [1991] ECR I-5469, paragraph 15, emphasis added).

[39] *Kadi* and *Al Barakaat, cit.*, n. 28, paragraphs 280 to 372.

[40] *Kadi* and *Al Barakaat, cit.*, n. 28, paragraphs 335 to 352. The Court thereby endorsed the Opinion of Advocate General Poiares Maduro (Opinion delivered on 16 January 2008, on Case C-402/05 P, *Yassin Adbullah Kadi v Council and Commission* [2008] ECR I-6351). Following *Kadi* and *Al Barakaat*, see *Othman, cit* n. 28.

terrorism. The weight that the nature of the act has in upholding or denying the right to be heard also varies, being different in *Atlanta*, *Pfizer*, and *Alpharma*, on the one hand, and in *Yusuf* and *Kadi*, on the other.

All have in common the fact that they have either introduced, developed, or dwelt upon limitations placed by the Courts on the right to be heard of adversely affected persons in procedures leading to the adoption of measures of general scope. Arguably, in all cases, the limits placed on the right to be heard derive from forceful formal arguments that are blind to the effective consideration of the rights and interests involved.[41] *Pfizer* and *Alpharma* are direct 'heirs' to the principle defined in *Atlanta* according to which the right to be heard in an administrative procedure affecting a specific person cannot be transposed to the context of a legislative process leading to the adoption of general laws involving a choice of economic policy. *Yusuf* and *Kadi*, although paying tribute to the same principle, depart from it, given the fact that the acts contested are of direct and individual concern to the applicants. However, the argument on the basis of which the Court of First Instance rejected their right to be heard also did not take heed of the substantive interests and rights at issue, much less of the possibility of reaching a balance between them.[42] While the Court of Justice corrected this flaw on appeal, it did not directly address the relationship between the presence or absence of a discretionary power and the recognition of the right to be heard.

One could argue that the *Yusuf* and *Kadi* line of cases complements the *Atlanta* rule with a different one: the right to be heard is applicable in the context of procedures leading up to the adoption of general rules, even in the absence of a Treaty basis, whenever the general rule is of direct and individual concern to certain persons identified in the procedure. As such, whether an act is a regulation or a decision is only relevant, for the purposes of recognizing or denying a right to be heard, to the extent that in the former case the person's direct and individual concern has to be proven,

[41] This remark does not apply to the limits put by the Court of Justice to the right to be heard in *Kadi and Al Barakaat*. On this see, above, Chapter 2, Section 2.6.

[42] Compare the approach in *Yusuf* and *Kadi*, on the one hand, with the reasoning in *Modjahedines* and *Sison*, on the other, even if the types of sanctions are different in each case (the latter relate to autonomous sanctions). In the latter, the Court, considering that the right to be heard was applicable, sought to strike a balance between the need to ensure procedural protection to the applicant's fundamental rights and the public interest that had justified the adoption of the contested acts (*Modjahedines*, *cit.*, n. 28, paragraphs 99 to 108 and 137; *Sison*, *cit.*, n. 28, paragraphs 147–155 and 184).

whilst in the latter it is assumed (certainly if addressed to the person). However, as was seen above, this possible complementary rule was rejected in *Pfizer* and *Alpharma*, where the applicants' direct and individual concern gave them access to Court but no access to the decisional procedure that led to the adoption of the act. The contrast between the rulings in these two cases and the approach adopted in *Yusuf* and *Kadi* therefore turns the direct and individual concern requirement into a fortuitous element when it comes to defining the scope of participation rights.

In the absence of any express provision requiring compliance with the right to be heard, the main dividing line to decide whether such a right is applicable or not is the general or the individual nature of the act at issue, possibly, but not necessarily, nuanced by the direct and individual concern of the persons affected. Cutting across different areas of law, general acts fall under the *Atlanta* rule, unless they effectively contain individual acts (which is actually the case of the regulations establishing restrictive measures against suspects of terrorist association), while individual acts are covered by the fundamental principle of EU law according to which all those liable to be adversely affected by a measure must be placed in a position in which they can effectively make known their views on the truth and relevance of the facts adduced on the documents that form the basis of the said measure. The next section examines to what extent this is a 'just' distinction.

5.2 Participation Rights between Normative and Individual Acts

5.2.1 *The* Atlanta *rule, 'legislative' and 'normative' acts*

Together with Paul Craig, one may start by acknowledging that the rule stated in *Atlanta* is defensible. It is grounded in the premise that there is a clear distinction between the way individuals are adversely affected by a normative act and by an individual act.[43] This distinction has been accepted and followed in many legal systems.[44] In addition, it is coherent with the Courts' stance regarding the right to be heard in procedures leading to the

[43] Paul Craig (2006) *EU Administrative Law*, Oxford: Oxford University Press, p. 319.

[44] On the principles and rules of selected EU legal systems, see, above, Chapter 2, Section 2.4.

adoption of individual decisions, as characterized above.[45] Indeed, returning to the Opinion of Advocate General Mischo on *Atlanta*, according to whom the link of the individual to the act is different in each case, the *Atlanta* rule confirms that the bilateral relationship established between a natural or a legal person and the decision-maker is the decisive structural element to trigger participation rights. Nevertheless, there are sufficient reasons to contest the Courts' position.

One first point of criticism pertains to the fact that the principled exclusion of participation rights from procedures leading to the adoption of general acts applies without distinction to legislative and to administrative normative acts (as defined above). This becomes clear not so much on the basis of *Atlanta* itself, but taking into account both *Federolio* and rulings that have subsequently relied on *Atlanta*, such as *Bergaderm*, *Pfizer*, or *Alpharma*. It is worth analysing this point more closely, in particular the grounds and terms for excluding participation rights in each case. Indeed, it will be shown that the reasoning followed by the Court in *Atlanta* may ground the exclusion of legislative acts from the scope of the *audi alteram partem* principle, but it is immaterial for the denial of participation rights in relation to other normative acts.

Risking repetition, it is useful to revisit the statements of the Court of First Instance, leaving aside for the moment the argument that draws on the principle of representative democracy:

> [T]he right to be heard in an administrative procedure affecting a specific person cannot be transposed to the context of a *legislative process* leading to the adoption of *general laws*.... [The case law according to which undertakings suspected of having infringed rules of the Treaty must be heard before any measures, and particularly sanctions, are taken against them] must be considered in its proper context and should not be extended to the context of a Community *legislative process* culminating in the enactment of *legislation* involving a choice of economic policy and applying to the generality of the traders concerned.
>
> In the context of a procedure for the adoption of a Community act based on an article of the Treaty, the only obligations of consultation incumbent on the *Community legislature* are those laid down in the article in question....[46]

It should be pointed out, at the outset, that the language terms used are likely to confuse the interpreter seeking support for their arguments in the formulation of the rule at issue. Indeed, prior to the entering into force of

[45] See Chapter 4, Sections 4.2 (in particular Sub-section 4.2.3) and 4.3.

[46] *Atlanta*, *cit.*, n. 2, paragraphs 70 and 71. Emphasis added.

the Lisbon Treaty, it was even less easy to discern the meaning of the use of terms with legislative connotations. In this case, moreover, 'legislative process' and 'Community legislator' are the only such terms common to the other language versions analysed.[47] 'General laws' and 'legislation' correspond to the more neutral '*Maßnahmen allgemeiner Art*' and '*Rechtsvorschriften*' in the original language of the case, which were also preferred in the other language versions considered.[48]

Despite these discrepancies, the use of the 'legislative language' is an indication that the scope of the rule formulated in *Atlanta* is effectively circumscribed to legislative acts. First, in the language of the case, the Court mentions normative acts adopted as a result of a legislative procedure by the (then) Community legislator, instead of simply making reference to acts of a general nature. It thus alludes to a procedural and organic criterion in delimiting the acts to which it refers.[49] Secondly, a long-standing strand of case law that distinguishes individual acts from general acts on the basis of a criterion different from a procedural or organic one, and that notes that general acts may be of direct and individual concern to certain persons, was ignored by the CFI. It was laconically addressed by the ECJ only to tersely deny that the applicants could deduce a right to be heard from former

[47] They correspond to the original '*Gesetzgebungsverfahren*' and '*Gemeinschaftsgesetzgeber*', also used by the ECJ judging on appeal and also uniformly translated into the other languages (*Atlanta* (appeal), *cit*., n. 3, paragraph 37). In *Federolio* the term 'legislative procedure' is also the only one common to all the versions checked (with the exception of the Italian term '*processo normativo*' translated as '*legislative*' in the other languages), as in *Bergaderm* ('*procédures législatives*') and in *Pfizer* and *Alpharma* ('*legislative procedure*'). On this, see notes 15 to 18 and 23 above.

[48] French, Italian, Portuguese, and Spanish. With the exception of the Spanish version that uses both '*medidas de carácter general*' and '*medidas de carácter legislativo*' (paragraph 70). The same applies to the ECJ ruling, '*generelle Rechtsnorm*' being translated into the equivalent '*normative acts*' except in English (where 'legislative act' shows up once again). Discrepancies in referring to the acts adopted and to their nature are also common to *Federolio and Bergaderm* (see notes 15 to 18 above), while in *Pfizer* and *Alpharma* there is an agreement on the use of '*measures of general application*' (paragraphs 487 and 388, respectively). Overall, it seems that the English versions tend to accentuate the legislative nature of the acts at issue, irrespective of the terms used in the original language and of the basis on which the act is adopted (i.e. irrespective of it being grounded directly in a Treaty article or being an implementing act).

[49] This use of 'legislative language' to refer to acts adopted directly on the basis of the Treaty and following the procedures therein enshrined was not a novelty in the Courts' case law. Yet, the 'legislative language' often did not refer specifically to acts adopted on the basis of the Treaty. Thus, in *Simmenthal*, the Court mentioned the 'Community legislative power' without distinguishing the type of acts adopted in the use of this power (Case 106/77, *Amministrazione delle Finanze dello Stato v Simmenthal SpA* [1978] ECR 629) and in *Germany v Commission*, it referred to the Commission as the 'Community legislature' when adopting implementing regulations (Case C-240/90, *Germany v Commission* [1992] ECR I-5383, paragraph 20).

Article 230(4) EC (now Article 263(4) TFEU).[50] The applicants sought the assimilation of the regulation challenged to an individual decision in what concerned its effects on their legal sphere, but, as mentioned above, the Court did not enter into the analysis of the regulation to determine its possible direct and individual concern with regard to the applicants, preferring to focus its analysis on institutional arguments.

Admittedly, these observations alone do not make a strong case in favour of the assertion that the *Atlanta* ruling only excluded participation rights specifically in relation to legislative procedures. In fact, this position is more solidly based on the arguments invoked by the Court in *Atlanta*, which will now be considered. The core of the *Atlanta* ruling, as it has been repeated in subsequent cases, is that 'the right to be heard . . . cannot be transposed to a legislative procedure leading . . . to the adoption of a measure of general application'.[51] This has been grounded in three arguments, which have already been presented above.[52] To begin with, the case law sustaining the right to be heard 'must be considered in its proper context', that is, in the context of 'administrative procedure[s] taken against a specific person'.[53] At first sight, this line of reasoning seems to draw a distinction between, on the one hand, individual acts and, on the other, general measures (to be faithful to the original term '*Rechtsvorschriften*') involving a choice of economic policy, and applied without distinction to the persons affected, not between legislative acts and other normative acts. However, the Court specifies that the case law on the right to be heard cannot be extended 'to the context of a *Community legislative process*' culminating in the enactment of such general measures.[54] In addition, the second and third arguments invoked—the principle of representative democracy combined

[50] Cf. *Atlanta*, *cit.*, n. 2, paragraph 67 and *Atlanta* (appeal), *cit.*, n. 3, paragraphs 34–36. The differences between the two Treaty provisions are considered in Chapter 4, Sub-section 4.1.1.

[51] As stated in *Pfizer* and *Alpharma*, *cit.*, n. 20, paragraphs 487 and 388, respectively.

[52] See Sub-section 5.1.1 above.

[53] *Pfizer*, *cit.*, n. 20, paragraph 487, and *Alpharma*, *cit.*, n. 20, paragraph 388. 'Proper context' cannot be intended to refer to the areas where it has been developed, but to the type of procedures in relation to which it has been asserted. This is suggested by the contraposition contained in paragraph 70 of the CFI judgment in *Atlanta* (supported by the ECJ, paragraphs 36 and 37), as well as in the cited passages of *Pfizer* and *Alpharma*, and in *Bergaderm*, *cit.*, n. 17, paragraph 58 ('[the *audi alteram partem* principle], which applies in all administrative procedure initiated *against a person* which are liable to culminate in a measure adversely affecting *that person*, is a fundamental principle of Community law . . . but it does not apply in the context of the legislative process . . . ', emphasis added).

[54] *Atlanta*, *cit.*, n. 2, paragraph 70, emphasis added.

with the authority of the specific procedures defined in the Treaty—are clearly restricted to the acts that are directly adopted on the basis of a Treaty article.[55] Hence, the three arguments in which the Court grounded the exclusion of participation rights from procedures leading to the adoption of normative acts are effectively restricted to legislative acts.

Nevertheless, essentially by the effect of subsequent judgments (analysed in the section above), the rule formulated in Atlanta ended up covering all normative acts.[56] This aspect, and the problems it raises, will be resumed below. For now, given the scope of the *Atlanta* rule as stated in *Atlanta*, two related aspects will be analysed in turn. First, given that at the time of the judgment, it was all but clear what 'Community legislative procedures' were and who the 'Community legislator' was, this section will try to make sense of the references to a combined organic and procedural criterion used in the judgment. This will confirm and reinforce the argument that the rule formulated in *Atlanta* was restricted to legislative acts, defined on the basis of this combined criterion. Secondly, the pertinence of an argument based on the principle of representative democracy will be analysed. This is an oft-invoked principle to contest the possibility of participation rights in procedures conducing to the adoption of legislative acts, in particular, and of normative acts, in general.

Before entering this analysis, one clarification is due. Both the Treaty on European Union (after Lisbon) and the TFEU contain provisions that impact, in different ways, on these two aspects of the *Atlanta* judgment. First, as is widely known, the TFEU introduced in the Treaties the distinction between legislative and non-legislative acts (Articles 289, 290, and 291 TFEU) following essentially an organic and procedural criterion, thereby confirming the combined criterion adopted by the Court in *Atlanta* (Article 289(3) TFEU).[57] Secondly, the principle of participatory democracy—

[55] *Atlanta* (T-521/93), *cit.*, n. 2, paragraph 71. This argument is developed below, Sub-section 5.2.3.

[56] This was perhaps favoured by the Court of Justice on appeal, which, when contradicting the applicants' argument, stated that 'no right to be heard prior to the adoption of a [general norm] can be deduced from [Article 230 (4)]' (*Atlanta* (appeal), *cit.*, n. 3, paragraph 35). As mentioned above, the English version uses the expression 'legislative act' in the place of '*generelle Rechtsnorm*'. Given that German is the language of the case and that the other language versions stick closely to the original term, I preferred to use 'general norm' in the quotation.

[57] On this and on the ensuing problems see, among others, Michael Dougan (2008) 'The Treaty of Lisbon 2007: Winning minds, not hearts', *Common Market Law Review*, Vol. 45, n. 3, pp. 617–703, at pp. 637–52; and Herwig Hofmann (2009) 'Legislation, delegation and implementation under the Lisbon Treaty: Typology meets reality', *European Law Journal*, Vol. 15, n. 4, pp. 482–505.

although not expressly named—is now explicitly one of the democratic foundations of the Union (Article 11 TEU). Bearing in mind the relevance of these changes, the purpose of the following sub-sections is to provide a solid basis to scrutinize critically the Courts' reasoning that led to the exclusion of participation rights from rule-making procedures. For this reason, and because at the time of the writing it is still unclear what impact the new constitutional setting may have in this matter, the following analysis is based on the rules in force at the time this judgment was issued, but taking the new Treaties into account. This will show the lines of continuity between those rules and the current constitutional framework.

5.2.2 *(Pre-Lisbon) Community legislative acts*

At the time the judgment at first instance was delivered (December 1996), the revision of the classification of Community acts and of a hierarchy of norms had been put on the agenda of the Amsterdam Intergovernmental Conference (held in June 1997) by the Sixteenth Declaration annexed to the Maastricht Treaty.[58] According to two commentators, this declaration reflected effective demands of the Community institutional system as it had evolved since the beginnings of European integration.[59]

Then, the criterion adopted by the Treaties to distinguish the types of legal instruments relied exclusively on the structure and effects of the act adopted (whether it is directly applicable or not, whether it is binding in its entirety or leaves scope for choice of further forms and methods, requiring in this case a two-tier normative definition of a given legal regime, whether

[58] The 'Declaration on the hierarchy of Community acts' reads as follows: 'The Conference agrees that the Intergovernmental Conference to be convened in 1996 will examine to what extent it might be possible to review the classification of Community acts with a view to establishing an appropriate hierarchy between the different categories of acts' ('*categories de norms*' in the French version; the other versions analysed used the equivalent to '*categories of norms*').

[59] Antonio Tizzano (1995) 'La hiérarchie des normes communautaires', *Revue du Marché Uniques Européen*, n. 3, pp. 219–32, at pp. 222–6 (defending the introduction of such an 'order', though recognizing its difficulties); Pierre-Yves Monjal (1996) 'La Conférence intergouvernamentale de 1996 et la hiérarchie des norms communautaires', *Revue Trimestrielle de Droit Européen*, Vol. 32, n. 4, pp. 681–716, at pp. 685–700, in particular p. 700 (proposing possible solutions for a hierarchy of norms). On this matter, see also the collective work Gerd Winter (ed.) (1996) *Sources and Categories of European Union Law. A Comparative and Reform Perspective*, Baden Baden: Nomos, in particular the chapter by Gerd Winter, 'Reforming the sources and categories of European Union Law: a summary', pp. 13–65, mapping the 'state of the art' at the time and putting forward a concrete proposal for a hierarchy of norms.

it is addressed to a Member State or an individual) and not on the author of the act and its democratic importance (former Article 249 EC).[60] This posed problems to a categorization of acts based on a democratic organizational principle. Yet, this was precisely what is alluded to in the Court's reasoning in *Atlanta*, given the reference to the organic and procedural criteria mentioned and the invocation of the principle of representative democracy as underpinning the Community legislative process.

Until the entry into force of the Lisbon Treaty, Article 207(3) EC, introduced in the Amsterdam revision, remained the only legal basis in the Treaty on which it was possible to identify a category of legislative acts.[61] It determined that the Council must 'define [in its rules of procedure] the cases in which it is to be regarded as acting in its legislative capacity, with a view to allowing greater access to documents in those cases, while at the same time preserving the effectiveness of its decision-making process'. Therefore, the purpose of this identification was clearly one of transparency. The same provision also determined that, as a consequence of the Council acting in its legislative capacity, 'the results of votes and explanations of vote as well as statements in the minutes shall be made public'. This provision was concretized by Article 7 of the Council's rules of procedure, in force at the time, according to which:

> the Council acts in its legislative capacity . . . when it adopts rules which are legally binding in or for the Member States, by means of regulations, directives, framework decisions or decisions, on the basis of the relevant provisions of the Treaties, with the exception of discussions leading to the adoption of internal measures, administrative or budgetary acts, acts concerning interinstitutional or international relations or non-binding acts (such as conclusions, recommendations or resolutions).[62]

[60] Among many others, see Jean-Victor Louis (1995) *The Community Legal Order*, 3rd edn, Luxembourg: Office for Official Publications of the European Communities, p. 100 and Tizzano, *op. cit.*, pp. 221–2.

[61] There were scattered references in the EC Treaty to 'Community legislation' (Article 67(5) of the English version), to 'législation communautaire' (Articles 67(5) and 116(2)(b) of the French version), 'legislazione comunitaria' (Articles 57(1) and (2) and 116(2)(b) of the Italian version), 'legislação comunitária' (Articles 57(1) and (2), 67(5) and 116(2)(b) of the Portuguese version) 'legislación comunitaria' (Articles 57(2), 67(5) and 116(2)(b) of the Spanish version). These, however, could be understood as referring, generally, to the Community legal order.

[62] This wording was first introduced by the 1993 Council's rules of procedure (Article 7(5) of Council Decision No. 93/662/EC and respective annex, OJ L 304/1 10.12.1993) and maintained throughout the several versions which succeeded until Council Decision No. 2006/683/EC, Euratom (also Article 7; OJ L 285/47, 16.10.2006, amended). In a way, it anticipated the wording of the Treaty amendment introduced by the Amsterdam revision (before Amsterdam, Article 151

Thus, all binding acts adopted by the Council on the basis of a Treaty article were legislative acts, or at least, acts adopted by the Council in its legislative capacity. This determined—and still determines today[63]—which documents should be publicly accessible and which should not. Transparency, not the democratic quality of the author of the acts, was at the core of such a broad concept of 'legislator' and the aim of the definition of Article 7 was to broaden the scope of documents of public access. As such, Article 7 did not allow us to draw a distinction between legislative and administrative normative acts, unless one were to exclude the latter from this transparency intent. Today, this conclusion would go against the Treaty, specifically against Article 298(1) TFEU. Further, the list of acts expressly excluded from the legislative realm indicated that the main purpose was to distinguish legislative acts, defined in light of the criterion mentioned, from acts of a political nature.[64]

This was the definition of legislative acts in force at the time of the *Atlanta* judgment. Further, the 1993 Council's rules of procedure, applicable at the time, included a specification of situations in which the Council acted in its legislative capacity, which disappeared in the subsequent versions. The annex of the Council decision approving those rules mentioned that the Council acted as a legislator 'in particular' when adopting acts on the basis of Article 43 (later Article 37 EC, now replaced by Article 43 TFEU) and 'in the framework of the procedures of Article 189b and 189c' (later Article 251 EC, now replaced by Article 294 TFEU, and Article 252 EC, repealed by the Lisbon Treaty). Given the uncertainty of which

EC merely habilitated the Council to adopt its rules of procedure, without further specification, similarly to today's Article 240(3) TFEU, which replaced Article 207(3) EC). The 2000 rules of procedure (Council Decision No. 2000/396/EC, ECSC, Euratom, OJ L 149/21, 23.6.2000) introduced a second paragraph to Article 7 which bounded the Council as to the forms of the acts it must adopt when acting in its legislative capacity and ensured compliance with the principle of transparency that inspired the definition of the Council's legislative capacity. These are the forerunners of current Article 7 of the rules of procedure (Council Decision No. 2009/937/EU, of 1 December 2009, OJ L 325/35, 11.12.2009), which deals exclusively with the openness of legislative procedures (nn. 1 to 4) and with the forms of legislative acts (n. 5).

[63] See Articles 16(8) TEU and 15(2) TFEU, as well as Article 7 of Council Decision No. 2009/937/EU, *cit.*

[64] These considerations draw on Jacques Ziller's analysis in Comité des Régions (2006), *Le Comité des Régions dans la mise en oeuvre et le contrôle des principes de subsidiarité et de proportionalité à la lumière de la Constitution pour l'Europe*, Luxembourg: Office des publications officielles des Communautés européennes, pp. 121–2. Under Article 7 of the current rules of procedure, acts of a political nature are still today excluded from the openness requirements that apply to legislative acts.

acts could be classified as legislative acts under the EC Treaty, this exemplification meant that at least these cases ought to be encompassed by the transparency rule.[65]

It results from the exemplification contained in the 1993 Council's rules of procedure that acting in a 'legislative capacity' presupposed, naturally, a body or institution to which this capacity was recognized, but also the enactment of formal binding acts through specific procedures. The procedures singled out by Article 7 of the rules of procedure, in its 1993 version, were, on the one hand, the procedure defined in the Treaty for the adoption of acts creating common agricultural markets, according to which the Council acted on the basis of a Commission proposal after consulting the Parliament, and, on the other hand, the co-decision and cooperation procedures, where the Council shared its legislative power with the Parliament, in the first case, or was bound by the Parliament's intervention, in the second case. This reflects the fact that, at the time, the Community legislative body '*par excellence*' was the Council. Further, this indicates that the legislative procedures were, cumulatively, those where the Parliament intervened, though with different roles in relation to the weight of its intervention in the final act adopted, and those that were triggered by a Commission proposal. This could have been a normative element to base the Court's finding that the regulation under challenge in *Atlanta*—a regulation adopted by the Council on the basis of Articles 42 and 43 of the EC Treaty at the time—was a legislative act. An act therefore subject to a minimal transparency rule but not to participation rights.

Thus, on this basis, a 'legislative act'—or a normative measure issued from a legislative procedure—could be intended in Community law at that time as referring to acts containing legally binding rules adopted on the basis of a Treaty article as a result of the particular combination defined therein of the intervention of the three Community institutions that share normative power in different qualities and to different degrees, as resulting from the institutional balance defined in the EC Treaty.[66] Arguably, this is the meaning that the term also had in *Atlanta*. This excluded from the category of legislation those binding rules not adopted directly on the basis

[65] According to Article 7(5) of the 1993 Council's rules of procedure, 'the record of the votes shall be made public [. . .] when the Council is acting as legislator within the meaning of the term given in the Annex to these Rules of Procedure, unless the Council decides otherwise'.

[66] This is the meaning given to 'legislative act' by Koen Lenaerts (1993) 'Regulating the regulatory process: "delegation of powers" in the European Community', *European Law Review*, Vol. 18, n. 1, pp. 23–49, at p. 27.

of a Treaty article, or adopted on the basis of the Treaty but, in any case, not resulting from the combined will of the three institutions endowed with rule-making power following the rule-making procedures defined in the EC Treaty. This was already in 1996 a basis to identify administrative normative acts, even if the distinction between these and legislative acts remained—and still remains—problematic.[67] The latter were the type of acts at issue in *Bergaderm*, *Pfizer*, and *Alpharma*, where participation rights were denied without much ado by invoking the *Atlanta* rule.

As results from current Article 289(3) TFEU, this definition, based on an organic and procedural criterion, remains valid today, albeit with reference to the ordinary and special legislative procedures (also defined by the cumulative intervention of the Commission—with the exception of Articles 17(2) TEU and 289(4) TFEU—the European Parliament, and the Council). This norm is the result of a series of normative developments that have over the years solidified the distinction between legislative and non-legislative acts in EU law along the formal lines mentioned.[68] However, this embeddedness does not mean that the combined organic and procedural criterion adequately grasps the diversity of EU acts or that it is apt to exclude participation rights from the realm of legislative acts.

5.2.3 *The 'fundamental' representative principle and institutional balance*

According to the Court, the only obligations of consultation incumbent on the EU legislature, when adopting an act based on a Treaty article, are those laid down in the respective Treaty basis. Further, the EU decisional procedures as defined in the Treaty, envisaging the intervention of the Parliament, abide by the principle according to which 'people should take part in the exercise of power through the intermediary of a representative assembly'.[69] According to the Court, this excludes other forms of participation in the exercise of power.

[67] Dougan, *op. cit.*, n. 57, pp. 646–8, Hofmann, *op. cit.*, n. 57, pp. 487–91.

[68] Namely, the early introduction in the Community's legal system of the distinction between basic regulations (directives) and implementing regulations (directives), consolidated by the *Köster* case law, and furthered by the Lisbon Treaty (Article 291 TFEU); the progressive legislative role that the European Parliament acquired first through the creation and then through the extension of the co-decision procedure, continued by the Lisbon Treaty; the clarification of the Commission's executive role with the amendment of Article 145 of the Treaty (later Article 202 EC, now repealed) by the Single European Act and a constant institutional practice of assigning the Commission the implementing powers of the acts adopted by the Council or by the Council and the European Parliament (see, now, Article 290 TFEU).

[69] *Atlanta*, *cit.*, n. 2, paragraph 71. Echoing this, see Case T-532/08, *Norilsk Nickel Harjavalta Oy and Umicore SA/NV v Commission* [2010] nyr., paragraph 113.

In favour of this argument, the Court invoked the ECJ's judgment in *Roquette Frères*. Here, the Court of Justice had stated that the participation of the European Parliament in the legislative process reflects the principle of representative democracy at Community level, *although in a limited manner*.[70] This qualification, absent from the *Atlanta* judgment, is important, since it better reflects the reality of the EU institutional balance and is more faithful to the allocation of normative tasks between institutions, certainly as this was defined at the time of the judgment but, arguably, also as it is defined today. In fact, despite the successive Treaty amendments (including the most recent one) that have conferred greater influence on the European Parliament in the EU decisional processes, there are still significant instances in which the Council adopts normative acts—legislative acts according to the definition above—following procedures where the opinion of the Parliament, despite being compulsory, does not bind the Council.[71] Such was the case of the procedure behind the regulation challenged in *Atlanta*. In this particular instance, the regulation had suffered considerable amendments during the legislative procedure, after the consultation of the Parliament, without this having justified additional Parliament scrutiny. Called in another case to appreciate the validity of the same regulation, the Court sanctioned the choice of the Council not to refer the regulation back to the Parliament, thus favouring the good functioning of the decisional procedure over consideration for democratic concerns.[72] This was not an anomaly but a reflection, first, of the functioning of the consultation procedure and, second, of the way the legislative power of the EU is conceived, even if the Parliament has stronger powers in other instances (and despite the expansion of the ordinary legislative procedure—co-decision—across more legal bases). Indeed, still today, the notion of legislative power in EU law stems more from the cooperation among institutions with different legitimacy sources than from the power conferred on an elected body that ensures democratic representation. According to one commentator, referring to EU law prior to Lisbon,

[70] Case 138/79, *SA Roquette Frères v Council* [1980] ECR 3333, paragraph 33.

[71] See, for example, Articles 21(3), 77(3), 81(3), 115, 118(2), 153(2), third paragraph (the passarelle clause notwithstanding), and 192(2) TFEU.

[72] Case C-280/93, *Germany v Council* [1994] ECR I-4973, paragraphs 38 to 42. See also the comment by Ulrich Everling (1996) 'Will Europe slip on bananas? The bananas judgment of the Court of Justice and national courts', *Common Market Law Review*, Vol. 33, n. 3, pp. 401–37, at pp. 425–6.

'the notion of legislative power should be conjugated in a participatory form. It is the convergence of the collective or common action of dynamic bodies that reveals the Community legislator'... 'the notion of legislative procedure, which covers that of legislative power and legislative act, must rely on a triple legitimacy: integrative, through the Commission; democratic, by way of the Parliament; relying on the state, due to the Council'... 'organically, the legislator is the trio formed by the dynamic institutions, the functional and dialectic co-existence of legitimacies'.[73]

This remains valid today. The principle of representative democracy is therefore confined by the particular institutional balance resulting from the Treaty norms. This diminishes its strength as an argument against participation rights in legislative procedures. Besides, the argument is, in any case, week. First, elements of participatory democracy may be combined with the predominant representative institutions. Today, denying this is inconsistent with the principle of participatory democracy enshrined in the EU Treaty.[74] This is mostly the recognition of the long-standing practices of EU institutions fostering interest representation.[75] In addition, the Court has characterized the involvement of social partners in the acts adopted under Articles 138(4) and 139 EC (current Articles 154(4) and 155 TFEU) as an alternative source of democratic legitimacy, although admittedly as a means of compensating the absence of the intervention of the European Parliament during the respective procedure.[76] Secondly, and more importantly, the recognition of participation rights in procedures leading up to the adoption of general acts does not stem exclusively from a principle of participatory democracy. Being related to an ideal of participatory democracy, the recognition of participation rights also in procedures leading to the adoption of general acts has deeper legal grounds in the rule of law: participation rights may be required in normative procedures as a means of ensuring the material justice of the act adopted.[77]

[73] Pierre-Yves Monjal (1998) 'Remarques sur l'emploi de la notion de fonction législative en droit communautaire', *Revue de la Recherche Juridique, Droit Prospectif*, Vol. 23, n. 3, pp. 1117–62, at pp. 1141, 1148, and 1149, respectively (author's translation). See also Denys Simon (2001) *Le système juridique communautaire*, Paris: Presses Universitaires de France, p. 263.

[74] Article 11 TEU.

[75] See Chapter 3. The Court mentioned the interest representation that takes place through the Economic and Social Committee, but only to reject the idea that any other form of participation could be admitted, an aspect that will be contested below.

[76] Case T-135/96, *Union européenne de l'artisanat et des petites et moyennes entreprises (UEAPME) v Council* [1998] ECR II-2335, paragraphs 88 and 89. On this, see Loïc Azoulai (2000) *Les garanties procédurales en droit communautaire. Recherches sur la procédure et le bon gouvernement*, PhD Thesis, European University Institute, Florence, pp. 488–92.

[77] See, above, Chapter 2, Section 2.2 and Section 2.5.

In this line of reasoning, the issue is not so much one of respecting the principle of representative democracy as such, but that of respecting the decisional procedures defined in the Treaty. This may be a different justification for the Court's statement that the obligations of consultation impinging on the Community (now Union) institutions are solely those defined in the Treaty article on which their action is based. Arguably, this is a stronger argument than one based purely on the principle of representative democracy. In fact, defending a procedural duty of the Council to hear parties particularly concerned by an act adopted on the basis of a Treaty article could be interpreted as breaching this provision, insofar as the procedure to be followed does not entail any such procedural step. However, this is also not a decisive argument. To begin with, additional procedural steps may arise from customary institutional practices not necessarily initially envisaged by the drafters of the Treaty without this implying a violation of the Treaty provisions. Further, it is not excluded that the lack of an express provision may constitute in certain cases a lacuna which requires the creation of a new norm of judicial origin. Still, it could be argued in favour of the Courts' stance that imposing duties of consultation beyond the Treaty provisions could breach the principle of institutional balance. However, the argument only holds if the sort of consultation envisaged potentially impacts on the concrete institutional balance defined by each legal basis when setting out the procedure to be followed in the adoption of an act. The recognition of a right to participate, as a procedural guarantee which needs to be complied with by the deciding institutions when their acts impact particularly on the rights or interests of natural and legal persons, does limit the procedural action of the legislator and, eventually, its discretion. This limitation, however, pertains to the relations between natural and legal persons, on the one hand, and the EU institutions, on the other. It does not necessarily impact on the relations or distribution of power between the latter, which are ensured by the Treaty. Further, as mentioned elsewhere in this work, if participation in decisional procedures aims to influence their outcomes, the deciding body is not bound by the opinions expressed by the persons affected.

The transposition of this reasoning to administrative normative acts, as done in *Bergaderm*, *Pfizer*, and *Alpharma*, is even less justifiable. First, while the dialectical relationship between the three normative institutions is also present in the adoption of administrative normative acts (or implementing acts, an expression that in the pre-Lisbon terminology encompassed all secondary derivative acts), the combination of their roles at this level changes considerably. Namely, the weight of the Parliament in procedures leading up to their adoption is considerably lower, virtually insignificant at the time of the adoption of the regulation at issue in the *Bergaderm* judgment. This was where the *Atlanta* ruling was first invoked by the Court to ground the exclusion of participation rights in procedures leading to the adoption of administrative normative acts, without any other argument apart from resort to the *Atlanta* rule.[78] Thus, an exclusion of participation rights based on respect for the principle of representative democracy as a fundamental principle of EU law was not only unfitted, as argued above, but also misplaced in this context, especially considering that the legislative basis for the adoption of secondary derivative acts is often a *carte blanche* conceded to the Commission.[79] Secondly, such acts are adopted following rule-making procedures created by primary legislation on the basis of a Treaty article and there is no higher principle of EU law which would hinder the creation of participatory procedures for their adoption (as it, in fact, occurs),[80] or the Courts in considering that in certain circumstances higher principles of EU law, such as the rule of law, require that concerned parties are given the opportunity to express their own views in procedures affecting their rights and interests. In this respect, the Courts' stance is very likely due more to self-restraint vis-à-vis choices of legislative policy implicitly or expressly assumed by the Council alone or together with the Parliament, as well as by the Commission, than to the constitutional arguments expressly invoked by the Courts.

To conclude, the principled exclusion of participation rights in relation to legislative acts, on the basis of the two main arguments adduced—the principle of representative democracy combined with the EU institutional balance—may be defended but is contestable on the basis of the arguments presented above. The principles invoked by the Court are not forceful arguments, even if they may be in tension with the recognition of participation rights.

[78] The Eightieth Commission Directive No. 95/34/EC (OJ L 167/19, 18.7.1995), challenged by Bergaderm, was adopted on the basis of Article 10 of Council Directive No. 76/768/EEC of 27 July 1976 on the approximation of the laws of the Member States relating to cosmetic products (OJ L 53/30, 25.2.77), which envisaged comitology procedure of the regulatory type (this classification would only be introduced later, in the first comitology decision, Decision No. 87/373/EEC), deprived of any form of parliamentary input.

[79] They often only determine the procedural aspects of the implementing regulation, by reference to the comitology decision (for example: 'the amendments necessary for adapting Annex II to technical progress shall be adopted in accordance with the [regulatory] procedure'—Article 8(2) of Council Directive No. 76/768/EEC, *cit.*).

[80] See Chapter 7, on participation rights in food law.

In any case, these arguments are clearly immaterial to deny participation rights in relation to administrative normative acts. To begin with, institutional balance is not as formally strict in relation to procedures conducive to acts that are not adopted on the basis of a Treaty article as it is in relation to those based on a Treaty article. Further, the principle of representative democracy, for the reasons mentioned, is considerably weaker in relation to secondary derivative acts than in relation to acts adopted directly on the basis of the Treaty.

The question then is whether there is any other element in the case law that could ground the exclusion of participation rights in procedures leading to the adoption of administrative normative acts.

5.2.4 '*The very nature of the process*'

As results from the above, in *Bergaderm*, *Pfizer*, and *Alpharma* the Court denied rights of participation in the procedures leading to the adoption of administrative normative acts simply by invoking the *Atlanta* ruling, without considering the institutional differences between the acts challenged in each case and overlooking the fact that the *Atlanta* reasoning was almost exclusively based on institutional arguments that are not transposable to administrative normative acts.[81]

In *Federolio*, a case that preceded the *Atlanta* judgment, the exclusion of participation rights seems to have been grounded in a slightly different argument, which was also present in the Court's reasoning in *Atlanta*. As mentioned above, the Court held in this case that 'the *very nature of the process* of preparing [normative] acts *and of such acts themselves* as measures of general application' is such that it does not require the participation of the persons affected.[82] Without further specification, this is a circular argument: the general principles of EU law do not require participation rights in these circumstances because the nature of the process and the nature of the acts at issue do not require participation.

[81] As was already referred to above, the Court of Justice, at the instance of the applicants, also mentioned their lack of direct and individual concern, although it reached this conclusion without entering into analysis of the regulation.

[82] *Federolio, cit.*, n. 15, paragraph 74, emphasis added. In line with the original language of the case, I replaced the term '*legislative*' used in the English version with the term '*normative*' (see note 15 above). The same line of argument has been more recently reiterated in the Order of the Court of First Instance in Case T-369/03, *Arizona Chemical BV and others v Commission* [2005] ECR II-5839, paragraph 73, and in *Norilsk Nickel, cit.*, n. 69, paragraph 113.

What in 'the very nature of the process' prevents the recognition of participation rights on the basis of general principles of EU law? On the basis of the case law on the right to be heard in relation to individual determinations, one could argue that the scope of this right is delimited by the basic bilateral scheme characterized above and that this is non-existent in normative procedures. Here, there is no initiative taken against a person or that has the person's situation as an object nor, given the procedure's structure and object, can one consider that the measure adopted at the end of such a procedure affects specific persons. This would still be a strictly formal argument, but one that would be in line with the Courts' conception of participation rights. This was not the ground chosen by the Court in *Federolio*. Instead, apparently, the Court resorted implicitly to the institutional arguments that were later used in *Atlanta*, just by invoking the nature of the legislative process.[83] The Court seems to have added to this an argument based on the nature of the normative acts themselves 'as measures of general application', these being such that the interests of the persons affected are 'deemed to be represented by the political authorities called upon under the Treaty to adopt those acts'.[84]

Thus, both in what concerns legislative acts, as defined above, and administrative normative acts, the reasoning of the Court stuck to the formality of the procedures, invoking the same arguments for both types of act. The recognition or otherwise of participation rights depends on the nature of the act, the dividing line being drawn between individual acts, on the one hand, and normative acts, on the other. However, the reasons for excluding participation rights are based solely on institutional arguments that, especially in the case of administrative normative acts, are inappropriate for this purpose.

Therefore, one needs to have a closer look at what is understood by normative acts in EU law and, in particular, how these can be distinguished from individual acts, thereby addressing the argument based on the nature of the 'acts themselves', detached from the principles of political representativeness. In doing so, the following pages will both present the shortcomings of a blunt denial of participation rights in rule-making procedures that does not take into consideration the content of the act and reinforce the

[83] *Federolio*, *cit*., n. 15, paragraph 77. See n. 16 above.
[84] *Federolio*, *cit*., n. 15, paragraph 74.

inadequacy of organic and procedural criteria to exclude participation rights from rule-making procedures.

5.2.5 *Normative acts*

There is a long-standing strand of case law on the distinction between individual and normative acts, mainly developed to determine the *locus standi* of private parties in the action for annulment directed against acts of the Council, the Parliament, and the Commission, in the terms of former Article 230(4) EC.[85] Beyond its specific context, and the purpose in view of which it was elaborated, this line of case law reveals the Courts' interpretation on the characteristics of normativity, and, therefore, provides a criterion to distinguish normative from non-normative acts.[86]

The starting point of this case law is a ruling of 1962, where the Court defined the criterion to distinguish between regulations and decisions. According to the Court, this criterion 'must be sought in the general "application" or otherwise of the measure in question'. A regulation has '*essentially*' a normative nature, therefore being 'applicable not to a limited number of persons, defined or identifiable, but to categories of persons viewed abstractly and in their entirety'. However, there might be doubtful cases. In these situations, 'it is necessary to ascertain whether the measure in

[85] As noted in Chapter 4, the corresponding Article 263(4) TFEU only changes the rules on private standing with regard to self-executing regulatory acts, therefore maintaining the requirements of individual and direct concern for all other actions of annulment brought by natural or legal persons (only a person challenging an act addressed to them does not need to demonstrate these requirements). Their interpretation of the standing requirements in all other cases is likely to remain valid law. See, in this respect, Case T-539/08, *Etimine SA and Ab Etiproducts Oy v Commission* [2010] nyr., paragraphs 97 to 119, and Norilsk Nickel, *cit.*, n. 69, paragraphs 101 to 121, judgments issued after Lisbon but still applying Article 230 (4) EC on the basis of the rule *tempus regit actum*.

[86] Even if the nature and the scope of normative acts was defined in light of former Article 230 (4) (now Article 263(4) TFEU), the interpretations of the Court have been guided by former Article 249 EC (Article 288 TFEU). On this basis, one may argue that the significance of this case law is not restricted to the issue of access to Court. Broader implications may be drawn from it. In this sense, Robert Kovar (1999) 'L'identification des actes normatifs en droit communautaire', in Marianne Dony and Aline De Walsche, *Mélanges en Hommage à Michel Waelbroeck*, Bruxelles: Bruylant, Vol. I, pp. 387–422, at pp. 387–8 and Rosa Greaves (1996),'The nature and binding effect of decisions under Article 189 EC', *European Law Review*, Vol. 21, n. 1, pp. 3–16, at pp. 4–5, in relation to decisions. Further, the same case law has been used by the Courts to determine the scope of application of liability rules (until *Bergaderm*; on the relevance of this case as a turning point in the case law on liability, see Takis Tridimas (2001) 'Liability for breach of Community law: growing up and mellowing down?', *Common Market Law Review*, Vol. 38, n. 2, pp. 301–32).

question is of individual concern to specific individuals'.[87] In this respect, the Court determined that:

if a measure entitled by its author a regulation contains provisions which are capable of being not only of direct but also of individual concern to certain natural or legal persons, it must be admitted, *without prejudice to the question whether that measure considered in its entirety can be correctly called a regulation*, that in any case those provisions do not have the character of a regulation and may therefore be impugned by those persons under the terms of the second paragraph of article 173 [later fourth paragraph of article 230].[88]

This kind of reasoning was later extended to other acts such as directives and decisions addressed to Member States that are capable of having a normative scope.[89] According to subsequent case law, an act is normative if the scope of persons to whom it applies is delimited according to objective conditions, in such a way that every person whose legal or factual situation corresponds to the objective scope determined in the regulation is thereby included in the category therein defined. However, as has been noted by one commentator, the causality between the indeterminate number of persons affected by the act and its normativity is not absolute, since the normative character of an act is not put into question when it is possible to identify, with more or less precision, the number or even the identity of the subjects to whom it can apply at a given moment. It suffices that this same identification is not due to specific qualities of these subjects (which would put them in a situation similar to that of an addressee of an individual decision), but emerges from an objective factual or legal situation identified by the act in question in relation to its aim.[90]

Thus, an act directed at a closed group of persons *identifiable at the moment at which it was adopted* can have a normative nature, as long as the definition of the subjects affected results from objective criteria determined in accordance with the aim of the act. The analysis of this aim may allow the interpreter to determine the weight that the possible knowledge of individual situations

[87] Joined Cases 16/62 and 17/62, *Confédération nationale des producteurs de fruits et légumes and others v Council* [1962] ECR 471, at 478.

[88] *Idem, ibidem*. Emphasis added.

[89] On this Kovar, *op. cit.*, n. 86, pp. 394–6.

[90] Kovar, *op. cit.*, n. 86, pp. 396–7. In the same sense, Greaves, *op. cit.*, n. 86, p. 6, although the latter underlines the inconsistencies of the Court in this respect. More recently, see, for example, *Yusuf, cit.*, paragraph 185, and Case T-418/04, *Confcooperative, Unione regionale della Cooperazione Friuli-Venezia Giulia Federagricole and Others v Commission* [2007] ECR II-24, paragraphs 45 to 48. See also *Etimine, cit.*, n. 85, paragraph 101.

had in the adoption of the act.[91] However, this knowledge is, by itself, not enough to classify the act as a decision. The act only loses its normative character—or at least, it may be considered to be of individual concern to certain persons—if its author, when defining its content, has taken into account their specific circumstances in such a way that the characteristics of the act are due to this consideration. In these circumstances, it may be concluded that the aim of the act was to regulate those specific circumstances.[92]

This means that only the *analysis of the object and content of the act* allows us to determine its normative nature. The qualification of an act is therefore dependent upon its intrinsic characteristics. More importantly, this also means that a normative act may concern identifiable persons. In order to assess the normative nature of a given act, the Courts consider both its general character, the abstract definition of its scope of application, and its aim. Abstraction seems to be the predominant factor to determine the normative nature of the act. Its application to every person that falls within the categories objectively defined therein is a consequence of its normativity.[93] Once it has been defined, on this basis, that the act has a normative nature, it is immaterial for its characterization whether it affects the legal sphere of identifiable persons.[94] Moreover, it should be borne in mind that whether the act is normative or not is often the result of a choice between alternative regulatory techniques.[95]

[91] Kovar, *op. cit.*, n. 86, p. 410.

[92] Kovar, *op. cit.*, n. 86, pp. 401–2 and pp. 405–8. See also Denis Waelbroeck and A.-M. Verheyden (1995) 'Les conditions de recevabilité des recours en annulations des particuliers contre les actes normatifs communautaires', *Cahiers de Droit Européen*, Vol. 31, n. 3–4, pp. 399–441, at pp. 400–1. For a recent application of this reasoning, see *Etimine*, *cit.*, n. 85, paragraphs 106 and 107, and Case T-16/04, *Arcelor v European Parliament and Council* [2010] nyr., paragraphs 106 and 107.

[93] Kovar, *op. cit.*, n. 86, p. 398–400. Cf., among many other examples, T-91/07, *WWF-UK Ltd v Council* [2008] ECR II-81, paragraphs 62 and 63.

[94] Kovar, *op. cit.*, n. 86, p. 409 and Greaves, *op. cit.*, n. 86, p. 7. In *Extramet* (Case C-358/89, *Extramet Industrie v Council* [1991] ECR I-2501) and *Codorniu* (Case C-309/89, *Codorniu v Council* [1994] ECR I-1853), the effect that the act had on the applicants, and not the object of the act, grounded their *locus standi* on the basis of Article 230(4) (as noted by Waelbroeck and Verheyden, *op. cit.*, p. 401). However, none of the cases dwelt upon the nature of the act in issue, namely whether it was still to be considered a regulation or an act equated with a decision (on this, Tim Corthaut and Frédéric Vanneste, (2006) 'Waves between Strasbourg and Luxembourg: the right of access to a Court to contest the validity of administrative and legislative measures', *Yearbook of European Law*, Vol. 25, pp. 475–514, at pp. 494–5). For more recent applications of this rule, see Joined Cases T-295/04 to T-297/04, *Centro Provincial de Jóvenes Agricultores de Jaén (ASAJA) and Others v Council* [2005] ECR II-3151, paragraphs 35 to 37; Case T-287/04, *Lorte SL and Others v Council* [2005] ECR II-3125, paragraph 43; and *Yusuf*, *cit.*, n. 28, paragraph 186.

[95] See Chapter 7, Sub-section 7.3.1.

This case law had the immediate effect of closing the doors on an action of annulment to private parties even in circumstances in which they were clearly affected in a differentiated way when compared to the general public (that is the case, for example, of regulations that excluded certain producers from the entitlement to aid as a result of newly established calculation criteria or of regulations that impede given producers to use a certain denomination for its products).[96] While normativity coincides with abstraction of the object, private parties can still relate to that act in a differentiated way, although not being in a position identical to that of the addressees of a decision. This could still require a right to intervene in the respective procedure. Here lies one of the gaps regarding the protection of the subjective rights and legally protected interests of the individuals.

Indirectly, this case law had the effect of enlarging the universe of the acts that can be qualified as normative. A large number of normative acts have been enacted that, given their nature (economic intervention), have a special effect in relation to a group or groups of individuals to whom are denied both the possibility of attacking them in Court, because they are not in a position similar to that of the addressee of a decision, and the possibility of acceding to the decisional procedure through the recognition of participation rights, because according to the *Atlanta* rule there are no such rights in procedures leading to the adoption of normative acts.

Subjective rights and legally protected interests can be particularly affected by acts that were meant to have a general and abstract scope, even in cases that according to the case law of the Courts cannot be considered to be individual decisions adopted under the form of a regulation.[97] Therefore, the argument according to which the nature of the normative acts themselves 'as measures of general application' does not require the participation of the persons affected is not enough of a reason for excluding participation rights altogether from rule-making procedures. One may argue that it is more difficult to identify the persons concerned by a normative act than to identify those affected by an individual act. In this sense, the nature of the act does make a difference. Nevertheless, when the Courts deny participation rights in relation to normative acts they also deny *a priori* that these may have effects

[96] *Lorte*, *cit.*, n. 94, for the first example, *Confcooperative*, *cit.*, n. 90, for the second. See also *Etimine*, *cit.*, n. 85, paragraph 106, where the General Court reiterated that 'the possibility that the applicants will suffer economic disadvantage—even a serious one—as a result of the contested [act] is not enough to show that [this act distinguishes] them individually from all other operators who might be exposed to similar consequences'.

[97] See note above.

similar to individual acts. In doing so, they flatly disregard their case law on the distinction between general measures and individual acts, which is based on an analysis of the content of the act (the most evident cases are *Pfizer* and *Alpharma* in which the individual and direct concern of the applicants was not considered to be capable of grounding participation rights). Therefore, the Courts have ignored, or disregarded as irrelevant, the cases in which individuals' rights and interests may be particularly affected by normative acts, beyond the specific cases in which these can be considered to be of individual concern to certain persons.

Another aspect should be highlighted. While defining the normativity of Union acts on the basis of their object and admitting that an '*essentially*' normative act may in fact contain concrete provisions concerning certain natural or legal persons, this strand of case law regarding the distinction between normative and individual acts reveals the limits of an exclusively organic and procedural approach to basing a typology of Union acts.[98] This is due to the specificities of the EU legal system, in which the exercise of the EU competences is essentially defined by the determinations contained in the Treaty legal bases. The content of the latter may determine, beyond organic and procedural aspects, a specific combination of elements stemming both from the exercise of a normative and of an administrative function in a narrow sense, which is in turn determined by the aim to be achieved by a given act in the context of a specific policy. Depending on the 'density' of the Treaty rules in question, on the concrete aim to be achieved by the normative act, or simply on the policy option of the legislator, it is possible that 'first rank' norms, adopted directly on the basis of the Treaty have, in fact, an executive function, at least in part of their content (e.g. organization of agricultural common markets; adoption of lists of persons suspected of having terrorist connections; harmonization of legislation entailing the identification of the products which may be marketed and the exclusion of others). In turn, the secondary derivative acts—or administrative normative acts—are determined by the content of the primary norm (or by a specific policy choice within the framework of this norm) on the basis of which they are adopted. In these circumstances, both legislative and non-legislative acts, irrespective of their normative nature, may have concrete provisions impacting on the legal sphere of natural and legal persons. Finally, the relevance of the content of the act is revealed by

[98] In a similar sense, see Monjal, *op. cit.*, n. 59, p. 1121.

another aspect of the EU legal system: the definition of direct effect of EU acts. Irrespective of their normative nature or institutional rank, the direct effect of an EU provision is established, among other requirements, on the basis of the unconditional and sufficiently precise nature of the provisions at issue. Therefore, the analysis of the content of the act is a decisive element to attribute to the act characteristics that would in principle be denied on the basis of its formal classification.

In sum, for certain effects of EU law—namely access to justice of private applicants and the production of direct effect of the provisions of given acts—it is important to take into account the content of the act, irrespective of its author and the procedure followed for its adoption. It is argued, on the basis of the above, that this should also be the case in order to determine whether or not participation rights apply in administrative rule-making. In fact, only an analysis of the content of the act can determine whether it gives rise to a legal administrative relationship, to the extent that it shapes the advantageous and disadvantageous positions of the persons involved, thereby justifying the recognition of participation rights. This applies both to legislative and administrative normative acts and is without prejudice to the institutional developments that allow us to distinguish legislative from other normative acts.

5.2.6 *Weaknesses of* Atlanta: *breaches in the dividing line*

This section has demonstrated the feeblenesses of the Courts' argumentation in denying *a priori* the possibility of granting participation rights in procedures that lead to the adoption of normative acts. First, the reasoning of the *Atlanta* judgment, namely the resort to the principle of representative democracy, is only capable of denying these rights in relation to legislative acts. In fact, on the basis of the rules in force at the time of the judgment, it was possible to single out legislative acts from the other normative acts and thus clarify the scope of application of the *Atlanta* rule. Secondly, in a system in which the legislative role of the Parliament is still limited, the strength of the argument based on the principle of representative democracy is necessarily limited; moreover, this is not a forceful argument to deny the recognition of participation rights in the realm of rule-making procedures, given the *de facto* participatory features of EU decisional processes and the grounds on which participation rights may be defended. Thirdly, despite the fact that the argument drawn on the principle of institutional balance could be more convincing to deny participation rights in rule-making procedures, it is still not decisive. In fact, procedural steps other than those specified on the procedures defined on the Treaty may be developed as customary institutional practices, or required to fulfil lacunae, as long as they do not hinder the balance of powers between the institutions involved. In principle, the recognition of participation rights to persons substantively affected in their rights and interests only impinges upon the relationship between the latter and the EU institutions. Nevertheless, the possibility that participation rights could disrupt the decisional procedure should not be entirely disregarded. Certainly, if participation rights were granted in first level normative procedures, the concrete design of participatory procedures would need to take this risk into account.

If the arguments used in *Atlanta* to deny participation rights in rule-making procedures are weak in relation to legislative acts then they are wrong in relation to administrative normative acts. If at all, the arguments invoked by the Court only serve to deny participation rights in relation to legislative acts. The inaccuracy of the extension notwithstanding, they were equally applied in cases where the applicants sought the recognition of participation rights in relation to administrative normative acts.

Also the argument drawing on the very nature of the normative act, as an act of general application, cannot uphold the denial of participation rights in rule-making procedures. While it should be acknowledged that normative acts tend to affect natural and legal persons in a different way than individual decisions addressed to them, the impact that they may have in their legal sphere may also ground the recognition of participation rights in this case. This impact is likely to occur in the EU legal system, since the content of the act is concretely determined by a Treaty basis. The latter's object, aim, and policy context may require or favour that the acts adopted contain sufficiently precise provisions which substantively affect the legal sphere of natural and legal persons. From this perspective, the contestation of participation rights relying essentially on institutional arguments is even more inadequate. In these cases, by analogy, the persons affected should be granted a right to participate in the procedure that affects their rights and interests, irrespective of the formal nature of the act. Besides, going beyond the formal nature of the act to acknowledge that it may have legal effects that in principle it would not have is coherent with other features of the EU legal system. Therefore, bearing in mind the rationales of participation, participation rights should be granted whenever an act, irrespective of its status or legal qualification, affects substantively the rights and interests of certain persons, subject to the limits that should be put to these procedural rights.[99]

5.3 Beyond Formal Boundaries: Legal Protection and Participation

The above analysis has demonstrated the limits placed by the Courts on participation rights. These limits pertain essentially to the persons and acts excluded from the scope of these rights. First, the bilateral scheme according to which the right to be heard is granted to those affected by an act in an equivalent way to that of an addressee of an individual decision, had the effect of excluding access to the decisional procedure of those who cannot be regarded to be in such a position but who are nonetheless substantively affected by an act. Secondly, participation rights have been refused altogether in relation to normative acts, irrespective of whether their content is liable to produce substantial adverse effects in the legal sphere of natural and legal persons. Whenever there is no express provision requiring participation, the only possible exception to this outright refusal are the cases where the normative act may be considered to be of individual and direct concern to certain persons. However, as was demonstrated above, the consequences to derive from this assessment in terms of participation rights are not always consistent. Therefore, be it because of their position in relation to an individual decision or because of the normative nature of the act at issue, holders of rights and of legally protected interests, who are substantively affected by the act and should on this basis be given access to the decisional procedure, are denied legally protected and judicially enforceable participation rights.

The Courts' construction of the right to be heard and their approach to participation rights in rule-making procedures are intertwined. The refusal of similar procedural rights in rule-making is *prima facie* logical, given that the bilateral relationship established between a person and the decision-maker is the decisive structural element of the right to be heard and is inseparable from the adverse effect produced in the person's legal sphere, which places them in the position of an addressee.[100] From this perspective,

[99] See, above, Chapter 2, Section 2.6.
[100] Chapter 4, Sub-section 4.2.3 and Section 4.3.

the interplay between the Courts' stance with regard to participation rights in relation to individual acts, on the one hand, and to normative acts, on the other, is perhaps one of the most consistent and stable aspects of the EU Courts' case law on the matter, contrasting with the impression of incoherence that was highlighted elsewhere in this book.[101]

The message is clear: not all acts and not every degree of adversity require the procedural protection of the persons concerned through the recognition of participation rights. This principled position is, as such, defensible. Participation rights need to be placed within certain objective limits, if for no other reason than because they tend to conflict with the effectiveness of decisional procedures. Nevertheless, the Courts' stance denies participation rights in situations that are substantively analogous to those that ground the right to be heard, or at least to persons whose interests are 'perceptibly affected' by EU acts.[102] This is first and foremost due to the fact that the Courts have in general maintained a formal approach to participation rights, notwithstanding their groundbreaking contribution to the furtherance of the right to be heard, in particular during the 1970s and 1990s.[103] With regard to individual decisions, as shown above, the bilateral scheme described prevails over the adverse effect that an act may produce on the legal sphere of private persons. A formal approach is, in any case, much stronger regarding participation in rule-making, where, as a rule, participation rights are denied irrespective of their impact on the person's rights and interests. Thus, the relevance of the distinction between acts of general and individual scope—a consequence of the bilateral scheme—is one of the major hindrances to an adequate procedural protection of the persons affected by EU acts and the factor that most contributes to a mismatch between the powers exercised by EU regulatory and administrative entities and this procedural protection. This is all the more contestable as the very distinction between the two different types of acts is far from being straightforward. An additional factor contributing to this restrictive stance lies in the abovementioned prevalence of the dignitarian rationale and the purpose of defence that ground the procedural intervention of affected persons.

The shortcomings of the Courts' case law could be overcome if participation rights were conceived as reflecting the material administrative

[101] Chapter 4, Sub-section 4.2.1.

[102] To use the formulation of the right to be heard as stated in *Transocean Marine Paint Association*, *cit.*, n. 26, paragraph 14.

[103] Chapter 4, Sub-section 4.2.2.

relationship which underlies the procedure and were not determined by the type of act that shapes or rules this administrative relationship. Their entitlement would thus reflect the links of advantageous and disadvantageous positions established by force of the regulatory intervention between the decision-maker, public, and private persons. This corresponds essentially to the concept of participation put forward in Chapter 2. From this perspective, the decisive factor to trigger the recognition of participation rights is not the type of act or the structure of the procedure followed for its adoption, but effectively the material connection of the persons concerned to the procedure given the ability of the ensuing act to cause a change in their legal position. It is not a requirement that they be directly and individually concerned by an act as if they were its addressees, but that the participants have a legally protected material interest that may be substantively affected by the outcome of the procedure. Further, if one considers that participation as defence, underpinned by the protection of the person's dignity, and participation as collaboration, grounded in its role as facilitator of more accurate and efficient decision-making, are intertwined and not easily severable, the justification for procedural intervention is not limited to defending the stakes of the persons concerned in the outcome of the procedure.[104] Their contribution to decision-making, namely to the appropriateness and accurateness of the final decision, may equally underpin participation rights. If this is capable of extending the range of persons that may access the procedure claiming a right to participate,[105] it is nevertheless submitted that only those with a particular connection to the material relationship underlying the procedure are in a position that allows them to make the aforementioned contribution.

This position breaks with the bilateral scheme that has formally delimited the scope of the right to be heard. Participation rights remain, in any case, grounded in the particular relation of the participants with the material situation which motivated the procedure, or, in other words, in the degree to which their substantive rights and legally protected interests are affected. Participation rights are justified where the regulatory activity of the EU institutions and bodies shapes legal administrative relationships between public and private entities. This occurs when EU acts either define or decisively determine the content of the rights, interests, duties, and charges that are recognized or impinge upon the persons concerned. This

[104] See, in a similar sense, Azoulai, *op. cit.*, n. 76, pp. 393–5.

[105] See the analysis above (Chapter 4, Sub-section 4.2.2) regarding the judgment in *Technische Universität München*.

should be assessed independently of the form of the act. The fact that this type of effect may be more likely to occur as a result of individual decisions does not imply that it cannot occur as a result of a normative act. Instead, the verification of this effect depends on the convergence of two variables. First, the type of power exercised by the EU institutions and bodies needs to be such as to interfere with the rights, interests, duties, and charges that private persons enjoy or endure. Secondly, the participants need to have a sufficiently close connection with the material situation that is the subject of regulation. The persons concerned are therefore holders of subjective rights and legally protected interests that are affected by the exercise of those powers, i.e. holders of substantive rights or of interests protected by the legal system, which are touched by the procedure and which, by force of the pertinent legal norms and principles, are relevant to the material situation at issue. As such, they should be considered in the final decision.[106]

The fact that participation rights are granted to persons other than those formally or substantively targeted by the procedure does not mean that persons affected cannot be treated differently *inter se*. Not all legal positions are protected in the same way by the legal system. In particular, the stronger substantive protection of subjective rights may justify that their holders have 'privileged access' to the communication with the decisional entities.[107] Situations in which sanctions or penalties may be imposed on a person or in which decisions are taken that impose restrictions on their fundamental rights correspond to the very core of participation rights, or to the right to be heard as this has been conceived by the Courts. Here the dignitarian rationale prevails over the instrumental rationale of participation and this may require that they are afforded reinforced procedural guarantees, such as a right to an oral hearing, the right against self-incrimination, the right to be assisted by a lawyer, and legal privilege. These guarantees, in turn, are likely not to be required in cases where the participation of affected persons is legally valued essentially on the basis of their ability to voice interests that need to be taken into account by the decision-maker as part of the overall assessment that grounds the final decision—for example, when a traders' or consumers' association intervenes to voice the collective or diffuse interests affected by the outcome of the procedure, for the defence of which they were created. In this last instance, and according

[106] See below Chapter 7, Sub-section 7.3.3 and Chapter 8, Sub-section 8.2.3.

[107] On the distinction between holders of subjective rights and holders of legally protected interests, see Chapter 2, Section 2.3.

to the circumstances of the case, the deciding body may delimit the subject matter in relation to which it hears these interested parties. They might therefore not be given access to all the information. This might, for example, lead to different standards of interpretation of the exception on access to documents defined in Article 4(3) of Regulation No. 1049/2001.[108] Moreover, while the statement of reasons should take into account the interest which the addressees of the measure and other persons affected in their subjective rights may have in obtaining explanations, the duty to give reasons does not require the specific situation of holders of legally protected interests.[109] Between the two poles in which it is possible to identify a prevailing rationale, different degrees of procedural protection stemming from participation rights may be envisaged depending on the specific circumstances of each case, in particular on the type of subjective position affected and on the type of constraint or effect produced by the final act, as well as on the relevant applicable rules. Concretely, the circles of interest which need to be considered by the decision-maker, the position of their holders, and their corresponding degree of procedural protection result from the principles and norms which regulate the substance of the subject matter.

As mentioned elsewhere in the book, this distinction is part of the balancing exercise that the decision-maker needs to perform while assessing a given situation. It should be defined in each concrete case, taking full account of the normative scope of protection that arises from the applicable norms.[110]

The argument that the nature of the act does not interfere with the recognition or otherwise of participation rights does not, however, amount to denying that the recognition of these rights in procedures leading to the adoption of normative acts may be problematic. Some of the related difficulties and the possible ways to tackle them have already been mentioned in this book, namely with regard to the great number of people who, on the basis of the conception sustained in this book, may be entitled to

[108] Regulation No. 1049/2001, of the European Parliament and the Council, of 30 May 2001, regarding public access to European Parliament, Council and Commission documents (OJ L 145/43, 31.5.2001). On the applicability of these rules in circumstances in which access to information serves participation in decisional procedures, see below, Sub-section 5.4.1.

[109] As will be see in more detail below, this results from the case law of the Courts on the duty to give reasons (Sub-section 5.4.2). These different procedural statuses are substantiated in the sector studies (see below, Chapter 7, Sub-section 7.3.3 and, in particular, Chapter 8, Sub-section 8.2.3).

[110] See Chapter 2, Section 2.3.

participate.[111] Another problem pertains to the fact that it may be more difficult to identify those who are sufficiently concerned and therefore should be granted participation rights. However, these are not insurmountable difficulties. To begin with, in some cases the normative act may refer to the persons concerned by name, in which case it is likely that it in fact contains an administrative decision. In others, particularly affected persons may have been identified beforehand, given the 'concreteness' of the act.[112] Others may be identified because they have informally contacted the Commission exposing their situation. This is more likely to occur with more powerful lobbyists, but it might also happen that Member States communicate the particular situation of certain persons to the competent EU institution before the adoption of regulatory acts that might harm national markets or specific producers.[113] Limiting access to these persons would favour inequality of access to the procedure, in particular in the first case. There are, however, alternatives to broaden the scope of persons identified during the procedure. If it comes to the attention of the decision-maker during sessions of public discussion that other persons may be affected by the proposed act, the decision-maker should accord them a right to participate. In any case, these persons are those entitled to participation rights on the basis of the rules presented above and should justify this entitlement. On this basis, those who until then had not had access to the procedure could be thus identified.

Countering one of the main criticisms of public participation, it is submitted that granting participation rights in the terms proposed could have the effect of countervailing the influence of the more powerful lobbyists, at least to a certain extent. The argument is as follows. Communication channels to decision-makers, privileged in some cases, exist independently of participation rights. Providing the persons concerned by a given act with a legal channel to express their views on the possible future decision would create legal conditions for equal access, broaden the possibilities of access, while at the same time filtering access by the need to demonstrate a sufficient connection to the material relationship that is shaped by the

[111] See, Chapter 2, Section 2.6.

[112] For example, in a procedure leading to the adoption of a Commission decision adopting the list of sites of EU relevance for purposes of environmental protection, the landowners affected are identifiable by the Commission, since the areas of land covered may be identified according to geographical criteria (cf. Opinion of Advocate General Bot, delivered on the 23 October 2008, in Case C-362/06 P, *Markku Sahlstedt and Others v Commission*, [2009] ECR I-2903, paragraph 112).

[113] See, for example, *Lorte*, *cit.*, n. 94, paragraph 62.

act to be adopted.[114] A sufficient connection to the material relationship may be established, for example, when a legal person was constituted to defend the promotion of sustainable use of natural resources and operates in a geographical area that is affected by a regulation defining the allowable catches of certain fish stocks;[115] or when, by virtue of a decision addressed by the Commission to an exporting third country, a group of undertakings is prevented from complying with previously agreed contracts established with exporters from that country.[116]

In addition, it is noteworthy that practices similar to notice and comment, at least for some types of acts, already exist in EU rule-making, which means that this solution would not represent a disproportionate burden to the EU institutions.[117] The possible effects of the proposed extension of participation rights are twofold. First, the possibility of excluding participation in acts that are liable to have adverse effects in the legal sphere of natural and legal persons would no longer be left to the discretionary choice of the Commission. Secondly, this would generalize a practice that already exists in some cases, where the Commission is committed to ensuring the effectiveness of existing consultation procedures: the information provided by holders of participation rights would be treated and reported, revealing where necessary how the different aspects implicated in the examination of the case were considered in the final act, as well as demonstrating that the legally protected interests involved were sufficiently taken into account. Before concluding this point, it should be noted that the decision-maker is not required to be aware of all potential impacts of the envisaged act and to take them into account in the final decision. The decision-maker ought to

[114] It should be noted that empirical studies suggest that the lack of formal rules of participation has been one of the pitfalls of the practices of consultation in which the Commission has engaged so far. See Sandra Kröger (2008) 'Nothing but consultation: the place of organised civil society in EU policy-making across policies', European Governance Papers (EUROGOV) No. C-08-03, <http://www.connex-network.org/eurogov/pdf/egp-connex-C-08-03.pdf> p. 23. This is suggested also by Maria Paola Ferretti (2008) 'Participatory strategies in the regulation of GMO products in the EU', in Jens Steffek, Claudia Kissling, and Patricia Nanz (eds), *Civil Society Participation in European and Global Governance. A Cure for the Democratic Deficit?*, Basingstoke, New York: Palgrave Macmillan, pp. 166–84, pointing out the failures of the due consideration model of consultation followed by the Commission.

[115] See the facts of Case T-91/07, *WWF-UK Ltd v Council and Commission* [2008] ECR II-81.

[116] See the facts of Case T-238/07, *Ristic and Others v Commission* [2009] ECR II-117.

[117] For example, for certain cases, impact assessments could be extended and adapted for these purposes (in this sense, Ian Bartle (2006) 'Legitimising EU regulation: procedural accountability, participation, or better consultation?', in Richard Bellamy, Dario Castiglione, and Jo Shaw (eds), *Making European Citizens: Civic Inclusion in a Transnational Context*, Basingstoke, New York: Palgrave Macmillan pp. 133–53, at p. 148).

demonstrate that they assessed carefully the material situation on which they need to decide. Within the limits of the principle of care, the different public and private interests at issue should be known and considered by the decision-maker, not to satisfy them, but to consider and balance them, thereby ensuring that decisions are taken with respect for the rights and interests of private persons.

The approach to participation rights put forward here raises one additional problem. Once one identifies, by reference to the rule of law, the situations that should give rise to participation rights, the procedural relationship that intervenes between decision-maker and participants is put within the realm of judicial review (except where the rules of standing block access to courts). In fact, being a matter of procedural rights, it should be possible to control the correctness of the decision-maker's conduct in this regard, in order to ensure respect for the legal positions of the persons concerned. This amounts to extending the power of the courts to decisions that would otherwise remain outside their reach, an effect that may be unwelcome both to courts and decision-makers.[118] This could harm both judicial decision-making, as a result of possible workload increases, and administrative decision-making, since administrative decisions may be invalidated on procedural grounds, an effect that is likely to entail high costs.[119]

Two main arguments may counter the assumption that 'judicialization' of administrative decision-making should be rejected by denying an extension of participation rights. First, the procedural protection of subjective

[118] The dangers associated with a 'judicialization' of the administrative activity have been widely debated in other legal systems. In particular in the United States, this has been discussed with respect to the 'hard look' approach adopted by US courts when reviewing informal rule-making in light of possible 'arbitrary, capricious, or abuse of discretion', one of the grounds that may lead to setting aside informal rules, according to the US Administrative Procedure Act of 1946. On this and other causes for 'ossification' see, among others, Thomas O. McGarity (1992) 'Some thoughts on 'deossifying' the rulemaking process', *Duke Law Journal*, Vol. 41, n. 6, pp. 1385–462. For a divergent opinion, see Mark Seidenfeld (1997) 'Demystifying deossification: rethinking recent proposals to modify judicial review of notice and comment rulemaking', *Texas Law Review*, Vol. 75, n. 3, pp. 438–524 (which led to a response from McGarity in the same year—'Courts and the ossification of rulemaking: a response to Professor Seidenfeld', *Texas Law Review*, Vol. 75, n. 3, pp. 525–58). For a broader view of the debate, see William S. Jordan III (2000) 'Ossification revisited: does arbitrary and capricious review significantly interfere with agency ability to achieve regulatory goals through informal rulemaking?', *Northwestern University Law Review*, Vol. 94, n. 2, pp. 393–450.

[119] In general on the advantages and disadvantages of securing participation by law and of leaving it to the policy process Paul Graig, *op. cit.*, n. 43, pp. 328–9.

rights and legally protected interests should not be made contingent upon the effectiveness or efficiency of decision-making.[120] Secondly, there are ways of circumventing undesirable effects of increased judicial powers over decisional procedures stemming from the exercise of participation rights. To begin with, one may defend a model of judicial review that ensures control over the decision-maker's assessment as to the legitimacy of interested persons to intervene in the procedure, as to the respect of the conditions upon which depends the effectiveness of participation (e.g. access to information), and as to whether or not the views expressed were effectively taken into account, in similar terms to those followed by the Court in the *Fern Olivieri* case, discussed in Chapter 7.[121] Although the boundaries between procedural and substantive review are difficult to draw,[122] it is submitted that this standard of judicial review could avoid excessively intrusive control by the Courts. Moreover, with regard to legal acts where the personal factor is not determinant in the underlying material situation—the decision does not target identifiable individuals nor does the decision-maker need to consider the individual position of specific persons—the possible annulment of the act on the basis of an infringement of procedural rules can be made dependent on the harmless error rule (i.e. the act is only annulled when it is proved that, had the infringement not occurred, the final outcome would have been a different one).

Note that this does not amount to defending the application of the harmless error rule as the Courts have applied it so far. This rule provides the judiciary a fair margin of manoeuvre to safeguard decisions which are otherwise sound but nonetheless vitiated by procedural flaws. The Courts have used it rather inconsistently, at times resulting in a depletion of the right to be heard. Here, it is defended within specific limits. First, it cannot be applied when the personal position of an affected person needs to be assessed as such by the decision-maker. Secondly, the decision-maker should demonstrate that they have nonetheless performed a diligent assessment of the legal interests affected by the final act.

In a similar vein, one may argue that only in cases where the substantive rights and interests of concerned persons have been harmed by the vitiated

[120] The effectiveness of decision-making may impact on the scope and forms of exercising participation rights, but sufficient safeguards are still required in order not to deplete completely the content of such rights. On this, see above Chapter 2, Section 2.6.

[121] Sub-section 7.3.3.

[122] On this, Craig, *op. cit.*, n. 43, pp. 396–7.

act is its annulment justified. Moreover, in certain cases, one may resort to an excusable error rule, for example, when an entity representative of legally protected interests involved in the decision-making claims to have been illegitimately excluded from the procedure, while the decision-maker has nonetheless sought to ensure the presence of the persons affected and the inclusiveness of the procedure. This may be grounded in the constraints which the administration, operating normally, is objectively subject to. However, similarly to what was defended above, the decision-maker ought to show that, despite the procedural flaw, they have diligently assessed the material situation under examination. This may be envisaged for situations in which it is more difficult to identify the persons whose subjective rights and legally protected interests may be affected by the act, as might be the case in rule-making procedures.

One further difficulty with the extension of participation rights proposed in this book pertains to the restricted rules of private standing in the EU legal system, which remain in place (with the exception of self-executing regulatory acts). In particular, holders of legally protected interests whose participation rights are breached (supposing a scenario in which the proposed extension would be endorsed) would be very likely denied standing, unless they could prove their direct and individual concern with regard to the act adopted. This could be countered by recognizing a direct and individual concern to those who were given access to the procedure or were denied access although they had a legal claim thereto, on the bases explained above. While this has been recognized by the Courts in some instances, it has been denied in relation to acts of a general nature, in particular when the intervention in the decisional procedure is not backed by an enabling legal provision.[123] However, this would admittedly be excessive in the case of those persons whose procedural intervention is legally assessed not so much on the basis of their being individually affected as of the objective interests that they voice in the procedure.[124] Even though one can discuss whether a substantial adverse effect could be a legitimate reading of individual concern,[125] in the absence of broader rules of standing and of class actions, compliance with participation rights, in certain cases,

[123] On this, Craig, *op. cit.*, n. 43, p. 134. More recent examples are *Etimine*, *cit.*, n. 85, paragraphs 108 to 110, and *Norilsk Nickel*, *cit.*, n. 69, paragraphs 102 to 103.

[124] On this, see below, Chapter 7, Sub-section 7.3.3 and, in particular, Chapter 8, Sub-section 8.2.3.

[125] Craig, *op. cit.*, n. 43, p. 343.

can in principle only be scrutinized by the European Ombudsman, to the extent that non-compliance with these rights may be considered a form of maladministration.[126]

As mentioned, Article 263(4) TFEU introduced one significant change with regard to the standing of natural and legal persons in actions for annulment: they are not required to demonstrate individual concern when pleading for the annulment of self-executing regulatory acts. The limitation and imprecision of this new rule notwithstanding,[127] this opens new possibilities to private litigants seeking enforcement of participation rights in rule-making.[128] These will be narrower or broader depending on the Courts' interpretation of 'regulatory acts'. Together with other provisions of the Lisbon Treaty—namely Article 11(1) to (3) TEU, Articles 15(1) and 298(1) TFEU—this might spur a change in the Courts' principled denial of participation rights in rule-making. Nevertheless, it is as yet uncertain if this will occur and which views the Courts will adopt in this matter. For current purposes, it suffices to underline that the possible mismatch between the recognition of participation rights defended in the book and the possibilities of judicial review is potentially narrower under the current rules on private standing.

To conclude, it is contended that a concept of participation rights defined by reference to the persons whose intervention is considered legally relevant, in the terms presented above, and to the functions of this intervention intended as a convergence between a dignitarian and an instrumental rationale, is capable of exceeding the boundaries of the Courts' case law on this matter without extending them to an unreasonable extent. Exceeding these boundaries is essential if EU administrative law is to respond to a paradigm that is respectful of the person's rights and interests while ensuring a proper exercise of the administrative power. Keeping participation within legal boundaries is essential if one aims to propound the recognition of judicially enforceable rights, since, for this purpose, these need to be

[126] See Chapter 4, Sub-section 4.1.1, n. 27.

[127] See Chapter 4, Sub-section 4.1.1.

[128] See, for instance, the action brought on January 2010, by Inuit Tapiriit Kanatami e.a. against the Parliament and the Council (OJ C 100/41, 17.4.2010), where the applicants contest the validity of a regulation on trade in seal products on the basis, *inter alia*, that they were not heard in the respective procedure despite the impact of this regulation on their subsistence possibilities. Admittedly filing an action does not amount to having standing. However, should the Courts grant them standing, the fact that litigants are invoking participation rights in this case provides the Court with the opportunity to revise its case law on participation in rule-making procedures.

grounded in legal principles and substantive rights or legally protected interests. Participation in this sense is therefore distinct from other uses that have been made of this concept, particularly in the governance initiatives of the EU and, especially, by the Commission.

The last section of this chapter will dwell upon the question of how other procedural rights and duties, ancillary to the exercise of participation rights, contribute to the legal protection of persons affected by EU regulatory activity. The following pages will therefore focus on the relationships between these rights and duties, on the one hand, and participation rights, on the other. Its goal is to illustrate how the proposed extension of participation rights impacts on these relationships and demonstrate the extent to which it may be considered to 'match' these other rights and duties. It will be concluded that, with some nuances and adaptations regarding the duty to give reasons, and with the exception of the duty of careful and impartial examination, the proposed extension of participation rights does not require an expansion of these ancillary procedural rights. As a rule, their scope is broad enough to accommodate this extension.

5.4 The Other Facets of Procedural Protection

Where recognized, participation rights constitute the ability of the persons affected to express their views 'on the truth and relevance of the facts and circumstances alleged as well as on the documents used by the Commission' to support its decision.[129] This is their generally acknowledged minimum content, which sets out the ability of persons affected to influence the possible outcome of the procedures.[130] Participation rights require, in particular, that

[129] Case 85/76, *Hoffmann-La Roche & Co. AG v Commission* [1979] ECR 461, paragraph 11. This reference in this case is restricted to the right to be heard in individual procedures.

[130] Referring specifically to the right to be heard, see Maria C. Baruffi (2001) *La tutela dei singoli nei procedimenti amministrativi comunitari*, Milano: Giuffrè, p. 87; Craig, *op. cit.*, n. 43, pp. 363–5; and Takis Tridimas (2006) *The General Principles of EU Law*, Oxford: Oxford University Press, pp. 385–6 (noting that, beyond general observations, 'the precise requirements of the right to be heard depend on the type of procedure at issue and the particular circumstances of the case', p. 386); Barbier de la Serre (2006) 'Procedural justice in the European Community case-law concerning the rights of the defence: essentialist and instrumental trends', *European Public Law*, Vol. 12, n. 2, pp. 225–50, at p. 233. For a more detailed account of the technical rules which organize the possibility of influencing the content of the act, Azoulai, *op. cit.*, n. 76, pp. 154–64, by reference to the regulations ruling the main areas of EU economic law (competition, antitrust, state aid, and anti-dumping).

the persons concerned are informed, in 'good time', of the existence of the procedure, of the envisaged decision, and of the supporting documents.[131] On the other hand, the persons affected by a given measure need to be aware of the reasons that grounded it, so as to 'enable them to defend their rights and to enable the Court to exercise its supervisory jurisdiction'.[132] As such, participation rights require at least two ancillary procedural guarantees the absence of which deprives them of their substance: the right of access to information and the duty to give reasons. Apart from this 'logical and chronological inseparable whole',[133] the duty of care and impartial examination in dealing with decisional procedures as well as the right to communicate with the EU institutions in one of the languages of the Member States also need to accompany participation rights, if these are to be effective.

These are rights and duties *a se stante* that, as mentioned, are taken here in a very specific perspective: their relationships with participation rights. These have been either shaped or reflected by the Courts' case law on the basis of the right to be heard, in the strict meaning established by the EU Courts. Hence, the term 'right to be heard' will be used whenever pertinent to refer to the specific scope of participation rights recognized by the EU Courts. It should be noted that the relevance of the distinction between the stricter scope coincident with the judge-made right to be heard and the wider meaning of participation rights argued for in this work is not uniformly relevant for the considerations that follow. For example, while, for the sake of precision, one needs to make this distinction when mentioning access to information, this is virtually immaterial for the purpose of analysing the relationship between participation and language rights.

5.4.1 *Access to information, access to the file, and access to documents*

The right of access to information is a fundamental prerequisite for an effective exercise of participation rights. This axiom has been acknowledged by the Courts and highlighted in the literature with regard to the specific relations between access to file and right to be heard, and it is now enshrined in Article 41(2) of the Charter of Fundamental Rights.[134] When the

131 *Transocean*, *cit.*, n. 26, paragraph 15.

132 *Technische Universität München*, *cit.*, n. 38, paragraph 26.

133 Azoulai, *op. cit.*, n. 76, p. 103, n. 582.

134 For a recent account on the Courts' case law, see *Alrosa*, *cit.*, paragraph 197. See, among others, Koen Lenaerts and Jan Vanhamme (1997) 'Procedural rights of private parties in the Community administrative process', *Common Market Law Review*, Vol. 34, n. 3, pp. 531–69, at

former is taken as an ancillary guarantee to the latter, it requires that the holder of the right to be heard is 'at least... able to put his own case on the documents taken into account by the Community institution' in the case made against them.[135] In other words, the person concerned should be given 'the opportunity to examine all the documents in the investigation file which may be relevant for its defence'.[136]

However, as is widely known, the right of access to file associated with the rights of the defence is only one of the dimensions of the right of access to information in EU law. The right of access to documents, currently enshrined in Article 15(3) TFEU and Article 42 of the Charter of Fundamental Rights, entitles 'any citizen of the Union, and any natural or legal person residing or having its registered office in a Member State' to have access to documents held by the Union institutions, bodies, offices, and agencies.[137] As conceived in the EU legal system, this right

p. 541. 'Right of access to information' is taken here, perhaps inexactly, as a broad term encompassing both the right of access to the file and the right of access to documents.

[135] Case T-42/96, *Eyckeler & Malt AG v Commission* [1998] ECR II-401, paragraphs 79 and 80.

[136] This was first stated as such in Case T-30/91, *Solvay SA v Commission* [1995] ECR II-1775, paragraphs 81 and 83, and Case T-36/91, *Imperial Chemical Industries plc (ICI) v Commission* [1995] ECR II-1847, paragraphs 91 and 93. It was more recently reiterated in Joined Cases C-204/00 P, C-205/00 P, C-211/00 P, C-213/00 P, C-217/00 P, and C-219/00 P, *Aalborg Portland A/S and Others v Commission* [2004] ECR I-123, paragraph 68, which contains the quoted sentence; and in Case T-410/03, *Hoechst GmbH v Commission* [2008] ECR II-881, paragraph 145. On the relevance of the *Solvay* and *ICI* judgments, as well as on the previous status of the right of access to the file see, in particular, Hanns Peter Nehl (1999) *Principles of Administrative Procedure in EC Law*, Oxford: Hart Publishing, pp. 45–55, and Azoulai, *op. cit.*, n. 76, pp. 174–81. See also, Koen Lenaerts (2004) 'In the Union we trust: trust-enhancing principles of Community law', *Common Market Law Review*, Vol. 41, n. 2, pp. 317–43, at pp. 324–9, and Craig, *op. cit.*, n. 43, pp. 365–9, the latter explaining the origins and consolidation of the right.

[137] Circumscribing this right to the documents *held* by the Union institutions implies referring to the latter period of evolution of the right in the EU legal order, subsequent to the adoption of Regulation No. 1049/2001 (quoted below note 143). Only with the TFEU has this been widened to bodies, offices, and agencies (although in practice many of them were already bound by the regulation by force of EU legislation). The literature covering the right of access to documents and, especially, transparency, is extensive. On this evolution, covering the different stages, see in particular Claudia Morviducci (2000) 'Diritto di accesso ai documenti delle istituzioni e Trattato de Amsterdam' *Rivista Italiana di Diritto Pubblico Comunitario*, Vol. 10, n. 4, pp. 665–718; Steven Peers (2003) 'The new regulation on access to documents: a critical analysis', *Yearbook of European Law*, pp. 385–442; Marc Maes (2007), Vol. 22, 'L'accès du public aux documents des Institutions de la Communauté européenne: vers une révision du règlement (CE) 1049/2001', *Revue du Droit de l'Union Européenne*, n. 2, pp. 411–32. On the developments and current status of the right, underlining its fundamental nature, see moreover Opinion of Advocate General Poiares Maduro delivered on 18 July 2007 in Case C-64/05 P, *Kingdom of Sweden v Commission* [2007] ECR I-11389, paragraphs 38–43.

is not a procedural guarantee that serves the procedural intervention of interested persons in a specific decisional procedure that concerns them. Being linked to the principle of transparency, it is more broadly 'intended to secure a more significant role for citizens in the decision-making process and to ensure that the administration acts with greater propriety, efficiency and responsibility vis-à-vis the citizens in a democratic system'.[138] It therefore 'helps to strengthen the principle of democracy and respect for fundamental rights',[139] while giving 'citizens the opportunity to monitor more effectively the lawfulness of the exercise of public powers'.[140] Thus, it is not excluded that access to documents may take place after a given administrative procedure has been closed so as to allow public scrutiny, or, at least, scrutiny by persons interested in the institutions' conduct.[141]

It follows that the rationales behind the right of access to file and the right of access to documents are different. Their scope also varies. As a procedural guarantee ancillary to the right to be heard, the concrete scope of the right of access to file is defined in secondary sector legislation, it has been refined by the Courts' judgments in light of the purpose of defence, and, subject to a few exceptions, it is limited to the file, that is, to the documents that might be relevant to the defence of the person concerned.[142] By contrast, access to documents under Regulation No.

[138] Case T-211/00, *Kuijer v Council* [2002] ECR II-485, paragraph 52; Case T-84/03, *Maurizio Turco v Council* [2004] ECR II-4061, paragraph 53; Case T-403/05, *MyTravel Group plc v Commission* [2008] ECR II-2027, paragraph 49.

[139] *Kuijer*, *cit.*, paragraph 52; *Turco*, *cit.*, paragraph 53, reiterated in Joined Cases C-514/07 P, C-528/07 P, and C-532/07 P, *Sweden v Association de la Presse International ASBL (API) and Commission, Association de la Presse International ASBL (API) v Commission, and Commission v Association de la Presse International ASBL (API)* [2010] nyr., paragraph 68.

[140] Joined Cases T-391/03 and T-70/04, *Yves Franchet and Daniel Byk v Commission* [2006] ECR II-2023, paragraph 112.

[141] Case T-194/04, *The Bavarian Lager Co. Ltd v Commission* [2007] ECR II-4523, quashed on appeal on the grounds that the Court of First Instance (General Court) wrongly interpreted the exception of Article 4(1) (b) of Regulation No. 1049/2001 and did not respect the EU legislation on data protection with regard to the request to access the document at issue in its entirety (Case C-28/08 P, *Commission v The Bavarian Lager Co Ltd* [2010] nyr.; see in particular paragraphs 56 to 65 and 76 to 80). Moreover, access to file may also be still relevant after adoption of the decision for the purposes of judicial review (Craig, *op. cit.*, n. 43, p. 365).

[142] On the meaning of file, see Matthew Levitt (1997) 'Access to the file: the Commission's administrative procedures in cases under Articles 85 and 86', *Common Market Law Review*, Vol. 34, n. 6, pp. 1413–44, at pp. 1420–3 and Sandra Bartelt (2006) in her commentary to Case T-2/03, '*Verein für Konsumenteninformation* v. *Commission*', *Common Market Law Review*, Vol 43, n. 1, pp. 191–206, at pp. 200–1.

1049/2001 refers to any document irrespective of the applicant's interest in having access to the documents requested. In fact, the person interested in the disclosure does not need to state the reasons for disclosure in the application.[143] The regime of the respective exceptions also differs. With regard to access to the file, the 'legitimate interests of confidentiality and of professional and business secrets' need to be balanced with the right of every person to have access to their file. These exceptions, now contained in Article 41(2) of the Charter of Fundamental Rights, result from the combination between the consolidated practices of the Commission and the Courts' case law developed in particular in the field of competition law.[144] In this field, limitations to accessing the file allow us to distinguish the procedural status of different parties concerned on the basis of the role that they are assigned within the procedure, complainants and other third parties having more limited access to information than the persons who are targeted by the decision. In contrast, under Regulation No. 1049/2001, refusal of access to documents is possible on the grounds listed in this regulation and is subject to a specific examination following demanding procedural rules that have been successively refined, especially by the Court of First Instance.[145]

Despite their different background, rationale, scope, and regime, one may argue that, in the current state of development of EU law, these two rights partially overlap. They overlap in the 'inner circle' where access to documents may be attached to the purpose of procedural intervention in a given decisional procedure. From a different perspective, one could consider that, in this respect, access to the file and access to documents consubstantiate the same right, albeit with different scopes that are delimited according to the rationale prevailing in each case.[146] Or, more accurately, that 'they are legally distinct, but... lead to a comparable situation from a

[143] Articles 2(3) and 6(1) of Regulation No. 1049/2001, *cit.*, n. 108.

[144] On this, Levitt *op. cit.*, pp. 1424–40 (the author highlights an excessive restrictive practice of the Commission in interpreting these exceptions, at the time). On the background of Article 41(2) of the Charter of Fundamental Rights, see 'Explanations relating to the Charter of Fundamental Rights', now in OJ C 83/389, 30.3.2010, p. 28. Specifically on the balancing between access and protection of secrets, see Azoulai, *op. cit.*, n. 76, pp. 185–98.

[145] On these rules, see, for example, Case T-2/03, *Verein für Konsumenteninformation v Commission* [2005] ECR II-1121, paragraphs 69 and 75.

[146] Adopting this latter construction, see Opinion of Advocate General Trstenjak delivered on 13 March 2008, in Case C-204/07 P, *CAS SpA v Commission*, [2008] ECR I-6135, paragraphs 93 and 94, quoting Opinion of Advocate General Tesauro in Case C-58/94 *Netherlands v Council* [1996] ECR I-2169, points 13 to 15.

practical point of view'.[147] This aspect is important when considering whether current rules on access to documents could match an extension of participation rights, in particular given the existence in some areas of law of restrictive rules on access to file of the so-called third parties. In fact, persons concerned by administrative procedures may avail themselves of the rules on access to documents under Regulation No. 1049/2001 if the rules of access to file turn out to be too restrictive in their regard. This has been admitted by the Court of First Instance in *Verein für Konsumenteninformation*. In this instance, a consumer association obtained the annulment of a Commission decision refusing it access to documents, on the basis of an infringement of the procedural rules of Regulation No. 1049/2001. Nevertheless, the documents at issue pertained to an antitrust procedure and, under the applicable legal regime, a consumer association can only be considered a third party to whom access to file is not recognized.[148] In *Franchet and Byk*, the Court of First Instance did not expressly distinguish between the right of access to file and the right of access to documents (a distinction that, moreover, had been invoked by one of the parties), admitting that the rules governing the latter could be used for purposes of defence in administrative procedures.[149] Nevertheless, it held that the application to access documents under Regulation No. 1049/2001 filed by applicants that have a direct interest in the disclosure 'must be examined in the same way as an application from any other person', therefore denying any privileged position to those who resort to the regime of access to documents as persons affected in the course of administrative proceedings.[150] Moreover, in *MyTravel Group*, the Court of First Instance held that

> the fact that an undertaking which is party to a concentration does not have the right of access to the internal documents in the administrative file by virtue of Article 17 (3) of Regulation n. 802/2004 [setting the procedural rules on the control of concentrations] does not mean that it can be ruled out that any person, whoever it

[147] Case C-139/07 P, *Commission v Technische Glaswerke Ilmenau GmbH* [2010], nyr., paragraph 59.

[148] *Verein für Konsumenteninformation*, *cit.*, n. 145. See commentary by Bartelt, *op. cit.*, n. 142, pp. 205–6, who highlights the problems that might follow for the regime of access to file in competition law procedures from an enhanced procedural protection of third parties under Regulation No. 1049/2001. See also Herke R. Kranenborg (2006) 'Is it time to revise the European regulation on public access to documents?', *European Public Law*, Vol. 12, n. 2, pp. 251–74.

[149] *Franchet and Byk*, *cit.*, n. 140, paragraph 22 (referring to the contested decision).

[150] *Yves Franchet and Daniel Byk v Commission*, *cit.*, n. 140, paragraph 82.

may be, may have a right of access to those documents on the basis of the principles laid down in Regulation n. 1049/2001.

It thereby rejected the Commission's argument that the exclusion set by the sector regulation defining the scope of the right of access to file could have an impact in interpreting that undertaking's right of access to documents under Regulation No. 1049/2001.[151] The European Court of Justice recently countered the tendency of the (now) General Court to allow access to documents irrespective of specific rules on access to the files. Contrary to the General Court, it has held that sectoral rules on access to the file must be taken into account for the purposes of interpreting the provisions of Regulation No. 1049/2001, in particular the exceptions that it establishes.[152] While the rules on access to documents remain applicable, this requirement may make it more difficult for third parties possibly excluded from accessing the file to have access to documents on the basis of Regulation No. 1049/2001. For example, the exclusion of interested persons other than the addressee of a decision from the scope of the right to access the file may mean that there is a 'general presumption that disclosure of documents in the administrative file in principle undermines protection of the objectives of investigation activities'.[153] In this case, the interested person who resorts to Regulation No. 1049/2001 to avoid the limits placed on access to the file by specific rules will have to demonstrate that the presumption is not applicable in a given instance or that there is, in any case, an overriding public interest justifying the disclosure.[154]

On the basis of both the judgments of the Court of First Instance and the more recent position of the European Court of Justice, one can identify two main limitations of the request to access documents under Regulation No. 1049/2001 for purposes of participation in decisional procedures. First, irrespective of specific rules on access to file that could impact on the interpretation of Regulation No. 1049/2001, the fact that a request to access documents serves the defence of a person in the context of administrative or judicial procedures is irrelevant for the decision of granting access. According to the Courts' case law, the purpose of Regulation No.

[151] *MyTravel Group*, *cit.*, n. 138, paragraphs 86 to 91 (the quotation is from paragraph 89), in particular, paragraphs 86 and 89. This judgment was under appeal at the time of writing (Case C-506/08 P, *Appeal brought by the Kingdom of Sweden*, OJ C 55/6, 7.3.2009).

[152] *Technische Glaswerke Ilmenau*, *cit.*, n. 147, paragraphs 58, 60, and 61.

[153] *Idem* paragraph 61.

[154] *Idem* paragraph 62.

1049/2001 is to 'guarantee access for everyone to public documents and not merely access for the requesting party to documents concerning him', and, therefore, the applicant's particular interest in accessing documents that personally concern them cannot be taken into account.[155] Likewise, the Court of First Instance has considered that the right to a fair hearing in the context of national judicial proceedings and EU staff disciplinary processes does not constitute an overriding public interest that could justify disclosure, when access is denied on the basis of one of the exceptions of Article 4 (2) of Regulation No. 1049/2001.[156] However, it is not excluded that participation in a decisional procedure could be an important factor to weigh in the decision regarding access to documents, if this purpose does not consist solely of a private interest of defence.[157] Secondly, while Regulation No. 1049/2001 remains an alternative path of accessing information for purposes of participation, specific rules on access to file may remain as a hindrance to broader access sought by persons who are not the addressees of administrative decisions, and who would otherwise be straightforwardly denied access to documents in an administrative file.

Outside these two situations—access to documents with a purely private purpose of defence and specific rules on access to file that continue to restrain broader access to administrative files in procedures leading to individual decisions—the scope of the rules on access to documents is, in principle, broad enough to match an extended scope of participation rights, in particular in rule-making procedures. The right of access to documents has acquired a secure place in the EU legal system, and is crucial for the enhancement of participation rights, as has been implicitly recognized by the Court when stating that the principle of transparency is 'intended to secure a more significant role for citizens in the decision-making

[155] *Franchet and Byk*, *cit.*, n. 140, paragraphs 136 and 137; Case C-266/05 P, *Jose Maria Sison v Council* [2007] ECR I-1233, paragraphs 43 to 48, upholding the Court of First Instance judgment—Joined Cases T-110/03, T-150/03 and T-405/03, *Sison v Council* [2005] ECR II-1429, paragraphs 52 to 55.

[156] In *Franchet and Byk*, the Court held that, while 'the right to a fair hearing is in itself a general interest', in this case, Mr Franchet and Mr Byk invoked a private interest in defending themselves (*cit.*, n. 140, paragraph 138).

[157] See note above. Moreover, the Court has admitted that, in assessing when there is an overriding public interest in disclosure under Article 4(2) of Regulation No. 1049/2001, it is for the institution concerned to strike a balance between 'the public interest in disclosure and the interest which is served by a refusal to disclose in the light, where appropriate, of the arguments put forward by the applicant in that connection' (Case T-36/04, *Association de la presse internationale a.s.b.l. (API) v Commission* [2007] ECR II-3201, paragraph 94, emphasis added).

process'.[158] Indeed, access to documents should be wider 'in cases where the institutions are acting in their legislative capacity, *including under delegated powers*'.[159] While inspired by democratic concerns, this principled position would also allow a broad enough access to documents to the 'new' holders of participation rights in the construction proposed in this book.

5.4.2 *The duty to give reasons*

The duty to state reasons also has, in the EU legal system, an 'independent life' beyond participation rights; in particular it is independent of the right to be heard as it stands in current case law. First, as is widely known, and has been mentioned above, the duty to state the reasons on which the acts of the institutions are based covers all the formally binding instruments of the Union,[160] although the Courts have stressed that the respective requirements are less stringent in relation to normative acts than in relation to individual decisions. Secondly, the applicability of the duty to motivate decisions does not depend on the possible adverse effect of the act with regard to the person or persons concerned by it.[161]

The duty to give reasons is essentially conceived as a requirement of control. First, it is a means to allow, chiefly, Member States and also other persons concerned to ascertain the circumstances in which the Treaty has been applied. This rationale has been largely absent from the Courts' judgments, but seems to be the basic reason grounding the enshrinement of this duty in the Treaty.[162] Secondly, the duty to give reasons is intended as an 'essential connecting element between administrative and judicial procedure'.[163] It enables the persons concerned to access judicial review 'in the

[158] *Kuijer*, *cit.*, n. 138, paragraph 52.

[159] Regulation No. 1049/2001, *cit.*, n. 108, recital 6, reiterated by the European Court of Justice in *Technische Glaswerke Ilmenau*, *cit.*, n. 147, paragraph 60.

[160] Article 296, second paragraph TFEU. On this, See Fernand Schockweiler (1989) 'La motivation des décisions individuelles en droit communautaire et en droit national', *Cahiers de Droit Européen*, Vol. 25, n. 1–2, pp. 3–40, at p. 35; Jean-Victor Louis, Georges Vandersanden, Denis Waelbroeck, and Michel Waelbroeck (1993) *Commentaire Mégret. La Cour de Justice. Les actes des institutions*, Bruxelles: Éditions de l'Université de Bruxelles, pp. 525–30; Jürgen Schwarze (2006) *European Administrative Law*. Revised 1st edn, London: Sweet and Maxwell, pp. 1407–16. For a recent example in the case law, see Case C-310/04, *Spain v Council* [2006] ECR I-7285, paragraphs 57 to 60, and 64 to 65.

[161] Cf. Article 41(2), third indent of the EU Charter of Fundamental Rights. Jill Wakefield (2007) *The Right to Good Administration*, The Netherlands: Kluwer Law International, p. 78.

[162] This is suggested by Schwarze (*op. cit.*, p. 1401).

[163] Lenaerts and Vanhamme, *op. cit.*, n. 134, pp. 562–6, in particular p. 563.

best conditions possible' as to the knowledge of the decisions that affect them, while at the same time facilitating the Courts' judgment in assessing whether the acts have been lawfully adopted.[164] This has been reiterated by the Courts, on several occasions, upholding that

> the statement of reasons required by Article 253 EC [269, second paragraph, TFEU] must disclose in a clear and unequivocal fashion the reasoning followed by the institution which adopted the measure in question in such a way as to enable the persons concerned to ascertain the reasons for the measure and to enable the competent court to exercise its power of review of the lawfulness thereof.[165]

As such, the duty to give reasons functions as 'an indicator of substantive defects in the decision to be examined'.[166] Thirdly, the statement of reasons serves the interest of the decisional body insofar as it contributes to ensuring that all the relevant circumstances were duly balanced and taken into account.[167] In this sense, it serves the principle of care.

This being said, the duty to give reasons may also function as a procedural guarantee ancillary to participation rights, that is, it may contribute to the effectiveness of participation insofar as the persons concerned may be able to infer from the reasons given for the adoption of an act how their interests were weighed in the final decision. This does not mean that all the issues raised by interested parties during a decisional procedure need to be taken into account in the final decision, nor that the views expressed ought to be reflected therein. If the autonomy of the decision-maker is to be preserved, the relationship between these two procedural guarantees needs to be a different, more modest one: the statement of reasons reveals the thrust, the grounds of fact and law that based the decision and, in doing so, reveals the weighing of interests that determined it. In this respect, the duty to give reasons allows both the decisional body and those who are concerned by the decision to verify, from different perspectives, that all the relevant aspects of the case were duly considered.

164 The quotation is from Schockweiler, *op. cit.*, n. 160, p. 33.

165 E.g. Case T-229/02, *Osman Ocalan, on behalf of the Kurdistan Workers' Party (PKK) v Council*, [2008] ECR II-45, paragraph 62. In this case, the Court considered that the above conditions were not complied with and annulled the Council decision inserting the name of the applicant in the list of the persons, groups and entities suspected of terrorist association. This decision merely stated that 'it is "desirable" or that it has been "decided" to adopt an up-to-date list' (paragraph 65). Similarly, Case T-253/04, *Kongra-Gel and others v Council* [2008] ECR II-45, paragraphs 95 and 98, and *Pye Phoy Tay Za*, *cit.*, n. 28, paragraph 95.

166 Schwarze, *op. cit.*, n. 160, p. 1403.

167 Schockweiler, *op. cit.*, n. 160, p. 34; Louis et al., *op. cit.*, n. 160, 524; Schwarze, *op. cit.*, n. 160, p. 1401.

Concretely, the relationship between the duty to give reasons and participation rights is delimited by two fundamental rules that guide the Courts' case law when assessing compliance with what is now the second paragraph of Article 269 TFEU. On the one hand, 'the requirement of a statement of reasons must be assessed in light of the circumstances of the case, in particular of the content of the measure, the nature of the reasons given *and the interest which the addressees of the measure, or other parties to whom it is of direct and individual concern, may have in obtaining explanations*'.[168] On the other, 'it is not necessary for the reasoning to specify all the relevant matters of fact and law, inasmuch as the adequacy or otherwise of the reasoning is to be evaluated with regard not only to its wording but also to its context and to all the legal rules governing the matter in question'.[169]

The protective role of the duty to give reasons

The first rule endorses the protective role of the statement of reasons. Moreover, it may lead one to consider whether persons concerned by the procedure but not having access to it under the right to be heard, in the strict meaning conveyed by the Courts, could seek in the duty to give reasons a compensation for their limited procedural protection.[170] The argument is that those affected by a given act but having a weak procedural protection in comparison to holders of the right to be heard are at least entitled to have their interest in having explanations considered in the motivation of the act. This issue has been dealt with mainly in the context of state aid cases. *British Airways* is perhaps the most paradigmatic ruling in this respect. The Court considered that the applicant—a person concerned in a state aid procedure within the meaning of current Article 108(2) TFEU—had a limited right to participate in the procedure.[171] Yet, in light of the Courts' case law, the Commission, in motivating its final decision, could not limit itself to considering the interest that the Member State to which the decision is addressed may have in obtaining information on the decision:

[168] See, for recent examples, *inter alia*, Joined Cases T-246/08 and T-332/08, *Melli Bank plc v Council* [2009] ECR II-2629, paragraph 145, emphasis added; and Joined Cases T-309/04, T-317/04, T-329/04, and T-336/04, *TV 2/Danmark A/S and others v Commission* [2008] ECR II-2935, paragraph 178.

[169] Again, *Melli Bank*, *cit.*, paragraph 145, *TV 2/Danmark*, *cit.*, paragraph 178, and *Pye Phoy Tay Za*, *cit.*, n. 28, paragraph 95.

[170] On this, Azoulai, *op. cit.*, n. 76, pp. 203–4.

[171] This is further developed below in Chapter 8, Section 8.1.

it 'must address all the complaints which parties directly and individually concerned by that decision have made either on their own initiative or as a result of information supplied by the Commission'.[172] Later, in *Ufex*, stressing that 'a statement of reasons must be assessed by reference to the circumstances of each case', the Court held, in the case at hand, that several circumstances justified a more detailed statement of reasons. Namely, 'the fact that the applicants [complainants in the state aid procedure under judgment] submitted several economic studies during the administrative procedure should also have led the Commission to prepare a *thorough statement of reasons* while *responding to the essential arguments of the applicants*, as substantiated by those economic studies'.[173]

In short, the statement of reasons may indeed have the effect of protecting the so-called third parties in administrative procedures. In particular, not being entitled to express their points of view during the procedure in the same terms as the addressee of the act, they should be able to infer from the statement of reasons how their arguments were weighed by the decision-maker in the final decision. Yet, it should be stressed that the possibility of the statement of reasons compensating for weak procedural protection is in current EU law limited to 'persons directly and individually concerned' within the meaning of Article 263(4) TFEU.[174] Further, it seems that the decision-maker is only obliged to take account of the interests of such persons when they are in some way legally entitled to intervene in the procedure.[175]

[172] Joined Cases T-371/94 and T-394/94, *British Airways and Others v Commission* [1998] ECR II-2405, paragraphs 64 and 89–96. See further, Chapter 8, Sub-section 8.1.4.

[173] Case T-613/97, *Union française de l'express (Ufex) and others v Commission* [2000] ECR II-1531, paragraph 97, emphasis added. This cannot be seen as a return to the first judgment in *Sytraval*, since the Court carefully based its judgment on the specific circumstances of the case. (Case T-95/94, *Sytraval v Commission* [1995] ECR II-2651; see Chapter 8, Sub-section 8.1.4). In particular, the fact that the Commission's decision was dealing with a new, complex matter—another circumstance that required a detailed explanation—seems to have weighed in the part of the ruling quoted in the text. In any case, *Commission v Sytraval* (refused below, n. 179), *British Airways* and the *Ufex* ruling seem to embody a 'dialogue requirement' in the sense and with the risks of 'invasive' substantial judicial review pointed out by Martin Shapiro (Shapiro (1992) 'The giving reasons requirement', *The University Chicago Legal Forum*, pp. 179–220, at pp. 186, 203–5). Arguably, this effect is limited by the rules presented next in the text.

[174] Joined Cases 296/82 and 318/82, *Netherlands and Leeuwarder Papierwarenfabriek v Commission* [1985] ECR 809, paragraph 19; *British Airways*, *cit.*, paragraph 90.

[175] Case T-266/94, *Foreningen af Jernskibs- og Maskinbyggerier i Danmark and others v Commission* [1996] ECR II-1399, paragraph 238, where the Court held that third parties' interests need not be taken into account in the statement of reasons of a state aid decision adopted under current Article 108(3) TFEU, which does not require the intervention of any other person apart from the Member State concerned (on this procedure, see Chapter 8 below).

While the extension of participation rights defended in the book may enlarge the scope of those who are legally entitled to intervene in the procedure, not all holders of participation rights would benefit from the requirement that their individual interests in obtaining explanations should be considered in the motivation of the act. Only holders of subjective rights affected by the act adopted, whose personal position needs to be taken into account by the decision-maker, could benefit from this requirement. In this case, the motivation of the act would not have, in their regard, a compensatory function for a weaker procedural position. It would, instead, reflect their procedural position, and, hence, their substantive position in relation to the act adopted. This means that the protective role of the statement of reasons would encompass not only those directly and individually concerned by the act but, more broadly, holders of subjective rights concerned by it.

Caveats

This protective effect of the statement of reasons is, in any case and by force of the Courts' case law, subject to a few caveats. The first follows from the second rule mentioned above. In particular, the decision-maker is not expected to take into account all the factual and legal elements that were raised by each interested person during the administrative procedure.[176] This stems from the main functions of the statement of reasons, mentioned above, but also reveals a 'pragmatic understanding of the notion of adequate reasoning' intended to avoid or limit the annulment of sound decisions on formal grounds, as well as to avoid substantial review under the guise of procedural review.[177] Insofar as affected persons are concerned, this statement only needs to 'provide [them] with an adequate indication as to whether the decision is well founded or whether it may be vitiated by some defect enabling its validity to be challenged'.[178] A different solution would distort the main functions of the duty to give reasons and impair the efficiency of the institution's decisional capacity. This protective role of the duty to state reasons has thus a forceful limit; and the overall relevance of this

[176] Case T-149/89, *Sotralentz SA v Commission* [1995] ECR II-1127, paragraph 73; Case T-49/95, *Van Megen Sports Group BV v Commission* [1996] ECR II-1799, paragraph 55; Case T-231/99, *Colin Joynson v Commission* [2002] ECR II-2085, paragraph 166; Case C-301/96, *Germany v Commission* [2003] ECR I-9919, paragraph 140).

[177] Lenaerts and Vanhamme, *op. cit.*, n. 134, pp. 563–4; Azoulai, *op. cit.*, n. 76, pp. 204–5 and 210. The later aspect mentioned is however ambiguous in the Courts' case law (see Azoulai, *op. cit.*, n. 76, pp. 210–13).

[178] *Van Megen*, *cit.*, paragraph 51.

requirement as a procedural guarantee associated with participation rights exists only within these boundaries.

In addition, the decision-maker is not required to 'define its position on matters which are manifestly irrelevant or insignificant or plainly of secondary importance'.[179] In particular, they are not required to 'reply point by point to arguments lacking in any relevance relied on by the national authorities concerned or by intervening third parties'.[180] The thrust is clear and the position defensible: this precision is intended to preserve the economy and efficiency of the administrative action. In any event, it stresses the 'sovereign role of the Commission in defining the object of debate in the case at issue',[181] although there is some power of judicial review over what are relevant and absolutely irrelevant arguments.[182] In this sense, this rule may diminish the effect of procedural guarantee attached to reason-giving.

Finally, another aspect conditions the relationship between the duty to motivate decisions and participation rights. The Court has consistently held that when the persons concerned were closely associated to the procedure and were thus aware of the reasons behind the final decision, standards of compliance with the duty to give reasons can be less stringent.[183] The reasoning is straightforward, at least from the point of view of a 'judicial conception' of the duty to give reasons.[184] If the function of this duty is to ensure that persons concerned have the possibility of defending adequately their rights before the courts and the latter of exercising their power of review, a more flexible stance when the persons concerned have participated not only does not hinder the function of giving reasons, but also favours the economy and efficiency of administrative decision-making. Furthermore, it seems that this cannot be detrimental to the procedural

[179] Case C-367/95 P, *Commission v Sytraval and Brink's France SARL* [1998] ECR I-1719, paragraph 64, reiterated in *Ufex*, *cit.*, n. 173, paragraph 64.

[180] Joined Cases T-239/04 and T-323/04, *Italy and Brandt Italia SpA v Commission* [2007] ECR II-3265, paragraph 119.

[181] Azoulai, *op. cit.*, n. 76, p. 205, quoting Advocate General Vesterdorf in his Opinion delivered on 10 July 1991, on Case T-1/89, *Rhône-Poulenc v Commission* [1991] ECR II-867.

[182] On this, Lenaerts and Vanhamme, *op. cit.*, n. 134, p. 566.

[183] Case T-132/96 and T-143/96, *Freistaat Sachsen and others v Commission* [1999] ECR II-3663, paragraphs 150, 258; T-54/99, *max.mobil Telekommunikation Service GmbH v Commission* [2002] ECR II-313, paragraph 79; Case T-277/03, *Vlachaki v Commission* [2005] ECR II-243, paragraphs 83 to 85 (in the literature, see Schockweiler, *op. cit.*, n. 160, p. 35; Louis *et al.*, *op. cit.*, n. 160, pp. 525; Lenaerts and Vanhamme, *op. cit.*, n. 134, p. 565).

[184] The expression is a free translation from Azoulai, *op. cit.*, n. 76, p. 200 ('une conception « contentieuse » de la motivation').

protection of persons concerned different from the addressee.[185] However, one may argue that this rule risks impairing the other functions of giving reasons, namely the 'self-regulation' of the decisional body in the sense pointed out above,[186] as well as the reflexive function that was argued for above, i.e. the duty to give reasons as a procedural guarantee which enables those who participated to assess whether and how the interests they voiced were taken into account. Although the presumption is precisely that these persons do not need the statement of reasons in order to be aware of the reasons behind the decision and how their interests were accounted for, 'caution is necessary when applying this reasoning' in order not to jeopardize the protection due to other interested persons.[187] Moreover, the transparency of the decisional process facilitated by the statement of reasons is, as a result of this rule, limited to those directly involved in it; in this sense, it paradoxically stresses the element of procedural protection as a requirement that is supposed mainly to ensure the conditions for proper decision-making.

This same element of defence comes to the fore when the Court implicitly argues that the effect the decision has on the person affected influences the content of the statement of reasons (this is an instance of the rule according to which the statement of reasons must be appropriate to the nature of the measure at issue). As such, the Court has held that 'the grounds for a decision entailing serious consequences for the recipient of Community aid must clearly show the grounds justifying the measure

[185] Case 294/81, *Control Data Belgium NV SA v Commission* [1983] ECR 911, paragraph 15 (where the Court held that 'it is not sufficient that the Member States, as addressees of the decision, are aware of the reasons as a result of their participation in the preliminary procedure and that the applicant, the person directly and individually concerned, is able to deduce these reasons by comparing the decision in question with similar earlier decisions. It is further necessary that the applicant should be enabled in practice to defend its rights and the court should be able effectively to exercise its power of review on the basis of the statement of reasons').

[186] The quoted expression is borrowed from Schwarze (*op. cit.*, n. 160, p. 1401). See, in relation to what is stated in the text, the Opinion of Advocate General Roemer in Case 24/62 *Germany v Commission* [1963] ECR 63, at p. 73: '[O]ne must not forget the useful function which the obligation to state reasons performs for the purposes of a logical strengthening of the protection afforded by the law, in so far as it forces the Executives, when they formulate the statement of reasons for a decision, to give careful consideration to the conditions giving rise to the decision.'

[187] Opinion of Advocate General Poiares Maduro delivered on 21 October 2004 in Case C-141/02 P, *Commission of the European Communities v max.mobil Telekommunikation Service GmbH* [2005] ECR I-1283, paragraph 97. The Advocate General points out that 'there must be no doubt at all that the person concerned has actually acquired knowledge' and 'in particular where the Commission has a broad discretion in complex economic situations ... the persons concerned have a legitimate interest in being notified in due form of the reasons which led the Commission to adopt a measure' (paragraph 97).

adopted against it by the administration'.[188] In the same sense, it considered that when 'a decision taken in application of Article 81 EC [101 TFEU] relates to several addressees and raises a problem with regard to liability for the infringement, it must include an adequate statement of reasons with respect *to each of the addressees*, in particular those of them who according to the decision must bear the liability for the infringement'.[189]

In sum, although it can be deduced from the Courts' case law that the duty to motivate decisions may have the role of a procedural safeguard, the protective function of the statement of reasons is limited in view of its objective functions and of the balance sought between the efficiency of the institutions' decisional capacity, the possibility of judicial review, and the preserve of decisional bodies, chiefly the Commission, in exercising their discretion. As such, in light of the impact that a possible expansion of participation rights may have on this duty, one may argue that this expansion would not substantially increase the risks of 'intrusive judicial review'.[190] However, the recognition of participation rights in normative procedures would require more stringent requirements to give reasons in relation to normative acts than those that have been so far accepted by the Courts. In these cases, the rule is that a general act only needs to reveal the essential part of the aim pursued and that it would be excessive to require a specific reason for each of the choices it entails.[191] While this should, as a rule, be maintained, it is nevertheless argued that the protective role of the statement of reasons should not be different in view of the different nature of the act in cases where it can be asserted that an act affects the legal sphere of certain persons in an analogous way to an individual decision. This may be grounded in the rule according to which the requirements to be satisfied by the statement of reasons depend on the circumstances of each case, in particular on the content of the measure. In this respect, judicial review of normative acts would come closer to that of individual decisions.

[188] Case T-306/00, *Conserve Italia Soc. coop. rl v Commission* [2003] ECR II-5703, paragraphs 37–38.

[189] Case T-330/01, *Akzo Nobel NV v Commission* [2006] ECR II-3389, paragraphs 49-51. See also Case T-174/05, *Elf Aquitaine v Commission* 2009 ECR II-183, paragraphs 79–80.

[190] On these risks, see Shapiro, *op. cit.*, n. 173, pp. 184–9 and 201–17.

[191] *Spain v Council*, *cit.*, n. 160, paragraphs 58 and 59. The Courts' stance regarding the motivation of acts of general application has recently been reiterated in *Ayadi*: '[I]n the case of a measure intended to have general application, [...] the preamble may be limited to indicating the general situation which led to its adoption, on the one hand, and the general objectives which it is intended to achieve, on the other' (*cit.*, n. 28, paragraph 166).

5.4.3 *Careful and impartial examination*

The meaning of the principle of care for the procedural protection of persons concerned by the administrative action of the EU institutions has been thoroughly examined by Nehl and Azoulai, in particular in relation to the landmark rulings on this matter: *Nölle*, *Technische Universität München*, and *Commission v Sytraval*.[192] In the view of the Court, the principle of care is a 'rule protecting individuals'. It entails 'the duty of the competent institution to examine carefully and impartially all the relevant aspects of the individual case', which is all the more important in cases where the institutions have a wide power of appreciation.[193] This principle has been particularly important in reinforcing the procedural position of complainants in competition and state aid procedures, requiring the Commission 'to conduct a diligent and impartial examination of the complaint, which may make it necessary for it to examine matters not expressly raised by the complainant'.[194]

The relationship between the principle of care and the right to be heard is not simple. As noted by Nehl, the first may be considered to give complementary protection to persons who have access to the procedure making use of their right to be heard as well as to have a protective effect of the interests of those who were not recognized to have such a right but nonetheless had access to the procedure.[195] The Court of First Instance has not been fully clear on this matter.[196] Nevertheless, it has acknowledged that the principle of care, being essentially an objective standard of procedure, affords procedural protection to persons concerned by EU acts against negligence or misconduct on the part of the deciding body in handling the case before it. For example, in *Industrias Químicas del Vallés*, the Court held that the Commission committed a manifest error of appraisal insofar as it took no account of the applicant's circumstances, thereby (it is implicit in the

[192] Nehl, *op. cit.*, n. 136, Chapters 8 and 9; Azoulai, *op. cit.*, pp. 213–29.

[193] Respectively, Case T-167/94, *Detlef Nölle v Council and Commission* [1995] ECR II-2589, paragraph 76, and *Technische Universität München*, *cit.*, n. 38, paragraph 14. The protective role of the duty of diligence has been more recently reiterated in *MyTravel Group*, *cit.*, n. 138, paragraph 49.

[194] See Case C-367/95 P, *Commission v Sytraval and Brink's France SARL*[1998] ECR I-1719, paragraph 62, for the case of state aid; CFI judgment in *max.mobil*, *cit.*, n. 183, paragraph 49 and the case law quoted therein, for other procedures in the area of economic law. On this, Craig, *op. cit.*, n. 43, pp. 375–8.

[195] Nehl, *op. cit.*, n. 136, pp. 110–11 and p. 124. Backing this view, see Case C-349/07, *Sopropé v Fazenda Pública* [2008] ECR I-10369, paragraph 50.

[196] Nehl, *op. cit.*, n. 136, pp. 131–2 and p. 137, referring to *Nölle* and *France-Aviation* (Case T-346/94, *France-Aviation v Commission* [1995] ECR II-2841).

judgment) infringing its duty of examining carefully and impartially all the relevant facts of the individual case.[197] In another case, the Court held that impartiality is a rule which is intended to confer rights on individuals for the purposes of awarding damages, insofar as it 'is intended, as well as ensuring that the public interest is respected, to protect the persons concerned and confers on them a right as individuals to see that the corresponding guarantees are complied with'.[198] Hence, the duty to carefully and impartially examine all the relevant facts of a case obliges, in principle, the deciding body to take into due account the facts and views brought into the procedure by the persons thereby concerned, who were entitled to access it on different grounds. This is valid not only in relation to the addressees of a decision, or to those who are in a similar position, and therefore are granted a right to be heard, but also in relation to the so-called third parties to the procedure.

There are, however, limits to the extent to which individuals may avail themselves of the duty of careful and impartial examination in order to defend their own interests.[199] In fact, the consideration of the private interest of the persons concerned in handling the case during the procedure is limited by objective considerations pertaining to efficient decision-making and must be weighed against the other interests that the decision-maker needs to consider. Exactly how a balance should be achieved is not clear in the Courts' case law. Admittedly, this fundamentally depends on the concrete circumstances of each case. In one instance, the Court of Justice has held that a decision defining a prerequisite for the attribution of a marketing authorization 'may be adopted by the Commission pursuant to the principle of sound administration and the duty of care, after the interests of all the parties concerned have been weighed, namely, on the one hand, the interest of the institution in not having to follow a highly burdensome decision-making procedure..., and, on the other hand, the

[197] Case C-326/05 P, *Industrias Químicas del Vallés, SA v Commission* [2007] ECR I-6557, paragraphs 77 to 89, especially 77, 83, 84, 88. See, moreover, *Arizona*, *cit.*, n. 82, paragraphs 88 and 89, insofar as they stress the protective effect of the duty of care in relation to procedures leading up to the adoption of individual measures.

[198] Case T-309/03, *Manel Camós Grau v Commission* [2006] ECR II-1173, paragraph 102. Chiefly at issue was a conflict of interest on the part of the European Anti-Fraud Office (OLAF) officials in investigating a case of financial mismanagement, a conflict of interest which was not duly tackled by OLAF. Impartiality has thus a very precise meaning in this case, commensurate with the natural law principle *nemo iudex in causa sua*. More broadly, the principle of care is called into question insofar as OLAF's conduct in addressing this problem was also at stake.

[199] Nehl, *op. cit.*, n. 136, p. 111.

legitimate interest of an undertaking in not having to delay the implementation of its marketing plans . . .'.[200] In some cases, the objective rationale seems to prevail. Thus, in state aid cases, the Court of First Instance has stressed that the diligent and impartial examination of the complaints in the context of the preliminary procedure of Article 108(3) TFEU is carried out 'in the interests of sound administration of the fundamental rules of the Treaty relating to state aid'.[201] In others, the protective role of the duty of care seems to be predominant. For example, in an anti-dumping procedure, the Court of First Instance considered that the Commission, as a correlative of the duty of the parties concerned to cooperate with it, is required to verify, 'as far as possible', the accuracy of the information provided by the parties concerned, on which its conclusions are based. This may require it to dispel a contradiction between data in the proceedings and to carry out a subsequent analysis of the applicant's submissions. Not having done so, according to the Court, the Commission infringed its obligation 'to take account of all the relevant circumstances and to appraise the facts of the matter with all due care' and adopted a measure that was detrimental to the applicant. Although stressing the 'particular circumstances' of the case at hand, the Court annulled the Council regulation imposing anti-dumping duties insofar as it concerned the applicant.[202]

Two cases help to delimit the outer boundaries of the protective effect of this principle. On the one hand, the final outcome of the *max.mobil* case made it clear that the protective effect of the principle of care cannot reach as far as to ground a subjective right to a specific result nor a right to bring proceedings before the Court.[203] On the other, in a case related to the procedural guarantees of individuals in the framework of the adaptation of a directive to technical progress, the Court held that the operators concerned

[200] Case C-248/99 P, *France and Monsanto v Commission* [2002] ECR I-1, paragraph 92.

[201] Case T-210/02, *British Aggregates Association v Commission* [2006] ECR II-2789, paragraph 177.

[202] Case T-413/03, *Shandong Reipu Biochemicals v Council* [2006] ECR II-2243, paragraphs 82 to 85, 87, 95, and 96. The quotations are from paragraphs 87 and 96, respectively.

[203] Case C-141/02 P, *max.mobil v Commission* [2005] ECR I-1283, paragraphs 66 to 75. See Opinion of Advocate General Poiares Maduro delivered on this case (*cit*, n. 187), according to whom 'the requisite diligent and impartial examination is not carried out in relation to [the person concerned], but first of all by reference to the general interest in sound administration and the proper application of the rules of the Treaty'. As such, 'this obligation is not comparable to the rights which may be conferred on interested parties to intervene directly in the procedure for the adoption of measures concerning them, such as the right to be heard and the right of access to the file' (paragraph 56).

by the ensuing classification of certain products cannot 'rely on the duty of diligence in the context of a procedure resulting in the adoption of measures of general application in the same way as they may rely on procedural guarantees in the context of a procedure resulting in the adoption of an administrative act of individual application'.[204]

Accordingly, in the context of procedures leading up to the adoption of regulations or directives, 'the duty of diligence is essentially an objective procedural guarantee arising from an absolute and unconditional obligation on the Community institution relating to the drafting of an act of general application and not the exercise of any individual right'.[205] Different standards of procedural protection resulting from the principle of care are thus clearly drawn by the Court in relation to individual decisions, on the one hand, and to normative acts, on the other. This means that the protective effect that persons concerned who participated in the procedure may draw from the principle of care, insofar as it may function as a procedural guarantee to persons affected by EU acts, cannot be extended to the context of normative procedures. While this can be accepted as a rule, in light of the different 'nature' of the two types of act, this is disputable when normative acts directly shape the content of the ensuing material relationship, defining the rights and duties of the persons concerned, or at least, when they in fact contain decisions that concern certain persons individually.[206] As a result, in these cases, and contrary to what has been so far acknowledged, the protective role of the principle of care should be extended to the realm of normative procedures.

In short, the enhanced procedural protection that persons concerned and involved in the procedure may draw from the principle of care is restricted by the objective facet of sound administration. This is particularly strong in normative procedures, to the point of excluding the protective function of the principle of care in these cases. This should be limited to cases in which the normative act does not impact decisively on the rights and duties of private persons. In any event, the protective effect that they may draw from the principle of care is limited to the conduct of the decision-maker during the procedure, i.e. it is not extended to the outcome of the procedure.

[204] *Arizona*, *cit.*, n. 82, paragraph 86.

[205] *Idem*, *ibidem* (see also paragraph 89).

[206] This is arguably the case in *Arizona*, where a directive adapting a 'mother directive' to technical progress determined that a given product has certain scientific characteristics that entail risks for human health that must be specified in the respective labelling.

5.4.4 *Language and access rights*[207]

In the multilingual context of the European Union, the right of every person—according to the Charter of Fundamental Rights—or of every citizen—according to the Treaty (TFEU)—to address the EU institutions in one of the languages of the Member States and to receive an answer in the same language is an essential part of the procedural guarantees of those concerned by acts of the institutions.[208] This principled formulation notwithstanding, the Court has refused to consider this as a general principle of EU law.[209] Its scope and limits as a procedural guarantee result from the practice of the institutions and, especially, from the case law of the Courts.

The language rules of the EU institutions in their relationships with Member States and the 'persons subject to [their] jurisdiction' were initially defined in Council Regulation No. 1/58. There it is specified that the documents sent to the institutions 'may be drafted in any of the official languages selected by the sender' and the reply must be drafted in the same language.[210] Further, documents sent by the institutions to a Member State or to a person subject to the jurisdiction of a Member State must be drafted in the 'language of such State'.[211] The legal significance of these rules as procedural guarantees in the context of administrative procedures is

[207] For current purposes, the analysis is restricted to the impact of the language regime on procedural guarantees of persons affected by EU rules or decisions. This topic is summarily addressed by Lenaerts and Vanhamme, *op. cit.*, n. 134, pp. 553–4. For a broader analysis of the regime of the use of languages in the European Union within its institutions and bodies as well as in the relationships with Member States and natural and legal persons, see Diana-Urania Galetta and Jacques Ziller (2008) 'Il regime linguistico della Comunità' in Mario P. Chiti e Guido Greco (eds), *Trattato di Diritto Amministrativo Europeo. Parte Generale. Tomo II*, Milano: Giuffrè, 2nd edn, pp. 1067–113.

[208] Cf. Article 41(4) of the Charter of Fundamental Rights and Article 24, fourth paragraph TFEU (previous Article 21 EC, third paragraph, EC). This and other differences between the two provisions are analysed in detail by Galetta and Ziller, *op. cit.*, pp. 1093–5 (referring to Article II-101(4) of the Constitutional Treaty, the wording of which is identical to that of Article 41(4) of the Charter). Bruno de Witte points out the exclusion of regional and minority languages from this right (de Witte, (2004) 'Language law of the European Union: protecting or eroding linguistic diversity?' in Rachael Craufurd Smith (ed.), *Culture and European Union Law*, Oxford: Oxford University Press, pp. 205–41, at p. 224).

[209] Case T-120/99, *Christina Kik v Office for Harmonisation in the Internal Market (Trade Marks and Designs) (OHIM)* [2001] ECR II-2235, paragraph 58, upheld on appeal (Case C-361/01 P, *Christina Kik v Office for Harmonisation in the Internal Market* [2003] ECR I-8283, paragraph 82).

[210] Article 2 of Council Regulation No. 1/58, determining the languages to be used by the European Economic Community (OJ L 17/385, 6.10.1958), as amended.

[211] Article 3 of Council Regulation No. 1/58, *cit.*

measured by the consequences attached to its infringement. In this respect, the Court has held that failure of compliance is a mere irregularity which is only capable of affecting the procedure's validity if harmful consequences are produced in the legal sphere of the person concerned.[212] This amounts to the 'harmless error rule' that the Court has applied in several instances in relation to the right to be heard. It is clear that language rights as procedural guarantees should essentially ensure that access and procedural rights are not hindered by the use of language that is not accessible to the persons concerned or hinders their full comprehension of procedural acts.

The scope of the rules mentioned is limited by the meaning of 'document' for the purposes of defining the scope of language rights. Thus, in competition procedures, the Court has drawn a distinction between documents as to the effect of Article 3 of Regulation No. 1/58 and evidence on which the Commission relies. In particular, documents that do not emanate from the Commission (used as 'supporting documentation') are considered to fall under the latter category and are subject to an opposite rule: they must 'be brought to the attention of the addressee as they are, so that the addressee can appraise himself of the interpretation of them which the Commission has adopted and on which it has based both its statement of objections and its decision'.[213] In this line of reasoning, documents annexed to the statement of objections, which defines the Commission's position vis-à-vis undertakings targeted by the procedure, do not need to be translated and, indeed, *should not* be translated.[214] Moreover, the statement of objections may contain 'various untranslated quotations from documents emanating from undertakings and associations of undertakings' and the Commission is also not obliged to provide translations of the minutes of the hearings.[215] According to the Court, 'observance of the rights of the defence ... requires that addressees of the [statement of objections]

[212] Case 41/69, *ACF Chemiefarma NV v Commission* [1970] ECR 661, paragraphs 47 to 53. This has been reiterated in Joined Cases T-25/95, T-26/95, T-30/95 to T-32/95, T-34/95 to T-39/95, T-42/95 to T-46/95, T-48/95, T-50/95 to T-65/95, T-68/95 to T-71/95, T-87/95, T-88/95, T-103/95, and T-104/95, *Cimenteries CBR and Others v Commission* [2000] ECR II-491, paragraph 643 ('Where an institution sends a person within the jurisdiction of a Member State a document which is not drawn up in the language of that State, the irregularity, however regrettable, vitiates the procedure only if it gives rise to harmful consequences for that person in the administrative procedure'). A similar stance is adopted by the Court of Justice in *Kik*, *cit.*, n. 209, paragraph 96.

[213] Case T-148/89, *Tréfilunion SA v Commission* [1995] ECR II-1063, paragraph 21.

[214] *Idem, ibidem.*

[215] *Cimentries, cit.*, paragraphs 634 and 636.

should have access during the administrative procedure to all the incriminating documents in their original versions . . . ', but this does not 'require the Commission to translate documents cited in the [statement of objections] or used in support of it into the language of the Member State where [its] addressees are established'.[216] It is doubtful to what extent these findings are compatible with the principle that language should not constitute an obstacle to an adequate exercise of access rights. If the underlying reasoning is that competition procedures impinge upon undertakings that are capable of supporting translation costs, it is submitted that the application of such rules should at least take into account this very capacity, which may change from undertaking to undertaking.

These findings apply the general rule according to which both the Treaty references to the use of languages in the European Union and the rules contained in secondary legislation, 'cannot be regarded as evidencing a general principle of Community law that confers a right on every citizen to have a version of anything that might affect his interests drawn up in his language in all circumstances'.[217] This rule was formulated by the Court of Justice in *Kik*, a case concerning the language rules of the Office for Harmonization in the Internal Market.[218] In this case, a distinction was drawn between 'procedural documents' and 'written communications' in order to establish the validity, in light of the principle of non-discrimination, of the rule according to which the Office may send written communications to the parties in a second language chosen by them.[219] It is important for current purposes to indicate the principles that grounded the Court's reasoning and its interpretation of the language rules. Although recognizing that some of the aspects of the language regime adopted by OHIM may be problematic, the Court considered that this regime is

> the result of a difficult process which seeks to achieve the necessary balance between the interests of economic operators and the public interest in terms of the cost of proceedings, but also between the interests of applicants for Community trade marks and those of other economic operators in regard to access to translations of

[216] *Cimentries*, *cit.*, paragraph 635.

[217] See the ECJ judgment in *Kik*, *cit.*, n. 209, paragraph 82, as well as CFI judgment in *Kik*, *cit.*, n. 209, paragraph 58.

[218] On this case, see Galetta and Ziller, *op. cit.*, n. 207, pp. 1087–9; also de Witte, *op. cit.*, n. 208, pp. 222–3 (on the CFI judgment). The OHIM is particularly restrictive in what concerns the use of languages, limiting the languages of the procedures before it to five.

[219] ECJ judgment in *Kik*, *cit.*, n. 209, paragraphs 45 to 48.

documents which confer rights, or proceedings involving more than one economic operator.[220]

The fact that the EU trade mark regime applies to economic operators, not to citizens in general, weighed in the Courts' reasoning and led to the conclusion that the choice to limit the use of languages to those which are most widely known is 'appropriate and proportionate'; implicitly then it is assumed that these operators must bear the translation costs.[221] As mentioned above, this reasoning is transposable to the rulings on the language rights of persons concerned in the context of competition procedures. Accordingly, analogous limitations of language rights should not apply when the persons concerned are individuals or not-for-profit organizations, although in fact this remains an open question in the current case law.

Two other aspects of the Court of Justice's ruling in *Kik* are worth mentioning. First, it confirms that former Article 21, third paragraph, EC requires that the duty of institutions, the advisory committees, and the Ombudsman to correspond with the citizens 'in one of the languages mentioned in Article 55 (1) of the Treaty on the European Union' does not extend to the 'all bodies in the Union'. This has been modified by the fourth paragraph of Article 24 TFEU.[222] Secondly, it specifies that, contrary to acts of general application, individual decisions need not be drafted in all the official languages, '*even though [they] may affect the rights of a citizen of the Union other than the person to whom [they are] addressed*, for example a competing economic operator'.[223] This conclusion, based exclusively on economic reasons, considerably limits access rights and, in particular, participation rights in procedures that involve complex administrative relationships and in those having normative effects. It is particularly problematic regarding decisions touching upon diffuse interests, such as the authorization of genetically modified organisms. In principle, it should at least not be considered valid in case secondary legislation expressly affords

[220] ECJ judgment in *Kik*, *cit.*, n. 209, paragraph 92; see also paragraph 86.

[221] *Idem*, paragraphs 88 and 94 (even though the Court rather emphasized the profit that these economic operators take out of a trademark right, and the voluntary character of their resort to the Office's services, to hold that they should bear the operating costs of the Office itself—paragraphs 89 and 91).

[222] *Idem*, paragraph 83. Article 24 TFEU is reinforced by Article 20(2)(d) TFEU, according to which citizens have the right to 'petition the European Parliament, to apply to the European Ombudsman, and to address the institutions and advisory bodies of the Union in any of the Treaty languages and to obtain a reply in the same language'.

[223] *Idem*, paragraph 85. Emphasis added. See Article 4 of Regulation No. 1/58.

other persons rights to intervene in the procedure. Yet, this is precisely the case of the trademark opposition, revocation, and invalidity procedures, in which several persons of different nationalities may be concerned and may have access to the decisional procedure. It is submitted that such a rule needs to be subject to a proportionality test in order to avoid different treatment between different interested persons.

Similar problems arise when decisional procedures are subject to public consultation, in view of the distinction between working languages and official languages. As pointed out by Creech, 'the institutions are more linguistically inclusive when dealing with the public and individual Member States and more restrictive when internal matters are concerned'.[224] However, the distinction between internal documents and documents having external effects becomes particularly blurred in view of consultation procedures.[225] The fact that many of the working documents of the institutions are limited to a few languages may hinder the involvement of persons concerned by the acts subject to discussion and of the public in general. This has been reported in relation to the consultation procedures undertaken under the so-called Lamfalussy procedure: a specific problem felt by consumers and small businesses in accessing the consultation procedures, on which the Lamfalussy regulatory approach is largely based, was the fact that the consultation documents had been produced only in English. This, in conjunction with the highly technical nature of these documents, is a factor of inequality between consumers and small businesses, on the one hand, and organizations representing market participants and larger businesses on the other.[226] These difficulties are particularly acute in relation to normative procedures, but also, as results from the above, in relation to decisions that may have normative effects or, in any case, effects that extend beyond the legal sphere of its addressee.

As results from the considerations set out above, the rules enshrining language rights mentioned at the outset of this section are far from

[224] Richard L. Creech (2005) *Law and Language in the European Union. The Paradox of a Babel 'United in Diversity'*, Gronigen: European Law Publishing, p. 24.

[225] Galetta and Ziller, *op. cit.*, n. 207, p. 1076. On the different rules and practices of the institutions and agencies, idem, *op. cit.*, n. 207, pp. 1077–89. On language as an element of democracy and on the democratic significance of multilingualism in the EU, see Alain Fenet (2001) 'Diversité linguistique et construction européenne', *Revue Trimestrielle de Droit Européen*, Vol. 37, n. 2, pp. 235–69, at pp. 256–60.

[226] 'Third report monitoring the Lamfalussy Process', Brussels, 17 November 2004, p. 21. On the Lamfalussy regulatory approach, see Chapter 6, below.

resolving 'all the linguistic difficulties encountered by citizens in the context of the activities of the Union's institutions and bodies', as has been rightly acknowledged by the Court.[227] Multilingualism may in fact hinder the exercise of participation rights, whether they be restricted to the right to be heard or extended in the terms proposed in this book. In this sense, it remains a challenge to the procedural rights of persons dealing with the EU administration.

5.5 Unbinding Participation Rights

This chapter has confirmed the Courts' restrictive stance with regard to participation rights, which is essentially due to the bilateral conception of the administrative procedure characterized in the previous chapter. It has been shown that the denial of such rights in normative procedures is a mere logical consequence of the Courts' formalistic approach to the right to be heard in adjudicative procedures, which, moreover, confirms its adherence to a formal position. A substantial adverse effect produced in the legal sphere of natural or legal persons by the effect of a normative act does not entail any right of participation, even where an analogy between the situation of persons affected by an individual decision and that of persons affected by a normative act could be established. This thereby demonstrates that, according to the Courts' case law, the lack of convergence between this effect and the structural element of the right to be heard, characterized in Chapter 4, impedes the recognition of participation rights.

As a result, the nature of the act, whether individual or normative, becomes the main criterion to decide on the recognition or otherwise of participation rights. This choice is contestable. First, the institutional arguments invoked by the Courts to support this normative option are not only feeble but also cannot encompass all types of normative acts adopted by the EU institutions. In fact, they are not capable of explaining the exclusion of administrative normative acts from the scope of application of participation rights. Secondly, adhering to the formalism of this distinction, the Court deliberately ignores that, on the basis of its case law and by reason of the powers exercised in each case by the EU institutions, the classification of an act as normative encompasses situations in which natural

[227] ECJ judgment in *Kik*, *cit.*, n. 209, paragraph 86.

and legal persons, possibly even identified during the procedure, are sufficiently differentiated from the public at large in what concerns the effects produced by the act.

This formalistic approach should be overcome. It is in contradiction with a paradigm of EU administrative law that is respectful of the persons' rights and interests. It prevents the extension of participation rights to situations where they would be justified and required in light of their rationales. In fact, the scope of these rights may be critically reviewed on the basis of the functions that participation rights carry out in the decisional procedures. Participation rights facilitate the achievement of materially just decisions, grounded in the consideration of the opposing private and public interests that come together therein, enabling both the procedural protection of those substantively affected and an accurate representation of the underlying factual situation. As such, their recognition should reflect the material administrative relationship that is created or modified by force of the act adopted, irrespective of its formal characterization. It should, moreover, take into account the set of interests that are considered legally relevant by force of the applicable substantive rules. Therefore, access to the decisional procedure should be granted to those whose legal sphere will be modified by the effect of the links between advantageous and disadvantageous positions that result from the regulatory intervention, including those whose intervention is legally valued essentially on the basis of their objective contribution to the procedure.

Broader access to the decisional procedures in the terms proposed is, moreover, 'matched' by the scope of other procedural rights and duties that are recognized in EU law, although it would impact on some of the currently accepted rules, namely on the duty to give reasons and on the duty of care. Thus, extended participation rights may impact on the content of the duty to give reasons, insofar as the latter may have a protective role vis-à-vis holders of subjective rights in the terms and with the limits that result from current case law. If extended possibilities of participation were ensured, the scope of persons interested in obtaining explanations would possibly broaden, even if this interest would not need to be satisfied in relation to all participants. In relation to the duty of care, the Court has argued that the protective effect associated therewith cannot be extended in the same way to the realm of normative procedures. While this can be accepted as a rule, in cases where normative acts do impact on the legal sphere of certain persons so as to shape their rights and duties with regard to a certain material situation, this duty should be equally conceived as a 'rule protecting individuals', to return to the Court's statement in *Nölle*. As for the other two rights addressed above, first, it was argued that the rules on access to documents ensure, in principle, that holders of participation rights in the terms proposed may have access to the information they need in order to exercise their procedural rights; secondly, as far as language rights are concerned, it was seen that the problems that language diversity may cause to participation rights are common both to a restrictive and to a broader concept of such rights.

Chapter 6

The 'Lamfalussy Process', Consultation, and Participation Rights

The regulatory process proposed by the Committee of Wise Men on the Regulation of European Securities Market, chaired by Alexandre Lamfalussy (henceforth, the Lamfalussy Committee)—the so-called 'Lamfalussy process'—is one example of EU governance arrangements where 'participation at large', in the form of consultation, is given considerable weight. The concrete design of the 'Lamfalussy process', as far as consultation is concerned, highlights the difference between, on the one hand, participation rights as they have been characterized in the previous chapters and, on the other, consultation practices as they have been envisaged by the Commission in its governance initiatives. In other words, the 'Lamfalussy process' illustrates the difference between a rights-based approach to participation that underlies the concept of participation propounded in this work and the forms of public involvement in decisional processes that have been sustained by the EU institutions under the impetus of the Commission. This distinction was briefly sketched in Chapter 2 and, in part, concretized by the analyses presented in Chapters 3 and 4. Consultation should nevertheless be recalled here. It was said that consultation is a way of allowing for the involvement of persons situated outside the formal, public decision-making structures typical of a representative system, while ensuring that the 'external input' received is filtered by the latter (it is hence a form of 'participation at large', as explained in Chapter 2). Consultation involves the creation of public discussion periods in which either the public in general or particularly interested persons are called upon to express their views on a given regulatory proposal, regardless of the form this proposal may take. In general, this form of procedural intervention does not entail the emergence of a procedural legal relationship between participants and decision-maker(s), that is, the former are not recognized rights inherent in their intervention that would require the latter to follow a specific course of conduct. Explaining how consultation came to the foreground of EU financial services regulation is particularly illustrative of the reasons that made consultation and, with it 'participation at large', one of the characteristic features of EU governance. Moreover, this analysis reveals how much the creation of participatory procedures is due to regulatory specificities of the sector at hand, even if some concerns are common to different fields.

In order to analyse the role of consultation in the realm of financial services, one needs first to consider the reasons that led to the adoption of this regulatory approach (Section 6.1) and to situate the *fora* of participation envisaged in their novel and other not so innovative features (Section 6.2). These are the starting points for the analysis that follows, which will therefore focus on the policy documents that were issued following the adoption of the 1999 Financial Services Action Plan, in particular the Lamfalussy Report.[1] The core of the chapter highlights the rationales and characteristics of participation as established in the EU regulation of financial services following the recommendations of the Lamfalussy Report and the subsequent institutional practices (Section 6.3). This contributes to better distinguishing this type of participation from the rights-based concept defended in the book. Further, a few observations are made on how consultation procedures have been perceived and conducted in practice, as far as this is possible on the basis of the available documents (Section 6.4). This sheds light on the limits of law with regard to some problems ensuing from the practice of participation. Next, the features of consultation are contrasted with the features of a rights-based concept of participation (Section 6.5). This last section of the chapter presents the differences and points of contact of the two concepts. In addition, by resorting to one aspect of the market abuse regime—the decisional process that underlies the definition of accepted market practices—it illustrates the type of situations in which participation rights should be recognized in the realm of securities market regulation. The difficulties that arise from the proposed extension

[1] Communication of the European Commission, 'Financial services: implementing the framework for financial markets: action plan', COM (1999) 232, 11.5.99. Final Report of the Committee of Wise Men on the Regulation of European Securities Market', Brussels, 15 February 2001, hereinafter the 'Lamfalussy Report' (available at <http://ec.europa.eu/internal_market/securities/docs/lamfalussy/wisemen/final-report-wise-men_en.pdf>).

of participation rights in this case are also addressed, as well as the possible ways of circumventing them.

Before proceeding, two facts should be noted. To begin with, the Lamfalussy process was originally conceived for securities market regulation and expanded to banking, insurance, financial conglomerates, and UCITS, where parallel regulatory structures were set up.[2] The analysis undertaken in the following pages is limited to securities market regulation, taken here as a reference field. In addition, EU financial regulation and supervision is undergoing a substantial reform process in the context of the current financial crisis.[3] The general sense of the reform, in what specifically concerns the structure of regulation and supervision, is to strengthen the role of the EU in this field, building upon existing structures. At the time of writing, the European Parliament and the Council had agreed, *inter alia*, with the Commission's proposal to transform the so-called Lamfalussy committees—the Committee of European Securities Regulators (CESR, analysed below) and its counterparts in the areas of banking, insurance, and occupational pensions—into independent agencies.[4] They will be part of a

[2] ECOFIN decision of 3 December 2002 (see Press release 361, 14368/02 on the 2471st Council meeting, Economic and Financial Affairs, p. 7, available at <http://www.consilium.europa.eu/ueDocs/cms_Data/docs/pressData/en/ecofin/73473.pdf>). Contradicting the assertion on sector specificities' conditionality, it has been pointed out that the Lamfalussy process might serve as a pilot for future changes in other policy fields (see Frédéric Varone, Christian de Visscher, Carl-Fredrik Bergström, and Josefin Almer, 2004, 'Governance and the EU Securities Sector', report produced in the context of the New Modes of Governance project, Project 7—Governance and the EU securities sector, Priority 7—Citizens and governance in the knowledge-based society, reference number 7/D1, p. 3—available at <http://www.eu-newgov.org/database/DELIV/D07D01_EU_securities_sector.PDF>).

[3] See, in general, Communication from the Commission, 'European financial supervision', COM (2009) 252 final, Brussels, 27.5.2009, hereinafter the '2009 Commission Communication on financial supervision' (in the follow-up of the 'Report' commissioned to the High-Level Group on Financial Supervision in the EU, Chaired by Jacques de Larosière, Brussels, 25 February 2009—hereinafter the 'Larosière Report'). See also Communication from the Commission, 'Review of the Lamfalussy process. Strengthening supervisory convergence', COM (2007) 727 final, Brussels, 20.11.2007 (hereinafter the '2007 Commission Communication on the review of the Lamfalussy process'). Only the aspects pertaining to consultation are taken into account in this chapter.

[4] Proposal for a Regulation of the European Parliament and of the Council establishing a European Banking Authority (COM (2009) 501 final, Brussels, 23.9.2009); Proposal for a Regulation of the European Parliament and of the Council establishing a European Insurance and Occupational Pensions Authority (COM (2009) 502 final, Brussels, 23.9.2009); Proposal for a Regulation of the European Parliament and of the Council establishing a European Securities and Markets Authority (COM (2009) 503 final, Brussels, 23.9.2009); Proposal for a Directive of the European Parliament and of the Council, amending Directives 1998/26/EC, 2002/87/EC,

network of supervisors (European System of Financial Supervisors) and cooperate with the European Systemic Risk Board, which is deprived of legal personality and responsible for macro-prudential supervision.[5] The reform builds on the Lamfalussy process, but affects the regulatory levels where consultation procedures have been in place (in particular, levels 2 and 3), mostly due to the enhanced powers that the new agencies will have. This is taken into account in the following sections. The impact the reforms will have on consultation is still uncertain. This will be analysed below (Subsection 6.3.6). For now it suffices to say that the references to consultation in the 2009/2010 documents are scant,[6] and this can be interpreted in different ways.

6.1 The Origins of the 'Lamfalussy Process'

The immediate origins of the 'Lamfalussy process' lie in a Commission Communication of 1999 that set up a Financial Services Action Plan, taking the introduction of the euro as the momentum for regulatory change. The fulfilment of this agenda was grafted onto the strategy for accomplishing a 'competitive and dynamic knowledge-based economy' defined by the

2003/6/EC, 2003/41/EC, 2003/71/EC, 2004/39/EC, 2004/109/EC, 2005/60/EC, 2006/48/EC, 2006/49/EC, and 2009/65/EC in respect of the powers of the European Banking Authority, the European Insurance and Occupational Pensions Authority and the European Securities and Markets Authority (COM (2009) 576 final, Brussels, 26.10.2009). Hereinafter, these will be generally referred to as the '2009 proposals'. The European Parliament's resolutions, at first and single reading, were adopted in 22 September 2010 following compromise agreements with the Council and introduced amendments to the Commission's proposal. The official resolutions were not yet available at the time of writing. The following compromise agreements will be considered in the text: COD/2009/0144, 'European Securities and Markets Authority (ESMA): establishment (political agreement on final act)', and COD/2009/0161, 'Financial supervision: powers of the European Banking Authority, the European Insurance and Occupational Pensions Authority and the European Securities and Markets Authority (political agreement on final act)'. Both are available in the Legislative Observatory database (<http://www.europarl.europa.eu/oeil/search_reference_procedure.jsp>)—hereinafter, 'compromise agreements'. At the time of writing (October 2010), a consolidated text of the reforms was still not available. Whenever pertinent, reference will be made to the Commission's proposals and, where applicable, to the compromise agreements.

5 Proposal for a Regulation of the European Parliament and of the Council on Community macro prudential oversight of the financial system and establishing a European Systemic Risk Board (COM (2009) 499 final, Brussels, 23.9.2009).

6 The Larosière Report, the 2009 proposals, and the compromise texts quoted above.

Lisbon European Council of 2000.[7] In the Action Plan mentioned, it was assumed that the economic benefits potentially stemming from free cross-border provision of financial services were hindered mainly by regulatory divergences among Member States.[8] The regulatory approach followed up to that point, based on the principle of mutual recognition, on minimum harmonization, and on the principle of home country control, had failed fully to achieve the purposes of integration, due to shortcomings in the regulatory process itself and to deficient—or lack of—enforcement.[9]

For this reason, according to the Commission, both the European legislative process and the process of implementation and enforcement should be placed under scrutiny. The legislative procedure (co-decision), as it stood, was deemed to be excessively slow and cumbersome. It was considered that it could not speedily adapt to changing market circumstances and had failed to produce the legislation needed. The deficiencies of the implementation and enforcement phase were attributed by the Commission mainly to the lack of uniform application and interpretation of Community rules by Member States.[10] On the basis of this assessment, among other proposals to deliver the Action Plan, the Commission strove for 'a more inclusive and consensual approach in shaping policies from an early stage and in advance of drafting legislation [...] [extensive] to all EU institutions, but also to representatives of market practitioners, consumers, users and employees'. This was deemed to favour swifter decisional processes.[11] Thus, with regard to the inclusion of non-institutional entities, it proposed the creation of 'a high level forum [...] to take soundings from bodies representing the principal EU interest groups which have an interest in the smooth and efficient operation of financial markets'.[12] In addition, it was

[7] See 'The Committee of Wise Men terms of reference given by the European Union's Economic and Finance Ministers on 17 July 2000' (p. 98 of the Lamfalussy Report).

[8] Financial Services Action Plan, *cit.*, n. 1, pp. 5, 9, and 10. This assumption and concern were, however, not new. See Damien Chalmers, Christos Hadjiemmanuil, Giorgio Monti, and Adam Tomkins (2006) *European Union Public Law: Texts and Materials*, Cambridge: Cambridge University Press, pp. 786–91.

[9] On this, Rosa Lastra (2003) 'The governance structure for financial regulation and supervision in Europe', *Columbia Journal of European Law*, Vol. 10, n. 1, pp. 49–68, at pp. 60–1; Matteo Ortino (2007) 'The role and functioning of mutual recognition in the European market of financial services', *International and Comparative Law Quarterly*, Vol 56, n. 2, pp. 309–38, in particular pp. 323–8.

[10] Financial Services Action Plan, *cit.*, n. 1, pp. 13–15 (regarding implemention) and 16–17.

[11] Financial Services Action Plan, *cit.*, n. 1, p. 16.

[12] Financial Services Action Plan, *cit.*, n. 1, p. 17.

underlined that the regulatory system should produce flexible solutions under proper oversight. Speed and flexibility should be the cornerstones of a new regulatory framework to be created in the field of financial services.

The diagnosis of regulatory failures in the field of the securities market, at both levels—decision-making, on the one hand, implementation and enforcement, on the other—was the basis of the process put forward by the Lamfalussy Committee, mandated by the Council to review the rule-making procedures in this field, in view of the agenda set out in the Action Plan.[13] The regulatory reform delineated in the Lamfalussy Report was endorsed by the Stockholm European Council of 23 March 2001 and by the European Parliament Resolution of 5 February 2002 on the implementation of financial services.[14] These resolutions reveal the high degree of inter-institutional compromise backing up the regulatory approach defined by the Committee. This put an end to an institutional conflict regarding the terms of delegation of powers to the Commission in this field.[15] This was only possible after the Commission, at the urging of the European Parliament, provided guarantees aimed at ensuring the respect of the principle of institutional balance and, specifically, of the European Parliament's role in this process.[16]

6.2 The Four-level Regulatory Structure

As summarized by one author, the Lamfalussy process essentially aimed at 'streamlining [. . .] the procedure for the adoption of substantive regulatory

[13] See 'The Committee of Wise Men terms of reference . . .', *cit.*, n. 7.

[14] European Council Resolution, of 23 March 2001, on more effective securities market regulation in the European Union (OJ C 138/1, 11.5.2001). European Parliament Resolution, of 5 February 2002, on the implementation of financial services legislation (OJ C 284 E/15, 21.11.2002). In addition, the specificity of the regulatory process is intended to be safeguarded by a declaration attached to the Treaty on the Functioning of the European Union, according to which 'the Conference takes note of the Commission's intention to continue to consult experts appointed by the Member States in the preparation of draft delegated acts in the financial services area, in accordance with its established practice.' (Declaration No. 39 on Article 290 of the Treaty on the Functioning of the European Union, Treaty of Lisbon, Final Act of the Intergovernmental Conference, OJ C 83/350, 30.3.2010).

[15] On the previous 'institutional deadlock', see Varone, de Visscher, Bergström, and Almer, *op. cit.*, n. 2, pp. 6–10.

[16] On the negotiation process behind the resolutions of the European Council and of the European Parliament, see Varone, de Visscher, Bergström, and Almer, *op. cit.*, n. 2, pp. 13–16.

standards ... as a means for ensuring more comprehensive harmonization and ... strengthening ... cooperation between existing national regulators and the coherent and equivalent application of the European norms by Member States'.[17] As mentioned, celerity and flexibility were the ultimate aims of this regulatory strategy.

In order to fulfil these purposes, the Lamfalussy Committee proposed a regulatory approach structured along four regulatory levels: framework principles, implementing measures (in the pre-Lisbon terminology, which will be used throughout the text), cooperation, and enforcement. This basic structure has shaped current law and is, in essence, maintained in the 2009 proposals, institutional changes notwithstanding.[18] At level 1, the European Parliament and the Council following co-decision—now ordinary legislative procedure—adopt framework principles.[19] These enshrine the basic political choices that are complemented by the level 2 detailed technical measures adopted through comitology procedures, following the intervention of the European Securities Committee (ESC), which is supported by the advice of the Committee of European Securities Regulators (CESR), soon to be replaced by the European Securities and Markets Authority (ESMA). The ESC is a comitology committee. It assists the Commission in the adoption of implementing measures following the regulatory procedure or the regulatory procedure with scrutiny defined in the comitology decision.[20] It is composed

[17] Chalmers *et al.*, *op. cit.*, n. 8, p. 817.

[18] See e.g. recital 15 of the Proposal for a Regulation establishing a European Securities and Markets Authority (*cit.*, n. 4), and recital 9 of the Proposal on the amendments to financial services directives in respect of the powers of the agencies (*cit.*, n. 4; hereinafter 'Omnibus directive' proposal), as well as the compromise agreement on this last text.

[19] The Lamfalussy Report and the Stockholm European Council Resolution had shown preference for the adoption of legislation through fast-track procedure, reduced to a single reading by the European Parliament. This procedure was followed in the adoption of the Transparency Directive (references in n. 20). Neither the Council nor the Parliament have shown willingness in making a more generalized use of this possibility ('Third report monitoring the Lamfalussy Process', Brussels, 17 November 2004, pp. 15–17, hereinafter, the 'Third report', available at <http://ec.europa.eu/internal_market/securities/docs/monitoring/third-report/2004-11-monitoring_en.pdf>). Nevertheless, in the context of the financial crisis, this was the procedure followed to adopt the amendments to level 1 directives (see compromise agreement on the 'Omnibus directive' proposal, *cit.*, n. 4). On the problems raised by this fast-track procedure, see Inter-institutional Monitoring Group, 'Third report ...', *cit.*, p. 16.

[20] Articles 5 and 5a of Council Decision No. 1999/468/EC, of 28 of June 1999, laying down the procedure for the exercise of implementing powers conferred on the Commission, as amended (OJ L 184/23, 17.7.1999), now under revision (see Chapter 7, n. 28). This is applied under Article 64 of the MiFid Directive (Directive No. 2004/39/EC of the European Parliament and of the Council of 21 April 2004 on markets in financial instruments, OJ L 145/38, 30.4.2004, as amended); Article 17 of the Market

of high level officials of Member States' Ministries of Finance and chaired by a Commission representative who participates in the meetings as an observer.[21] CESR was conceived as an independent advisory body,[22] outside the comitology process. It is composed of 'high level representatives from the national public authorities in the field of securities' designated by each Member State and by a 'high-level representative' from the Commission, who will soon integrate the Board of Supervisors of the ESMA.[23] At level 2, and at least until the end of 2010, it has been assisting the Commission, 'in particular' in the preparation of draft implementing measures in the field of securities, either on its own initiative or upon a Commission request. In this case, it has acted on the basis of a mandate given by the European

Abuse Directive (Directive 2003/6/EC of the European Parliament and of the Council of 28 January 2003 on insider dealing and market manipulation, OJ L 96/16, 12.4.2003, as amended); Article 24 of the Prospectus Directive (Directive 2003/71/EC of the European Parliament and of the Council of 4 November 2003 on the prospectus to be published when securities are offered to the public or admitted to trading, OJ L 345/64, 31.12.2003, as amended); and Article 27 of the Transparency Directive (Directive 2004/109/EC of the European Parliament and of the Council of 15 December 2004 on the harmonisation of transparency requirements in relation to information about issuers whose securities are admitted to trading on a regulated market, OJ L 390/38, 31.12.2004, as amended).

[21] Article 3 of Commission Decision No. 2001/528/EC, of 6 June 2001, establishing the European Securities Committee, as amended (OJ L 191/45, 13.7.2001).

[22] Article 1 of Commission Decision No. 2009/77/EC, of 23 January 2009, establishing the Committee of European Securities Regulators (OJ L 25/23, 29.1.2009, hereinafter 'the 2009 Decision'), repealing Commission Decision No. 2001/527/EC, of 6 June 2001 (OJ L 191/43, 13.7.2001, hereinafter 'the 2001 Decision'). This advisory role is in accordance with the proposals of the Lamfalussy Report (*cit.*, p. 32). Note, however, the strengthening of the CESR's role in the 2009 Decision, described below. The fact that the committee's chairperson is elected among its members is intended to stress the CESR's independence vis-à-vis the Commission (Article 7, paragraph 3 of the 2009 Decision and Article 2.1 of the CESR Charter, Ref.: CESR/08-375d, September 2008, available at <http://www.cesr.eu/index.php?docid=5192>. Until 2009, the CESR's budget was exclusively made up of its members' contributions (Article 8 of the 2002 Charter, reviewed in 2006, Ref.: CESR/06-289c, July 2006, available at <http://www.cesr-eu.org/index.php?page=document_details&id=348>, hereinafter 'the CESR Charter'). Since 2009, it can receive contributions or financing for specific projects from the European institutions (Article 9 of the Charter, quoted above, following the 2007 Commission Communication on the review of the Lamfalussy process, *cit.*, n. 3, pp. 12 and 13; see also the 2009 Commission Communication on financial supervision, *cit.*, n. 3, p. 13).

[23] Article 7 (1) and (2) of the 2009 Decision, *cit.*, n. 22; Article 25(1) of Proposal for a Regulation establishing a European Securities and Markets Authority (*cit.*, n. 4) indicates that the heads of the national competent authorities will integrate the Board of Supervisors. The compromise agreement of the European Parliament and the Council on this proposal indicates that changes were introduced regarding the composition of this body, but it does not specify which ones (see COD/2009/0144, *cit.*, n. 4).

Commission (following the advice of the ESC).[24] In essence, it is expected that the ESMA will maintain this advisory role at levels 1 and 2.[25] Nevertheless, a significant change will likely affect level 2: the ESMA will be entitled to develop technical standards that, subject to the Commission's enforcement, will then be adopted as delegated or implementing acts (Articles 290 and 291 TFEU).[26]

It follows from what has been said so far that the Lamfalussy process is very much grounded in comitology procedures. As such, it would risk being trapped by the doubts that cast gloom upon the new Articles 290 and 291 TFEU. This is avoided by Declaration 39 of the Treaty of Lisbon, according to which 'the Conference takes note of the Commission's intention to continue to consult experts appointed by the Member States in the preparation of draft delegated acts in the financial services area, in accordance with its established practice'. This safeguards the Lamfalussy process from such doubts.

At level 3, as originally conceived, coherent transposition into national law, uniform interpretation and application of EU and national rules, as well as convergence between supervisory practices need to be ensured. Up to the creation of the ESMA, these tasks have been decentralized, and entrusted to national regulators acting within CESR,[27] which has operated here under a different hat—no longer as an advisory body to the Commission in the implementing rule-making procedure, but as 'a fully independent' network coordinator acting on its own initiative.[28] This will fundamentally change with the creation of the ESMA.

The CESR's core task at level 3 has been to ensure coordinated transposition, as well as convergence among national regulators both in their

[24] Article 2 of the 2009 Decision *cit.*, n. 22, and Article 4.2 of the CESR Charter, *cit.*, n. 22.

[25] Article 19(1) of the Proposal for a Regulation establishing a European Securities and Markets Authority (*cit.*, n. 4) encompasses this advisory role and recital 8 of the preamble indicates that the new authorities will 'assume all of the tasks and competences of the [committees they replace]'. This last specification was reiterated in the respective compromise agreement (*cit.*, n. 4).

[26] Article 7 of the Proposal for a Regulation establishing a European Securities and Markets Authority (*cit.*, n. 4). It follows from the compromise agreement on the 'Omnibus directive' proposal (COD/2009/0161, *cit.*, n. 4) that the technical standards to which this Article refers are likely to affect both level 2 and level 3 measures. On this see, Sub-section 6.3.6 below.

[27] Lamfalussy Report, *cit.*, n. 1, p. 37; Articles 3 and 4 of the 2009 Decision n. 22; Articles 4.3 and 4.4 of the CESR Charter, *cit.*, n. 22.

[28] Lamfalussy Report, *cit.*, n. 1, pp. 37–8.

rule-making tasks (defining 'common approaches and standards in order to facilitate harmonized implementation of EU law') and in their supervision of the behaviour of financial firms.[29] This task will be taken over by the ESMA, endowed however with increased regulatory powers.[30] The CESR's role at level 3 has been progressively defined very much on the basis of CESR's practice. It has also been considerably strengthened, in particular after the 2009 decision that revised the CESR's legal status. Among other points, this decision, currently in force, opened the possibility of adopting decisions by qualified majority, where consensus cannot not be reached,[31] and established that the CESR members that do not follow the CESR guidelines are expected to state reasons for their choice.[32] This was intended to put pressure on non-complying members and to reinforce the CESR's authority over the choices of national regulators.[33] This was the first step of the ongoing trend to reinforce the role of the EU bodies in ensuring consistent application of EU rules. In fact, the future agency will be endowed with the power, *inter alia*, to issue draft binding technical standards 'designed to further develop, specify or determine the conditions of application of... level 2 measures'.[34]

[29] As explained by CERS in 'The Role of CESR at 'Level 3' under the Lamfalussy Process', Ref: CESR/04-527b, October 2004, pp. 5–12 (the quotation is from p. 5), at <http://www.cesr-eu.org/index.php?docid=2550>). Hereinafter, 'The Role...'. On the distinction between regulation and supervision, see Lastra, *op. cit.*, n. 9, pp. 49 and 60.

[30] Articles 8 and 9 of the Proposal for a Regulation establishing a European Securities and Markets Authority (*cit.*, n. 4). See also Articles 14 (which indicates the tasks that the ESMA will perform 'at a minimum' in order to ensure a common supervisory culture) and 15.

[31] See Article 14, 1st paragraph of the 2009 Decision (see Articles 5.5 to 5.7 of the 2002 CESR's Charter, *cit.*, n. 22) and Articles 6.2 (where consensus is defined as 'all members concurring with one or two exceptions') and 6.3 of the current CESR's Charter, *cit.*, n. 22. The fact that the CESR (in fact, all the so-called 'Level 3 Committees') has generally acted on the basis of consensus was perceived as one of the factors harming the efficiency and effectiveness of its action (see Commission Com munication, 'Review of the Lamfalussy process', p. 9, *cit.*, n. 3). The 2009 Proposal for a Regulation establishing a European Securities and Markets Authority shifts to decision-making by qualified or simple majority (see Article 29(1) and (2) of the Proposal, *cit.*, n. 4).

[32] See, respectively, Articles 3 and 14, second paragraph, of the 2009 Decision, *cit.*, n. 22. See also Article 6.4 of the CESR's Charter, where the reasons not to apply a CESR decision are spelt out, as well as the procedure that should be followed in this case.

[33] See the 2007 Commission Communication, Review of the Lamfalussy process, *cit.*, n. 3, pp. 9–10.

[34] Compromise agreement on the 'Omnibus directive' proposal (COD/2009/0161), *cit.*, n. 4. The text of the agreement refers to 'binding technical standards'. It is not clear to which Article of the proposal this refers, but very likely this corresponds to Article 7, which rules the conditions under which ESMA issues technical standards.

Finally, regulatory action at level 4 as conceived in the Lamfalussy Report was entrusted to the Commission, which should boost the enforcement of EU rules, performing its traditional role of 'guardian of the Treaties' (in principle with the cooperation of Member States, regulators, private actors, and the European Parliament).[35] The reform will endow the ESMA with considerable powers of enforcement, even if it is specified that these are without prejudice to the powers of the Commission under Article 258 TFEU (former Article 226 EC).[36]

In short, in view of the aims of the Lamfalussy process, two main features were of fundamental importance. First, the clear distinction between the 'core principles' and the technical character of level 2 implementing measures was considered a key aspect to speed up the adoption of legislation. Secondly, the coordination activity carried out by the CESR at level 3 was crucial in order to ensure greater supervisory convergence and address shortcomings in the uniform application and interpretation of EU rules that could otherwise hinder the cross-border provision of services. The first feature was far from being a novel issue in EU law. In fact, the dividing line between basic and implementing acts has long since been a battleground for defining the contours of inter-institutional balance (and is likely to remain so, given the doubts on how to apply Articles 290 and 291 TFEU). At the same time, this was, from the outset, one of the thorny points of the process.[37] It is in the second feature—the creation of an independent expert committee at level 3 (soon to be succeeded by the ESMA)—that the main innovation of the Lamfalussy process lay.

Both aspects contend with the legitimacy and accountability of the whole process. These two issues have been very much present in the conception, setting up (mainly due to the European Parliament's objections), and

[35] Lamfalussy Report, *cit.*, n. 1, p. 40.

[36] See, in particular, Articles 9(6) and 1(3) of the Proposal for a Regulation establishing a European Securities and Markets Authority (*cit.*, n. 4).

[37] See, Lastra, *op. cit.*, n. 9, p. 64; Karel Lannoo (2005) 'The transformation of financial regulation and supervision in the EU', in Donato Masciandro (ed.), *Handbook of Central Banking and Financial Authorities in Europe. New Architectures in the Supervision of Financial Markets*, Cheltenham, Northampton: Edward Elgar, pp. 485–511, at pp. 491–2). Relating the Courts' jurisprudence in this matter to financial services regulation, see Yannis V. Avgerinos (2002) 'Essential and non-essential measures: delegation of powers in EU securities regulation', *European Law Journal*, Vol. 8, n. 2, pp. 269–89. See also the 2007 Commission Communication, Review of the Lamfalussy process, n. 3, p. 4).

evolving dynamics of the Lamfalussy process.[38] Consultation was, from the outset, proposed as one possible means of ensuring both. However, this provides only part of the explanation on the importance acquired by consultation in this context. Indeed, the specific characteristics of the regulated markets provided an additional impetus to the creation of consultative procedures.

6.3 'Active, Well Defined Involvement of Market Participants and Consumers'

Two main sets of reasons justify the relevance attributed to consultation in the Lamfalussy regulatory framework.[39] First, as suggested above, fears of technocratic regulation and deficient democratic accountability of decision-making stemmed from the creation of swift rule-making procedures relying on extensive delegation and, perhaps to a lesser extent, from the creation of an administrative regulatory structure of fluid contours inserted in the formal Community (now Union) regulatory process. Arguably, these concerns remain after the current ongoing reform, perhaps to an increasing degree, given the powers of the agencies. Secondly, anticipated consensus on the existence and meaning of rules was perceived as a factor favouring the effectiveness of regulation. This is in part due to the neo-functionalist logic of reaching out to those interested 'in the smooth and efficient operation of financial markets', reflected in the Financial Services Action Plan.[40] In part, this

[38] Pinning down the whole procedure to institutional links and controls was a concern present in the Lamfalussy Report: it insisted on the need to safeguard the institutional balance and the decisional process defined in the Treaty, and advised the early involvement of the Parliament in the definition of the borderline between level 1 and level 2 measures (see, for example, pp. 19–20, 25, 30, 34). On the European Parliament's resistances regarding the risks posed by the Lamfalussy process to the inter-institutional balance and on the ensuing guarantees, see John F. Mogg (2002) 'Regulating financial services in Europe: a new approach', *Fordham International Law Journal*, Vol. 26, n. 1, pp. 58–81, at pp. 77–80, Lastra, *op. cit.*, n. 9, pp. 62–3, Chalmers *et al.*, *op. cit.*, n. 8, pp. 810–11. On the way this problem has been perceived by the CESR, see Niamh Moloney (2007) 'Innovation and risk in the EC financial market regulation: new instruments of financial market intervention and the Committee of European Securities Regulators', *European Law Review*, Vol. 32, n. 5, pp. 627–63, at pp. 644–63. Similar concerns are revealed by the compromise agreements on the Commission's 2009 proposals, which insist on the 'genuinely technical' nature of the standards adopted by the agencies and on the intervention of the European Parliament in their adoption (see compromise agreements, *cit.*, n. 4).

[39] The sentence in the title is taken from the Lamfalussy Report, *cit.*, n. 1, p. 42.

[40] Financial Services Action Plan, *cit.*, n. 1, p. 17.

results from specific regulatory characteristics of the securities field that pushed for the desired inclusive approach, namely its fragmented and hybrid nature.[41] These two sets of reasons are analysed in the following sections, while presenting also how consultation was conceived in the Lamfalussy Report and in other related documents. Only the documents that preceded the current reform allow us to understand the relevance that consultation acquired in this sector in more recent years. It is thus justified that, despite the envisaged replacement of CESR by the ESMA, the following analysis will refer to the regulatory framework still in place at the end of 2010. This section ends with an overview of the possible impact of the envisaged reform on current consultation practices.

6.3.1 *Level 1: minimum standards*

According to the Lamfalussy Report, consultation must be ensured throughout the rule-making process. In a first phase, 'there should be a strengthened and open dialogue with market participants and end-users so as to advise the Commission on a continuous basis on level 1 work'.[42] To achieve this, the Commission should hold 'open, transparent and systematic' consultations and, 'where necessary, open hearings'. The Lamfalussy Committee considered that minimum guarantees should be adopted to safeguard the usefulness of consultation: it proposed the clear definition of deadlines and the elaboration of a summary of the consultation process undertaken to be made available with the final proposal.[43]

Far from being a novelty, consultation at this level represented the continuation of the long-standing practice of consultation preceding the Commission's legislative proposals. The proposals of the Lamfalussy Committee merely underlined aspects that needed to be corrected in order to take the full benefits from consultation procedures, and, in a way, heralded some of the 'good governance' measures that the Commission later proposed in the White Paper on Governance.

Alongside this, the Lamfalussy Report also underlined that Member States and their regulators, on the one hand, and the European Parliament, on the other, should be consulted as early as possible on any Commission proposal for level 1 legislation. Therefore, both inter-institutional agreement and

[41] These two characteristics are pointed out by Julia Black (2003) 'Enrolling actors in regulatory systems: examples from the UK financial services regulation', *Public Law*, pp. 63–91.

[42] Lamfalussy Report, *cit.*, n. 1, p. 25.

[43] All quotations are from p. 25.

anticipated consensus were considered crucial to achieving the desired goals of the regulatory process.

6.3.2 *Level 2: bringing participation to the realm of comitology*

At the second level of regulation, the Lamfalussy Committee recommended that the CESR, following a request by the Commission for technical advice, should engage in consultation with market participants, consumers, and end-users 'according to a fixed, preferably mandatory set of [previously established] procedural rules'. The Lamfalussy Committee defined both the principles and the essential steps of the consultation procedures, according to the following basic principles:

> market practitioners must be involved . . . at every level . . . in a continuous process . . . with particular weight given to those with knowledge and expertise on the subject in question . . . in an open process, using, inter alia, the internet . . . with end-users being considered at the same time.[44]

The consultation procedure should be designed along the following lines. First, in the face of complex issues, the CESR should delineate the appropriate regulatory approach following consultation on the basis of a 'concept release', where the problem and the several options are outlined, thereby asking for public input on the desirable approach. Secondly, the CESR should submit a draft proposal to consultation. Each of these two phases should last for a maximum period of three months. Thirdly, it was suggested that, where necessary, the CESR should complement this consultation procedure with hearings or roundtables. Lastly, the Committee advised that the CESR's final recommendations should be accompanied by a summary of the comments received.[45] Particular care was taken to insist on the involvement of the European Parliament also during the level 2 regulatory process.

Both the Council and the European Parliament were favourable to consultation. The Council endorsed the proposals of the Lamfalussy Committee in this respect, considering that the Commission should '[strengthen] its dialogue with consumers and market participants' and that the CESR 'should consult extensively, in an open and transparent manner . . . and . . . have the confidence of market participants'.[46] The European Parliament urged the Commission to 'guarantee market operators and consumers wide-

[44] Lamfalussy Report, *cit.*, n. 1, pp. 32–3.

[45] *Ibidem.*, p. 33.

[46] European Council Resolution of 23 March 2001, *cit.*, n. 14, paragraphs 2 and 6.

ranging consultation by setting up an advisory committee under the supervision of the Regulators Committee [the CESR]'.[47] In addition, in line with the recommendations of the Lamfalussy Committee and the European Council's receptivity, the Commission imposed on the CESR a legal obligation to consult, at the same time defining some parameters of action. Thus, according to the first paragraph of Article 12 of the 2009 Decision (which reproduces the corresponding provision of the 2002 Decision), 'before transmitting its opinion to the Commission, the Committee shall, *at an early stage*, consult market participants, consumers and end-users *extensively* and in an *open and transparent manner*'.[48] Moreover, as a rule, the Committee ought to publish the results of the consultations.[49] Clearly, consultation was considered to be intrinsic to the function of the CESR, at least in relation to its role at level 2.[50] Finally, since this consultation takes place in one of the sub-phases of the procedure for the adoption of level 2 measures, the Lamfalussy Committee, in addition to the insistence on consultations carried out by the CESR, recommended the Commission 'to maintain a similar level of transparency and openness as these proposals move to the Securities Committee [ESC]'.[51]

It is interesting to compare this approach to consultation with the one that, a few months after the publication of the Lamfalussy Report, was adopted by the Commission in its White Paper on Governance, which was later developed in the Communication on 'a reinforced culture of consultation' setting forth a code of conduct on consultation practices. In the main, the Lamfalussy process anticipated the Commission's more 'structured' approach to consultation presented in the White Paper on Governance and in the communication mentioned.[52] Two aspects are, however, strikingly different. First, the

[47] European Parliament, Report on the implementation of financial services regulation (2001/2247(INI)), Committee of Constitutional Affairs, Rapporteur: Karl von Wogau, Final A5-0011/2002, 23 January 2002, point 11 and point 2 of the conclusions.

[48] Emphasis added. The 2009 Decision will be repealed by effect of the entry into force of the regulation establishing the ESMA. This point will be resumed below.

[49] Article 12, second paragraph, of the 2009 Decision, *cit.*, n. 22.

[50] The scope of Article 12 is limited to the decisions that the CESR needs to transmit to the Commission. Its wording does not encompass the non-binding decisions addressed to national regulators, which form most of the work that the CESR has developed at level 3 up to now.

[51] Lamfalussy Report, *cit.*, n. 1, p. 33.

[52] Commission of the European Communities, 'European Governance. A White Paper', COM (2001) 428 final, Brussels, 25.7.2001; 'Towards a reinforced culture of consultation and dialogue—General principles and minimum standards for consultation of interested parties by the Commission', COM (2002) 704 final, Brussels, 11.12.2002.

obligation to consult imposed on the CESR by the Commission, under Article 12 of the decision establishing the CESR, is seemingly at odds with the position according to which the Commission should not rely on legal rules to ensure consultation. The main concern of the Commission, when stating its general approach to consultation, was to prevent judicial review on procedural grounds. Article 12 certainly prevents a hypothetical inversion of policy with regard to consultation—and, to this extent, consolidates the Lamfalussy recommendations.[53]

Secondly, and more importantly, consultation was strengthened at the regulatory level that, as a rule, stayed outside of the scope of the Commission's code of conduct on consultation practices: in the procedures leading up to the adoption of implementing regulations and directives by the Commission. This different treatment can be explained on the basis of the two specific features of the Lamfalussy process that distinguish it from 'traditional comitology procedures'. One of those features was the blunt and overt assumption that in order to ensure one of the main goals of the whole regulatory set-up—speed in decision-making—rules adopted under the then co-decision procedure should be restricted to 'essential issues' and leave out 'technical implementing details'. While this aspect merely corresponded to the well-known reality of EU regulation, here it was stated as a principle on which the success of the whole process rests. As such, it seemed to limit the Council and the Parliament's power in favour of less democratic and less transparent procedures perhaps more than in other fields. A second specificity of the Lamfalussy strategy, alluded to above, added to the fear of technocratic decision-making: national regulators, through the CESR, were directly involved in the decisional procedure in an advisory role to the Commission. Again, this was nothing fully unknown to comitology procedures, where often the consultation of expert committees takes place in parallel with the intervention of committees composed of representatives of national governments. The CESR's independence, however, raised specific issues of accountability, as will be seen in the next section.

More broadly, it should be recalled that during this period (in the aftermath of the mad-cow disease crisis) the comitology system was, more than ever, under scrutiny. Furthermore, at a time at which the Commission was undergoing an overhaul of its governing practices, the Parliament kept struggling for an equal recognition of its institutional rights at the level of

[53] See, however, Sub-section 6.3.6 below.

implementing regulation. Moreover, the EU institutions were in general increasingly concerned with citizens' detachment from European matters. This context could be an indication that the need to ensure the legitimacy and accountability of the regulatory process was one of the concerns justifying the relevance attributed to consultation in the Lamfalussy Process.[54] Still, in general, this did not lead to reinforced consultation practices in comitology procedures, which, as noted, remained outside the scope of the consultation standards published in 2002. In this respect, the contrast of the Lamfalussy Process with 'normal' comitology procedures is noteworthy, in particular, the degree of detail of the Lamfalussy Report with regard to consultation procedures undertaken at level 2.

Times have changed, and despite the fact that similar issues of legitimacy and accountability are very likely to remain after the present reform, no provision similar to Article 12 of the 2009 Decision is presently envisaged with regard to the ESMA. In the Commission's 2009 proposal, the correspondent provision to Article 12 entails a looser duty of consultation, applicable to draft technical standards according to which 'before submitting them to the Commission, the Authority shall, *where appropriate*, conduct open public consultations on technical standards and analyse the potential costs and benefits'.[55]

6.3.3 *Level 3: facing accountability and legitimacy deficits*

In contrast to the detail with which consultation was considered at level 2, and despite the insistence on ensuring consultation throughout the regulatory process, the Lamfalussy Report omitted any reference to the involvement of interested parties in the CESR level 3 activities. Indeed, the very definition of the CESR role at level 3 was left quite open. At any rate, it was clear from the outset that, in contrast to its role at level 2, its tasks at this level did not imply issuing an opinion that should be transmitted to the Commission, but the adoption of acts and measures that have the national regulators and authorities as addressees.[56] As such, they do not fall under the obligation to consult in current Article 12.[57] Nevertheless, there was a

[54] Chalmers et al., *op. cit.*, n. 8, pp. 810–11.

[55] Article 7(1), second paragraph, emphasis added, of the Proposal for a Regulation establishing a European Securities and Markets Authority (*cit.*, n. 4). The analysis of this provision will be resumed below in Sub-section 6.3.6.

[56] See Article 8 of the Proposal for a Regulation establishing a European Securities and Markets Authority, *cit.*, n. 4).

[57] See note above.

self-commitment on the part of the CESR to extend the consultation processes envisaged in level 2 to the activity in level 3. As one can read in the document where the CESR defined its role at level 3, the 'CESR follows the same consultation practices at level 2 and level 3' and 'the CESR Charter and CESR Public Statement on Consultation Practices... do not distinguish between level 2 and level 3 in [the] CESR's approach to consultation'.[58]

Hence, in addition to the recommendations of the Lamfalussy Committee, the CESR created a market participants' consultative panel and established consultative working groups, working together with its expert groups. The consultative panel, according to information available on the CESR's website, resulted from suggestions of both the European Parliament and the Lamfalussy Committee. At present, this panel assists the CESR but it also has a sort of surveillance role in particular in what concerns the committee's consultation policy, its priorities, and working methods.[59] The possibility of creating consultative working groups was envisaged in the CESR's Charter, 'for the purpose of facilitating the dialogue with market participants, consumers and other end users of financial services'.[60] According to the CESR's website, the members of the working groups are drawn from across the Member States and are not intended to represent national or specific firms' interests. Their role is to provide technical advice to the expert groups and their intervention does not replace consultations with all market participants. Information on the processes and criteria to choose the members both of the consultative panel and of the working groups cannot be found either in the legal texts or in the documents available on the CESR's website, although, in some cases, the

[58] 'The Role...', *cit.*, n. 29, p. 5. Note that Article 12 of the 2009 Decision continues to exclude the duty of the CESR to consult at level 3, despite the fact that one of the concerns underlying the 2009 revision of the CESR's legal status (and that of the other level 3 Committees) was to adapt its original founding decision in order to better reflect its role and functioning at level 3 (see the 2007 Commission Communication on the revision of the Lamfalussy process, *cit.*, n. 3, p. 8; see also recitals 4 and 6 of the preamble of the 2009 Decision, as well as its Article 4 to 6, without correspondence in the previous Decision). Article 7 of the Commission's proposal (*cit.*, n. 4) covers the adoption of technical standards intended to further develop level 3 measures. Arguably, the looser requirement of consultation enshrined therein could also apply to level 3 measures. On this, see Sub-section 6.3.6. below.

[59] For more information, see <http://www.cesr-eu.org>. Similarly, the Proposal for a Regulation establishing a European Securities and Markets Authority (*cit.*, n. 4) envisages the creation of a Securities and Markets Stakeholder Group, which will cover some of the tasks now performed by the consultative panel (Article 22, on this see Sub-section 6.3.6 below).

[60] Article 5.9 of the CESR's Charter.

list of members is public[61] (as are the reports of the consultative panel meetings).

Concerns for legitimacy and accountability are likely to have determined the role of consultation at this regulatory level. In fact, the CESR was a novel 'institution' which needed to prove sufficient 'democratic qualities' beyond its ability to perform effectively the role that was assigned to it. At the same time, its 'hybridity' is not unproblematic in terms of accountability. It is an 'independent advisory group'[62] deprived of legal personality but, at the same time, it is more than just a network of regulators: it was created by a European decision and given the status of independence in the framework of a regulatory approach that was endorsed at the highest political level. While CESR's level 3 activity is already potentially highly influential on financial markets, it is, arguably, not adequately limited by the controls envisaged at the EU level. The only explicit mechanism formally envisaged is the CESR's duty to 'periodically and *at least annually* inform the Council, the European Parliament and the Commission on the achievement of the activities set out in the work program'.[63] However, it is not clear what the consequences of this duty to report may be, in particular taking into account the CESR's status of independence and its composition. Given that the CESR is composed of representatives of national regulators, one may argue that it is accountable mainly to the Council as well as to national parliaments and governments. Yet, *how* these controls are concretized is not envisaged in any of the documents ruling the institutional aspects of the CESR. Alongside this, its members are also independent vis-à-vis their national governments, and the ability of national mechanisms of accountability to ensure control over the activity that the CESR performs at the EU level is likely to vary. Not surprisingly, the CESR has 'shown itself very sensitive to accountability charges' and carefully built its links with the European Parliament and the Council.[64] To this, one could add the fact

[61] This is true for the consultative panel (see <http://www.cesr-eu.org/template.php?page=contenu_groups&id=24&keymore=1&BoxId=2> and for some of the expert groups (see <http://www.cesr-eu.org/template.php?page=contenu_groups&id=5&keymore=1&BoxId=2>).

[62] Article 1 of the 2009 Decision, *cit.*, n. 22.

[63] Article 13 of the 2009 Decision, emphasis added; see also Article 6 of the CESR's Charter, *cit.*, n. 22. In its Charter CESR further defined that it submits its annual report to the Commission and this is sent to the European Parliament and the Council. However, the Chair of the Committee reports to the European Parliament upon request and maintains strong links with the European Security Committee.

[64] Moloney, *op. cit.*, n. 38, p. 659. For other remarks regarding accountability, see *idem*, pp. 650–3, 658–62.

that, at least until recently, the role of the CESR at level 3 remained relatively undefined. This was vaguely sketched in the Lamfalussy Report, which was endorsed as such by the EU institutions, and virtually absent from the 2002 Decision that established the committee.[65] In this normative vacuum, it was essentially the CESR itself that defined what its role would be at this regulatory level, until the adoption of the 2009 Decision, which largely built upon previous practices.[66]

Uncertain accountability mechanisms and the uncertain legal mandate that prevailed until recently could have hindered the perceived legitimacy of the CESR. In addition, legitimacy concerns may arise from the possibility that, in the course of regulatory creation and adaptation, level 3 standards may determine or pre-empt choices to be taken at levels 1 and 2, thus inverting the logic of the procedure, and overstepping the institutional prerogatives of the European institutions.[67] In these circumstances, opening up CESR's decisional processes to input from interested parties, transparently revealing the results of consultation as well as showing which contributions were taken into consideration in the final decisions, was very likely perceived as a means of countervailing legitimacy claims.

One should add that, arguably, similar accountability concerns that were raised up to now by the CESR will apply also to the ESMA, to the extent that it is doubtful whether the envisaged mechanisms of control will suffice to hold it accountable, in particular in view of its reinforced independence.[68] Yet, the future of consultation in the new regulatory framework is uncertain.[69]

[65] These concerns underlie the 'Final report monitoring the Lamfalussy process', delivered by the second inter-institutional monitoring group in 15 October 2007, available at <http://ec.europa.eu/internal_market/finances/docs/committees/071015_final_report_en.pdf>, pp. 17–18 (hereinafter 'Final Report...'). The inter-institutional monitoring group pleaded for a clear legal mandate of the Level 3 Committees, including CESR's, and related this to the committees' accountability.

[66] On the way the CESR has developed its role at level 3, see Moloney, *op. cit.*, n. 38, pp. 644–63. See n. 58 above.

[67] Moloney, *op. cit.*, n. 38, p. 662. This risk is confirmed by the care taken in the compromise agreement on the 'Omnibus directive' proposal (COD/2009/0161, *cit.*, n. 4) to clarify that 'in cases where the technical standards are designed to further develop... level-2 measures, they should be adopted only once the relevant level-2 measure has been adopted and should respect the content of the level-2 measure'.

[68] See, on the one hand, Articles 27, 31, 33(1), 34, 35(1), 37 and, on the other, Articles 28(4) and (5), 32(6), and 35 of the Proposal for a Regulation establishing a European Securities and Markets Authority (*cit.*, n. 4), as well as the specification, added by the compromise agreement, that technical standards shall be forwarded by the Commission to the European Parliament (*cit.*, n. 4).

[69] See Sub-section 6.3.6 below.

6.3.4 *Consultation: matching legitimacy and accountability?*

How can consultation, in the way it was envisaged in the Lamfalussy Report, enhance legitimacy and accountability of the regulatory process? The answer to this question depends on the concepts of legitimacy and accountability that are adopted. It is not appropriate to enter here into the extensive debates on legitimacy and accountability deficits of the EU institutional set-up, nor on the discussion on which values and qualities these concepts should ensure.[70] For our purposes, the relations between the three concepts at hand will only be considered in the context of the Lamfalussy process. In other words, the observations that follow take the Lamfalussy process as a frame of reference. As previously noted, one should underline that in the primary sources concerning this procedure there are no indications that consultation procedures were at any point associated with legitimacy and accountability. This assumption results from the interpretation presented above.

If legitimacy means the perception by decision-makers and the recipients of decisions that an institution has the 'right to rule',[71] then consultation *may* enhance legitimacy in four different ways. First, it is perceived to further the effectiveness of the regulatory process, insofar as it facilitates anticipated consensus regarding the content and meaning of rules. From this perspective, consultation also ensures responsiveness in a double sense. It allows not only the creation of rules that speak to the needs of the regulated but, in addition, these rules are grounded in a combined deployment of regulatory resources in order to allow for better policy solutions to which both national regulators and regulated contribute.[72] Next, and in the same vein, consultation may contribute to adding expertise to the regulatory

[70] For a synthetic overview of the legitimacy debate and the problems of some of the academic contributions in this regard see Wolfgang Wessels (2003) 'On the EU legitimacy debate: approaches and desiderata', in Georges Vandersanden and Aline de Walsche (eds), *Mélanges en hommage a Jean-Victor Louis*, Vol I, Bruxelles: Éditions de l'Université de Bruxelles, pp. 627–37. On accountability in the EU, see the works quoted below at notes 72, 74, 75, 77, 78, and 83. See also Madalina Busuioc (2010) *The Accountability of European Agencies. Legal Provisions and Ongoing Practices*, Delft: Eburon, Chapter 3.

[71] This draws on the concept of legitimacy used by Black, *op. cit.*, n. 41, p. 76. In similar terms, drawing on Harbermas, Amaryllis Verhoeven (2002) *The European Union in Search of a Democratic and Constitutional Theory*, The Hague, London, New York: Kluwer Law International, p. 11.

[72] To this extent, the Lamfalussy process resembles the responsive regulation model developed by Ian Ayres and John Braithwaite (1992) *Responsive Regulation: Transcending the Deregulation Debate*, Oxford: Oxford University Press, pp. 4–5.

process, thereby aiming at better regulatory outcomes.[73] These seem to have been the predominant concerns underlying the design of the Lamfalussy process.[74] Finally, by adopting an inclusive approach to consultation—if possible, embracing all those with a stake in the rules to be adopted—decision-makers (in this case, the Commission, and up to now the CESR) seek to ensure support for regulation and 'create a public', thus broadening their legitimacy basis throughout the varied range of interests and communities to which their regulatory activity relates. Indeed, consultation, in the way it was conceived by the Lamfalussy Committee, presupposes open and transparent procedures, in which, first, information is publicized in advance, secondly, any person with a relation to financial markets is granted access as a means of seeking inclusiveness and, thirdly, a summary of the input received is made public together with the final decision (ideally, it should be possible to deduce from there the reasons why a certain rule has been adopted and to trace which input influenced the outcome). In this shift, consultation as a means to improved problem-solving could probably mutate into a possible source of 'normative legitimacy', i.e. the acceptance of the entity in question as legitimate in light of democratic standards,[75] insofar as it creates the potential for 'democratizing destabilization' through practices that resemble some aspects of democracy.[76] However, this can only be verified on the basis of a deeper empirical study, tested against the background of normative theories of legitimacy.[77] Admittedly, building

[73] 'Third report...', *cit.*, n. 19, p. 20.

[74] See Sub-section 6.3.5 below.

[75] Achim Hurrelmann (2007) 'Multilevel legitimacy: conceptualizing legitimacy relationships between the EU and national democracies', in Joan DeBardeleben and Hurrelmann (eds), *Democratic Dilemmas of Multilevel Governance. Legitimacy, Representation and Accountability in the European Union*, Basingstoke, New York: Palgrave MacMillan, p. 17–37, at p. 17.

[76] Charles Sabel and Jonathan Zeitlin (2008) 'Learning from difference: the new architecture of experimentalist governance in the EU', *European Law Journal*, Vol. 14, n. 3, pp. 271–327, at p. 277, who argue that 'the diffusion of procedural commitments to transparency and participation in the EU networked governance has had the democratizing destabilization effect in terms of stimulating demands to widen the circle of actors and alternatives involved in policy making at the national as well as the European level' (pp. 315–16).

[77] The Lamfalussy procedure could be tested in light of theories of deliberative democracy, assessing to what extent 'initial preferences are transformed through discussion by the force of the better argument' (Sabel and Jonathan, *op. cit.*, p. 272). This is, partially, the object of a doctoral project that was undertaken in the University of Bamberg by Eva Ruffing, who compared the legitimacy of regulatory decisions from the perspective of the liberal and the deliberative democratic theory (at the time of the writing its working title was 'Die legitimität europaïscher Regulierungsentscheidungen am Beispiel der Wertpapierregulierung'—'The legitimacy of European regulatory decisions using as an example the securities regulation'). In a way, this is inserted

links with market participants (as well as with international organizations operating in the field), the CESR in particular has sought to create the constituencies that might consider the regulatory options adopted to be legitimate, thereby strengthening its market and institutional position.[78]

It is conceivable that these potential advantages of consultation were envisaged by the designers of the Lamfalussy process. Nevertheless, the extent to which these are effective advantages depends on empirical evidence that might support these assumptions. While this falls outside the realm of this book, a limited account of how these procedures have worked in practice is given below (Section 6.4), with a view to illustrating the practical problems that might hinder consultative procedures. In any event, as it emerges from the above characterization, consultation is a means of enhancing the technical legitimacy of regulatory options, hardly their political legitimacy grounded in democratic values.

Arguably, it is less evident how the consultation procedures proposed, adopted, and furthered in practice could enhance accountability of the actors involved. At first sight, one could claim that consultation procedures constitute a channel of accountability. Responsiveness, which may be considered one of the aims of this new institutional and procedural design, may be seen as one way of ensuring accountability to the public. Indeed, where decision-makers are deemed to be or become responsive to a particular public's needs, it may be considered that they are accountable to the public they serve.[79] Consultative procedures, in the way envisaged in the Lamfalussy process, could be seen as a means of ensuring both. Furthermore, the legitimacy concerns associated with this regulatory strategy might make it tempting to attribute this role to consultation procedures.[80] This would be in line with the Commission's White Paper on Governance, which suggested that better involvement and broad consultations could be a source of

in a broader strand of research that undertakes to assess participation in EU decisional processes in light of deliberative democracy and other democratic theories (see Beate Kohler-Koch and Barbara Finke (2007) 'The institutional shaping of EU-society relations: a contribution to democracy via participation?', *Journal of Civil Society*, Vol. 3, n. 3, pp. 205–21).

[78] Moloney, *op. cit.*, n. 38, pp. 647–9.

[79] This relationship is analysed by Richard Mulgan, who indicates that the two terms have been taken as synonyms in particular in public sector reform literature: Richard Mulgan (2000) "Accountability': an ever-expanding concept?', *Public Administration*, Vol. 78, n. 3, pp. 555–73, at p. 568.

[80] Underlining the associations between accountability to the public and particular conceptions of democracy, in particular deliberative democracy, Mulgan, *op. cit.*, pp. 569–70.

accountability.[81] The idea is that involving external actors in the decisional process and publicizing documents at their various stages provides opportunities for public control that would not exist otherwise. Indeed, in a way, the consultation procedures undertaken in the realm of the Lamfalussy process may be considered to constitute a type of community-based control,[82] insofar as they involve regulators, regulated, and other potentially interested persons in the making of norms and in the definition and monitoring of how they are transposed into each legal system. This is, however, something different than considering that those external actors or the public in general can call decision-makers to account.[83]

Countering such arguments, a few authors have recently called attention to the need to distinguish participation (in the sense of 'participation at large', following the terminology presented in Chapter 2) from accountability, denying that the former can bring about the latter. Accountability, in a narrow but still somewhat vague sense, presupposes 'ex post calling by one person of another actor to account for his prior conduct'.[84] In a commonly used formula, this implies defining who is accountable, to whom, for what, with which consequences, and through which procedures.[85] In this sense, accountability may be a synonym for political responsibility as well as for liability, equally embracing other forms of judicial control.[86] As such, the 'public' or the interested persons consulted during decisional procedures cannot constitute an 'accountability forum', to use

[81] 'European Governance. A White Paper', *cit.*, n. 58, p. 17. Carol Harlow (2002) *Accountability in the European Union*, Oxford: Oxford University Press, p. 185.

[82] See, in this respect, Colin Scott (2002) 'The governance of the European Union: the potential for multi-level control', *European Law Journal*, Vol. 8, n. 1, pp. 59–79, at p. 65. Scott considers the Lamfalussy process and regards it as a hybrid between hierarchy and community-based control (p. 68).

[83] On the distinction between accountability and control, presenting the former to be narrower than the latter, see Mulgan, *op. cit.*, n. 79, pp. 563–6. Distinguishing both terms differently, Harlow, *op. cit.*, p. 10. See also Madalina Busuioc (2009) 'Accountability, Control and Independence: The Case of European Agencies', *European Law Journal*, Vol. 15, n. 5, pp. 599–615, and Deirdre Curtin (2009) *Executive Power of the European Union. Law, Practices and the Living Constitution*, Oxford: Oxford University Press, p. 252.

[84] Richard Stewart (2006) 'Mars or Venus? US and European models for regulatory governance and the discontents of globalization', Discussion paper presented at the Transatlantic Program, Robert Schumann Centre for Advanced Studies, European University Institute, 27 April 2006, p. 8.

[85] *Idem*, pp. 8–9. Similarly, Mark Bovens (2007), 'Analysing and assessing accountability: a conceptual framework', *European Law Journal*, Vol. 13, n. 4, pp. 447–68, at pp. 454–5.

[86] For a flavour on the use of these concepts and on how much they are dependent on national traditions, see Harlow, *op. cit.*, n. 81, pp. 13–18.

Bovens' expression. Consultation procedures lack the structural element of accountability, namely that of retrospective control. They do not allow decision-makers to be held to 'account to a forum *after the fact*'.[87] This is intrinsically linked to the fact that consultation procedures have a different purpose than that of holding decision-makers to account. Even if they may allow some control over the decision-makers' conduct, this is an effect marginal to the goal of ensuring that the persons consulted contribute to the outcome of the decisional procedures. As a result, consultation procedures also lack substantive elements of accountability.[88] To begin with, the object of consultation procedures is not to require explanations and justifications pertaining to the conduct of the decision-maker in order to pass a judgment on their actions. Next, they do not entail sanctions attached to possible misconduct of the decision-maker. There may be mechanisms for holding the decision-maker to account for their conduct regarding consultation procedures, but these mechanisms do not themselves constitute a channel of accountability.[89] Insofar as they do not encompass the possibility of applying a sanction attached to a right to demand answers, consultation procedures do not fit the concept of accountability.[90] Therefore, the idea that accountability to the public could result from consultation procedures should be discarded. This putative form of accountability does not satisfy the requirements that channels of holding decision-makers to account should fulfil.

Lastly, a few words on transparency are due, since they are likely to better elucidate the question analysed here. Transparency stands at the intersection between legitimacy and accountability and permits clarification of the relationships between these concepts, on the one hand, and consultation

[87] Bovens, *op. cit.*, p. 453, emphasis added.

[88] The terminology (structural and substantive elements of accountability) is Stewart's, *op. and loc. cit.*, n. 84.

[89] *Idem, ibidem.*

[90] There is no general agreement on whether accountability presupposes the possibility of applying sanctions. Nevertheless, it is assumed here that any process of calling to account would be incomplete without it. In this sense, Mulgan, *op. cit.*, n. 79, pp. 555–6; Stewart, *op. cit.*, n. 84, pp. 2 and 19. Less assertively, Bovens, *op. cit.*, n. 85, pp. 450–2 and, in line with the latter, Carol Harlow and Richard Rawlings (2006) 'Promoting accountability in multi-level governance: a network approach', European Governances Papers (EUROGOV), No. C-06-02, available at <http://www.connex-network.org/eurogov/pdf/egp-connex-C-06-02.pdf>, p. 4. Bovens, Harlow, and Rawlings argue that mechanisms that are 'effective in securing redress or reparation' (Bovens, *op. cit.*, n. 85, p. 452) or that operate as 'to put matters right if it should appear that errors have been made' (Olivier quoted by Harlow and Rawlings, p. 4) suffice to ensure accountability. See also, Curtin, *op. cit.*, n. 83, pp. 271–2.

(and participation), on the other. Transparency is understood here as knowledge about how decisions are made, or, more broadly, as understandability of decisional processes, encompassing access to information, knowledge of decision-making procedures, and the giving of reasons.[91] As such, it is a premise of participatory procedures in a double sense.[92] First, those who participate need to have access to the relevant information. In particular if participatory procedures are conceived as a means to ensure inclusiveness and to enable a comprehensive view of the interests involved in decision-making, they compel the public availability of the relevant information. Secondly, if participation is to be effective, participants should, as much as possible, become aware of which factors weighed in the decision adopted. At the same time, transparency enables the attribution of accountability and creates one condition of legitimacy.[93] The giving of reasons and the public provision of information facilitate, in principle, the process of bringing the decision-maker to account, since the 'decisional path' is clear and publicly known. In any case, as such, the giving of reasons and public provision of information do not enable the participants to hold the decision-maker to account

[91] This concept of transparency draws both on Adam Tomkins (2000) 'Transparency and the emergence of a European administrative law', *Yearbook of European Law* 1999/2000, Vol. 19, pp. 217–56, at p. 220, and on Jacob Söderman (1998),'The role and impact of the European Ombudsman in access to documents and transparency of decision-making' in Veerle Deckmyn and Ian Thomson (eds), *Openness and Transparency in the European Union*, Maastricht: European Institute of Public Administration, pp. 75–83, at p. 75. For alternative views, see Andrea Santini (2004) *Il principio di trasparenza nell'ordinamento dell'Unione Europea*, Milano: Giuffrè, pp. 7–11.

[92] In contrast, transparency does not require participation. Access to information and justification of decisions on the basis of publicly available information (to return once more to Söderman's formulation) may suffice to ensure openness and understandability. For a contrary view, see Bo Vesterdorf (1999), 'Transparency—not just a vogue word', *Fordham International Law Journal*, Vol. 22, n. 3, pp. 902–29, at p. 903. In addition, as is known, the term transparency has broader implications than the ones mentioned in the text (on this, among others, see Kieran Bradley, 1999, 'La transparence de l'Union Européenne: une évidence ou un trompe l'œil?', *Cahiers de Droit Européen*, Vol. 35, n. 3–4, pp. 283–362, at pp. 285–6, and Peter Dyrberg (2002) 'Accountability and legitimacy: what is the contribution of transparency?' in Anthony Arnull and Daniel Wincott (eds), *Accountability and Legitimacy in the European Union*, Oxford: Oxford University Press, pp. 81–96.

[93] On the first limb, Armin von Bogdandy (2006) 'Constitutional principles' in Bogdandy and Jürgen Bast (eds), *Principles of European Constitutional Law*, Oxford and Portland: Hart Publishing, pp. 3–53, at p. 28; Dyrberg, *op. cit.*, p. 83; Bovens, *op. cit.*, n. 85, pp. 450 and 453; Deirdre Curtin (2007) 'Holding (quasi-) autonomous EU administrative actors to public account', *European Law Journal*, Vol. 13, n. 4, pp. 523–41, at p. 532. On the second, Dyrberg, *op. cit.*, p. 83; Deirdre Curtin (1996) 'Betwixt and between: democracy and transparency in the governance of the European Union' in Jan Winter, Deirdre Curtin, Alfred Kellermann, and Bruno de Witte (eds), *Reforming the Treaty on the European Union—The Legal Debate*, The Hague, Boston, London: Kluwer Law International, pp. 95–121, at pp. 95–6.

for the latter's decisions. However, the possibility of enhanced control over decision-making that may derive from consultation is intrinsically linked to the conditions of legitimacy. In fact, perceivable decisional processes, that, at another level, may enable the attribution of accountability, are one of the conditions for the exercise of decisional power to be considered legitimate, as individuals need to understand the decisional processes in order to consider them legitimate.[94] Beyond this basic condition of legitimacy, there is not a unique answer as to which other values or qualities decisional procedures and decision-makers need to respect in order to be considered legitimate.

In sum, consultative procedures such as the ones created in the realm of the Lamfalussy process may enhance the technical legitimacy of decision-making insofar as they favour effectiveness and responsiveness, as well as better regulatory outcomes through the incorporation of expertise and inclusiveness. Possibly, they may also favour political legitimacy, to the extent that they enhance consideration of a variety of conflicting interests. At any rate, even in the instances regarding which such an argument can be made, this is *per se* not sufficient to ensure political legitimacy *grounded in democratic values*. Moreover, while consultation procedures may enhance the control exerted over decision-makers, they do not provide a channel for holding them to account. The transparency of decisional procedures required by participated procedures is a condition both of legitimacy and of accountability exerted through other means.

It is interesting to note that consultation was considered sufficiently important to prevail over concerns of delay that are usually associated with participation. While swiftness was one of the stated justifications and aims underlying the whole Lamfalussy process, the extensive processes of consultation throughout the rule-making process may add quite a few more months to the length of the procedure. The reason why this was accepted lies, possibly, in the assumptions regarding the contribution of consultation to mitigating the perceived legitimacy and accountability problems raised by this decisional process. In addition, as was mentioned above, beneath these concerns, specific characteristics of the sector at issue contribute to explaining the creation and commitment to consultation in the realm of the Lamfalussy process. These are explained next.

[94] Similarly, Curtin, 'Betwixt and between...', *cit.*, pp. 95–6.

6.3.5 *Beneath legitimacy*

The perceived need to overcome the legitimacy problems of the Lamfalussy process, enhanced by the particular political salience of this regulatory approach, is only part of the explanation for the peculiarly high degree of commitment to consultation that characterizes it. One also needs to look beneath the regulatory set up and examine the specific features of financial services that might have influenced this aspect of the process.

The stated aim of consultation, at least as it has been conceived by the CESR, is to 'favour market participants' adherence' to regulation.[95] As mentioned, this ties in with the concern for warranting legitimacy and effectiveness. It is assumed that anticipated consensuses and responsive regulation ensure better results in implementation and compliance. At a deeper level, however, specific characteristics of financial services help to better explain the salience of this concern. Given the way capital markets have developed, regulatory functions—typically rule-making or standard-setting, information gathering, and ensuring modification of behaviour in accordance with the regulatory goals—are spread among a myriad of regulatory actors, public and private, national and international, commercial and non-commercial.[96] As a result, 'financial services regulation is characterised by a network of inter-locking rules, both at the national and international level'.[97] From the point of view of harmonization and cross-border provision of financial services, the fact that various actors possess different regulatory capacities means that it is particularly important not only to gather spread resources (namely information, expertise, and strategic position in relation to the aims of regulation),[98] but also, for this very

[95] 'The role...', *cit.*, n. 29, p. 9.

[96] Lastra, *op. cit.*, n. 9, pp. 61–2. Black, *op. cit.*, n. 41, p. 70 (see also pp. 67–9). Julia Black's analysis refers specifically to UK financial services (see, in addition, Julia Black (2003) 'Mapping the contours of contemporary financial services regulation', CARR Discussion Paper No. 17, London School of Economics and Political Science). The UK undoubtedly has one of the most dynamic financial markets in Europe (perhaps only matched by that of Germany). Despite the national specificities, it is submitted that, at least to a certain extent, her mapping of the regulatory actors in the UK may be extended to other settings, in particular given the degree of internationalization of financial markets.

[97] Black, 'Enrolling actors in regulatory systems...', *op. cit.*, n. 41, p. 89.

[98] Black defines regulatory capacities as 'a composite notion, consisting of the actual or potential conditions that make it likely that those resources will be deployed both now and in the future in such a way as to further the identified goals of those seeking to regulate or resolve identified problems' (*ibidem*, p. 72). She identifies six key resources for the performance of regulatory functions (information, expertise, financial and economic resources, authority and

reason, to warrant their adherence in order to ensure that their actions buttress the interest of market integration. The earlier this engagement starts, the more likely adherence is. Its continuity—one of the principles of consultation underlined by the Lamfalussy Committee—ideally ensures adherence throughout the regulatory chain. In addition, the interdependence of the EU regulatory process with international standards also favours consultation. On the one hand, EU regulation is, in a way, framed by standards defined by international bodies. On the other, given that financial markets are highly internationalized, an *a priori* reaction of international regulatory actors to EU rules is relevant.

In a word, the high 'fragmentation and hybridisation' of financial markets regulation make the way in which the various regulatory actors respond to EU regulation and the goals of convergence a crucial factor for the success of integration.[99] This is particularly relevant when maximum harmonization is sought, which was one of the ultimate goals to be achieved through the Lamfalussy process. In this light, consultative procedures that potentially involve all interested parties in the regulatory process become an essential instrument to achieve the desired level of integration in this field.

In the Lamfalussy institutional framework, this is not unproblematic. As has been implemented thus far, the advice given by the CESR at level 2 has been, in principle, based on wide consultations with market participants, consumers, and end-users. Arguably, not only does this represent an agreed solution among national regulators[100]—which, in addition, can be supported by the ESC's vote—but it is also meant to be the result of the aggregate views of market participants and, possibly, represents an accepted and expected practice. In these conditions, it is fair to assume that the Commission's right of initiative might be constrained, since it is unlikely that its final decision will substantially deviate from the CESR's advice. To this extent, the Lamfalussy regulatory design has not been without risks for the principle of institutional balance and for the Treaty regulatory framework, which the Committee purported to uphold, thereby respecting the limits of its mandate. Against this, it could be argued that, even if the

legitimacy, strategic position, organizational capacity) and explains with detail the relative relevance of each (*ibidem*, pp. 73–81).

[99] The quoted expression is Black's.

[100] Consensus is still the general rule, despite the fact that the CESR's decisions can also be adopted by qualified majority. See Articles 14, paragraph 1 of the 2009 Decision and Articles 6.2 and 6.3, al. a) of the CESR's Charter, *cit.*, n. 22. See n. 31, above.

constraint of the Commission's power remains a possibility, still the Commission's control over the regulatory process has been ensured, as far as the CESR's intervention is concerned, by the fact that the CESR has acted at level 2 upon a mandate issued by the Commission, whereby the latter formalizes its request for advice. At the end, the content of the CESR's intervention depends on the Commission's will. However, a concrete example shows clearly that this is merely a formal argument. In the mandate that formalized the Commission's request for technical advice regarding the implementing measures of the MiFID Directive, the Commission asked the CESR to be 'detailed and precise in order to allow for a harmonised and uniform definition of the financial instruments that fall under the scope of this Directive' and charged the CESR with 'providing comprehensive advice on all subject matters covered by the delegated powers'. The terms of the mandate gave the CESR considerable leeway. In these conditions, the claim that the Commission's right of initiative cannot be affected and that an articulated proposal by the CESR cannot hinder the Commission from disagreeing with the proposal becomes merely a formal argument. The suggestion of the second inter-institutional monitoring group, supported by market participants, that the Commission should be obliged to justify the cases where it has not followed the CESR's advice (that of the level 3 Committees in general) seems to confirm this interpretation.[101]

Fragmentation and hybridization are not exclusive to financial services regulation, even if, to a lesser extent, they are likely to be present in other areas of EU law. At the margin of the Treaties, decisional procedures that entail consultations with the various persons with stakes in the regulatory processes, in particular industries concerned, have been perceived to be necessary to the fulfilment of market integration goals.[102] These procedures may be more or less formalized, more or less transparent, more or less exclusive, more or less favourable to the inclusion of all interested parties in the regulatory process. In essence, however, it is fair to assume that they fulfil the same purpose: gathering together different regulatory capacities and, if possible, facilitating the adherence of different actors to the market integration goals in each sector. The concrete shape of procedures or *fora* of consultation are designed accordingly. In this sense, fragmentation and

[101] 'Final report...', *cit.*, n. 65, pp. 10—point 19—and 24–5.

[102] This is referred to by Burkard Eberlein in relation to the energy market: Burkard Eberlein (2008) 'The making of European energy market: the interplay of governance and government', *Journal of Public Policy*, Vol. 28, n. 1, pp. 73–92, at pp. 77–8.

hybridization, on the one hand, and consultation as a form of enhancing the technical legitimacy of the decisional processes, on the other, are interrelated aspects of the same process.

6.3.6 *The 2009 proposals: the future of consultation*

As mentioned above, both the policy documents that launched the current reform of the EU regulation of financial services and the 2009 legislative proposals, as well as the respective compromise agreements have only scant references to consultation. In particular, contrary to the Lamfalussy Report, the Larosière Report hardly mentioned the role of consultation. There are, however, important specifications in this respect in the Commission's proposal.[103]

According to the Commission, when drafting technical standards which, once endorsed by the Commission, will have a binding legal effect, the ESMA must, 'where appropriate', open the procedures for consultation. The compromise agreement between the European Parliament and the Council on the amendments to financial services directives in respect of the powers of the agencies ('Omnibus directive proposal'), indicates that the draft technical standards adopted by the agencies will affect both level 2 and level 3 regulation. Indeed, it refers both to 'draft technical standards [adopted] by means of delegated or implementing acts' and to 'technical standards . . . designed to further develop, specify or determine the conditions of application of . . . level-2 measures'.[104] At the time of writing, it is not yet clear how this will be translated into the final legislative act. It is submitted that Article 7 could, in certain cases, apply by analogy to both level 2 and level 3 measures. This gives contrasting signs in relation to the future of consultation. Indeed, as mentioned above, Article 7 enshrines a much looser duty to consult than the current Article 12 of the 2009 Decision on the CESR, applicable to level 2 measures. In this respect, Article 7 will be less constraining with regard to the consultation practices of the ESMA and could mean a regression in current practices. However, if it could indeed apply to level 3 measures, these would for the first time be covered by a legal duty to consult, thereby consolidating, to a certain extent, what have so far been

[103] The following observations will focus on the European Securities and Markets Agency. Similar provisions are, nonetheless, also found in the proposals for the establishment of the European Banking Authority and the European Insurance and Occupational Pensions Authority.

[104] Compromise agreement on the 'Omnibus directive' proposal (COD/2009/0161), *cit.*, n. 4.

only self-imposed practices of the CESR. It remains, in any case, quite a loose duty of consultation that does not bind the ESMA to specific standards and gives it leeway to decide when to conduct open public consultations. Consultations restricted to specific groups of stakeholders remain a choice of the competent EU body.[105]

In addition to Article 7, the Commission's proposal indicates in the preamble that 'in its decision-making procedures, the Authority should be bound by Community rules and general principles on due process and transparency' and adds 'the right to be heard of the addressees of the Authority's decision should be fully respected'.[106] However, this does not seem to add any legally significant meaning to Article 7. First, the normative value of preamble provisions is questionable. Secondly, this is not significantly reflected in other provisions of the proposal,[107] and, as has already been said elsewhere in the book, in EU law principles of due process (contrany to transparency) are restricted to adjudicative procedures, except where legal provisions state otherwise. This indication in the preamble is not a legal provision intended or capable of extending due process rights to rule-making. The normative consequences of this reference remain obscure in this respect.

The creation of a stakeholder group is the second important measure of the 2009 proposal regarding consultation. According to the preamble of the proposed regulation, this is established for purposes of consultation on the adoption of technical standards, guidelines and recommendations, and 'for reasons of efficiency', and should 'actively work as an interface with other user groups'.[108] This is very much in line with some mechanisms that have been developed by the CESR (consultative panel and working groups) and the indications of Article 22 of the proposal reveal much of the inconveniences of organic participation that have been identified in Chapter 3.[109] Namely, the appointment of the members of this group, as

[105] See Proposal for a Regulation establishing a European Securities and Markets Authority, recital 33 of the preamble (*cit.*, n. 4), referring to consultation of 'interested parties', as well as Article 22 mentioned below.

[106] Proposal for a Regulation establishing a European Securities and Markets Authority, recital 35 of the preamble (*cit.*, n. 4).

[107] The right to be heard only shows up as a duty of the Commission in Article 9(4), third paragraph, referring to the Commission's power to take a decision requiring action in case of non-compliance with EU law, although in principle it applies also to the ESMA acting under Article 9(6) of the proposed regulation (see, in particular, Article 9(6), second paragraph).

[108] Proposal for a Regulation establishing a European Securities and Markets Authority, recital 33 of the preamble (*cit.*, n. 4).

[109] Sub-section 3.2.1.

well as its functioning, are dependent on the executive body it assists (in this case, the agency).[110] At the same time, there are also provisions that may have the effect of countervailing this dependence. As proposed by the Commission, the stakeholder group may issue opinions independently of an agency's request and the agency has the duty to make these opinions public. This applies also to the results of the group's contributions.[111] Furthermore, the group is autonomous in drafting its own rules of procedure.[112] These possibilities give the group a certain leeway to act somewhat independently of the agency.

In general, the scant references to consultation in the policy documents on which the current reform is based could be an indication that the same importance is no longer attached to the involvement of market participants. However, this may also reveal that consultation in financial market regulation is already considered a given. This last possibility is perhaps more likely. In fact, the two reports have different scope: while the Lamfalussy Committee was in charge of designing a new regulatory structure for the field, the Larosière Committee specifically dealt with the shortcomings of convergence in financial supervision and with the possibilities of strengthening the role of the EU in this respect (which affects in particular level 3 as originally conceived by the Lamfalussy Committee). Moreover, the Larosière Report explicitly acknowledged that the Lamfalussy process achieved 'good results' with regard to open consultation, transparency, and political accountability, highlighting only the difficulties in reaching agreement in practices of supervision.[113] In addition, as pointed out below, consultation has been perceived as one of the reasons for the success of the Lamfalussy process in ensuring the completion of the regulatory agenda set out in the 1999 Financial Services Action Plan. On this basis, and taking into account that the consultation practices in the field of financial services have largely developed outside legal frameworks, one can surmise that the provisions on consultation of the 2009 proposals will not impact negatively on current practices.[114] Also the fact that the characteristics of the financial services

[110] Article 22(3) of the Proposal for a Regulation establishing a European Securities and Markets Authority (*cit.*, n. 4).

[111] Article 22(5) and (7), *idem*. [112] Article 22(6), *idem*.

[113] Larosière Report, p. 75.

[114] See the 2007 Commission Communication on the review of the Lamfalussy process, *cit.*, n. 3, p. 5. Also defending that it is unlikely that the deciding bodies will deviate much from the practices followed so far, although writing before the 2009 proposals were presented, Moloney, *op. cit.*, n. 38, pp. 627–8.

sector, which have justified in part the relevance attributed to consultation, remain largely the same would indicate that consultation will retain a similar weight in EU financial regulations. Nevertheless, only time will tell if other factors—such as swiftness—will dictate a regression in the practices currently in place.

6.4 Consultation in Practice

The above considerations shed light on the reasons that determined the relevance attributed to consultation in the realm of the Lamfalussy process and also on why the Committee's recommendations were taken further. The empirical evidence and studies available on the functioning of the Lamfalussy process do not allow us to assert whether the assumptions on the role of consultation procedures with regard the technical legitimacy were concretized or not. Neither the reports of the inter-institutional groups nor the empirical studies consulted specifically address the grounds that were indicated above as justifying that consultation is one of the characteristic features of the Lamfalussy process.[115]

These reports and studies do, however, coincide in considering consultation as one of the several reasons for the effectiveness of the procedure.[116] The two inter-institutional monitoring groups, which were set up in order to assess the functioning of the whole procedure, pointed out the virtues and problems of the practice of consultation processes.[117] Their reports highlighted two aspects, in particular. First, consultation was perceived, more enthusiastically by the second monitoring group than by the first, as one of the cornerstones of the Lamfalussy process. The first group, while pointing out the problems faced in consultation procedures, deemed 'the use of earlier and more systematic consultation mechanisms' to be one of

[115] Of the empirical studies consulted, those undertaken in the realm of the New Modes of Governance project, Project 7—Governance and the EU securities sector, Priority 7—Citizens and governance in the knowledge-based society—come closer to the issues debated in the text.

[116] See the reports mentioned in nn. 19, 65, and below in n. 119, and Christian de Visscher, Olivier Maiscoq, and Frédérik Varone (2008) 'The Lamfalussy reform in the EU securities markets: fiduciary relationships, policy effectiveness and balance of power', *Journal of Public Policy*, pp. 36–7. Consultation is also praised in the 2007 Commission Communication on the review of the Lamfalussy process as one of the 'sound regulatory principles' that this process pioneered.

[117] The first was operational until 2004, the second up to 2007, after the extension of the Lamfalussy process to other areas of financial services. See IP/02/1452, Brussels, 10 October 2002 and IP/05/1002, Brussels, 25 July 2005.

the factors that facilitated the speedy adoption of level 1 legislation and, consequently, of level 2 measures.[118] The second group stressed that 'all respondents were generally positive about the improved transparency and consultation mechanisms, which were seen as a major achievement of the Lamfalussy process'.[119] Secondly, both groups pointed out problems of inclusiveness, especially in what concerns consumers, as well as problems related to procedures and outcomes. These two last aspects will be presented in turn.

The problems of inclusiveness pertain to the fact that both consumers and end-users (in particular, companies) are under-represented in consultation procedures. Two factors may explain this. First, there are not enough incentives to participate. One reason may be that most companies are 'infrequent users', as noted by the first monitoring group (this may be due to little integration in the financial markets until the implementation of the FSAP, or, more deeply, to lack of incentives to provide cross-border services). In these circumstances, many companies have 'little incentive to monitor events continuously'.[120] Another hindrance is the highly technical nature of financial services regulation. Indeed, according to the second group, 'it is necessary to be realistic about the extent to which consumers can collaborate in the development of technical requirements'.[121] Secondly, lack of resources, the production of consultation documents only in English, and the non-availability of documents addressed to non-professionals were pointed out as obstacles to the involvement of consumers and small businesses.[122] These two factors roughly correspond to some of the drawbacks of consultation pointed out by the literature: lack of involvement and limitations on information available.[123] Nevertheless, according to the

[118] 'Third report...', *cit.*, n. 19, pp. 5 and 10. This is equally underlined by Varone, de Visscher, Bergström, and Almer (2006) 'Final Report' produced in the realm of the New Modes of Governance project, Project 7—Governance and the EU securities sector, Priority 7—Citizens and governance in the knowledge-based society, reference number 7/D06, pp. 16–18—available at <http://www.eu-newgov.org/database/DELIV/D07D06_Final_Report.pdf>.

[119] 'Second interim report monitoring the Lamfalussy process', delivered by the (second) inter-institutional monitoring group in 26 January 2007, available at <http://ec.europa.eu/internal_market/finances/docs/committees/070126_second_interim_report_en.pdf> (hereinafter 'Second interim report...'), p. 9.

[120] 'Third report...', *cit.*, n. 19, p. 210 [121] 'Final report...', *cit.*, n. 65, p. 11.

[122] 'Third report...', *cit.*, n. 19, p. 21.

[123] See, for example, Ian Bartle (2006) 'Legitimising EU regulation: procedural accountability, participation or better consultation?' in Richard Bellamy, Dario Castiglione, and Jo Shaw (eds), *Making European Citizens: Civic Inclusion in a Transnational Context*, Basingtoke, New York: Palgrave Macmillan, pp. 133–53, at p. 148.

second group, 'representation of consumers and end-users in expert groups is increasing'.[124] The lack of inclusion of some interests together with the concern of the Commission to ensure the desired inclusiveness in financial services regulation led to the creation of two groups: the Forum of User Experts in the Area of Financial Services (FIN-USE) and the Financial Services Consumer Group (FSCG).[125] While these initiatives are a sign of the Community's efforts to promote access to all interested parties to rule-making procedures in this field, they reveal not only the inequalities inherent in consultation processes but also the interest of the administration in pushing for inclusiveness in order to benefit from the ensuing regulatory advantages.[126]

As mentioned, the monitoring groups pointed out deficiencies in the consultation practices of the Commission and the CESR. In particular, their reports reveal that market participants, although generally satisfied with the improvements of consultation processes under the Lamfalussy approach, considered that the length of consultation periods is not always commensurate with the volume and technical nature of the matter, and feedback statements of comments received should be improved.[127] Moreover, market participants raised issues regarding the methods used for analysing comments, but it is not clear from the wording of the report whether the problem is lack of clarity or contestation over the methods used.[128] Finally, in what concerns the outcomes of the regulatory process, the first group has shown concern for possible inconveniences deriving from consultation practices under the Lamfalussy process. Namely, it

[124] 'Second interim report...', *cit.*, n. 119, p. 10.

[125] Moloney has observed that 'FIN-USE has emerged as a robust actor in policy-making, if somewhat a lone voice among the dominant market interests' (Moloney (2006) 'Financial market regulation in the post-financial services action plan era', *International and Comparative Law Quarterly*, Vol. 55, n. 4, pp. 982–92, at p. 985, footnote 20. The Charter of the FIN-USE can be consulted at <http://www.ec.europa.eu/comm/internal_market/fin-use_forum/charter/index_en.htm>. The FSCG is a sub-group of the European Consumer Consultative Group (created by Commission Decision No. 2003/709/EC, of 9 October 2003, OJ L 258/35, 10.10.2003). Information is available at <http://ec.europa.eu/internal_market/finservices-retail/fscg/index_en.htm>.

[126] In this respect, the second monitoring group suggested an additional measure: the Commission and the level 3 Committees, where that is considered necessary after a cost-effectiveness analysis, should seek consumers' direct opinions ('Final report...', *cit.*, n. 65, p. 11)

[127] 'Third report...', *cit.*, n. 19, pp. 19–20, and 'Final report...', *cit.*, n. 65, pp. 24–5. The Commission in its 2007 Communication on the review of the Lamfalussy process also acknowledged these problems (*cit.*, n. 3, p. 5).

[128] 'Final report...', *cit.*, n. 65, p. 25.

pointed out that too much consultation and lobbying might lead to more amendments of the original text, possibly hindering its internal logic and quality.[129]

In these consultation procedures, respect for the self-imposed procedural rules regarding consultation, as well as consideration for the flaws pointed out by the inter-institutional monitoring groups depend merely on the will of the rule-making bodies that conduct consultation, namely the Commission and, up to now, the CESR (or, broadly, the level 3 Committees). Under current rules, the exception is the provision imposing consultation at level 2. At the same time, they seem to have had the utmost interest in ensuring the openness, transparency, and effectiveness of the process for the reasons stated above. The reports of the inter-institutional monitoring groups show that both the Commission and the CESR have, in fact, remained committed to the spirit of the Lamfalussy recommendations, problems of inclusiveness notwithstanding.[130]

Finally, some of the problems pointed out in these reports also reveal the limits of law in tackling shortcomings of participation. While issues pertaining to the availability of documents in only one language and, within certain limits, to the length of consultation periods or to the lack of consideration of inputs could be countered by judicial control over decisional procedures, others such as under-representation due to lack of material resources and the quality of legislative drafting can hardly be tackled through legal rules.

6.5 Consultation and Rights-based Participation

6.5.1 *Dividing and connecting lines*

The differences between the type of 'participation at large' (consultation) just described, on the one hand, and the rights-based approach to

[129] 'Third report…', *cit.*, n. 19, p. 12. Differently, another study indicates that there is 'more consistency in the proposals submitted by the Commission to the Council and the European Parliament, thanks to extensive consultation' (Christian de Visscher, Olivier Maiscocq, and Frédéric Varone (2008) 'The Lamfalussy reform in the EU securities markets: fiduciary relationships, policy effectiveness and balance of power', *Journal of Public Policy*, pp. 19–47, at p. 39).

[130] Varone, de Visscher, Bergström, and Almer analysed the process for the adoption of the Market Abuse Directive and concluded that, at least at level 2 (where the process stood at the time of their analysis), the consultation standards had been fulfilled (*op. cit.*, n. 118, pp. 19–21).

participation endorsed in this book, on the other, become clearer after the above analysis. Their core functions are different and therefore also the scope of persons legitimated or called to intervene may differ in the two cases. A rights-based approach to participation is grounded in specific values warranted by the rule of law, which can ultimately be pinned down to a concern for material justice. It results from the combination of the subjective and objective functions of participation explained in Chapter 2 that the persons entitled to intervene in the procedure are holders of a substantive right or legally protected interest that is potentially affected by the outcome of the procedure. In other words, holders of participation rights are those whose legal spheres are affected by a decision taken by a public entity.

Consultation as envisaged in the Lamfalussy process, and present in other sectors where similar regulatory structures or institutional arrangements prevail,[131] has a different meaning. Respect for the person's dignity is not an issue here, nor is the instrumental rationale of consultation informed by an ideal of material justice. Consultation is a tool designed to achieve certain regulatory outcomes, but detached from the values that ground a rights-based participation. It results from the awareness that key resources relevant to the exercise of power are spread between different public and private persons and that the achievement of the regulatory goals intended requires assembling them in the decisional procedures. As such, consultation is one among several means of responding to this need. At the same time, it may contribute to the perception that the decisional procedures are legitimate in the ways pointed out above. Access to the procedures may either be restricted to those whose contribution is considered relevant for previously set regulatory goals or extended to the public in general. Access to consultation procedures does not reflect the substantive legal positions that might be affected by the ensuing decisions (although, for consultation to make sense, interveners must have some knowledge of the issue being regulated and, hence, some proximity to the situation being regulated), nor does consultation ground procedural rights (unless the decision-maker has a legal obligation to hear representatives of the interested sectors, in which case they have at least the procedural right to intervene). Consultation procedures are the product of policy choices. They exist where the

[131] On these, see David Coen and Mark Thatcher (2008) 'Network governance and multi-level delegation: European networks of regulatory agencies', *Journal of European Public Policy*, Vol. 28, n. 1, pp. 49–71, at p. 64.

decision-maker considers that the characteristics of the sector being regulated and the outcomes to be achieved justify opening the procedure to the views of those concerned. This form of participation is therefore more vulnerable to policy change than one that is grounded in legal values and, ideally, ensured through legal rules.

In a sense, consultation and rights-based participation are two different concepts, pertaining to two different ways of understanding the administrative phenomenon. The former accompanies 'modes of governance' designed to gather together spread regulatory capacities with a view to delivering the desired outcomes. The latter is a well-known category of traditional administrative law, underpinned by command-and-control processes of decision-making, where rights-based participation ensures the due consideration of legally protected interests affected by public decisions, both from a subjective and from an objective standpoint. Nevertheless, they are inter-related. The instrumental rationale of participation rights brings them closer to the intervention of interested parties in consultation procedures. This is clearer in cases where the personal factor is not predominant in the situation that is subject to regulation. In borderline situations, there may be a continuum between participation rights and the intervention of interested parties in consultation procedures. However, in the absence of legal rules that endorse consultation and in the absence of substantive rights and interests that may give rise to the right to participate, the procedural intervention in the latter case remains in the realm of the political.[132]

Given their different rationales and functions, there might be occasions in which both types of procedural intervention are justified. As mentioned, the intervention in consultation procedures, such as those analysed above, is not primarily designed to ensure the protection of legally protected interests, certainly not of individual legal positions.[133] This justifies the decision-maker being left with the option of defining, in each case, the treatment given to the persons heard, as well as who is heard (except if this aspect is determined by legislation), without being bound by procedural legal rules. However, it is argued here that in cases where the legal sphere of persons concerned is directly affected by decisions adopted following a consultation procedure, there should be room for the exercise of participation rights. Moreover, holders of affected rights and interests that are limited or removed from their legal sphere or indeed persons on whom

[132] See, further, Chapter 7, Section 7.2, Sub-section 7.2.2.

[133] See, above, Section 6.3.

duties or charges may be imposed should be granted a differentiated procedural position from that accorded to the public in general or to representatives of the interests involved in the regulatory regime that is being decided.

In other words, there might be a case for participation rights also in the realm of 'governance arrangements', since the decisive criterion for granting such rights lies in the ability of regulatory decisions to cause a change in the legal sphere of persons concerned. Where this is the case, the basic principles that ground participation rights are valid across the spectrum of decisional procedures and of EU actors with decision-making powers. Admittedly, the type of situation that gives rise to participation rights is rarer in general regulatory procedures than in adjudicative decision-making. At any rate, where participation rights are justified, the fact that there was a consultation procedure with representatives of the interests affected by the regulatory process should not pre-empt the right of affected persons to be heard.[134]

6.5.2 *An illustration: the legal regime on market abuse*

Consultations similar to those analysed in the sections above are expressly foreseen in the legal regime regarding market abuse. An overview of some of the provisions of the directives that constitute this legal regime helps to clarify the type of situations that may give rise to participation rights. This contributes to separating them from other situations in which rights and interests of market participants may be affected by certain rules without, however, this justifying a legally protected right to intervene in the procedure. This sub-section is thus dedicated to some of the EU rules on market abuse, examined here only with the purpose of illustrating the distinction between consultation and rights-based participation.

To begin with, a few words are due on the 'framework directive' (level 1). This sets the basic principles regarding inside dealing and market manipulation. For the most part, it defines in general and abstract terms the types of behaviour that must be forbidden by Member States or that must be observed by market participants in order to avoid those forms of market abuse.[135] The way this definition of forbidden behaviours relates to the

[134] Takis Tridimas (2006) *The General Principles of EU Law*, Oxford: Oxford University Press, p. 408.

[135] The core provisions are Articles 2 to 6 of Directive No. 2003/6/EC of the European Parliament and of the Council of 28 January 2003 on insider dealing and market manipulation (*cit.*, n. 21). Articles 7 to 10 detail the scope of application of these rules.

legal sphere of the persons concerned is remote. These would be those who, by reason of their participation in the securities markets, may have access to inside information or could engage in market manipulation. The directive sets the general framework within which market participants should operate, in the form of obligations incumbent upon Member States and upon market participants and in view of the stability and integrity required of financial markets. This entails provisions that are liable to shape the content of the legal relationships that will emerge between market participants and regulators and between the latter two groups and EU institutions, thus conditioning their respective rights and duties. To this extent, the rules of the directive *concern* or *affect* private persons. However, the duties they define are supposed to be further concretized by rules adopted, first, by the Commission and, secondly, by the national regulators following the recommendations that, up to now, have been issued by the CESR at level 3 and will be issued by the ESMA in the future.[136] The rules of the directive are drafted in terms that do not pre-empt, but rather suppose further substantive concretization of the rights and duties of the persons concerned. Therefore, they are not capable of directly affecting the legal sphere of those who come under its realm of application.

Consultation in the definition of accepted market practices

Contributing to the legal certainty of market participants, the level 1 directive envisages the possibility of certain market practices being defined as accepted on given markets. Accordingly, these will not be penalized as market manipulation. The definition of accepted market practices is a task of national regulators, but, as had been determined in the level 1 directive,

[136] One of the level 2 acts is Commission Directive No. 2004/72/EC, of 29 April 2004 (accepted market practices, definition of inside information in relation to derivatives on commodities, drawing up of lists of insiders, notification of managers' transactions and of suspicious transactions), OJ L 162/70, 30.4.2004. For details on the decisional procedure regarding the adoption of level 2 measures, see Guido Ferrarini (2004) 'The European market abuse directive', *Common Market Law Review*, Vol. 41, n. 3, pp. 711–41, at p. 712). The CESR adopted three level 3 documents: Market Abuse Directive, Level 3—first set of CESR guidance and information on the common operation of the Directive (CESR/04-505b), 11 May 2005, (available at <http://www.cesr.eu/index.php?docid=3282>); CESR, Market Abuse Directive, Level 3—second set of CESR guidance and information on the common operation of the Directive to the market (CESR/ 06-562b), 12 July 2007 (available at <http://www.cesr.eu/index.php?docid=4683>); Guidelines—Market Abuse Directive, Level 3—Third set of CESR guidance and information on the common operation of the Directive to the marke (CESR/09-219), 15 May 2009 (available at <http://www.cesr.eu/index.php?docid=5727>).

the Commission identified in one of its implementing directives the factors against which market practices must be assessed for this purpose and the procedure that national regulators should follow in this respect.[137] According to this procedure, national regulators 'consult as appropriate relevant bodies such as representatives of issuers, financial services providers, consumers, other authorities and market operators'.[138] Arguably, the rationales for this consultation are similar to those that ground consultations during the adoption of EU legislation. They are also the same as those that justify another consultation duty incumbent upon Member States: the latter must establish 'effective consultative arrangements and procedures with market participants concerning possible changes in national regulation'.[139] The rules adopted by national regulators define which practices market participants may adopt and, *a contrario*, those which may be considered unacceptable with a view to safeguarding the integrity of the market that is made up of their decisions. These rules guide the action of market participants in view of the public interests of market stability and market integration. It is deemed that the hearing of their representatives in the making of these rules is essential to their acceptability and effective operation. At the same time, the Commission also determined that the revision of accepted market practices needs to follow the same procedure.[140]

While Member States must ensure that national regulators consult, the latter are also given enough margin of manoeuvre to decide when consultation is appropriate and define the modes of consultation.[141] Moreover, the duty to consult refers only to the 'relevant' entities that represent the categories mentioned in Article 3(2). Despite the advantages of consultation, the Commission seems to have foreseen that there might be situations in which national regulators consider that consultation may hinder more than favour the effectiveness of the decisional procedure. Thus, the absence of consultation in some instances does not seem to breach the duty to consult as foreseen in Article 3(2). On the contrary, a national regulator that never consults or that only rarely does so would cause the respective

[137] Article 1, point 5 of Directive No. 2003/6/EC, *cit.*, n. 21, and Articles 2 and 3 of the Commission Directive No. 2004/72/EC, *cit.*

[138] Article 3(2) of the Commission Directive No. 2004/72/EC, *cit.*

[139] Article 11(2) of the Directive No. 2003/6/EC, *cit.*, n. 21. Although this duty does not refer specifically to the transposition process, it may be understood that this is encompassed by Article 11(2), insofar as adaptations to national legislation are required by the transposition.

[140] Article 3(5) of the Commission Directive No. 2004/72/EC, *cit.*, n. 136.

[141] Article 3(2) of the Commission Directive No. 2004/72/EC, *cit.*, n. 136.

Member State to be in breach of Article 3(2). Likewise, considering the overall system of consultation in which it is embedded, the express exclusion from consultation procedures of one of the groups mentioned would equally violate this provision. It should, moreover, be noted that it might be problematic to restrict consultation to 'relevant bodies', since there are no criteria to define who constitutes a relevant body under Article 3(2).

Before arriving at the stage at which national regulators decide on accepted market practices, the CESR adopted guidance on how national regulators should interpret the directive's provisions in order to ensure 'the proper operation of the regime for accepted market practices'.[142] As such, the CESR served as an intermediary between the decisions of each national regulator and the rules defined by the Commission in the implementing directive. This 'guidance' corresponds to level 3 of the Lamfalussy process, which means that it has equally been subject to consultation at the EU level. In a sense, there is a double consultation. Nevertheless, the rules agreed by the CESR should have a different content from those adopted by each national regulator, even if the former are agreed by the CESR members and, hence, are very likely to be followed by each regulator when concretely deciding which practices it will consider acceptable.[143] In this case, the CESR chose not to publish the accepted practices that were agreed upon. Instead, it laid down 'types of practice that the CESR members would consider to constitute market manipulation', thereby leaving apparently more room for national regulators' decisions to adapt to the specific characteristics of the market they supervise.[144] As such, the object of the consultation at the European level is delimited by the goal of convergence that has been the *raison d'être* of the CESR's decisions at this phase.

[142] Market Abuse Directive, 'Level 3—second set of CESR guidance...', *cit.*, n. 136, p. 4. On this, see Moloney, 'Innovation and risk in the EC financial market regulation...', *cit.*, n. 38, pp. 655–7.

[143] Despite the fact that the 2009 Decision has opened the door for enlarging the possibilities of CESR adopting decisions by qualified majority (Article 14, 1st paragraph of the 2009 Decision; also Article 6.3 of the CESR's Charter; cf. Articles 5.6 and 5.7 of the previous Charter, all *cit.*, n. 22), at present the rule is still that decisions are taken by consensus. Qualified majorities, at least at level 3, remain a solution of last resort (see Article 6.3, al. d) of the CESR's Charter). The 2009 proposal for the establishment of a European Securities and Markets Agency will change this (*cit.*, n. 4 Article 29). As mentioned, this proposal also envisages that technical standards developed by the new agency are binding upon endorsement by the Commission (Article 7).

[144] 'Level 3—second set of CESR guidance...', *cit.*, n. 136, p. 5 and Section IV.

When participation rights step in

Should there be any room for participation rights in the adoption of accepted market practices? The answer to this question depends on the possible content and effects of the respective decision.

The decision of the national regulator is applicable to all market participants. It needs to be published and it must contain the 'appropriate description' of the practices that have been accepted, thereby delimiting the scope of application of the norms on market manipulation and indicating the legal choices of the regulator regarding the treatment of related practices.[145] The decision adopted has a permissible character. Nevertheless, in order to benefit from the consequences of the accepted practice, i.e. avoid the risk of being subject to penalties for market abuse, the persons who follow them need to abide by the concrete indications of the national regulator contained in the 'appropriate description'. For example, in the case of liquidity contracts which were considered as an accepted practice by the Spanish securities market regulator, the rights and duties that may be defined in individual contracts are determined in great detail in the act that accepted this market practice.[146] This includes the maximum prices at which buy and sell orders may be made, the maximum percentage of average daily trading, the restrictions in trade to which the issuer is subject, as well as rules on the internal organization of the financial intermediary so as to ensure the independence of its employees.[147] In practice, the regulator's act creates a substantive legal relationship between the national regulator and the different persons that need to follow its determinations in order to benefit from the respective advantages. The rights and duties of the latter are concretely defined and the powers of the former in relation to that market practice are constrained, insofar as the regulator cannot engage in punitive action if the terms of the practice are followed by the contracting parties. The conduct of the persons that wish to engage in this type of contract is conditioned by the act's determinations to the point where practically the only elements lacking for the effective constitution of the legal relationship are the actual signing of the contract by the issuer and the financial

[145] Article 3(2) of Commission Directive No. 2004/72/EC, *cit.*, n. 136.

[146] See note below.

[147] See second, third, and fifth rules of Circular 3/2007, by the Comisión Nacional del Mercado de Valores on liquidity contracts for the purposes of their acceptance as a market practice (available at <http://www.cesr.eu/index.php?docid=4949>).

intermediary, where the object and trading price are defined, as are the rate and frequency of the intermediary's remuneration. As for the rest, the will of the contracting parties is almost limited to signing (or not) a contract the terms of which were previously defined.

According to the rights-based approach to participation defended in this book, given the content and effects of this type of measure, participation rights ought to be granted in the respective decisional procedure. In fact, the rights and duties of the persons who wish to engage in the accepted market practice, as well as those directly affected by their conduct (i.e. investors), are *a priori* defined by the national regulator on the basis of the assessment of the market in which they operate. The exercise of participation rights by those affected should be ensured in parallel to, or simultaneously with, the consultation phase that, according to Article 3, needs to be followed by national regulators when deciding on accepted market practices. In other words, in view of the possible content of the decisions adopted and the impact that they have in the concerned persons' legal spheres, it can be argued that this consultation phase should be accompanied by or accommodate a form of participation different from the one envisaged by the Commission when defining this procedural step. This is not envisaged in the scheme of the directive and it certainly does not follow from its written provisions, nor arguably from its spirit. Nevertheless, one may elaborate on the claim that this type of measure should lead to the recognition of participation rights.

Several problems follow from this claim, namely: how would this affect the effectiveness of decision-making? How could holders of participation rights be identified? What consequences should be attached to the breach of such rights? In fact, admitting that the conditions for the recognition of participation rights are fulfilled, there are still other aspects of the decisional procedure that need to be taken into account. In addition, the practicability of participation should also be considered. It follows from the directive's provisions on consultation that the involvement of interested persons might not always be compatible with the effectiveness of the procedure. In particular, the definition of accepted market practices may need to be based on complex economic assessments of the characteristics of the market. In such circumstances, there might not be room to accommodate the concerns possibly voiced by the interested persons that intervene in the procedure. On the other hand, as a rule, this is not the type of decision where the individual position of those affected would need to be considered by the decision-maker. In fact, in principle, the decision-maker is not assessing the specific conduct of given market participants. The decision is taken on the basis of an assessment of the market and affects the respective participants in their quality of market operators. It was defended earlier in this book that, in these circumstances, the decision-maker should be given the possibility to dispense with a participatory phase, but needs to justify this decision. Moreover, the act adopted should also reveal that the legally protected interests of the persons concerned were sufficiently taken into consideration.[148] Note that this assumption may be inverted, in case the conduct of specific operators is effectively considered in the overall assessment.

At any rate, once it is asserted that the decision-making procedure should encompass a rights-based participation, the decision-maker needs to be able to identify the persons who are entitled to participate and whose exclusion from the procedure could have legal consequences for the validity of the act adopted. In this case, depending on the size of the market, the definition of accepted market practices potentially concerns a great number of persons: issuers, financial services providers, investors operating on the national market (consumers, according to the terminology of the directive). In line with Article 3(2) of the Commission's directive, participation should be restricted to the representatives of these interests. However, contrary to what stems from this provision, the definition of who is a 'relevant' entity for these purposes should not be a free choice of the decision-maker, given the possible effects of an act defining accepted market practices. 'Relevant' entities should be those who aggregate the interests of the persons concerned by the decision at issue. The decision-maker should be bound to ensure the representativeness of the interests concerned during the consultative procedure. Namely, they should certify that, on the whole, the entities who participate are able to represent the legally protected interests at issue (in similar terms to the concept of 'sufficient collective representativity' used by the Court of First Instance in the *UEAPME* case).[149] Where necessary, they should urge persons who

[148] These conditions have been specified in Chapter 2, Section 2.6.

[149] Case T-135/96, *Union européenne de l'artisanat et des petites et moyennes entreprises (UEAPME) v Council* [1998] ECR II-2335, paragraphs 90 to 100. In this case, however, the requirement mentioned applied not to the consultation of interest representatives (in this case, social partners) but to access to the negotiation procedure conducive to agreements that may have the value of law, currently adopted under Articles 154 and 155 of the Treaty on the Functioning of the European Union (former Articles 138(4) and 139 EC).

may voice similar interests to coordinate their intervention, for example, requiring them to nominate a representative for the purposes of participation.[150]

As for the consequences that are attached to the exercise of participation rights conceived in these terms, it is clear that the recognition of participation rights limits the discretion of the decision-maker as to their procedural conduct vis-à-vis interested persons. Following a model of 'pure consultation', they may consult whoever they consider to be appropriate for the purposes of consultation, as they may define the scope of consultation according to the aspects regarding which input is considered necessary. Likewise, the treatment of the input received is largely the decision-maker's choice (whether to write a report on the consultation procedure or not—even though, at present, Article 12 of the 2009 Decision obliges the CESR to publish the results of consultation—which information to include, which treatment to give to such information). On the contrary, the exercise of participation rights means that the decision-maker is constrained by stricter rules of procedure. These pertain to the persons who are entitled to participate, to the scope of consultation, to the motivation of the decision adopted, to the duty of care in considering the various competing interests touched by that decision, to the moment at which the holders of participation rights are heard (the envisaged act must be available to consultation before it is adopted but at a moment at which it is still possible to incorporate the views manifested by the persons concerned). In a word, there are a series of procedural choices that are no longer left to the discretion of the decision-maker and that may be controlled by the Courts. Nevertheless, it should be acknowledged that the effects stemming from covering participation with a 'legal cloak' may equally result from 'non-legalized' consultation procedures: the fulfilment of the goals of consultation may urge the decision-maker to adopt similar procedural conduct to that just described as resulting from the exercise of participation rights. The main difference then is that, in the latter case, their conduct is not subject to judicial review, which, from one perspective, may be considered an advantage.

Effectively what is entailed in a claim for participation rights is the 'judicialization' of administrative decisions.[151] Which consequences

[150] On the conditions that should be placed on the possibility of representation, see Chapter 2, Section 2.6.

[151] On this, see above, Chapter 5, Section 5.3.

should then be attached to the breach of participation rights? This point has already been addressed in this book. It results from what was defended in Chapter 5 that, with regard to decisions such as the definition of accepted market practices, where the personal factor is not determinant in the underlying material situation, the harmless error rule would apply. In addition, in cases in which one person claims to have been excluded from the procedure, in violation of the access rules suggested above, an excusable error rule might cover the procedural failure of the decision-maker.[152]

Before concluding, reference should be made to other instances in the market abuse regime that give rise to participation rights. At the other end of the spectrum from the regulatory competences of national regulators are the 'supervisory and investigatory powers that are necessary for the exercise of [their] functions', the 'right' (*sic*) to 'require the cessation of any practice that is contrary to the provisions adopted in the implementation of the [market abuse] directive', 'suspend trading of the financial instruments concerned', 'request the freezing and/or sequestration of assets', and 'request temporary prohibition of professional activity'.[153] These are administrative sanctions applied to unlawful behaviour. Typically, such powers are exercised according to national administrative law procedures, which, as a rule, entail the right to be heard of the persons against whom the sanctions are aimed. As has been seen elsewhere in this book, the procedural intervention of the persons concerned in these cases corresponds to the core of the participation rights, where the 'personal factor' is stronger and where the dignitarian rationale as a justification for that intervention prevails over instrumental considerations.

These two examples of instances where participation rights should be recognized lead to the conclusion that, in the field of financial services regulation, procedural protection of rights and legally protected interests is, in principle, a matter that only needs to be taken into account at the administrative level of execution of the substantive legal regimes that were created according to the Lamfalussy process.

The fact that the decision is adopted by a national entity does not exempt it from the scope of EU administrative law. It is, however, not without consequence for possible participation rights. In fact, in the absence of EU rules on this matter, national rules of procedure apply to the extent that they

152 See, further, Chapter 5, Section 5.3.

153 Article 12(1) and (2)(e) to (h) of Directive No. 2003/6/EC, *cit.*, n. 21.

are no less favourable than those ruling national situations and do not render impossible or excessively difficult the exercise of rights conferred by EU law.[154]

This scenario will change in the future, given that binding technical standards will be adopted by the EU. If the level of concreteness of its decisions is such as to enable the emergence of an administrative relationship, participation rights should then also be acknowledged at the EU level. Certainly so, when it addresses decisions to market participants.[155]

6.6 Concluding: Legal and Non-legal Dimensions of Participation

It results from the above that two fundamental aspects allow us to distinguish consultation, as it has been envisaged in the Lamfalussy process, and the rights-based participation propounded in this book: first, their rationales and functions; secondly, the persons who are entitled to intervene and, especially, the way access is defined as well as their procedural status. Consultation, in this case, has been perceived as a means of circumventing the legitimacy and accountability shortcomings of the Lamfalussy regulatory structure, although, as has been explained in the third section of this chapter, one should be cautious when linking consultation to these concepts. At the same time, consultation responded to the regulatory characteristics of the securities markets that could hinder market integration based on purely unilateral regulation. In fact, consultation enables gathering together regulatory resources that are spread throughout various public and private, national, European, and international actors, thereby ensuring responsiveness and market participants' adherence to the rules adopted. Given these rationales, consultation is destined to encompass representatives of all groups involved in financial markets regulation. Even if it is implied that participants have a material connection to the substance of the matter under regulation, procedural intervention is not linked to the possibility of the participants' substantive rights and legally protected interests being affected

[154] See Chapter 4, Sub-section 4.1.2.

[155] See Article 9(6) of the Proposal for a Regulation establishing a European Securities and Markets Authority (*cit.*, n. 4). See also n. 116 above.

or to the degree to which they are affected—indeed, consultation is open to whoever wishes to comment on the regulatory initiatives.

Despite the sector's specificities, it is likely that similar reasons have motivated the choice of participation as one of the principles of EU governance. Interestingly, but not surprisingly given the characteristics of the Lamfalussy process, two aspects differentiate consultation undertaken in the fields covered by the latter from consultation rules and standards that have been defined in the Commission's White Paper on Governance and in its Communication 'Towards a reinforced culture of consultation': the CESR, at present, has a legal obligation to consult, as well as to publish the results of consultation; and consultation is envisaged in procedures leading up to the adoption of implementing/delegated regulations or directives by the Commission.

The 'structural' differences between consultation and rights-based participation justify the different procedural status of interested persons in each case. Participants in consultation procedures are not recognized as having procedural rights that would require the decision-maker to follow a specific conduct subject to judicial control. Nevertheless, this difference may be mitigated by the degree of commitment of the deciding bodies to the standards of consultation chosen. In fact, their adherence to the goals of consultation may ensure that persons who intervene in a consultation procedure have *de facto* a similar procedural status to the one that would result from rights-based participation.

The identification of situations that could result in the recognition of participation rights in the realm of securities regulation has led us to examine the place of participation in decisional procedures grounded in complex technical assessments. It was concluded that concerns pertaining to the effectiveness of the decisional procedure as well as to the practicability and consequences of the exercise of participation rights should not lead to the complete exclusion of some form of procedural protection, where this is justified. Possible negative consequences of 'judicialization' may also be circumvented by attaching to the infringement of participation rights effects other than the annulment of the vitiated decisions.

On the basis of the identification of the situations that in the field of securities regulation could lead to the recognition of participation rights, it was also seen that procedural protection in the realm of the Lamfalussy procedures may be an issue to be tackled at the administrative level of implementation that, in this regulatory scheme, and at the time of writing, is still left to the national authorities.

Lastly, it should be mentioned that the practical problems of consultation detected in the realm of the Lamfalussy process, analysed in the fourth section of this chapter, not only illustrate problems that may be common to other forms of participation, but in particular they reveal the limits of legal rules in tackling issues such as the under-representation of certain groups.

Chapter 7

Participation Rights in EU Food Law

EU food regulation has led to the creation of EU decisional powers that contend directly with the legal sphere of private persons. The analysis of some procedures in this sector confirms that the EU legal order does not only affect the distribution of competences between Member States and the EU institutions and bodies, as it is generally assumed. It is also capable of affecting directly private persons in their relationships with the administrative entities that are part of the EU administration in areas which go beyond those traditionally situated in the realm of direct administration.

This chapter is structured as follows. To begin with, an account is given of the factors that constitute the development of such powers and of the models of administrative action that can generally be identified in the field of EU food law (Section 7.1). This first part sets the scene for the analysis undertaken in this chapter. Next, different procedures pertaining to EU market authorizations are examined. This not only illustrates the type of decisions formed at the EU level that impact on private legal spheres, but also demonstrates that little attention was paid to the procedural protection of persons concerned in the design of such procedures (Section 7.2). How are the procedures organized in terms of involvement of potentially affected parties and how should they be? This is the question that guides the analysis of the different procedures and of the ensuing acts. Finally, the last part of the chapter reconstructs the procedures analysed in light of the conception of participation rights defended in this book (Section 7.3). This is guided by two basic arguments. First, the clear-cut distinction between general and individual acts does not fit market authorizations, which embody the prior administrative controls in this sector. This distinction is therefore unsuitable to determine the scope of participation rights. Secondly, the bilateral scheme that has traditionally underpinned the right to be heard is also not consistent with the effects ensuing from the legal acts analysed in this chapter. They give rise to multilateral administrative relationships, affecting the legal spheres of persons other than the addressee of the act. This should ground the recognition of participation rights beyond the limits that have been set by the Courts.

7.1 Contextualizing: EU Food Law and Models of Administrative Action

EU food law originated from the need to remove trade barriers that could hamper free movement of goods within the internal market. Harmonization of national legislations directed at the protection of public health and safety that defined different protection standards was initially the main thrust behind integration in the food sector. In principle, health and safety issues remained a Member State competence; in particular, their administrative competences were not hampered by the harmonization of legislation. However, the line between ensuring free trade and pursuing consumer health protection soon became difficult to draw.[1] In the view of the EU institutions, regulating the free trade of food in the internal market meant defining the composition of foodstuffs, the conditions under which they can be placed on the market (e.g. food additives, foodstuffs for particular nutritional uses, novel foods, genetically modified organisms), ensuring an informed choice by the consumer (labelling), setting up hygiene requirements and rules to be respected when handling food, and creating mechanisms of enforcement of food law (official controls of foodstuffs).

Successive Treaty amendments expanded the EU competences in the protection of public health and consumer protection, but did not create a specific competence to adopt measures related to food safety.[2] Article 95

[1] Renaud Dehousse (1994) 'Some reflections on the crisis of the harmonisation model', in Francis Snyder (ed.), 'A regulatory framework for foodstuffs in the internal market', EUI Working Paper Law No. 94/4, p. 48. On the argument that the internal market implies the Europeanization of product safety law, Christian Joerges, Joseph Falke, Hans-W. Micklitz, and Gert Brüggemeier (1991) 'European Product Safety, Internal Market Policy and the New Approach to Technical Harmonisation and Standards', EUI Working Paper Law 91/10-14 (13, p. 81). Generally, on the pursuance of non-market values in internal market regulation, see Bruno de Witte (2006) 'Non-market values in internal market legislation', in Niamh Nic Suibhne (ed.), *Regulating the Internal Market*, Cheltenham, Northampton: Edward Elgar Publishing, pp. 61–86.

[2] See Articles 168 and 169 TFEU (former Articles 152 and 153 EC). In this sense, Ellen Vos (1999) *Institutional Frameworks of Community Health and Safety Regulation. Committees, Agencies and*

EC—today Article 114 TFEU—remained the core basis for the Community intervention in these matters, even where this meant providing the Commission with powers of decision regarding the trading of specific products.[3] Meanwhile, Treaty amendments introduced additional rules regarding the conduct of the Community institutions when adopting harmonization measures concerning health, safety, environmental, and consumer protection. The Single European Act determined that the Commission proposals for harmonization measures need to be based on a 'high level of protection'; the Amsterdam Treaty added that the Commission should, in particular, take into account 'any new development based on scientific facts' (Article 95(3) EC, current Article 114(3) TFEU). Both indications were extended to the European Parliament and the Council 'within their respective powers' (Article 95(3) EC, now Article 114(3) TFEU).

Nevertheless, the limits of product regulation based merely on legislative harmonization were clear.[4] In 1997, in its Green Paper on 'The general principles of food law in the European Union', the Commission stated:

> ...Experience suggests that the Community does not possess the instruments which are necessary to respond to the quickening pace of innovation and the ever increasing range of scientific knowledge....
>
> For example, in the field of food additives, any amendment to add or withdraw an additive from the positive list, or to enlarge or restrict the conditions of use of an additive, must be adopted using the co-decision procedure.... An average of about 5 years is necessary to complete the procedure at Community level. This increases to 6-7 years if allowance is also made for the time necessary for the adoption of national implementation measures. In contrast, in most if not all Member States a similar decision would be taken rapidly by a ministerial decision, on advice from the competent scientific advisory committee, and without the need for primary legislation.

Private Bodies, Oxford, Portland: Hart Publishing, p. 35. Article 168 TFEU allows for the expansion of Union competences in the area of public health (Article 168(4)(c) and (5)), but this does not contend with the above statement.

[3] Such as the so-called rapid alert system created by the product safety directive to cope with emergency situations that threaten the health and safety of consumers (Articles 7 to 12 of Council Directive No. 92/59/EEC, of 29 of June, on general product safety, OJ L 228/24, 11.8.1992, Article 9 of which has been challenged by Germany—Case C-359/92, *Germany v Council* [1994] ECR I-3681; this directive has been repealed by Directive No. 2001/95/EC of the European Parliament and of the Council of 3 December 2001, OJ L 11/4, 15.1.2002).

[4] Dehousse, *op. cit.*, n. 1, p. 47.

Even if powers are delegated to the Commission, they are often subject to procedures which are inappropriately burdensome. . . .[5]

The suggestion that the Community needed to have instruments that would go beyond the legislative intervention with a view to harmonization was clear. This seems to have been seconded by the European Parliament which, reacting to the Green Paper in the midst of the BSE crisis, drew 'attention . . . to the importance of prompt and efficient adjustment of existing legislation to new scientific findings' and urged 'the Commission to adopt a coordinating structure to prevent the marketing of foodstuffs posing a potential threat to the consumer'.[6] The Economic and Social Committee, in a later opinion, stated that its constitutive groups would support a food policy with 'genuine intervention capability'.[7] At the same time, it can be argued that, by the end of the 1990s, the possible reluctance of Member States in transferring competences in this area to the Community weakened, given the difficulties in tackling food crises at the national level and, likely, also given a certain unwillingness in assuming the political costs possibly entailed in crisis situations.[8]

[5] COM (97) 176 final, Brussels, 30.04.1997, pp. 24–5. The procedure described as an example of the lack of adequate regulatory powers was only modified by effect of Regulation No. 1331/2008, of the European Parliament and of the Council, of 16 December 2008, establishing a common authorisation procedure for food additives, food enzymes and food flavourings (OJ L 154/1, 31.12.2008; cf. Articles 16, second paragraph, and 9, for its entry into force), together with Regulation No. 1333/2008, of the European Parliament and of the Council, of 16 December 2008, on food additives (OJ L 154/16, 31.12.2008). Under the new rules, amendments to positive lists are adopted by the Commission following the regulatory procedure with scrutiny (Article 10 (3) of Regulation No. 1333/2008, and Articles 9(4) to (6) and 14 of Regulation No. 1331/2008). This will be analysed below (Sub-section 7.2.2).

[6] European Parliament Resolution on the Commission Green Paper on the general principles of food law in the European Union (COM (97) 0176, C4-0213/97), OJ C 104, 6.4.1998, points 25 and 18, respectively.

[7] Opinion of the Economic and Social Committee on the 'White Paper on Food Safety' (2000/C 204/06), OJ C 204/21, 18.7.2000, point 2.10. In the White Paper on Food Safety, however, the Commission focused its claim for enhanced regulatory powers on the need to streamline existing decision-making procedures and called for the use of secondary legislation in certain fields (such as food additives). Moreover, it claimed intensified Community powers in the control of the functioning of the market (*ex-post* administrative action, e.g. inspections).

[8] The fact that the alert mechanism of Regulation No. 178/2002 did not cause a judicial reaction similar to the one relating to the product safety directive may be a sign of this 'relaxation', in particular taking into account that the limits placed on the Commission's powers in the latter case are considerably less than those attached to the emergency measures adopted under the product safety directive (Article 53(1) of Regulation No. 178/2002, laying down the general principles and requirements of food law, establishing the European Food Safety Authority and

In general, the difficulties in foreseeing possible risks to health and safety and the respective responses; the limited resources of the legislator in terms of expertise in this field; the need for scientifically based assessments; as well as the need to adapt regulation to technological developments, to the most recent scientific knowledge, and to the changing normative social perceptions of risk, gave rise to other forms of regulatory intervention that complement, give form and action to the general objectives, concepts, and principles defined in legislative acts. As these were being enshrined in Community legislation, the centre of gravity of health and safety regulation, both of a legislative and an administrative nature, progressively shifted from the national to the European level. This occurred essentially on the basis of Article 95 EC (now Article 114 TFEU), disrupting the balance between Community harmonization and national regulation that underlies this norm. More recently, as harmonization is completed in some areas of food law, the tendency is to replace the original directives by new regulations. Being adopted on the basis of the same Treaty provision, they define authorization procedures in which decisions are adopted by the Commission following the advice of the European Food and Safety Authority.[9] This means that the regulatory intervention of Member States is reduced to their participation in EU bodies, in particular in the committees that prepare the final decision.[10] The next section of the chapter points out how decisional powers have been conferred on EU institutions or bodies. Arguably, their

laying down procedural in matters of food safety, OJ L 31/1, of 1.2.2002, amended; see below note 11). It should be noted that this regulation was adopted in the aftermath of the BSE crisis.

[9] In the area of food additives, see Regulations No. 1331/2008, *cit.*, n. 5 (adopted following the Commission proposal for a regulation of the European Parliament and of the Council establishing a common authorisation procedure for food additives, food enzymes and food flavourings, COM (2006) 423 final, Brussels, 28.7.2006) and 1333/2008, *cit.*, n. 5 (adopted following the Commission proposal for a regulation of the European Parliament and of the Council on food additives, COM (2006) 428 final, Brussels, 28.7.2006). The Commission stated that 'the area of food additives is fully harmonised in the EU' and clarifies that the proposal 'combines current framework Directives and specific Directives to a single instrument to facilitate the use of food additives in the EU' (p. 8 of the last cited document). In the area of novel foods, see Commission proposal for a regulation of the European Parliament and of the Council on novel foods and amending Regulation No. XXX/XXXX [common procedure], COM (2007) 872 final, Brussels, 14.1.2008 (hereinafter, 'the Commission's 2008 proposal'; at the time of the writing, the Commission had adopted its opinion on the amendments proposed by the European Parliament to the Council's position—Opinion of the Commission pursuant to Article 294, paragraph 7, point c) of the Treaty on the Functioning of the European Union, COM (2010) 507 final, Brussels, 11.10.2010). See Sub-sections 7.2.1 and 7.2.2, below.

[10] See Sub-section 7.2.2, below.

outcomes stray beyond mere harmonization and, as will be shown subsequently, they may lead to decisions that impact directly in the private persons' legal spheres. As mentioned, this has occurred essentially on the basis of Article 95 EC (now Article 114 TFEU). It is therefore relevant to show how the Court's interpretation of this Treaty article has endorsed this development (Sub-section 7.1.1), as well as to situate the analysis that follows in the context of the models of administrative action that emerge from EU food legislation (Sub-section 7.1.2). These are underpinned to a great extent by former Article 95 EC, even if not always solely on this provision.

7.1.1 *Building on 'measures for the approximation' of legislative and administrative acts*

The Court of Justice considered well-founded, on the basis of former Article 95, the creation of the Commission's direct powers in the fields of consumer safety and food regulation, as well as the design of legislative schemes that give broad leeway to the Commission's implementing acts. Two cases, in particular, illustrate the Courts' stance in this respect.

In a case pertaining to the so-called rapid alert system created by the product safety directive to cope with health and consumer safety emergency situations[11]—*Germany v Council*—the Court sustained that:

> [i]n certain fields, and particularly in that of product safety, the approximation of general laws alone may not be sufficient to ensure the unity of the market. Consequently, the concept of 'measures for the approximation' of legislation must be interpreted as encompassing the Council's power to lay down measures relating to a specific product or class of products and, if necessary, individual measures concerning those products.[12]

The contested mechanism allowed the Commission to adopt a decision requiring Member States to take temporary measures, in order to comply

[11] Council Directive No. 92/59/EEC, *cit.*, n. 3 (since repealed, see n. 3). The scope of this directive was not food regulation, but the underlying concerns resemble those of food safety. In particular, the rapid alert system the legality of which was challenged in the case mentioned in the text was analogous to the one envisaged in Regulation No. 178/2002, also based on former Article 95 EC, even though the Commission's powers are broader in the latter case: the Commission can adopt emergency measures on its own initiative; in doing so it is not limited to measures contained in a restrictive list and, depending on the gravity of the situation, the comitology procedure may or may not be followed before the adoption of the Commission's decision (see Article 53(1) of Regulation No. 178/2002, *cit.*, n. 8, and Articles 9 and 10 of the Council Directive No. 92/59/EEC). On comitology after Lisbon, see n. 28.

[12] *Germany v Council*, *cit.*, n. 3, paragraph 37.

with the general safety requirement defined in the directive. These ranged from the publication of special warnings to the prohibition of placing on the market the product that was considered dangerous or the withdrawal and eventual destruction of a product already placed on the market. These measures were, as a rule, adopted by the Member States.[13] The fact that different elements of the procedure for the adoption of the measures were still in the hands of the Member States seems to have weighed in the Court's decision. On the one hand, the Commission's power was triggered by the notification or information provided by a Member State and it was limited by the intervention of Member States' representatives in the comitology committee. On the other, the decision was addressed to the Member States and, according to a declaration contained in the preamble of the directive, was deprived of direct effect.[14] In these conditions, according to the Court, the Commission's competence under the product safety directive could still be pinned down to the concept of 'measures for the approximation' and, hence, based on Article 95.

The same expression of 'measures for the approximation' that was at the centre of this case was subject to another extensive interpretation a decade later in a case opposing the United Kingdom to the European Parliament and to the Council.[15] This time, the Court was called upon to judge the validity of a regulation that creates a two-stage harmonization procedure, by which the legislative act merely lays down the procedures for the adoption of a Community list of authorized products and for the adaptation of that list whilst the harmonization effect is only produced by a Commission act—either a regulation or a decision—pursuant to this procedure.[16] The United Kingdom alleged that 'the legislative power conferred by Article 95 EC [now Article 114 TFEU] is a power to harmonize national

[13] According to the directive, Member States needed to ensure that products placed on the market are safe and that producers and distributors comply with their obligations under the directive (Articles 3 to 6). Article 8 defined the duties of Member States in emergency situations and the Annex of the directive contained the detailed procedures for rapid exchange of information.

[14] *Germany v Council*, *cit.*, n. 3, paragraph 35.

[15] It is defended in the text that the judgment on *Germany v Council* meant an extensive interpretation of the concept of 'measures for the approximation'. This position assumes that the creation of decisional powers directed at the adoption of individual measures or regarding specific products was not envisaged by the Member States when signing the Treaty of Rome, nor later when revising it.

[16] Case C-66/04, *United Kingdom v European Parliament and Council* [2005] ECR I-10553, on the validity of Regulation No. 2065/2003, of the European Parliament and of the Council, of 10 November 2003 on smoke flavourings used or intended for use in or on foods (OJ 2003 L 309/1, 26.11.2003).

laws, not a power to establish Community bodies or to confer tasks on such bodies, or to establish procedures for the approval of lists of authorized products' and, in addition, denied that this resulted in harmonization.[17] The Court, however, considered that:

> by the expression 'measures for the approximation' in Article 95 EC the authors of the Treaty intended to confer on the Community legislature a discretion, depending on the general context and the specific circumstances of the matter to be harmonized, as regards the harmonization technique most appropriate for achieving the desired result, in particular in fields which are characterized by complex technical features.[18]

The Court was of the opinion not only that the regulation contains the essential elements of the harmonization measure,[19] but also that the procedure designed for the implementation of the regulation is shaped in such a way that it allows for a harmonization effect, despite the fact that this effect does not result directly from the basic regulation. In the Court's view, it was enough that the powers of the Commission are clearly defined as to assigning to the (then) Community the decision-making competence in this respect.[20] The definition of the essential elements of the harmonization act and a final harmonization effect are, hence, the threshold fixed by the Court to ensure the legality of acts based on former Article 95 EC (current Article 114 TFEU).

As is demonstrated below, Article 95 EC served as a legal basis to create procedures the outcomes of which contend directly with the legal sphere of private persons, bypassing to a great extent the two-tier legislative system that underlies the harmonization of national legislative, regulatory, and

[17] *United Kingdom v European Parliament and Council, cit.*, paragraphs 18 and 21. The allusion to the creation of Community bodies on the basis of Article 95 EC is a reference to another Community act contested by the UK, which established the European Network and Information Security Agency (Case C-217/04, *United Kingdom v European Parliament and Council* [2006] ECR I-3771). Arguably, the same reasoning is applicable to Regulation No. 178/2002, which created the EFSA and defined its tasks in the framework of the general rules and principles of food law, on the basis of former Article 95 EC but also of Articles 37, 133, and 152(4)(b) EC.

[18] *United Kingdom v European Parliament and Council, cit.*, n. 16, paragraph 45. The argumentation put forward by the European institutions in this case bluntly confirms the limits of the legislature when regulating scientific complex matters. The European Parliament, Council, and Commission agreed in this respect (paragraphs 31, 35, and 39, respectively).

[19] *United Kingdom v European Parliament and Council, cit.*, n. 16, paragraphs 53–59.

[20] *United Kingdom v European Parliament and Council, cit.*, n. 16, paragraphs 49–50 and 60–63.

administrative measures. The Court's interpretation of the meaning of 'measures for the approximation' of legal regimes has sanctioned this use.

7.1.2 *Models of administrative action*

The distribution of the regulatory tasks involved in food regulation varies from sub-sector to sub-sector and, hence, both the powers attributed to EU institutions or left to Member States' authorities and the way these affect the rights and interests of the persons concerned by food regulation also vary from case to case. In general, however, one may argue that EU food law has given rise to three different models of administrative action in which decisional procedures and administrative decisions are controlled, coordinated, or supervised by the EU institutions, usually the Commission, with the assistance of the European Food and Safety Authority (henceforth 'the EFSA').

First, the public intervention in the food market may be structured on the basis of *ex-ante* controls embodied in market authorizations. These regulate the internal market by defining the conditions that a certain product has to fulfil in order to be admitted to trade, consequently defining also the rights and duties of producers and traders. Next, regulatory intervention may be focused on *ex-post* controls. In this case the conditions and requirements for producing given products are previously defined in EU legislation, regulations, or guidelines and the bulk of the administrative activity lies in controlling the respect for those rules (this model underlies, for example, the hygiene regulations).[21] Finally, procedures to act in emergency situations or to react to imminent risks form a third type of regulatory action. In this case, ensuring safety and public health requires the adoption of measures that, even if temporary, have regulatory effects resembling those of the market authorizations. These measures often modify the conditions that had been previously defined in prior authorizations and impose duties

[21] Regulation No. 852/2004, of the European Parliament and the Council, of 29 April 2004, on the hygiene of foodstuffs (OJ L 226/3, 25.6.2004), as amended; Regulation No. 853/2004, of the European Parliament and the Council, of 29 April 2004, laying down specific hygiene rules for food and animal origin (OJ L 226/22, 25.6.2004), as amended; Regulation No. 854/2004, of the European Parliament and the Council, of 29 April 2004, laying down specific rules for the organisation of official controls on products of animal origin intended for human consumption (OJ L 226/83, 25.6.2004), as amended; Regulation No. 882/2004, of the European Parliament and the Council, of 29 April 2004, on official controls performed to ensure the verification of compliance with feed and food law, animal health and animal welfare rules (OJ L 191/1, 28.5.2004).

of conduct on private operators in the field as well as on public authorities. All three types of public intervention typically correspond to forms of administrative action.

This distinction reveals only the basic matrix of the regulatory model. In fact, the three types of controls co-exist in most sub-sectors, albeit in different degrees. Thus, where administrative activity is focused on *ex-ante* controls, monitoring the activity performed might determine a change of the conditions previously defined, given the need to face a previously unknown risk before the end of the period for which the authorization was granted. Moreover, procedures for the adoption of emergency measures are nowadays horizontal to different legal regimes on foodstuffs.[22] The above classification is, in any case, relevant for analytical purposes. In fact, the position of the persons affected by the exercise of the administrative powers differs in each case, as does the balance between the protection of public and private interests that the regulatory decision requires.

In the first case, the authorization to market a given product entails *prima facie* the creation of a relationship established between a market operator and the administrative authority competent for delivering the authorization upon which depends the possibility of trading that product. In the case of EU procedures, the latter is usually the most visible entity of an administrative network, created and formalized by the procedure that underpins the final decision. This decision, in turn, has a decisive bearing on the rights and interests of the applicant, since the right to market a product and the conditions under which they may exercise that right are dependent on this decision. Its effects have, however, a broader reach. Other producers operating in the internal market will be able to trade the same product under the same conditions, other distributors might also be interested in the possibility of trading it, consumers and their associations want to be reassured that the product is safe for public health, while environmentalists very likely want to ensure that environmental risks were sufficiently accounted for. These are simultaneously public interests that are protected under EU law and that, therefore, need to be balanced in the procedure leading to the authorization or to its refusal. The decision-maker is, therefore, entangled in a net that reaches beyond the bilateral relation that links it to the applicant. Arguably, allowing the holders of the different interests to intervene in the decisional procedures may contribute to a better composition of

[22] Articles 53 and 54 of Regulation No. 178/2002, *cit.*, n. 8.

the interests that should be reflected in the final decision, and enables an anticipated legal protection of the persons affected. This point is further developed below.

In the second case, the competent administrative entities enjoy the typical powers that pertain to a 'police' function, such as carrying out inspections and applying sanctions for eventual infringements of the applicable rules. Ensuring the respect for rules previously established is the traditional core of the administrative authority. In principle, the relationship resulting from the exercise of this type of power merely involves the decision-maker and the person or persons in respect of whom they are exercised. The exercise of these powers, although naturally involving a power of appreciation of each case, does not entail the balancing of divergent interests in a similar way to the kind of administrative intervention identified above. In principle, potentially interested parties, other than those against whom certain decisions are taken, have a general interest that the law is effectively applied and that, where infringements have occurred, the corresponding sanctions are applied. The composition of interests lies elsewhere. The procedural guarantees that should be ensured to the persons targeted by the procedures are often a matter of respect for fundamental rights in carrying out an administrative action (e.g. respect for the right of property, correspondence, or protection against arbitrary or disproportionate intervention by the public authorities, which has been defined in *Hoechst* as a general principle of EU law).[23]

In the third model, the need to balance competing and potentially conflicting interests is also present but, in the face of a concrete risk situation, the composition of interests is secondary to the need to adopt in the shortest possible time adequate and appropriate measures to tackle the risk in question. In emergency situations, the involvement of holders of affected interests is likely to be overridden by a unilateral definition of what best suits the public interest. This is also suggested by Article 9 of Regulation No. 178/2002, according to which 'where the urgency of the matter' justifies it, the public authority is exempted from the general duty of opening decision-making to public consultation. Where participation rights exist, the possibility of intervening in the decision-making procedure, if not feasible before the adoption of the measure, should be offered after its implementation.[24]

[23] Joined Cases 46/87 and 227/88, *Hoechst AG v Commission* [1989] ECR 2859.

[24] See Case C-28/05, *G.J. Dokter and others v Minister van Landbouw, Natuur en Voedselkwaliteit* [2006] ECR I-5431, paragraph 76.

In general, the issue of legal protection of the interests affected by the final decision is shifted to remedies: there needs to be the possibility of challenging the measure before the courts and affected parties must be made aware of the remedies available as well as of the time limits that apply to such remedies.

The first model offers the more interesting possibilities for analysing the way EU administrative procedures structure the diverse interests involved or affected by the final decisions, as well as for considering in which situations participation rights should or not be recognized to the persons concerned. In the third model this aspect is likely to be displaced to a moment subsequent to the adoption of the decision. It has in common with the second model the fact that the issue of legal protection is, in these cases, more pressing and compelling: the administrative powers may be quite 'invasive' and are exercised on previously constituted rights. This is, therefore, the type of situation that is in principle covered by the right to be heard, as defined by the jurisprudence of the EU Courts. Hence, the type of administrative action involved in the first model allows better testing of the hypothesis of extension that is discussed in this book.

7.2 Administrative Procedures

EU laws that regulate the food markets by defining *ex-ante* administrative controls nowadays cover various aspects of the composition of food: food additives, foodstuffs for particular nutritional uses, food supplements, novel foods, genetically modified organisms, genetically modified food and feed. The EU has resorted to different ways of combining the distribution of powers between national and EU bodies dealing with these matters. These were, mostly, arranged in different authorization procedures that can be grouped in the following types: national procedures implementing EU law, decentralized EU procedures, and centralized EU procedures.

The first type corresponds *grosso modo* to the 'ideal model' of indirect administration. The procedure is initiated and completed by the national administrations implementing EU law, following national administrative law rules. However, because they implement EU law, EU bodies also intervene at a certain point, either actively during the procedure (issuing opinions that may be binding on the final decision) or, in a perhaps more passive role, after its conclusion (Member States may be required to inform the Commission of the decisions taken). It should be noted that the constraints dictated by EU law to national autonomy in each case may question the characterization of the procedure as national, despite the apparent clear allocation of procedural and decision-making competences. This model corresponded to the first food additives legislation,[25] which was enacted in the period of completion of the internal market in the food sector. As was mentioned above, it is being replaced by EU centralized procedures, which strengthens the Commission decision-making powers in this field.

The second—decentralized EU procedures—are equally started and concluded by the national administrations. Nevertheless, contrary to the procedures that fall under the first category, the national decision-maker is also the face of a network that involves the other Member States' competent bodies and the Commission (usually accompanied by advisory committees and the EFSA). The interventions of the latter are decisive for the final outcome. Moreover, the different phases of these procedures are defined with detail in an EU legal act, while that is in principle not the case with the national procedures of EU function. This is the case of the novel food regulation still in place at the time of writing, which came about in a period in which public health and consumer protection had already become a prominent Community task in the food sector.[26] Also here, following the Commission proposal for a new regulation in this field, it is likely that this form of procedure will be replaced by a centralized procedure, largely the same as the one created for the authorization of food additives.[27]

Finally, centralized EU procedures are those where an EU institution, irrespective of the collaboration and intervention of national administrative

[25] Council Directive No. 89/107/EEC, of 21 December 1988, on the approximation of the laws of the Member States concerning food additives authorized for use in foodstuffs intended for human consumption (OJ L 40/27, 11.02.1989), replaced (together with the so-called daughter directives that complemented it) by Regulation No. 1333/2008, *cit.*, n. 5 (see also n. 9).

[26] Regulation No. 258/97, of the European Parliament and of the Council, of 27 January 1997, concerning novel food and novel food ingredients (OJ L 43/1, 14.2.1997), as amended (hereinafter, 'the novel foods regulation').

[27] See Articles 7 and 19 of the Commission's 2008 proposal on novel foods, *cit.*, n. 9. See also Article 8 of the Position of the European Parliament adopted at first reading on 25 March 2009 with a view to the adoption of Regulation (EC) No . . . /2009 of the European Parliament and of the Council on novel foods, amending Regulation (EC) No 1331/2008 and repealing Regulation (EC) No 258/97 (P6_TA(2009)0171); as well as Articles 6, 16, and 28 of Position No. 6/2010, of the Council at First Reading, with a view to the adoption of a Regulation of the European Parliament and of the Council on novel foods, amending Regulation No 1331/2008 and repealing Regulation No 258/97 and Commission Regulation No 1852/2001, adopted by the Council on 15 March 2010 (OJ C 122/E/38, 11.5.2010).

bodies or entities, formally and substantively takes the final decision. Usually, national administrative bodies or entities are also involved in the administrative procedure, but their action is merely ancillary to that developed at the EU level (sometimes, the role of national administrations is limited to receiving the application for authorization). The main preparatory acts are produced either by the EFSA as such or by a network of national entities coordinated by this agency. The final decision is usually taken by the Commission following a comitology procedure.[28] Member States can influence the course of the procedure only through their participation in EU bodies. The procedure is, therefore, developed and decided at the EU level. Besides the new procedure for the authorization of food additives, already mentioned, another example of this model is the procedure for the approval of genetically modified food and feed. The regulation that defines it was approved after the fundamental change that occurred in the EU administrative organization in this field—the creation of the EFSA—which was in turn accompanied by transparency concerns and partially determined by the need to ensure public trust in food regulation.[29]

To the extent that these three models of combining the distribution of powers between national and EU administrative bodies have coincided in time, it is likely that the legislative choice for one or the other was essentially conditioned by the outcomes of the negotiations between the converging or diverging views of the Member States, the Parliament, and the Commission, and maybe also influenced by the perceived level of risk entailed in each category of foodstuffs and by the scientific and technological knowledge required. However, the current stage of integration in this field seems to clearly favour the last model mentioned.

[28] The likely impact of the new framework for implementing acts in the Lisbon Treaty will be considered below, when analysing the specific legal regimes for the market authorization of food products. For now, it suffices to say that, under the new constitutional framework, comitology procedures will be applicable only in the realm of implementing acts (Article 291 TFEU). Note that the Commission Proposal for a Regulation of the European Parliament and of the Council laying down the rules and general principles concerning mechanisms for control by Member States of the Commission's exercise of implementing powers (COM (2010) 83 final, Brussels, 9.3.2010), in essence, envisages the continuity between current and the new procedures, with the exception of the regulatory procedure with scrutiny.

[29] Regulation No. 1829/2003, of the European Parliament and of the Council, of 22 of September 2003, on genetically modified food and feed (OJ L268/1, 18.10.2003), as amended, hereinafter 'the genetically modified food regulation'. Regulation No. 178/2002 laid down the general principles and requirements of food law, as well as food safety procedures, and established the European Food Safety Authority (*cit.*, n. 8).

The analysis that follows illustrates the functioning of the two last models, examining the procedures regarding the market authorizations of novel foods, food additives, and genetically modified food and feed.[30] Its purpose is to assess the scope of procedural protection afforded to the persons concerned by the ensuing decisions. Two factors should, therefore, be examined. First, what kind of procedural relationship—bilateral, involving the addressee of the decision and the decision-maker, or multilateral, encompassing procedural links with other interested persons—emerges from the procedural design chosen in each case. This will focus on the relationships established between public entities, on the one hand, and private persons, on the other, disregarding the sometimes complex interrelations between the different public entities involved in the procedure. Secondly, given that in current EU administrative law, the procedural protection of individuals is largely dependent on the form of the act adopted, attention is also paid to the type of acts that in each case embody the market authorization. Anticipating what will be said with regard to each of the procedures, the following analysis will show that these acts are either individual decisions or general acts—in the new framework of non-legislative acts introduced by the Lisbon Treaty, the latter will be either implementing or delegated acts (Articles 290 and 291 TFEU).[31] The question of whether there is a case for the possible extension of participation rights, beyond the typical situations in which the right to be heard is applied, constitutes the second phase of analysis. This occupies the next section

[30] Note that the procedure for the authorization of food additives is contained in Regulation 1331/2008 (*cit.*, n. 5), which defines a common procedure applicable also to the authorization of food enzymes and food flavourings. Moreover, a reference in recital 22 of this regulation reveals that this might in the future be extended to other areas of food law (this is envisaged in the Commission's 2008 proposal on novel foods–see n. 27). The other procedures have mentioned already been described in other earlier works. In particular, the authorization of genetically modified food has attracted much academic attention (see, *inter alia*, Caoimhín Macmaoláin (2007) *EU Food Law. Protecting Consumers and Health in a Common Market*, Oxford, Portland: Hart Publishing, pp. 248–9; Damian Chalmers (2005) 'Risk, anxiety and the European mediation of the politics of life', *European Law Review*, Vol. 30, n. 5, pp. 649–74, at pp. 653–4; Theofanis Christoforou (2004) 'The regulation of genetically modified organisms in the European Union: the interplay of science, law and politics', *Common Market Law Review*, Vol. 41, n. 3, pp. 637–709, at pp. 657–61; the latter also presents the procedure for the authorization of novel foods, *idem*, pp. 649–51). However, in view of purposes of analysis stated in the text, it is opportune to also describe this procedure here.

[31] Indeed, under the new rules of the Lisbon Treaty, individual decisions cannot be adopted as delegated acts (Article 290(1) TFEU expressly applies to 'non-legislative acts of general application').

(Section 7.3), where the characteristics of the acts ensuing from the procedures are also examined.

Despite the envisaged replacement of the novel food regulation currently in force, its analysis is still considered pertinent for two main reasons. First, this regulation illustrates a different way of conceiving market authorization procedures that is still valid today. Secondly, the intricacies of the procedure envisaged therein show the need to identify, in composite procedures, the level at which the final decision is effectively formed in order to delimit the cases in which participation rights should be exercised directly before EU institutions or bodies or, in any event, at the EU level of decision-making.[32] At the same time, the contrast with the now predominant centralized procedures is interesting to understand the evolution that has occurred in this field. The Commission's 2008 proposal is taken into account where pertinent, as well as the positions of the Parliament and the Council in this regard.[33] The procedure envisaged in the new regulation is, indirectly, covered by the analysis of the food additives procedure that occupies the following subsection. As mentioned, this procedure will also apply to novel foods.[34]

7.2.1 *Novel foods*

The novel foods regulation originated from the perceived need to ensure a 'single safety assessment through a Community procedure before [novel foods or food ingredients] are placed on the market within the Community'.[35] The main reasons behind the adoption of the regulation were to ensure the protection of public health and the free movement of foodstuffs, as well as to contribute to the development of the biotechnology industry

[32] Case T-42/96, *Eyckeler & Malt AG v Commission* [1998] ECR II-401, paragraphs 84–88; Case T-50/96, *Primex Produkte Import-Export GmbH & Co and others v Commission* [1998] ECR II-3773, paragraphs 67–71. On these cases, see Chapter 4, Sub-section 4.2.2. It results from these judgments that participation rights should be recognized at the EU level of decision-making when the final act is effectively adopted by an EU institution. However, as was noted above in the book, there are signs that the Courts' case law is not 'stable' in this respect, since in a later judgment, the Court implicitly defended that the right to be heard should in any case be exercised before the national administrations.

[33] The Opinion of the Commission on the European Parliament's amendments to the Council position on the proposal for a new regulation on novel foods contains provisions on the procedure only to the extent that it indicates the acts that, in the Commission's opinion should be adopted as implementing acts under Article 291 TFEU (see Opinion of the Commission, *cit.*, n. 9, p. 7).

[34] See n. 27.

[35] Second recital of the preamble of Regulation No. 258/97, *cit.*, n. 26, (in this sub-section also simply referred to as 'the regulation').

in the food sector.[36] Novel food or food ingredients are those resulting from non-natural processes of production and that have not been used for human consumption to a significant degree within the common market.[37] According to the regulation, three conditions need to be respected for their placement on the market to be allowed: the novel foods or food ingredients must not present a danger to, nor mislead the consumer, nor be nutritionally disadvantageous for the consumer.[38] Novel foods, and, concomitantly, the respective legal regime, are a highly relevant area of food law, embracing production processes such as cloning or nanotechnology, which are capable of engendering considerable controversy.[39]

The placement on the market of novel foods or food ingredients depends on an evaluation made by public authorities, which currently follows either a simplified procedure of notification or an authorization procedure. The former applies, by way of exception, to situations in which the legislator believes that fewer safety risks are raised, given the substantial equivalence between the novel foods or food ingredients and existing foods or food ingredients 'as regards their composition, nutritional value, metabolism, intended use and the level of undesirable substances contained

[36] The first two rationales mentioned are documented in the first and second recitals of the preamble (and correspond also to the first recital of the Commission's 2008 proposal, Article 1 of which also mentions consumer protection as one of the goals to be achieved; note that the European Parliament has proposed a new drafting emphasizing food safety, consumer and environmental protection, as well as animal health and welfare as the main concerns that should underpin this legal regime—see Report on the proposal for a regulation of the European Parliament and of the Council on novel foods and amending Regulation (EC) No XXX/XXXX [common procedure] (2008/0002(COD), Committee on the Environment, Public Health and Food Safety, Rapporteur Kartika Tamara Liotard, A6-0512/2008, 18 December 2008, p. 23 and pp. 5–6). The third is supported by Gwenole Cozigou, at the time Head Commission's Food Industry Unit in 'Un nouveau cadre juridique pour les applications biotechnologiques dans le secteur alimentaire: le règlement 'Nouveau aliments", *Revue du Marche Unique*, n. 2, pp. 67–80, at p. 73.

[37] Article 1(2) (cf. Article 3(2)(a) of the Commission's 2008 proposal, *cit.*, n. 9). The realm of application of this regulation was considerably reduced when, by effect of the genetically modified food regulation, examined below, the authorization of 'foods and food ingredients containing or consisting of genetically modified organisms', as well as those 'produced from, but not containing, genetically modified organisms' was subtracted from the legal regime of novel foods (Article 38 of the genetically modified food regulation (Regulation No. 1829/2003, *cit.*, n. 29)). This change is one of the grounds on which the Commission based its 2008 proposal (p. 2, *cit.*, n. 9).

[38] Article 3(1) of the novel foods regulation (these are maintained in Article 6 of the Commission's 2008 proposal, as well as in the Positions of the Council—Article 8—and of the European Parliament—see, however, Article 7; *cit.*, n. 27).

[39] See, for example, 'Public strongly against cloned animal meat, study reveals', *The Guardian*, 06.06.2008.

therein'.[40] For the purposes of this book, only the standard authorization procedure is relevant and, therefore, considered in the following analysis. Suffice it to say that the simplified procedure is a centralized bilateral procedure that involves the Commission (possibly supported by the Standing Committee on the Food Chain and Animal Health) and the applicant. Being grounded in an assessment of a controversial concept dependent on scientific evidence—the 'substantial equivalence' of a novel food to a 'conventional' food—this procedure is not unproblematic.[41] The possibility of a simplified procedure was, therefore, written out of the Commission's 2008 proposal.[42]

Standard authorization procedure

Novel food or food ingredients are subject to a full safety assessment through a procedure that involves Member States and their scientific bodies in direct collaboration with the EU administrative bodies. As mentioned, those substantially equivalent to 'conventional food' are, under current rules, exempted from this procedure.

According to the novel foods regulation, the producer who wishes to place a novel food on the market must submit a request to the Member States in the territory of which they intend to release it for the first time, while also forwarding this request to the Commission.[43] Gathering the information to support the request is primarily a task for the applicant; they have the onus of demonstrating that the general safety and labelling requirements have been complied with.[44] This, however, is subject to an

[40] Article 3(4). This can apply only to two of the categories of novel foods that fall within the scope of the regulation (Article 1(2)(d) and (e)).

[41] See Opinion of Advocate General Alber, delivered on 13 March 2003, Case C-236/01, *Monsanto Agricoltura Italia SpA and Others v Presidenza del Consiglio dei Ministri and Others* [2003] ECR I-8105 [2003] ECR I-8105, paragraph 34. The concept of 'substantial equivalence' was at the centre of the judicial conflict between Monsanto and Italy that culminated in the intervention of the ECJ by means of a preliminary ruling. At issue was the use of this procedure for products derived from genetically modified organisms, a possibility that no longer exists (since the genetically modified food regulation excluded foods containing genetically modified organisms from the realm of the novel food regulation).

[42] See Commission's 2008 proposal, *cit.*, n. 9, p. 7. However, the official explanations for this choice (among which, clarity, transparency, and the need to effectively ensure a separation between risk assessment and risk management) are found elsewhere: see the Commission's proposal for a regulation of the European Parliament and of the Council on genetically modified food and feed, COM (2001) 425 final, Brussels, 25.7.2001, p. 7.

[43] Article 4(1) of the novel foods regulation, *cit.*, n. 26.

[44] Article 6(1) of the novel foods regulation and Commission Recommendation No. 97/618/EC of 29 July 1997 concerning the scientific aspects and the presentation of information

initial assessment carried out by the Member State's food assessment authority.[45] It is the national food assessment authority that has the competence to carry out the initial report, which is determinant for the next steps of the procedure. The national authority either decides that the authorization requires an additional assessment, which, this time, will be carried out by the Commission following a comitology procedure, or that there is no need for a further assessment, in which case the final decision will be taken by the Member State concerned. In any event, the report is equivalent to an intermediate procedural decision.

In fact, in either case, the Commission informs the other Member States that the procedure is being carried out, and identifies the competent national authority.[46] The initial report also needs to be communicated 'without delay' by the Member State concerned to the Commission, which, in turn, circulates it among the other national administrations. Both these and the Commission can comment on or object to the marketing of the novel food or food ingredient at issue. Moreover, any of the Member States can request information from the applicant.[47] The time limits are well defined: the initial report has to be delivered within three months of receipt of the request, while the comments and objections have to be submitted and circulated among Member States within a further two months from the date of circulation of the report by the Commission. In addition, any reasoned objection raised by the Commission has to be supported by an opinion of the EFSA, under Article 11 of the novel food regulation and Article 29(1)(a) of Regulation No. 178/2002.[48]

When the national food assessment authority decides that no further assessment is required and when no reasoned objection is raised within the time limit defined in the regulation, the Member State's competent

necessary to support applications for the placing on the market of novel foods and novel food ingredients and the preparation of initial assessment reports under Regulation No. 258/97 of the European Parliament and of the Council (OJ L 253/1, 16.9.1997).

[45] Article 6(2) and (3) of the novel foods regulation.

[46] Article 6(2), second paragraph, *idem*.

[47] Article 6(4), *idem*.

[48] According to the first provision, 'the Scientific Committee for Food [the EFSA, by force of Article 62(1) of Regulation 178/2002] shall be consulted on any matter falling within the scope of this regulation likely to have an effect on public health'. According to the second, 'the Authority shall issue a scientific opinion at the request of the Commission, in respect of any matter within its mission, and in all cases where Community legislation makes provision for the Authority to be consulted'.

authority takes the final decision.[49] Even when the initial assessment concludes that there is no need for a further assessment, the national authority must wait another two months before it can notify its positive decision to the applicant. This decision is hence the result of the consent of all Member States and the Commission regarding the marketing of that particular novel food product. It is necessarily a positive decision. This results in general from the scheme of the regulation and corresponds to the wording of Article 4(2), according to which the national authority 'shall inform the applicant without delay that he may place the food or food ingredient on the market, where the additional assessment [...] is not required, and that no reasoned objection has been presented [...], or that, in accordance with Article 7, *an authorization decision* is required.'[50]

If the authorization to market the novel food is refused the procedure must continue at EU level. At this point, the procedure changes its nature: here, a centralized EU procedure is grafted on to what had been until then a procedure largely left to Member States' administrations. This mutation, however, is not fully in the hands of the latter, since, in the first stage, the Commission can also raise a reasoned objection that provokes this shift.[51] The applicant is, in any case, informed.[52] From here on, the decision is left to an EU body—the Standing Committee on Food Chain and Animal Health—functioning under the chairmanship of the Commission. This remains, in any case, a procedure that develops between the applicant and the administrative body that is the face

[49] This results from the wording of Articles 4(2), 6(4) and, *a contrario sensu*, from Article 7(1) of the novel foods regulation, *cit.*, n. 26. It is not clear from the regulation if the same authority that produced the report is competent to take this final decision. The regulation only requires that Member States 'notify to the Commission the name and address of the food assessment bodies responsible in its territory for preparing the initial assessment reports referred to in Article 6(2)' (Article 4(3)). When referring to the authorization to be delivered by the national authorities on the basis of Article 4(2), it merely mentions 'the Member State referred to in paragraph 1', i.e. the one that received the application, without any further specification. However, admitting that the principle of severing risk assessment from risk management (Article 6(2) and (3), recitals 17 and 18 of Regulation No. 178/2002, *cit.*, n. 8) is equally applicable to the Member States' action in the field of food safety, these are, in principle, two different entities.

[50] Emphasis added (this wording corresponds to other language versions, namely the French, German, Italian, Portuguese, and Spanish texts). This can only be understood in the sense that, in this case, an authorization *taken at EU level* is required.

[51] In fact, this can either follow directly from the conclusion of the initial report or from an objection raised in the first stage of the procedure of Article 7(1) of the novel foods regulation.

[52] The applicant is either immediately notified, in the case where the initial report concludes that an additional assessment is required, or after the period of three months, in the event of a reasoned objection (Article 4(2) of the novel foods regulation, *cit.*, n. 26).

of a network of administrations (at this stage, the Commission). The final 'authorization decision' is taken following a comitology procedure.[53] Admitting that the current novel food regulation will still be in force once the new procedural rules that implement Article 291 TFEU are enacted, the respective market authorizations will most likely be implementing decisions under new Article 291 TFEU.[54] This decision 'shall define the scope of the authorization and shall establish, where appropriate, the conditions of use of the food or food ingredient, the designation of the food or food ingredient, and its specification [and] specific labelling requirements...'.[55] Moreover, besides the necessary notification to the applicant, the decision needs to be published in the Official Journal.

Bilateral relationship with a network of administrative entities

It results from the provisions of the novel food regulation that the core procedural relationship external to the 'network' of administrative authorities is established between the applicant and the national administration of the Member State where the applicant intends to market the novel food for the first time. Nevertheless, the applicant knows when their request circulates among other Member States and they may be questioned by one of them or by the Commission during the instruction phase, thereby entering into direct contact with the other administrative entities that function as a network. The applicant's request may even be assessed by a different national administration: the Member State that received the application may ask the Commission to arrange for the report to be prepared by a food assessment body of another Member State. This is, therefore, an EU procedure, which is decentralized when a positive decision is envisaged at an early stage. It involves all Member States, linked with each other and with the Commission by a duty of cooperation, and requires a food safety assessment undertaken by a public authority. The silent consent of the Commission and of the other Member States can lead to a positive decision issued by the Member State that has received the application.

There is no express provision for participation rights during this procedure. While any of the Member States involved may request information from the applicant, this does not constitute the exercise of a right to be heard. It merely corresponds to the possibility of clarifying specific points of the

[53] Articles 7(1) and 13, *idem*. See n. 28 above.

[54] See n. 31 above.

[55] Article 7(2), *idem*.

application, if further clarifications on the documents filed with the application are needed. Hence, this does not allow the applicant to set forth their views on the expected decision, although it is admittedly a possibility that endows the applicant with a certain degree of control over the procedure.[56] If there are grounds to recognize participation rights in the situations covered by this regulation (e.g. in cases of negative decisions), the terms in which the intervention of interested persons could occur are those resulting from the Courts' case law on the *audi alteram partem* principle, which, in principle, in this case, encompasses only the applicant.[57]

The recognition of possible participation rights in this context—and of the right to be heard in particular—should take into account the structure of the procedure. In particular, it should reflect the fact that the decision of the Member State to whom the request was presented is conditioned by the assessments made by the latter and also the fact that, ultimately, the final decision may be adopted by the Commission. Concretely, the effective procedure followed and its final outcome are not dependent only on the decision of the Member State.[58] Therefore, one cannot rely for the purposes of participation on the application of national rules of procedure. Even if the possibility of hearing interested parties, in accordance with national legislation, may still be accommodated within the time frame defined in the novel food regulation, the final decision may be the result of the converging opinions of the other competent national bodies and of the Commission. In these circumstances, the exercise of participation rights at the national level, or at least in a phase of the procedure in which all competent public bodies have not yet intervened, is potentially ineffective. In a word, since participation rights should be ensured at a moment of the procedure in which the decision-maker has a high degree of certainty about

[56] Arguably, not questioning the applicant in case of doubts may, in certain conditions lead to a breach of the principle of care and may therefore affect the legality of the procedure.

[57] Above Chapter 4, Section 4.2.

[58] For example, the Commission Decision of 25 July 2005 refusing the placing on the market of betaine as a novel food or novel food ingredient (OJ L 199/89, 29.7.2005) was adopted in the sequence of a negative opinion of the EFSA, while the Finnish initial assessment report had concluded that the safety of betaine for the intended use as proposed by the applicant had been established. This is one of the three negative decisions, of a total of 45, that have been issued so far (October 2010) by the Commission following the procedure of the novel food regulation (the others are: Commission Decision No. 2000/196/EC, of 22 February 2000 refusing the placing on the market of Stevia rebaudiana Bertoni: plants and dried leaves, OJ L 61/14, 8.3.2000; Commission Decision No. 2001/17/EC, of 19 December 2000, on refusing the placing on the market of 'Nangai nuts', OJ L 4/35, 9.1.2001).

the outcome (i.e. after the intervention of other national assessment bodies and of the Commission), the corresponding procedural rules need to reflect the reality of the composite procedure. This seems to result from the judgments in *Eyckeler & Malt* and *Primex Produkte*, to the extent that the Court has argued in these rulings that, in view of the power of assessment of the Commission at a second stage of a composite procedure, the persons concerned should be heard by the Commission before the adoption of the ensuing decision, in the cases where this entails a different assessment from the one made at an earlier stage by the national administration. Moreover, in both cases, the Court insisted on the need to satisfy 'the fundamental purpose of the right to be heard', an observation that might be considered as accommodating the need for participation to occur at a moment of the procedure where it can be effective.[59] However, as was seen in Chapter 4, the Court has not been consistent in this respect. As such, one may argue that there are no steady EU rules in this regard.

At any rate, opening the procedure to the intervention of potentially interested persons, besides the applicant, was not a regulatory choice of the EU legislator. This is confirmed by the Commission regulation that set out the details of the authorization procedure. This regulation only concerns the need to balance the transparency of the procedure regulated in Article 4 with the need to protect the confidentiality of the information provided by the applicant, even if the 'mandate' of the basic regulation could cover other aspects of the procedure.[60] As is shown below, a similar conclusion may be drawn in relation to the food additives authorization procedure that, in case the Commission's 2008 proposal is accepted on this point, will be extended to the authorization of novel foods. The question of whether there is a case for extended participation rights is addressed in the section below.

7.2.2 *Food additives and genetically modified food*

The authorization procedure established in the new food additives regulation roughly resembles the procedure for the authorization of genetically

[59] *Eyckeler & Malt*, *cit.*, n. 32, paragraph 87; *Primex Produkte*, *cit.*, n. 32, paragraph 70.

[60] Article 2 of Commission Regulation No. 1852/2001, of 20 September 2001, laying down detailed rules for making certain information available to the public and for the protection of information submitted pursuant to European Parliament and Council Regulation No. 258/97 (OJ L 253/17, 21.9.2001), adopted on the basis of Article 4(5) of the novel foods regulation (according to which 'any detailed rules for implementing this Article shall be adopted in accordance with the [comitology] procedure laid down in Article 13').

modified food and feed. This is the case with regard to the distribution of powers between the Commission and the Member States that underlies its main steps as well as to the principles on which it is founded (those defined in Regulation No. 178/2002). In both cases, and in line with Regulation No. 178/2002, the EFSA is in charge of the risk assessment of the product at issue and the Commission is entrusted with risk management that bases the final decision on the requested authorization. Therefore, this section examines both procedures in parallel.

Food additives are defined as substances that are 'not normally consumed as food itself' and that are intentionally added to food 'for a technological purpose'.[61] Genetically modified food and feed, on the other hand, contain, consist of, or are produced from genetically modified organisms.[62] The basic requirements that both have to fulfil in order to be traded within the internal market are similar to those laid down for novel foods. In order to be placed on the market, they cannot cause adverse effects on human health, nor to animal health (in the case of genetically modified food), must not mislead the consumer, nor should normal consumption thereof be nutritionally disadvantageous for the consumer.[63] Adverse effects on the environment are an impediment to placing genetically modified food on the market, while, in relation to the authorization of food additives, 'environmental factors' need to be considered, where relevant, by the decision-maker before the inclusion of a substance in the EU list. Apart from pursuing these public interests, both regulations are intended to ensure the effective functioning of the internal market.[64]

[61] Article 3(2)(a) of Regulation No. 1333/2008 (*cit.*, n. 5), hereinafter 'the food additives regulation'.

[62] Article 2(6) and (7) of the genetically modified food regulation (*cit.*, n. 29), hereinafter 'the genetically modified food regulation' (although its provisions apply also to genetically modified feed). Note that, even though the following analysis, while referring to this regulation, will encompass only the procedure for the authorization of trading food, this is almost faithfully mirrored by the procedure for the authorization of trading feed; thus what is expounded in the following pages applies equally to the latter. As is widely known, this regulation is only a limited part of the EU legal framework on genetically modified organisms. For an overview, see, among others, Christoforou, *op. cit.*, n. 30, pp. 639–69.

[63] Article 4(1) of the genetically modified food regulation. Article 6(1) of the food additives regulation adds to the requirements mentioned a 'reasonable technological need' unachievable by other means; moreover, food additives also must have 'advantages and benefits for the consumer' and follow one of the purposes stated in Article 6(2) of the latter regulation.

[64] This goal seems to be more prominent in the wording of Article 1 of the food additives regulation than in the drafting of Article 1(a) of the genetically modified food regulation.

The key principle is that no person shall place such products on the market without having adequately and sufficiently demonstrated that they satisfy the general safety and public interest requirements, and without this having been authorized and the respective conditions of use specified.[65] It should be noted, at the outset, that, if the request is positively assessed, the procedure for the authorization of genetically modified food culminates with the adoption of a decision addressed to the applicant. This is issued pursuant to a regulatory comitology procedure, is published in the Official Journal, and then entered into an official register. This is different from the procedure for the authorization of food additives. Here, the authorization to market a substance or a modification to the trading conditions of an authorized substance takes the form of an update to previously established lists of authorized products and leads to the adoption of a regulation that gives effect to this update.[66] The initial lists of authorized food additives are established in accordance with a procedure that, in essence, does not differ much from the procedure to update the lists that is considered below: they are defined by the Commission (or by the Council, where this is envisaged in the comitology decision) pursuant to a comitology regulatory procedure with scrutiny.[67] This difference has an impact on defining whether, under the new rules of the Lisbon Treaty, these acts will be delegated or implementing acts (Articles 290 and 291 TFEU). In fact, despite the doubts that still remain on the delimitation of these two provisions, one thing is certain: individual decisions will necessarily be implementing acts adopted under Article 291 TFEU, since Article 290 TFEU clearly delimits its scope to 'non-legislative acts of general application'.[68] Therefore, all other things remaining equal, and irrespective of the rules that will be adopted under

[65] Article 4(2) and (3) of the genetically modified food regulation (*cit.*, n. 29); Article 4(1), (2), and (5) and Article 5 of the food additives regulation (*cit.*, n. 26).

[66] Cf Article 7(3) to (5) of the genetically modified food regulation, on the one hand, and Article 3(3) of Regulation No. 1331/2008 (*cit.*, n. 5), hereinafter 'the procedural regulation'.

[67] Article 30 of the food additives regulation (*cit.*, n. 26) and Article 5a(1) to (4) of Council Decision No. 1999/468/EC, of 28 June 1999, laying down the procedures for the exercise of implementing powers conferred on the Commission, as amended (OJ L 184/23, 17.7.1999).

[68] This is confirmed by the Commission Communication to the European Parliament and the Council, 'Implementation of Article 290 of the Treaty on the Functioning of the European Union' (COM (2009) 673 final, Brussels, 9.12.2009, p. 4) and, implicitly, by the European Parliament (Resolution of 5 May 2010 on the power of legislative delegation, P7_TA-PORV (2010)0127), and by the Council (Council Declaration on the Commission Communication on Article 290 of the Treaty on the Functioning of the European Union COM (2009) 673 final, Brussels, 14 December 2009, 17512/09).

Article 291(3) TFEU, the market authorizations of genetically modified food will be implementing acts, while the market authorizations of food additives can be delegated acts.[69]

Authorization procedures

Member States have a minor role during both procedures.[70] In the procedure for the authorization of genetically modified food, the Member States' competent authorities receive the application but from this moment, on the whole, procedure is developed at the EU level.[71] The competent national authorities need to be duly informed throughout the procedure, but, as a rule, they do not perform an active role unless the EFSA requires their intervention. Differently, the procedure for the authorization of food additives may be initiated by the Member States (or by an interested person who may represent other interested persons) by sending an application directly to the Commission.[72] The Member States need to be informed of the development of the procedure, but, as in the authorization of genetically modified food, national administrations are not an active part of it.[73]

The EFSA, on the other hand, has a prominent position in both procedures, even if this is regulated in slightly different terms in both cases. In the authorization procedure of genetically modified food, it informs the other Member States and the Commission at the beginning of the procedure, it publishes a summary of the dossier of the application, it collects the necessary information that grounds the final decision, and, for this purpose, it coordinates the intervention of the scientific national entities that collaborate with it and that of the EU bodies.[74] More importantly, the EFSA's opinion on the application is decisive for the outcome of the procedure. The core of this opinion is the assessment of the EFSA's scientific panel on genetically modified organisms. If the panel is favourable to the authorization of the food subject to the procedure, this is complemented with additional information (including, *inter alia*, conditions or restrictions

[69] See further, below, Sub-section 7.3.1.

[70] Note that what will be said regarding the authorization of food additives applies, *mutatis mutandis*, to the authorization of food enzymes and food flavourings (see n. 30 above).

[71] Article 5(2)(a) of the genetically modified food regulation (*cit.*, n. 29).

[72] Article 3(1) of the procedural regulation (*cit.*, n. 66).

[73] See Article 4 (note that the procedure may also be initiated by the Commission, in which case, Member States also need to be informed—Article 4(2)); Articles 5(2), 6(4), 8(1) *in fine*, 10 *in fine*, 12(3) and (7), as well as Article 3(4) of the procedural regulation (*cit.*, n. 66).

[74] Article 5(2)(b) and 6(3) of the genetically modified food regulation (*cit.*, n. 29).

which should be imposed on the placing of the food or feed on the market) in order to form the EFSA's global opinion.[75] Reasons must be provided in this opinion: the EFSA has to indicate the information on which the opinion is based; this is then forwarded to the Commission, the Member States, and the applicant.[76] In the authorization procedure of food additives, the EFSA gives its opinion at the request of the Commission, and forwards it to the Commission, the Member States and, where applicable, the applicant.[77] The general rules on the collaboration with national food assessment authorities defined in Regulation No. 178/2002 apply, as well as those regarding the motivation of its decisions.[78] Significantly, in this case, the Commission may dispense with the opinion of the EFSA when it intends to add, remove, or change the conditions, specifications, or restrictions related to an authorized substance or when it intends to remove a substance from the EU list of authorized additives, if 'the updates in question are not liable to have an impact on human health'.[79] Therefore, the Commission may be much more autonomous in this case.

This opinion is made public upon its adoption in accordance with the general obligation of transparency that binds the EFSA by force of Regulation No. 178/2002.[80] The scope of the information disclosed may be limited in order to protect the applicant's commercial interests: upon the latter's request and after consulting them, the Commission decides which information should be kept confidential within the limits defined in each regulation.[81] According to the genetically modified food regulation, the

[75] Article 6(5) of the genetically modified food regulation (*cit.*, n. 29). Stressing the need to distinguish the EFSA's scientific panel opinion and EFSA's global opinion, see 'Report from the Commission to the Council and the European Parliament on the implementation of Regulation No. 1829/2003 of the European Parliament and of the Council on genetically modified food and feed', COM (2006) 626 final, Brussels, 25.10.2006, p. 7.

[76] Article 6(6) of the genetically modified food regulation (*cit.*, n. 29).

[77] Articles 3(2), first paragraph, and 5 of the procedural regulation (*cit.*, n. 66, see also Article 6).

[78] Article 22(9) of Regulation No. 178/2002 (*cit.*, n. 8). According to Article 4(3) of the Decision of the EFSA's Management Board concerning implementing measures of transparency and confidentiality requirements (MB 10.03.2005–10, Parma, 10 March 2005, available at <http://www.efsa.europa.eu/EFSA/DocumentSet/mb_transparency_confidentiality_requirements 1,0.pdf?ssbinary= true>), EFSA's scientific opinions for publication must refer to information on which they are based, without prejudice to confidential information.

[79] Article 3(2), second paragraph.

[80] Article 6(7) of the genetically modified food regulation, Article 11 of the procedural regulation, and Article 38(1) of Regulation No. 178/2002.

[81] Article 30 of the genetically modified food regulation and Article 12 of the procedural regulation.

public can comment on the EFSA's opinion to the Commission within a period of thirty days after its publication.[82] Both the EFSA and the Commission decide on the forms and means through which consultation takes place. In fact, while they have the duty to ensure consultation, the regulation is silent in respect to any other aspect (namely form and consequences) of the public inquiry. Nothing similar is envisaged in the procedural regulation applicable to the authorization procedures of food additives. Arguably, the same obligation flows from the general provision of Article 9 of Regulation No. 178/2002, according to which public consultation should, in principle, be ensured in the preparation, evaluation, and revision of food law, a term which embraces administrative measures.[83] Given the transparency concerns that dominate food law, it is, nonetheless, bizarre that a similar provision has not been envisaged in this case, in particular because one cannot discard the possibility of casting away the application of Article 9 on the basis of the *lex specialis derogat legi generalis* rule.[84]

In both cases, the Commission, when drafting its decision, needs to take into account 'the opinion of the Authority, any relevant provisions of Community law and other legitimate factors relevant to the matter under consideration'.[85] In addition, it has to justify any deviations from the EFSA's opinion.[86] After receiving the latter, the Commission forwards a draft decision (in the case of the authorization of genetically modified food) or a draft regulation (in the case of the authorization of a food additive) to the Standing Committee in the Food Chain and Animal Health.[87] Thereafter, the final decision is taken either by the Commission or by the Council, depending on the concrete functioning of the regulatory comitology procedure.[88]

[82] Article 6(7) of the genetically modified food regulation (*cit.*, n. 29). Contrary to what was initially envisaged in the Commission's proposal, public consultation applies also in the cases of modification, suspension, and revocation of the authorization (Article 11 of the Commission's proposal on this matter made no reference to a public discussion period—Proposal for a Regulation of the European Parliament and the Council on genetically modified food and feed, 2001/0173 (COD), COM (2001) 425 final, Brussels, 25.7.2001).

[83] See n. 109, below. The meaning of these public consultations is analysed below in this subsection.

[84] See n. 107 below.

[85] Article 7(1) of the genetically modified food regulation (*cit.*, n. 29); Article 7(1) of the procedural regulation.

[86] Article 7(1) of the genetically modified food regulation (*cit.*, n. 66); Article 7(3) of the procedural regulation.

[87] See observations above on the impact of the Lisbon Treaty (p. 343).

[88] Articles 7(3) and 35(2) of the genetically modified food regulation; Articles 7(1) and 14(4) of the procedural regulation. See n. 28 above.

Both authorizations are precarious acts. The authorization to market genetically modified food is valid for ten years, after which it can be renewed for 10-year periods by a decision of the Commission or the Council, following, *mutatis mutandis* the primary authorization procedure just described.[89] However, during the validity period of the authorization, the EU administration may adjust its terms in light of new developments and perceived risks. Accordingly, the authorization can be modified, suspended, or revoked, if it no longer meets the safety conditions defined in the genetically modified food regulation. The corresponding decisions are taken upon the EFSA's initiative, that of any Member State, or of the Commission, always on the basis of an EFSA's opinion, following a comitology procedure, and in the terms defined for the primary authorization procedure.[90] Finally, the authorization can still be subject to emergency measures when an authorized product is likely 'to constitute a serious risk to human health, animal health or the environment'.[91] The authorization of food additives may be subject to modifications or may be removed from the list of authorized substances. With a few particularities, these decisions are adopted pursuant to the same procedural steps followed for the authorization.[92] They are also subject to emergency measures, in general terms.[93]

Bilateral relationships

The considerations outlined above with regard to the type of procedural relationship established by the novel foods regulation, as well as to the scope for participation rights in the respective authorization procedure, apply *mutatis mutandis* to the procedure just described. In fact, the core procedural relationship established by the effect of the applicable procedural rules involves the applicant and the decision-maker. Without prejudice to the subsequent inquiries made by the competent assessment bodies, the procedure is based on the information provided by the applicant. The latter is the interlocutor of the EFSA and of the Commission during the course of the procedure.[94] Only they can be considered to be in a

[89] Article 11 of the genetically modified food regulation (*cit.*, n. 29).

[90] Article 10 of the genetically modified food regulation. See n. 28 above.

[91] Article 34 of the genetically modified food regulation and Articles 53 and 54 of Regulation No. 178/2002, *cit.*, n. 8.

[92] Articles 2(b) and (c); 3(2), second paragraph; 7(1), second paragraph of the procedural regulation (*cit.*, n. 66).

[93] Article 13 of the procedural regulation.

[94] The EFSA may ask the applicant to supplement the application where appropriate (Article 6(2) of the genetically modified food regulation); the EFSA's opinion is notified to the

procedural relationship with the EU administration. The main difference with the novel foods procedure analysed earlier is that the decision-maker is not a national administrative body that functions as the face of a network of public entities, or the Commission in a subsequent phase of the procedure, but simply a European institution in any possible variant of the procedure: either the Commission or the Council depending on the concrete path that the corresponding comitology procedure follows.[95] The option to keep the procedural relationships within the boundaries of a bilateral scheme is, therefore, maintained in the more recent changes in the structure of procedures from decentralized to centralized ones. No express provision for participation rights is made, either in relation to the applicant—who is nonetheless covered by the general *audi alteram partem* principle—or in relation to other persons potentially affected by the outcome of the procedure, even if the interests they might represent could fall within the scope of the interests protected by the legislative act (e.g. consumers' associations striving for high standards of public health protection). However, the fact that the market authorizations, irrespective of the form they adopt, need to be published in the Official Journal is a clear indication, at least, of the public interest involved in these decisions, but also, arguably, of their ability to affect persons other than the holder of the authorization.[96]

As mentioned, contrary to other procedures analysed, a period of public consultation is explicitly envisaged in the procedure for the authorization of genetically modified food. It is worth having a closer look at the meaning of this procedural step, since the intervention of the public may change the structure of the relationship established by the effect of the procedure. Even if, for the reasons mentioned, the applicant retains a privileged position, the intervention of the public may entail additional procedural duties on the part of the deciding bodies that could indirectly endow interested persons that intervene in the public consultation with a sufficiently formalized position. In other words, depending on the way in which this sub-stage of the procedure is conceived, and, specifically, on the ensuing duties impinging upon the deciding body, the public consultation period could bring

Commission, the Member States, and the applicant (Article 6(6)), the latter being also notified of the Commission's decision, as mentioned above (Article 7(4)). See also Article 5(3), on the content of the application.

[95] Article 7 and 14(2) of the Commission 2008 proposal for a common procedure, *cit.*, n. 9; Article 7(3) and 14(2) of the 2006 Commission proposal for a new regulation on novel foods.

[96] Article 7(3) of the novel foods regulation (*cit.*, n. 26), Article 7(4) of the genetically modified food regulation (*cit.*, n. 29).

about a surrogate form of participation rights, thereby potentially transforming the bilateral procedural relationship into a multilateral one.

Nothing in the genetically modified food regulation suggests that this could be the case. The provision for public consultation is scant as to the duties of the EFSA and of the Commission in complying with the norms that ensure the openness of the procedure. The only indications regarding consultation provided by these norms, in the various stages of the 'life' of the authorization, are the object of consultation (the EFSA's opinion), the time limit within which comments by the public can be submitted (thirty days), and the entity to which they are submitted (the Commission).[97]

More information can be found in the 'Report from the Commission to the Council and the European Parliament on the implementation of Regulation No. 1829/2003',[98] which gives an account of the action taken by the Commission to comply with the legal duty impinging on it under the genetically modified food regulation. There one can read that the Commission created a website dedicated to consultations that relate to the authorization of genetically modified food and feed,[99] where the public can find information on when a given public inquiry period is open, as well as a form for the submission of the comments. Care seems to have been taken to ensure accessibility to the procedure. The Commission states in this report that the consultation is advertised throughout the full period on the first page of the website 'Food safety—from the farm to the fork'.[100] The opening of that period is also announced through an email service ('sanco news'). In addition, there is a link on the webpage of the Health and Consumer Protection Directorate General to the EFSA's webpage, where the relevant opinions are published.

The system is similar to the 'inter-active policy making' mechanisms adopted by the Commission to collect the public's opinions during the preparation of Commission's rule-making proposals.[101] In this respect, the

[97] Articles 6(7) and 10(1) of the genetically modified food regulation. On the option of submitting the EFSA's opinion to public consultation and putting the Commission in charge of receiving them, see Patrycja Dąbrowska (2006), *Hybrid Solutions for Hybrid Products? EU Governance of GMOs*, PhD Thesis, European University Institute, Florence, p. 230. Dąbrowska analyses the procedure for deliberate release of genetically modified organisms, but this feature is common to the procedure for the authorization of genetically modified food.

[98] *Cit.*, n. 75, at pp. 8–9.

[99] <http://ec.europa.eu/food/food/biotechnology/gmo_authorisation_en.htm>.

[100] <http://ec.europa.eu/food/consultations/index_en.htm>.

[101] An account of this mechanism is given in Paul Craig (2006), *EU Administrative Law*, Oxford: Oxford University Press, pp. 326–7.

legal obligation to consult enshrined in the genetically modified food regulation is meaningful only to the extent that it binds the Commission to respect a procedural phase that it was, in principle, interested in following.[102] It adds little in terms of the procedural guarantees accorded to persons who may hold a legitimate interest in the outcome of the procedure. The rationale of this public consultation period lies more in improving the transparency of the decisional procedure (and also possibly in appeasing public concern regarding the authorization of genetically modified food) than in shaping a procedure in terms of ensuring an accurate consideration of the competing interests affected by the final decision, which is instrumental both in an anticipated legal protection of those interests and in the diligent conduct of the decision-maker.

The fact that the Commission, when drafting its decision on the basis of the EFSA's opinions, needs to take into account 'other legitimate factors relevant to the matter' could be interpreted as entailing a duty to consider the comments received that signal those legitimate factors.[103] This is, however, a far-fetched argument. In fact, even if some of the comments received may alert the Commission to the 'legitimate factors' that should be pondered, whether to consider such comments and how to treat them is entirely in the hands of the Commission (and, at a second stage, of the Member States during the comitology procedure). The legality threshold is respected as long as the public is effectively able to submit comments on the EFSA's opinion. Nothing in the wording of the genetically modified food regulation points to the duty to consider the comments received or to indicate in the motivation of the decision how they might have influenced the final decision.[104] Besides, as mentioned, the object of consultation is the

[102] This can be inferred from the fact that this discussion period, as it is envisaged in the genetically modified food regulation, was included in the respective Commission's proposal (see Article 7 of this proposal, *cit.*, n. 82).

[103] Article 7(1) of the genetically modified food regulation (*cit.*, n. 29). On this, Dąbrowska, *op. cit.*, n. 97, p. 198, concurring that, in any event, the consideration of public comments as belonging to the 'legitimate factors' mentioned is not legally enforceable.

[104] According to the report on the implementation of the genetically modified food regulation (*cit.*, n. 29), the practice of the Commission is to communicate 'without delay' the comments received to the national competent authorities, so that both the Commission and the Member States 'can take these documents into consideration for the last phase of the authorization process' (i.e. during the comitology procedure). In addition, the comments received are also made public in the webpage of Health and Consumer Protection Directorate General (report quoted above, n. 75, at p. 9; webpage referred above, n. 100). Contrary to the genetically modified food regulation, the preamble of the directive on the deliberative release of genetically modified organisms determines that the 'comments by the public should be taken into consideration in the drafts of measures

EFSA's opinion, not the Commission's draft. The fact that the latter needs to take into account other legitimate factors, apart from the results of the scientific risk assessment, is an intrinsic part of weighing different policy alternatives. This is the basis of risk management envisaged in EU law on the assumption that scientific risk assessment alone cannot always provide all the information in which a risk management decision should be grounded.[105] On these grounds it may be argued that overlooking these legitimate factors may infringe the duty of care.

In sum, the public consultation phase of the procedure for the authorization of genetically modified food does not change the structure of the procedural relationship. This remains bilateral.

The observations presented above apply also to the general rules of consultation enshrined in Regulation No. 178/2002. In fact, the genetically modified food regulation is dependent on the rules and principles defined in this regulation. Transparency through public consultation in decisional procedures pertaining to food is a basic principle of EU food law. According to Article 9,

> there shall be open and transparent public consultation, directly or through representative bodies, during the preparation, evaluation and revision of food law, except where the urgency of the matter does not allow it.

Moreover, the EFSA should 'develop effective contacts with consumer representatives, producer representatives, processors and any other interested parties'.[106] In which forms, circumstances, and for which purposes these 'effective contacts' are made, and at which stage of the procedures of preparation, evaluation, and revision of food law public consultation shall occur, in which forms and with which consequences are all decisions of the EFSA and of the Commission. Therefore, in the absence of any specific provision for participation rights in specific legislation, these rules cannot be considered to be a source of participation rights of holders of legally protected interests, in the event that they are justified in these instances.[107]

submitted to the regulatory committee' (recital 46 of Directive No. 2001/18/EC, OJ L 106/1, 17.4.2001). Nevertheless, it is equally doubtful that this is a legally enforceable duty.

[105] Article 3(1)(12) as well as Articles 6(3) and 7(2) of Regulation No. 178/2002, *cit.*, n. 8. See also recital 19 of the same regulation.

[106] Article 42 of Regulation No. 178/2002 *cit.*, n. 8.

[107] Regarding the combined application of the rules and principles of Regulation No. 178/2002 and those defined in specific legislation on certain categories of foodstuffs, the Court has applied the general rule according to which *lex specialis derogat legi generalis*. This has been decided

This type of participation ensures broad access to the procedure, since it does not discriminate between the persons who are entitled to intervene. 'The public' is, potentially, anybody. However, the lack of distinction between the potential commentators blurs the position of those who could have a direct interest in the outcome of the procedure. This interest stems from the effects of the ensuing decision on their legal sphere: for example, the duties and responsibilities defined in the authorization are also extended to them (e.g. other producers who need to comply with safety measures defined in the marketing authorization), or possible participants were created to represent the interests that are affected by the final decision (e.g. consumer and environmentalist associations). This aspect could be singled out by providing other forms of participation, complementing public consultations as to ensure the exercise of legally enforceable participation rights, without prejudice to the mechanisms of transparency already envisaged. Whether and when this is justified is an aspect that will be developed in the section below.

Concretely, it will be argued that there is a case for extending participation rights to procedures leading to the authorization of marketing of foodstuffs, given the ability of these acts to generate multilateral relationships and affect interests which are legally protected by the applicable legislation. First, however, it will be demonstrated that the fact that the authorization acts can be either individual administrative decisions addressed to the authorization holder or acts that amend the positive lists of authorized foodstuffs annexed to the respective directive or regulation is immaterial for the recognition or otherwise of participation rights. These should be granted irrespective of the formal nature of the acts resulting from these procedures.

7.3 Market Authorizations and Administrative Relationships

What has been written so far demonstrates that EU administrative action in the food sector has evolved in such a way that the effects produced in the

in a preliminary ruling regarding the food supplements directive (Directive No. 2002/46/EC, OJ L 183/51, 12.7.2002; Joined Cases C-211/03, C-299/03, C-316/03, C-317/03, and C-318/03, *HLH Warenvertriebs GmbH and Orthica BV v Bundesrepublik Deutschland* [2005] ECR I-5141, paragraphs 35 to 39).

legal sphere of private persons are the direct result of administrative decisions taken by EU institutions or bodies.

As has been stressed before, in EU law, procedural guarantees that afford anticipated legal protection to rights or legitimate interests affected by EU decisions are, by force of the *audi alteram partem* principle, and in the absence of specific rules, restricted to the recognition of a right to be heard to the addressees of unfavourable decisions or, more broadly, to persons who are substantively in a position equivalent to that of the person with regard to whom the procedure was initiated. In the procedures analysed above, this covers the position of the applicant in the cases in which the procedure is likely to culminate in a negation of the authorization. In the absence of provisions expressly recognizing the right to intervene in the procedure, and taking into account the type of procedural relationship created by the applicable rules, it is not certain to what extent persons other than the applicant or authorization holder would be granted access to the procedure by way of application of the general *audi alteram partem* principle.[108] As was argued elsewhere in this book, participation rights could be understood in broader terms. In particular, following the *Technishes Universität München* judgment, they need not be limited to a pure rationale of defence. However, as was also mentioned the Courts did not follow this stance in subsequent cases. In addition, the ability of regulatory decisions to shape the legal positions of persons other than the addressee of an act should be taken into account.

Nevertheless, the outcomes of the procedures analysed are decisions the effects of which are not exhausted in creating a favourable or unfavourable situation to the applicant who wishes to place a product on the market. The acts in question are instrumental to the regulation of the internal market of foodstuffs, and, as such, they involve persons other than the authorization holder—namely, traders of the product authorized. These are bound to the duties and conditions defined in the authorization. In fact, according to Article 17(1) of Regulation No. 178/2002,

> food and feed business operators at all stages of production, processing and distribution within the businesses under their control shall ensure that foods or feeds satisfy the requirements of food law which are relevant to their activities and shall verify that such requirements are met.[109]

[108] See Chapter 4, Sub-section 4.2.3.

[109] Food law, according to point 1 of Article 3 of Regulation No. 178/2002, *cit.*, n. 8, 'means the laws, *regulations and administrative provisions* governing food in general, and food safety in

Moreover, authorizations to trade foodstuffs touch upon consumer and environmental protection. The effects that decisions adopted regarding specific foodstuffs may have in both types of interest need to be considered by the decision-maker. Consumer protection is one of the objectives of EU food law in general, as well as of the specific legal regimes that have been analysed.[110] Moreover, the general food law determines that, where appropriate, environmental protection should be taken into account in food regulation.[111] This concern comes clearly to the fore in the genetically modified food regulation and in the food additives regulation.[112] Therefore, consumer protection and, in some instances, environmental protection are part of the scope of interests that are legally protected by the food law regimes.

The question is then whether the broad effects of market authorizations should be formally reflected in the way the procedural relationships underlying their adoption are conceived. It is argued here that this should be the case where legal material relationships stem from the act adopted. This would mean that potentially affected parties, other than the applicant, could be recognized as having a right to intervene in the procedure. First, however, it is pertinent to examine the nature of the acts that authorize the trading of foodstuffs. This serves two purposes: first, it demonstrates the general effects produced by these acts, irrespective of their form; secondly, it concomitantly highlights the limitations of making the recognition of participation rights dependent upon the nature of the act.

7.3.1 *Individual acts, general acts, and regulations*

Formally, market authorizations may be one of two types. They are either adopted under the form of a decision addressed to a specified food business operator,[113] or under the form of an EU list that contains information on

particular, whether at Community or national level; it covers any stage of production, processing and distribution of food, and also of feed produced for, or fed to, food-producing animals' (emphasis added).

[110] Article 5 of Regulation No. 178/2002 (*cit.*, n. 8), Article 3(1) of the novel foods regulation, Article 1(a) of the genetically modified food regulation (*cit.*, n. 29), and Article 1 of the food additives regulation (*cit.*, n. 26).

[111] Article 5(1) of Regulation No. 178/2002, *cit.* (n. 8).

[112] Article 1(a) of the genetically modified food regulation (see also Article 4(1)) and Article 1, first paragraph of the food additives regulation (see also Article 6).

[113] On the different types of decisions in EU law see Armin von Bogdandy, Felix Arndt, and Jürgen Bast (2004) 'Legal instruments in European Union Law and their reform: a systematic approach on an empirical basis', *Yearbook of European Law*, Vol. 23, pp. 91–136, at pp. 101–6.

the foodstuffs that may be traded to the exclusion of all others. In this second case, two situations should be distinguished. First, the EU list can be inserted in an annex of the legislative act regulating certain types of foodstuffs. This was the case of the food additives listed in the daughter directives, which will, after re-evaluation, be inserted in the annexes of the 2008 food additives regulation.[114] In this case, subsequent restrictions to the substances referred to therein require an amendment to the legislative act (which, in the case of the food additives, will follow the procedure analysed above). Alternatively, the list may be adopted in the form of an implementing regulation issued by the Commission at a later stage (this is the case of the smoke flavourings regulation).[115] Arguably, under the new Lisbon rules, in both cases, these can either be adopted as delegated or as implementing acts. Currently, there are no indications in this respect. As is known, the delimitation of delegated acts and implementing acts is, in most aspects, far from clear, although of great institutional relevance.[116] At first sight, the first case mentioned—amendments to the annex of a legislative act—would very likely correspond to delegated acts, since they amend non-essential elements of the basic act. However, so far, the institutions have given contradictory signs in this respect. According to the Commission, delegated acts apply as soon as the Commission is empowered to amend 'an annex containing measures of general application'.[117] However, on the other hand, the Council, in its Position on the new novel food regulation, envisages a specific authorization procedure according to which the updating of Union lists will take place following a comitology

[114] Article 30 of the food additives regulation (*cit.*, n. 26). See, in this respect, Commission Regulation No. 257/2010 of 25 March 2010, setting up a programme for the re-evaluation of approved food additives in accordance with Regulation No. 1333/2008 of the European Parliament and of the Council on food additives (OJ L 80/19, 26.3.2010).

[115] As was mentioned above, the smoke flavourings regulation establishes the procedures for the authorization of smoke flavourings—in particular, a procedure for the elaboration of an initial list of authorized products (Articles 6(1) and 10 of Regulation No. 2065/2003, *cit.*, n. 16) and one for the addition of products to this list (Articles 6(2) and 7 to 9 of the same regulation)—a task which is entrusted to the Commission, that adopts the corresponding regulations and decisions (Articles 10(2) and 9(1)). This technique has been confirmed by the Court of Justice to be legitimately based on former Article 95 EC (above, Sub-section 7.1.1).

[116] See, in particular, Paul Craig (2008) 'The Role of the European Parliament under the Lisbon Treaty' in Stefan Griller and Jacques Ziller (eds), *The Lisbon Treaty: EU Constitutionalism without a Constitutional Treaty?*, Wien: Springer, pp. 110–34, and Herwig Hofmann (2009) 'Legislation, delegation and implementation under the Lisbon Treaty: Typology meets reality', *European Law Journal*, Vol. 15, n. 4, pp. 482–505, at pp. 497–8.

[117] Commission Comunication, 'Implementing Article 290', *cit.* n. 68. p. 4.

procedure, hence, as an implementing act, whereas the Parliament considers that this type of act should be adopted as a delegated act.[118] This should be borne in mind when attempting to predict the future of non-legislative acts in the area of food additives.

Despite the extreme institutional significance of the adoption of a delegated or of an implementing act, given the different conditions defined in Articles 290 and 291 TFEU, this distinction is not relevant for our purposes. What is of interest here is to analyse the continuity between individual and general acts in view of their content and effects and demonstrate that, contrary to what is at present the case in EU law, the distinction between individual and general acts ought not to form the basis for the recognition or otherwise of participation rights.

The market authorizations adopted under the form of individual decisions have as their main characteristics those of individual acts: the procedures are initiated by a given applicant to whom the final decision is addressed; moreover, the purpose of the act is the placement of a concrete product on the market and the definition of its conditions of use. Nevertheless, as mentioned above, there is a regulatory effect attached to the permissibility of producing and trading the product.[119] Indeed, besides the more diffuse impacts on consumer and environmental protection, all food business operators wishing to make use of the authorized food product—using it in the production of other foods or trading it—are bound by the requirements defined in the authorization. They can benefit from this

[118] Article 16(3) of Postion No. 6/2010 (*cit.*, n. 27). In this position delegated acts are reserved only to the definition of criteria for assessing whether a food fulfils the criteria of novel food (Article 20 of this Position). See the European Parliament Recommendation for second reading on the Council Position at first reading for adopting a regulation of the European Parliament and of the Council on novel foods, amending Regulation (EC) No. 1331/2008 and repealing Regulation (EC) No. 258/97 and Commission Regulation (EC) No. 1852/2001 (11261/3/2009 – C7-0078/2010 – 2008/0002(COD)), Committee on the Environment, Public Health and Food Safety Rapporteur: Kartika Tamara Liotard, A7-0152/2010, 10.5.2010, amendments 70 and 100). Contrary to what it indicated in the Communication quoted in the note above, the Commission concurs with the Council on this (see Opinion of the Commission pursuant to Article 294, paragraph 7, point c) TFEU, *cit.*, n. 9, p. 7).

[119] These can be considered general authorizations that 'flank a permissive dimension to one that is properly regulatory' (Giacinto della Cananea, 2000, *Gli atti amministrativi generali*, Cedam: Padova, p. 94, author's translation). Placing on the market means 'the holding of food or feed for the purpose of sale, including offering for sale or any other form of transfer, whether free of charge or not, and the sale, distribution, and other forms of transfer themselves' (Article 3(8) of Regulation No. 178/2002 *cit.*, n. 8).

decision, developing an economic activity that otherwise would not be possible, provided that they respect the terms of the authorization granted.

While this stems, in general, from the responsibility rule enshrined in Regulation No. 178/2002, in the case of genetically modified food, the *erga omnes* effect of the market authorization is further acknowledged by Article 9(1) of the respective regulation, according to which

> the authorization-holder *and parties concerned* shall comply with any conditions or restrictions which have been imposed in the authorization and shall in particular make sure that products not covered by the authorization are not placed on the market as food or feed.[120]

This general effect is even clearer in the case of the authorization of smoke flavourings, defined in Regulation No. 2065/2003. This determines that after the authorization has been issued, it will be valid 'throughout the Community' and

> the authorization holder or any other food business operator using the authorized primary product or derived smoke flavourings shall comply with any condition or restriction attached to such authorization.[121]

Moreover, as mentioned above, the fact that the market authorizations are published in the Official Journal is an additional indication of their general effects.[122]

Formally, these market authorizations stand between individual administrative acts—in that their addressee is specified and is bound by specific duties—and general administrative acts—given their ability of producing effects vis-à-vis an *a priori* undetermined group of individuals, as indicated by the requirement of publication.[123] With regard to market authorizations, this ability results in particular from the effects EU law attaches to the use of

[120] Emphasis added. Arguably a similar effect stems from the combination of Articles 4(1) and 5 of the food additives regulation (*cit.*, n. 26).

[121] Article 9(3) and (4) of Regulation No. 2065/2003, (*cit.*, n. 16).

[122] This is the case of market authorizations for novel foods and for genetically modified food (*cit.*, n. 96). Also market authorizations issued in application of Article 18(1) of the Directive No. 2001/18/EC *cit.*, n. 104, need to be published. Authorizations of food additives, on the other hand, are adopted under the form of a regulation (while the refusal of the application is adopted in the form of a decision addressed to the applicant—Article 3(3) and (4) of the food additives regulation; the same happens in the case of the authorization of smoke flavourings: cf. Article 9(1) and (2) of Regulation No. 2065/2003, *cit.*, n. 16). Although nothing is said with regard to their publication, this results from the general rules regarding publication of Union acts (Article 297(2) TFEU).

[123] See, further, Chapter 2, Sub-section 2.4.3.

authorized products, concretely, from the duties it imposes on business operators. This effect reveals that the authorization 'is conceived with regard to a category of persons, who must respect certain requirements', despite the fact that, in some cases, it is addressed to an individual.[124]

The elaboration of positive lists for products that can be marketed to the exclusion of all others, approved directly in a directive or basic regulation or at a later stage in a (delegated or implementing) regulation issued by the Commission, are an alternative regulatory technique to the issuing of market authorizations through 'individual acts' in the terms just characterized. In the first case, the legislative act determines rules and principles that apply to the objects that it already identifies. An act changing this list to adapt it to technological and scientific developments is an act of an administrative nature, irrespective of the form it assumes, to the extent that it does not change the rules and principles defined in the primary act, but only the object to which they apply. This happens, for example, when the Commission withdraws a product from a list of authorized products or restricts the conditions for its use.[125] An act extending the scope of a positive list by adding one product or substance is also an act of an administrative nature.[126] By the same token, the act that creates the list is of an administrative nature, even if inserted in a legislative act. Such lists allow for the application of the general principles and rules to specific goods. They ascertain that the substances inserted therein conform to the applicable legislation, while also defining the conditions that need to be respected for that to be the case (e.g. definition of the maximum concentrations and other levels of food additives). They may be preceded by market authorizations addressed to a specific producer who is responsible for the placement of the substance or the product on the market (as results from the Commission's proposal on a new regulation on novel foods regarding the insertion in a list of the authorizations that have been issued under the current regulation),[127] or they may be enacted directly in a (delegated or implementing) regulation (e.g. food additives). In the first case, they may include information on the authorization holder (e.g. the name and address). In this case, this should be considered as additional information that helps to characterize the product in question and, particularly, to identify the person who controls

[124] Giancinto della Cananea, *op. cit.*, n. 119, p. 95 (author's translation).

[125] For example, pursuant Article 10(3) of the food additives regulation (*cit.*, n. 26) and Article 2(2) of the procedural regulation (*cit.*, n. 66).

[126] *Idem, ibidem.*

[127] See Article 17 of the Commission's 2008 proposal (*cit.*, n. 9).

the full information regarding the safety of the product.[128] The identification of which foods are tradable within the Union and the respective specifications are, in any event, non-essential elements of a legislative act.[129] The content and effects of the acts that set them out are the same irrespective of whether it is considered that they are better defined by the Commission under the use of delegated powers or that these would be in principle implementing tasks of Member States, which are only exercised by the Commission given the need for ensuring uniform implementation.

The inclusion of the product in a positive list has the same effects as the market authorization addressed to a specific producer: the products therein identified may be commercialized in the internal market provided that the respective conditions of use are respected. In certain cases, the authorization *is* the insertion of a new entry in a EU list of authorized products.[130] The only difference is that it is not addressed to an identified person. The effects of both acts are exactly the same, since market authorizations proper (those addressed to a specific producer) also affect persons who are not named in the decision and who may be identified by their inclusion in a general category, defined by their quality and function ('food business operator'). In view of these effects, and according to what was said above, the EU lists can be assimilated to general administrative acts. But they can also be considered to be proper administrative regulations. The option for one classification or another has essentially to do with the relevance to be attributed to abstractness as a characteristic of general administrative acts and to the interpretation of these lists as containing norms or not (if one considers that general administrative acts are not normative acts), which are both contentious issues.[131] Yet, the decisive question, for our purposes, lies not so much in delimiting the nature of these acts—or in assessing whether they will be delegated or implementing acts under the new Articles 290 and

[128] E.g. Article 6(2) of Regulation No. 2065/2003, *cit.*, n. 16.

[129] The introduction of the regulatory procedure with scrutiny for the amendment of these elements first contributed to distinguishing the nature of the two types of provisions that may be inserted in a legislative act (recital 7a, Articles 2(2) and 5a of Council Decision No. 1999/468/EC laying down the procedures for the exercise of implementing powers conferred on the Commission—OJ L 184/23, 17.7.1999, as amended—still in force at the time of the writing).

[130] This is envisaged in Article 3(3) of the procedural regulation; see also, regarding the authorization of smoke flavourings, Article 9(1) of Regulation No. 2065/2003, *cit.*, n. 16. In both cases, the authorization decision in which the procedure culminates is a regulation updating the list.

[131] See works quoted in n. 110 of Chapter 2. See also Vezio Crisafulli (1959) 'Atto normativo', in *Enciclopedia del Diritto*, Vol. IV, Milano: Giuffrè, pp. 238–61.

291 TFEU—than in highlighting the similarity of the effects in the two cases and the continuity between individual decisions and general acts beyond the form under which they are adopted. Both market authorizations proper and EU lists of tradable products, or substances, concretize aspects that were not decided upon in the primary norm—which products comply with the safety requirements defined in that norm—with the effect of rendering unlawful the actions that go against this secondary determination. In the cases in which the elaboration of a positive list is based on single market authorizations previously issued this continuity is even stronger. Then the inclusion of the product in a positive list (arguably done for reasons of public certainty) implies the formal recognition that the authorization issued has effects vis-à-vis an undetermined group of individuals, who need to act on the basis of the specifications enshrined in these lists.

The regulatory option of concretizing *a priori* administrative controls through market authorizations or through positive lists, which may or may not be elaborated on the basis of those authorizations, derives from the fact that the legislator, while setting out a given regime, and administrative authorities, when enacting it, have difficulties in defining in advance the concrete products to which this regime will apply. In some cases, such as the legal regimes regarding most biotechnological products, this is manifestly impossible, since, in these areas, public authorities cannot know which products will be created. But this is also true in other fields where the technical and scientific complexity of the processes involved prevents an anticipated evaluation of the substances that should be approved or not (e.g. smoke flavourings, some food additives).

So far, the choice between the three possibilities—individual market authorization, positive lists included in primary or in implementing legislation, and positive lists based on market authorizations—essentially depends on the degree of scientific complexity in determining the risks associated with a given product. The argumentation of the EU institutions in the *Smoke Flavourings* case is clear in this respect. As mentioned, the smoke flavourings regulation was challenged by the United Kingdom, which argued against the legitimacy of a harmonization regulation that left to a later date the adoption of the positive lists. Justifying the regulatory option taken, in view of the United Kingdom's pleadings for the annulment of the smoke flavourings regulation, the Parliament argued that:

the absence of a common approach to evaluating the safety of smoke flavourings means that the Community legislature was unable, for objective scientific reasons, to draw up an exhaustive list of approved products in the text of the contested regulation itself. In those circumstances, and to ensure a high level of protection of human health and at the same time guarantee the free movement of products containing smoke flavourings, the Community legislature was forced to provide that the list of authorized products would be drawn up on the basis of a toxicological evaluation of each of the products concerned, and to entrust the Commission with that task.[132]

It was seconded by the Council and the Commission.[133] Admittedly, post-Lisbon, and given the fact that only general acts can be adopted as delegated acts, the choice between these different possibilities to grant market authorizations will necessarily take into account the institutional implications of adopting an act under Article 290 or Article 291 TFEU.

At any rate, although the legal form varies, the essence of these acts is the same, notwithstanding the differentiated position that the authorization holder retains by way of fact (because, for example, they possess the information related to the process of production of a substance) or law (given the legal duties that accordingly impinge on them), when an individualized authorization is required. They all have the effect of regulating the internal market. By defining which products can be traded and under which conditions they can be used, they influence the actions of private operators to comply with those conditions and, hence, ensure that throughout the EU the same products are authorized or prohibited, on the basis of the same safety requirements. In doing so, these acts have in common the fact that they have *erga omnes* effects, even when they are embodied in an act formally addressed to a given individual.

These similarities would require the recognition of participation rights to the affected persons, a consequence that is denied by the Courts' case law on the right to be heard. This would also apply across the distinction between delegated and implementing acts introduced by the Lisbon Treaty. In this respect, the Commission in its Communication on 'Implementing Article 290' attempts a distinction between 'quasi-legislative' acts and 'purely

[132] Case C-66/04, *United Kingdom v European Parliament and Council*, *cit.*, n. 16, paragraph 31.

[133] The Council argued: 'authorization for the entire Community of products such as smoke flavourings requires complex scientific evaluations. It would be practically impossible to draw up a legislative instrument in which all the technical parameters were described in such detail that all discretion could be ruled out in the making of those evaluations' (paragraph 35). The Commission maintained that 'having regard to the many technical constraints of the necessary toxicological evaluations, the Community legislature was obliged to provide for a system incorporating a case-by-case evaluation of the safety of primary products and the progressive establishment of a harmonized list, on the basis of the substantive criteria set out in the contested regulation.' (paragraph 40, *idem*).

executive' acts.[134] Again, the institutional relevance of this distinction notwithstanding, this is irrelevant to decide on the scope of participation rights. On the basis of the concept of administrative relationships and on the assumption that these may emerge from general acts, as well as from individual acts, it is possible to argue that such rights should be recognized, not only to the addressee of the authorizations (where applicable), but also to other interested persons whose legal spheres are equally affected by the act adopted, irrespective of their form.

7.3.2 *Bilateral or multilateral procedural relationships?*

Considering the *erga omnes* effects produced by the market authorizations, to limit access to the procedure to the addressee of the administrative act implies adopting a restrictive approach to the procedural protection of the persons and interests affected by these decisions. This is particularly evident when the persons affected can be identified, since, in these circumstances, it is perhaps easier to establish the contours of the administrative relationship that emerges from the adoption of the act. It has been argued elsewhere in this work that administrative legal relationships may arise from the adoption of acts that have general effects.[135] The point will now be made that, with regard to the market authorizations analysed above, the bilateral structure of the relationship shaped as such by the respective procedures is unsuitable in view of the effects stemming from the respective acts.

The inadequacy of conceiving the procedural relationship emerging by force of the administrative procedure as a bilateral relationship in situations where the legal spheres of other individuals are effectively involved is well illustrated in the *Fern Olivieri* case.[136] This concerned the authorization of medicinal products, but the parallels between this type of authorization and those of foodstuffs make it relevant for current purposes: in both cases, the procedures are designed to regulate the market with the aim of ensuring the pursuance of a public interest and, in both cases, bilateral procedures can potentially affect the rights and interests of other persons who are not entitled to intervene in the procedure.[137]

[134] *Cit.*, n. 66, p. 3.

[135] Chapter 2, Sub-section 2.5.3.

[136] Case T-326/99, *Nancy Fern Olivieri v Commission and the European Agency for the Evaluation of Medicines (EMEA)* [2003] ECR II-6053.

[137] The procedure for the authorization of medicinal products has been analysed by Edoardo Chiti (2002) *Le agenzie europee. Unità e decentramento nelle amministrazioni comunitarie*, Padova: Cedam, pp. 195–219.

Nancy Fern Olivieri is a doctor specialized in developing pharmacological therapy for a rare disease. This research had been sponsored by Apotex, a multinational pharmaceutical company. Her participation in the research was interrupted by Apotex, after she had reached a preliminary conclusion on the ineffectiveness of the substance that was being tested (deferiprone). Having become aware that Apotex had submitted an application to obtain a market authorization for a medicinal product containing that substance as an active ingredient, she intervened *de facto* in the administrative procedure. She submitted observations on the favourable opinion that had been issued by the competent committee of the European Agency for the Evaluation of Medicinal Products (EMEA), alerting it to the risks associated with the substance in question.[138] The market authorization was granted, although Dr Olivieri's observations were taken into consideration during the procedure and ultimately led to a revised opinion of the competent committee.[139] She sought the annulment of that decision before the Court of First Instance, invoking her interest in safeguarding her professional reputation, as well as in seeking the protection of public health.[140]

The Court considered the action inadmissible on the basis that, unlike other EU procedures (in the field of competition law), the regulation laying down market authorization procedures for medicinal products establishes a purely bilateral procedure (which is a centralized EU procedure).[141] According to the Court, this 'is a procedure between the applicant for marketing authorization and the administration, during which the administration must take into account the applicant's interest in obtaining marketing authorization and the public interest in the protection of human health', pursued by the Commission (on the basis of the opinion of the EMEA). Hence, Dr Olivieri, being a third party, 'is not entitled to participate in that procedure or set herself up as interlocutor of the [competent committee of the EMEA] and of the Commission in regard to the assessment of the

[138] The applicable regulation contained no provision regarding the publicity of the committee's opinion, nor the public intervention during the authorization procedure (Council Regulation No. 2309/93, of 22 July 1993, laying down Community procedures for the authorization and supervision of medicinal products for human and veterinary use and establishing a European Agency for the Evaluation of Medicinal Products, OJ L 214/1, 24.8.1993). This regulation was repealed by Regulation No. 726/2004, of the European Parliament and the Council, of 31 March 2004 (OJ 136/1, 30.4.2004), which determines that the opinion of the committee responsible for drawing up the opinion of the agency needs to be made public (Article 5(3) thereof).

[139] *Fern Olivieri, cit.*, n. 136, paragraphs 28–36.

[140] *Idem*, paragraphs 56–57.

[141] *Idem*, paragraph 94.

scientific data relating to the product in question'.[142] The Court further considered that 'as a result, the applicant has no interest in bringing proceedings to challenge the legality of the contested decision in order to protect public health in so far as concerns the scientific assessment of deferiprone'.[143]

Still, the Court was of the opinion that it was important to assess whether the duty to safeguard public health, which, under EU law, should guide the Commission's decision, had been effectively fulfilled. Therefore, the Court analysed the substance of the case. In its reasoning, compliance with this duty implied that the Commission had to consider all the information available, which in this case meant taking into account the information made available by Dr Olivieri. Underlining the prominence of public health as a public interest that needs to be protected in this instance, the Court held that the bilateral relationship defined in the regulation 'cannot prevent the Commission from obtaining information from a third party where such a course of action is indispensable in order to safeguard public health'.[144] It thus deemed it necessary to examine the role played by Dr Olivieri throughout the administrative procedure 'in order to determine if she [had] any interest in bringing this case'.[145] In contradiction to its conclusion that Dr Olivieri was not entitled to participate in this procedure, but coherently with its concern with the pursuance of public interest, the Court assessed the validity of the Commission's decision in light of its consideration for the information submitted by Dr Olivieri.[146] More importantly, it recognized that she was 'entitled to make sure that [the scientific committee] and the Commission examined the information which she had sent ... in order to contribute to the scientific assessment of deferiprone and to ensure the authenticity of the results obtained in the course of [the scientific trial]'. However, it did not clarify on which grounds she was entitled to this right. Furthermore, it held that this 'right ended at the moment when that information was examined and taken into account in the course of that assessment procedure', again without clarifying how she could control the utility of her intervention since, formally, she had no procedural rights in the

[142] *Idem*, paragraph 94.

[143] *Idem*, paragraph 95.

[144] *Idem*, paragraph 73. Nevertheless, in the Court's opinion this did not bear upon the adequacy of the structure of the regulation in order to ensure the pursuance of its aims (see also paragraph 72).

[145] *Idem*, paragraph 74. [146] *Idem*, paragraphs 75 to 88.

procedure, given its bilateral structure.[147] While the Court considered that, in the circumstances of the case, Dr Olivieri had no *locus standi*, it admitted that, had there been an 'implicit decision to reject' the information provided by Dr Olivieri, she would have had a right to stand.[148] Again, it is not clear on which grounds this right would be ascertained. Because she 'played an essential role in the work towards the perfecting of deferiprone'?[149] Because of her effective role during this authorization procedure?[150] Since her intervention was instrumental in the protection of the public interest pursued by the applicable legal regime? And, then, why recognize this right only in the face of a decision that refused to consider the information provided by Dr Olivieri?

This case demonstrates the difficulties in which the Court found itself once it considered the procedure strictly from the perspective of the bilateral structure that emerged from the applicable regulation. While sticking to the formality of the procedure, the Court also considered that the crucial point was to determine whether the public interest pursued by this procedure was effectively ensured, placing this interest in the core of its analysis. In fact, on the one hand, the Court sought refuge in the formal structure of the procedure to deny Dr Olivieri a participation right as well as her *locus standi*. On the other hand, throughout its analysis, it acted as if Dr Olivieri effectively had a right to submit observations and, more than that, to be assured that these observations had been taken into account. Relying on substantive concerns, i.e. the need to ensure that the protection of public health was correctly considered in this case, the Court held that the Commission was required to carefully consider the information submitted by a third party. On formal grounds, however, it denied her the right to intervene in the procedure and to be recognized as having *locus standi*, on the basis that the information provided by her had been taken into account.

The same duality is present in the Court's appreciation of Dr Olivieri's interest to defend her professional reputation. The Court considered that the decision of the Commission taken on the basis of the scientific committee's opinion did not harm Dr Olivieri's professional reputation insofar as the information she provided was taken into consideration in the final

[147] *Idem*, paragraph 91.
[148] *Idem*, paragraph 81. [149] *Idem, ibidem*.
[150] In fact the Court found that 'the information which she sent to the CPMP [the Committee for Proprietary Medicinal Products] enabled the Commission to confirm, in the interest of public health, that the particulars and documents on the basis of which the marketing authorization was authorized were both complete and correct.' (paragraph 81).

decision. However, here the Court fully clarified its position: even if that had not been the case, Dr Olivieri would still not have been recognized to have standing, given the fact that the applicable regulation does not allow the Commission to take such considerations into account.[151] This seems to confirm that Dr Olivieri's possible standing, in case there had been a decision to reject the information provided by her, would be based on her contribution to the pursuance of the public interest the protection of which is the *raison d'être* of the applicable regulation. Given her material connection to the procedure, she could provide useful information regarding the impact of the decision on public health, even if the latter's effect on her legal sphere could not be differentiated from the impact it could have with regard to other persons.

In this judgment, the Court was influenced by the bilateral structure of the procedure, in light of which Dr Olivieri's interest could not be considered 'equivalent to that of an applicant ... who participates in the administrative procedure by virtue of a right which [the marketing authoriszation rules] have conferred on it'.[152] Moreover, the fact of her intervention being instrumental to the pursuance of the public interest could not ground her participation rights and, subsequently, *locus standi*, since this would be opening the doors to public interest litigation. The Court, therefore, reduced Dr Olivieri's position to a mere information provider, formally deprived of any procedural guarantees under the applicable regulation. Had the Court considered the possibility of recognizing broader participation rights on the basis of her connection to the material situation underlining the procedure and of her ensuing capacity to voice legally protected interests it could have been more consistent with its substantive position.

7.3.3 *Legal protection of persons concerned: extending participation*

As argued above, the interconnections of rights, interests, and duties emerging from the regulation of food markets stray beyond the bilateral structure of the relationship formally established between the decision-maker, on the one hand, and the applicant—later, authorization holder—on the other.

In the food law procedures analysed, it is possible to identify two different circles of possible affected persons, who, being implicated in

[151] *Idem*, paragraphs 97 and 98. [152] *Idem*, paragraph 93.

the underlying material situation that is regulated by the decision-maker, should in principle, be granted access to the decisional procedure. There is, in the first place, a group of persons that for professional reasons have a link to the activity that is being evaluated as permissible or not. Such is the case of food business operators who, under general rules and principles of EU food law, are bound to comply with the conditions defined for the authorized product. The practical meaning of this possibility may vary according to the type of conditions defined in the authorization, and in particular on whether there are restrictions of use or duties of control attached to the authorization that can be considered also to impinge on persons other than the authorization holder.[153] Arguably, their interests are voiced in the procedure through the intervention of the applicant, since in principle those interests are convergent with the latter's concerns. Nevertheless, considering that they will be bound by the duties that may be defined in the authorization, they should be granted the possibility of intervening in the procedure, if they find it useful to do so. These are persons whose subjective rights and interests may, in certain circumstances, be adversely affected by the outcome of the procedure. In fact, this produces a change in their legal position, to the extent that duties and charges may emerge therein.

It may be argued that the genetically modified food regulation recognizes the possibility of at least some of these persons intervening in the authorization procedure, since it envisages that the administrative review of decisions taken and omissions committed by the EFSA can be triggered by 'any person directly and individually concerned'.[154] Since these decisions or

[153] An overview of the authorizations adopted on the basis of the genetically modified food regulation during 2008 and until October 2010 reveals that in none of the cases checked did the EFSA consider it necessary to define specific conditions or restrictions for the placing on the market or for the use and handling of the products authorized (Commission Decisions No. 2010/432/EU of 28 July 2010, OJ L 202/11, 4.8.2010, recital 9—this is one of five decisions adopted on the same day, all authorizing in similar terms the placing on the market of products containing, consisting of, or produced from different types of genetically modified maize; No. 2010/139/EU of 2 March 2010, OJ L 55/68, 5.3.2010, recital 13; No. 2010/136/EU, of 2 March 2010, OJ L 53/15, 4.3.2010, recital 4; No. 2009/866/EC, of 30 November 2009, OJ L 314/102, 1.12.2009, recital 8; No. 2009/813/EC, of 30 October 2009, OJ L 289/21, 5.11.2009, recital 8; No. 2009/184/EC, of 10 of March, OJ L 68/28, 13.09.2009, recital 13; No. 2008/933/EC, of 4 of December, OJ L 333/7, 11.12.2008, recital 8; No. 2008/730/EC, of 8 of September, OJ L 247/50, 16.09.2008, recital 9). However, in light of the rules that have been mentioned above, the contrary situation may also occur.

[154] Article 36 of the genetically modified food regulation, *cit.*, n. 29.

omissions necessarily refer to preparatory acts (as was mentioned, the EFSA's task is to prepare the decision to be adopted following a comitology procedure), this is a means for affected persons other than the applicant to react against the EFSA's opinion during the procedure.[155] Nevertheless, the goal of this mechanism is to enable the Commission to control the EFSA's conduct and, in addition, resort to this possibility is only recognized, apart from the Member States and the Commission itself, to those who can demonstrate a direct and individual concern. This formulation, influenced by former Article 230(4) EC (which, in this respect, remains unchanged in Article 263(4) TFEU), may excessively restrict the scope of persons who are entitled to intervene in the procedure resorting to this means.

A second circle of interested persons are those who are affected by the decision adopted to the extent that the latter may be detrimental to legally protected interests. By reason of a certain proximity to the material situation being regulated, these persons can voice concerns that coincide with the public interest, which, under the applicable legislation, should be considered in the decisional procedure. In a way, they can be identified on the basis of an overlap between the interests which are concretely pursued by these persons and those which, for the reasons mentioned, are objectively relevant for the decision to be adopted. These may be consumer and environmentalist associations, whose constitutive aims coincide with the public interests that, in view of the relevant legal determinations, need to be pursued by the decision-maker. They may be individuals who have a sufficient or qualified knowledge regarding the matter being decided and whose intervention is therefore relevant to the attainment of an accurate decision which respects the interests that have been defined by the legislator as being relevant in the case under appreciation (this encompasses situations similar to the *Fern Olivieri* case, for example). They should, in any case, demonstrate their connection to the case being decided and the utility of their intervention.

Reasoning by analogy with the broadest interpretation of the right to be heard, and taking the *Technische Universität München* judgment as a

[155] The combination of the time frame within which this administrative control may be triggered (two months, according to Article 36, third paragraph), on the one hand, and that within which the Commission must adopt its draft decision to submit to the committee that will negotiate the final decision (three months, according to Article 7(1)), on the other, allows this administrative control to be triggered during the procedure for the adoption of the authorization. Its outcomes can therefore be considered in the final decision.

reference, the recognition of a participation right requires that an adverse effect may be produced by the outcome of the procedure in the legal sphere of the persons concerned (e.g. the denial of an advantageous position, the imposition of duties or charges, a restriction of the scope of protection).[156] Assessing this negative impact may be more difficult in relation to acts that have general effects or, at any rate, when the procedural intervention consists of voicing a public interest which is legally protected by the applicable rules. In these cases, one may argue that the adverse effect may consist of the lack of consideration or of a manifest disproportionate weighing of the interests at issue, which, in itself, could cause harmful effects.[157] In these circumstances, it is also harder to identify those who are entitled to participate, although, arguably, holders of subjective rights or the persons upon whom a duty or hardship may be imposed may be identified on the basis of categories or groups targeted by the duties or hardships defined (e.g. certain producers). Furthermore, given that the relevance of the personal situation of those affected is not predominant in this type of procedure, the participation of interested persons is also valued accordingly. Thus, moving away from the core of participation rights—formed by the cases where a bilateral relationship is established between a private person and the decision-maker that justifies the intervention of the latter, mainly in order to defend their position in that context—in these outer circles in which participation rights may still be recognized, the purpose of the procedural intervention of interested persons gradually shifts from securing individual positions to ensuring due consideration for the competing public and private interests that, irrespective of this participation and under the applicable rules, need to be balanced by the decision-maker.[158] In any case, as mentioned, participation rights depend on a legal connection to the material situation underlying the procedure.

[156] Even if the recognition of the right to be heard is eventually not triggered by this adverse effect, this element is nonetheless a condition thereof, as was the case in *Technisches Universität München* (on this, see Chapter 4, Section 4.2).

[157] On the balancing tasks the decision-maker needs to perform in order to respect the rights and interests of the persons concerned, José Joaquim Gomes Canotilho (1994) 'Relações jurídicas poligonais, ponderação ecológica de bens e controlo judicial preventivo', *Revista Jurídica do Urbanismo e Ambiente*, n. 1, pp. 55–65, at p. 61.

[158] It was argued in Chapter 2 (Section 2.2) that these two dimensions of participation cannot be fully detached from one another. This is maintained here. The *Fern Olivieri* case exemplifies precisely this. Dr Olivieri considered that her professional reputation was harmed by the Commission's decision, but also that certain aspects regarding the risks at stake had not been taken into account in this decision. It was only to the extent that she had been involved in the research

Depending on the effects of the act, this task of balancing competing interests in light of the aims defined as pertinent by the legislator should be performed after hearing the persons concerned by the material situation under appreciation. Now, in order to discharge the decisional competence in compliance with the rights and interests of the persons concerned, the decision-maker must comply with certain procedural duties. Given that the persons concerned may not be easily identified, the procedure should be open by publicizing the envisaged decision as well as other pertinent information (e.g. the opinion of the EFSA, possibly accompanied by a summary of the relevant information thereof), together with the time within which comments can be submitted and the categories of persons whose interests need to be considered in the procedure. Secondly, the information received should be examined, assessed in light of its pertinence to the matter being decided, and eventually taken into account by the decision-maker. Thirdly, the motivation of the decision adopted should reveal the weighing of interests that was determinant for the final act and, where applicable, which changes have resulted from the intervention of concerned persons.

As such, this model of administrative conduct does not fundamentally differ from the consultation procedures that the Commission has been developing in the last few years (in particular in the framework of regulatory impact assessments), of the type envisaged in the genetically modified food regulation. The difference is that compliance with the model outlined above corresponds to a bundle of procedural duties of the decision-maker that should be subject to judicial review: notice, access to documents, and reasoned decision that pays heed to the comments submitted. These are the correlative duties of participation rights.

It results from the above that holders of participation rights are the persons who are involved in the web of links of advantageous and disadvantageous positions that emerge from the adoption of an act and whose legal sphere may be perceptibly affected by such act. Even if legally protected interests are voiced by associations or other representative legal persons, these intervene in the procedure to defend the interest of a group to pursue

for developing the substance in issue and, on this basis, submitted information which was relevant for the protection of public health that her intervention in the procedure was considered legally relevant. The former claim was discarded as irrelevant for the purposes of authorization. This example shows that the difference between participation fundamentally grounded in one aspect or the other may only be a matter of what, in each case, is considered relevant in legal terms.

the socio-economic goals for which the legal person was created. This is still a subjective position protected by the legal system, especially in the case in which the individual members of the legal person are targeted by the act adopted.[159] When this is not the case, but the legally protected interests that they represent may, at any rate, be affected by the decisional procedure, and this impacts in their legal sphere, they have at least a legitimate interest that the order of interests that the decision-maker should pursue in light of the applicable legislation is duly considered in the decisional procedure. They should, therefore, be involved in the corresponding procedural relationship. In this case, their intervention in the procedure is essentially evaluated on the basis of their possible contribution to an adequate outcome, even if, as mentioned, their subjective position may be adversely affected insofar as the lack of an adequate consideration of the interests they defend may have harmful effects. In a way, their entitlement to participate is justified by the need to ensure the due consideration of the competing interests involved in the adoption of the act, although still dependent on an adverse effect that the final decision may produce, or, in other words, on the ability of the act to produce a change in their legal position. In essence, this only differs from the procedural interests of those who intervene primarily to defend their subjective rights to the extent that holders of legally protected interests cannot aspire to have their personal situation considered as such by the decision-maker. The difference stems from the degree of legal protection that is afforded by the legal system in both cases. Nevertheless, given the values in which participation rights are grounded and the functions of participation, these persons should also be recognized as possessing participation rights, even if they might have a weaker procedural position than the one recognized to holders of subjective interests.

The procedural status of those affected in their subjective rights should be considered analogous to that of the applicant or authorization holder, although the latter may retain a dominant position by reason of fact and law.[160] The procedural position of the applicant needs to be situated in the broader context of the relationships established also with other persons

[159] In a similar sense, Riccardo Villata (1992) 'Riflessioni in tema di partecipazione la procedimento e legittimazione processuale', *Diritto Processuale Amministrativo*, Vol. 9, pp. 171–205, at p. 191.

[160] The applicant is often the holder, and even the producer, of the information that forms the basis of the preparatory acts and the final decision adopted.

affected by the act adopted.[161] Moreover, at the end, in some cases, the applicant may not be the person targeted by the procedure. This is the case in which market authorizations are granted by adopting or adapting a regulation that contains the list of authorized substances and products. It is more difficult to argue that holders of 'simple' legally protected interests should have the same procedural status as the applicant or authorization holder, given that, as mentioned, their particular legal position need not be taken into consideration by the decision-maker and their intervention is legally valued mostly on the basis of their contribution to the procedure. In food law, the assessment of adverse effects produced in the legal sphere of certain persons cannot be detached from the examination of the public interests that need to be pursued by the rules and decisions that implement legislative determinations. The intervention of this second group of persons is valued in this light. Therefore, even if a certain connection to the underlying material situation can be ascertained, ultimately they are defending the interest of a community to benefit from a common good (e.g. health, environment) not a subjective right requiring specific legal protection.

It is the decision-maker's task to assess whether the criteria that ground participation rights have been met, as well as to weigh the relevance of the contribution of each interested person to the final decision.[162] However, from the moment at which the procedure is open to consultation, be it because it is difficult to identify *a priori* who are the holders of participation rights or because this is considered relevant to collecting all the information that might be pertinent to the final act, consultation must be open to all those who may be affected by the outcome of the procedure.[163] The identification of the interested persons is, therefore, made during the procedure, if this was not feasible before. Whether they may be adversely affected by its final outcome and whether this adverse effect is legally relevant is also assessed by the decision-maker in the latter's appreciation of the input received and on the basis of the arguments put forward by the persons concerned.[164]

[161] A similar argument is sustained by Chiti, referring to the activity of national independent regulatory agencies (Edoardo Chiti (2004) 'La disciplina procedurale della regolazione', *Rivista Trimestrale di Diritto Pubblico*, Vol. 54, n. 3, pp. 679–736, at p. 687). Arguably, the argument can be extended to any situation in which the administrative activity implies, directly or indirectly, mediating between different private interests.

[162] In this sense, see Chiti, *op. cit.*, p. 715.

[163] Similarly, *idem*, p. 695.

[164] On this, see Chapter 5, Section 5.3.

Supporting the intervention of the holders of rights and legally protected interests in this way corresponds to the defence of an extended adversarial model as the adequate form of participation in relation to market authorizations adopted in the field of food law. This is justified on the basis of the effects of the latter and of the balancing of interests that the legislator puts forward in these matters. In fact, even if the specific legislation applicable to given substances or products envisages merely the establishment of a bilateral relationship between the applicant and the decision-maker, at the end, the protection of the interests of the former needs to be situated in the broader context of the inter-relationships ensuing from the market authorization and of the interests pursued by the latter.

Drawing inspiration from Chiti's analysis on the procedural regime of regulation, undertaken with respect to Italian law, one could say that this form of participation would

> bind both public and private entities to observe an argumentative method on the basis of which each party is called to provide the reasons for his or her own position; the various arguments are cross-examined and discussed with a view to identify possible incoherences; the adopted solution is rationally justifiable, i.e. accepted by the interested persons and by the public in general.[165]

The goal of this argumentative process would be the adoption of a measure that 'is presumed reasonable and may be shared in neutral terms as long as the need for a different determination is not argued in convincing terms', in light of interests protected by the applicable legal regime.[166] In this sense, both public and private persons are bound by duties of conduct in view of the goals of the procedure.[167]

[165] Chiti, *op. cit.*, n. 161, p. 700 (author's translation). This corresponds to Chiti's re-interpretation of models of consultation undertaken in the realm of the general activity of national independent regulatory authorities and is presented as a specificity of the procedural regime of regulation (contrasted to traditional forms of administrative intervention). It is argued here that this is applicable to the forms of regulatory action under analysis in this chapter. First, this has in common with the activity of independent regulatory authorities the fact that the decision-maker needs to arbitrate between competing private interests in light of the public interest the latter is seeking to pursue. Secondly, one of the core principles of EU food law is the independence of the scientific analysis that grounds the decisions and rules adopted in this field. Arguably, also, the decision-maker, while balancing the pertinent 'legitimate factors' that need to be taken into account in the risk management task entrusted to them, is equally bound by a duty of neutrality and impartiality vis-à-vis the competing interests involved.

[166] Chiti, *op. cit.*, n. 161, p. 703.

[167] Chiti, *op. cit.*, n. 161, p. 701. Note also his considerations on the parallels and the differences with regard to an interest representation model (pp. 702–3).

Arguably, in these terms, the model of participation proposed is likely to reinforce the impartiality of the decision-maker vis-à-vis the interests involved,[168] and, thereby, also to underpin public trust in the decisions and rules that implement the general rules and principles of EU food law, which is one of the regulatory concerns in this field.[169] This is particularly relevant in the case of market authorizations, since the dominance of the applicant, by force of factual circumstances, should be tempered by the legal duty to consider other public and private interests that are legally protected.[170]

The proposed model of participation, insofar as it restricts the intervention in the procedure to holders of subjective rights or legally protected interests, may also be a way of countering some deficiencies and inconsistencies of current consultation practices.[171] In particular, this would avoid dealing with contributions that are objectively not legally pertinent to the final decision, which can ultimately lead to the discredit and uselessness of participatory procedures, since access to participation is delimited and not open to the public in general.[172] The proposed model of participation cannot tackle other deficiencies of consultation practices, which have been pointed out in the literature. In particular, participation, as proposed here, cannot redress the imbalance between the applicant and other interveners.[173]

[168] In a similar sense, underlining the importance of the principles of participation and transparency in the regulatory activity carried out by independent administrative authorities, see Chiti, *op. cit.*, n. 161, pp. 687 and 691.

[169] See, for example, recital 9 of the preamble of Regulation No. 178/2002, *cit.*, n. 8.

[170] On the dominant position of the applicant, see n. 160 above.

[171] These have been studied by, among others, Maria Paola Ferretti (2008) 'Participatory strategies in the regulation of GMO products in the EU', in Jens Steffek, Claudia Kissling, and Patricia Nanz (eds), *Civil Society Participation in European and Global Governance. A Cure for the Democratic Deficit?*, Basingstoke, New York: Palgrave Macmillan, pp. 166–84. A literature review in these matters is provided by Sandra Kröger (2008) 'Nothing but consultation: the place of organised civil society in EU policy-making across policies', European Governance Papers (EUROGOV) No. C-08-03, <http://www.connex-network.org/eurogov/pdf/egp-connex-C-08-03.pdf>, with a focus on consultation procedures carried out by DG SANCO (pp. 19–22).

[172] Ferretti draws attention to the incongruence of asking for comments from the public in general given the incapacity of making sense of some of these comments for regulatory purposes and the lack of competence of lay people to communicate with the institutions in some matters (*op. cit.*, pp. 172–5). To be sure, as the author points outs, the fact that certain comments are not legally relevant does not mean that they cannot be taken into account by the decision-maker insofar as they might express tendencies or opinions that the latter would wish to consider (Ferretti, *op. cit.*, p. 174). In any event, the submission of such comments is deprived of the legal effects envisaged in the model proposed in this chapter.

[173] This is another aspect pointed out by Ferretti (*op. cit.*, p. 178).

Tempering the dominance of the applicant, as sustained above, does not mean that it is possible to overcome it. The applicant or the authorization holder retains, *de facto* and *de jure*, a privileged position, which is reflected in the qualified duties and responsibilities that impinge upon them by effect of the market authorization. In any event, *formal* equality between the different interveners must be ensured, to the extent that they participate in the procedure in similar capacities: either as holders of affected subjective rights, or as holders of legally protected interests who, by reason of their proximity to the material situation being regulated, may have a contribution to the procedure.

Defending an extended adversarial model of participation in the terms proposed does not imply arguing the inadequacy of consultations to the public in general. On the contrary, in the way they are put into practice, there are overlaps between public consultation periods,[174] on the one hand, and participation as conceived in this book, on the other (e.g. both require there to be a public notice opening the procedure to participation). Nevertheless, these public consultations serve different purposes from those that underlie the model presented here.[175] This model should rather be understood as a means of complementing the existing public consultations with a view to enforcing participation rights of the persons whose legal spheres are affected by the decision-making process. In fact, as it stands, participation in food regulation is as much limited as it is extended by the model of public consultations chosen. It allows for the intervention of whoever wants to have a say in the procedure, but, in doing so, the different 'qualities' of the interveners are *prima facie* indistinct and blurred in the midst of the various manifestations of 'the public'. From the view point of participation rights, this model is limited precisely for this reason: it does not reflect the specificities emerging from the material situation that is under appreciation; it does not ensure that the different subjective positions affected by it are duly taken into account. Moreover, it does not allow for the recognition of legally enforceable procedural rights, nor does it create the conditions for an argumentative process that favours the weighing of the competing public and private interests that are involved in the procedure.

[174] Such as those envisaged in the genetically modified food regulation, as well as the general provisions on participation enshrined in Regulation No. 178/2002, *cit.*, n. 8.

[175] See above Sub-section 7.2.2.

7.4 Matching Administrative Powers and Participation

The creative use of former Article 95 EC (now Article 114 TFEU), which has been supported by the case law of the Court of Justice, has led to the creation of decisional powers, entrusted essentially to the Commission, that are capable of producing effects of law directly in the legal sphere of private persons. The fact that this is not backed by the Treaty has not prevented the creation of direct decisional powers of the Commission in the field of food law. These were prompted by the perceived need for new techniques of regulatory intervention in this field, which in turn derives both from the related technical and scientific developments and from the fact that the protection of public health became one of the tasks assumed by the EU. Independently of the decentralized or centralized nature of the procedure chosen to regulate the aspects of food law examined here, and of the ensuing distribution of competences between Member States and EU institutions or bodies, the effects of the final act, in all the cases analysed, are determined by an act adopted at the EU level. However, these developments were not accompanied by the creation of the corresponding procedural guarantees. On the one hand, this aspect was, as a rule, not considered by the EU legislator (perhaps with the exception of the mechanism for administrative review envisaged in the genetically modified food regulation). On the other, the rules on participation rights stemming from the Courts' case law are inadequate to confer procedural protection on the persons affected by the exercise of these powers as well as to ensure an adequate consideration for the interests involved. This chapter has demonstrated, first, that an extended recognition of participation rights exercised before the EU decision-maker is justified in the field of food law and, secondly, how this may be conceived.

The fact that the decisions taken by the Commission are decisive in shaping the rights and duties of the interested persons requires that, where applicable, participation rights are exercised directly before the Commission, even if Member States also have decisional competences in the matter. Alternatively, if these rights are exercised before national administrations on the basis of national procedural rules, the intervention of the interested persons needs to occur at a moment in the procedure in which other competent public bodies, national or European, have already intervened with a view to shaping the final decision (as was suggested for the procedure regarding the authorization of novel foods). The former rule results from the case law of the Court of First Instance (now General Court), albeit it has not been stated as such. The latter, however, can only be deduced from the desired effectiveness of the exercise of participation rights. In fact, if the recognition of participation rights in the procedures for market authorizations does not take into account the decisional structure of these procedures, the exercise of these rights may be deprived of any meaning and utility (an idea that has already been conveyed by the Courts). The examination of the procedure enshrined in the novel foods regulation illustrated that, while it seems clear that securing procedural guarantees at the EU level of decision-making has not been a concern of the EU legislator, the structure of rather complex procedures and the place and moment at which the bulk of the decision is formed should be taken into account, when considering the recognition of participation rights in such instances. The analysis of the procedures for the authorization of food additives and of genetically modified food further confirmed that ensuring the procedural protection of persons affected by decisions adopted by the EU administration is an aspect that has not been taken into account in the design of the respective decisional procedures.

The study of the procedure for the authorization of genetically modified food pointed out how the existing rules and practices of public consultation are shallow in terms of legal protection of the persons affected by decisional powers of the EU institutions, when these affect persons other than the one who triggered the procedure, i.e. the addressee of the final decision. Furthermore, they do not embody or reflect any rule as to the due consideration of the interests that need to be balanced before the adoption of a decision on this matter, which could ensure an anticipated protection of the interests involved and diligent conduct by the decision-maker. In fact, public consultation periods have been designed to perform a different function from the one that underlies the recognition of participation rights: to improve the transparency of the decisional procedure in sensitive issues bound to raise public concerns. As such, the binding legal rules applicable to the public consultation period in the authorization of genetically modified foods do not provide any basis for grounding participation rights, nor do the procedural rules on transparency and public scrutiny enshrined in Regulation No. 178/2002, where applicable to specific procedures.

In all these cases, the acts adopted produce general effects, irrespective of the form they assume. Procedures for the authorization of foodstuffs may lead to the adoption of individual market authorizations as well as positive lists that can be considered administrative regulations and may either be inserted in the basic legislative act itself or be adopted as implementing (or delegated) regulations. In some cases, these positive lists are elaborated on the basis of previously issued market authorizations. In others, the market authorization requested by a given applicant is adopted under the form of a regulation or by introducing changes to prior lists. The choice between these different regulatory techniques has so far been essentially a matter of the scientific and technical complexity associated with the creation of certain products and of the assessment of the risks they entail. On the basis of the similarity of the effects produced by these different acts, one may argue that there is a continuity between individual and general acts. Therefore, where participation rights are applicable, there is no reason to distinguish them according to the formal nature of the acts.

As defended in this book, participation rights should be granted when an act adopted by the EU institutions creates rights, duties, and hardships that link the legal spheres of two or more public and private persons, to those who are adversely affected by this act. On the basis of the study undertaken in this chapter, it is possible to identify two groups of persons who would be entitled to participate in the procedure. First, those who, by force of the general responsibility rule of EU food law are bound to comply with the conditions defined for the authorized product. When these are sufficiently precise in relation to specific products, one may argue that an administrative relationship arises from the adoption of market authorizations, which also embraces the food business operators dealing with the products at issue, to the extent that charges and duties may emerge in their legal spheres. A second group of interested persons consists of those who have a sufficient connection to the material situation being decided and have therefore the capacity to voice interests that are legally protected by the applicable legal regime and are affected by the act envisaged. Their intervention in the procedure is mainly valued as a means to ensure the due consideration for the objective interests that, by force of law, need to be balanced by the decision-maker and that might be adversely affected by the procedure. Thus, market authorizations of foodstuffs have the ability to give rise to multiple material relationships. This should be mirrored by the procedural relationship that is established under the corresponding decisional procedure, between the respective interveners. Moreover, this procedural relationship should be conceived in light of the substantive regime that it serves and, therefore, encompass persons who, fulfilling the requirements identified above, may have a valid contribution to the procedure.

In light of the above, an extended adversarial model of participation in the terms proposed in this chapter ensures that decision-making is carried out with respect for the rights and interests of the persons concerned. Moreover, if built into the procedure, this enhances the correct fulfilment of the order of interests protected by the legislator that need to be respected by the decision-maker and reinforces the impartiality of the latter vis-à-vis those interests. Thereby, this may contribute to ensuring public confidence in food regulation. This supplements a model of decision-making in which the logic of argumentation is restricted to the consideration of national interests, virtually excluding the persons who are affected by the final decision. In fact, the decisional procedures analysed were created to ensure that the relevant national authorities are present in the EU procedures. Indeed, in the absence of an EU competence in these matters, these would have been the entities and bodies competent to adopt decisions in the cases analysed. Their presence at the EU level is ensured both in decentralized administrative procedures (by the possibility of Member States and the Commission raising objections to a first assessment made by the Member State competent to adopt a final decision) and in centralized EU procedures (essentially via the comitology procedures, the scope of which is very likely to be more limited after Lisbon).[176] However, given the direct relationship established between the EU administration and the individuals affected by its decisions, the exclusion from the procedure of affected persons that are external to this 'network' of public entities can no longer hold, if one follows a model of administrative law that values procedural fairness and material justice.

[176] At the time of the writing, the future of comitology is still under discussion (see Commission Proposal for a Regulation laying down the rules and general principles concerning mechanisms for control by Member States of the Commission's exercise of implementing powers, *cit.*, n. 28). For a discussion on the impact of Articles 290 and 291 TFEU on comitology, see Paul Craig, 'The Role of the European Parliament under the Lisbon Treaty', in Griller and Ziller (eds), op. *cit.*, n. 116, in particular pp. 123–5 and Paolo Ponzano (2008) '"Executive" and "delegated" acts: The situation after the Lisbon Treaty', in the same volume, pp. 135–41.

Chapter 8

Participation Rights in State Aid

The Commission's powers in the field of state aid provide an interesting case for the purposes of the book. The Commission's competences in this field expressly envisaged in the Treaty are framed by a participatory procedure. This is the rare case in which a duty to give notice to parties concerned by the possible outcome of an administrative procedure is enshrined in primary EU law. However, the Commission's powers with regard to state aid control have expanded beyond the Treaty's provisions: the Commission has *de facto* been entrusted with both decision- and rule-making competences in this field, having different instruments at its disposal to enforce its state aid policy.

Insofar as its powers of control over notified aid are concerned, the Commission needs to follow the procedure of Article 108 TFEU. According to its second paragraph, the Commission gives notice to the parties concerned to submit their comments before issuing a decision that, on the basis of the Commission's appreciation of a given aid in light of Article 87, finds this aid incompatible with the common market or considers that it is being misused.[1] This corresponds to the second phase of the administrative procedure concerning the examination of new aid.[2] It follows the

[1] 'Parties concerned' are, in other language versions, 'les intéressés', 'gli interessati', '[die] Beteiligten', 'os interessados', 'los interesados'. Although the Treaty references follow those of the Lisbon Treaty, all the developments mentioned on the procedure for state aid control have been grounded in former Article 88 (Article 93, in the original numeration of the EC Treaty). Its paragraphs (2) and (3) are reproduced in current Article 108(2) and (3) TFEU.

[2] The Courts have expressly qualified the procedure of current Article 108(2) and (3) TFEU as an administrative procedure (see, among others, Case 40/85, *Belgium v Commission* [1986] ECR 2321, paragraph 28 and Case T-354/99, *Kuwait Petroleum (Nederland) BV v Commission* [2006] ECR II-1475, paragraph 80). 'New aid' refers to aid which was non-existent prior to the entry into force of the Treaty in the respective Member State or that, in any case, has not been approved by the Commission or by the Council.

preliminary examination subsequent to the notification by the concerned Member State, pursuant Article 108(3), when the Commission considers that aid to be incompatible with the common market.[3] Although, according to the Treaty, control of existing aid relies on the cooperation between Member States and the Commission (Article 108(1)), resort to Article 108 (2) occurs when the Member State concerned resists to accept the proposals of the Commission.[4]

The first part of the chapter scrutinizes the motivations of the drafters of the EC Treaty when enshrining such a provision. This is followed by an examination of the scope of 'parties concerned' within the meaning of Article 108(2) TFEU, as well as of the rationale and meaning of their participation rights, as interpreted by the Courts (Section 8.1). A critical analysis of the Courts' case law is the basis for the second part of the chapter. Elements stemming from this case law substantiate the general framework that underpins the definition of participation rights presented in this book. In fact, judicial interpretations of Article 108 TFEU provide important elements to confirm the theoretical construction followed in this work (Section 8.2). This reconstruction of participation rights under Article 108(2) TFEU frames the analysis undertaken in the third and last part of the chapter. Here, the fact that the powers expressly assigned to the Commission are, in the scheme of the Treaty, intended to be framed by a participatory procedure, which is conceived in light of the specific problems posed by state aid regulation, is confronted with the existing regulatory

[3] Article 108(3) TFEU. For a complete overview of this procedure, see, among others, Michel Waelbroeck and Aldo Frignani (1997) *Commentaire Mégret. Le Droit de la CE*, vol 4 (Concurrence). Bruxelles: Editions Université de Bruxelles, pp. 368–83; Andrea Blasio and Francesco Munari (2004) 'Aiuti concessi dagli Stati' in Antonio Tizzano (ed.), *Trattati dell'Unione Europea e della Comunità Europea*, Milano: Giuffrè, p. 608–14.

[4] Article 19(2) of the Council Regulation No. 659/1999, of 22 March 1999 (OJ L 83/1, 27.3.99), hereinafter the 'procedural regulation'. See, on this, Case T-354/05, *Télévision française 1 SA (TF1) v Commission* [2009] ECR II-471, paragraphs 63 to 67 (displaying, however, somewhat contradictory views regarding resort to former Article 88(2) in these cases; see Case T-152/06, *NDSHT Nya Destination Stockholm Hotell & Teaterpaket AB v Commission* [2009] ECR II-471, paragraphs 58 and 63). For the period before the entry into force of the said regulation, see Waelbroeck and Frignani, *op. cit.*, p. 370. In addition, this interpretation is confirmed by the procedural regulation of 1999 while concretizing former Article 88(2) in relation to the procedure on notified aid (Article 6(1)), that on misuse of aid (Article 16), that on existing aid (Article 19(2)). The contradictory procedure does not apply in cases of unlawful aid, according to the fourth type of procedure defined in this regulation (Articles 10 to 15). For more developments on these procedures, see Adinda Sinnaeve and Piet Jan Slot (1999) 'The New Regulation on State Aid Procedures', *Common Market Law Review*, Vol. 36, n. 6, pp. 1153–94.

structure in this field. It is questioned whether the other forms of regulatory intervention of the Commission in this field should equally follow a notice and comment procedure. The differences between the type of powers regulated by Article 108(2) and (3) TFEU, on the one hand, and other regulatory powers of the Commission, on the other, are duly taken into account, thus testing the very possibility of analogy. Nevertheless, it is once more stressed that the distinction between individual acts and acts of general scope is not a necessary argument for denying the possibility of participation in relation to the latter. In fact, where an analogy can be established between the two situations the nature of the act should not be an impediment to the recognition of participation rights (Section 8.3).

8.1 Participation Rights: The Treaty and the Case Law

8.1.1 *The history of Article 108(2) TFEU*

The specific reasons that determined the choice as to whether to introduce a participatory procedure in the field of state aid control remain unclear. The formulation that corresponds to the current wording of Article 108(2) TFEU appeared for the first time in the course of the negotiations of the EEC Treaty in a project drafted by an expert group, at the demand of the Common Market Group, which was presented at the Intergovernmental Conference for the Common Market and EURATOM held in Brussels in November 1956. The wording of the provision proposed was the following:

> Si, après avoir mis les intéressés en demeure de présenter leurs observations, la Commission constate qu'une aide accordée par un Etat membre ou au moyen de ressources d'un Etat membre est incompatible avec le Marché commun aux termes de l'article 44 [107 TFEU], ou que cette aide est appliqué de façon abusive, elle en décide la suppression ou la modification et fixe un délai à cet effet.[5]

The same wording is repeated in the subsequent projects and made its way into the Treaty of Rome. There is no documentation available on the

[5] Article 44a § 2, 'Projet de rédaction concernant les articles 44 à 44a relatifs aux aides accordées para les Etats établi le 28 novembre 1956 par un Groupe d'experts à l'intention du Group du Marché Comum', Intergovernmental Conference for the Common Market and the EURATOM, Brussels, 28 November 1956 (MAE 661 f/56 mp, Historical Archives of the European Union, CM3/NEGO-238).

meetings of this group, nor any notice on possible debates between the delegations of the future Member States regarding this specific point.

Apparently, the Member States involved in the drafting of the Treaty considered that the specificity of the problems raised by Community control of aid granted by the Member States justified a notice and comment phase in the administrative procedure that gives effect to this competence of the Commission. The fact that the Commission's powers of appreciation are framed by a principled prohibition of state aid might have influenced the creation of a participatory procedure, on the assumption that negative effects could emerge for the persons concerned, namely the aid recipients. The relevance of this guiding rule in the definition of the Community legal system of state aid control is evidenced in the discussions between the members of the national delegations over a previous draft.[6] This interpretation may be confirmed by the fact that the project presented by the French delegation included a proposal for giving standing to the 'entreprises intéressés' to challenge a Commission or Council decision on the aid concerning them.[7]

Nevertheless, without further documentation, any interpretation of this provision on the basis of the preparatory works of the Treaty of Rome remains in the realm of supposition. Only one firm conclusion may be defended: the powers expressly assigned to the Commission, in the scheme of the Treaty, were intended to be framed by this particular procedural rule. Beyond this assertion, concrete indications on the legal interpretation of this norm can only be provided by the Courts' case law on the matter.

8.1.2 *Procedural guarantees in a 'special procedure'*

The Court has considered the procedure of current Article 108(2) and (3) TFEU to be a special procedure that allows the Commission to keep state aid under constant review, designed both to ensure the effectiveness of the general prohibition of Article 107(1) TFEU and to warrant the pursuance of the Union's general interest, as well as to grant the protection of the interests of the persons concerned.[8] In particular, the Court has held that:

[6] 'Memento interne du Groupe du Marché Commun', 14 septembre 1956, MAE/Sec 34/56 js, Historical Archives of the European Union, CM3/NEGO-238.

[7] 'Tableau synoptique des projects d'articles soumis par les experts des délégations concernant les règles de concurrence applicables aux aides accordées par les Etats', Bruxelles, le 26 septembre 1956 (MAE/Sec. 51 mb, p. 4 and 5, Historical Archives of the European Union, CM3/NEGO-238).

[8] In Case C-256/97, *Déménagements-Manutention Transport SA (DMT)* [1999] ECR I-3913, paragraph 14, the Court stated that 'Article 93 of the EC Treaty [now Article 108 TFEU]

the procedure laid down in [Article 108 (2)] provides all the parties concerned with guarantees that are specifically adapted to the special problems created by state aid with regard to competition in the common market.... [9]

The Court has sought to protect these guarantees in three ways. First, it prevented the Commission from resorting to the preliminary procedure of the action for infringement (now Article 258 TFEU) as an alternative to the procedure of Article 108(2) TFEU. Since the procedure of Article 258 TFEU only involves the Commission and the Member State concerned, using it as an alternative to Article 108 could circumvent the procedural guarantees accorded by this last provision to the individuals concerned. Although Article 108(2) *per se* does not prevent the use of Article 258, the Court has determined that when the Commission wishes to establish that a given aid is incompatible with the internal market it must use the former procedure.[10]

Secondly, in view of the interplay between Article 108(3) and (2), the Courts defined that opening of the procedure of Article 108(2) is essential whenever the Commission has 'serious difficulties' in determining the compatibility of an aid with the internal market.[11] Ultimately, this is grounded in the

provides for a special procedure by which the Commission is to keep state aid under constant review'; in Case C-404/00, *Commission v Spain* [2003] ECR I-6695, paragraph 20, the Court held that the Commission's role in state aid procedures of current Article 108(3) is to ensure the effectiveness of the prohibition of Article 107. In Joined Cases 91/83 and 127/83, *Heineken Brouwerijen v Inspecteur der Vennootschapsbelasting, Amsterdam and Utrecht* [1984] ECR 3435, paragraph 14, it stresses that the procedure in Article 108(3) is intended to allow the Commission to act in the 'general interest of the Communities', while Article 108(2) provides for the protection of the interests of any 'individuals concerned'. (All three cases are quoted by Jean-Paul Keppenne (2006) 'General questions on procedure. Control of state aid compatibility. Council's decision-making power', in Luis Ortiz Blanco (ed.), *European Community Competition Procedure*, Oxford: Oxford University Press, 2nd edn, pp. 785–954, p. 795).

[9] Case 290/83, *Commission v France* [1985] ECR 439, paragraph 17. On the relevance of this argument to frame the interpretation of Article 108(2) TFEU, see below Sub-section 8.2.2.

[10] *Idem*, paragraphs 17–19.

[11] Case 84/82, *Germany v Commission* [1984] ECR 1451, paragraph 13; Case T-49/93, *Société Internationale de Diffusion et d'Edition (SIDE) v Commission* [1995] ECR II-2501, paragraph 58; Case C-367/95 P, *Commission v Sytraval and Brink's France SARL* [1998] ECR I-1719, paragraph 39; Case T-95/96, *Gestevisión Telecinco SA v Commission* [1998] ECR II-3407, paragraph 52; Case T-46/97, *SIC—Sociedade Independente de Comunicação SA v Commission* [2000] ECR II-2125, paragraph 71-2; Case T-73/98, *Société chimique Prayon-Rupel SA v Commission* [2001] ECR II-867, paragraphs 41-42; Case T-158/99, *Thermenhotel Stoiser Franz Gesellschaft mbH & Co. KG and Others v Commission* [2004] ECR II-1, paragraphs 58–60; Case T 375/03, *Fachvereinigung Mineralfaserindustrie eV Deutsche Gruppe der Eurima v Commission* [2007] ECR II-121, paragraph 88; Case T-388/03, *Deutsche Post AG and DHL International v Commission* [2009] ECR II-199, paragraph 88; Case T-36/06, *Bundesverband deutscher*

different object and scope of the preliminary phase of the procedure (Article 108(3)), on the one hand, and of its formal stage (Article 108(2)), on the other. According to the Courts, while the former 'is intended merely to allow the Commission to form a *prima facie* opinion on the character of the measure in question as state aid and the partial or complete conformity of the aid in question with the common market', the latter 'is designed to enable the Commission to be fully informed of all the facts of the case' before taking its decision.[12] These differences justify the Courts' conviction as to the importance of the formal stage of the procedure: whenever there are difficulties in determining whether a given aid is compatible with the internal market, these have to be solved on the basis of all the information available including that which can be submitted by the economic and social sectors concerned and other Member States during the formal stage of the procedure.[13] Hence, the Commission has the duty to initiate the procedure of Article 108(2) under such circumstances. *A contrario*, the Commission can only restrict itself to the preliminary examination if it is convinced beyond any serious doubt that the aid is compatible with the Treaty. Any other justification on which the Commission could possibly rely to deny the initiation of the formal procedure is irrelevant to this effect, even if based on considerations that are legally pertinent (e.g. 'third party interests, considerations of economy of procedure or any other ground of administrative convenience').[14] Furthermore, the decision of the Commission to initiate the procedure of Article 108(2) is subject to judicial review.[15] Accordingly, the Courts have investigated thoroughly the conditions under which the Commission has refused to open the procedure of Article 108(2). For example, an excessive length of the

Banken eV v Commission [2010] nyr., paragraph 125, Case T-359/04, *British Aggregates Association and others v Commission* [2010] nyr., paragraph 55.

[12] *Germany v Commission*, *cit.*, paragraphs 11 and 13; Case C-198/91, *William Cook plc v Commission* [1993] ECR I-2487, paragraph 22; Case C-225/91, *Matra v Commission* [1993] ECR I-3203, paragraph 16; *Commission v Sytraval*, *cit.*, paragraph 38; *Gestevisión*, *cit.*, paragraph 51; *SIC*, *cit.*, paragraph 70; Case T-27/02, *Kronofrance SA v Commission* [2004] ECR II-4177, paragraph 70; Order of the Court of First Instance of 21 November 2005 in Case T-426/04, *Tramarin Snc v Commission* [2005] ECR II-4765, paragraphs 27-8; Case C-78/03 P, *Commission v Aktionsgemeinschaft Recht und Eigentum eV.* [2005] ECR I-10737, paragraph 34; *Fachvereinigung Mineralfaserindustrie*, *cit.*, paragraph 47; *Deutsche Post*, *cit.*, paragraph 41; Case T-375/04, *Scheucher-Fleisch GmbH and Others v Commission* [2009] ECR II-4155, paragraph 41.

[13] *Prayon-Rupel*, *cit.*, paragraph 42.

[14] *Prayon-Rupel*, *cit.*, paragraph 44; *Deutsche Post*, cit., paragraph 90; *Scheucher-Fleisch*, *cit.*, paragraph 72.

[15] Among others, Cook, *cit.*, paragraph 30, and *Prayon-Rupel*, *cit.*, paragraphs 43–47 (as well as *British Aggregates* [2010] *cit.*, n. 11, paragraphs 56 and 58).

preliminary examination procedure—two months was considered the reasonable time needed to form a *prima facie* opinion on the compatibility of the aid with the internal market—or concrete circumstances surrounding the negotiations between the Commission and the Member State concerned may indicate that the Commission had 'serious difficulties' in assessing the compatibility of the aid under assessment. These difficulties justify the opening of the formal investigative procedure.[16] Also the content of the contested decision may provide evidence that the Commission was faced with serious difficulties in assessing the compatibility of the aid with the internal market.[17] Where such difficulties can be asserted and, despite them, the Commission has decided not to initiate the formal stage of the procedure, it has infringed the procedural guarantees of concerned parties enshrined in Article 108(2). In addition, the Commission's decision not to open the procedure of Article 108(2) is subject to a duty of careful and impartial examination of the case put before it.[18]

The third step taken by the Court to protect the procedural guarantees of the persons concerned was to recognize *locus standi* in actions for the annulment of Commission decisions refusing to open the procedure of Article 108(2) to persons that could have otherwise been granted the possibility of submitting comments.[19] In the *Cook* and *Matra* judgments, the Court rightfully considered that these persons may only secure compliance with procedural guarantees from which they are intended to benefit if they are able to challenge such a decision before the Court.[20] They should

[16] *Germany v Commission, cit.*, n. 11, paragraphs 14–16; *Prayon-Rupel, cit.*, n. 11, paragraphs 93 and 98 (*Prayon-Rupel* is particularly illustrative of the Court's activism in protecting the procedural guarantees of persons concerned; see, in particular paragraphs 48 and 100); *Deutsche Post, cit.*, n. 11, paragraphs 96–106.

[17] *Deutsche Post, cit.*, n. 11, paragraphs 93–95 and 108–118.

[18] *Fachvereinigung Mineralfaserindustrie, cit.*, paragraph 90. Implicit also in *Scheucher-Fleisch, cit.*, n. 12, paragraph 73, and *Bundesverband deutscher Banken, cit.*, n. 11, paragraphs 126 and 127.

[19] The same requirement applies in actions for failure to act (see, for a recent example, Case T-167/04, *Asklepios Kliniken GmbH v Commission* [2007] ECR II-2379, paragraphs 45–48). On these and other aspects of remedies to secure procedural guarantees of Article 108(2) see Jan Winter (1999) 'The rights of complainants in state aid cases: judicial review of Commission decisions adopted under Article 88 (ex 93) EC', *Common Market Law Review*, Vol. 36, n. 3, pp. 521–68, in particular pp. 532–45.

[20] *Cook, cit.*, n. 12, paragraph 23. This was restated in *Matra, cit.*, n. 12, paragraph 17, in *Commission v Sytraval*, (*cit.*, n. 11) paragraph 47 and consistently reiterated by the Court (recently cf. *Asklepios, cit.*, paragraph 47; Case T-254/05, *Fachvereinigung Mineralfaserindustrie eV Deutsche Gruppe der Eurima v Commission* [2007] ECR II-124, paragraph 32—hereinafter quoted as *Fachvereinigung Mineralfaserindustrie II*—*Scheucher-Fleisch, cit.*, paragraph 42, Case T-193/06, *Télévision française 1 SA (TF1) v Commission* [2010] nyr., paragraph 70).

therefore be recognized as having 'individual and direct concern' for the purposes of former Article 230(4) EC, a requirement that is maintained, in these cases, in Article 263 TFEU. As a result, a distinction is made between standing in actions in which the applicants react against the Commission's decision not to open the formal phase of the procedure, thereby infringing the procedural rights of persons concerned, and actions in which the applicants seek the annulment of the Commission's decision adopted on the basis of Article 108(3) on substantive grounds. In the first case, the applicants' *locus standi* depends on the demonstration that they are parties 'concerned' within the meaning of Article 108(2). In the second, they need to comply with the general requirements defined in the *Plaumann* case, i.e. they need to prove that they are individually concerned in the terms that have been determined by the Courts and, thereby, show evidence that their competitive position in the market has been substantially affected by the Commission's decision.[21, 22]

The concept of 'parties concerned' is, therefore, determinant for the whole legal regime stemming from Articles 108(2) and (3). The vicissitudes of this concept are presented below and, in particular, it will be shown how the *Cook* and *Matra* rule, despite subsequent clarification of its scope of application, has influenced the Courts' interpretation of this concept.

8.1.3 *The concept of 'parties concerned'*

Intermills is the landmark case in this matter. Here, the Court considered that the concept of 'parties concerned' refers to 'an indeterminate group of persons to whom notice must be given', which includes 'not only the

[21] Case 25/62, *Plaumann & Co v Commission* [1963] ECR 95; Case T-114/00, *Aktionsgemeinschaft Recht und Eigentum eV v Commission* [2002] ECR II-5121, paragraphs 45 and 46 (hereinafter *ARE*); Case C-78/03 P, *Commission v Aktionsgemeinschaft Recht und Eigentum eV* [2005] ECR I-10737, paragraphs 35, 37, 68–70. On this distinction regarding the conditions of standing, see, critically, Opinion of Advocate General Jacobs delivered on 24 February 2005 in Case C-78/03 P, *Commission v Aktionsgemeinschaft Recht und Eigentum eV* [2005] ECR I-10737, paragraphs 138–142, as well as Opinion of Advocate General Bot delivered on 6 March 2008 in Joined Cases C-75/05 P and C-80/05 P, *Germany v Kronofrance SA* and *Glunz AG, OSB Deutschland GmbH v Kronofrance SA* [2008] ECR I-6619, paragraphs 101–113.

[22] An additional norm grants standing to persons who have taken an active part in the procedure that led to the adoption of the rules applicable to the contested aid and whose position as a negotiator could be affected by the decision not to open the procedure of Article 108(2) (Case C-313/90,*CIRFS and Others v Commission* [1993] ECR I-1125, paragraphs 29 and 30) and also to persons who have taken an active part in the procedure for the adoption of a decision under Article 108(2) (Joined Cases 67/85, 68/85, and 70/85,*Van der Kooy and Others v Commission* [1988] ECR 219, paragraphs 19–25).

undertaking or undertakings receiving aid but equally the persons, undertakings or associations whose interests might be affected by the grant of the aid, *in particular* competing undertakings and trade associations'.[23] In this respect, the Court followed the Opinion of the Advocate General, who considered that 'parties concerned' can include 'the recipients of the aid in question... [,] undertakings which may be placed at a competitive disadvantage by such aid, not to mention customers, suppliers, employees and trade associations'.[24] This understanding, encompassing a potentially broad range of persons, is coherent with the practice of publishing a notice in the Official Journal to inform possible interested persons that a procedure has been initiated. As stressed by the Advocate General in the said opinion, this form of giving notice ensures the observance of the principle of equal treatment among parties concerned. As a result, and considering that Article 108(2) aims to ensure that 'all persons who may be concerned are notified and given an opportunity of putting forward their arguments', the Court overruled the applicant's claim according to which Article 108(2) requires individual notice to be given by a decision addressed to particular persons.[25]

Although one can say that this broad concept of parties concerned is, at least in its wording, undisputedly accepted in the case law,[26] it has been subject to restrictions as a result of the *Cook* and *Matra* rule. These judgments relied on *Intermills*,[27] and the Court felt the need to reconcile such a rule, which is based on a broad concept of persons concerned, with the requirement of individual and direct concern now enshrined in Article 263 (4) TFEU. As a result, on occasion, it ended up restricting the very concept of persons concerned. The main difficulties arose with regard to cases in which the applicant, as a person concerned within the meaning of Article 108(2) sought the annulment of the Commission's decisions that assessed general aid schemes. The Court not only considered that the *Cook* and *Matra* rule is inapplicable in these cases, but it also suggested that only

[23] Case 323/82, *SA Intermills v Commission* [1984] ECR 3809, paragraph 16. Emphasis added.

[24] Opinion of Advocate General Van Themaat, delivered on 11 July 1984 on Case 323/82, *SA Intermills v Commission* [1984] ECR 3834, at p. 3837.

[25] *Intermills*, *cit.*, n. 23, paragraph 17.

[26] Moreover, it was 'given expression' in the notion of 'interested parties' as defined in Article 1(h) of the procedural regulation, quoted above, note 4 (Case T 395/04, *Air One SpA v Commission* [2006] ECR II-1343, paragraph 36; *Asklepios*, *cit.*, n. 19, paragraph 49). For a recent application of this notion, see *TF1*, *cit.*, n. 4 paragraph 71.

[27] *Cook*, *cit.*, n. 12, paragraph 24; *Matra*, *cit.*, n. 12, paragraph 18.

undertakings in effective competition with the beneficiary of the aid can qualify as parties concerned within the meaning of Article 108(2).[28] The argument is the following: considering that the existence of competing undertakings presupposes an actual beneficiary of the aid, there cannot be undertakings which could invoke the procedural guarantees of Article 108 (2) before general aid schemes have been put into practice by the grant of individual aids.[29] This restriction of the concept of 'parties concerned' was confirmed in *Waterleiding*, where the Court clearly stated that '*in order to demonstrate its status as a party concerned within the meaning of [Article 108(2)] of the Treaty*, the applicant is required to establish that the aid . . . affects its competitive position on the market'.[30] But, this time, this restriction was based on a more thorough analysis of the interpretation of Article 108(2) enshrined in *Intermills*. In fact, the Court stated:

> Although the use by the Community judicature of the phrase 'in particular' might suggest that an undertaking which is not a direct competitor of the beneficiary of aid may have the status of a person concerned within the meaning of [Article 108 (2)], it must nevertheless be emphasized that, in Intermills v Commission, the applicant was the beneficiary of an individual aid measure declared incompatible with the common market, whilst in Cook v Commission, Matra v Commission and Sytraval and Brink's France v Commission the applicants were or represented competitors of the beneficiary of the individual State measure impugned. The action in Intermills v Commission was declared admissible on the ground that, in its capacity as beneficiary of the aid in question, the applicant was directly and individually concerned by the Commission's decision (at paragraph 5 of the judgment). In Cook v Commission, Matra v Commission, and Sytraval and Brink's France v Commission, the applicants, as direct competitors of the beneficiaries of the impugned State measure, clearly had the status of persons concerned within the meaning of [Article 108(2)] of the Treaty. . . .[31]

Therefore, the Court considered the circumstances in which the judgments mentioned were issued to be determinant for the interpretation of the definition given in *Intermills* and, concomitantly, for the scope of the

[28] Case T-398/94, *Kahn Scheppvaart BV v Commission* [1995] ECR I-2651, n. 12, paragraphs 48 and, especially, 49.

[29] *Idem*, paragraph 49.

[30] Case T-188/95, *Waterleiding Maatschappij NoordWest Brabant NV v Commission* [1998] ECR II-3713, paragraph 67, emphasis added (see also paragraph 62). As it had done in *Kahn* (paragraph 50), the Court considered that a different, more embracing, interpretation 'would be clearly incompatible with the interpretation of [Article 108(2)] given in the jurisprudence', quoting *Intermills*, *Cook*, *Matra* and *Kahn* (*Waterleiding*, *cit.*, paragraph 68).

[31] *Waterleiding*, *cit.*, paragraph 61.

Cook and *Matra* rule. Admittedly, the wording of Article 108(2) gives room to broader or narrower interpretations, since it is not possible to deduce from any of its written elements any further indication on what exactly is meant by 'parties concerned'. The reasoning of the Court is, however, feeble. First, guided by the need to restrict the *Cook* and *Matra* rule, it restricted the range of the procedural rule of Article 108(2), without duly interpreting it, in particular without considering the meaning or the rationale of this norm. Moreover, this interpretation encroaches upon the wording of the judgments in *Intermills*, *Cook*, and *Matra*, where no element is found that can support the restricted interpretation defended by the Court in *Kahn* and *Waterleiding*.[32] Contrary to the Court's argumentation, the rules formulated in these prior judgments transcend, in the terms used therein, the specificities of the cases under judgment. Finally, the restrictive meaning of 'parties concerned' does not follow from the fact that in the *Cook* and *Matra* cases the applicants 'clearly had the status of persons concerned': *per se*, this argument does not exclude that persons other than those directly and effectively affected can qualify as 'parties concerned', as is implicit in *Kahn* and explicitly stated in *Waterleiding*.[33]

In a word, as a result of the *Waterleiding* judgment the concept of 'parties concerned' would no longer refer to an indeterminate group of people whose interests might be affected by the granting of a given aid (*Intermills*), but to those whose competitive position is affected by such aid. In order to preserve the meaning of the requirement of 'individual concern' now transposed to Article 263(4) TFEU, in the interpretation consistently held by the Court, and possibly to avoid the gap between the recognition of a procedural right and the absence of a remedy, the Court restricted indirectly the scope of possibly affected people, in relation to the effect of Article 108(2), to those who have a restricted economic interest qualified by a given position in the market. While, in later cases, contrary to the *Waterleiding* reasoning, the Court sought to separate clearly the criterion to ascertain who are 'parties concerned' (Article 108(2)) from that underlying the determination of persons individually concerned (Article 263(4)), in effect, however, it often also ended up conflating both concepts. This was the case, for

[32] This restricted interpretation violates the wording of the precedent judgments ('notamment' and 'in particular' are adverbial forms that have an illustrative meaning, highlighting one object out of a number which deserves notice—see Le Robert Dictionnaire de la Langue Française, Vol. VI; The Oxford English Dictionary, Vol. VII).

[33] *Kahn*, *cit.*, n. 28, paragraph 50, and *Waterleiding*, *cit.*, n. 30, paragraph 64.

example, in *Hamburger Hafen- und Lagerhaus* where the Court held that 'it is settled case-law that parties concerned within the meaning of [Article 108 (2)] of the Treaty include... persons, undertakings or associations *whose interests might be affected* by the grant of the aid, in particular competing undertakings and trade associations'.[34] And it added: '[I]t is also settled case-law that, in order for its action to be admissible, the competitor of the recipient of the aid must demonstrate that its competitive position in the market is affected by the grant of the aid. *Where that is not the case, it does not have the status of a party concerned within the meaning of [Article 108(2)] of the Treaty*.'[35] Clearly, in these cases, the Court was not able to detach access to the administrative procedure from access to court, and defined the former in light of the latter.

Nevertheless, subsequent judgments corrected this. To begin with, the Court continued to rely on the *Intermills* formulation to determine the scope of parties concerned within the meaning of Article 108(2).[36] Although this is not *per se* meaningful, this was the basis of other rulings that countered the consequences of *Waterleiding*. Firstly, as mentioned above, in *ARE*, the Court of Justice clarified the distinction between, on the one hand, actions in which persons concerned within the meaning of Article 108(2) contest the refusal of the Commission to open the formal phase of the procedure, thereby claiming an infringement of their procedural rights, and, on the other hand, actions in which applicants seek the annulment of the Commission's decision on substantive grounds.[37] In doing so, it resolved the issue of standing, settling that only in the latter case do applicants need to demonstrate that their market position is substantially affected by the contested aid. It thus eased the distinction

[34] Case T-69/96, *Hamburger Hafen- und Lagerhaus and Others v Commission* [2001] ECR II-1037, paragraph 40 (quoting *Intermills*, *Cook*, *Matra*, and both *Sytraval* cases) emphasis added. Exactly the same statement is found in the judgment of the Court of First Instance in *ARE*, *cit.*, paragraph 51.

[35] *Idem*, paragraph 41 (quoting *Waterleiding*; emphasis added). It should be noted that this judgment refers to two different aids, one is a general aid scheme, the other not (see paragraphs 1–4 and 23).

[36] This was the case in *Thermenhotel*, where the Court considered that '*among the parties concerned referred to in [Article 108(2)]*, who are, as such, entitled to the procedural safeguards afforded in the course of the formal investigation procedure of aid projects under that provision, are undertakings *whose interests might be affected* by the grant of the disputed aid, *including* undertakings competing with the recipient of the aid' (*Thermenhotel*, *cit.*, n. 11, paragraph 70, emphasis added). Nevertheless, also in this case, the applicants were direct competitors of the beneficiary of the aid.

[37] See n. 21.

between parties concerned within the meaning of Article 108(2) and persons directly and individually concerned for purposes of what is now Article 263(4), since, in the former case, the condition of being a person concerned, in the *Intermills* formulation, whose interests might be affected is enough to ensure standing.[38] Secondly, in the *Air One* judgment, the Court not only maintained the *Intermills* formulation, but also expressly stated that 'the status of "party concerned" is not... restricted to undertakings that are substantially affected by the grant of aid'.[39] Thirdly, the Court of Justice, held in *3F v Commission* that a trade union may be considered a person concerned within the meaning of Article 108(2) if it shows that 'the aid is likely to have a real effect on its situation or that of the [persons] it represents'. The resilience of *Waterleiding* notwithstanding, in this case the Court implicitly admitted that demonstrating that the competitive position of a trade union in relation to others operating in the same market is hindered by the aid at issue is one possible way of showing the requisite legal standard.[40] Following the distinction settled in *ARE*, and on the assumption that the applicants in this case were seeking standing in order to secure their procedural rights under Article 108(2), the Court set aside the CFI judgment that had dismissed their action at first instance on the basis of lack of standing.[41]

[38] The stance adopted in *ARE* has been recently reiterated: cf. *Deutsche Post*, *cit.*, n. 11, paragraphs 42–44; Case C-487/06 P, *British Aggregates Association v Commission* [2008] ECR I-10505, paragraphs 28–30; *Scheucher-Fleisch*, *cit.*, n. 12, paragraphs 42 and 44; *TF1*, *cit.*, n. 4, paragraphs 70, 72, and 76. However, despite *ARE*, this clear distinction between persons concerned within the meaning of Article 108(2) and persons individually concerned for the purposes of standing still seems to be a difficult one to draw, at least in certain cases (this difficulty is revealed, for example, in Case C-319/07 P, *3F, formerly Specialarbejderforbundet i Danmark (SID) v Commission* [2009] ECR I-5963, paragraph 35). In cases where the applicant has challenged a state aid decision both on procedural and substantive grounds, the Courts have either applied the stronger test (*British Aggregates* [2008] *cit.*, paragraphs 35, 37) or sought to distinguish the procedural from the substantive grounds, applying different criteria in each case (*Deutsche Post*, *cit.*, n. 11, paragraphs 46–57; *Scheucher-Fleisch*, *cit.*, n. 12, paragraph 50).

[39] *Air One*, *cit.*, n. 26, paragraph 36.

[40] *3F v Commission*, *cit.*, n. 38, paragraphs 33 and 59. In particular, the Court of Justice held that 'excessively restrictive interpretation of the concept of "market" in connection with the question of the status of party concerned within the meaning of [Article 108(2) TFEU] of an organization such as a trade union' would counter the social policy objectives of the EU (paragraph 59).

[41] *3F v Commission*, *cit.*, n. 38, paragraph 36.

This overview of the Court's stance regarding the concept of 'parties concerned' reveals the stalemate in which the Court found itself[42] when dealing with the connection between granting access to an administrative procedure and ensuring *locus standi* to secure the resulting procedural guarantees, in the face of the requirements of what is now Article 263(4) TFEU. Confronted with the *Cook* and *Matra* rule, the Court followed one of three possible paths on different occasions. In one approach, it secured that rule, following a principled position according to which procedural rights should be covered by remedies. However, this implied restricting the concept of 'parties concerned' to those who have a competitive position affected by the decision at issue, in order to contain standing within the limits of Article 263(4) (*Waterleiding*), a result that was only tempered in recent judgments (in particular, in *3F*). Alternatively, the Court maintained a broad concept of 'parties concerned', but, as a consequence, abandoned the rule formulated in the *Cook* and *Matra* judgments, or, at least, failed to avoid a contradiction with its terms (*Hamburger Hafen- und Lagerhaus*). Finally, it settled at drawing a distinction between the standing requirements of persons concerned depending on the type of pleas they presented with regard to a Commission's decision not to open the formal procedure of Article 108(2) (*ARE*). This gives rise to two different types of action, even if the goal pursued by the applicant is ultimately the same in both cases.[43]

More important for our purposes is the fact that, as noted above, in the cases in which the Courts' reasoning regarding the interplay between Article 108(2) and 263(4) impacted upon the concept of parties concerned, the Courts did not duly consider the meaning of this procedural norm in light of the substantive legal regime that it serves and the type of material situations that it regulates.[44] Nevertheless, the clarification of the meaning of this concept can only be consistently defined on the basis of the function of this participatory procedure, assessed in light of the corresponding substantive regime. Indeed, the range of persons encompassed by Article 108(2) is broader or more restricted according to the nature of this procedural step and the due consideration of the material situations that it

[42] The cases analysed are all from the Court of First Instance (now General Court), except *Intermills*, *Cook*, and *Matra*, where these difficulties do not arise, and naturally, the *ARE* and the *3F*, which were judgments issued on appeal.

[43] In this regard, see Opinion of Advocate General Kokkot, delivered on 1 February 2007, Case C-260/05 P, *Sniace SA v Commission* [2007] ECR I-5, paragraphs 15–17, and Opinion of Advocate General Bot, delivered in *Germany v Kronofrance*, *cit.*, n. 21, paragraph 106.

[44] As is shown below, *3F* is an exception.

encompasses. The surrounding administrative procedural aspects—guarantees, rules, or practices—should also follow from this principled characterization. Reducing the concept of parties concerned to those holding a 'competitive position' hindered by a Commission decision on state aid should only be a conclusion of the interpretation of Article 108(2) and not an assertion predetermined by the requirements of Article 263(4). This analysis is undertaken in the next sub-section, on the basis of the Courts' interpretation of this norm.

8.1.4 *The rationale of participation under Article 108(2) TFEU*

Parties concerned as information sources

The clear distinction between the two phases of the administrative procedure delineated in Article 108(2) and (3), according to which the first phase is merely intended to allow the Commission to form a *prima facie* opinion on the measure at issue and the second is destined to provide the Commission with all the information available before adopting a decision, indicates, in principle, that the intervention of parties concerned is set to be a mere additional vehicle for this information.[45] This argument is reinforced by the fact that, whenever the Commission is faced with 'serious difficulties' in assessing the compatibility of a given aid with the internal market, it is obliged to open a formal procedure where the respective interested parties intervene. Accordingly, in principle, any person affected by a Commission decision adopted on the basis of Article 108 who may validly contribute to clarifying such difficulties may be considered to be a person concerned.

The position according to which the aim of the notice and comment of Article 108(2) is to obtain from the interested parties all the information needed to ground the Commission's decision dates back to the 1970s. In an infringement action over state aid granted by the German government to the mining industry and mining regions, the Court considered that the communication of Article 108(2) has the function of acquiring information: its 'sole aim . . . is to obtain from persons concerned all information required for the guidance of the Commission with regard to its future action'.[46] Accordingly, it denied that this communication could affect the rights of the individuals concerned by the aid at issue. Specifically, the Court refuted the Commission's contention that, after becoming aware of the procedure,

45 On the distinction between these two phases, see above the introduction to this chapter.

46 Case 70/72, *Commission v Germany* [1973] ECR 813, paragraph 19.

the parties concerned could no longer rely on the legality of the legal provisions under which the aid was being granted.

In line with this view, the Court ruled in the *British Airways* judgment that the Commission may 'validly prefer to use other sources of information and thereby reduce the significance of participation of interested parties'.[47] Hence, it may opt to limit the content of this notice to the aspects on which doubts still remain after the information has been gathered during the first phase of the administrative procedure (Article 108(3)).[48] Interestingly, however, it also held that in motivating its final decision the Commission 'must address all the complaints which parties directly and individually concerned by that decision have made either on their own initiative or as a result of information supplied by the Commission'.[49] In any case, as results from the Court's reasoning, the care taken in defining sufficiently 'dense' requirements of the duty to motivate the decision is more a means to frame the Commission's discretion and allow for a sufficient degree of control than to ensure that procedural guarantees accorded to interested parties are complied with.[50]

A similar stance was followed in *Ufex*.[51] Yet, the Court introduced here a slightly different perspective of analysis which was pursued in subsequent cases.[52] As in the *British Airways* case, it held that 'the parties concerned have [under Article 108 (2)] only the right to be involved in the administrative

[47] Joined Cases T-371/94 and T-394/94, *British Airways and Others v Commission* [1998] ECR II-2405, paragraph 64.

[48] *Idem*, paragraphs 59–62.

[49] *Idem*, paragraph 64. A similar stance had been adopted by the Court of First Instance in *Sytraval* (the Commission is 'obliged to give a reasoned answer to each of the objections raised in the complaint', Case T-95/94, *Chambre Syndicale Nationale des Entreprises de Transport de Fonds et Valeurs and Brink's France SARL v Commission* [1995] ECR II-2651, paragraph 62). The ECJ upheld the CFI in this point, although it drafted the Commission's duty using a less tight formulation: 'the Commission must at least... provide the complainant with an adequate explanation of the reasons for which the facts and points put forward in the complaint have failed to demonstrate the existence of State aid' (*Commission v Sytraval, cit.*, n. 11, paragraph 64).

[50] More extensively, on the interplay between participation rights and the duty to give reasons, see above Chapter 5, Sub-section 5.4.2.

[51] Case T-613/97, *Union française de l'express (Ufex) and Others v Commission* [2000] ECR II-4055, paragraphs 89–90.

[52] Joined Cases C-74/00 P and C-75/00 P, *Falck SpA and Acciaierie di Bolzano SpA v Commission* [2002] ECR I-7869, paragraphs 79–83; Joined Cases T-228/99 and T-233/99, *Westdeutsche Landesbank Girozentrale and Land Nordrhein-Westfalen v Commission* [2003] ECR II-435, paragraphs 121–132; Case T-198/01, *Technische Glaswerke Ilmenau GmbH v Commission* [2004] ECR II-2717, paragraphs 191–198; Case T-156/04, *Électricité de France (EDF) v European Commission* [2009] ECR II-4503, paragraph 102.

procedure to the extent appropriate in light of the circumstances of the case'.[53] Consequently, they are 'far from enjoying the same rights to a fair hearing as those which individuals against whom a procedure has been instituted are recognized as having'.[54] The Court hence conceived the procedure of Article 108(2) as an *inter partes* procedure involving primarily the Member State concerned and the Commission (probably drawing upon the conception introduced in the judgment on the *Sytraval* appeal, according to which decisions assessing the compatibility of an aid with the common market are always addressed to the Member State concerned).[55] Therefore, it rejected any similarities between the right to be heard as a principle of law established by the Courts' case law and the procedural position that these 'parties concerned' enjoy under Article 108(2).[56] This reasoning allowed the Court to dismiss the applicants' claim that the refusal of the Commission to disclose the documents supporting the notice published in the Official Journal hindered their right to participate in the procedure. Although the Court acknowledged the link between the right to be heard and the right to access the file,[57] this was simply not considered relevant in relation to the applicants, given that they have a different procedural status.[58] As stated in *Technische Glaswerke*, responding to a different but similar claim, 'since the interested parties other than the Member State concerned *cannot rely on a right to participate in an adversarial procedure with the Commission*', access to the non-confidential part of the file on the administrative procedure can be refused

[53] *Ufex*, *cit.*, n. 51, paragraph 89.

[54] *Idem, ibidem*. 'Right to a fair hearing' is the translation of the French expression 'droits de la défense'.

[55] *Idem*, paragraph 86.

[56] In this respect, note the Court's assertive statement in *Technische Glaswerke*: 'it should be pointed out that the Community Court cannot, on the basis of general legal principles relied on by the applicant, such as those of the right to due process, the right to be heard, sound administration or equal treatment, extend the procedural rights which the Treaty and secondary legislation confer on interested parties in procedures for reviewing State aid' (*Technische Glaswerke*, quoted above, paragraph 194). Similarly, Joined Cases T-227/01 to T-229/01, T-265/01, T-266/01, and T-270/01, *Territorio Histórico de Álava—Diputación Foral de Álava and Comunidad autónoma del País Vasco—Gobierno Vasco and Others v Commission* [2009] nyr., paragraph 269, and Case T-62/08, *ThyssenKrupp Acciai Speciali Terni SpA v Commission* [2010] nyr., paragraphs 163 and 167.

[57] *Ufex*, *cit.*, n. 51, paragraph 85. On the interplay between participation rights and access to information, see above Chapter 4, Sub-section 5.4.1.

[58] Not even the quality of the applicant as a trade association competing with the beneficiary of the aid and its competitive position affected as a result of the granting of the aid seem to have been considered by the Court as a possible basis to grant it a stronger procedural position.

and the Commission is under no obligation to send to the interested party the comments or replies to the Commission's questions submitted by their competitor.[59]

In *Technische Glaswerke*, moreover, the Court attached a further consequence to this conception of the interested parties' procedural role. It held that, in order to comply with the duty to give reasons, 'the Commission is not obliged to adopt a position on all the arguments relied on by the parties concerned'; 'it is sufficient if it sets out the facts and the legal considerations having decisive importance in the context of the decision'. Further, it underlined that the parties concerned by a procedure on state aid measures initiated against a Member State 'cannot themselves seek to debate the issues with the Commission in the same way as [the latter] may'.[60] Accordingly, it defended that the duty to state reasons for the rejection of arguments raised during the procedure is not as exhaustive vis-à-vis parties concerned as it must be with regard to the Member State addressee of the decision.[61] Although the Court here clearly departed from its position in *British Airways* regarding the giving of reasons, it effectively did not leave parties concerned 'uncovered' from any guarantee in respect to the giving of reasons. In fact, the Court analysed the reasoning of the Commission that grounded its decision and asserted that it 'enabled the applicant, as a party concerned, to understand why its argument had been rejected'.[62]

While access to file is limited, the Commission being lawfully able to refuse access to the file at issue, the statement of reasons requirement seems at least to entail consideration of the arguments put forward by those parties concerned. In contrast to the latter rule, the limits to access the file can effectively constrain the procedural role of parties concerned, in cases where such limits impede them from adequately presenting their point of view on the facts and arguments assembled during the procedure that precedes the Commission's decision. If this consequence is coherent with the conception of parties concerned as information providers, it can be argued that even from this perspective this position on access to file can

[59] *Technische Glaswerke*, *cit.*, n. 52, paragraph 197, emphasis added. Similarly, Joined Cases T-427/04 and T-17/05, *French Republic and France Télécom SA v Commission* [2009] ECR II-4315, paragraph 149.

[60] *Idem*, paragraphs 60 and 61.

[61] *Idem*, paragraph 64. This was confirmed by the ECJ on appeal (Case C-404/04 P, *Technische Glaswerke Ilmenau GmbH v Commission* [2007] ECR I-1, paragraph 31).

[62] *Idem*, paragraph 67. Equally confirmed on appeal (judgment quoted in the note above, paragraph 35).

harm the utility of the intervention of these persons. Possibly aware of this effect, the Court pointed out in *Kuwait* that 'the Commission is obliged *duly* to place the interested parties in a position to put forward their comments in the course of a formal investigation procedure on state aid'.[63]

In short, two combined factors decide the procedural position and, hence, the procedural guarantees that are recognized to parties concerned when intervening in a procedure under Article 108(2): the perspective according to which they are mere information providers and the conception of the procedure as an *inter partes* adversarial procedure involving the Commission and the Member State concerned.[64] The consequently limited nature of the right of parties concerned to participate in the administrative procedure also limits the guarantees that accompany this right, although the Court is not always consistent in defining the scope of these guarantees.

'An opportunity to make their views known': a right of defence?

At the beginning of the 1980s, in another case involving a dispute between Germany and the Commission, the Court seemed to hint at a different view on the meaning of the Commission's duty to give notice to parties concerned to submit their comments. While analysing the lawfulness of the Commission's procedural conduct in the case at issue, the Court considered that the notice of Article 108(2) 'guarantees the other Member State and the sectors concerned an opportunity to make their views known *and* allows the Commission to be fully informed of all the facts of the case before taking its decision'.[65] Accordingly, other informal means of consultation with the Member States do not 'offer those concerned or the Commission itself the same guarantees and advantages which the formal consultations provided for in [Article 108(2)] offer'.[66] This wording could point in a direction different from the one presented above. However, the possible violation of the procedural rights granted by Article 108(2) was not the principal matter in question. Following the pleas put forward by the applicant, this matter was mentioned as one aspect of the whole procedural

[63] *Kuwait, cit.* (n. 2) paragraph 83, emphasis added. See also Case T-291/06, *Operator ARP sp. z o. o. v Commission* [2009] ECR II-2275, paragraph 38, and *France Télécom, cit.*, n. 59, paragraph 148.

[64] Both factors have been recently reiterated by the Court: e.g. *Operator, cit.*, paragraphs 35 and 36; *France Télécom, cit.*, n. 59, paragraphs 146 and 147; *EDF, cit.*, n. 52, paragraphs 102 and 103, *ThyssenKrupp, cit.*, paragraph 163. They are also restated in the Commission's Code of best practice for the conduct of state aid control procedures (OJ C 136/13, 16.6.2009), point 34.

[65] *Germany v Commission* (*cit.*, n. 11) paragraph 13, emphasis added.

[66] *Idem*, paragraph 18.

regime of Article 108(2) and (3), not being further developed. A similar stance was taken up a few months later in *Intermills*, where the Court held that the 'sole purpose [of the notice of Article 108(2)] is to oblige the Commission to take steps to ensure that all persons who may be concerned are notified and given an opportunity of putting forward their arguments'.[67]

This reasoning could ground a conception of the procedural requirement of Article 108(2) as being also correlated with a dignitarian rationale and a way of ensuring procedural defence. A reference in another judgment issued in that same year could be seen as a confirmation of this position: 'the interests of any individuals concerned are protected by [Article 108(2)], which requires the Commission, when it initiates the procedure provided for in that paragraph, to give notice to the interested parties to submit their comments'.[68] Nevertheless, the judgment in *Germany v Commission* was not sufficiently assertive in this sense and gave room to different interpretations. It was quoted in future judgments, without notice having been taken of the possibility of giving a different meaning to the intervention of parties concerned in state aid procedures.[69]

Nor did the 'revolutionary' CFI judgment on the *Sytraval* case contribute to a major shift in this regard. The Court sought to extend the scope of the duty to hear concerned parties so as to encompass the preliminary phase of the administrative procedure (Article 108(3)), grounding this claim on the Commission's duty of diligence and impartiality. It deemed that compliance with this duty implied 'eliciting' the complainant's views 'as may be necessary', which could require an 'exchange of views and arguments' with the latter.[70] However, the Court based its reasoning on the view that the decision under judgment was directed at the complainant, a perspective that was reversed by the ECJ on appeal,[71] and that impedes an analysis of this judgment from the perspective of third parties' participation rights and of the meaning of their intervention.

[67] *Intermills*, *cit.* (n. 23) paragraph 17.

[68] Joined Cases 91/83 and 127/83, *Heineken Brouwerijen BV v Inspecteur der Vennootschapsbelasting, Amsterdam and Utrecht* [1984] ECR 3435, paragraph 14.

[69] See, for example, *British Airways*, *cit.*, n. 47, paragraph 58; also, *Falck*, *cit.*, n. 52, paragraph 80; Case T-109/01, *Fleuren Compost BV v Commission* [2004] ECR II-127, paragraph 41; *EDF*, *cit.*, n. 52, paragraph 106 (this adopts a similar wording to *Germany v Commission*, *cit.*, n. 46, but does not afford the applicant—the beneficiary of the aid—any privileged procedural position in comparison to other persons concerned); *ThyssenKrupp*, *cit.*, n. 56, paragraph 174.

[70] *Sytraval v Commission cit.*, n. 49, paragraph 78. The argument was rejected by the ECJ on appeal (*Commission v Sytraval*, *cit.*, n. 11, paragraphs 58 and 59).

[71] *Sytraval v Commission*, *cit.*, n. 49, paragraph 51; *Commission v Sytraval*, *cit.*, n. 11, paragraph 45.

More recently, *Le Levant* confirmed this second interpretation of Article 108(2). At issue here was a decision of the Commission declaring that an aid granted by the French government to the construction of a cruise vessel was incompatible with the common market. Accordingly, the decision also determined the recovery of the unlawful aid.[72] The investors had not been mentioned in the notice that opened the procedure pursuant to Article 108(2) and the terms of that notice made it seem that they were not targeted by the procedure.[73] They were, however, mentioned in the Commission's final decision as beneficiaries from whom the French government should recover the unlawful aid.[74] In the face of these facts, the Court considered that the absence of any reference to the beneficiaries in the decision to open the procedure led to a procedural failure. In fact, in cases of unlawful aid, the identification of its beneficiaries constitutes one of the elements of fact that 'must, under Article 6(1) of Regulation No. 659/1999, be contained in the decision to open the procedure if that is possible at that stage . . .'.[75] The possible outcome of the procedure vis-à-vis the beneficiaries according to Article 14 of the abovementioned regulation seems to have been decisive in this respect: in the case of a decision declaring the aid incompatible with the common market, the Member State concerned is required to recover the aid from its beneficiaries.[76] Another crucial factor is the role that the beneficiaries of the aid have in the material administrative relationship underlying the procedure: it is on the basis of the identification of the beneficiaries of the aid that the Commission is able to adopt the recovery decision.[77] Hence, the Court ruled that the absence of reference to the beneficiaries, either in the notice that opens the procedure or at a later stage, enabling them to submit their comments prior to the adoption of the Commission's final decision, constitutes a violation of the right to be heard that, as a matter of principle, should be granted to 'any person against whom an adverse decision may be taken'.[78] In addition, the Court stated that, in the absence of such reference, '*that type of interested party cannot be regarded as having been duly called on to submit his comments*, because he may legitimately believe that such comments are not necessary, since he is not named as the beneficiary of the aid to be recovered'.[79]

[72] Case T-34/02, *EURL Le Levant 001 v Commission* [2006] ECR II-267, paragraphs 27 and 32.

[73] *Idem*, paragraph 88. [74] *Idem*, paragraph 32. [75] *Idem*, paragraph 82.

[76] *Idem*, paragraphs 80 to 84. [77] *Idem*, paragraph 82.

[78] *Idem*, paragraph 97.

[79] *Idem*, paragraph 83. Emphasis added. In line with this reasoning, and answering a similar claim to the one submitted by Le Levant, in another case the CFI examined whether the

The judgment is not necessarily in contradiction with the position according to which parties concerned within the meaning of Article 108(2) are called to participate in the procedure as information providers.[80] The change introduced by this judgment lies in the fact that the Court considered that, among those interested parties, the substantive position of some of them is differentiated. This ruling singles out from the circle of potential parties concerned the beneficiaries of the aid under judgment that were identified by the Commission. A similar consequence stems from the *Ferriere Nord* ruling. While confirming the *Ufex* reasoning according to which participation rights of persons concerned are different from the right to be heard,[81] both Courts considered that the right of these persons to be associated with the procedure 'to the extent appropriate in light of the circumstances of the case' requires a new consultation when the Commission wishes to base its decision on new principles that could alter the criteria for the assessment of the aid.[82] This departs, at least in part, from the consideration of interested parties as mere information providers. In fact, the Commission sought, unsuccessfully, to contest this reasoning on appeal, alleging precisely that the rationale of the participation of persons concerned within the meaning of Article 108(2) does not contend with purposes of defence.[83]

Commission's decision pursuant to the former Article 88(2) EC enabled the applicant to understand that they might have been required to repay the grant received (*Operator*, *cit.*, n. 63, paragraphs 38 to 42). However, the Court also considered that 'the review stage under [Article 108(2) TFEU] is designed to enable the Commission to be fully informed of all the facts of the case' (paragraph 36), while in another judgment issued on the same day by the same Chamber, the Court held that 'the sole purpose of the procedure provided for in [Article 108(2) TFEU] is to oblige the Commission to take steps to ensure that all persons who may be concerned are notified and given an opportunity of putting forward their arguments' (Joined Cases T-81/07, T-82/07, and T-83/07, *Jan Rudolf Maas and Others v Commission* [2009] ECR II-2411, paragraph 177). The Court, therefore, seems to indicate that there is no contraction between the two functions of participation of persons concerned.

[80] See note above and also *Deutsche Post*, *cit.*, n. 11, paragraph 87.

[81] Case T-176/01, *Ferriere Nord SpA v Commission* [2004] ECR II-3931, paragraph 74.

[82] *Ferriere Nord v Commission*, *cit.*, paragraphs 75 and 81; C 49/05 P, *Commission v Ferriere Nord SpA*, [2008] ECR I-68, paragraph 74. See, however, *EDF*, where the Court held that, even if the Commission ends up making a substantive analysis of the state aid different from the one provisionally communicated in the decision to initiate the formal procedure, this does not hinder the procedural rights of the only beneficiary of the aid as a party concerned (*EDF*, *cit.*, n. 52, paragraphs 110–114).

[83] *Commission v Ferriere Nord*, *cit.*, paragraphs 58–61.

In one point, though, this strand of case law does deviate from the previous case law: the state aid procedures, even if involving primarily the Commission and the Member State concerned, are not exclusively *inter partes* procedures. Or, at least, even if conceived as such, the legal position of some of the so-called third parties may distinguish them from other potentially interested persons and they should, therefore, be granted a qualified procedural position. This had been recognized previously by the Court with regard to rules relating to undertakings (now Article 106 TFEU) but had been thus far denied in state aid cases.[84] An attempt to draw a parallel between the circumstances of this case and the position of the beneficiaries of state aid had already been made by applicants in previous state aid cases, not meeting with much success. Sticking to the formal structure of the administrative procedure, the Court held that beneficiaries of state aid are to be regarded as any other concerned party.[85] In *Le Levant*, however, the Court was clear: 'the Commission cannot entrench itself behind a formalist interpretation of its state aid obligations'.[86]

To conclude, it results from the above that, even if the main aim of the intervention of concerned parties is to gather all the information needed to base a substantiated decision, some persons may also intervene in order to defend a qualified legal position based on a particular link that they have to the material situation being decided upon. As shown by the *Le Levant* and *Ferriere Nord* cases, their subjective position on the underlying material situation is legally protected, at least to a certain extent. Consequently, it should be possible to distinguish between different types of persons concerned and different procedural statuses. This is, however, a point that is not wholly accepted by the Courts, as is shown below.

[84] Joined Cases C-48/90 and C-66/90, *Netherlands v Commission* [1992] ECR I-565, paragraphs 50 and 51. Here, the Court considered that undertakings that are the direct beneficiaries of a State measure, being expressly named by the pertinent law and directly affected by the challenged decision and the economic consequences thereof, have the right to be heard in the administrative procedure that leads up to a decision addressed to the Member State under what is now Article 206(3).

[85] That was the case in *Westdeutsche Landesbank*, *cit.*, n. 52, paragraphs 108 and 122.

[86] *Le Levant*, *cit.*, n. 72, paragraph 96. It should be noted that, after *Le Levant*, the Court continued to stress the bilateral structure of the state aid procedure as involving primarily the Commission and the Member State concerned (see *Operator*, *cit.*, n. 63, paragraph 35; Joined Cases T-309/04, T-317/04, T-329/04, and T-336/04, *TV 2/Danmark A/S and Others v Commission* [2008] ECR II-2935, paragraph 137). This is particularly clear in *EDF*, where the Court upheld the bilateral structure of the procedure and was not sensitive to the arguments of the applicant—the beneficiary of the aid—that highlighted its distinctive circumstances in the procedure of state aid control (*EDF*, *cit.*, n. 52, paragraphs 88, 90, 93, 96, 97, 104, 110, and 114).

8.2 Participation Rights, Rationales, and 'Parties Concerned' Reconstructed

8.2.1 *The state of the art*

The case law of the Courts regarding the rights of procedural intervention enshrined in Article 108(2) allows us to distinguish two different layers of participation rights. Undisputedly, the Courts separate the right to be heard from other participation rights, in this case, those enshrined in Article 108(2). The former, as has been analysed elsewhere in this book, is granted to persons against whom an adverse decision may be taken and essentially consists of giving them the opportunity to effectively make their views known in respect of the facts held against them by a public entity. The latter, in the case of Article 108(2), consists of the right to be associated to the decisional procedure 'to the extent appropriate in light of the circumstances of the case'. Consequences in terms of procedural guarantees follow from this distinction: the right of access to the file and a statement of reasons that takes into consideration the arguments raised are denser with regard to adversely affected persons to whom the decision is addressed. In state aid cases, this position is occupied by the Member State concerned. Accordingly, the Commission cannot, for example, use facts or documents to base its decision without previously giving the Member State the opportunity to express its views on them,[87] while in principle this is not the case regarding other interested persons. In addition, the comments gathered by the Commission are communicated to the Member State concerned, who may reply to those comments,[88] but the same opportunity is not given to third parties that have intervened on the basis of Article 108(2).

This distinction essentially stems from the assumption that these procedural rights of intervention have different rationales in the two cases. As was examined in Chapter 4, despite some oscillations, the Courts have fundamentally underpinned the right to be heard in individual procedures to the protection of the dignity of the person and to the function of defence attached to the procedural intervention.[89] As a consequence of the characterization of

[87] *Belgium v Commission*, *cit.*, n. 2, paragraph 30.
[88] Article 6(2) of the procedural regulation, *cit.*, n. 4.
[89] See above, Chapter 4, Section 4.2.

the procedural rights of Article 108(2), as well as of their very formulation, these rights are essentially perceived as a means of ensuring a correct discharge of the Commission's functions in the appreciation of the compatibility of an aid with the internal market rules. This is confirmed by the role that the procedural regulation attributes to persons concerned: only from this perspective is it possible to understand that one of the rights of interested parties is to 'inform the Commission of any alleged unlawful aid and any alleged misuse of aid'.[90] While this assumption on the different rationales of rights of procedural intervention leads to a broad concept of persons concerned—embracing all those who may have a valid contribution to the procedure—it also conditions their procedural capacity, in particular the procedural guarantees that are granted to these persons.

This assumption is very likely determined by the bilateral scheme that has underlain the recognition of the right to be heard in the Courts' case law. In fact, the right to be heard has been understood as the procedural consequence of a bilateral administrative relationship that is established between the author and the addressee of an individual decision, as a result of the latter. Where the right to be heard has been recognized to persons other than the addressee of a decision, these are deemed to be in a position substantially analogous to that of the addressee. Therefore, the bilateral construction of the procedure that frames the right to be heard is maintained, since it is still the recognition that another person may be targeted by the procedure in a similar way to the addressee of the decision that grounds their right to be heard. For example, in *Lisrestal*, also a state aid case, the Court took into account the effective links established by such a decision and admitted that the adverse effects that justify the right to be heard can be produced in the legal sphere of a person who is not the addressee of the act.[91] The fact that this person was consequently granted a right to be heard in parallel terms to the addressee of the decision did not

[90] Article 20(2) of the procedural regulation (*cit.*, n. 4). The other rights enshrined in Article 20 are the following: the right to submit comments, concretizing current Article 108(2) and adding that those who have submitted comments as well as the aid beneficiaries are sent a copy of the Commission's decision (Article 20(1)); when informing the Commission of misconducts, private parties have the right to be informed of the Commission's appreciation and of the result of their complaint (Article 20(2)); and the right to obtain a copy of the Commission's decision regarding the preliminary examination of a State aid notification, of the decision closing the formal investigation procedure, of the request for information (information injunction) addressed to the Member State concerned in procedures regarding unlawful aid, and of the injunction to suspend or provisionally recover aid (Article 20(3)).

[91] This case is analysed above Chapter 4, Section 4.2.2.

contradict the bilateral scheme nor could it ground the extension of the personal scope of the right to be heard. *Le Levant* and *Ferriere Nord*, to a certain extent, follow from this same conception: like the applicants in *Lisrestal*, Le Levant and Ferriere Nord were the beneficiaries of the contested state aid and therefore were directly affected by a decision to reduce this aid or declare it incompatible with the internal market. However, contrary to *Lisrestal*, where the Commission had decided to reduce the aid previously accorded due to misuse, the Commission's decisions in *Le Levant* and *Ferriere Nord* were adopted on the basis of Article 108(2) TFEU and the corresponding provisions of the procedural regulation. As such, the rights of procedural intervention of these persons fell necessarily within the scope of the procedural rights enshrined in this Treaty article. Given the bilateral scheme that in EU law underlies the recognition of the right to be heard, in principle the procedural rights of persons concerned within the meaning of Article 108(2) could not be assimilated to this right. Nevertheless, this was exactly what the Court did in *Le Levant*.[92]

One of the significant aspects of the *Le Levant* judgment was the Court's assertion that the Commission should not cling to a formalist interpretation of its state aid obligations.[93] This suggests that the procedural protection of the persons involved in the material situation being decided should mirror the effects that the final decision may have in the legal sphere of the persons concerned. In other words, the intervention of parties concerned in the administrative procedure should be linked to the legal position occupied by parties concerned in the material situation that is being decided upon. However, this implies distinguishing between different types of persons concerned, something that, despite the *Le Levant* judgment, the Court continues to deny. In fact, in *Scott*, the Court considered that:

> ...the procedure for review of State aid accords no special role to the recipient of State aid as compared with all interested parties. It is clear, moreover, that the procedure for reviewing State aid is not a procedure initiated 'against' the recipient

[92] *Le Levant*, *cit.*, n. 72, paragraph 97.

[93] There are enough examples of cases in which the Court did exactly the opposite: see, for example, *Télévision française 1* (*cit.*, n. 4), where Court clung to the strict bilateral scheme that underlies the case law on the right to be heard. The fact that a decision was capable of affecting the interests of a so-called third party was not relevant for the recognition of participation rights in the absence of a written provision endowing such rights (paragraphs 79–81, 89, and 99–104).

of aid giving rise to rights on which it could rely which are as extensive as rights of defence as such....[94]

In the same judgment the Court stressed the different nature of the procedural rights of persons concerned, stressing that where persons concerned (in this case, the recipient of the aid) are granted 'certain procedural rights', these 'are designed to enable [them] to provide information to the Commission and to put forward its arguments'.[95] The Court therefore denied any continuity between the right to be heard and other procedural rights of participation. Nevertheless, the judgment issued in *Scott* is illustrative of the difficulties that a clear-cut distinction between these different entitlements poses. In fact, once again the Court stressed that 'the Commission cannot shelter itself behind a formalist interpretation of its state aid obligations'. In particular:

> Even though the procedure for reviewing state aid is a procedure initiated against the Member State responsible..., the Commission cannot ignore the fact that a potential order for recovery could have significant financial consequences for the recipient of aid.[96]

Specifically, the Court resorted to the duty of careful and impartial examination to reinforce the procedural position of the person concerned: it upheld the applicant's claim, concluding that 'the Commission might be obliged, in certain circumstances, to take into account the observations of the recipient of aid after the expiry of the time laid down by the decision to open the procedure'.[97]

It follows that, beyond the distinction between the right to be heard, on the one hand, and participation rights of persons concerned, on the other—which essentially stems from the bilateral scheme that underlines the right to be heard—the Courts do not formally admit a further distinction

[94] Case T 366/00, *Scott SA v Commission* [2007] ECR II-797, paragraph 54. This judgment was set aside on appeal in Case C-290/07 P, *Commission v Scott* [2010] on the basis of the CFI's review of the Commission's duty to conduct a diligent and impartial examination in determining the amount of state aid in question. The procedural rights of persons concerned were not an issue and the point quoted was not rebutted.

[95] *Idem, ibidem*. This judgment follows a European Court of Justice judgment of 2005, pertaining to the same Commission decision, in which the Court had again stressed the bilateral nature of the procedure of Article 108(2) (Case C-276/03 P, *Scott SA v Commission* [2005] ECR I-8437, paragraphs 33 and 34).

[96] *Scott v Commission* [2005], *cit.*, n. 94, paragraphs 58 and 59.

[97] *Scott v Commission* [2007], *cit.*, n. 94, paragraph 56.

between different persons interested in the outcome of the procedure on the basis of their legal positions in the material situation under appreciation. Nonetheless, in certain circumstances, this last aspect is considered a relevant factor to determine the procedural status of these persons. Still, the Courts do not draw from it any conclusions regarding the conception of participation rights.

8.2.2 *Reconstruction: premises*

It was argued above that the definition of persons concerned within the meaning of Article 108(2) can only be consistently drawn in light of the substantive legal regime that it serves, considering the material situations that it regulates. While the participatory procedure serves the purpose of assisting the Commission in its assessment regarding the compatibility of the aid with the internal market, it cannot be excluded that certain persons who have a differentiated legal position in the material situation being regulated seize this opportunity to defend their position in the procedure. This is an effect that should be legally recognized. This acceptance, however, requires that they are granted procedural guarantees that effectively enable them to put forward their views. This is equivalent to acknowledging continuity between their participation rights and the addressee's right to be heard. As results from the above, this effect has been refused by the Court essentially on the basis of a bilateral characterization of the procedure of Article 108(2), involving only the Commission and the Member State. Nevertheless, the right of persons concerned to be associated with the procedure 'to the extent appropriate in the light of the circumstances of the case' should require that, where appropriate, some are recognized as having a different procedural status. This necessarily implies a different conception of this procedure.

The design and ensuing conception of the procedure for the review of state aid should reflect the functions it fulfils, that is, it should be conceived in light of the substantive legal regime that it serves, disregarding any preconceptions that essentially derive from the Courts' construction of the right to be heard. In this respect, it should be recalled, resorting to the Court's words, that the procedure of Article 108(2) was designed in view of the 'special problems created by state aid with regard to competition in the common market'.[98] The Commission's review of state aid limits the

[98] See above, Sub-section 8.1.2.

Member States' capacity to award benefits to support specific companies or sectors, to the extent that they may hinder trade between Member States. Hence, by the effect of a Commission decision that deems an aid to be incompatible with the internal market, the Member State concerned will no longer be able to pursue an action that it had considered to be of public interest, or, at least, such action will be subject to certain conditions. The specificity of state aid control lies precisely here, in the political sensitiveness of the EU intervention in these matters: the object of the Commission's decisions pursuant to Article 108(2) are political economy measures that Member States have adopted or wish to adopt. This stems from Article 107, which defines the exceptions to the principled prohibition of state aid. Potentially, not only persons whose competitive position is affected by a Commission's decision that, in itself is directed at safeguarding or restoring the 'natural' conditions of competition, are concerned by such a decision, even if, admittedly, these can have a particularly protected position in the regime of state aid.

In fact, going beyond a formalist interpretation of the Commission's state aid obligations, as the Court has required, implies paying heed to the varied range of interests involved in these procedures. This range of interests is to a large extent determined by the rule that guides the whole discipline of state aid: the incompatibility clause of Article 107(1). Now, notwithstanding the fact that avoiding distortions or threats of distortions to competition has been erected as the main goal of the Commission's intervention in these matters, the breadth of interests that should be protected by procedures that underpin state aid control cannot be reduced to defining a level playing field for undertakings operating within the internal market or to safeguarding individual competitive positions, given the broader effects that such decisions may have. These are reflected in the exceptions defined in Article 107(2) and (3). As stated by the Court, specifically with regard to the exception in Article 107(3)(c), the exercise of the Commission's power of appreciation in these cases involves complex assessments of an economic, social, and technical character (this reasoning may be extended to other exceptions defined in this provision).[99] Arguably, restricting state aid control only to a matter of competition has become particularly unsustainable with the boosting of horizontal aid policies after the Single European Act, which 'take as their starting-point the desirability of aid to

[99] *Fachvereinigung Mineralfaserindustrie*, *cit.*, n. 11, paragraph 89.

accomplish certain goals', beyond the strict maintenance of the competition conditions in the internal market.[100] Moreover, the widening of the EU's competences to non-economic fields indicates that the state aid policy should be situated within the broader aims of integration,[101] or, at least, the Commission when controlling state aid cannot disregard non-economic interests protected by EU law. This has been recently acknowledged by the Court of Justice.[102]

In light of the above, the 'special problems created by state aid with regard to competition in the common market' evolve as a result of the integration process. They also vary according to the functions that state aid policy assumes in different contexts. Consequently, the type of interests that need to be balanced in the procedure vary from case to case. In view of its prevailing instrumental rationale, the right of persons concerned to be associated to the procedure 'to the extent appropriate in the light of the circumstances of the case' also needs to be determined taking notice of the different legally relevant interests involved. This is particularly relevant since the Commission's decision comprises complex assessments and the balancing of economic and non-economic interests, the Commission being required 'in the interests of sound administration of the fundamental rules of the Treaty relating to state aid' to deliver a decision based on a diligent and impartial examination of the facts at issue.[103]

[100] This aspect of state aid is underlined by Andrew Evans and Stephen Martin (1991) 'Socially acceptable distortion of competition: Community policy on state aid', *European Law Review*, Vol. 16, n. 2, p. 79–111, at p. 110. Examples of horizontal aid policies (mentioned by the authors) are regional policy, environmental policy, and the programme for small and medium-sized enterprises. Quoting the Commission's Eighteenth Report on Competition Policy of 1988, they conclude that, in the context of wider policies, 'state aid is increasingly seen as vehicle for making the completion of the internal politically acceptable'. In fact, they add that 'suitably controlled, state aid can bolster political consensus in favour of economic union, by ensuring that the benefits produced by such a union are distributed in a way that is perceived as fair' (*idem, ibidem*).

[101] The 'Community framework for state aid for research and development and innovation' (OJ C 323/1, 30.12.2006) is an example of the multiple goals that may be pursued by state aid policy. Adopted on the assumption that 'promoting Research and Development and Innovation [R&D&I] is an important objective of common interest', the Commission refers to the Treaty legal basis that grounds the European research and technological development policy and asserts that state aid for these purposes 'shall be compatible if the aid can be expected to lead to additional [research, development and innovation] and if the distortion of competition is not considered contrary to the common interest' (point 1.1 of the framework).

[102] *3F, cit.*, n. 38, paragraph 58.

[103] *Commission v Sytraval, cit.*, n. 11, paragraph 62; *Fachvereinigung Mineralfaserindustrie, cit.*, n. 11, paragraph 90.

An additional aspect of the procedure of Article 108(2) needs to be taken into account in the context of state aid control: the Commission's regulatory intervention covers national decisions that were taken in respect of a sufficiently identified situation. Therefore, often, they touch upon interests whose holders may be identified during the administrative procedure developed at EU level. Moreover, it should be borne in mind that the Commission opens the formal investigative procedure of Article 108(2) at a moment in which it has already formed a preliminary negative assessment as to the compatibility of the aid with the internal market rules (information that has to be included in the notice published in the Official Journal that opens the call for comments).[104] This facilitates the identification of the persons concerned by the procedure that should be entitled to intervene. The possibility of identifying the persons affected highlights the similarities with the situations of those persons to whom the Court has recognized a right to be heard, i.e. the addressee of an adverse decision and the persons otherwise identified therein.

The interpretation of the participatory procedure of Article 108(2) should be based on this approach to the basic set of rules that underpin the control of state aid. The notice thereof is intended to acquaint parties who have a legally protected interest in upholding the aid (or in its suppression) with the beginning of the EU procedure and enable them to put forward their views. Their procedural intervention should provide the Commission with the full information regarding the circumstances of the case that is put before it. In fact, when opening the procedure of Article 108 (2), the Commission relies essentially on the information provided by the Member State concerned or by possible complainants. Opening up the procedure to parties concerned may bring into the Commission's inquiry new information that might be relevant to the final decision. In light of the applicable rules and of the particular case before it, the Commission is, in principle, able to distinguish, within the broad range of persons who are entitled to intervene in the procedure, those persons whose legal sphere is affected by the procedure and who have a stronger role in the underlying material position (e.g. those from whom the unlawful aid can be recovered). These should be granted a differentiated procedural status. It might be misplaced to consider them simply as mere information providers.

[104] Article 6(1) of the procedural regulation, cit., n. 4.

This presupposes that the relationship established between the Commission and the persons affected by its decisions adopted on the basis of Article 108(2) and (3) cannot be considered a bilateral relationship that involves the decision-maker and the Member State, all other persons being considered third parties, but a complex relationship that is composed of the links between rights and duties that emerge from the Commission's intervention with regard to state aid control. Given the nature of such decision, this necessarily includes the effective or potential beneficiaries of the aid, and their competitors, as well as their respective associations, but not necessarily only these, as shown by the ECJ in *3F*.[105]

8.2.3 *The concept of 'parties concerned': proposal*

It follows from the above that persons concerned may be identified on the basis of their material connection to the procedure, which grounds the ability of the ensuing act to affect their legal spheres. Since not all legal positions are protected in the same way by the legal system, their participation might be valued in different ways and they may be afforded a different procedural treatment. In their assessment, the decision-maker should take into account the varied range of legally protected interests that might be affected by the final decision. On this basis, reducing the concept of parties concerned to those holding a competitive position is manifestly inadequate. This is an excessively restrictive interpretation of Article 108(2) in particular in cases where the state aid measure under appreciation contends with interests, other than safeguarding competition, which are also legally protected by EU law and, as such, pertinent to the decision at issue.[106]

[105] As stated below, these correspond to the categories of persons who have been recognized by the Court to be individually concerned by a Commission decision adopted on the basis of Article 108(2) or (3). See n. 110.

[106] This has been acknowledged by the ECJ in 3F, *cit.*, n. 38, paragraphs 57 and 58. This judgment is still, nevertheless, a derivative of the conception according to which parties concerned are those who are affected in their competitive position by the Commission's decision (indeed, the ECJ does not contest the starting point of the CFI in its analysis of parties concerned, i.e. whether the appellant's competitive position in the market was affected; see also the wording of paragraph 59; the allegations of the parties in the judgment at first instance may justify this—Case T-30/03, *Specialarbejderforbundet i Danmark (SID) v Commission* [2007] ECR II-34, paragraphs 17 and 20). See also, by analogy, the situation underlying the judgments in Case T-585/93, *Stichting Greenpeace Council (Greenpeace International) and others v Commission of the European Communities* [1995] ECR II-2205 and Case C-321/95 P, *Stichting Greenpeace Council (Greenpeace International) and Others v Commission of the European Communities* [1998] ECR I-1651.

'Parties concerned', therefore, includes both those who, being likely to be affected in their subjective rights and interests by the outcome of the procedure, have essentially a functional role of providing the Commission with all the relevant information on the basis of which it can reach an impartial and reasoned decision, as well as those who should be given the opportunity to have their personal interests voiced in the procedure and, therefore, granted a stronger procedural protection. The latter form a particular category of 'parties concerned' qualified by the fact that they have a differentiated substantive legal position. They have, therefore, a personal interest in intervening, which is defined on the basis of their substantive interests and rights likely to be affected by the final decision. While 'parties concerned' may be, at the stage in which they are called to express their views—the very beginning of the formal investigative procedure—an indeterminate group of persons, the abovementioned differentiation is likely to become evident during the procedure, in particular through the information brought into the procedure as a result of the notice and comment period.

It is possible to trace in the Courts' case law a basis for this distinction. The differentiation between different categories of persons concerned stems from the body of case law dwelling upon the *locus standi* of persons concerned. As was explained above, the need to reconcile the *Cook* and *Matra* rule and the restrictive conditions of standing for individuals under Article 263(4) led the Court to limit the scope of the concept of parties concerned within the meaning of Article 108(2). It was also argued that this restriction cannot be upheld, in light of the rationales of the participatory procedure of Article 108(2). Nevertheless, the need to distinguish persons concerned within the meaning of Article 108(2) and persons individually concerned within the meaning of Article 263(4) led the Court to distinguish those who 'clearly [have] the status of persons concerned', in the formulation used in *Waterleiding*,[107] from persons who are 'only indirectly and potentially affected'.[108] This distinction was maintained in subsequent case law that clarified the different conditions of standing, settling that only those who seek the annulment of a Commission decision stemming from Article 108(3) on substantive grounds need to demonstrate that their market position is substantially affected by the contested aid.[109]

[107] *Waterleiding*, *cit.*, n. 30, paragraph 61. [108] *Kahn*, *cit.*, n. 28, paragraph 50.

[109] Judgment of the ECJ in *ARE*, *cit.*, n. 21, paragraph 37. See above n. 38.

As summarized by Advocate General Ruiz-Jarabo Colomer, the persons concerned that the Court of Justice has considered to be individually affected (or, in other words, that have a distinct legal position) are those who 'are specified, or are at least capable of being specified, in relation to the disputed measure' and may be classified in three groups: '(a) undertakings currently or potentially in receipt of the state aid in question, (b) competitors of the recipient undertaking and their trade associations, and (c) certain associations of economic operators concerned in their capacity as a negotiator'.[110] The first two categories correspond to 'economic operators whose position in the market is significantly affected by the relevant decision'; the latter are persons who are entitled to participate as negotiators in the preparation of a decision and are affected in this quality by the decision adopted.[111] In both cases, they are persons whose particular situation the decision-maker is legally bound to consider in the adoption of the decision.[112] Flanking this category of persons concerned are those who voice interests that the Commission should take into account as part of the overall assessment upon which its decision is based. In state aid cases, the Courts have included in this second category bodies representing the employees of the beneficiary of the aid and trade unions: this is, arguably, extended to those representing the employees of the competitor.[113] While these, being persons concerned within the meaning of Article 108(2), may submit comments to the Commission 'which could be taken in account by the latter if appropriate',[114] their individual position does not require particular consideration, even if they are affected by the decision. In fact, under the state aid substantive legal regime, their legal position does not deserve specific protection. The interests they voice in the procedure are

> part of an overall assessment which includes a large number of considerations of various kinds, linked in particular to the protection of competition, regional development, the promotion of culture or again to the protection of the environment.[115]

[110] Opinion of Advocate General Ruiz-Jarabo Colomer, delivered on 9 November 1999, in Case C-106/98 P, *Comité d'Entreprise de la Société Française de Production and Others v Commission* [2000] ECR I-3659, paragraph 17. On this last category see above, n. 22.

[111] Opinion of Advocate General Ruiz-Jarabo Colomer, *cit.*, paragraph 27.

[112] *Idem*, paragraphs 29 and 30.

[113] Case T-189/97, *Comité d'Entreprise de la Société Française de Production and Others v Commission* [1998] ECR II-335, paragraph 41.

[114] CFI judgment in *Comité d'Entreprise*, *cit.*, paragraph 41.

[115] Case C-106/98 P, *Comité d'Entreprise de la Société Française de Production and Others v Commission* [2000] ECR I-3659, paragraph 52. In *3F*, the ECJ uses the same formulation,

In these cases, the capacity of persons concerned to participate derives from the fact that they defend legally protected interests, in relation to which the decision may produce an adverse effect, and should therefore be considered by the decision-maker. As noted by the ECJ in *3F*, denying them access would risk undermining the legal protection of these very interests.[116] Holders of such interests should, in any case, have a certain connection to the material situation being regulated (e.g. trade unions representing the workers of the undertakings involved in the dispute, or, in any event, effectively concerned by the aid at issue, but not trade unions as such). Their access also depends on their legal spheres being affected by the decision.

This distinction arises also in another case, where, however, the Court of First Instance contradicted the construction that is being defended here, basing its judgment on a restrictive concept of the parties concerned within the meaning of Article 108(2).[117] In fact, in *Pérez Escolar*, the Court held that:

> a natural or legal person, *in order to be recognized as having the status of a party concerned within the meaning of Article [108(2) TFEU]*...*must be able to establish that it has a legitimate interest* in whether or not the aid measures in question should be put into effect, or maintained if they have already been granted. In the case of an undertaking that legitimate interest may, in particular, consist in protecting its competitive position on the market, in so far as that position is adversely affected by the aid measures.[118]

As a result, it took the view that:

> [t]o recognize any person *having a purely general or indirect interest* with regard to the State measures to which objection is taken as having the status of a party concerned . . . would amount to recognizing that any taxpayer is a party concerned . . . in relation to aid financed through the general tax resources of a Member State.[119]

mentioning 'the Community maritime policy, the promotion of Community maritime transport, or the promotion of employment' (paragraph 64).

[116] *3F*, *cit.*, n. 38, paragraph 57. The applicant—a trade union—had sought to establish *locus standi* on the basis of its competitive position (see n. 106, above). The ECJ refuted the position of the CFI, according to which the action was inadmissible because the social aspects involved in this specific case were 'only indirectly linked to the subject-matter of the contested decision' (*Specialarbejderforbundet i Danmark (SID)*, *cit.*, n. 38, paragraph 36; *3F*, *cit.*, n. 38, paragraphs 54–59).

[117] Case T-41/01, *Rafael Pérez Escolar v Commission* [2003] ECR II-2157.

[118] *Pérez Escolar*, *cit.*, paragraph 35, emphasis added.

[119] *Idem*, paragraph 36, emphasis added.

In the Court's view, this would be 'clearly incompatible with the provisions of Article [108(2) TFEU]' and, when applied to actions for annulment, 'it would have the effect of depriving the concept of a person individually concerned for the purposes of the fourth paragraph of Article [263 TFEU] of all legal significance [as stated in *Waterleiding*] by transforming that remedy into a sort of *actio popularis*'.[120] Again, it is clear that the interplay between Article 108(2) and Article 263(4) TFEU led the Court to conflate the two concepts, as it had done before in *Waterleiding*. It is this conflation that underpins the conclusion that persons concerned within the meaning of Article 108(2) need to demonstrate a *legitimate interest* pertaining to the decision that they contest. Both this reasoning and the ensuing conclusion have been sufficiently contested above.[121] However, the Court's judgment in *Pérez Escolar* is relevant for current purposes, despite the fact that the Court reaches conclusions that diverge from the construction defended in this book. First, when confronted with this construction, this judgment helps to clarify that, as suggested in this work, holders of legally protected interests who may qualify as persons concerned are not just any interested persons without further qualification. In fact, taxpayers cannot be considered as persons concerned who have participation rights under Article 108(2): their interests are not part of those that the Commission needs to take into account in its assessment, given that they are not legally protected under EU law. This confirms that holders of legally protected interests need to prove an adverse effect that can be considered legally relevant, and, thereby, have a sufficient connection to the procedure that grounds their procedural intervention.[122] Secondly, the distinction between a 'general interest' and a 'legitimate interest', and, especially, the way in which the Court defined legitimate interest, contribute to refining the distinction between the two categories of persons concerned identified for purposes of participation. In fact, the Court considered that, for the purposes of standing under Article 263(4) TFEU, an adverse effect to a legitimate interest would need to consist in a loss which has a '*connection with the interests Article [108] is designed to protect*' and there should be a causal link 'between such a loss and the measure that might fall within the Community rules on state aid'.[123] The applicant was a minority

[120] *Idem, ibidem.* [121] Sub-section 8.1.3.

[122] This results from the ECJ ruling in *3F* (*cit.*, n. 38, paragraphs 54–59).

[123] *Idem*, paragraphs 42 and 44, respectively (see, for a comprehensive view of the Court's reasoning, paragraphs 41–45).

shareholder who, as a result of this aid, had been prevented from exercising his right to preferential allotment when the beneficiary's capital was increased. He did not demonstrate any of the aforementioned conditions, although he had admittedly been adversely affected by the contested aid. Therefore, this criterion contributes to singling out one type of person concerned among others affected: using the terminology adopted in the book, holders of endangered subjective positions (subjective rights), that are as such protected by the legal system.

It should be kept in mind that the conditions that underpin the concept of relevant legitimate interest defined by the Court in this case have been defined in order to assert the applicant's *locus standi* and not for the purposes of delimiting the realm of participation rights under Article 108(2). It reflects, therefore, a particularly demanding criterion, more exacting than the demonstration of an endangered competitive position that can underpin the definition of a sufficiently individualized position in relation to the contested decision, since, following this criterion, the Court does not require proof of an effective loss suffered.[124] Therefore, for the purposes of defining the personal scope of participation rights, the criterion defined by the Court in *Pérez Escolar* may be considered one criterion among several. Still with regard to the Court's analysis in *Pérez Escolar*, what again should be underlined is the connection between the interests voiced by the persons concerned and the interests that, under Article 108, may be considered legally relevant. The same occurs in *3F*.[125] Returning to the point made above, this confirms the suitability of defining the persons concerned on the basis of the range of interests that are legally protected by the applicable rules, and that, therefore, should be considered and duly balanced in the Commission's decision.

One should point out that, although the Court has, at least implicitly, recognized the criterion of the range of interests legally protected by the applicable norms to ground the concept of persons concerned, the

[124] See, namely, *Asklepios*, *cit.*, n. 19, paragraph 50, where the Court considered that 'even a future or simply a potential competitor of the beneficiary of the contested aid must be deemed to be a party concerned within the meaning of Article [108(2) TFEU]'. See also Opinion of Advocate General Bot delivered on 6 March 2008 in *Germany v Kronofrance*, *cit.*, n. 21, paragraph 117, according to whom, in light of the Courts' previous case law, the Court of First Instance did not need to examine whether the applicant's interests were '*substantially affected*', it being sufficient to assert that Kronofrance's market position '*might be affected*' by the granting of the aid (emphasis in the original).

[125] *Cit.*, n. 38, paragraphs 57 and 58.

argument developed in the pages above according to which the substantive legal regime of state aid includes the protection of non-economic interests has, until recently, only been hesitantly recognized, in particular by the CFI. In *Comité d'Entreprise* the Court of First Instance repudiated the applicants' claim that the 'action by the Commission is intended to reconcile the competition rules with considerations of a political nature, so that the review of legality must also be carried out in light of the social objectives of the Treaty'.[126] In the absence of other factors that demonstrate individual concern, this was, admittedly, a far-fetched argument for establishing standing.[127] However, the Court recognized that trade unions could be considered parties concerned within the meaning of Article 108(2) and, as such, 'submit comments to the Commission on considerations of social nature which *could be* taken into account by the latter *if appropriate*'.[128] Nevertheless, in the Court's view, the interests voiced by the applicants *did not need to be* considered by the Commission, since, as underlined by the Court, '[Articles 107 and 108] are intended to prevent intervention by a Member State from resulting in distortion of competition in the common market'.[129] This was more strongly asserted by Advocate General Colomer, according to whom:

> There is nothing in either the treaties or the case-law of the Court of Justice which supports the idea that, so far as state aid is concerned, the Commission should act and monitor the legality of such aid in accordance with the general objectives of the Community, in particular the social objectives, to any greater extent than in other areas of Community activity, such as the monitoring of concentrations of undertakings. In both areas the primary objective of Community policy is to maintain an effective level of competition.[130]

[126] CFI judgment in *Comité d'Entreprise*, *cit.*, n. 113, paragraphs 38 and 39.

[127] In *Comité d'Entreprise* the applicants were not pleading for the annulment of a Commission decision adopted on the basis of what is now Article 108(3) TFEU, on the grounds of an infringement of their procedural rights. Therefore, their standing depended on the fulfilment of the *Plaumann* requirements under Article 263(4) TFEU.

[128] CFI judgment in *Comité d'Entreprise*, *cit.*, n. 113, paragraph 41. See also *3F*, *cit.*, n. 38, paragraph 102.

[129] *Idem*, paragraph 39.

[130] Opinion of Advocate General Ruiz-Jarabo Colomer delivered on 9 November 1999, *Comité d'Entreprise*, *cit.*, n. 110, paragraph 8. He also observed that claiming that competition rules need to be reconciled with social concerns would make the Community system of state aid 'subject to social policy considerations' (paragraph 9) and 'the applicants statements, although interesting, are more like proposals for legislative policy than an interpretation *de lege lata* of the current legal position' (paragraph 7). See, however, *3F*, *cit.*, n. 38, paragraph 58.

For this reason, Advocate General Colomer denied that trade unions can 'in the context of [Articles 107 EC and 108 TFEU], occupy a position similar to that occupied by those actually involved in competition, namely the undertakings'.[131] On the contrary, the Courts' rulings with regard to *locus standi* of persons concerned within the meaning of Article 108(2) 'quite logically favour the persons who are naturally involved in free competition'.[132] These are the ones whose particular situation needs to be considered by the Commission when adopting its decision.[133]

However, arguably, this opinion does not amount to claiming that considerations of a non-economic nature should be ignored when dealing with state aid matters, but to admitting that there is an order of interests that are mainly protected by the applicable rules. That the Commission, when deciding on state aid issues, should consider non-economic considerations was precisely the position of the ECJ in *3F*. Here, the Court held that '...since the Community has not only an economic but also a social purpose, the rights under the provisions of the Treaty on state aid and competition must be balanced, *where appropriate*, against the objectives pursued by social policy...'.[134] As such, the Commission should take into account the social implications of state aid policy as part of the overall assessment it performs when assessing the compatibility of state aid.[135] In other words, social interests are legally protected interests that, depending on the circumstances of the case, need to be taken into account by the Commission in its state aid decisions. Importantly, according to the Court, this has consequences for defining the universe of persons concerned by the Commission's decisions.[136]

This reinforces the argument defended in this book that the scope of holders of participation rights should be defined on the basis of their connection to the procedure (i.e. those who can be adversely affected by the measures at issue), taking into account the substantive interests that are legally protected by the applicable norms. Moreover, it is in line with the argument put forward in this book that the legal criteria stemming from the substantive rules relevant in each case contribute to distinguishing different categories of participants. While this does not follow directly from the ECJ judgment in *3F*, arguably it results from the procedural rules that apply in state aid procedures, as the Courts have developed them. It follows in

[131] *Idem*, paragraph 9. [132] *Idem*, paragraph 23. [133] *Idem*, paragraph 30.
[134] *3F*, *cit.*, n. 38, paragraph 58. Emphasis added. See also paragraphs 57 and 59.
[135] *Idem*, paragraph 64. [136] *Idem*, paragraphs 57 and 69.

particular from the precision that certain legally protected interests should be considered by the decision-maker (in these cases, the Commission) as part of the overall assessment that grounds the final decision. This means that some persons concerned may be admitted to the decisional procedure not because the decision-maker needs to take into account their personal stakes and assess their specific legal position, but because they are holders of legally protected interests that the decision-maker needs to weigh in the decision. Their intervention is a means to ensure the achievement of a decision that is just, in the sense that it is the result of a full representation of the interests in dispute. In state aid cases, they must therefore be considered persons concerned within the meaning of Article 108(2). However, they may be refused the status of persons individually concerned within the meaning of Article 263(4). As results from the Courts' case law and from what was argued above, this is not an incongruity, since these concepts obey different modes of access.[137]

The different position of these persons justifies that they are afforded a different procedural status, weaker when compared to those persons whose particular situation needs to be specifically assessed. Thus, the intervention of persons concerned, which is legally relevant insofar as it contributes to the achievement of appropriate decisions, is, within the limits imposed by the principle of care, compatible with the power of the Commission to choose its sources of information, such as it considers to be more adequate in light of the cases it is called upon to assess. This means that the significance of participation of these persons can be reduced in a given procedure.[138] Nevertheless, interested parties, even if their legal position cannot be differentiated from that of other persons, have to be given access to all the information that is required in view of the utility of their intervention. The scope of the information disclosed is determined by the Commission, not only in light of the legitimate interests or rights that require legal protection (e.g. professional secrecy), but also taking into consideration the doubts and problems that the Commission needs to clarify. Moreover, the statement of reasons that accompanies the decision should reveal the reasoning and the sources of information taken into account by the Commission, but does not need to pay heed to the specific interest of each holder of legally protected interests in obtaining explanations.

[137] See what was said in this respect in Chapter 4, Sub-section 4.1.1.

[138] As mentioned above, this corresponds to the stance adopted by the Court of First Instance in the *British Airways* case (*cit.*, n. 47).

In contrast, the non-consideration of the view put forward by a party concerned whose particular situation the decision-maker is legally bound to consider, given their distinguished legal position and the protective scope of the applicable substantive norms, should be considered unlawful if it infringes the person's dignity. Accordingly, an interested person intervening in these circumstances should be given access to all the information that is relevant for effectively putting forward their views on the facts of the case (including, if such is needed, comments from other parties received by the Commission), within the legal limits of confidentiality and of professional and business secrecy, but without restrictions pertaining to the usefulness of their contribution to the outcome of the procedure.[139] In addition, persons concerned who have a qualified subjective entitlement in the administrative procedure, i.e. those whose subjective position needs to be considered as such by the decision-maker, should be able to understand why their argument has been rejected by the Commission when adopting the final decision.[140] In other words, their position should be adequately taken into account in the statement of reasons of the final decision. In short, given their stronger substantive position protected by the applicable norms, the procedural guarantees of holders of subjective rights who may be adversely affected by the procedure are more densely construed than those accompanying the intervention of persons whose legally protected interests should be considered as part of the overall assessment that bases the final decision.

It follows from the above that, even if formally a decision adopted on the basis of Article 108(2) is addressed to the Member State responsible for the contended aid, in light of its effects, the ensuing material relationship does not fit within the bilateral scheme that has been supported by the Courts. The corresponding procedural relationship, formed during the course of

[139] This is contrary to Article 6(2) of the procedural regulation, *cit.*, n. 4, whereby the comments received shall be submitted to the Member State concerned, and to the case law of the Courts that denies the possibility defended above in the text on the grounds that the state aid procedure of Article 108(2) is an adversarial procedure involving uniquely the Commission and the Member State concerned. However, this conception has been sufficiently contested above. Moreover, in cases where the rights of third parties require legal protection, sticking to that view would amount to maintaining a strict formalistic view of the procedure. In respect to the provision of the procedural regulation, it may be argued that this norm does not prohibit the Commission from forwarding the comments received to certain third parties when the circumstances of the case so require, even though, as a rule, the Commission is not required to transmit to third parties comments received during the notice and comment period.

[140] See *Technische Glaswerke*, *cit.*, n. 52, paragraph 67.

the procedure, should reflect the reality of the complex network of rights and duties effectively shaped by the decisions adopted and should be conceived in light of the substantive regime that it serves. This requires distinguishing between different types of persons concerned and recognizing them to have different procedural statuses that should reflect their normative connections to the situation being decided. Therefore, it should be possible to distinguish between three different layers of participation rights that, by displaying continuity, are not necessarily neatly distinguished from one another: the right to be heard of the addressee of the decision, participation rights of holders of subjective rights (which are analogous to the right to be heard), and participation rights of holders of legally protected interests.

8.2.4 *'Parties concerned' and the* Cook *and* Matra *rule*

The proposed distinction between the two categories of persons concerned within the meaning of Article 108(2) TFEU, to a certain extent, may also provide a useful path to come to terms with the *Cook* and *Matra* rule in its interplay with Article 263(4) TFEU. It can be argued that the Court, when defining in those two judgments the rule according to which 'the persons intended to benefit from [the] procedural guarantees [of Article 108 (2)] may secure compliance therewith only if they are able to challenge [the Commission's decision] before the Court', envisaged only the situations in which a person wishes to intervene in a procedure to defend a distinct subjective position.[141] In other words, 'procedural guarantee', in the sense of this rule, would imply a protection of this distinct subjective position. This interpretation would leave holders of legally protected interests who voice objectivized interests deprived of judicial remedy, in the case of breach of Article 108(2), if the Commission should choose to adopt its decision on the basis of Article 108(3) irrespective of serious difficulties in assessing the compatibility of the aid.

This is, admittedly, not an ideal situation, but one that is in line with the requirement of individual concern, as the Courts have interpreted it for the purposes of standing. One may support this solution, which results from the requirement mentioned, on the basis that the entitlement of holders of legally protected interests to intervene in the procedure is not underlain by a qualified subjective entitlement: it essentially derives

[141] *Cook*, *cit.*, n. 12, paragraph 17; *Matra*, *cit.*, n. 12, paragraph 23.

from the objective protection of the interests they voice, even though their legal sphere needs to be somehow implicated in the decisional procedure. As such, the questions relating to compliance with their procedural rights could be left to the control of the Ombudsman. Access to the Omdusman could be an open door to minimize the undesirable effects of excluding holders of legally protected interests from standing altogether. This is especially important since, as mentioned in Chapter 2, the distinction between holders of subjective rights and holders of legally protected interests is not clear-cut: it depends essentially on an assessment of the decision-maker in light of the circumstances of the case and of the applicable legal rules.

This interpretation eases the task of reconciling the *Cook* and *Matra* rule with the Court's strict interpretation of Article 263(4). In fact, this would dispense with the need to distinguish between different grounds of appeal in order to define *locus standi*, an aspect that has been criticized as being excessively confusing.[142] Coherently with the individual concern requirement of Article 263(4), it would still be a sufficiently individualized position that would ground access to judicial review. Nevertheless, the requirement of individual concern should not be interpreted as strictly as it results from the *Plaumann* test, in the way the Courts have applied this.[143] On the basis of the *Cook* and *Matra* rule, the likelihood that a qualified subjective position is affected by a given decision or procedure could, as such, be enough to fulfil the requirement of individual concern for purposes of standing.

[142] Both Advocate General Jacobs and Advocate General Bot argue that access to courts should not be distinguished on the basis of the legal grounds of the action, albeit with opposite conclusions. The former argues for the application of the test of individual and direct concern to all the cases where the applicant challenges a decision adopted under Article 108(3) (Opinion of Advocate General Jacobs delivered on 24 February 2005 on *Commission v Aktionsgemeinschaft Recht und Eigentum eV*, *cit.*, n. 21, paragraph 141). The latter argues that the *Cook* and *Matra* rule should be maintained and applied to all actions challenging decisions under Article 108(3) (Opinion of Advocate General Bot delivered on 6 March 2008 on *Germany v Kronofrance*, *cit.*, n. 21, paragraphs 104–110, in particular 110). This was the position followed by the ECJ in *3F*.

[143] That this test does not 'have to be interpreted as narrowly as it was in Plaumann' has been defended by Advocate General Jacobs, not only in his famous opinion in the *UPA* case, but also in the Opinion referred to in the note above (*cit.*, n. 21, paragraph 141). In this case he reinforces his argument invoking that 'the Community Courts have rightly taken a somewhat broader view of the test for standing of complainants in other related areas, namely under the competition rules applying to undertakings [Articales 101 and 102 TFEU] and in cases of dumping' (*idem, ibidem*).

8.2.5 *'Parties concerned' and general aid schemes*

In light of the above, in particular on the basis of a broad concept of persons concerned for the purposes of Article 108(2) TFEU, one may argue that a sufficient link that grounds access to the procedure as enshrined in this provision can be established also by the effect of decisions that appreciate the compatibility of general aid schemes with the internal market.

It is worth addressing this issue, since the Courts' temptation to conflate the concept of persons concerned within the meaning of Article 108(2) with that of persons individually concerned within the meaning of Article 263(4) TFEU was greater in cases involving general aid schemes.[144] As mentioned above, the Court of First Instance held in *Kahn* that the existence of an actual beneficiary, with whom a relation of competition could be established, 'presupposes the practical application of the aid scheme by the grant of individual aids', suggesting also that only in these circumstances could there be persons concerned within the meaning of Article 108(2).[145] In *Waterleiding*, also a case in which the dispute was related to a general aid scheme, the Court confirmed that persons concerned within the meaning of Article 108(2) need to demonstrate, for the purposes of this norm, that their competitive position on the market has been adversely affected by the aid at issue.[146] Nevertheless, contrary to *Kahn*, this time the Court admitted that the competitive position of persons concerned could be affected by a general aid scheme.[147]

Later, in *Hamburger Hafen und Lagerhaus* the Court of First Instance, deciding on the applicants' standing, did not seem to attribute any significance to the fact that one of the measures at issue was a general aid scheme.[148] More significantly, in *ARE*—when clarifying where the line should be drawn in order to reconcile the *Cook* and *Matra* rule with the

[144] Above, Sub-section 8.1.3.

[145] *Kahn*, *cit.*, n. 28, paragraph 49. See above Sub-section 8.1.3, where it is explained that underlying this judgment was the view that the condition of 'person concerned' requires the demonstration that the person has a competitive position that may be endangered by the measure adopted.

[146] *Waterleiding*, *cit.*, n. 30, paragraphs 62 and 67.

[147] *Waterleiding*, *cit.*, n. 30, paragraphs 65, 79–81, 85, and 86.

[148] *Hamburger Hafen- und Lagerhaus*, *cit.*, n. 34, paragraphs 42–52. As mentioned above, in this case the Court conflated the concept of persons concerned within the meaning of Article 108(2) and of persons individually concerned for purposes of Article 263(4) (see Sub-section 8.1.3). In the reasoning of this judgment, there is no reference to the difficulties in determining the existence of a 'competitive position' in relation to a decision approving a general aid scheme.

requirements of former Article 230(4) EC, and hence solidifying the distinction between persons concerned within the meaning of Article 108(2) TFEU, on the one hand, and persons individually concerned within the meaning of the current Article 263(4) TFEU, on the other—the Court of Justice did not accord any relevance to the fact that the decision challenged in this case consisted of the appreciation of the compatibility of a general aid scheme with the rules of the internal market.[149] Therefore, it implicitly assumed that, even if the Commission's decision pertains to a general aid scheme, this decision is capable of affecting the rights and interests of persons concerned.[150] There is no reason why one should take a different stance when assessing the conditions of access to administrative procedures, instead of access to courts. In another case, the Court of First Instance confirmed that this type of aid might affect the competitive position of certain undertakings operating in the relevant market. This happens when the object of the aid at issue is to render some specific products more competitive than others in the same market. Therefore, it may be held that, in such cases, since the adoption of the general aid scheme, the act's ability to affect the competitive position of producers is certain and no longer just potential.[151] The CFI thereby dismissed the Commission's contention according to which (drawing on *Kahn*), in order to consider

[149] ECJ judgment in *ARE*, *cit.*, n. 21, paragraphs 44–47 and 65–68. See also *TF1*, *cit.*, n. 4, paragraph 73.

[150] Specifically regarding standing, this seems to apply both when the persons concerned seek annulment of a Commission decision pursuant Article 108(3) on procedural and on substantive grounds (see Case T-210/02, *British Aggregates Association v Commission* [2006] ECR II-2789, paragraphs 50–52 and 54–63; also the ECJ judgment on this case, *cit.*, n. 38, paragraphs 28–31, 55, and 56). Nevertheless, also on this point the Courts have oscillated. In *Asklepios*, referring to a situation in which the applicant would be entitled to bring an action for annulment in order to secure their procedural rights, the Court of First Instance held that the fact that the aid concerned a great number of beneficiaries 'is not such as to affect the admissibility of the action, since the allegedly unlawful aid was *in fact granted . . . and as such does not constitute a general aid scheme*' (*cit.*, n. 19, paragraph 56). Moreover, in a recent line of cases where the applicants sought the annulment, on substantive grounds, of a Commission decision on a general aid scheme adopted under former Article 88(2) EC, the Court of First Instance held that standing can only be granted if the applicant 'is an actual recipient of individual aid granted under a sectoral aid scheme, recovery of which has been ordered by the Commission' (see Case T-292/02, *Confederazione Nazionale dei Servizi (Confservizi) v Commission* [2009] ECR II-1659, paragraph 59; Case T-297/02, *ACEA SpA v Commission* [2009] ECR II-1683, paragraph 45; Case T-300/02, *Azienda Mediterranea Gas e Acqua SpA (AMGA) v Commission* [2009] ECR II-1737, paragraph 49; Case T-301/02, *AEM SpA v Commission* [2009] ECR II-1757, paragraph 45; Case T-309/02, *Acegas-APS SpA v Commission* [2009] ECR II-1809, paragraph 49; Case T-189/03, *ASM Brescia SpA v Commission* [2009] nyr., paragraph 43).

[151] *Fachvereinigung Mineralfaserindustrie*, *cit.*, n. 11, paragraph 62.

undertakings that compete with the beneficiaries of the aid as persons concerned, the general aid scheme would need first to be implemented.[152]

With regard to this line of case law, it is noteworthy that a decision approving a general aid scheme is, in terms of EU law, an individual act. It is a decision 'binding in its entirety upon those to whom it is addressed' and it does not lose its defining characteristics by the fact that its object is an aid scheme approved by a national act of a general nature. What changes is the universe of people potentially concerned by that measure. The oscillations of the Court regarding the relevance of the object of a state aid decision for purposes of access highlight the artificiality of the distinction between acts of a general nature and acts of an individual nature to define the scope of participation rights, denying them in the first case and supporting them in the latter. In a way, these oscillations demonstrate the effective importance of assessing the material connections of the persons with the procedure and the ability of the act to produce a change in their legal sphere, in order to determine access both to procedures and remedies in a way that is mindful of their substantive rights and interests.

Admittedly, in certain cases, the identification of parties concerned entitled to participate in the procedure might be more difficult with respect to measures of general application than in relation to individual measures with clearly identified beneficiaries. However, as shown above, it cannot be excluded that general measures may have an actual impact in the legal sphere of third parties, by reason of their concrete circumstances and attributes.

Therefore, one may conclude that there is no reason to distinguish procedures of Article 108(2) according to the object of each decision. Both decisions contending with individual aid and those assessing general aid schemes fall within the realm of this provision and no distinction should be made in defining access to the procedure in the two cases. Given the possible effects of decisions assessing general aid schemes, these can contend both with qualified substantive entitlements and with legally protected interests.

8.3 Participation Rights in Administrative Rule-making

The judicial developments regarding the participation of interested persons in state aid decisions are based on, and limited to, the provision of

[152] This, however, seems to remain a valid argument for purposes of standing (see n. 150).

Article 108(2) TFEU. The above considerations are, as such, naturally limited to the Commission's powers of enforcement under the Treaty and, hence, to the individual decisions that it is entitled to enact vis-à-vis Member States on the basis of this norm. This is confirmed by the fact that the rights of interested parties, as they have been defined in the procedural regulation laying down the rules for the application of Article 108, are limited to individual decision-making procedures.[153] The regulatory powers of the EU in this field that are arguably capable of impinging upon the legal sphere of private persons have strayed beyond the limits of this provision. However, there does not seem to be any basis to claim that participation rights could also be recognized in other instances not covered by the procedure defined in the Treaty. While Regulation No. 994/98 envisages a participatory phase in the procedure for the adoption of implementing regulations (in the pre-Lisbon terminology) defining the rules for certain categories of horizontal state aid—and thereby demonstrates the importance attached to participation also in the rule-making realm—there are no indications that this norm could be interpreted in a similar way to Article 108(2).[154]

Nevertheless, one may argue that Article 108(2), as interpreted above, provides a normative basis for establishing participation rights also in relation to rule-making in the field of state aid, on the grounds of an analogy argument. The premises of such reasoning are as follows. First, as stated, according to the scheme of the Treaty, the Commission's regulatory powers in this field were intended to be framed by a procedure involving not only the Member States concerned but also the persons who may be affected by the final decision. Secondly, as is often the case, the reality of state aid regulation was revealed to be much richer than what could be perceived strictly on the basis of a reading of the Treaty. In particular, since the outset of the integration process, the Commission's powers in this field have expanded considerably, encompassing a long-standing *de facto* task of defining the applicable rules in state aid matters. Thirdly, the argument according to which the rationales of participation rights in individual determinations are also capable of grounding similar rights in rule-making procedures is also valid here. As results from the above analysis, Article 108 (2) participation rights are grounded in the need to ensure both that the

[153] Article 20 of the procedural regulation (*cit.*, n. 4).

[154] Article 6 of Council Regulation No. 994/98, of 7 May 1998 (OJ L 142/1, 14.5.98), hereinafter 'the block exemptions regulation'. On the meaning of this provision, see below, Sub-section 8.3.3.

Commission has all the information needed to issue a substantiated decision (in view of the political sensitivity of the matters that it is called upon to decide) and that those who may be adversely affected by this decision are given the possibility of putting forward their views before its adoption. Where it may be established that general rules may impinge on the legal spheres of persons in a similar way to individual determinations, participation rights should, in principle, also be granted in the respective procedures.

In fact, the rationale for the intervention of persons concerned pursuant to Article 108(2) is an essential factor in determining the possibility of analogy. If one considers a legal norm to be the result of a valued-based assessment of the facts that it intends to rule, discovering its rationale might lead to extending this norm to cover a different hypothesis where this same rationale can also be deemed to apply. The assessment that grounds the norm is made in relation to a given historical moment on the basis of values that persist beyond that historical situation. Thence, the norm is inserted in a legal system, but it requires observation in view of those values and of changing societal demands. If there is a substantial similarity between the facts regulated by a given norm and other facts that are not covered by it, both of which are determinant for the legal treatment accorded in the first case, then the two factual situations are sufficiently similar and it may be concluded that they require similar legal treatment.[155] In this case, and for our purposes, the analogy is justifiable if the rationales behind the regulated form of participation and the one not envisaged by the legal system are sufficiently similar. However, at first sight, the parallels between the two factual situations have certain immediate constraints: first, individual decisions and general rules are different in scope and meaning; secondly, their structure differs (the former are unilateral decisions by the Commission while the latter are often negotiated rules); thirdly, if the requirement of a notice and comment period is related to the assumption that a possible adverse outcome may issue from the Commission's decision, this same conjecture might not hold vis-à-vis a general measure. As examined elsewhere in this work, the first argument has been elevated to a general and principled objection to the recognition of participation rights in rule-making procedures. Although it has been already refuted in another chapter

[155] Emilio Betti (1971), *Interpretazione della legge e degli atti giuridici. Teoria generale e dogmatica*, Milano: Giuffrè, p. 163–79, at pp. 166 and 169–170, quoting Norberto Bobbio, *L'analogia nella logica del diritto* (1938).

of the book,[156] this point is resumed here in the specific context of state aid. The other arguments are also developed and criticized below. It is argued that they do not constitute insurmountable obstacles to the recognition of rights of participation in rule-making that supports the Commission's state aid policy. This extension is grounded in an analogy with Article 108(2).

Before proceeding with this analysis, the second premise enunciated above—i.e. the acquisition of regulatory powers by the Commission at the margin of the Treaty powers—requires further elaboration. In effect, this study should be based on a more accurate understanding of the Commission's powers in this field, in order to define the scope of the analogy, namely to determine in relation to which rule-making procedures participation rights should equally be envisaged, if the analogy can effectively be established. The following section, therefore, examines the regulatory structure of this sector and recalls the reasons that resulted in the expansion of the Commission's intervention beyond the powers expressly assigned to it under the Treaty.

8.3.1 *Regulatory structure in the field of state aid*

Institutional framework

As results from the procedure of Article 108 TFEU, the Treaty assigns to the Commission a central role in the implementation of the rules on state aid control. The Commission was endowed with supervision powers over Member States' action in this field, which can either result in proposing to them 'appropriate measures required by the progressive development or by the functioning of the common market'[157] or consist of investigative powers framed by the two-stage procedure for the assessment of existing and intended aid that has been, in part, analysed above.[158] On the other hand, according to the Treaty, the competence to define general and abstract norms is entrusted to the Council, which formally has the power to enact regulations for the application of Articles 107 and 108 TFEU.[159]

Nevertheless, in contrast to the institutional framework defined in the Treaty, the EU state aid policy evolved mostly on the basis of soft law rules,

[156] Above Chapter 4, Sub-section 4.3.2.

[157] Article 108(1) TFEU. [158] Article 108(2) and (3) TFEU.

[159] Article 109 TFEU. The Parliament only gained a voice in state aid matters after 1992, when the Maastricht revision defined that consultation of the European Parliament had to precede the adoption of measures under former Article 89 EC. This remains unchanged in Article 109 TFEU and was already in force at the time the first regulations were adopted on the basis of this provision.

issued by the Commission at the margin of the competences formally attributed to it, apart from the individual decisions enacted on the basis of what are now paragraphs 2 and 3 of Article 108 TFEU. The former frame and limit the Commission's discretionary power in the appreciation of each individual case and often codify and perpetuate the Commission's practice that the latter embody. 'Guidelines', 'disciplines', 'frameworks', 'codes', 'notices', and 'letters' define the activities that can be aided, the criteria for eligibility of aid, its purposes and maximum levels, methods of calculation, as well as procedural rules (e.g. requirements of notification procedures).[160] Soft law instruments have been seen to have the advantage of structuring the Commission's internal work, coordinating the activity of the different Directorates General that deal with state aid,[161] overall enabling the Commission to work more efficiently.[162] A case-by-case approach is deemed to be not only impractical in the face of the amount of cases to be decided, but also to give rise to possible discrimination. Moreover, it is regarded as clearly unsatisfactory in terms of legal certainty. By contrast, spelling out the Commission's policy in frameworks and guidelines is considered to increase transparency and legal certainty, since they inform governments and industry of the Union's intended practice. In addition, these instruments are thought to discipline the Commission in the authorization of aid.[163] These claimed advantages, however, do not explain the adoption of a soft law approach to rule-making in this sector as an alternative to the use of hard law instruments. This, instead, seems to have had its origins in the balance of power that was achieved between Council and Commission, after a bitter period in their institutional relations between the late 1960s and early 1970s, during which the Commission launched two failed initiatives for the adoption

160 On this, see Frank Rawlinson (1993) 'The role of policy frameworks, codes and guidelines in the control of state aid' in Ian Harden (ed.), *State Aid: Community Law and Policy*, Cologne: Bundesanzeiger, pp. 52–60, at p. 55; Michelle Cini (2001) 'The soft law approach: Commission rule-making in the EU's state aid regime', *Journal of European Public Policy*, Vol. 8, n. 2, pp. 192–207, at p. 200; Herwig C.H. Hofmann (2006) 'Administrative governance in state aid policy', in Herwig Hofmann and Alexander Türk (eds), *European Administrative Governance*, Cheltenham, Northampton: Edward Elgar, pp. 185–214, at p. 194.

161 Hofmann, *op. cit.*, p. 194.

162 Rawlinson, *op. cit.*, p. 56.

163 *Idem*, pp. 57–8. The advantages first mentioned are documented in the Commission's 'Proposal for a regulation on the application of Articles 92 and 93 of the EC Treaty to certain categories of horizontal aid', where it states the following: 'Over the years the Commission has devoted much effort to develop an efficient, coherent and more transparent state aid control as regards both procedure and substance. For this purpose the Commission has developed and published comprehensive guidelines and communications spelling out Commission policies' (COM (97) 396 final, Brussels, 15.07.1997, p. 2).

of regulations under former Article 89 EC (now Article 109 TFEU).[164] Only in the late 1990s, did the Commission again exercise its power of initiative under this provision, finally using this legal basis.

The legality of the Commission's power to issue non-binding rules has been debated in the literature, in particular in view of the lack of a clear legal basis.[165] Two arguments have been put forward in its favour. First, the power of the Council is a non-mandatory one: current Article 109 TFEU, in contrast with the parallel legal basis in the fields of merger control and anti-trust, only defines that the Council 'may' adopt regulations for the application of Article 107 and 108 TFEU. It may be held that if the Council does not follow suit on the Commission's proposals, the latter can legitimately step in. Secondly, it may be argued that the enactment of such guidelines stems from the Commission's discretionary power conferred by Articles 107 and 108 as well as from its 'right to self-organization ... as institution of the [EU]'.[166] However, this claim does not hide the difficulties of the matter: the only undisputable legal basis could be Article 108(1), whereby the Commission has the power to propose 'appropriate measures required by the progressive development or by the functioning of the internal market'. Nevertheless, this power is expressly associated with the Commission's competence of supervising existing systems of aid; it is not a general regulatory power. The use of soft law instruments by the Commission remains, therefore, problematic, not least because it allows for a concentration of the regulatory powers in this institution.[167] Furthermore,

[164] These are analysed by Inda Bevis (2002) *The Legal Effect of EC Appropriate Measures and ECSC State Aid Codes*, PhD Thesis, Florence: European University Institute, pp. 69–72. She gives an account of the institutional relations between the Council and the Commission at that time and explains the failure to follow up those proposals in light of this context. This is also mentioned by, among others, Giancinto della Cananea (1993) 'Administration by guidelines: the policy guidelines of the Commission in the field of state aids', in Ian Harden (ed.), *State Aid: Community Law and Policy*, Cologne: Bundesanzeiger, pp. 61–75, at p. 62, n. 8; Cini, *op. cit.*, n. 160, p. 197; Sinnaeve and Slot, *op. cit.*, n. 4, p. 1999, n. 3.

[165] Cananea, *op. cit.*, pp. 69–70. Cini, *op. cit.*, n. 160, p. 200.

[166] Hofmann, *op. cit.*, n.160, p. 194; see also Herwig C.H. Hofmann (2006), 'Negotiated and non-negotiated administrative rulemaking: the example of EC competition policy', *Common Market Law Review*, Vol. 43, n. 1, pp. 153–78, at p. 168. Opinion of Advocate General Lenz, delivered on 23 May 1996, on Case C-311/94, *Ijssel-Vliet Combinatie v Minister van Economische Zaken* [1996] ECR I-5023, paragraph 15. For a different interpretation, see Mona Aldestam (2004) 'Soft law in the State aid policy area', in Ulrika Mörth, *Soft Law in Governance and Regulation. An Interdisciplinary Analysis*, Cheltenham, Northampton: Edward Elgar, pp. 11–36, at pp. 19–20.

[167] Cananea, *op. cit.*, n. 164, pp. 72–4;Hofmann, 'Administrative governance ...', *cit.*, n. 160, p. 200.

despite the codifying intent, the flexibility that soft law rules permit is likely to be contradictory with the same principles of transparency and legal certainty that these in principle seek to ensure. However, in this last respect, the inconveniences attached to the use of soft law have been, at least to a certain extent, overcome by effect of the Court's case law. In fact, the Courts have bound the Commission to its own guidelines, on the basis of the commitment that they represent, and reviewed its acts and actions in light of general principles of law, namely the principle of legitimate expectations and the principle of equal treatment.[168]

Difficulties notwithstanding, there seems to have been an implicit institutional consensus that left the Commission with a preponderant role both in the definition of state aid rules and in their enforcement. At least, the absence of proposals by the Commission after the early 1970s that could trigger the use of what was then Article 89 EC was accompanied by the silence of the Council which did not urge the Commission to act (a power bestowed then on it by former Article 208 EC, now Article 241 TFEU). In substantive terms, the flexibility required by a highly sensitive area in political terms, where the goal of granting undistorted competition within the internal market has to be balanced against the need to take into account the particularities of a given economic situation that can have disparate origins (underemployment, regional characteristics, disturbances in a given economic sector, the public interest of an innovative project, etc.) might be at the origin of the quasi-absence of formal legislation.[169]

The Commission's 'renewed' regulatory power

Despite the dominance of a soft law approach in the development of state aid policy, a process of 'gradual formalization of both substantive policy and procedures' came about mostly through the interplay between the Commission's decisions and the Courts' case law.[170] Since the beginning of the

[168] Hofmann, 'Administrative governance . . .', *cit.*, n. 160, pp. 194–5. See also, Leigh Hancher (1994) 'State aids and judicial control in the European Community', *European Competition Law Review*, Vol. 15, n. 3, pp. 134–50, at pp. 141–2.

[169] This seems to be suggested by Rose D'Sa (1998) *European Community Law on State Aid*, London: Sweet and Maxwell, p. 19. On the function of state aid policy, see, Cini, *op. cit.*, n. 160, p. 198.

[170] Cini, *op. cit.*, n. 160, p. 200. According to Rawlinson in 1993, at that time principal administrator in the Commission's state aid directorate, 'the margin of discretion the Commission has depends on the actual provisions of the frameworks, not their legal form' (*op. cit.*, n. 160, p. 59). He argued that there is 'no difference in practice' in the Commission's attitude while applying policy frameworks that take the form of legislation and those that do not.

1990s, however, the process of 'hardening' the Commission's regulatory power acquired a new shape, due to two main factors.

First, the Commission showed that it was willing to resort to its investigative powers under the Treaty to compel dissident Member States to conform to the terms of frameworks and guidelines. That was the case in the dispute that opposed the Commission to Spain and Germany over the 'Community Framework on State Aid to the Motor Vehicle Industry'.[171] As has been reported by other scholars, in this case the Commission countered Germany's resistance to complying with this framework by issuing a decision in which it reiterated Germany's obligations, as they had been defined in the said framework in relation to all Member States. The Commission thereby attributed a formal binding effect to duties that had been defined in negotiations between itself and the Member States, abidance by which relied until that point on the voluntary conduct of the former.[172]

Secondly, as mentioned, in the late 1990s two regulations were proposed and approved on the basis of what was then Article 89 EC. The first framed the rules for group exemptions from the notification requirement to be applied to certain categories of horizontal state aid, thereby paving the way for the adoption of implementing regulations by the Commission in relation to this subject matter.[173] References in the preamble indicate that the regulation builds on the Commission's previous rules and decisions and that it is essentially destined to enable the Commission to enact formally binding regulations that can be directly applied by national courts.[174] The second laid down detailed rules for the application of Article 88 EC (now 108 TFEU), with the aim of codifying the procedural rules that had been defined by the Commission and the Courts as well as strengthening the Commission's control of aid.[175] Both regulations were the result of the Commission's initiative to overhaul state aid control, which was motivated by a perceived need to secure efficiency in a context of escalating work load,

[171] OJ C 123/3, 18.5.1989. This case is analysed in Bevis, *op. cit.*, n. 164, pp. 171–90. See also Cini, *op. cit.*, n. 160, p. 201–2. The continuation of this practice is suggested by the analysis of Keppenne, *op. cit.*, n. 8, p. 804.

[172] Commission Decision No. 90/381/EEC of 21 February 1990 on all the German aid schemes applicable to the automobile sector (OJ L 188/55, 20.07.1990).

[173] Block exemption regulation, *cit.*, n. 154.

[174] Recitals 4 and 5 of the preamble. See also the new paragraph 4 of Article 108 TFEU.

[175] Procedural regulation (Council Regulation No. 659/1999), *cit.*, n. 4, referred to in this chapter as 'the procedural regulation'. See recital 2 of the preamble. Sinnaeve and Slot point out the twofold aim of the regulation mentioned in the text (*op. cit.*, n. 4, p. 1156).

to increase transparency and legal certainty,[176] as well as to deal with the pressure of the Courts, in particular the Court of First Instance, which had imposed stricter procedural rules on the Commission. By proposing to define those rules in a regulation, the Commission sought to deter an activist stance by the Court in this respect.[177]

After forty years of state aid policy that had allowed the Commission to shape and reinforce its role in aid control vis-à-vis Member States, this institution has since the late 1990s also been entitled to enact implementing regulations.[178] Furthermore, it appears to be 'legitimized' by a clearer and more transparent procedural framework.

According to Cini, these developments represent two main trends: first, there is a move away from the use of soft law in the definition of procedural rules, while substantive regulation continues to rely on this type of rule; secondly, hard law is used as a complement to soft regulatory instruments whenever this is deemed necessary to ensure Member States' compliance.[179] As a result, the Commission continues to use regulatory instruments that are based on Member States' voluntary agreement and compliance, but associates them with formal decisions in order to enforce them. Hard law hence 'serves as a shadow of hierarchy compelling member state authorities to seek consensus'.[180]

This provides the Commission with a 'mix of appropriate policy instruments',[181] consisting of soft rules and formal decisions, as well as implementing regulations issued under the block exemptions regulation. Both formal rule-making and informal rule-making, as well as formal decisions and informal settlements (e.g. agreements reached between Member State and Commission putting an end to the first stage of the investigative procedure defined in Article 108(3)) make up the specific set of legal and policy instruments used by the Commission in state aid control. Therefore, the possibility of an analogy between Article 108(2) and rule-making procedures followed in the field of state aid needs to consider the procedure underlying the adoption of

[176] This is stated in the preamble of both regulations (paragraph 5 of the block exemption regulation, *cit.*, n. 154, and paragraph 3 of the procedural regulation, *cit.*, n. 4). Also the concern of ensuring efficient action results implicitly from paragraph 4 of the former regulation and from paragraph 2 of the latter.

[177] Sinnaeve and Slot (*op. cit.*, n. 4, p. 1154) as well as Cini (*op. cit.*, n. 160, p. 203) refer to the *Sytraval* ruling of the Court of First Instance as a judicial event that gave impetus to the Commission's proposal for a procedural regulation.

[178] 'Implementing regulations', here and in the subsequent pages, is pre-Lisbon terminology to refer to regulations adopted on the basis of primary acts of the Council or of the Parliament and the Council.

[179] Cini, *op. cit.*, n. 160, pp. 203–4. [180] *Idem*, p. 204. [181] Cini, *op. cit.*, n. 160, p. 193.

implementing regulations as well as the procedures preceding the adoption of soft rules. These two instances are considered in turn below, after establishing the very possibility of an argument of analogy in order to defend the extension of participation rights to rule-making procedures.

8.3.2 *Extending rights by analogy*

As mentioned, the rationales of participation rights ensuing from Article 108(2) are also applicable to possible participation rights in rule-making procedures. However, three features differentiate the two situations. First, the objects of the decisions adopted on the basis of Article 108(2) are Member States' administrative or legislative acts adopting state aid measures, which means that Commission decisions are taken in respect to sufficiently defined situations, or, in other words, to already established legal relationships to the extent that these may be created by the primary act. They are a sort of 'meta-decision', which assess the compatibility of the national political will with EU law. By contrast, EU formal or informal rules on state aid policy are first level arrangements aimed at ruling an undetermined number of situations that fall within their scope. Secondly, the procedure regulated in Article 108(2) is an adversarial procedure, whilst the soft law instruments adopted by the Commission are often the product of negotiations between Member States and the Commission, even if ultimately the obligations therein defined will impinge on the latter and be enforced precisely through this procedure.[182] Thirdly, as mentioned above, Article 108(2) is the formal stage of an investigative procedure that is opened by the Commission when, after a preliminary examination, it finds that the aid at issue is incompatible with the functioning of the common market and it has serious difficulties in assessing this aid. Thus, the notice and comment period has behind it an assumption of the likelihood of a negative decision by the Commission, an assumption that in principle is not present in rule-making.

The possibility of analogy therefore depends on the verification of three conditions. First, it must still possible to assert that the act at issue has the ability to establish concrete links between the decision-maker and the persons affected, and, thereby, demonstrate that the fact that the decisions

[182] In this sense, see Rawlinson, *op. cit.*, n. 160, p. 60 and Keppenne, *op. cit.*, n. 8, p. 804. Hofmann distinguishes two types of rule-making: unilateral and negotiated, the latter's realm being the control of existing aid under current Article 108(1) TFEU (Hofmann, 'Negotiated and non-negotiated administrative rulemaking...', *cit.*, n. 166, p. 156 and pp. 165–9).

based on Article 108(2) impact on national measures and do not constitute a primary composition of interests is not an impediment to the parallelism between participation in individual determinations and participation in rule-making. In addition, one needs to demonstrate that the structure of both types of procedures does not hinder the possibility of analogy. Lastly, the feasibility of an argument based on analogy depends on the meaning to be given to the third feature pointed out above, i.e. the assumption that a negative position of the Commission will issue from the procedure is a factor that favours the recognition of participation rights.

With regard to this last point, on may argue that this feature is only determinant to the relative importance of the rationales of the notice and comment period. As has already been stressed, it is not possible to fully detach the two rationales of participation rights. The fact that the intervention of the so-called third parties occurs at a phase of the procedure in which there is the assumption of a possible negative decision of the Commission underlines the preponderance of the dignitarian rationale over the instrumental rationale of participation. It does not exclude the hearing of persons concerned for purposes of information gathering and sound decision-making. Paradoxically, the latter has been the rationale most underlined by the Courts. Moreover, the wide concept of persons concerned defended above supports this interpretation, since, in any event, not only holders of subjective rights adversely affected by the decision at issue are granted access to the procedure by the effect of Article 108(2). Furthermore, the possibility of an adverse effect, which is one of the requirements of participation rights, can also be assessed in relation to rule-making procedures. As argued in Chapter 7, this adverse effect may result from the lack of consideration for legally protected interests involved in the dispute. The fact that a presumption of incompatibility of the aid underlies the procedure of Article 108(2) does not, therefore, constitute an obstacle to the intended analogy: it does not preclude the similarity of the *fattispecie* under comparison nor that between the rationales behind the provision of Article 108(2) and the recognition of rights of participation in administrative rule-making.

The second feature mentioned—the structure of the procedure as a possible objection to analogy—can be easily refuted. In fact, behind the unilateral decision of the Commission based on Article 108(2), there is a negotiation process, the unilateral decision being often the formal ending of a negotiated solution.[183] Often even, due to an exchange of views between the Commission and the Member State, either formally framed by Article 108(3) or on an informal basis, the Commission might not adopt a formal decision on the basis of Article 108(2).[184]

The different object of individual decisions based on Article 108(2) and of general rules enacted by the Commission raises more complicated questions. First, it touches again upon the issue of the different meaning and scope of abstract rules and individual determinations. Secondly, its refutation entails the demonstration that measures of general scope are also capable of giving rise to administrative relationships.

With regard to the former point, it should be noted that, notwithstanding their different scope, both individual decisions taken on the basis of Article 108(2) and abstract rules enacted by the Commission in light of the substantive provisions of Article 107 are capable of having a general regulatory effect. This effect stems precisely from the fact that the Commission's decisions in the realm of state aid policy touch upon measures that Member States wish to adopt in order to face concrete socio-economic situations and, therefore, affect those directly involved in the situations being regulated. For this reason, it cannot be argued, with a view to denying the general regulatory effect of the Commission's decision, that when it upholds a Member State measure or when it rejects it as incompatible with the common market it is issuing a decision that has a precise effect solely in respect to the Member State's margin of manoeuvre in putting into effect a political economy measure, in terms comparable to the cases in which it applies a sanction to an undertaking for violation of competition rules. This is particularly clear regarding those decisions that assess general aid schemes adopted by Member States, but may equally apply to individual state aid measures.[185] The argument that the simple fact that a measure of general scope is directed at an indeterminate group of individuals is *per se* reason enough to deny the possibility of any parallelism between Article 108(2) and the recognition of eventual participation rights in rule-making

[183] Keppenne, *op. cit.*, n. 8, p. 789. This practice is currently reflected in the Notice from the Commission on a simplified procedure for the treatment of certain types of state aid (OJ C 136/3, 16.06.2009), points 13–16.

[184] In this event, persons concerned within the meaning of Article 108(2), who can be granted standing, may secure their procedural guarantees by bringing actions for failure to act under Article 265 TFEU (e.g. *Air One*, *cit.*, n. 26, paragraph 25), if the conditions for the admissibility of this action are fulfilled.

[185] For example, decisions confirming aid for the realization of works that may not respect environmental protection standards.

procedures is, therefore, rejected. Hence, the decisive point lies in the second issue raised: drawing this parallel depends on whether it is possible to assert that the general measure at issue has a sufficient impact on the legal sphere of the persons concerned, namely that it has the ability to give rise to legal administrative relationships.

The answer to this question depends on the concrete content of the norms. In abstract terms, both a positive and a negative answer are possible. It cannot be *a priori* excluded that there may be cases where it is possible to identify with a sufficient degree of precision the interests affected by a given rule. This is an indication that the act at issue might be sufficiently concrete to have the ability to produce by itself a change in the legal position of affected persons. The fact that the Commission's guidelines or frameworks often reflect the content of previous decisions or build upon the Commission's knowledge of problems that might be raised in certain areas, given previous practices, can be an indicator that, in some cases, the Commission is sufficiently informed about an identifiable circle of interests that will be affected by its policy frameworks. In fact, the content of certain norms might reflect the knowledge of concrete situations that the Commission was previously called upon to assess. Even if this does not hinder the general nature of the measure adopted, the Commission may be in the position to know that a given norm affects the interests and the position of a sufficiently indentified group of persons. In these cases, where it is possible to establish a sufficient similarity between the facts underlying the provision of Article 108(2) and an analogous factual situation in respect to procedures leading up to the adoption of administrative rules, the analogy with the notice and comment period enshrined in Article 108(2) is justified.

Admittedly, this might not be the most common situation. In most cases, while setting out the rules in policy frameworks, the Commission is not able to determine *a priori* with sufficient precision the range of interests that will be affected by these norms. In some cases even, it publishes beforehand consultation papers destined to have practitioners' feedback on concrete policy choices, thence gathering not only information on their eventual adherence or opposition to the Commission's proposed policy, but also factual information needed to better adjust this policy in conformity with its goals.[186] In these cases, it might be contended that the argument of analogy

[186] For example, in October 2005, during the process of revision of the 'Guidelines on State aid for Environmental Protection' the Commission launched a questionnaire for public consultation (at <http://ec.europa.eu/comm/competition/state_aid/reform/00910_questionnaire_env_

does not apply and these consultation procedures may be seen as pertaining exclusively to the realm of policy definition and political choice.[187] Note, however, that, as mentioned, the possibility of identifying affected persons is not in itself decisive in determining whether participation rights apply or not. It is merely an indication of the degree of concreteness of the act.

8.3.3 *Participation in implementing regulations*

The approach followed to analyse the possibility of extension of participation rights to implementing regulations and informal rules needs to be different. In the first case, the respective procedure envisages a period of consultation, the question being how to construe this procedural stage and to what extent the respective norm may be interpreted as embracing the exercise of participation rights. Article 6 of the block exemptions regulation determines the following:

> Where the Commission intends to adopt a regulation, it shall publish a draft thereof to enable all interested persons and organizations to submit their comments to it within a reasonable time limit to be fixed by the Commission and which may not under any circumstances be less than one month.

It is very likely that this provision was drafted with a view to enabling the Commission to have access to all the information needed in order to create rules that are adequate to the fulfilment of the regulatory goals that the Commission wishes to pursue. This is, at the same time, the view that prevailed in the Courts' case law regarding participation based on Article 108(2), which has equally been reflected in the respective codifying regulation. This has also been the position consistently defended by the Commission in the Court cases analysed above and it has presumably influenced the enshrinement of a consultation period in the Commission's proposal that formed the basis of the block exemptions regulation.[188]

The regulation does not give any indication as to how the procedure is to develop, in particular with regard to the sequence between the public

en.pdf>). It asked *inter alia*, for information on 'identified market failures, which have a negative impact on environmental protection, and which could be remedied through state aid' as well as for 'views about other justifications that have been used to grant State aid for Environmental Protection' (p. 2 of the questionnaire).

[187] See, below, Sub-section 8.3.4.

[188] Article 7 of the 'Proposal for a regulation on the application of Articles 92 and 93 of the EC Treaty to certain categories of horizontal aid', *cit.*, n. 163.

consultation and the intervention of the advisory committee, and whether the comments received from the public may still be 'filtered' by the opinion of this committee. According to Article 8 of the regulation, this advisory committee (composed of Member States' representatives and chaired by a Commission representative) is consulted by the Commission both before publishing a draft regulation and before adopting the regulation, which indicates that it needs to be consulted also after the public consultation period.[189] This interpretation may be reinforced by the fact that in its proposal, the Commission specified that it intended to inform the advisory committee of the views of interested parties before the adoption of an implementing regulation.

It is unlikely that this provision was drafted with the intention of also providing procedural guarantees to persons possibly affected by the provisions of the implementing regulations. The only procedural guarantee expressly mentioned in the regulation is that there must be a reasonable time period of at least one month, the concrete duration of which is fixed by the Commission according to the circumstances. This, however, is a necessary condition to ensure the utility of any participation phase, irrespective of its prevailing rationale.

Whether or not this provision should be interpreted in analogous terms to Article 108(2) depends on the verification of the abovementioned conditions for establishing the analogy. In view of what was defended above, considering in particular the similarity of rationales of participation rights with regard to individual determinations and to general rules, the main question that remains open is whether the norms of the implementing regulations are sufficiently precise and capable of giving rise to administrative relationships. The fact that the implementing regulations must mention the categories of beneficiaries, the thresholds, and the conditions governing the accumulation of aid may be an indication that this may occur.[190] Nevertheless, this has to be determined in relation to each concrete case. Where the analogy can be established, in particular where the norms of the implementing regulation adversely affect a sufficiently identified scope of persons, participants in rule-making procedures should enjoy similar guarantees as those that have been developed by the Courts in

[189] The Commission has, in any case, the final say, being bound to take the 'utmost account of the opinion delivered by the committee' and to inform the committee 'of the manner in which its opinion was taken into account' (Article 8(5)).

[190] Article 1(2) of the block exemptions regulation, *cit.*, n. 154.

relation to Article 108(2) procedures. It cannot be excluded that, similarly to what has been defended in relation to the procedure of Article 108(2), during the consultation period, holders of subjective rights come to the fore and are identified as such by the Commission, being thereby accorded a corresponding differentiated procedural treatment from the one recognized to holders of legally protected interests. While, to date, there is no judgment on Article 6 of the block exemptions regulation from which one could draw any indication confirming or countering this possibility, in current EU law the very possibility of establishing an analogy in these circumstances is denied by the principled exclusion of participation rights from rule-making procedures.

8.3.4 *Participation in the elaboration of informal rules*

Outside the realm of formal rule-making procedures, there are additional difficulties to this kind of reasoning. The procedures for the adoption of informal rules are, logically, not formalized, the Commission being free to decide whether or not to open these procedures to public consultation. Notwithstanding the different degree of formality, the possibility that norms pertaining to policy frameworks are sufficiently concrete to shape the legal positions of the persons concerned is also present here. In such cases, the fact that these are considered to be procedures that, given their political nature, should not be subject to a legalized form excludes in principle any possibility of granting procedural guarantees to persons adversely affected by their provisions, unless the Court attributes them characteristics similar to formal rules, as it has done with regard to other issues regarding policy frameworks.

Where, considering the content of the informal rules, an analogy with Article 108(2) could be established, not recognizing the participation rights of affected persons in similar terms to those of Article 108(2) will lead to a de-formalization of these rights. This conclusion is supported by two related arguments, which were presented above. First, the Commission's power of adopting such frameworks was not envisaged in the Treaty, and is obviously not framed by the procedural rules set out therein. They result from the institutional practice developed since the early days of integration, expanded and maintained until today. Secondly, the powers that the Treaty attributed to the Commission in matters of state aid control are framed by a procedure that entails a notice and comment phase. Against this last argument in particular, it may be countered that these powers are very different in nature from those that the Commission is exercising while defining policy frameworks: the former are investigative powers, the latter pertain to the realm of policy definition. This possible objection can, however, be refuted on the basis of the characteristics of the regulatory structure in the field of state aid presented above. In fact, the interplay between individual decisions stemming from Article 108(2) and the enactment of guidelines cannot be underestimated: the latter often codify the Commission's stance with regard to state aid that was first revealed in those decisions. As such, resort to informal rules may merely embody a choice of a different regulatory strategy, deemed to be more practical, efficient, and certain, both in terms of the Commission's internal work and with regard to the external effects of the measures it adopts.

In addition, in certain circumstances, solving eventual conflicts involving state aid measures outside the formal adversarial procedure of Article 108(2) may circumvent the rights resulting from this norm. As results from the above, the function of these rules is precisely to structure certain aspects of the Commission's state aid that was policy, making the content of the latter's decisions more predictable than it would otherwise be and giving coherence to the treatment of individual situations. Both in light of this function and by force of the Court's case law—according to which the Commission cannot deviate in individual decisions from the rules that it set out on a purely voluntary basis—the content of these rules necessarily weighs in the Commission's individual decisions. In certain cases, the degree of detail of the Commission's rules may be such that they determine most of the content of the future individual decisions. As much as this situation may be desirable from the perspective of legal certainty, it impacts negatively on the participation rights of concerned persons that could otherwise be granted on the basis of the Treaty. In fact, the situations in which the Commission will be faced with serious difficulties that would justify triggering the Article 108(2) procedure will likely be much fewer, and the settlement of conflicts arising from state aid will more often be kept within the negotiations carried out between the Commission and the Member State concerned, under Article 108(3). As such, this is not at odds with the Treaty and it is moreover justified in light of procedural economy: procedures will be shorter and conflicts will be resolved faster, within the formal mechanisms envisaged by the Treaty. Nevertheless, if rights of intervention of concerned parties similar to those of Article 108(2) are not envisaged in the procedures leading up to the adoption of the rules that allow for that result, there will be a deviation from the Treaty rules, namely from the scheme of Article 108. As shown above, according to the Courts' interpretation, this provision requires that serious difficulties raised in the assessment of state aid measures must be solved with the intervention of parties concerned. The solution is to envisage a period of notice and comment leading to the adoption of those acts of a general nature. The differentiation of the various interests involved and the eventual different procedural treatment required by the diverse ways in which those interests are affected might only be possible after the analysis of the comments received.

There are, therefore, enough reasons to claim that participation should be a requirement of the procedure of enacting informal rules in the cases in which their content is sufficiently precise to determine the final composition of interests involved in solving a legal issue. However, this claim may be seen as a contradiction in terms, since, by definition, it should not be possible to formalize soft law or informal rule-making procedures. Even though the Courts' case law has given binding effect to policy frameworks and guidelines—thereby in a certain way diminishing the distance between formal and informal rules—this process of 'formalization' has not been extended to any aspect of the procedure for the adoption of these informal rules.[191] Yet, certain procedural requirements may be established on the basis of general legal principles. For example, publication requirements follow from the principle of transparency.[192] Participation rights recognized on the basis of an argument of analogy can be based on the principle of equal legal treatment, which requires that similar situations should result in similar legal consequences. To the extent to which it is possible to draw an analogy between a situation in which the legal sphere of an individual is particularly affected by a decision issued on the basis of Article 108(2) and others where rules contained in policy frameworks have a similar effect, particularly affected persons in the latter case should also be given the opportunity of putting forward their views before the final decision is issued and, therefore, should be accorded the guarantees explained above.

[191] On the process of formalization carried out by the Courts in the field of state aid, see, among others, Keppenne, *op. cit.*, n. 8, pp. 802–6. The landmark case in respect to the binding effect of Commission's guidelines on what regards the Commission's own decisions as well as those of Member States (to the extent in which they have agreed upon those guidelines) is Case C-313/90, *CIRFS and others v Commission* [1993] ECR I-1125 (paragraph 14 and 34–36).

[192] The example is drawn from Hofmann, 'Administrative governance . . .', *cit.*, n. 160, p. 195, who also points out the practical need for such publication for the effectiveness of guidelines as steering tools.

Consultation in the adoption of policy frameworks: the case of research, development, and innovation

What has been defended above pertains to the cases in which it is possible to establish an analogy between the enactment of informal rules and the adoption of individual determinations. As alluded to above, such an analogy cannot be defended in all cases. In fact, this essentially depends on the functions of the rules adopted and, in particular, on their content. As such, the argumentation presented above obviously does not rule out cases in which the intervention of interested persons can have a different scope and rationale from those grounding participation rights. These cases should also be considered here, since they point to a meaning of participation different from the one that has been argued for in this book. To a certain extent, they illustrate the Commission's stance with regard to participation that has been characterized in Chapter 3.

In the field of state aid, the origin of the Commission's consultation practice seems to be the 2005 'State Aid Action Plan', which launched the reform of the Commission's policy.[193] The range of soft law instruments is such that consultation practices that are apparently uniform may also diverge considerably in meaning. The fact that there is not a procedural framework similar to the one envisaged for the adoption of implementing regulations enhances this diversity. Nor is the treatment accorded to the different procedures in terms of inclusiveness and transparency uniform either. Some procedures are better documented on the Internet than others. For example, in the case of the 'Community framework for state aid for research and development and innovation',[194] the main documents of the consultation procedure are fully accessible online.[195] However, regarding other procedures, it is not possible to determine, on the basis of the information provided on the DG Competition webpage dedicated to consultation on state aid matters, how consultation proceeded.

In this case, in the document released for consultation, the Commission set out the main goals of its policy, the types of innovation-related activities targeted by it, and the corresponding measures that it intended

[193] 'State aid action plan. Less and better targeted state aid: a roadmap for state aid reform 2005–2009', COM (2005) 107 final, Brussels, 7.5.2005.

[194] OJ C 323/1, 31.12.2006.

[195] <http://www.ec.europa.eu/comm/competition/state_aid/reform/comments_innovation/index.html>.

to adopt.[196] It thereby asked for comments on these proposed measures as well as on other specific issues and announced that 'the results of the consultation will be used to formulate new clear rules for inclusion in the legal instruments on state aid and which will define the limits within which state aid to innovation might be seen to be compatible with the common market'.[197] The issues thereby addressed pertain to general policy choices, apparently not revealing the possibility of *a priori* determination of a specific range of interests eventually affected by the future norms (e.g. 'should the rules on state aid for innovation include regional bonuses for cohesion purposes?'; 'should they differ according to the geographical situation of the region, irrespective of cohesion issues?'),[198] but also not necessarily excluding this possibility (e.g. 'stakeholders are invited to provide empirical evidence about the appropriateness of authorizing state aid to non-technological innovation, notably in services sectors').[199]

The stated aim of this particular consultation process was to 'assess whether the Commission's proposed approach was adequate'.[200] To this effect, the Commission defined the contents of the future regulatory instrument and, more than testing the adherence of practitioners to the proposed norms, it seemed to intend to collect more information in order to flesh out and tune its regulatory choices in view of the goals that it wishes to attain. Accordingly, most of the questions posed were quite open. For example, in respect of measures that could support 'the development of poles of excellence through collaboration and clustering', the Commission stated that 'this is a new area in the field of state aid where there is no established practice, and previous experience is extremely limited'. Thus, it called for additional feedback on certain points. It asked, for example, whether 'state aid should be allowed to promote centres of excellence [and,] if so, what type of state aid, for what reasons, and subject to what conditions';[201] or 'whether large firms should be entitled to state aid, e.g. to establish research

[196] Communication from the Commission, 'Consultation document on State aid for innovation', COM (2005) 436 final, Brussels 21.9.2005.

[197] *Idem*, p. 4, paragraph 10.

[198] *Idem*, p. 8, question No. 6.

[199] *Idem*, p. 8, question No. 5.

[200] 'Results of the consultation on State aid for innovation—detailed summary', 05.05.2006 (available at <http://ec.europa.eu/competition/state_aid/reform/comments_innovation/summary_innovation.pdf>, last visited in July 2008), p. 5.

[201] *Idem*, p. 17, question No. 17.

facilities in a European pole of excellence' and 'what type of economic evidence should be requested to analyse the necessity of such state aid'.[202]

In this case, as mentioned, the treatment given by the Commission to this information was quite transparent. It published a detailed summary of the comments received, where it explained the methodology used for the treatment of this data, and indicated the number of answers received for each question or measure proposed, the degree of support, and the comments received.[203] Moreover, taking account of the difficulties in summarizing contributions addressing specific concerns of specific interest groups, the Commission invited the reader to consult also the individual contributions in order to have 'a full picture of the comments received'.[204] Ultimately, it could be possible in some cases to trace the influence that the comments received might have had in the final solution adopted.

This process, in particular the substance of these questions, reveals, at least in relation to certain points of the policy framework, a 'sharing' of rule-making powers with the relevant 'stakeholders', to use the Commission's jargon. Possibly, the concrete solutions ultimately adopted depend on the negotiations carried out between the Commission and the Member States. Still, it cannot be ruled out that consultation procedures such as this lead to situations of co-regulation, more than participation, in public rule-making procedures. The lack of any procedural rules that tailor the role of participation in rule-making procedures, even if only scantly defined, may favour this shift, which is solely in the hands of the Commission. However, ultimately, this depends on the concrete circumstances that the Commission is faced with and, in particular, on the information resources or 'in-house' knowledge that it possesses.

The rationales that underlie participation rights, in particular the dignitarian rationale, are absent in this case. The contents of the regulatory instrument were not yet sufficiently precise and commentators were asked to give their opinions on broad policy choices. It may be argued that the representatives of the interests that, nonetheless, may be identified as being linked to the subject matter subject to consultation, should be given an

[202] *Idem*, p. 17, question No. 20.

[203] In accordance with standard E of the Commission's code of practice—Communication from the Commission, 'Towards a reinforced culture of consultation and dialogue—General principles and minimum standards for consultation of interested parties by the Commission' (COM (2002) 704 final, Brussels, 11.12.2002), p. 21.

[204] The detailed summary is quoted in note 201. The list of the several contributions is equally available on the Internet (*cit.*, n. 195).

opportunity to express their views on the issues consulted and be given equal conditions of access. Nevertheless, the meaning of their intervention differs from the situations of participation that have been analysed so far; in particular, they cannot be passed off as participation rights. In these circumstances, interest representatives are called upon to define a regulatory policy in collaboration with the decision-maker. They do not express their views on a regulatory measure that defines the composition of interests involved with enough precision effectively to determine the content of the advantageous and disadvantageous positions that the persons they represent will be endowed with. Their intervention is not a means to ensure compliance with the principle of care that the decision-maker should respect when considering different alternatives that will shape the rights and duties of the persons concerned by the decision.

This essentially amounts to acknowledging that the recognition or otherwise of participation rights requires a distinction between the realm of political decision-making and that of legal decision-making. In this respect, for the purposes of this work and on the basis of what has been defended so far, one criterion may be put forward: there is a shift from the political to the legal when there is an impact on the legal spheres of persons, which are thereby shaped by public decisions.

8.4 Weaving Loose Threads

Different aspects of the Courts' interpretation of the participatory procedure of Article 108(2) TFEU constitute relevant indications that confirm the suitability of the construction of participation rights proposed in this book.

First, as if forced to admit the existence of participation rights beyond the strict bilateral scheme that underlies their conception of the right to be heard, the Courts (mostly the CFI, now General Court, but also the Court of Justice on appeal) made a clear distinction between the right to be heard of the addressee of individual decisions and the participation rights of the persons concerned defined by Article 108(2). Nevertheless, they were not able fully to maintain such a neat distinction with regard to persons other than the addressee whose substantive legal position can also be differentiated from that of other persons concerned. Secondly, the vicissitudes of the concept of 'persons concerned', which has been restricted due to the need to reconcile the conditions of access to decisional procedures with the EU rules on private standing, confirm that the standing requirements have influenced the Courts' stance with regard to participation rights. At the same time, they are illustrative of the difficulties posed by the extension of participation rights proposed in this work. Thirdly, the Courts have distinguished persons whose specific position the decision-maker is bound to consider from persons who may be adversely affected by the procedure and are, therefore, entitled to intervene on the basis of Article 108(2), but whose intervention is legally relevant insofar as they voice interests that, in light of the applicable rules, should be taken into account by the decision-maker. Fourthly, in some of the cases analysed, the Courts have established a link between the qualification of certain persons as being concerned by the decisions adopted on the basis of Article 108(2) and the interests that state aid rules are designed to protect. Fifthly, the fact that a decision adopted under Article 108(2) may impinge upon individual aid measures with concretely identified beneficiaries and counter-interested undertakings, or that it may assess general aid schemes regarding which the identification of the persons concerned may not be immediate, confirms the continuity between individual and general acts and the unsuitability of using a criterion based on the nature of the act to determine the scope of participation rights.

To a certain extent, these are loose threads in the Courts' case law. This chapter has woven them together in light of the conception of participation rights defended here, in order to demonstrate that it is possible to ground it in elements of positive law. It was pointed out that the Courts have not given these aspects the meaning that they were attributed in the construction of participation rights this book proposes. In particular, they have refused to overcome the conception of the procedural relationship stemming from a state aid control decision as involving only the Commission and the Member State concerned—still, they were mindful of the effects that such a decision has on the legal sphere of the beneficiaries of state aid and their competitors. They maintain that there is no room to distinguish different categories of persons concerned, even where they recognized that some of the persons concerned outside this bilateral relationship should be accorded a differentiated procedural treatment. Moreover, the Courts certainly did not go as far as to suggest that the procedure should reflect the material effects produced by the Commission decision in the legal sphere of the persons concerned. This last aspect has only implicitly and partially been accepted by the Courts.

Arguably, the judicial interpretation of Article 108(2) is, at least in certain respects, preconceived by the bilateral scheme that underlies the Courts' case law on the right to be heard. It was argued that, instead, the structure of the procedure for the review of state aid should be conceived in light of the substantive legal regime that it serves and of the effects that the Commission's decision may have on legally protected interests. Persons who may be adversely affected should be entitled to participate in the procedure, either to defend their subjective legal positions or to voice concerns related to the set of interests that the decision-maker needs to balance. In the former case, they should be granted stronger procedural protection, since their position can be distinguished from that of other persons concerned. To this extent, their stake might not be different from that of the addressee of a decision, and they should be granted similar procedural guarantees.

Another aspect examined in this chapter was the possibility of extending participation rights in the field of state aid to other decisional procedures of which the Commission is in charge in this sector. The basis of the analogy is threefold: the rationales of participation rights, as defined in relation to Article 108(2), are also applicable to rule-making procedures; the material effects stemming from individual decisions may be similar to those arising from the adoption of general rules; the differences between the type of powers regulated under Article 108(2) and others acquired by the Commission are not such as to impede *a priori* the possibility of analogy. A distinction was made in this regard between implementing regulations adopted under the block exemptions regulation and informal rules. In the first case, where it is possible to establish this analogy, the provision for consultation enshrined in Article 6 of the block exemptions regulation should be interpreted as providing persons concerned with similar guarantees to those that stem from Article 108(2). In the second case, the informal nature of the procedures represents an additional difficulty to an argument of analogy, although the Courts have steadily diminished some of the differences between formal and informal rules. In any event, where analogy can be ascertained, denying the recognition of the procedural rights based on Article 108(2) may amount to a de-formalization of such rights. In fact, solving conflicts over state aid measures outside the formal adversarial procedure of Article 108(2) may, in certain circumstances, circumvent the rights resulting from this norm.

Chapter 9

Conclusions

9.1 Pervasive Participation, Fading Participation Rights

Participation is ubiquitous in EU law and governance and yet participation rights are not sufficiently comprehensive in current EU administrative law. The two parts of this statement recall the two different meanings and veins of participation in EU law: participation as a trait of the EU institutional form as well as of its regulatory processes (interest representation) and participation in decisional procedures that may adversely affect the individual (rights-based participation). Despite the fact that participation has featured prominently in recent institutional and political developments that have shaped the EU's constitutional framework, little attention has been paid to participation rights as a means of ensuring the procedural protection of persons affected by EU regulation in the diverse forms that the latter may assume. Both the legislator and the EU Courts have largely ignored this dimension of the rule of law.

Participation, in the first sense, is perceived as an important means of acquiring specialized knowledge and information, of ensuring responsive regulation as well as of facilitating compliance with the enacted rules. Participation enables the deciding bodies to scrutinize beforehand how their regulatory proposals may be received by market participants, in order to accommodate the perceived social and economic needs of the sector in question, to forge consensus or, at least, to enhance adherence to the regulatory choice of the decisional body. In a word, participation represents a means of securing the efficient and effective deployment of the EU's regulatory functions. It has, therefore, a 'legitimizing' function, to the extent that it contributes to the technical appropriateness of the decisions adopted by the EU institutions and to enhancing the confidence of the 'interested public' in the decisional procedures. The different participatory practices that pervade EU decision-making may be pinned down to these meanings and functions.

In this vein, participation has both resulted from the specific political-institutional characteristics of the EU—and, before it, of the European Communities—and has been a reflexive and constitutive feature of the EU polity throughout the integration process. Originally, two factors led to participation becoming an institutional feature of the Communities: the reduced apparatus of their administrations—a trait that comes from the way the administration of the European Coal and Steel Community was conceived—and the neo-functionalist logic of the Commission. As the integration process advanced, the involvement of interested parties in EU decision-making procedures, recognized in the founding Treaties by way of the 'grand' advisory bodies, was reproduced, widened, and furthered in practice. The creation of committees exclusively or partially composed of interest representatives, the provision for organic participation within the structure of some agencies, and, especially, the multiple consultation procedures organized by the Commission are manifestations of the pervasiveness of participation in EU decision-making. Interest representation, understood as the involvement of representatives of the interests affected in the regulatory processes that concern them, has thereby become intrinsic to different levels of decision-making across different regulatory fields, powers, and forms of delivering the EU administrative functions.

On this basis, one may claim that participation is a constitutional feature of the EU. This is reinforced by the fact that it has accompanied the constitutional transition from market building to the creation of a political union. In the contemporaneous overhaul of the regulatory policy of the EU, participation was not only heralded as one of the principles of European governance, but was also considered to be one of the ways to tackle the ever more salient legitimacy problems faced by the EU. From being mainly a means of ensuring the performance of the EU regulatory functions, participation became a tool for 'public-making', for reaching out to the 'European citizens' and 'civil society'. Nevertheless, in essence, this did not deviate much from the neo-functionalist logic that had grounded participatory mechanisms since the beginning of the integration process. Although changes in the EU political-institutional context have resulted in alterations to the way participation is perceived, little has changed in the nature of the participatory mechanisms in place. In the main, these have kept the same functions and the same characteristics of the long-standing participatory practices of the European Community. In particular, the deciding bodies have maintained the prerogative of choosing which segments of policy- and rule-making and which matters are subject to participatory procedures, as well as the relevance attributed to participation. One such choice was to largely leave out the regulatory activity pertaining to the Commission's executive powers from the participatory procedures fostered by the Commission in the aftermath of its White Paper on Governance.

These long-standing participation practices are now, after Lisbon, the substratum of Article 11 of the Treaty of the European Union, which enshrines the principle of participatory democracy. Article 11 is mostly the culmination of the institutional evolution that was described and analysed in Chapter 3. Far from being an innovation proper, this 'principle' provides formal constitutional recognition to those previous practices (with the exception of the provision for citizens' legislative initiative). As such, it also incorporates their constitutive features. Undoubtedly, Article 11 reflects the intent of providing these practices with a new normative cloak: participatory democracy is now formally one of the democratic principles on which the Union stands.[1] This, however, cannot hide the fact that, at least until now, the participation practices on which this 'principle' builds have little to do with the political legitimacy of decisional processes grounded in democratic values, one that would be based on a fundamental choice of the political system as to how to ensure the democratic basis for decision-making. As it has been construed in the EU political system, this 'principle' ultimately stems from and is embedded in the endeavour to ensure the technical legitimacy of regulatory decisions. Therefore, it is detached from normative considerations regarding the place of the citizen or the individual in the political system and their participation in the decisions of the representative bodies of a community. This last aspect was developed in Chapter 6, when analysing the consultative procedures in the field of financial services. The study of the so-called Lamfalussy process revealed that participation may be an instrument to tackle regulatory characteristics of a given sector, which need to be addressed in order to ensure the desired regulatory outcomes, rather than ensuring the yardsticks of democratic legitimacy. In the case of financial services, these characteristics—the spread of regulatory resources among various actors with different regulatory capacities, situated

[1] As mentioned previously in the book, despite the fact that, contrary to its predecessor in the Constitutional Treaty, the heading 'Principle of Participatory Democracy' does not figure in this article, there is little doubt that this is the meaning and purpose of this provision.

at different regulatory levels (national, European, and international)—closely resemble the original features of the European Communities that have led to the mushrooming of participation practices.

While Article 11 of the Treaty of the European Union is not per se an innovation, the fact that participatory democracy is now a Treaty norm is not without consequences. At the very least, what was a discretionary choice of the institutions based on long-standing and commonly accepted practices is now a norm of conduct by which the institutions and bodies need to abide. Naturally, it is still up to the EU institutions and bodies to decide in which instances and under which forms they will give effect to the determinations of Article 11. At any rate, a hypothetical regression of current practices could hardly be justified in light of this norm.

In the second sense mentioned above, participation refers to legally enforceable procedural rights that are recognized to persons adversely affected by the decisions of the EU bodies and institutions, mainly the Commission, in the exercise of its administrative powers. Participation follows from the recognition of legally regulated procedural guarantees directed at ensuring respect for the person's rights and legally protected interests, as well as the due consideration and balancing of the public and private interests involved in decisional procedures with a view to achieving just and technically appropriate decisions. Participation rights are grounded both in the dignity of the person and in the attainment of materially just decisions and are, therefore, an important dimension of the rule of law. This legal facet of participation stems from the legal principles common to the laws of Member States and adds a different 'thicker' constitutional dimension to participation. However, it has remained insulated from the broader regulatory developments that have occurred in European governance.

The difference between participation practices, in particular consultative procedures organized by the Commission, and a rights-based participation was illustrated by the procedures developed in the realm of the Lamfalussy procedures (Chapter 6). This difference was also shown by the analysis of the rules and practices of consultation in force in the field of EU food law, namely the procedure for the authorization of genetically modified food (Chapter 7) and by the examination of the consultation procedures that precede the adoption of the so-called 'policy frameworks' in the field of state aid (Chapter 8). While consultative procedures may be valuable in terms of achieving previously set regulatory goals and, thus, of ensuring the effective performance of the EU regulatory functions, they are largely meaningless for upholding the values that justify the recognition of participation rights. They are, in particular, inadequate to safeguard the legal protection of the rights and interests of persons affected by EU regulation. Therefore, EU governance arrangements, which entail participation as a tool designed to achieve regulatory outcomes, have largely ignored the thicker meaning of participation inherent in participation rights. In other words, the deployment of the regulatory functions by the EU institutions with respect for the rights and interests of affected persons, through participation rights, has not been a major concern, or at least not a consistent one, in the delineation of regulatory decision-making structures and procedures. This contention was demonstrated by the food law decisional procedures examined in Chapter 7, where the legislator does not seem to have considered the position of the persons affected by their decisions. In addition, where the EU has been active in fostering participation rights (e.g. in the field of the environment), these have been essentially conceived as duties of Member States. These rights do enhance the procedural guarantees of persons affected by decisions that fall within the realm of EU law. However, they do so in their relationships with Member State administrations, not with the EU institutions and bodies.

The lack of concern for the procedural protection of persons affected by EU decisions that is evident in the delineation of regulatory procedures is mainly due to the influence of the model of executive federalism. According to this model, the procedural and judicial protection of the rights and legally protected interests of persons affected by EU decisions remained essentially a task entrusted to the national rules of procedure (as was explained in Chapter 4). The argument that this form of conceiving the distribution of administrative power between the EU and the Member States has influenced the relevance attributed to the procedural protection of persons in the context of EU administrative law is reinforced by the contrast between the ECSC Treaty and the EC Treaty with regard to participation rules, as highlighted in Chapter 3. And yet, it may hardly be possible to insulate indirect administration by Member States from the exercise of effective decisional powers on the part of EU institutions or bodies, as demonstrated in particular by the analysis of the procedure for the authorization of novel foods still in force. In this sense, the specific division of powers that characterizes the EU administration should not influence the granting of participation rights. These ought to be recognized in procedures the outcome of which is liable to affect the legal sphere of natural or legal persons, independently of the concrete combination of administrative decisions that gives effect to EU legal acts.

9.2 The Right to be Heard: The Matrix of Individual Procedures

The neglect of administrative procedural protection in EU law has been partially countered by the Courts' case law, according to which the right to be heard is a 'fundamental principle of Community law which must be guaranteed even in the absence of any rules governing the proceedings in question'.[2] The procedural protection via the recognition of participation rights made its way into the EU legal system through this right, established and developed by the Courts' case law, and thereby recognized in 'all proceedings initiated against a person, which are liable to culminate in a measure adversely affecting that person'.[3] Nevertheless, while the Courts' elaboration of this principle has filled important lacunae of procedural protection in EU administrative law, the Courts have maintained an unduly formalistic approach to participation rights. This was argued and demonstrated in Chapters 4 and 5. In current EU administrative law, the scope of participation rights is mainly that endorsed in the Courts' jurisprudence. However, in developing their approach to participation rights, the Courts have not been sufficiently mindful of the multifaceted reality of EU regulation and, in particular, of the range of situations in which the regulatory activity of the EU institutions and bodies may adversely affect the rights and legally protected interests of natural and legal persons. They have adhered to excessively formal conceptions of participation rights that are premised on the right to be heard in individual procedures, as well as to a restrictive view regarding the relationships between the citizens and the administration.

The limits of the Courts' case law in this matter are essentially of two types: subjective, referring to the persons who are recognized as possessing the right to be heard, and objective, pertaining to the nature of the acts at issue. First, as a rule, in order to access the procedure, the person concerned needs to be in a position substantially equivalent to that of the person against whom a procedure has been initiated. Secondly, the right to be heard is granted in procedures leading to the adoption of individual decisions. Although it has also been extended to regulations of an individualized nature ('hybrid' regulations), the only cases in which, for purposes of

[2] This is the current formulation used by the Courts (see Chapter 4, n. 66).

[3] *Idem.*

participation, the Courts have consistently admitted that acts of a general nature may produce effects similar to those entailed in individual decisions of the type mentioned above are anti-dumping regulations. In other cases in which a general act, without losing its normative nature, could be considered to be of direct and individual concern to adversely affected persons, in the sense that it effectively embodies an individual decision, the Courts have both accepted and denied the recognition of participation rights. Outside these situations, the degree to which persons concerned by a normative act are affected is immaterial to their procedural rights.

These limits follow from the structural setting which determines the Courts' stance with regard to the right to be heard: while the adverse effect produced by the act adopted is the substantive element of this right, this effect can only engender a right to be heard within the framework of a bilateral relationship established between a natural or a legal person and the decision-maker. This is the constant thread of the Courts' case law in this matter. According to the Courts, the convergence of the substantive and structural elements is immediate if the act is an individual decision or equivalent thereto and the person concerned is its addressee or is in a substantively equivalent position. This undoubtedly forms the core of the right to be heard, but, as a rule, this is also the scope of the fundamental principle that must be recognized even in the absence of a written rule or when the existing rules do not ensure a sufficient degree of procedural protection. This book has shown that where the Court has widened the personal or objective scope of the right to be heard, the corresponding expansions have only been possible in cases that could still be brought within the basic structural framework mentioned (Chapter 4). Therefore, one may argue that the decisive criterion for the recognition of this right is not the adverse effect of a measure in the legal sphere of a natural or legal person as such, but the production of this adverse effect within the framework of a bilateral relationship. Indeed, the Courts have not taken as much care in defining what type of adverse effect may justify the procedural intervention of the person concerned as they have in delimiting the boundaries by reference to the structural element underlying the right to be heard.

Another aspect complements this structural scheme: the case law of the Courts on participation rights enhances the subjective element inherent in the dignity of the person and the function of procedural protection of individuals attached to their intervention in the procedure. This strengthens the subjective and objective limits of the right to be heard, since this right needs to be exercised where an individual decision negatively impacts on the legal sphere of an identified addressee. In most cases—at least regarding the more fundamental choices on the recognition of participation rights—the Courts seem to downplay the instrumental rationale of participation rights, i.e. their contribution to the material justice and technical correctness of the decision. The Courts' interpretation of the procedural intervention of persons concerned under former Article 88(2) EC—the wording of which is reproduced in Article 108(2) TFEU—could contradict this assertion, since it reflects the fact that the functions of participation cannot be reduced to an element of defence. However, the judicial interpretation of this norm was underpinned by the conception that the procedural right it enshrines and the right to be heard are two distinct rights.

The study of the case law on what is now Article 108(2) TFEU also revealed the difficulties the Courts are faced with when sticking unconditionally to a bilateral conception of the procedure. While maintaining the characterization of the state aid control procedures as involving a bilateral relationship established between the Commission and the Member State concerned, the Courts admitted that the ensuing decisions may decisively impact on the legal sphere of private persons, other than the Member State targeted by the Commission's decision. Nevertheless, the predominance of the bilateral scheme prevented them from distinguishing the different categories of the so-called 'third parties' concerned by the outcome of the procedure on the basis of their effective substantive position in the underlying material situation and of the legal effects produced in their legal spheres. In particular, this prevented the Courts from consistently recognizing a proper right to be heard to persons whose subjective rights are adversely affected, but who stand outside the bilateral scheme mentioned.

9.3 Participation Rights in EU Rule-making: Exclusion on Formal Grounds

The denial of participation rights in rule-making procedures is a mere logical consequence of the Courts' adherence to a formal stance regarding the right to be heard. In this interpretation, the institutional arguments that have been invoked in support of the normative option of excluding participation rights from procedures conducive to the adoption of general acts are solely ancillary to the underlying Courts' construction of the right to be heard. Furthermore, the institutional arguments invoked are feeble. As was argued in Chapter 5, the argument according to which the EU decisional procedures abide by the principle of representative democracy, and the contention that this would exclude other obligations of consultation incumbent upon the EU legislator apart from those enshrined in the Treaty, is inappropriate to deny participation rights in EU rule-making procedures. Moreover, it was defended that it is also unconvincing to argue that the only obligations of consultation incumbent upon the EU legislator are those explicitly enshrined in a Treaty article and that this would be needed to preserve the Union's institutional balance. In addition, it was argued that none of these two principles is capable of justifying the exclusion of participation rights from procedures which precede the adoption of normative acts not directly based on a Treaty article and not resulting from the combined will of the Commission, the Council, and the Parliament shaped according to the procedures defined in the Treaty. Therefore, in this last case, grounding the exclusion of participation in rule-making procedures on those institutional arguments is wrong. This is particularly true after Lisbon, given that, irrespective of how Article 11 is to be interpreted, it is now difficult to argue that the principle of representative democracy would exclude duties of consultation whenever these are not formally enshrined. For this reason, Article 11, together with other Treaty provisions, might ultimately contribute to overcoming the limits currently placed on participation rights. In particular, the looser standing requirements for the annulment of self-executing regulatory acts may open new possibilities to private litigants seeking enforcement of participation rights in rule-making and invoking Article 11 as a basis for their pleas.

The combination between the Courts' conceptual construction of the right to be heard and this principled exclusion of participation rights from rule-making procedures demonstrates the Courts' excessive formalism in their approach to participation rights. Outside the formal boundaries placed on participation rights, the procedural protection of the persons concerned by the adoption of an act is overlooked even where this would be required in light of the effects of the act adopted and the rationales of participation rights. This ignores that individual decision-making is one of many regulatory techniques that are capable of changing the legal positions of natural and legal persons, and, thus, limits the procedural protection of their substantive rights and interests to one specific form of regulation.

Three arguments were presented in this book to sustain the unsuitability of the distinction between individual administrative acts and general normative acts as a decisive criterion to determine whether participation should be a legal requirement of a decisional procedure. First, the legal divide between general and individual acts rests largely on a legal fiction. In fact there are different shades of the general and abstract characteristics of regulations. Apart from the cases in which the analysis of the content of the general act reveals that it effectively contains an individual decision, in other cases general acts may define very precise entitlements and duties. This may occur in such a way that after their adoption, the possibility of their affecting the persons who fall within their realm is effective and not merely potential. The fact that general provisions may directly create rights and duties in the legal spheres of individuals is demonstrated, in EU law, by the cases in which EU institutions incur non-contractual liability as a result of the adoption of regulations. While, in current EU administrative law, participation rights are excluded in these instances, given the form of the act and its generality, some of these acts may produce actual and certain damage in the legal sphere of natural and legal persons. In light of the rationales of participation rights, as put forward in this book, this is unjustifiable if grounded only in the nature of the act.

Secondly, the continuity between individual administrative acts and general normative acts is reinforced by the way the Courts have characterized EU normative acts. According to the Courts' case law, the normative character of an act is not called into question when it is possible to identify the number or even the identity of the subjects to which it can apply at a given moment, as long as this same identification emerges from an objective factual or legal situation identified by the act in question in relation to its aim. The fact that an act directed at a closed group of persons, identifiable at the moment at which it was adopted, can still be recognized as a normative act, hence maintaining its characteristics of abstractness and generality, narrows down the distance between general and individual acts. It cannot be excluded that a normative act may produce a legal change in the legal sphere of identifiable persons, thereby having effects which are analogous to those emerging from an individual decision. Even if the scope of the act is defined according to objective criteria, the possible knowledge of individual situations may weigh in the definition of its content. This shows the similarities that individual and general acts may have in certain circumstances. However, the Courts largely ignore these possibilities. The only exceptions are the cases in which they assess the direct and individual concern of the persons affected and consider this to be of relevance for granting them participation rights. The fact that, outside these cases, a substantial adverse effect produced in the legal sphere of natural or legal persons by the effect of a normative act is irrelevant for the recognition of participation rights—even if such an analogy could be established—reinforces the conclusion that the bilateral scheme mentioned above is the ultimate determinant factor in defining the scope of participation rights in EU administrative law.

Thirdly, the choice of resorting either to individual or to general acts may be only a consequence of a regulatory option that does not interfere with the legal effects actually stemming from the act. This is demonstrated by the example of the market authorizations of foodstuffs, analysed in Chapter 7. In this case, it was shown how acts that have very similar effects may be adopted either under the form of an individual administrative act addressed to a specified food business operator or under the form of a EU list. The latter contains information on the authorized foodstuffs, which may either be inserted as an annex into the basic legislative act or be adopted as an implementing regulation. So far, the choice between these different legislative techniques has depended essentially on the technical and scientific knowledge available in the pertinent field at the moment at which the primary act is adopted and on the complexity of the assessments involved in the authorization of each product. Under Lisbon, the institutional implications of adopting an individual or a general act—the latter can only take the form of implementing acts adopted under Article 291 TFEU—will very likely weigh on the concrete form chosen in each case. The fate of participation rights should not be dependent on either of these choices. The fact that the form of the act may be immaterial for the effects that it actually produces is also confirmed by what was said in Chapter 8 regarding Commission decisions on general aid schemes. The objects of these state aid decisions are general measures adopted by Member States and, despite their being formally individual decisions addressed to the Member State concerned, they produce legal effects in the legal spheres of the persons who are intended to benefit from such schemes and of those whose interests are contrary to the latter. Participation rights defined in current Article 108 (2) TFEU apply both to these cases and to state aid decisions impinging upon individual aid measures with concretely identified beneficiaries. This is an element of positive law that reinforces the conclusion according to which the nature of the act and the form of the act are inappropriate to ground the recognition of participation rights.

The claim that the nature of the normative acts themselves 'as measures of general application' is not a sufficient reason for excluding participation rights altogether from rule-making procedures is in tune with the general characteristics of EU law. Apart from the abovementioned conception of normative acts adopted by the EU Courts, the Treaty rules that define the competences of the EU may favour the convergence in the same act of elements stemming both from the exercise of a normative and of an administrative function in a narrow sense. Depending on the 'density' of the Treaty rules in question, on the concrete aim to be achieved by a given normative act, or simply on the policy option of the legislator, it is possible that norms adopted directly on the basis of the Treaty have, in fact, an executive function, at least as to part of their content. This is illustrated by the food law procedures analysed in Chapter 7, in particular by the fact that the primary act itself may include the list of authorized products to the exclusion of all others (even if this technique is increasingly being replaced by the adoption of implementing regulations, in the pre-Lisbon terminology). This has in fact a similar value to the individual authorization of those products. In turn, the secondary or administrative normative acts are shaped by the content of the basic act and, in the case mentioned, may be restricted to the technical adaptation of the primary act to technical and scientific developments. Therefore, it cannot be *a priori* excluded that both legislative and administrative normative acts, irrespective of their normative nature, may have concrete provisions that impact upon the legal sphere of natural and legal persons.

Several factors may have contributed to the Courts' general construction of participation rights. First, the judicial origins of this procedural right are clear in the common constitutional traditions of the Member States, which constitute the source of the *audi alteram partem* principle in EU law. This was seen in the comparative note presented in Chapter 2. Arguably, the restrictive formula used in *Hoffman-La Roche* and in subsequent case law—insisting on the individuality of the harm resulting from the EU administrative decisions—accentuated the parallel between judicial and administrative procedures where the right to be heard is deemed to be justified. Secondly, this has shaped the EU administrative procedures in the field of competition that have been influential in the design of other administrative procedures, in particular in areas of economic regulation. Thirdly, it is very likely that restrictive rules on private standing before the EU Courts have limited the range of persons who could claim participation rights and thereby possibly instigate further developments on this matter. Moreover, more generous rules of access to decisional procedures would probably strain the current rules of standing and this might have hindered a different stance regarding participation rights. The argument that this interplay might have influenced the Courts' approach to participation rights is confirmed by the interaction between the interpretation of current Articles 108(2) TFEU and 263(4) TFEU that, as demonstrated in Chapter 8, led the Court to conflate the concept of parties concerned for the purposes of access to the decision-making procedure with the concept of direct and individual concern relevant for purposes of standing.

9.4 A Rights-based Approach

With a view to overcoming the limits placed by the Courts on participation rights, it was argued in this book that these ought to be extended on the basis of the effective legal links resulting from an act, irrespective of its form, and, hence, taking into account the substantive legal positions of those affected. For this purpose, and depending on the case at issue, the interpreter might need to abandon the bilateral scheme that has traditionally underlain the recognition of the right to be heard. To be sure, not all acts and not every degree of adversity require the procedural protection of the persons concerned through the recognition of participation rights. Nevertheless, the limits placed on the scope of participation rights should be such that they allow coverage of a broader range of situations in which subjective rights and legally protected interests of the persons concerned require procedural protection. They need to be underpinned by a particular relation of the participants with the material situation that motivated the procedure, that is, primarily by the ability of an act to affect their substantive rights and legally protected interests. Participation rights are therefore understood as advantageous procedural positions conferred upon natural or legal persons, which allow their holders to influence the exercise of the decisional power with a view to fulfilling the underlying substantive interest that they voice in the procedure. Only in such a way can the functions of participation which stem from the rule of law be properly performed, namely the respect of the persons' dignity, by enabling them to defend their rights and interests in the procedures that concern them, and the achievement of materially just and technically correct decisions through an accurate consideration and balancing of the public and private interests involved in the decisional procedures. Participation rights are thus justified as a means to ensure respect for the rule of law values in the decisional procedure.

Extending the scope of participation rights beyond the limits that have been defined by the Courts—i.e. recognizing them to persons other than the addressee of the act (or those in an analogous position thereto) and in procedures leading to the adoption of both individual and general acts whenever subjective rights and legally protected interests are adversely affected—risks extending the realm of participation rights beyond a concept of participation that is still tenable on legal grounds. The underpinnings of participation rights by the construction proposed in this book—i.e. the connection of the person to the material situation being regulated and the functions of participation—counter this risk, but may not be sufficiently precise to delimit the persons and the situations in which participation rights ought to arise. The concept of legal administrative relationship, framed by the set of public and private interests legally protected by the applicable norms, helps to delimit the proposed subjective and objective scope of participation rights.

On this basis, participation rights are justified where the regulatory activity of the EU institutions and bodies shapes legal administrative relationships between public and private entities, in the sense that their acts either define or decisively determine the content of the rights, interests, duties, and charges recognized to, or impinging upon, the persons concerned. As mentioned, this requires exceeding the bilateral conception that dominates the legislative and judicial approaches to EU administrative procedures, since, as a rule, these do not take into account the effects that are actually produced by the adoption of an act. Hence, the procedural relationship (the one that emerges during the decisional procedure) should be conceived as a multilateral relationship in many cases where currently a bilateral conception of the procedure prevails. This is exemplified by the different procedures in the field of food law, as well as the state aid control procedures examined, respectively, in Chapters 7 and 8. The procedural relationship ought to reflect the effective links between different advantageous and disadvantageous legal positions that will likely be established by effect of the envisaged act. These links cannot always be pinned down to a bilateral relationship that involves the decision-maker and the immediate recipient of the decision. In addition, the procedural relationships ought to be interpreted in light of the substantive regime that the procedure serves. In other words, the way in which the procedural relationship is conceived cannot be isolated either from the material effects produced by the act or from the substantive criteria that, according to the applicable rules, need to guide the substantive regulatory choices in each case.

Moreover, resort to the concept of legal administrative relationship contributes to ordering the different connections between the legal spheres touched by the adoption of the act, as well as to structuring the roles of the participants during the procedure, in light of their relation to the subject matter of the procedure and of the substantive criteria legally defined for the resolution of the matter. In principle, it is possible to distinguish two categories of persons concerned: holders of subjective rights and holders of legally protected interests affected by the final decision. The former are persons who, in light of the applicable norms, may aim to acquire a certain good or advantage through the decision that is being adopted or prevent an effect that this decision is intended to produce in their legal sphere. The latter, while being sufficiently connected to the material situation under examination, voice 'objectivized interests' the fulfilment of which is, at the same time, one of the goals of the legal system and should therefore be considered in the exercise of the decisional function. Holders of legally protected interests cannot aspire to having their personal situation considered as such by the decision-maker, since their intervention is legally valued on the basis of their contribution to the procedure. Provided that they have a substantive link to the material situation, their capacity as persons concerned—on the basis of which they are given access to the procedure—derives from the fact that they defend legally protected interests which may be adversely affected by the decision and which ought to be considered by the decision-maker as part of the overall assessment that forms the basis of the decision. On the contrary, holders of subjective rights who might be adversely affected by the decision have a qualified subjective entitlement vis-à-vis the decision-maker. The latter needs to consider their subjective position as such while assessing the material situation that is being regulated.

The difference between the two categories of participants mentioned has essentially to do with the specific aims of protection and degrees of legal protection that derive from the applicable norms in each case, i.e. with the way the legal system values and protects their position in the material relationship that emerges from the act. This, in turn, essentially depends on the relevance of the personal factor in each case. Either the participants' legally relevant interests are protected as subjective rights—i.e. as a specific form of protection of the individual in particular before the exercise of public power—or as public interests relevant for a given community, which resonate also in the legal sphere of the respective members and are hence worthy of legal protection. In a way, this has been recognized by the Courts in the case law regarding the interpretation of current Article 108(2) TFEU. It is at least possible, on the basis of this case law, to distinguish between persons whose particular situation the decision-maker is legally bound to consider, in the adoption of the decision, from others who voice interests that should be taken into account as part of the overall assessment that forms the basis of this decision. The Court has, implicitly, recognized the criterion of the range of interests legally protected by the applicable norms to ground the scope of persons concerned for the purposes of Article 108(2) TFEU.

It results from the above that the differentiation between different categories of persons concerned is essentially a matter of interpretation. It depends on the way the material situation is assessed by the decision-maker within the limits of the legal criteria by which they are bound. In other words, it is part of the balancing exercise that the decision-maker needs to carry out when assessing the private and public interests at stake in a given material situation, as well as the link of the interested persons with the procedure at issue. This means that this distinction is not a clear-cut one, certainly not one that can be applied *a priori* to a given situation. The criteria that ground the distinction mentioned, as presented above, should then be understood as legal criteria that guide the decision-maker and the judge in assessing each material situation. This assessment should be directed at ensuring, through the procedure, the legal protection of those affected and a sound consideration of the interests that need to be balanced in each case, i.e. at ensuring the adoption of procedurally fair and materially just decisions.

The different degree of substantive protection may justify that different procedural statuses are recognized to holders of subjective rights and to holders of legally protected interests. Persons whose position the decision-maker is legally bound to take into consideration should be granted a stronger procedural status. The Courts have indirectly acknowledged this consequence in the case law on current Article 108(2) TFEU, albeit with hesitations and inconsistencies.

This is concretized, first, by the different density of the procedural rights and guarantees that accompany the participation rights of holders of subjective rights and of holders of legally protected interests, namely in what concerns possible restrictions to the right to access information and the scope of the protective role of the statement of reasons (i.e. to what extent this statement should consider the interest of the person concerned in obtaining explanations regarding specific points of the act adopted). This was developed, in particular, in Chapters 5 (Section 5.3), 7 (Sub-section 7.3.3), and 8 (Sub-section 8.2.3). Secondly, respect for the procedural position of holders of subjective rights requires different forms of accommodating participation rights, on the one hand, and other requirements of decision-making procedures (such as swiftness and effectiveness of decisions), on the other, than does the procedural protection of holders of legally protected interests. Also in this respect the procedural position of the former is stronger than that of the latter. As has been argued in Chapter 2 (Section 2.6), in duly justified circumstances, the decision-maker may decide not to hear holders of legally protected interests or may require that they nominate a representative. Thirdly, given that, under current rules, private standing depends on the demonstration of individual concern, except in the annulment of self-executing regulatory acts, only holders of subjective substantive rights may be recognized as having access to courts in order to ensure respect for their participation rights. Other persons concerned need to rely on the control of the European Ombudsman over the decisional procedures of the EU institutions and bodies. This is not an ideal situation. However, the looser requirements of Article 263(4) TFEU with regard to self-executing regulatory acts open new possibilities to private litigants seeking enforcement of participation rights in rule-making and may, to a certain extent, bridge the mismatch between the broader scope of participation rights defended in this book and the possibilities of judicial review to enforce those rights. Nevertheless, it remains to be seen how the Courts will interpret this provision. A fourth aspect pertains to the consequences that should be attached to the infringement of participation rights. For example, in a scenario in which *locus standi* could be recognized to holders of legally protected interests, a harmless error rule could apply to the infringement of procedural rights of holders of legally protected interests, but should not be valid in cases where subjective rights are adversely affected by the measures adopted by the EU institutions and bodies, where the decision-maker is bound to consider the individual position of interested persons.

This differentiation between procedural statuses, while granting the decision-maker a certain degree of flexibility in the treatment of procedural rights, entails risks for the legal protection of holders of legally protected interests. For this reason, it has been argued in this book that these rules need to be accompanied by sufficient guarantees to avoid the depletion of participation rights in these cases. Specifically, the procedural decisions need to be justified in each case and the decision-maker is bound to demonstrate that the legally protected interests that would otherwise have been voiced by the putative participants have been sufficiently and duly taken into account in the decisional procedure.

The proposed extension of participation rights might contend with the goal of effectiveness and result in an increased 'judicialization' of administrative decision-making. The assumption that these are enough reasons to deny *a priori* an extension of participation rights has been rejected in this book on the grounds of the normative value of participation rights. The recognition of limits to participation rights in given circumstances, and in the terms proposed, demonstrates that it is possible, within certain limits, to accommodate participation rights with the effectiveness of decisional procedures and the boundaries of judicial control over such procedures (see further Chapter 2, Section 2.6; Chapter 5, Section 5.3; Chapter 6, Subsection 6.5.2). In general terms, these limits are the reflection of the fact that participation rights are more limited the more attenuated the dignitarian rationale is in each case, or the weaker the relevance of the person or of the personal conduct is in each procedure. Seen from a different perspective, respect of subjective rights, in particular fundamental rights, sets the limits to the contingency of participation.

Another aspect considered in this book was the impact that the proposed extension of participation rights may have in the scope of the procedural rights and guarantees that need to accompany the exercise of participation rights (access to information, the duty to give reasons, the duty of care, and language rights). It was concluded that the current scope of these procedural rights and guarantees is broad enough to accommodate an extension of participation rights (Chapter 5, Section 5.4). Therefore, as a rule, the proposed extension of participation rights does not require an expansion of these ancillary rights and guarantees. However, some nuances and one exception qualify this statement. First, the proposed extension contends with the protective role of the statement of reasons, since this would be extended to the holders of subjective rights affected by an act, and not only to those individually concerned by it, as is currently the case. Secondly, the more stringent requirements of the statement of reasons defined for individual acts should be transposed to the realm of the general normative acts, in cases in which these impact on the persons' legal sphere in a similar way to individual decisions. Thirdly, and analogously, in these cases, the protective role of the principle of care would also need to be extended to rule-making procedures. The Courts have so far denied these effects. The first is, nevertheless, encompassed by the general rule according to which the requirements to be satisfied by the statement of reasons depend on the circumstances of each case, in particular on the content of the measure. The second would constitute a true exception to the conclusion that the extension of participation rights proposed would not require a concomitant extension of their ancillary rights and guarantees. As for the third consequence mentioned, needless to say, the same limits placed by the Court on the protective role of the principle of care in relation to individual acts would also apply in relation to general acts.

If one compares the current scope of the two essential supporting guarantees of participation—the right of access to information (backed up by the rules on access to documents) and the duty to motivate decisions—with that of participation rights, one may conclude that only the latter are restricted to the adoption of individual decisions. However, this is illogical. It is generally assumed that the broader scope of the former is justified by the 'objective' rationales that underpin them and by the fact that they are not necessarily linked to the procedural protection of natural and legal persons before acts adopted by the EU institutions and bodies. In light of what was defended in this book, it is not acceptable that the same justification is not extended to participation rights. A broader scope of the latter ought to be recognized. Not only do participation rights also have a protective role that extends beyond the subjective interests of the persons entitled to access the procedure, but the way participation rights are currently conceived in EU administrative law precludes procedural protection being afforded to the persons affected in cases where this would be justified in view of the effects of the regulatory acts adopted by the EU institutions and bodies. In a way, the final missing link in the procedural protection of natural and legal persons in their relationships with the EU administration lies in the limits placed on participation rights in current EU administrative law.

This book proposes an alternative normative model for participation rights in EU administrative law, one that would overcome these limits. This model should in general underlie the interpretation of participation rights. Therefore, some aspects of the proposed reform should be implemented through the combined action of the legislator and the Courts' judicial review. Both, in particular the legislator, should be aware of the importance of grappling with issues of procedural protection in decision-making at the EU level, since reliance on the principle of procedural autonomy inspired by a model of executive federalism is increasingly inadequate to come to grips with the effects of EU administrative action in the legal spheres of natural and legal persons. Furthermore, in order to concretize the proposed reform, a consistent approach by the Courts with regard to the procedural protection of persons concerned would be needed, which would also require a unitary conception of composite procedures. In addition, participation rights should be recognized according to the degree to which substantive rights and legally protected interests are affected by regulatory acts. This would imply departing from the structural scheme that has so far underpinned the judicial conception of participation rights.

Crucially, however, this change in the overall approach of the legislator and the Courts would need to be reflected in sector-specific regulation, since the differences from sector to sector are very likely to impact on the way concrete solutions are conceived. The scope and meaning of participation rights and the forms of exercising them (e.g. written or oral hearings, the possibility—or not—of opposition) may differ according to the regulatory specificities of each sector. It is, in any case, not excluded that sector-specific solutions may navigate from sector to sector. However important, sector specificities should not be overrated and inter-sector analysis may indicate interesting paths for reform.

9.5 A Matter of Paradigm and Normative Coherence

Several reasons may be invoked to justify the proposed extension of the scope of participation rights. To begin with, this contributes to overcoming the mismatch between the powers exercised by the EU regulatory and administrative entities, on the one hand, and the procedural protection of the persons who are affected by their acts, on the other.

Next, participation rights with the scope defended in this book contribute to the fulfilment of the rule of law requirements that should inform the functions of the administrative procedure. In fact, grounding participation in the material effects actually produced, or envisaged to be produced, by an act in the legal sphere of private persons is a way of ensuring that the deployment of the administrative function respects not only the rights and interests of the persons affected but also the set of interests that have been defined as legally protected in the applicable substantive norms. In this sense, the conditions to achieve materially just and technically appropriate decisions are enhanced.

Furthermore, the proposed extension would favour a paradigm of EU administrative law that is respectful of the rights and legally protected interests of natural and legal persons falling within the purview of the EU regulatory action as well as more consonant with constitutional features of EU law that have placed the individual as centrally important to legal principles such as direct effect, primacy, state liability for breaches of EU law, and respect for fundamental rights.

Moreover, the construction of participation rights proposed allows us to overcome the distinction between acts of general and individual scope as an essential basis for the recognition of participation rights in EU administrative law. Together with the preconception that administrative procedures are binary, this is a major hindrance to an adequate procedural protection of the persons affected by Union acts and it is based on arguments that are inconsistent with the effective features of the EU institutional system. The distinction between legislative and administrative acts in formal organic and procedural terms, as well as between general and individual acts, is not adequate to be held as the main criterion that supports the recognition of participation rights.

In addition, broader legal access to the procedure may favour equal conditions of access of persons whose rights and legally protected interests are at issue. At least in formal terms, more encompassing conditions of access, filtered in any case by legal criteria, provide a tool that may counter the privileged access of more powerful interest groups. At the same time, it ensures a voice to holders of affected rights and legally protected interests irrespective of their factual influence. It is, nevertheless, acknowledged that certain important factual conditions of inequality are beyond legal reach, as illustrated by some of the difficulties regarding under-representation of certain groups detected in the operation of the Lamfalussy consultative procedures (Chapter 6).

Finally, and returning to the opening of these conclusions, the proposed construction of participation rights finds support in the institutional characteristics of the EU described above. Participation rights, as sustained in this book, are embedded in the institutional-constitutional tradition of European integration. They are partially related to the mechanisms of participation that pervade the EU decisional structures, to the extent that the technical appropriateness of the decisions adopted is also one of their rationales. Indeed, this feature brings participation rights closer to the output-oriented forms of participation that pervade the EU regulatory structures. Therefore, exceeding the boundaries of participation rights defined by the Courts' case law is not only consonant with the legal values proclaimed by the EU legal system, but also with this constitutive feature of the EU institutional system.

In summary, this book has demonstrated that the scope of participation rights in current EU administrative law is unsuitably and unjustifiably narrow. Their extension to situations left outside their purview is required by legal values that underpin the EU legal order, it is coherent with principles and rules of EU law, and it is consonant with the fact that participation is a constitutionally relevant feature of the EU legal and political system. In particular this latter aspect is highlighted in the Treaty of Lisbon. This greater visibility may be the trigger for reform in the sense proposed in the book. In the face of these values, principles, and constitutional features, the possible negative consequences that could derive from this extension (i.e. an excessive strain on the effectiveness of decisional procedures and disproportionate powers of judicial control) are not *per se* reason enough to refuse the extension proposed.

BIBLIOGRAPHY*

Adinolfi, Adelina (1994) 'I principi generali nella giurisprudenza comunitaria e la loro influenza sugli ordinamenti degli Stati membri', *Rivista italiana di diritto comunitario*, Vol. 4, n. 3–4, pp. 521–79

Albors-Llorens, Albertina (2003) 'The standing of private parties to challenge Community measures: has the European court missed the boat?', *Cambridge Law Journal*, Vol. 62, n. 1, pp. 72–92

Aldestam, Mona (2004) 'Soft law in the State aid policy area', in Ulrika Mörth, *Soft Law in Governance and Regulation. An Interdisciplinary Analysis*, Cheltenham, Northampton: Edward Elgar, pp. 11–36

Almeida, José Carlos Moitinho de (1995) 'Le recours en annulation des particuliers (article 173, deuxième alinéa, du traité CE): nouvelles réflexions sur l'expression 'la concernent... individuellement', in Ole Due, Marcus Lutter, and Jürgen Schwarze (eds) *Festshrift für Ulrich Everling*, Vol. I, Baden-Baden: Nomos, pp. 849–74

Armstrong, Kenneth A. (2002) 'Rediscovering civil society: the European Union and the White Paper on Governance', *European Law Journal*, Vol. 8, n. 1, pp. 102–132

—— and Bulmer, Simon (1998) *The Governance of the Single European Market*, Manchester and New York: Manchester University Press

Arnull, Anthony (2001) 'Private applicants and the action for annulment since *Codorniu*', *Common Market Law Review*, Vol. 38, n. 1, pp. 7–52

—— (2002) 'Introduction: the European Union's accountability and legitimacy deficit', in Anthony Arnull and Daniel Wincott (eds) *Accountability and legitimacy in the European Union*, Oxford: Oxford University Press, pp. 1–12

—— (2006) *The European Union and its Court of Justice*, Oxford: Oxford University Press

Auby, Jean-Bernard (2007) 'Procédure administrative et garantie des droits des citoyens en droit français', in Alberto Massera (ed.) *Le tutele procedimentali. Profili di diritto comparato*, Napoli: Jovene Editore, pp. 31–49

—— and Dutheil de la Rochère, Jacqueline (2007) 'Introduction générale', in Auby and Dutheil de la Rochère (eds) *Droit administratif européen*, Bruxelles: Bruylant, pp. 1–22

* The list is ordered by the authors' surname. The Spanish authors are entered according to their first surname, the Portuguese authors by their last surname.

Avgerinos, Yannis V. (2002) 'Essential and non-essential measures: delegation of powers in EU securities regulation', *European Law Journal*, Vol. 8, n. 2, pp. 269–89

Ayres, Ian and Braithwaite, John (1992) *Responsive Regulation: Transcending the Deregulation Debate*, Oxford: Oxford University Press

Azoulai, Loïc (2000) *Les garanties procédurales en droit communautaire. Recherches sur la procédure et le bon gouvernement*, PhD Thesis, European University Institute: Florence

Azzi, Giuseppe Ciavarini (1999) 'Comitology and the European Commission' in Christian Joerges and Ellen Vos (eds) *EU Committees: Social Regulation, Law and Politics*, Oxford: Hart Publishing, pp. 51–7

Bailey, David (2007) 'Damages actions under the EC merger regulation', *Common Market Law Review*, Vol. 44, n. 1, pp. 101–39

Baldwin, Robert (1995) *Rules and Government*, Oxford: Clarendon Press

Bartelt, Sandra (2006) 'Commentary—Case T-2/03, *Verein für Konsumenteninformation* v. *Commission*', *Common Market Law Review*, Vol. 43, n. 1, pp. 191–206

Bartle, Ian (2006) 'Legitimising EU regulation: procedural accountability, participation or better consultation?' in Richard Bellamy, Dario Castiglione, and Jo Shaw (eds) *Making European Citizens: Civic Inclusion in a Transnational Context*, Basingstoke, New York: Palgrave Macmillan, pp. 133–53

Baruffi, Maria C. (2001) *La tutela dei singoli nei procedimenti amministrativi comunitari*, Milano: Giuffrè

Battini, Stefano, Mattarella, Bernardo G., and Sandulli, Aldo (2007) 'Il procedimento' in Giulio Napolitano (ed.) *Diritto Amministrativo Comparato*, Milano: Giuffrè, pp. 107–74

Beljin, Saša (2008) 'Right in EU Law', in Sacha Prechal and Bert van Roermund (eds) *The Coherence of EU Law. The Search for Unity in Divergent Concepts*, Oxford: Oxford University Press, pp. 91–122

Bellamy, Richard and Castiglione, Dario (2004) 'Normative theory and the EU: legitimising the Euro-polity and its regime', in Lars Trägardh (ed.) *After National Democracy. Rights, Law and Power in America and the New Europe*, Oxford and Portland Oregon: Hart Publishing, pp. 9–40

Bergström, Carl Fredrik (2005) *Comitology: Delegation of Powers in the European Union and the Committee System*, Oxford: Oxford University Press

Betti, Emilio (1971) *Interpretazione della legge e degli atti giuridici. Teoria generale e dogmatica*, Milano: Giuffrè, p. 163–79

Bevis, Inda (2002) *The Legal Effect of EC Appropriate Measures and ESCS State Aid Codes*, PhD Thesis, Florence: European University Institute

Bibier, Ronald, Dehousse, Renaud, Pinder, John, and Weiler, Joseph H. H. (1988) 'Back to the future: policy, strategy and tactics on the White Paper on the creation of a single European market' in Ronald Bibier, Renaud Dehousse, John Pinder, Joseph H. H. Weiler (eds) *1992: One European Market? A critical analysis of the Commission's internal market strategy*, Baden-Baden: Nomos, pp. 13–31

Bignami, Francesca (1999) 'The democratic deficit in European Community rulemaking: a call for notice and comment in comitology', *Harvard International Law Journal*, Vol. 40, n. 2, pp. 453–515

—— (2005) 'Creating European rights: national values and supranational interests', *Columbia Journal of European Law*, Vol. 11, n. 2, pp. 241–353

Bitsch, Marie-Thérèse (2004) *Histoire de la construction européenne*, Bruxelles: Editions Complexe

Black, Julia (2003) 'Enrolling actors in regulatory systems: examples from the UK financial services regulation', *Public Law*, pp. 63–91

—— (2003) 'Mapping the contours of contemporary financial services regulation', CARR Discussion Paper No. 17, London School of Economics and Political Science

Blasio, Andrea and Munari, Francesco (2004) 'Aiuti concessi dagli Stati' in Antonio Tizzano (ed.) *Trattati dell'Unione Europea e della Comunità Europea*, Milano: Giuffrè

Blumann, Claude (2005) 'Article II-103: Médiateur européen' in Laurence Burgorgue-Larsen, Anne Levade, Fabrice Picod (eds) *Traité établissant une Constitution pour l'Europe. Part II. La Charte des droits fondamentaux de l'Union, Vol. 2*, Brussels: Bruylant, pp. 551–66

Bogdandy, Armin von (2006) 'Constitutional principles' in Armin von Bogdandy and Jürgen Bast (eds) *Principles of European Constitutional Law*, Oxford and Portland: Hart Publishing, pp. 3–52

——, Arndt, Felix, and Bast, Jürgen (2004) 'Legal instruments in European Union Law and their reform: a systematic approach on an empirical basis', *Yearbook of European Law*, Vol. 23, pp. 91–136

Bonnor, Peter (2001) *The European ombudsman: a novel rule-source in Community administrative law*, PhD Thesis, European University Institute, Florence

Boulouis, Jean (1986) 'Représentation et participation dans la vie politique et administrative', in *La participation directe du citoyen à la vie politique et administrative. Travaux des XXIes Journées d'études juridiques Jean Dabin sous la direction de Francis Delpérée*, Bruxelles: Bruylant, pp. 49–67

Bovens, Mark (2007) 'Analysing and assessing accountability: a conceptual framework', *European Law Journal*, Vol. 13, n. 4, pp. 447–68

Bradley, Kieran (1999) 'La transparence de l'Union Européenne: une évidence ou un trompe l'œil?', *Cahiers de Droit Européen*, Vol. 35, n. 3–4, pp. 283–362

Bremejo Latre, José Luis (2004) 'Procedimiento administrativo común y elaboración de disposiciones administrativas', *Revista Española de Derecho Administrativo*, n. 124, pp. 611–29

Búrca, Gráinne de (1996) 'The quest for legitimacy in the European Union', *The Modern Law Review*, Vol. 59, n. 3, pp. 349–76

—— (2003) 'The constitutional challenge of new governance in the European Union', *European Law Review*, Vol. 28, n. 6, pp. 814–39

Búrca, Gráinne de and Scott, Joanne (2007) 'Introduction', *Columbia Journal of European Law*, Vol. 13, n. 3, pp. 513–17

Burgorgue-Larsen, Laurence (1997) 'L'élaboration d'une doctrine consultative par le Comité des Régions', in Jacques Bourrinet (ed) *Le Comité des Régions de l'Union Européenne*, Paris: Economica, pp. 191–229

Busuioc, Madalina (2009) 'Accountability, Control and Independence: The Case of European Agencies', *European Law Journal*, Vol. 15, n. 5, pp. 599–615

—— (2010) *The Accountability of European Agencies. Legal Provisions and Ongoing Practices*, Delft: Eburon

Cadeddu, Simone (2004) 'The proceedings of the European Ombudsman', *Law and Contemporary Problems*, Vol. 68, n. 1, pp. 161–80

Cadin, Raffaele, (2004) 'Il Comitato Economico e Sociale', in Antonio Tizzano (ed.) *Trattati dell'Unione europea e della Comunità europea*, Milano: Giuffrè, pp. 1206–20

Cafaggi, Fabrizio (2006) 'Rethinking private regulation in the European regulatory space', in Fabrizio Cafaggi (ed.) *Reframing Self-regulation in European Private Law*, The Netherlands: Kluwer Law International, pp. 3–75

Calandri, Elena (2000) 'Le genesi del Comitato Economico e Sociale: forze professionali e strategie nazionali' in Antonio Varsori (ed.) *Il Comitato Economico e Sociale nella costruzione europea*, Marsilio Editori: Venezia, pp. 47–65

Cananea, Giancinto della (1993) 'Administration by guidelines: the policy guidelines of the Commission in the field of state aids', in Ian Harden (ed.) *State Aid: Community Law and Policy*, Cologne: Bundesanzeiger, pp. 61–75

—— (2000) *Gli atti amministrativi generali*, Cedam: Padova

—— (2004) 'The European Union's mixed administrative proceedings', *Law and Contemporary Problems*, Vol. 68, pp. 197–217

Canotilho, José Joaquim Gomes (1994) 'Relações jurídicas poligonais, ponderação ecológica de bens e controlo judicial preventivo', *Revista Jurídica do Urbanismo e Ambiente*, n. 1, pp. 55–65

Caranta, Roberto, Ferraris, Laura, and Rodriguez, Simona (2005) *La partecipazione al procedimento amministrativo*, 2nd edn, Milano: Giuffrè

Cardi, Enzo (1995) 'Procedimento amministrativo', *Enciclopedia Giuridica*, Roma: Treccani, Vol. XXIV, pp. 1–8

Cartabia, Marta (1991) *La tutela nel procedimento amministrativo. La legge n. 241 del 1990 alla luce dei principi comunitari*, Milano: Giuffrè

Cassese, Sabino (1970) 'Il privato e il procedimento amministrativo', in *Archivio Giuridico Filippo Serafini*, pp. 25–147

—— (1986) 'Les conditions de participation du citoyen à la vie administrative', in *La participation directe du citoyen à la vie politique et administrative. Travaux des XXIes Journées d'études juridiques Jean Dabin sous la direction de Francis Delpérée*, Bruxelles: Bruylant, pp. 273–82

—— (2007) 'La partecipazione dei privati alle decisioni pubbliche. Saggio di diritto comparato', *Rivista trimestrale di diritto pubblico*, Vol. 57, n. 1, pp. 13–41

Castellà Andreu, Josep Mª (2001) *Los derechos de constitucionales de participación política en la Administración Pública*, Barcelona: Cedecs Editorial

Caunes, Karine (2007) 'Et la fonction exécutive européenne créa l'administration à son image... Retour vers le futur de la comitologie', *Revue trimestrielle de droit européen*, Vol. 43, n. 2, pp. 297–346

Chalmers, Damian (2005) 'Risk, anxiety and the European mediation of the politics of life', *European Law Review*, Vol. 30, n. 5, pp. 649–74

——, Hadjiemmanuil, Christos, Monti, Giorgio, and Tomkins, Adam (2006) *European Union Public Law: Texts and Materials*, Cambridge: Cambridge University Press

Chapus, René (2000) *Droit administratif général*, Tome I, 14th edn, Paris: Monchrestien

—— (2001) *Droit administratif général*, Tome I, 15th edn, Paris: Montchrestien

Chiti, Edoardo (2000) 'The emergence of a Community administration: the case of European agencies', *Common Market Law Review*, Vol. 37, n. 2, pp. 309–43

—— (2002) *Le agenzie europee. Unità e decentramento nelle amministrazioni comunitarie*, Padova: Cedam

—— (2004) 'Decentralisation and integration into the European administrations: a new perspective on European agencies', *European Law Journal*, Vol. 14, n. 3, pp. 402–38

—— (2004) 'La disciplina procedurale della regolazione', *Rivista Trimestrale di Diritto Pubblico*, Vol. 54, n. 3, pp. 679–736

—— (2009) 'An important part of the EU's institutional machinery: features, problems and perspectives of European agenzie', *Common Market Law Review*, Vol. 46, n. 5, pp. 1395–442

—— (2009) 'The administrative implementation of European Union law: a taxonomy and its implications' in Herwig C.H. Hofmann and Alexander H. Türk (eds) (2009) *Legal Challenges in EU Administrative Law. Towards an integrated administration*, Cheltenham: Edward Elgar, pp. 9–33

—— and Franchini, Claudio (2003) *L'integrazione amministrativa europea*, Bologna: Il Mulino

Chiti, Mario (1977) *Partecipazione popolare e pubblica amministrazione*, Pisa: Pacini Editore

Chittenden, Francis, Ambler, Tim, and Xiao, Deming (2007) 'Impact assessment in the EU', in Stephen Weatherill (ed.) *Better Regulation*, Oxford: Oxford University Press, pp. 271–86

Christiansen, Thomas (1995) 'Second thoughts—The Committee of the Regions after its first year' in Renaud Dehousse and Thomas Christiansen (eds) (1995) 'What model for the Committee of the Regions? Past experiences and future perspectives', EUI Working Paper EUF n. 95/2, pp. 34–64

Christoforou, Theofanis (2004) 'The regulation of genetically modified organisms in the European Union: the interplay of science, law and politics', *Common Market Law Review*, Vol. 41, n. 3, pp. 637–709

Cini, Michelle (2001) 'The soft law approach: Commission rule-making in the EU's State aid regime', *Journal of European Public Policy*, Vol. 8, n. 2, p. 192–207

Cloos, Jim, Reinesch, Gaston, Vignes, Daniel, and Weyland, Joseph (1993) *Le Traité de Maastricht. Genèse, analyse, commentaries*, Bruxelles: Bruylant

Coen, David and Thatcher, Mark (2008) 'Network governance and multi-level delegation: European networks of regulatory agencies', *Journal of Public Policy*, Vol. 28, n. 1 pp. 49–71

Cohen, Joshua and Sabel, Charles (1997) 'Directly-deliberative polyarchy', *European Law Journal*, Vol. 3, n. 4, pp. 313–42

Cole, Tony (2005) 'The Committee of the Regions and subnational representation to the European Union', *Maastricht Journal of European and Comparative Law*, Vol. 12, n. 1, pp. 49–72

Comité des Régions (2006) *Le Comité des Régions dans la mise en oeuvre et le contrôle des principes de subsidiarité et de proportionalité à la lumière de la Constitution pour l'Europe*, Luxembourg: Office des publications officielles des Communautés européennes

Coombes, David (1970) *Politics and Bureaucracy in the European Community*, London: George Allen and Unwin Ltd

Corthaut, Tim and Vanneste, Frédéric (2006) 'Waves between Strasbourg and Luxembourg: the right of access to a Court to contest the validity of administrative and legislative measures', *Yearbook of European Law*, Vol. 25, pp. 475–514

Cozigou, Gwenole (1997) 'Un nouveau cadre juridique pour les applications biotechnologiques dans le secteur alimentaire: le règlement 'Nouveau aliments'', *Revue du Marché Unique*, n. 2, p. 67–80

Craig, Paul (1990) *Public Law and Democracy in The United Kingdom and in the United States of America*, Oxford: Clarendon Press

—— (1997) 'Democracy and rulemaking within the EC: an empirical and normative assessment', *European Law Journal*, Vol. 3, n. 2, pp. 105–30

—— (2003) 'Standing, rights and the structure of legal argument', *European Public Law*, Vol. 9, n. 4, pp. 493–508

—— (2006) *EU Administrative Law*, Oxford: Oxford University Press

—— (2008) *Administrative Law*, 6th edn, London: Sweet and Maxwell

—— (2008) 'The role of the European Parliament under the Lisbon Treaty' in Stefan Griller and Jacques Ziller (eds) *The Lisbon Treaty: EU Constitutionalism without a Constitutional Treaty?*, Wien: Springer, pp. 110–34

Creech, Richard L. (2005) *Law and Language in the European Union. The paradox of a Babel 'united in diversity'*, Gronigen: European Law Publishing

Crisafulli, Vezio (1959) 'Atto normativo', in *Enciclopedia del Diritto*, Vol. IV, Milano: Giuffrè, pp. 238–61

Curtin, Deirdre (1996) '"Civil society" and the European Union: opening spaces for deliberative democracy?', *Collected Courses of the Academy of European Law*, Vol. VII, Book 1, The Hague: Kluwer International Law, pp. 185–280

—— (1996) 'Betwixt and between: democracy and transparency in the governance of the European Union' in Jan Winter, Deirdre Curtin, Alfred Kellermann, and Bruno de Witte (eds) *Reforming the Treaty on the European Union—The Legal Debate*, The Hague, Boston, London: Kluwer International Law, pp. 95–121

—— (2003) 'Private interest representation or civil society deliberation? A contemporary dilemma for European governance', *Social and Legal Studies*, Vol. 12, n. 1, pp. 55–75

—— (2007) 'Holding (quasi-) autonomous EU administrative actors to public account', *European Law Journal*, Vol. 13, n. 4, pp. 523–41

—— (2009) *Executive Power of the European Union. Laws, practices and the living constitution*, Oxford: Oxford University Press

—— and Mortelmanns, Kamiel (1994) 'Application and enforcement of Community law by the Member States: Actors in search of a third generation script' in Deirdre Curtin and Ton Heukels (eds) *Institutional Dynamics of European Integration. Essays in honour of Henry G. Schemers*, Vol II, Dordrecht: Martinus Nijhoff Publishers, pp. 423–66

Dabrowska, Patrycja (2006) *Hybrid Solutions for Hybrid Products? EU Governance of GMO's*, PhD Thesis, European University Institute, Florence

Dehousse, Renaud (1988) 'Completing the internal market: institutional constraints and challenges', in Ronald Bibier, Renaud Dehousse, John Pinder, and Joseph H. H. Weiler (eds) *1992: One European Market? A critical analysis of the Commission's internal market strategy*, Baden-Baden: Nomos, pp. 311–36

—— (1994) 'Some reflections on the crisis of the harmonisation model', in Francis Snyder (ed.) 'A regulatory framework for foodstuffs in the internal market', EUI Working Paper Law no. 94/4

—— (1997) 'Regulation by networks in the European Community: the role of European agencies', *Journal of European Public Policy*, Vol. 4, n. 2, pp. 246–61

—— (2002) 'Misfits: EU Law and the transformations of European Governance', in Christian Joerges and Renaud Dehousse (eds) *Good Governance in Europe's Integrated Market*, Oxford: Oxford University Press

—— and Christiansen, Thomas (eds) (1995) 'What model for the Committee of the Regions? Past experiences and future perspectives', EUI Working Paper EUF n. 95/2

Dougan, Michael (2008) 'The Treaty of Lisbon 2007: Winning minds, not hearts', *Common Market Law Review*, Vol. 45, n. 3, pp. 617–703

D'sa, Rose (1998) *European Community Law on State Aid*, London: Sweet and Maxwell

Duarte, David (1996) *Procedimentalização, participação e fundamentação: para uma concretização do princípio da imparcialidade administrativa como parâmetro decisório*, Coimbra: Almedina

Due, Ole (1987) 'Le respect des droits de la défense dans le droit administratif communautaire', *Cahiers de Droit Européen*, Vol. 23, n. 4–5, pp. 383–96

Dumoulin, Michel (ed.) (2007) *The European Commission 1958–72. History and Memories*, Luxembourg: Office for Official Publications of the European Communities

Dyrberg, Peter (2002) 'Accountability and legitimacy: what is the contribution of transparency?' in Anthony Arnull and Daniel Wincott (eds) *Accountability and Legitimacy in the European Union*, Oxford: Oxford University Press, pp. 81–96

Eberlein, Burkard (2008) 'The making of European energy market: the interplay of governance and government', *Journal of Public Policy*, Vol. 28, n. 1, pp. 73–92

Eckes, Christina (2009) *EU Counter-Terrorist Policies and Fundamental Rights. The Case of Individual Sanctions*, Oxford: Oxford University Press

Eilmansberger, Thomas (2004) 'The relationship between rights and remedies in EC law: in search of the missing link', *Common Market Law Review*, Vol. 41, n. 5, pp. 1199–246

Eisenberg, Ewald (2000) *L'audition du citoyen et motivation des décisions administratives individuelles. Étude comparative en France et en Allemagne*, Paris: L'Harmattan

Evans, Andrew and Martin, Stephen (1991) 'Socially acceptable distortion of competition: Community policy on state aid', *European Law Review*, Vol. 16, n. 2, p. 79–111

Everling, Ulrich (1996) 'Will Europe slip on bananas? The bananas judgment of the Court of Justice and national courts', *Common Market Law Review*, Vol. 33, n. 3, pp. 401–37

Falcon, Giandomenico (2004) 'Separazione e coordinamento tra giurisdizioni europee e giurisdizioni nazionali nella tutela avverso gli atti lesivi di situazioni soggettive europee', *Rivista Italiana di Diritto Pubblico Comunitario*, Vol. 14, n. 5, pp. 1153–77

—— (2007) 'La tutela giurisdizionale', in Mario Chiti e Guido Greco (eds) *Trattato di Diritto Amministrativo Europeo*, Vol. II, 2nd edn, Milano: Giuffrè

Falke, Josef (1996) 'Comitology and other committees: a preliminary empirical assessment', in Robin H. Pedler and Günther F. Schäfer, *Shaping European Law and Policy. The role of committees and comitology in the political process*, Maastricht: European Institute of Public Administration, pp. 117–65

—— (1997) 'Achievements and unresolved problems of European standardisation: the ingenuity of practice and the queries of lawyers' in Christian Joerges, Karl-Heinz Ladeur, and Ellen Vos (eds) *Integrating Scientific Expertise into Regulatory Decision-making. National traditions and European innovations*, Baden-Baden: Nomos, pp. 187–224

Fanara, Elio (1970) 'Alta autorità', in Rolando Quadri, Riccardo Monaco, and Alberto Trabucchi (eds) *Trattato istitutivo della Comunità Europea del Carbone e dell'Acciaio: Commentario, Vol. I, Articoli 1–45*, Milano: Giuffrè, pp. 226–75

Fenet, Alain (2001) 'Diversité linguistique et construction européenne', *Revue Trimestrielle de Droit Européen*, Vol. 37, n. 2, pp. 235–69

Ferrarini, Guido (2004) 'The European market abuse directive', *Common Market Law Review*, Vol. 41, n. 3, pp. 711–41

Ferretti, Maria Paola (2008) 'Participatory strategies in the regulation of GMO products in the EU', in Jens Steffek, Claudia Kissling, and Patricia Nanz (eds) *Civil Society Participation in European and Global Governance. A cure for the democratic deficit?*, Basingstoke, New York: Palgrave Macmillan, pp. 166–84

Fracchia, Fabrizio (1996) 'Manifestazioni di interesse del privato e procedimento amministrativo', *Diritto Amministrativo*, Vol. 4, n. 1, pp. 14–50

Franchi, Marina (2004) 'Articolo 253', in Antonio Tizzano (ed.) *Trattati dell'Unione Europea e della Comunità Europea*, Milano: Giuffrè, pp. 1194–96

Franchini, Claudio (1993) *Amministrazione italiana e amministrazione comunitaria. La coamministrazione nei settori di interesse comunitario*, Padova: Cedam

Fromont, Michel (2006) *Droit administratif des États européens*, Paris: Presses Universitaires de France

Galetta, Diana-Urania (2002) *La legge tedesca sul procedimento amministrativo (Verwaltungsverfahrensgesetz). Traduzione con testo a fronte e commento introduttivo*, Milano: Giuffrè

—— and Ziller, Jacques (2008) 'Il regime linguistico della Comunità' in Mario P. Chiti and Guido Greco (eds) *Trattato di Diritto Amministrativo Europeo. Parte Generale. Tomo II*, Milano: Giuffrè, 2nd edn, pp. 1067–113

Gallego, Córcoles Isabel (2007) 'La instrucción del procedimiento administrativo común', in José Garberi Llobregat (ed.) *El procedimento administrativo común (comentarios, jurisprudencia, formularios)* Vol. II, Valencia: Tirant Lo Blanc, pp. 1305–88

Galligan, Denis J. (1996) *Due Process and Fair Procedures: A Study of Administrative Procedures*, Oxford: Clarendon Press

Galmot, Yves (1997) 'L'apport des principes généraux du droit communautaire à la garantie des droits dans l'ordre juridique français', *Cahiers de Droit Européen*, Vol. 33, n. 1–2, pp. 67–79

García Álvarez, Gerardo (2006) 'Los poderes normativos de las Administraciones independientes en el ámbito economico', *Revista de Administración Pública*, n. 171, pp. 139–79

García de Enterría, Eduardo (1989) 'Principios y modalidades de la participation ciudadana en la vida administrativa', in Rafael Gómez-Ferrer Morant (ed.) *Libro homenaje al Profesor José Luís Villar Palasí*, Madrid: Civitas, pp. 437–52

—— (1993) 'La ampliación de la competencia de las jurisdicciones conncioso-administrativas nacionales por obra del Derecho Comunitario. Sentencia *Borelli* de 3 diciembre de 1992 del Tribunal de Justicia y el articulo 5 CEE', *Revista Española de Derecho Administrativo*, n. 78, pp. 297–314

Gbikpi, Bernard and Grote, Jürgen R. (2002) 'From democratic government to participatory governance', in Jürgen R. Grote and Bernard Gbikpi (eds) *Participatory Governance. Political and social implications*, Leske and Budrich, Opladen, pp. 17–34

Geradin, Damien and Petit, Nicolas (2004) 'The development of agencies at the EU and national levels: conceptual analysis and proposals for reform', Jean Monnet Working Paper 01/04 (available at <http://www.jeanmonnetprogram.org/papers/papers04.html>)

Gerven, Walter van (2000) 'Of rights, remedies and procedures', *Common Market Law Review*, Vol. 37, n. 3, pp. 501–36

Giannini, Massimo S. (1981) *Istituzioni di diritto amministrativo*, Milano: Giuffrè

—— (1993) *Diritto Amministrativo*, Vol. II, 3rd edn, Milano: Giuffrè

Girerd, Pascal (2002) 'Les principes d'équivalence et de l'effectivité: encadrement ou désencadrement de l'autonomie procédural des Etats membres', *Revue Trimestrielle de Droit Européen*, Vol. 38, n. 1, pp. 75–102

Goffin, Léon (1980) 'La jurisprudence de la Cour de Justice sur les droits de la défense', *Cahiers de Droit Européen*, pp. 127–44

Greaves, Rosa (1996) 'The nature and binding effect of decisions under Article 189 EC', *European Law Review*, Vol. 21, n. 1, pp. 3–16

Greenwood, Justin (2003) *Interest representation in the European Union*, 1st edn, Houndmills: Palgrave Macmillan

—— (2007) *Interest representation in the European Union*, 2nd edn, Houndmills: Palgrave Macmillan

Groussot, Xavier (2000) 'The general principles of Community law in the creation and development of due process principles in competition law proceeding: from Transocean Marine Painting (1974) to Montecatini (1999)', in Ulf Bernitz and Joakim Nergelius (eds) *General Principles of European Community Law*, The Hague: Kluwer Law International, pp. 185–204

Hancher, Leigh (1994) 'State aids and judicial control in the European Community', *European Competition Law Review*, Vol. 15, n. 3, pp. 134–50

Harden, Ian (2009) 'The revision of Regulation n. 1049/2001 on public access to documents', *European Public Law*, Vol. 15, n. 2, pp. 239–56

Harlow, Carol (1996) 'Codification of EC administrative procedures? Fitting the foot to the shoe or the shoe to the foot', *European Law Journal*, Vol 2, n. 1, pp. 3–25

—— (1999) 'Citizen access to political power in the European Union', EUI Working Paper RSC no. 99/2
—— (2000) *Accountability in the European Union*, Oxford: Oxford University Press
—— (2006) 'Civil society organizations and participatory administration: a challenge to EU administrative law?', in Stijn Smismans (ed.) *Civil Society and Legitimate European Governance*, Cheltenham, Northampton: Edward Elgar, pp. 115–40
—— and Rawlings, Richard (2006) 'Promoting accountability in multi-level governance: a network approach', European Governances Papers (EUROGOV) no. C-06-02 (available at <http://www.connex-network.org/eurogov/pdf/egp-connex-C-06-02.pdf>)
Haas, Ernst B. (1968 [1958]) *The Uniting of Europe. Political, Social, and Economic Forces 1950–1957*, Stanford: Stanford University Press
Heede, Katja (2001) *European Ombudsman: Redress and Control at the European Level*, The Hague: Kluwer Law International
Hilf, Meinhard, Ciesla, Gritta, and Pache, Eckhard (1991) 'Rights vis-à-vis the administration at the Community level', in Antonio Cassese, Andrew Clapham, and Joseph Weiler (eds) *Human Rights and the European Community: Methods of Protection*, Baden-Baden: Nomos, pp. 455–91
Hofmann, Herwig (2006) 'Negotiated and non-negotiated administrative rulemaking: the example of EC competition policy', *Common Market Law Review*, Vol. 43, n. 1, pp. 153–78
—— (2006) 'Administrative governance in State aid policy', in Herwig Hofmann and Alexander Türk (eds) *European Administrative Governance*, Cheltenham, Northampton: Edward Elgar, pp. 185–92
—— (2009) 'Legislation, delegation and implementation under the Lisbon Treaty: Typology meets reality', *European Law Journal*, Vol. 15, n. 4, pp. 482–505
—— (2009) 'Composite decision making procedures in EU administrative law', in Herwig Hofmann and Alexander Türk (eds) (2009) *Legal Challenges in EU Administrative Law. Towards an integrated administration*, Cheltenham: Edward Elgar, pp.168–76
—— and Türk, Alexander (2006) 'Conclusions—Europe's integrated administration', in Herwig Hofmann and Alexander Türk (eds) *EU Administrative Governance*, Edward Elgar, pp. 573–96
—— and Türk, Alexander (2007) 'The development of integrated administration in the EU and its consequences', *European Law Journal*, Vol. 13, n. 2, pp. 253–71
Hooghe, Liesbet and Marks, Gary (1995) 'Channels of subnational representation in the European Union', in Renaud Dehousse and Thomas Christiansen (eds) (1995) 'What model for the Committee of the Regions? Past experiences and future perspectives', EUI Working Paper EUF no. 95/2, pp. 6–33

Hoskins, Mark (1996) 'Tilting the balance: supremacy and national procedural rules', *European Law Review*, Vol. 21, n. 5, pp. 365–77

Hurrelmann, Achim (2007) 'Multilevel legitimacy: conceptualizing legitimacy relationships between the EU and national democracies', in Joan DeBardeleben and Achim Hurrelmann (eds) *Democratic Dilemmas of Multilevel Governance. Legitimacy, representation and accountability in the European Union*, Basingstoke, New York: Palgrave MacMillan, p. 17–37

Isaac, Guy (1968) *La procédure administrative non contentieuse*, Paris: LGDJ

Jacqué, Jean-Paul (2006) *Droit institutionnel de l'Union Européenne*, 4th edn, Paris: Dalloz

——, Bibier, Rolin, Haag, Marcel *et al.* (2000) *Commentaire J. Mégret. Le Parlement européen, le Conseil, la Commission, la Cour des comptes, le Comité economique et social, le Comité des régions, la Banque européenne d'investissement, le fonds européen d'investissement*, Vol. 9, 2nd edn, Bruxelles: Editions de l'Université de Bruxelles

Joerges, Christian (1988) 'The new approach to technical harmonisation and the interests of consumers: reflections in the requirements and difficulties of a Europeanisation of product safety policy' in Ronald Bibier, Renaud Dehousse, John Pinder, and Joseph H. H. Weiler (eds) *1992: One European Market? A critical analysis of the Commission's internal market strategy*, Baden-Baden: Nomos, pp. 175–225

——, Falke, Joseph, Micklitz, Hans-W., and Brüggemeier, Gert (1991) 'European Product Safety, Internal Market Policy and the New Approach to Technical Harmonisation and Standards', EUI Working Paper Law 91/10–14

——, Schepel, Harm, and Vos, Ellen (1999) 'The law's problems with the involvement of non-governmental actors in Europe's legislative processes: the case of standardisation under the "New Approach"', EUI Working Paper no. 99/9

Jordan III, William S. (2000) 'Ossification revisited: does arbitrary and capricious review significantly interfere with agency ability to achieve regulatory goals through informal rulemaking?', *Northwestern University Law Review*, Vol. 94, n. 2, pp. 393–450

Joshua, Julian M. (1991) 'The right to be heard in EEC competition procedures', *Fordham International Law Journal*, Vol. 15, n. 1, pp. 16–91

Kakouris, Constantinos N. (1997) 'Do Member States possess judicial procedural 'autonomy'?', *Common Market Law Review*, Vol. 34, n. 6, pp. 1389–412

Karydis, Georges (1997) 'Le contrôle des concentrations entre entreprises en vertu du règlement 4064/89 et la protection des intérêts légitimes des tiers', *Cahiers de Droit Européen*, n. 1–2, pp. 81–139

Keppenne, Jean-Paul (2006) 'General questions on procedure. Control of state aid compatibility. Council's decision-making power', in Luis Ortiz Blanco (ed.) *European Community Competition Procedure*, Oxford: Oxford University Press, 2nd edn, pp. 785–954

Knaap, Peter van der (1996) 'Government by committee: legal typology, quantitative assessment and institutional repercussions of committees in the European Union', in Robin H. Pedler and Günther F. Schäfer, *Shaping European Law and Policy. The role of committees and comitology in the political process*, Maastricht: European Institute of Public Administration, pp. 83–116

Koch, Cornelia (2005) '*Locus standi* of private applicants under the EU Constitution: preserving gaps in the protection of individuals' right to an effective remedy', *European Law Review*, Vol. 30, n. 4, pp. 511–27

Kohler-Koch, Beate (1997) 'Organised interests in European integration: the evolution of a new type of governance', in Helen Wallace and Alasdair R. Young (eds) *Participation and Policy-making in the European Union*, Oxford: Clarendon Press, pp. 42–68

—— (2008) 'Does participatory governance hold its promises?' in B. Kohler-Koch and F. Larat (eds) *Efficient and Democratic Governance*, Connex Report Series n. 9 pp. 265–95

—— and Finke, Barbara (2007) 'The institutional shaping of EU-society relations: a contribution to democracy via participation?', *Journal of Civil Society*, Vol. 3, n. 3, pp. 205–21

—— and Rittberger, Berthold (2007) 'Charting crowded territory: debating the democratic legitimacy of the European Union' in Beate Kohler-Koch and Berthold Rittberger (eds) *Debating the Democratic Legitimacy of the European Union*, Lanham: Rowman & Littlefield Publishers, pp. 1–29

Korah, Valentine (1980) 'The rights of the defence in administrative proceedings under Community Law', *Current Legal Problems*, Vol. 33, pp. 73–97

Kovar, Robert (1999) 'L'identification des actes normatifs en droit communautaire', in Marianne Dony and Aline De Walsche, *Mélanges en Hommage à Michel Waelbroeck*, Bruxelles: Bruylant, Vol. I, pp. 387–422

Kranenborg, Herke R. (2006) 'Is it time to revise the European regulation on public access to documents?', *European Public Law*, Vol. 12, n. 2, pp. 251–74

Kröger, Sandra (2008) 'Nothing but consultation: the place of organised civil society in EU policy-making across policies', European Governance Papers (EUROGOV) no. C-08-03 (available at <http://www.connex-network.org/eurogov/pdf/egp-connex-C-08-03.pdf>)

Kuyper, P. J. and van Rijn, T. P. J. N. (1982) 'Procedural guarantees and investigatory methods in European law, with special reference to competition', *Yearbook of European Law*, Vol. 2, pp. 1–55

Labouz, Marie-Françoise, Burgorgue-Larsen, Laurence, and Daups, Thierry (1994) 'Le Comité des Régions: 'guardien de la subsidiarité'?', *Europe*, Vol. 4, n. 10, pp. 1–4

Lastra, Rosa (2003) 'The governance structure for financial regulation and supervision in Europe', *Columbia Journal of European Law*, Vol. 10, n. 1, pp. 49–68

Laubadère, André de, Venezia, Jean-Claude, and Gaudemet, Yves (1996) *Traité de droit administratif*, Tome 1, 14th edn, Paris: LGDJ

Lauwaars, Richard H. (1988) 'The 'Model Directive' on technical harmonisation', in Ronald Bibier, Renaud Dehousse, John Pinder, and Joseph H. H. Weiler (eds) *1992: One European Market? A critical analysis of the Commission's internal market strategy*, Baden-Baden: Nomos, pp. 151–73

—— (1994) 'Rights of the defence in competition cases', in Deirdre Curtin and Ton Heukels (eds) *Institutional Dynamics of European Integration. Essays in honour of Henry G. Schermers*, Vol. II, Dordrecht: Martinus Nijhoff Publishers, pp. 497–509

Lee, Maria (2005) *EU Environmental Law. Challenges, change and decision-making*, Oxford: Hart Publishing

Lenaerts, Koen (1993) 'Regulating the regulatory process: "delegation of powers" in the European Community', *European Law Review*, Vol. 18, n. 1, pp. 23–49

—— (2003) 'Interlocking legal orders in European and comparative law', *International and Comparative Law Quarterly*, Vol. 52, n. 4, pp. 873–906

—— (2004) 'In the Union we trust: trust-enhancing principles of Community law', *Common Market Law Review*, Vol. 41, n. 2, pp. 317–43

—— and Vanhamme, Jan (1997) 'Procedural rights of private parties in the Community administrative process', *Common Market Law Review*, Vol. 34, n. 3, pp. 531–69

—— and van Nuffel, Piet (2005) *Constitutional Law of the European Union*, 2nd edn, London: Sweet and Maxwell

Lannoo, Karel (2005) 'The transformation of financial regulation and supervision in the EU', in Donato Masciandro (ed.) *Handbook of Central Banking and Financial Authorities in Europe. New architectures in the supervision of financial markets*, Cheltenham, Northampton: Edward Elgar, pp. 485–511

Levi, Franco (1977) 'Partecipazione e organizzazione', *Rivista Trimestrale di Diritto Pubblico*, Vol. 27, n. 4, pp. 1625–47

Levitt, Matthew (1997) 'Access to the file: the Commission's administrative procedures in cases under Articles 85 and 86', *Common Market Law Review*, Vol. 34, n. 6, pp. 1413–44

Lodge, Juliet and Herman, Valentine (1980) 'The Economic and Social Committee in EEC decision-making', *International Organization*, Vol. 34, n. 2, pp. 265–84

López Menudo, Francisco (1993) 'Los principios generales del procedimiento administrativo', in Javier Barnés Vázquez, (ed.) *La justicia administrativa en el derecho comparado*, Madrid: Civitas, pp. 91–158

Louis, Jean-Victor (1995) *The Community Legal Order*, 3rd edn, Luxembourg: Office for Official Publications of the European Communities

——, Vandersanden, Georges, Waelbroeck, Denis, and Waelbroeck, Michel (1993) *Commentaire Mégret. La Cour de Justice. Les actes des institutions*, Bruxelles: Éditions de l'Université de Bruxelles

Machado, João Baptista (1982) *Participação e descentralização. Democratização e neutralidade na Constitutição de 76*, Coimbra: Almedina

Machete, Pedro (1995) *A audiência dos interessados no procedimento administrativo*, Lisboa: Universidade Católica Editora

Macmaoláin, Caoimhín (2007) *EU Food Law. Protecting consumers and health in a common market*, Oxford, Portland: Hart Publishing

Maes, Marc (2007) 'L'accès du public aux documents des Institutions de la Communauté européenne: vers une révision du règlement (CE) 1049/2001', *Revue du Droit de l'Union Européenne*, n. 2, pp. 411–32

Magnette, Paul (2003) 'European governance and civic participation: beyond elitist citizenship?', *Political Studies*, Vol. 51, n. 1, pp. 144–60

—— (2003) *Contrôler l'Europe. Pouvoirs et responsabilite´dans l'Union Europeéne*, Bruxelles: Éditions de l'Université de Bruxelles

Manin, Philippe (2005) *L'Union Européenne. Institutions, ordre juridique, contentieux*, Paris: Pedone

Margellos, Théophile M. (1997) 'L'émergence de la "région" dans l'ordre juridique communautaire', in Georges Vandersanden (ed.) *L'Europe et les régions. Aspects juridiques*, Bruxelles: Éditions de l'Université de Bruxelles, pp. 19–63

Maseo Seco, Luis F. (2004) 'I procedimenti composti comunitari: riflessioni intorno alla problematica della impossibilità di difendersi ed eventuali alternative', in Giacinto della Cananea and Matteo Gnes (eds) *I procedimenti amministrativi dell'Unione Europea. Un'indagine. Atti del convegno di Studio, Urbino, 14 Marzo 2003*, Torino: Giappichelli, pp. 11–32

Massera, Alberto (2007) 'I principi generali', in Mario P. Chiti and Guido Greco (eds) *Trattato di diritto amministrativo europeo*, Tomo I, 2nd edn, Milano: Giuffrè

Mattarella, Bernardo G. (2000) 'L'attività' in Sabino Cassese (ed.) *Trattato di Diritto Amministrativo. Diritto Amministrativo Generale*, Vol. I, Milano: Giuffrè, pp. 629–703

—— (2000) 'Il provvedimento', in Sabino Cassese (ed.) *Trattato di Diritto Amministrativo. Diritto Amministrativo Generale*, Vol. I, Milano: Giuffrè, pp. 705–925

—— (2006) 'Discrezionalità amministrativa', in Sabino Cassese (ed.) *Dizionario di Diritto Pubblico*, Vol. III, Milano: Giuffrè, pp. 1993–2003

Maurer, Hartmut (1994 [1992]) *Droit administratif allemand* (traduit par Michel Fromont) Paris: LGDJ

McGarity, Thomas O. (1992) 'Some thoughts on 'deossifying' the rulemaking process', *Duke Law Journal*, Vol. 41, n. 6, pp. 1385–462

—— (1997) 'Courts and the ossification of rulemaking: a response to Professor Seidenfeld', *Texas Law Review*, Vol. 75, n. 3, pp. 525–58

McLaughlin, Andrew M. and Greenwood, Justin (1995) 'The management of interest representation in the European Union', *Journal of Common Market Studies*, Vol. 33, n. 1, pp. 43–156

Meisse, Eric (2005) 'La démocratie administrative dans le traité établissant une Constitution pour l'Europe', in Vlad Constantinesco, Yves Gautier, and Valérie Michel (eds) *Le Traité établissant une Constitution pour l'Europe. Analyses et commentaires*, Strasbourg: Presses Universitaires de Strasbourg, pp. 397–417

Mestre, Christian (1997) 'Radioscopie du Comité des Régions: organization, fonctionnement, compétences', in Jacques Bourrinet (ed.) *Le Comité des Régions de l'Union Européenne*, Paris: Economica, pp. 47–83

Meuwese, Anne C. M. (2007) 'Inter-institutionalising EU impact assessment', in Stephen Weatherill (ed.) *Better Regulation*, Oxford: Oxford University Press, pp. 287–309

Meyer, Hans (1993) 'El procedimiento administrativo en la Republica Federal de Alemania', in Javier Barnés Vasquez (ed.) *El procedimiento administrative en el derecho comparado*, Madrid: Civitas, pp. 281–316

Mogg, John F. (2002) 'Regulating financial services in Europe: a new approach', *Fordham International Law Journal*, Vol. 26, n. 1, pp. 58–81

Möllers, Christian (2006) 'European governance: meaning and value of a concept', *Common Market Law Review*, Vol. 43, n. 2, pp. 313–36

Moloney, Niamh (2006) 'Financial market regulation in the post-financial services action plan era', *International and Comparative Law Quarterly*, Vol. 55, n. 4, pp. 982–92

—— (2007) 'Innovation and risk in the EC financial market regulation: new instruments of financial market intervention and the Committee of European Securities Regulators', *European Law Review*, Vol. 32, n. 5, pp. 627–63

Monjal, Pierre-Yves (1996) 'La Conférence intergouvernementale de 1996 et la hiérarchie des norms communautaires', *Revue Trimestrielle de Droit Européen*, Vol. 32, n. 4, pp. 681–716

—— (1998) 'Remarques sur l'emploi de la notion de fonction législative en droit communautaire', *Revue de la Recherche Juridique, Droit Prospectif*, Vol. 23, n. 3, pp. 1117–162

Morviducci, Claudia (2000) 'Diritto di accesso ai documenti delle istituzioni e Trattato de Amsterdam', *Rivista Italiana di Diritto Pubblico Comunitario*, Vol. 10, n. 4, pp. 665–718

Mulgan, Richard (2000) '"Accountability": an ever-expanding concept?', *Public Administration*, Vol. 78, n. 3, pp. 555–73

Nehl, Hanns Peter (1999) *Principles of Administrative Procedure in EC Law*, Oxford: Hart Publishing

Neri, Sergio (1970) 'Diposizioni generali. Articoli 46 e 47', in Rolando Quadri, Riccardo Monaco, and Alberto Trabucchi (eds) *Trattato istitutivo della Comunità Europea del Carbone e dell'Acciaio: Commentario, Vol. II, Articoli 45–100*, Milano: Giuffrè, pp. 597–642

Nigro, Mario (1980) 'Il nodo della partecipazione', *Rivista trimestrale di diritto e procedura civile*, Vol. 34, pp. 225–36

—— (1980) 'Procedimento amministrativo e tutela giurisdizionale contro la pubblica amministrazione (il problema di una legge generale sul procedimento amministrativo)', *Rivista di Diritto Processuale*, Vol. 35, pp. 252–78

—— (1987) 'Ma che cos'è questo interesse legittimo? Interrogativi vecchi e nuovi punti di riflessione', *Il foro italiano*, pp. 469–83

—— (1994) *Giustizia amministrativa*, 4th edn, Bologna: Il Mulino

Nihoul, Paul (1994) 'La recevabilité des recours en annulation introduits par un particulier à l'encontre d'un acte communautaire de portée générale', *Revue Trimestrielle de Droit Européen*, Vol. 30, n. 35, pp. 171–94

Noël, Emil (1963) 'Comment fonctionnent les institutions de la Communauté Économique Européenne', *Revue du Marché Commun*, n. 54, pp. 14–21

Obradovic, Daniela and Alonso Vizcaino, Jose M. (2006) 'Good governance requirements concerning the participation of interest groups in EU consultations', *Common Market Law Review*, Vol. 43, n. 4, pp. 1049–85

Occhiena, Massimo (2002) *Situazioni giuridiche soggettive e procedimento amministrativo*, Milano: Giuffrè

—— (2006) 'Partecipazione al procedimento amministrativo', in Sabino Cassese (ed.) *Dizionario di Diritto Pubblico*, Vol. V, Milano: Giuffrè, pp. 4128–38

Oliveira, Mário Esteves de, Gonçalves, Pedro Costa, and Amorim, João Pacheco de (1999) *Código do Procedimento Administrativo Comentado*, 2nd edn, Coimbra: Almedina

Ortino, Matteo (2007) 'The role and functioning of mutual recognition in the European market of financial services', *International and Comparative Law Quarterly*, Vol. 56, n. 2, pp. 309–38

Parada Vasquez, José Ramón (2007) *Derecho Administrativo. Vol. I, Parte general*, 16th edn, Madrid: Marcial Pons

Parejo Alfonso, Luciano, Jiménez-Blanco, Antonio, and Ortega Álvarez, Luis (1998) *Manual de derecho administrativo*. Vol. 1. 5th edn, Barcelona: Ariel

Peers, Steven (2003) 'The new regulation on access to documents: a critical analysis', *Yearbook of European Law*, Vol. 22, pp. 385–442

Pelkmans, Jacques (1987) 'The new approach to technical harmonisation', *Journal of Common Market Studies*, Vol. 25, n. 3, pp. 249–69

Pescatore, Pierre (1980) 'Le recours dans la jurisprudence de la Cour de Justice des Communautés Européennes a des normes déduites de la comparaison des droits des États membres', *Revue Internationale de Droit Comparé*, Vol. 32, n. 2, pp. 337–59

Peterson, John (1995) 'Playing the transparency game: Consultation and policy-making in the European Commission', *Public Administration*, Vol. 73, n. 3 pp. 473–92

Pliakos, Asteris (1987) *Les droits de la defense et le droit communautaire de la concurrence*, Bruxelles: Bruylant

Ponzano, Paolo (2008) '"Executive" and "delegated" acts: The situation after the Lisbon Treaty', in Stefan Griller and Jacques Ziller (eds) *The Lisbon Treaty: EU Constitutionalism without a Constitutional Treaty?*, Wien: Springer, pp. 135–41

Prechal, Sacha (2005) *Directives in EC Law*, 2nd edn, New York: Oxford University Press

—— (2008) 'Protection of Rights: How Far?' in Sacha Prechal and Bert van Roermund (eds) *The Coherence of EU Law. The Search for Unity in Divergent Concepts*, Oxford: Oxford University Press, pp. 155–182

Prosser, Tony (2007) 'Administrative procedure and the protection of citizen's rights: report from the United Kingdom' in Alberto Massera (ed.) *Le tutele procedimentali. Profili di diritto comparato*, Napoli: Jovene Editore, pp. 71–95

Quittkat, Christine and Finke, Barbara (2008) 'The EU Commission Consultation Regime', in B. Kohler Koch, D. de Bievre, and W. Moloney, *Opening EU-Governance to Civil Society—Gains and Challenges*, CONNEX Report Series No. 5, pp. 183–222

Rasmussen, Hjalte (1980) 'Why is Article 173 interpreted against private plaintiffs?', *European Law Review*, Vol. 5, pp. 112–27

Rawlinson, Frank (1993) 'The role of policy frameworks, codes and guidelines in the control of State aid' in Ian Harden (ed.) *State Aid: Community Law and Policy*, Cologne: Bundesanzeiger, pp. 52–60

Reich, Norbert (1998) '"System der subjectiven öffentlichen Rechten" in the Union: A European Constitution for citizens of bits and pieces', *Collected Courses of the Academy of European Law*, Vol. VI, Book 1, pp. 157–236

Reuter, Paul (1953) *La Communauté Européenne du Charbon et de l'Acier*, Paris: LGDJ

Rideau, Joël (1993) 'Les groupes d'intérêt dans le système institutionnel communautaire', *Revue des Affaires Européens*, n. 3, pp. 49–73

Ritleng, Dominique (2009) 'L'identification de la fonction executive dans l'Union', in Jacqueline Dutheil de la Rochère (ed.) *Exécution du droit de l'Union, entre mécanismes communautaires et droits nationaux*, Bruxelles: Bruylant, pp. 27–51

Romano, Maria Chiara (2006) 'Atti amministrativi generali', in Sabino Cassese (ed.) *Dizionario di Diritto Pubblico*, Vol. I, Milano: Giuffrè, pp. 491–98

Sabel, Charles and Zeitlin, Jonathan (2008) 'Learning from difference: the new architecture of experimentalist governance in the EU', *European Law Journal*, Vol. 14, n. 3, pp. 271–327

Sanchéz-Moron, Miguel (1979) 'El principio de participación en la Constitución española', *Revista de Administración Pública*, n. 39, pp. 171–205

Sandulli, Aldo (1989) *Manuale di Diritto Amministrativo*, 15th edn, Napoli: Jovene

—— (2000) 'Il procedimento', in Sabino Cassese (ed.). *Trattato di diritto amministrativo. Diritto Amministrativo Generale*, Vol.II, Milano: Giuffrè, pp. 927–1215

Santamaria Pastor, Juan Alfonso (1988) *Fundamentos de derecho administrativo*, Vol. I, Madrid: Ramon Areces

Santini, Andrea (2004) *Il principio di trasparenza nell'ordinamento dell'Unione Europea*, Milano: Giuffrè

Savino, Mario (2005) *I comitati dell'Unione europea: la collegialità amministrativa negli ordinamenti compositi*, Milano: Giuffrè

Schäfer, Günther F. (1996) 'Committees in the EC policy process: a first step towards developing a conceptual framework', in Robin H. Pedler and Günther F. Schäfer, *Shaping European Law and Policy. The role of committees and comitology in the political process*, Maastricht: European Institute of Public Administration, pp. 3–23

Schepel, Harm (2005) *The Constitution of Private Governance. Product standards in the regulation of integrating markets*, Oxford, Portland: Hart Publishing

Schmidt-Assmann, Eberhard (2003) *La teoría general del derecho administrativo como sistema*, Madrid: Marcial Pons

Schneider, Catherine (1997) 'Morceaux choisis sur la composition du Comité des Régions', in Jacques Bourrinet (ed.) *Le Comité des Régions de l'Union Européenne*, Paris: Economica, pp. 15–45

Schockweiler, Fernand (1989) 'La motivation des décisions individuelles en droit communautaire et en droit national', *Cahiers de Droit Européen*, Vol. 25, n. 1–2, pp. 3–40

Schutter, Olivier De (2002) 'Europe in search of its civil society', *European Law Journal*, Vol. 8, n. 2, pp. 198–217

Schwarze, Jürgen (2004) 'The legal protection of the individual against regulations in European Union law', *European Public Law*, Vol. 10, n. 2, pp. 285–303

—— (2006) *European Administrative Law*. Revised 1st edn, London: Sweet and Maxwell

Scott, Colin (2002) 'The governance of the European Union: the potential for multi-level control', *European Law Journal*, Vol. 8, n. 1, pp. 59–79

Scott. Joanne and Trubek, David M. (2002) 'Mind the gap: law and new approaches to governance in the European Union', *European Law Journal*, Vol. 8, n. 1, pp. 1–18

Seidenfeld, Mark (1997) 'Demystifying deossification: rethinking recent proposals to modify judicial review of notice and comment rulemaking', *Texas Law Review*, Vol. 75, n. 3, pp. 438–524

Serre, Barbier de la (2006) 'Procedural justice in the European Community case-law concerning the rights of the defence: essentialist and instrumental trends', *European Public Law*, Vol. 12, n. 2, pp. 225–50

Shapiro, Martin (1992) 'The giving reasons requirement', *The University of Chicago Legal Forum*, pp. 179–220

—— (1996) 'Codification of administrative law: the US and the Union', *European Law Journal*, Vol. 2, n. 1, pp. 26–47

Silva, Vasco Pereira da (1996) *Em busca do acto administrativo perdido*, Coimbra: Almedina

Simon, Denys (2001) *Le système juridique communautaire*, Paris: Presses Universitaires de France

Simon, Denys (2006) 'Le principe de « bonne administration » ou la « bonne gouvernance » concrète', in *Le droit de l'Union Européenne en principes. Liber amicorum en l'honneur de Jean Raux*, Éditions Apogée, pp. 155–76

Sinaniotis, Dimitrios (2001) 'The plea of illegality in EC law', *European Public Law*, Vol. 7, n. 1, pp. 103–25

Sinnaeve, Adinda and Slot, Piet Jan (1999) 'The new regulation on State aid procedures', *Common Market Law Review*, Vol. 36, n. 6, pp. 1153–94

Smismans, Stijn (1999) 'An Economic and Social Committee for the citizen, or a citizen for the Economic and Social Committee?', *European Public Law*, Vol. 5, n. 4, pp. 557–82

—— (2004) *Law, Legitimacy, and European Governance. Functional participation in social regulation*, Oxford: Oxford University Press

—— (2007) 'New governance—the solution for active citizenship, or the end of citizenship?', *Columbia Journal of European Law*, Vol. 13, n. 3, pp. 595–622

—— (2008) 'New modes of governance and the participatory myth', *West European Politics*, Vol. 31, n. 5, pp. 874–95

Smith, Stanley A. de, Woolf, Harry, and Jowell, Jeffrey L. (1995) *Judicial Review of Administrative Action*, 5th edn, London: Sweet and Maxwell

Söderman, Jacob (1998) 'The role and impact of the European Ombudsman in access to documents and transparency of decision-making' in Veerle Deckmyn and Ian Thomson (eds) *Openness and Transparency in the European Union*, Maastricht: European Institute of Public Administration, pp. 75–83

Soto, Jean de (1958) *La Communauté européenne du charbon et de l'acier (C.E.C.A.)* Paris: Presses Universitaires de France

Stewart, Richard (1975) 'The reformation of American administrative law', *Harvard Law Review*, Vol. 88, n. 8, pp. 1667–813

—— (2006) 'Mars or Venus? US and European models for regulatory governance and the discontents of globalization', Discussion paper presented at the Transatlantic Program, Robert Schumann Centre for Advanced Studies, European University Institute, 27 April 2006

Strauss, Peter (2006) 'Rulemaking in the ages of globalization and information: what America can learn from Europe, and vice versa', *Columbia Journal of European Law*, Vol. 12, n. 3, pp. 645–94

Streeck, Wolfgang and Schmitter, Phillippe (1991) 'From national corporatism to transnational pluralism: organised interests in the Single European Market', *Politics and Society*, Vol. 19, n. 2, pp. 133–64

Sydow, Helmut Schmitt von (1988) 'The basic strategies of the Commission's White Paper', in Ronald Bibier, Renaud Dehousse, John Pinder, and Joseph H. H. Weiler (eds) *1992: One European Market? A critical analysis of the Commission's internal market strategy*, Baden-Baden: Nomos, pp. 79–106

Tizzano, Antonio (1995) 'La hiérarchie des normes communautaires', *Revue du Marché Uniques Européen*, n. 3, pp. 219–32

Töller, Annette (1998) 'The "Article 19 Committee": the regulation of the environmental management and audit scheme', in M.P.C.M van Schendelen (ed.) *EU Committees as Influential Policymakers*, Aldershot: Ashgate, pp. 179–206

Tomkins, Adam (2000) 'Transparency and the emergence of a European administrative law', *Yearbook of European Law*, Vol. 19, pp. 217–56

Toth, Akos G. (1978) *Legal Protection of Individuals in the European Communities. Volume I, The individual and Community law*, Amsterdam: North-Holland Publishing Company

Tridimas, Takis (2001) 'Liability for breach of Community law: growing up and mellowing down?', *Common Market Law Review*, Vol. 38, n. 2, pp. 301–32

—— (2006) *The General Principles of EU Law*, 2nd edn, Oxford: Oxford University Press

Trubek, David and Trubek, Louise (2007) 'New governance and legal regulation: complementarity, rivalry, and transformation', *Columbia Journal of European Law*, Vol. 13, n. 3, pp. 539–64

Tsadiras, Alexandros (2007) 'The position of the European Ombudsman in the Community system of judicial remedies', *European Law Review*, Vol. 32, n. 5, pp. 607–26

Türk, Alexander (2009) 'Judicial review of integrated administration in the EU', in Herwig Hofmann and Alexander Türk (eds) (2009) *Legal Challenges in EU Administrative Law. Towards an integrated administration*, Cheltenham: Edward Elgar, pp. 218–56.

Varone, Frédéric, Visscher, Christian de, Bergström, Carl-Fredrik, and Almer, Josefin (2004) 'Governance and the EU Securities Sector', report produced in the realm of the New Modes of Governance project, Project 7—Governance and the EU securities sector, Priority 7—Citizens and governance in the knowledge-based society, reference number 7/D1, p. 3 (available at <http://www.eu-newgov.org/database/DELIV/D07D01_EU_securities_sector.PDF>)

——, Visscher, Christian de, Bergström, Carl-Fredrik, and Almer, Josefin (2006) 'Final Report' produced in the realm of the New Modes of Governance project, Project 7—Governance and the EU securities sector, Priority 7—Citizens and governance in the knowledge-based society, reference number 7/D06, p. 16–18 (available at <http://www.eu-newgov.org/database/DELIV/D07D06_Final_Report.pdf>)

Varsori, Antonio (2000) 'Per una storia del Comitato Economico Sociale', in Antonio Varsori (ed.) *Il Comitato Economico e Sociale nella costruzione europea*, Venezia: Marsilio Editori, pp. 3–23

Verhoeven, Amaryllis (2002) *The European Union in Search of a Democratic and Constitutional Theory*, The Hague, London, New York: Kluwer Law International

Vesterdorf, Bo (1999) 'Transparency—not just a vogue word', *Fordham International Law Journal*, Vol. 22, n. 3, pp. 902–29

Villata, Riccardo (1992) 'Riflessioni in tema di partecipazione la procedimento e legittimazione processuale', *Diritto Processuale Amministrativo*, Vol. 9, pp. 171–205

Virga, Giovanni (1998) *La partecipazione al procedimento amministrativo*, Milano: Giuffrè

Visscher, Christian de, Maiscocq, Olivier, and Varone, Frédéric (2008) 'The Lamfalussy reform in the EU securities markets: fiduciary relationships, policy effectiveness and balance of power', *Journal of Public Policy*, Vol. 28, n. 1, pp. 19–47

Vogt, Matthias (2006) 'Indirect judicial protection in EC law—the case of the plea of illegality', *European Law Review*, Vol. 31, n. 3, pp. 364–77

Voort, Willem van der (1997) *In the Search of a Role. The Economic and Social Committee in European decision making*, PhD Thesis, Leiden University

Vos, Ellen (1999) *Institutional Frameworks of Community Health and Safety Legislation: Committees, Agencies, and Private Bodies*, Oxford, Portland: Hart Publishing

—— (1999) 'EU committees: the evolution of unforeseen institutional actors in European product regulation' in Christian Joerges and Ellen Vos (eds) *EU Committees: Social Regulation, Law and Politics*, Oxford: Hart Publishing, pp. 19–47

Waelbroeck, Denis and Verheyden, A.-M. (1995) 'Les conditions de recevabilité des recours en annulations des particuliers contre les actes normatifs communautaires', *Cahiers de Droit Européen*, Vol. 31, n. 3–4, pp. 399–441

Waelbroeck, Michel and Frignani, Aldo (1997) *Commentaire Mégret. Le Droit de la CE*, Vol. 4 (Concurrence) Bruxelles: Éditions de l'Université de Bruxelles

Wakefield, Jill (2007) *The Right to Good Administration*, The Netherlands: Kluwer Law International

Walker, Neil (2001) 'The White Paper in constitutional context', in Christian Joerges, Yves Mény, and Joseph H.H. Weiler (eds) 'Symposium: Mountain or Molehill? A critical appraisal of the Commission White Paper on Governance', Jean Monnet Working Paper no. 6/01

—— (2003) 'Postnational constitutionalism and the problem of translation' in Joseph H.H. Weiler and Marlene Wind (eds) *European Constitutionalism beyond the State*, Cambridge: Cambridge University Press, pp. 27–54

—— (2006) 'EU constitutionalism and new governance' in Gráinne de Búrca and Joanne Scott (eds) *Law and Governance in the EU and the US*, Oxford and Portland: Hart Publishing, pp. 15–36

Wallace, Helen (1997) 'Introduction', in Helen Wallace and Alasdair R. Young (eds) *Participation and Policy-making in the European Union*, Oxford: Clarendon Press, pp. 1–16

Ward, Angela (2007) *Judicial Review and the Rights of Private Parties in EU Law*, Oxford: Oxford University Press

Weatherill, Stephen (2007) 'The challenge of better regulation', in Stephen Weatherill (ed.) *Better Regulation*, Oxford: Oxford University Press, pp. 1–17

Weiler, Joseph H. H. (1991) 'Problems of legitimacy in post 1992 Europe', *Aussenwirtschaft*, Vol. 46, n. 3/4, pp. 411–37

Weiler, Joseph H. H. (1999) 'Epilogue—comitology as revolution: infranationalism, constitutionalism and democracy' in Christian Joerges and Ellen Vos (eds) *EU Committees: Social Regulation, Law and Politics*, Oxford: Hart Publishing, pp. 339–50

Wessels, Wolfgang (2003) 'On the EU legitimacy debate: approaches and desiderata', in Georges Vandersanden and Aline de Walsche (eds) *Melanges en homage a Jean-Victor Louis*, Vol I., Bruxelles: Éditions de l'Université de Bruxelles, pp. 672–37

Winter, Gerd (1996) 'Reforming the sources and categories of European Union Law: a summary', in Gerd Winter (ed.) *Sources and categories of European Union Law. A comparative and reform perspective*, Baden Baden: Nomos, pp. 13–65

Winter, Jan (1999) 'The rights of complainants in State aid cases: judicial review of Commission decisions adopted under Article 88 (ex 93) EC', *Common Market Law Review*, Vol. 36, n. 3, pp. 521–68

Witte, Bruno de (1999) 'Direct effect, supremacy, and the nature of the legal order', in Paul Craig and Graínne de Búrca (eds) *The Evolution of EU Law*, Oxford: Oxford University Press, pp. 177–213

—— (2004) 'Language law of the European Union: protecting or eroding linguistic diversity?' in Rachael Craufurd Smith (ed.) *Culture and European Union Law*, Oxford: Oxford University Press, pp. 205–41

—— (2006) 'Non-market values in internal market legislation', in Niamh Nic Suibhne (ed.) *Regulating the Internal Market*, Cheltenham, Northampton: Edward Elgar Publishing, pp. 61–86

Yataganas, Xénophon A. (2002) 'La gouvernance européenne: entre reformes administrative et institutionnelle. Articulation cohérente ou bricolage fortuit?' in Christian Joerges, Karl-Heinz Ladeur, and Jacques Ziller (eds) 'Governance in the European Union and the Commission White Paper', EUI Working Paper Law no. 2002/8, pp. 2–9

Zellentin, Gerda (1962) 'The Economic and Social Committee', *Journal of Common Market Studies*, Vol. 1, n. 1, pp. 22–8

Ziller, Jacques (2007) 'Introduction: les concepts d'administration directe, d'administration indirecte et de co-administration et les fondements du droit administratif européen', in Jean-Bernand Auby et Jacqueline Dutheil de la Rochère (eds) *Droit administratif européen*, Bruxelles: Bruylant, pp. 235–43

—— (2009) 'Exécution centralisée et exécution partagée: le fédéralisme d' exécution en droit de l'Union européenne', in Jacqueline Dutheil de la Rochère (ed.) *Exécution du droit de l'Union, entre mécanismes communautaires et droits nationaux*, Bruxelles: Bruylant, pp. 111–138

Zito, Alberto (1996) *Le pretese partecipative del privato nel procedimento amministrativo*, Milano: Giuffrè

Zito, Alberto (2002) 'Il diritto ad una buona amministrazione nella Carta dei Diritti Fondamentali dell'Unione Europea e nell'ordinamento interno', *Rivista Italiana di Diritto Pubblico Comunitario*, Vol. 12, n. 2–3, pp. 425–44

Zittel, T. (2008) 'Participatory Engineering: Promises and Pitfalls', in B. Kohler Koch, D. de Bievre, and W. Moloney (eds) *Opening EU-Governance to Civil Society—Gains and Challenges*, CONNEX Report Series No. 5, pp. 119–44

INDEX